THEORY AND PRACTICE OF FOREIGN AID

FRONTIERS OF ECONOMICS AND GLOBALIZATION

1

Series Editors:

HAMID BELADI
University of Texas at San Antonio, USA

E. KWAN CHOI
Iowa State University, USA

ELSEVIER

Amsterdam – Boston – Heidelberg – London – New York – Oxford – Paris
San Diego – San Francisco – Singapore – Sydney – Tokyo

THEORY AND PRACTICE
OF FOREIGN AID

Edited by

Sajal Lahiri

Vandeveer Professor of Economics,
Southern Illinois University at Carbondale, USA

160201

ELSEVIER

Amsterdam – Boston – Heidelberg – London – New York – Oxford – Paris
San Diego – San Francisco – Singapore – Sydney – Tokyo

Elsevier
Radarweg 29, PO Box 211, 1000 AE Amsterdam, The Netherlands
The Boulevard, Langford Lane, Kidlington, Oxford OX5 1GB, UK

First edition 2007

Notice
No responsibility is assumed by the publisher for any injury and/or damage to persons or property as
a matter of products liability, negligence or otherwise, or from any use or operation of any methods,
products, instructions or ideas contained in the material herein. Because of rapid advances in the medical sciences, in particular, independent verification of diagnoses and drug dosages should be made

Library of Congress Cataloging-in-Publication Data
A catalog record for this book is available from the Library of Congress

British Library Cataloguing in Publication Data
A catalogue record for this book is available from the British Library

ISBN-13: 978-0-444-52765-3
ISSN: 1574-8715

For information on all Elsevier publications
visit our website at books.elsevier.com

Printed and bound in The Netherlands

07 08 09 10 11   10 9 8 7 6 5 4 3 2 1

Working together to grow
libraries in developing countries

www.elsevier.com | www.bookaid.org | www.sabre.org

ELSEVIER   BOOK AID
            International   Sabre Foundation

In memory of my parents
Dipali and Samarendra Nath Lahiri

ABOUT THE SERIES:
FRONTIERS OF ECONOMICS AND GLOBALIZATION

This series is aimed at economists and financial economists worldwide and will provide an in depth look at current global topics. Each volume in the series will focus on specialized topics for greater understanding of the chosen subject and provide a detailed discussion of emerging issues. The target audiences are professional researchers, graduate students, and policy makers. It will offer cutting-edge views on new horizons and deepen the understanding in these emerging topics.

With contributions from leading researchers, each volume presents a fresh look at today's current topics. This series will present primarily original works, and employ references appropriate to the topic being explored.

Each volume will bring a set of highly concentrated articles that will provide in depth knowledge to a target audience, while the entire series will appeal to a wide audience by providing them with deeper knowledge on a broad set of emerging topics in the global economy.

The Frontiers of Economics and Globalization series will publish on topics such as:

- Frontiers of Trade Negotiations
- Frontiers of Derivative Pricing
- Frontiers of International Lending and Debt problems
- Frontiers of Economics Integration
- Frontiers of Trade and Environment
- Frontiers of Foreign Exchange
- Frontiers of International Finance
- Frontiers of Growth of Open Economies
- Frontiers of Futures Pricing
- Frontiers of International Financial Markets
- Frontiers of Investment Banking
- Frontiers of Mergers and Acquisitions
- Frontiers of Government Policy and Regulations
- Frontiers of Multi-Sector Growth Models
- Frontiers of Intellectual Property Rights
- Frontiers of Fragmentations and Outsourcing

Series Editors

Hamid Beladi
E. Kwan Choi

ABOUT THE VOLUME

About the Editor: Sajal Lahiri is the Vandeveer Professor of Economics at the Southern Illinois University – Carbondale; has worked as consultants to the FAO, IFAD, and the World Bank; has written extensively in top economics journals on issues related to development in general and to foreign aid in particular.

About the Volume: The volume contains contributions on both the theoretical and empirical sides of the literature on aid, and has equal emphasis on both. On the theoretical side, the analysis of the transfer paradox has evolved primarily in the context of traditional static models. However, given developments in the policy arena as well in the discipline itself, there is a need for further developments in the theoretical analysis of foreign aid. The theoretical contributions in this volume will do precisely that. For example, aid dependence, the impact of aid on saving, investment and growth calls for an intertemporal framework. Development of spatial economics calls for introduction of the spatial dimension to the analysis of foreign aid. Similarly, the potential role of aid in conflict resolution, in improving the environment, in public good (infrastructural) provision and in the establishment of good governance are some of the issues the theoretical contributions consider.

On the empirical side, the issue of the effectiveness of aid; fiscal implications of aid, the determinants of aid; the allocation criteria for aid; the relationship between aid and trade, and aid and poverty remain as important as ever. The contributions in this volume look at these issues from a number of different perspectives, using a number of different methodologies and different types of data sets (time series data from Africa, cross-country data, and panel data).

Aim and Scope of the Volume: This volume contains a comprehensive analysis of foreign aid from both theoretical and empirical perspectives, written by leading researchers in the field. The book should be an essential tool for both undergraduate and graduate students of development studies, researchers in the field, and policy makers trained in economics.

Acknowledgements: I would like to thank all the authors for their cooperation, to my wife Dipa for her support and understanding, and to Professor Hamid Beladi for immediate and helpful responses to all my queries.

LIST OF CONTRIBUTORS (IN ALPHABETICAL ORDER)

Channing Arndt	Associate Professor, Department of Agricultural Economics, Purdue University, USA, and National Directorate of Studies and Policy Analysis, Ministry of Planning and Development, Mozambique
Subhayu Bandyopadhyay	Associate Professor of Economics, Department of Economics, West Virginia University, Morgantown, WV, USA
Arabinda Basistha	Assistant Professor of Economics, Department of Economics, West Virginia University, Morgantown, WV, USA
Zsolt Becsi	Assistant Professor of Economics, Department of Economics, Southern Illinois University at Carbondale, IL, USA
Hamid Beladi	Professor of Economics, University of Texas at San Antonio, San Antonio, TX, USA
Arne Bigsten	Professor of Development Economics, Department of Economics, School of Business, Economics, and Law, Gothenburg University, Sweden
Steven Brakman	Professor of Economics, Department of Economics, University of Groningen, The Netherlands
Chir-Chur Chao	Department of Economics, Chinese University of Hong Kong, Shatin, Hong Kong, and Department of Economics, Oregon State University, Corvallis, OR, USA
Jai-Young Choi	Department of Economics and Finance, Lamar University, Beaumont, TX, USA
Kwan Choi	Department of Economics, Iowa State University, Ames, IA, USA, and Department of Economics and Finance, City University of Hong Kong

List of Contributors (in alphabetical order)

Shantayanan Devarajan	Chief Economist, South Asia Region, The World Bank, Washington, DC, USA
Slobodan Djajic	Professor of International Economics, the Graduate Institute of International Studies, Geneva, Switzerland
Gil Epstein	Professor, Department of Economics, Bar-Ilan University, Ramat Gan, Israel, and IZA Bonn, Germany
Ira Gang	Professor, Department of Economics, Rutgers University, New Brunswick, NJ, USA
Harry Garretsen	Professor of Economics, Utrecht School of Economics, University of Utrecht, The Netherlands
Scott Gilbert	Associate Professor of Economics, Department of Economics, Southern Illinois University at Carbondale, IL, USA
Panos Hatzipanayoto	Professor of Economics, Department of International and European Economic Studies, Athens University of Economics and Business, Greece, and CESifo, Germany
Bharat R. Hazari	Department of Economics & Finance, City University of Hong Kong, Kowloon, Hong Kong
Sam Jones	Economist, National Directorate of Studies and Policy Analysis, Ministry of Planning and Development, Mozambique
Jean-Pierre Laffargue	CEPREMAP, PSE and University of Paris I, Paris, France
Sajal Lahiri	Vandeveer Professor of Economics, Department of Economics, Southern Illinois University at Carbondale, IL, USA
Tim Lloyd	Reader in Economics, School of Economics, University of Nottingham, England, UK
Daniel M'Amanja	Deputy Director of Research in the Economics Department, Central Bank of Kenya, Nairobi, Kenya
Sugata Marjit	Reserve Bank of India Professor of Industrial Economics Centre for Studies in Social Sciences, Calcutta, India

Charles van Marrewijk	Professor of Economics, Department of Economics, Erasmus University Rotterdam, The Netherlands
George Mavrotas	Research Fellow & Project Director, World Institute for Development Economics Research, United Nations University, Helsinki, Finland
Michael S. Michael	Professor of Economics, Department of Economics, University of Cyprus, Nicosia, Cyprus, and CESifo, Germany
Katharina Michaelowa	Professor of Political Economy and Development, Institute for Political Science, University of Zurich, Switzerland
Oliver Morrissey	Director of CREDIT and Professor in Development Economics, School of Economics, University of Nottingham, England, UK
Vivekananda Mukherjee	Reader, Department of Economics, Jadavpur Universiy, Calcutta, India
Jonathan Munemo	Consultant, AFTPM Trade Team, Africa Region, The World Bank, Washington, DC, USA
Reza Oladi	Assistant Professor of Economics, Department of Economics, Utah State University, Logan, UT, USA
Yoshiyasu Ono	Professor of Economics, Institute of Social and Economic Research, Osaka University, Osaka, Japan
Andrew Sunil Rajkumar	Economist, Africa Region, The World Bank, Washington, DC, USA
Koji Shimomura	Professor of Economics, Research Institute of Economics and Business Administration, Kobe University, Kobe, Hyogo, Japan
Vinaya Swaroop	Lead Economist, South Asia Region, The World Bank, Washington, DC, USA
Kevin Sylwester	Associate Professor of Economics, Southern Illinois University at Carbondale, IL, USA
Finn Tarp	Professor of Development Economics, Department of Economics, University of Copenhagen, Denmark
Nikos Tsakiris	Department of International and European Economic Studies, Athens University of Economics and Business, Athens, Greece

Howard Wall   Assistant Vice President, and, Director, Center for
                             Regional Economics, Federal Reserve Bank of
                             St. Louis, St. Louis, MO, USA

Anke Weber   PhD student, Institute for Political Science,
                             University of Zurich, Switzerland

Howard White   Fellow, Institute of Development Studies, University
                             of Sussex, UK

Eden S.H. Yu   Department of Economics & Finance, City
                             University of Hong Kong, Kowloon, Hong Kong

CONTENTS

CHAPTER 6   WHEN CAN COMPETITION FOR AID REDUCE POLLUTION?

Nikos Tsakiris, Panos Hatzipanayotou and Michael S. Michael

CHAPTER 7   FOREIGN AID, INTERNATIONAL MIGRATION AND WELFARE

Slobodan Djajić

THEORY AND PRACTICE OF FOREIGN AID: INTRODUCTION

Sajal Lahiri

Department of Economics, Southern Illinois University at Carbondale, Carbondale, IL 62901-4515, USA
E-mail address: lahiri@siu.edu

The importance of foreign aid cannot be overstated.[1] Unprecedented integration of the world economy in recent years has brought the issue of poverty back in the policy debate at the international level. Some of the recent initiatives such as the United Nation's Millennium Development Goals and the report by the Africa Commission (set up by the British Prime Minister Tony Blair) which was discussed at length at G8 meetings, recognize this fact. The analysis of foreign aid is however fraught with controversies and paradoxes. This applies to both the theoretical and the empirical literature. There are two broad strands in the literature. First, in international trade theory, researchers have examined the welfare effects of foreign aid and, in particular, if aid can be donor-enriching and recipient-immiserizing – the so-called Transfer Paradox.[2] The main mechanism here is via changes in the international terms of trade. The primary benefit (loss) to the recipient (donor) can be offset by a secondary loss (gain) because of deterioration (improvement) in the international terms of trade. More recently, a number of studies have examined the possibility of strictly Pareto improving

---

[1] The repository of official information on aid is the Development Assistance Committee (DAC) of the OECD. DAC has two lists of countries. Members of list I are grouped into least developed countries (LLDCs), other low income countries (other LICs), low middle income countries (LMICs), upper middle income countries (UMICs) and high income countries (HICs). List II consists of countries who are in transition or reasonably advanced in the development process. These lists and classifications are updated on a regular basis. Aid given to members on list I is called official development assistance (ODA) and that to members of list II official aid (OA). ODA is further classified into bilateral (given directly by a donor country) and multilateral (given to international institutions like the World Bank for distribution). In most studies on aid, it is bilateral ODA that is examined. For aid to qualify as ODA, it has to satisfy three criteria: (i) it has to be undertaken by official agencies; (ii) it has to have the promotion of economic development as the main objective; and (iii) it has to have a grant element of 25% or more (more often than not, aid is simply a softer loan, rather than an outright grant. According to OECD convention, if the interest charged is more than 10%, the grant element is taken to be 0%, and the grant element is 100% for outright grants). There are two main points to be noted. First, private aid given via voluntary agencies is not counted as ODA. Second, military assistance is not counted either.

[2] Perhaps, this paradox had its inception in a debate between John Maynard Keynes and Bertil Ohlin in 1929 on the possibility of paradoxical effects of German reparations.

foreign aid, i.e., situations where both the donor and the recipient are better off as a result of the transfer.

The second strand in the literature comes from development economics, and the issue here is the effectiveness, or the lack of it, of foreign aid via mechanisms such as domestic savings and investment, foreign exchange, absorptive capacities, corruption, history, policies, etc. Some of the important questions asked in this strand of the literature are: why is aid often so ineffective? How can aid be made more effective? What factors determine the volume and the allocation of aid? How much aid should be provided by rich countries to poor countries? Should it be supply-determined such as the 0.7%-of-GDP rule or should it be demand-determined based on the needs of poor countries? How is aid distributed among recipients? Is the scaling up of aid necessarily good for the recipient countries? These are some of the important questions that one must have answers to before embarking on practical and effective aid policies.

This volume contains contributions on both sides of the literature and has equal emphasis to both sides. On the theoretical side, the analysis of the transfer paradox has evolved primarily in the context of traditional static models. However, given developments in the policy arena as well in the discipline itself, there is a need for further developments in the theoretical analysis of foreign aid. The theoretical contributions in this volume will do precisely that. For example, the impact of aid on saving, investment and growth calls for an inter-temporal framework, and this is done in Chapters 8–11.

In Chapter 8, Gil Epstein and Ira Gang develop a two-period model in which the donor can persuade the recipient to continue with the development project after aid is discontinued. Koji Shimomura in Chapter 9 analyzes the welfare effects of persistent aid in a fully dynamic two-country, two-good neoclassical growth model with borrowing constraints. He finds that it is possible that persistent untied aid benefits both the donor and the recipient. In Chapter 10, Yoshiyasu Ono also considers the possibility of consumption- and employment-increasing aid, but in a two-country, two-good fully dynamic monetary model that gives rise to liquidity trap. Finally, Chi-Chur Chao, Bharat Hazari, Jean-Pierre Laffargue and Eden Yu in Chapter 11 examine the possibility of recipient-immiserizing tied aid in the presence of import quota and externality from capital accumulation in the recipient country.

Recent development spatial economics in explaining core-periphery patterns calls for introduction of the spatial dimension to the analysis of foreign aid. In Chapter 3 Steven Brakman, Harry Garretsen and Charles van Marrewijk do precisely that. They examine the possibility/impossibility of Transfer Paradox in a number of settings including the presence and absence of a third bystander country that does not take part in transfers.

The issue of governance in the recipient country has been the subject of a large number of studies. In Chapter 2, Sugata Marjit and Vivekananda Mukherjee examine how foreign aid affects two aspects of governance, viz., adoption of "good" policies and corruption in the form of diverting away foreign aid from its intended use, and how these relationships are related to the level of development in the recipient country. The potential role of aid in conflict/war resolution is examined by Zsolt Becsi and Sajal

Lahiri in Chapter 1. In their model war is over some disputed land, and it is fought with soldiers (some of whom dies in the course of the war) and imported arms. They find that if the protective aspect of arms (protecting lives of soldiers) is significant, then foreign aid to two symmetric countries in a conflict would in fact increase the level of the conflict.

In Chapter 4, Hamid Beladi and Reza Oladi develop a three sector model with two private goods and one public, consumption good, the latter being financed by foreign aid. One of the private goods, viz., the sector producing the exportable, uses foreign capital. In this framework, they develop conditions under which foreign aid can lead to a reduction in foreign investment in the recipient country. Jai-Young Choi and Kwan Choi in Chapter 5 also consider a situation where foreign aid produces a public good, but unlike in Chapter 4, here the public good is a public input in a specific sector. They divide the urban sector into a formal and an informal one, allow for Harris–Todaro type unemployment, and examine the possibility of the Dutch Disease effect. Foreign aid finances a different kind of public good in Chapter 6 (written by Nikos Tsakiris, Panos Hatzipanayotou and Michael Michael), viz., the production of public abatement of pollution created by the producing sectors. There are polluting countries which are also the recipients of foreign aid from a donor country which suffers from cross-border pollution. Total amount of aid is fixed and the polluting countries compete for this aid. They show that whether the competition for aid reduces pollution or not depends on what policy instrument they compete with.

Finally, Chapter 7 by Slobodan Djajić examines the effect of foreign aid on emigration, welfare, and remittance flows in a two-country two good model with international mobility of labor.

Part II of this volume contains ten contributions. In Chapter 2, Howard White examines different methods of evaluating the impact of aid in reducing poverty. After discussing some of the methodologies, he presents three case studies in which project-level analyses at the country level are carried out. George Mavrotas in Chapter 13 examines the issue of recent call for scaled up foreign aid, particularly to countries in sub-Saharan Africa. A large increase in the flow of foreign aid opens up many opportunities, but it can also create many problems. He discusses most of the issues involved in a detailed and methodical way.

Chapters 14–17 are specifically about Africa. In Chapter 14, Channing Arndt, Sam Jones and Finn Tarp write comprehensively on the relationship between aid and development for Mozambique. They identify the specific mechanisms through which aid has influenced development in the country. With the help of both a growth accounting analysis and the micro-level analysis of intended and unintended effects of aid, they find that aid flows to Mozambique have made an unambiguous, positive contribution to rapid growth since 1992. They also find evidence that proliferation of donors and aid-supported interventions has burdened local administration in Mozambique. Arne Bigsten in Chapter 15 also identifies the overburdening of the recipient system as a key issue for Africa in general. This chapter reviews the determinants of, and the constraints to, growth in Africa, and how aid can potentially help relieve the constraints.

He pays particular attention to the choice of aid modalities, donor coordination, conditionality, and international integration.

In Chapter 16, Oliver Morrissey, Daniel M'Amanja and Tim Lloyd examine the aid-growth relationship for Kenya using annual time-series data for the period 1964–2002. They focus in particular on two channels in the said relationship, viz., the effect via changes in public spending and in public investment. They find that low productivity of public investment and the use of aid to finance budget deficits or aid fungibility are to a large extend responsible for the lack of positive effect of aid on growth. The issue of aid fungibility for the sub-Saharan African nations is at the heart of Chapter 17 (written by Shantayanan Devarajan, Andrew Sunil Rajkumar and Vinaya Swaroop) which uses Panel data for 18 sub-Saharan African countries for the period 1971–1995. They analyze the effect of aid on public spending, on current vis-à-vis capital spending, on debt servicing, and find varying degrees of fungibility. They also look at the fungibility of aid given to sectors such as energy, transport and communication, and education. They find nearly one-to-one effect for the education sector spending in sub-Saharan Africa. The effect of aid on primary enrollment and attainment is examined at length in Chapter 18 by Katja Michaelowa and Anke Weber. Using a dynamic panel analysis, they find positive effects. However, they find the magnitude of the effect to be small: an increase of current aid by 200% would raise primary enrollment by 2.5 percentage points.

The last three chapters use Panel data for a wider set of developing countries than only for sub-Saharan Africa, but focus on different issues. Subhayu Bandyopadhyay and Howard Wall in Chapter 19 examine the determinants of aid in the post-Cold War era. They find that, on the whole, countries with lower per capita income, higher infant mortality, better human rights record and more effective government, have received higher amount of aid. In Chapter 20, Scott Gilbert and Kevin Sylwester examines whether aid is better in promoting growth in historically advantaged as opposed to disadvantaged countries, and find that history does matter. Finally, the issue of scaling up of foreign aid and its potential effect on recipient countries are analyzed by Jonathan Munemo, Subhayu Bandyopadhyay and Arabinda Basistha in Chapter 21. In particular, they look at the long run effect on export performance and find evidence of large amount of foreign aid adversely affecting export performance for the whole sample as well as for sub samples.

PART I

Theory of Aid

CHAPTER 1

Conflict in the Presence of Arms Trade: Can Foreign Aid Reduce Conflict?

Zsolt Becsi and Sajal Lahiri

Department of Economics, Southern Illinois University at Carbondale, Carbondale, IL 62901, USA
E-mail adresses: becsi@siu.edu; lahiri@siu.edu

Abstract

We construct a specific-factor trade-theoretic model for two small open economies that are in conflict with each other and where war efforts are determined endogenously. War efforts involve the use of soldiers and imported military hardware. The purpose of war is to capture disputed land or some other resource, but with war lives are lost and production is sacrificed. In this framework, we examine the effect of foreign aid on the war efforts in the warring countries. We find, *inter alia*, that an increase foreign aid to the warring countries may increase war efforts when arms protect lives in a significant way.

Keywords: War, trade, conflict resolution, foreign aid, nash equilibrium, deaths

JEL classifications: F02, F11, H56, H77

1. Introduction

Compared to traditional labor-intensive wars, modern warfare has become much more capital intensive as weapons technology has become more deadly. Indeed, it is safe to say that the Twentieth Century was the bloodiest century ever, reaching an apex with World War II when approximately 40–55 million people died (Clodfelter, 2002). Since then wars have been fought on a smaller scale, shifting from international conflicts among a variety of nations to mainly intranational conflicts among developing nations.[1] Given the deadliness of modern warfare, we are interested in understanding

---

[1] According to Gleditsch (2004), there were 199 international wars and 251 civil wars between 1816 and 2002. International wars historically made up the bulk of all wars. However, since World War II, the number of international wars has steadily declined and they have been replaced by civil wars as the predominant form of violent conflict in the world.

THEORY AND PRACTICE OF FOREIGN AID
VOLUME 1   ISSN: 1574-8715
DOI: 10.1016/S1574-8715(06)01001-3

what economic forces can lead to conflict reduction. In particular, can the international community help reduce conflicts by using carrots such as foreign aid?[2]

How the arms trade affects conflict is not well understood. Anderton (1995) reviews the economic literature on the arms trade and concludes that it has not provided much in the way of theoretical or empirical understanding of how the arms trade is related to conflict. Though some attempts at modeling arms trade in trade theoretic models have been made, the focus has been more on the behavior of arms suppliers of major weapons systems (for instance, Levine and Smith, 1995) rather than the forces driving conflict and arms demand for light weapons which account for most of the fatalities in recent conflicts. International arms markets are such that most arms purchases are fairly easy to make. The international arms market is fairly open and competitive, with arms flowing from North to South that are encouraged by large subsidies from exporter governments and excess capacity after the end of the Cold War (Brzoska, 2001, and Markusen, 2004). However, the extent of the market is not well measured. While the legal world trade volume in weapons is roughly estimated at around $50 billion in the mid-1990s, the illegal trade volume (which includes illegal weapons sales and covert sales by governments) is unknown (Brzoska, 2001). Thus, the arms market appears to be small, but this does not mean that the arms trade has a small effect on conflict or that arms flows are any less deadly.

The arms trade tends to raise the costs of warfare relative to the benefits. If the benefits from warfare usually come from a gain of territory and resources, the costs of warfare are of two different types. The first cost of warfare is due to fore-gone production as resources are diverted towards warfare. This cost, which has been the focus of the recent trade theoretic literature on conflict (Skaperdas and Syropoulos, 2001, Syropoulos, 2004, Becsi and Lahiri, 2007),[3] has been estimated by Collier and Hoeffler (2007) as being roughly the equivalent of one years GDP for the typical developing country engaged in civil war. The second more visible cost of warfare is the human cost of warfare from death, disease, and displace-ment. The human cost has not been incorporated into modern analyses of conflict though it can easily exceed the production costs. The human cost of warfare has been estimated by Collier and Hoeffler (2007) as being roughly the equivalent of another one to two years of the initial GDP for the typical developing country en-gaged in civil war. Collier and Hoeffler acknowledge that the human cost may even

---

[2] According to Elbadawi and Sambanis (2000), there have been 89 external interventions in 139 civil wars since 1944 and if repeated interventions are counted then the total rises to 190 interventions.

[3] There is now a significant theoretical and empirical literature on the economics of conflict. The theoret-ical literature follows the seminal work of Hirshleifer (1988) and develops game-theoretic models where two rival groups allocate resources between productive and appropriative activities (see, for example, Brito and Intriligator (1985), Hirshleifer (1995), Grossman and Kim (1996), Skaperdas (1992), Neary (1997), and Skaperdas and Syropoulos (2002)). Recent contributions by Anderton *et al.* (1999), Skaperdas and Sy-ropoulos (1996, 2001), Garfinkel *et al.* (2004), and Findlay and Amin (2000) emphasize trade and conflict in two-country frameworks and Becsi and Lahiri (2007) consider a three-country model. Anderson and Marcouiller (2005) examine the consequences of endogenous transaction costs in the form of predation on international trade.

be higher because total war deaths are not always easily measured.[4] By failing to incorporate the human cost of warfare into previous analytical frameworks, the literature misses the humanitarian arguments that have shaped policies relating to war.

To explore the aid-arms trade-conflict nexus, we develop a two-good specific-factor trade-theoretic model. Our framework has two regions that trade with each other and are engaged in conflict. Our framework not only applies to civil wars but also to situations where two developing countries are engaged in conflict or two groups within a country are fighting each other.[5] The adversaries may choose to direct resources from productive activity to war where the conflict is over a factor of production (land). The conflict equilibrium is specified as a Nash one where each warring country decides on its war effort taking as given the war effort of the adversary as well as all international prices (small open economy case). The model is closely related to that of Becsi and Lahiri (2007, 2006), except that we add an additional input into conflict production (weapons) that is traded internationally. Though it is very common in the literature to consider a single input in a war production, having two inputs allows us to distinguish between inputs that are not traded internationally (soldiers) and those that are traded (weapons), with the effectiveness of one input affecting the other. Also, weapons now have two roles: an aggressive role in meeting the objectives of a war and a defensive role in protecting the lives of soldiers. Another difference with our previous work is that we also allow battle deaths to occur with the effect of reducing aggregate welfare. This consideration allows us to introduce 'income effects' in the war equilibrium. Although it widely believed that lack of resources and poverty is an important cause of war,[6] 'income effects' are usually missing from the specification of the war equilibrium in most existing theoretical models.[7] Thus, previous models are not very appropriate for analyzing, for example, the impact of foreign aid on war.[8]

---

[4] Recent work by Lacina and Gleditsch (2005) distinguishes between battle deaths, defined as civilians and soldiers killed in the course of combat, and total war deaths which also include deaths from disease, starvation, riots, and crime. They argue that battle deaths, while more easily measured than non-battle deaths, can significantly underestimate total war deaths as seen from the 1998–2001 civil war in the Democratic Republic of Congo where battle deaths were only one sixth of total war deaths.

[5] While some may think that civil wars and international wars are analytically distinct, we focus on features that are shared by both types of wars such as insecure property rights.

[6] See, for example, Tilly (1975), Dréze and Sen (1989), Homer-Dixon (1999), and Grossman and Mendoza (2003).

[7] Resources typically only affect the war equilibrium through changes in factor and commodity prices.

[8] An exception is Grossman (1992) although in his model aid works via a different mechanism, viz., aid increases conflict by increasing the size of the prize for rebels. In Collier and Hoeffler (2002) aid reduces conflict because governments divert aid towards greater protection against rebellion. That the effect of aid may vary according to the environment, was noted by Uvin (1999) who stresses that aid may have incentive or disincentive effects depending on the aid is administered.

The purpose of this paper is to address the above-mentioned shortcomings of the existing literature, and then examine the effects of foreign aid on conflicts.[9] We find that an increase in aid leads to an increase in soldiers and weapons for the adversaries and thus ultimately to an increase in conflict intensity as measured by greater battle deaths. Our results depend critically on a protective effect of weapons that is large with diminishing returns, which implies a higher value of life and also that indirect income effects of the various shocks determine the number of soldiers. This additional income effect is missing in Becsi and Lahiri (2007) who find that aid or terms of trade improvements reduces the number of soldiers and conflict intensity with only one input into conflict production. Although the underlying models are completely different, our current results resemble the findings of Grossman (1992) where aid also leads to more conflict, while in Becsi and Lahiri (2007) where there were no weapons and war deaths our conclusions resembled those of Collier and Hoeffler (2002).

The plan of the paper is as follows. In the next Section 2 we spell out our model structure. Section 3 derives the war equilibrium and performs initial analysis of the model. Section 4 will then be concerned with the analysis of the effect of foreign aid on the war equilibrium. Some concluding remarks are made in Section 5.

2. The model

We develop a two-region, two-good, many-factor model where the regions – labeled region a and region b – are engaged in a war with each other. All product and factor markets are perfectly competitive and the regions act like small open economies in international markets. There are many inelastically supplied factors of production; however, two of the factors play important roles in our analysis. For expositional ease, we shall call these factors labor and land although one could interpret them differently. A part of labor endowment is used in production and the rest is used to fight the war and land is what they fight for. Each region i ($i = a, b$) has an amount of land $\bar{V}^i$ that is undisputed, and the war is about a disputed amount of land denoted by X. For simplicity and without loss of any generality we shall assume that the disputed land is initially in possession of region b. Regions fight over the disputed land by employing soldiers L_s^a and L_s^b and buying military hardware A^a and A^b from the international market. We define $f(L_s^a, L_s^b, A^a, A^b)X$ as the net gain of land by country a from war. The net gain function for country a increases when more fighting forces and military hardware – L_s^a and A^a – are committed to conflict but decreases when the opposition increases its fighting forces L_s^b and hardware A^b. In other words, actions of adversaries create a negative externality through the net gain function. For this net-gain function we make the following assumptions.

---

[9] Hufbauer *et al.* (1990) provide a large number of case studies on the effect of external interventions on conflicts.

ASSUMPTION 1. The function $f(\cdot)$ satisfies: $f_1 > 0$, $f_2 < 0$, $f_3 > 0$, $f_4 < 0$, $f_{33} < 0$, $f_{44} > 0$, $f_{11} < 0$, $f_{13} > 0$, $f_{24} > 0$, and $f_{22} > 0$.

The assumption that $f_{13} > 0$ and $f_{24} > 0$ implies that soldiers and military hardware complement each other in war.

The production side of the economies indexed by $i = a, b$ is described by three revenue functions $R^a(p, \bar{L}^a - L_s^a, \bar{V}^a + f(L_s^a, L_s^b, A^a, A^b)X)$, and $R^b(p, \bar{L}^b - L_s^b, \bar{V}^b + (1 - f(L_s^a, L_s^b, A^a, A^b))X)$ where $\bar{L}^i$ and $\bar{V}^i$ are the endowments of labor and land respectively in country i, p is the international price of the non-numeraire goods.[10] We assume that the two factors are complements, i.e., $R_{23}^i > 0$, $i = a, b$.

Some of the soldiers die in the course of the war, and the representative consumers suffer some disutility from it. For analytical convenience, we assume that no civilians die. The number of soldiers that die is denoted by D^i and gives a measure of the intensity of conflict. Deaths of soldiers and the utility of the consumer u^i, in country i ($i = a, b$) are determined by

$$D^i = \bar{g}^i(L_s^a, L_s^b, A^a, A^b), \tag{1}$$

$$u^i = \tilde{u}^i - h^i(D^i) = \tilde{u}^i - g^i(L_s^a, L_s^b, A^a, A^b), \quad i = a, b, \tag{2}$$

where $\tilde{u}^i$ is the utility from the consumption of goods and the disutility function g^i is assumed to satisfy

ASSUMPTION 2. $g^i(L_s^a, L_s^b, A^a, A^b)$ is additively separable, i.e., $g^i(L_s^a, L_s^b, A^a, A^b) = \bar{g}_a^i(L_s^a, A^a) + \bar{g}_b^i(L_s^b, A^b)$ so that $g_{12}^i = g_{34}^i = g_{14}^i = g_{23}^i = 0$. It is also assumed to satisfy $g_1^i > 0$, $g_2^i > 0$, $g_3^i < 0$, $g_4^i > 0$, $g_3^b > 0$, $g_4^b < 0$, $g_{11}^i < 0$, $g_{22}^i < 0$, $g_{13}^i < 0$, $g_{33}^a > 0$, $g_{24}^a < 0$, $g_{33}^b < 0$, $g_{44}^a < 0$, $g_{44}^b > 0$ ($i = a, b$).

The assumptions that g_3^a, g_4^b, g_{13}^a and g_{24}^b are all negative capture the defensive or protective roles of military hardware. That is, military hardware is assumed to protect the lives of soldiers. This is in contrast to the net gain function $f(\cdot)$ which has an aggressive role in the sense that f_3^a, f_4^b, f_{13}^a and f_{24}^b are all positive.

Given the above utility function, the consumption side of the economies is represented by the expenditure functions $E^a(p, u^a + g^a(\cdot))$ and $E^b(p, u^b + g^b(\cdot))$.[11]

---

[10] All factors other than land and labor are suppressed in the revenue functions as they do not change in our analysis. As is well known, the partial derivative of a revenue function with respect to the price of a good gives the output supply function of that good. Similarly, the partial derivative of a revenue function with respect to a factor endowment gives the price of that factor. The revenue functions are positive semi-definite in prices and negative semi-definite in the endowments of the factors of production. In particular, they satisfy $R_{jj}^i \leq 0$, for $i = a, b, c$ and $j = 2, 3$. For these and other properties of revenue functions see Dixit and Norman (1980).

[11] The partial derivative of an expenditure function with respect to the price of a good gives the compensated demand function of that good, and that with respect to the utility level is the reciprocal of the marginal utility of income.

Normalizing $X = 1$, the income-expenditure balance equations of consumers in the two countries are given by:

$$E^a\left(p, u^a + g^a(\cdot)\right) = R^a\left(p, \bar{L}^a - L_s^a, \bar{V}^a + f(\cdot)\right) + R_2^a L_s^a + F^a - T^a, \qquad (3)$$

$$E^b\left(p, u^b + g^b(\cdot)\right) = R^b\left(p, \bar{L}^b - L_s^b, \bar{V}^b + 1 - f(\cdot)\right) + R_2^b L_s^b + F^b - T^b, \qquad (4)$$

where F^i is the amount of aid received by country i. The second term on the right-hand side of (3) and (4) – $R_2^a L_s^a$ and $R_2^b L_s^b$ respectively – is the income of the soldiers in the two countries. The terms T^a and T^b are lump-sum taxes on the consumers in the two countries.

We assume that the expenditure on war effort is paid for in the two warring countries by taxation of the consumers.[12] That is, the governments' budget-balance equations are given by

$$T^i = R_2^i L_s^i + p^A A^i, \quad i = a, b, \qquad (5)$$

where and p^A is the price of military hardware.

As for the international prices, the warring countries are assumed to be small open economies so that p and p^A are exogenous.

Although we refer to the adversaries a and b as countries, they can be interpreted as two different regions within a country and thus war in this paper can be interpreted as a civil war. However, this interpretation should not be taken to imply that the present model can explain all types of civil war which can be very heterogeneous. The type of civil wars that we model are those where the warring groups live in two distinct regions in a country with no mobility of labor between the two regions, and they fight over the ownership of a factor of production. There are some civil wars which satisfy the stylized facts of our model. For example, in the Tamil conflict in Sri Lanka the warring groups are restricted geographically with the Tamil rebels living mostly in the Jaffna region in the north of the country and with very limited mobility of labor. In other words, we are interested in conflicts with a sufficient amount of spatial separation or polarization amongst the population. Furthermore, for the civil war interpretation, we do not distinguish which side is the government side and which side is the rebel side. We assume that there is some form of governance for each side which can raise funds through taxation.

3. The War equilibrium

In this section, we derive the war equilibrium and perform some responses of that equilibrium of soldiers and imported arms.

---

[12] This particular aspect of financing war efforts makes war in our model a business of governments. In other words, we cannot model war process as being run by private firms (mercenaries) with no power over taxation.

We begin by substituting (5) into (3) and (4) and then differentiating Equations (3) and (4), we obtain

$$E_2^a \, du^a = \left[f_1 R_3^a - R_2^a - E_2^a g_1^a \right] dL_s^a + \left[R_3^a f_3 - E_2^a g_3^a - p^A \right] dA^a$$
$$+ \left[R_3^a f_2 - E_2^a g_2^a \right] dL_s^b + \left[R_3^a f_4 - E_2^a g_4^a \right] dA^b + dF^a, \tag{6}$$

$$E_2^b \, du^b = \left[-f_2 R_3^b - R_2^b - E_2^b g_2^b \right] dL_s^b + \left[-R_3^b f_4 - E_2^a g_4^b - p^A \right] dA^b$$
$$+ \left[-R_3^b f_1 - E_2^b g_1^b \right] dL_s^a + \left[-R_3^b f_3 - E_2^b g_3^b \right] dA^a + dF^b. \tag{7}$$

The first and the second terms in (6) and (7) give the effects of increased war efforts (both soldiers and imported arms) by a country on its own welfare. The benefit for the country of employing more soldiers is the additional output from appropriated land, while the costs are the loss of output because labor is diverted from the productive sector to the war sector and increased disutility from the death of soldiers. The third and the fourth terms in (6) and (7) give the international conflict externalities from war effort on the two warring countries. Higher war efforts by one country (either by the employment of more soldiers or by the imports of more arms), *ceteris paribus*, reduces the adversary's utility by reducing the adversary's endowment of land and by increasing fatalities. The direct effect of foreign aid is to increase welfare in the recipient countries, and these effects are given by the last term in (6)–(7).

We can now describe how war efforts in the two warring countries, L_s^a, L_s^b, A^a and A^b are determined. Following Skaperdas and Syropoulos (2001), we assume that each warring country decides on the levels of its own war effort by maximizing its welfare level, taking war efforts in the other country as given. The first order conditions are given by:

$$E_2^a \frac{\partial u^a}{\partial L_s^a} = f_1 R_3^a - R_2^a - E_2^a g_1^a = 0, \tag{8}$$

$$E_2^a \frac{\partial u^a}{\partial A^a} = R_3^a f_3 - E_2^a g_3^a - p^A = 0, \tag{9}$$

$$E_2^b \frac{\partial u^b}{\partial L_s^b} = -f_2 R_3^b - R_2^b - E_2^b g_2^b = 0, \tag{10}$$

$$E_2^b \frac{\partial u^b}{\partial A^b} = -R_3^b f_4 - E_2^a g_4^b - p^A = 0. \tag{11}$$

An increase in L_s^i, *ceteris paribus*, increases income in country i ($i = a, b$) by increasing the amount of land, but it also has costs in the sense that it reduces the amount of labor than can be used for producing goods and services, and increases the disutility from the death of soldiers. The first term in (8) and (10) is the marginal benefit of warfare, and the second term and third are the marginal costs. Similarly, an increase in the imports of arms has costs in terms of the direct costs of imports, but it also benefits the country by increasing the amount land and by reducing the death of soldiers. The first two terms in (9) and (11) are the marginal benefits, and the third terms are the marginal costs.

Henceforth we assume that the two countries are symmetric so that $L_s^a = L_s^b$, $A^a = A^b$, $f(\cdot) = 0$, $f_1 = -f_2$, $f_3 = -f_4$, $g_3 = -g_4$, $f_{12} = f_{14} = f_{32} = f_{34} = 0$.[13] Using the country-specific superscript a for variables in both countries, the first order condition (8)–(11) can be rewritten as:

$$f_1 R_3^a - R_2^a - E_2^a g_1^a = 0,\tag{12}$$

$$R_3^a f_3 - E_2^a g_3^a - p^A = 0.\tag{13}$$

These two equations can now be solved for L_s^a and A^a in terms of F^a.

Differentiating (12) and (13) we obtain respectively:

$$\left[f_{11}R_3^a - f_1 R_{32}^a + R_{22}^a - g_{11}^a E_2^a - g_1^a\left(g_1^a + g_2^a\right)E_{22}^a\right]dL_s$$
$$= g_1^a E_{22}^a du^a - \left[f_{13}R_3^a - E_2^a g_{13}^a\right]dA,\tag{14}$$

$$\left[R_3^a f_{33} - E_2^a g_{33}^a\right]dA$$
$$= g_3^a E_{22}^a du^a - \left[R_3^a f_{31} - E_2^a g_{31}^a - f_3 R_{32}^a - g_3^a\left(g_1^a + g_2^a\right)E_{22}^a\right]dL_s.\tag{15}$$

The above two equations tell us how an increase in the utility levels affect respectively the employment of soldiers (for a given level of A) and the imports of arms (for a given level of L_s). From (14) we find that $\partial L_s/\partial u^a < 0$ if E_2^a is not too large, i.e., if the warring countries are sufficiently poor so that their marginal utility of income $(1/E_2^a)$ is large enough.[14] The reason for the dominant negative effect of utility on L_s is that an increase in real income reduces the marginal utility of income and therefore increases the marginal cost of employment of soldiers arising due to death of soldiers (the last term in (12)). From (15) we find that $\partial A/\partial u^a > 0$. That is, the effect of an increase in real income on the imports arms is just the opposite of the effect on the employment of soldiers. The reason for this asymmetry is that where an increase in income reduces the marginal cost of employing soldiers, it increases the marginal benefit of importing arms by preventing the death of additional soldiers.

Substituting (12) and (13) in (6), we get a system of equations that determines the Nash responses

$$E_2^a du^a = dF^a + \left(R_3^a f_2 - E_2^a g_2^a\right)dL_s + \left(R_3^a f_4 - E_2^a g_4^a\right)dA.\tag{16}$$

Substituting (16) in (14) and (15), we obtain

$$\alpha_{11}\,dL_s + \alpha_{12}\,dA = \frac{g_1^a E_{22}^a}{E_2^a}\cdot dF^a,\tag{17}$$

$$\alpha_{21}\,dL_s + \alpha_{22}\,dA = \frac{g_3^a E_{22}^a}{E_2^a}\cdot dF^a,\tag{18}$$

---

[13] It can be verified that if the functions f and g take the form $f(L_s^a, A^a, L_s^b, A^b) = ((h^a(L_s^a) + k^a(A^a))/(h^a(L_s^a) + h^b(L_s^b) + k^a(A^a) + k^b(A^b)))X$ and $g(L_s^a, A^a, L_s^b, A^b) = (\bar h^a(L_s^a) + \bar k^a(A^a))/(\bar h^a(L_s^a) + \bar h^b(L_s^b) + \bar k^a(A^a) + \bar k^b(A^b))$, these restrictions will be satisfied under symmetry.
[14] If E_2^a is very large then the negative effect of an increase in soldiers on the marginal cost of employing a soldier given by $E_2^a g_{11}^a$ can be significant.

where

$$\alpha_{11} = f_{11} R_3^a - f_1 R_{32}^a + R_{22}^a - g_{11}^a E_2^a - \frac{g_1^a E_{22}^a (R_3^a f_2 - E_2^a g_1^a)}{E_2^a},$$

$$\alpha_{12} = f_{13} R_3^a - E_2^a g_{13}^a - \frac{g_1^a E_{22}^a (R_3^a f_4 - E_2^a g_4^a)}{E_2^a},$$

$$\alpha_{21} = R_3^a f_{31} - E_2^a g_{31}^a - f_3 R_{32}^a - \frac{g_3^a E_{22}^a (R_3^a f_2 - E_2^a g_1^a)}{E_2^a},$$

$$\alpha_{22} = R_3^a f_{33} - E_2^a g_{33}^a - \frac{g_3^a E_{22}^a (R_3^a f_4 - E_2^a g_4^a)}{E_2^a}.$$

We note that from the second order conditions relating the war equilibrium, we must have:

$$\alpha_{11} < 0, \alpha_{22} < 0 \quad \text{and} \quad \Delta = \alpha_{11}\alpha_{22} - \alpha_{12}\alpha_{21} > 0. \tag{19}$$

Furthermore, because of Assumptions 1 and 2 it follows that $\alpha_{12} > 0$.

It may be interesting to note the implications of the fact that $\alpha_{12} > 0$. A positive value of α_{12} means that an increase in the level of arms imports, *ceteris paribus*, will result in an increase the number of soldiers. That is, $dL_s/dA > 0$ along the L_s–A locus satisfying (17). This is because an increase in A reduces the utility level by increasing the negative externality from one country's war efforts on the utility level of the other country. This decrease in utility, *inter alia*, increases the marginal utility of income $(1/E_2^a)$ and therefore reduces the part of the marginal cost of employing soldiers which arises due to disutility from death (given by the third term on the left-hand side of (12)). An increase in the imports of soldiers will also reduce the utility level. However, in sharp contrast to the previous case, the resulting increase in the marginal utility of income decreases the part of the marginal benefit of arms imports which is given by the second term on the left-hand side of (12). Thus it is possible that $dA/dL_s < 0$ along the A–L_s locus satisfying (18) resulting in an negative value of α_{21}.

4. Foreign aid and conflict

Solving (17) and (18) simultaneously for dL_s and dA we can examine the effects of changes in foreign aid F^a on the levels of war activities measured by the number for soldiers L_s and amount of arms imports A, in the two warring countries. From (17) and (18) we get

$$\frac{E_2^a \Delta}{E_{22}^a} \cdot \frac{dL_s}{dF^a} = [g_1^a \alpha_{22} - g_3^a \alpha_{12}]$$

$$= R_3^a [g_1^a f_{33} - g_3^a f_{13}] + E_2^a [g_3^a g_{13}^a - g_1^a g_{33}^a]$$

$$= \frac{f_3 g^a R_3^a}{AL_s} \cdot [\epsilon_A^g \epsilon_{AL}^f - \epsilon_L^g \epsilon_{AL}^f] + \frac{g^a g_3^a E_2^a}{AL_s} \cdot [\epsilon_A^g \epsilon_{AL}^g - \epsilon_L^g \epsilon_{AA}^g], \tag{20}$$

$$\frac{E_2^a \Delta}{E_{22}^a} \cdot \frac{dA}{dF^a} = \left[g_3^a \alpha_{11} - g_1^a \alpha_{21} \right]$$

$$= g_3^a R_{22}^a + R_{32}^a \left[f_3 g_1^a - f_1 g_3^a \right]$$

$$+ R_3^a \left[g_3^a f_{11} - g_1^a f_{31} \right] + E_2^a \left[g_1^a g_{31}^a - g_3^a g_{11}^a \right]$$

$$= g_3^a R_{22}^a + R_{32}^a \left[f_3 g_1^a - f_1 g_3^a \right]$$

$$+ \frac{g^a f_1 R_3^a}{A L_s} \cdot \left[\epsilon_A^g \epsilon_{LL}^f - \epsilon_L^g \epsilon_{LA}^f \right] + E_2^a \left[g_1^a g_{31}^a - g_3^a g_{11}^a \right], \qquad (21)$$

where

$$\epsilon_L^g = \frac{\partial g^a}{\partial L_s^a} \cdot \frac{L_s}{g^a} = \frac{g_1^a L_s}{g^a}, \qquad \epsilon_A^g = -\frac{\partial g^a}{\partial A^a} \cdot \frac{A}{g^a} = -\frac{g_3^a A}{g^a},$$

$$\epsilon_{AA}^f = -\frac{\partial f_3}{\partial A^a} \cdot \frac{A}{f_3} = -\frac{f_{33} A}{f_3}, \qquad \epsilon_{AL}^f = \frac{\partial f_3}{\partial L_s^a} \cdot \frac{L_s}{f_3} = \frac{f_{31} L_s}{f_3},$$

$$\epsilon_{LL}^f = -\frac{\partial f_1}{\partial L_s^a} \cdot \frac{L_s}{f_1} = -\frac{f_{11} L_s}{f_1}, \qquad \epsilon_{LA}^f = \frac{\partial f_1}{\partial A^a} \cdot \frac{A}{f_1} = \frac{f_{13} A}{f_1},$$

$$\epsilon_{AA}^g = \frac{\partial g_3^a}{\partial A^a} \cdot \frac{A}{g_3^a} = -\frac{g_{33}^a A}{g_3^a}, \qquad \epsilon_{AL}^g = \frac{\partial g_3^a}{\partial L_s^a} \cdot \frac{L_s}{g_3^a} = \frac{g_{31}^a L_s}{g_3^a},$$

$$\epsilon_{LL}^g = -\frac{\partial g_1^a}{\partial L_s^a} \cdot \frac{L_s}{g_1^a} = -\frac{g_{11}^a L_s}{g_1^a}, \qquad \epsilon_{LA}^g = -\frac{\partial g_1^a}{\partial A^a} \cdot \frac{A}{g_1^a} = -\frac{g_{13}^a A}{g_1^a}.$$

From (20), we find that an increase in foreign aid will decrease the employment of soldiers if $\epsilon_A^g \epsilon_{AL}^f - \epsilon_L^g \epsilon_{AL}^f < 0$ and $\epsilon_A^g \epsilon_{AL}^g - \epsilon_L^g \epsilon_{AA}^g > 0$. Also, an increase in foreign aid will increase the employment of soldiers if $\epsilon_A^g \epsilon_{AL}^f - \epsilon_L^g \epsilon_{AL}^f > 0$ and $\epsilon_A^g \epsilon_{AL}^g - \epsilon_L^g \epsilon_{AA}^g < 0$. As for the imports of arms, it is clear that if α_{21} is negative, it follows from the first line of (21) that an increase in foreign aid will increase the amount of arms imports. In general, from the last line of (21) we find that $dA/dF^a > 0$ if, for example, $\epsilon_A^g \epsilon_{LL}^f \gg \epsilon_L^g \epsilon_{LA}^f$ so that the effect of the last terms in (21) (which is the only negative term) is outweighed. Combining the results, we can state that an increase in foreign aid will raise warfare by increasing both the employment of soldiers and the imports of arms if ϵ_A^g is sufficiently large. Formally,

PROPOSITION 1. *An increase in foreign aid to two symmetric warring countries will increase the employment of soldiers and the imports of arms in both countries if the effect of arms on the protection of the lives of soldiers is very significant.*

Intuitively, as we have seen before the direct effect of an increase in income (induced by foreign aid) will reduce the employment of soldiers and increase the imports of arms, and the magnitude of the increase in arms imports is positively related to the magnitude of ϵ_A^g which signifies the degree of protectiveness of arms (for soldiers' lives). As we have also discussed before, an increase in arms imports has a positive indirect effect on the employment of soldiers ($\alpha_{12} > 0$). If ϵ_A^g is sufficiently high the indirect effect will dominate the direct effect and an increase in foreign aid will increase both L_s and A.

5. *Conclusion*

Since military conflicts – whether between nations or between groups within a nation – are widespread, not surprisingly a rich body academic literature has developed in both political science and economics. In economics, a small but significant theoretical literature discussing various economic aspects of military conflicts has grown over the last twenty years or so. In this paper, we contribute to this theoretical literature by explicitly considering two factors. First, we consider the substitution possibilities between two inputs in warfare: soldiers and imported military hardware. Second, we allow for death of soldiers in warfare and disutility that such deaths entail. Under this framework we examine the effects of foreign aid on the levels of warfare in two symmetric warring countries or regions.

The second innovation mentioned above allows us to introduce income effects in the war equilibrium. For example, an increase in foreign aid to warring countries increases their income and therefore their marginal disutility from loss of life increases. This reduces soldiers employed in warfare. On the other hand, an increase in income (because of foreign aid by other means) and the resulting increase in the marginal disutility from death induces a country to import more military hardware which can protect the lives of soldiers. These contrasting effects of a higher income on the two inputs in warfare gives a number of interesting and surprising results. For example, we find that foreign aid to the two warring countries can actually increase both the employment of soldiers and the imports of military hardware in the two warring countries. This is clearly undesirable.

References

Anderton, C.H. (1995), Economics of arms trade. In: Hartley, K., Sandler, T. (Eds.), *Handbook of Defense Economics, vol. 1*. North-Holland, Amsterdam, pp. 523–561.

Anderson, J.E., Marcouiller, D. (2005), Anarchy and autarky: endogenous predation as a barrier to trade. *International Economic Review* 46, 189–213.

Anderton, C.H., Anderton, R.A., Carter, J.R. (1999), Economic activity in the shadow of conflict. *Economic Inquiry* 37, 166–179.

Becsi, Z., Lahiri, S. (2006), The relationship between resources and conflict: a synthesis, *Discussion Paper*, No. 2006-03, Department of Economics, Southern Illinois University Carbondale.

Becsi, Z., Lahiri, S. (2007), Bilateral war in a multilateral world: carrots and sticks for conflict resolution. *Canadian Journal of Economics*, in press.

Brito, D.L., Intriligator, M.D. (1985), Conflict, war, and redistribution. *American Political Science Review* 79, 943–957.

Brzoska, M. (2001), Taxation of the arms trade: An overview of the issues. Paper prepared for the United Nations ad hoc Expert Group Meeting on Innovations in Mobilizing Global Resources for Development, 25–26 June 2001.

Clodfelter, M. (2002), *Warfare and Armed Conflicts: A Statistical Reference to Casualty and Other Figures, 1500–2000*. McFarland, Jefferson, NC.

Collier, P., Hoeffler, A. (2002), Aid, policy and peace: reducing the risks of civil conflict. *Defense and Peace Economics* 13, 435–450.

Collier, P., Hoeffler, A. (2007), Civil war. In: Sandler, T., Hartley, K. (Eds.), *Handbook of Defense Economics, vol. 2*. Elsevier, Amsterdam, in press.

Dixit, A.K., Norman, V. (1980), *Theory of International Trade*. Cambridge University Press, Cambridge, UK.

Drèze, J., Sen, A. (1989), *Hunger and Public Action*. Clarendon, Oxford.

Elbadawi, I.A., Sambanis, N. (2000), External interventions and the duration of civil wars. Presented at the World Bank's Development Economic Research Group Conference on "The Economics and Politics of Civil Conflicts" at Princeton University, New Jersey, March 2000.

Findlay, R., Amin, M. (2000), *National Security and International Trade: A Simple General Equilibrium Model*. Department of Economics, Columbia University, New York.

Garfinkel, M.R., Skaperdas, S., Syropoulos, C. (2004), *Globalization and Domestic Conflict*. Department of Economics, Drexel University, Pennsylvania.

Gleditsch, K. (2004), A Revised list of wars between and within independent states, 1816–2002. *International Interactions* 30, 231–262.

Grossman, H.I. (1992), Foreign aid and insurrection. *Defence Economics* 3, 275–288.

Grossman, H.I., Kim, M. (1996), Swords or plowshares? A theory of the security of claims to property. *Journal of Political Economy* 103, 1275–1288.

Grossman, H.I., Mendoza, J. (2003), Scarcity and appropriative competition. *European Journal of Political Economy* 19, 747–758.

Hirshleifer, J. (1988), The analytics of continuing conflict. *Synthese* 76, 201–233.

Hirshleifer, J. (1995), Anarchy and its breakdown. *Journal of Political Economy* 103, 26–52.

Homer-Dixon, T.F. (1999), *Environment, Scarcity, and Violence*. Princeton University Press, Princeton, NJ.

Hufbauer, G.C., Schott, J.J., Elliott, K.A. (1990), *Economic Sanctions Reconsidered: History and Current Policy*, second ed. Institute for International Economics, Washington, DC.

Lacina, B., Gleditsch, N.P. (2005), Monitoring trends in global combat: a new dataset of battle deaths. *European Journal of Population* 21, 145–166.

Levine, P., Smith, R. (1995), The arms trade and arms control. *Economic Journal* 105, 471–484.

Markusen, A. (2004), The arms trade as illiberal trade. In: Brauer, J., Dunne, J.P. (Eds.), *Arms Trade and Economic Development: Theory, Policy, and Cases in ArmsTrade Offsets*. Routledge, London, pp. 66–88.

Neary, H.M. (1997), A comparison of rent-seeking models and economic models of conflict. *Public Choice* 93, 373–388.

Skaperdas, S. (1992), Cooperation, conflict, and power in the absence of property rights. *American Economic Review* 82, 720–739.

Skaperdas, S., Syropoulos, C. (1996), Competitive trade with conflict. In: Garfinkel, M.R., Skaperdas, S. (Eds.), *The Political Economy of Conflict and Appropriation.* Cambridge University Press, Cambridge, pp. 73–96.

Skaperdas, S., Syropoulos, C. (2001), Guns, butter, and openness: on the relationship between security and trade. *American Economic Review, Papers and Proceedings* 91, 353–357.

Skaperdas, S., Syropoulos, C. (2002), Insecure property and the efficiency of exchange. *Economic Journal* 112, 133–146.

Syropoulos, C. (2004), Trade openness and international conflict. Presented at the conference 'New Dimensions in International Trade: Outsourcing, Merger, Technology Transfer, and Culture,' held at Kobe University, Japan during December 11–12, 2004.

Tilly, C. (1975), Food supply and public order in modern Europe. In: Tilly, C. (Ed.), *The Formation of National States in Western Europe.* Princeton University Press, Princeton, NJ, pp. 380–455.

Uvin, P. (1999), *The Influence of Aid in Situations of Violent Conflict: A Synthesis and a Commentary on the Lessons Learned from Case Studies on the Limits and Scope for the Use of Development Assistance Incentives and Disincentives for Influencing Conflict Situations.* OECD DAC Informal Task Force On Conflict, Peace and Development Co-Operation, Paris.

CHAPTER 2

Poverty, Utilization of Foreign Aid and Corruption: The Role of Redistributive Politics

Sugata Marjit[a] and Vivekananda Mukherjee[b]

[a]Centre for Studies in Social Sciences, R-1, Baishnabghata, Calcutta 700094, India
E-mail address: smarjit@hotmail.com
[b]Department of Economics, Jadavpur University, Calcutta 700032, India
E-mail address: mukherjeevivek@hotmail.com

Abstract

This paper looks at the role of redistributive politics and corruption in the utilization of foreign aid. We find that the governments in relatively poor countries have incentive to adopt 'bad policies' which do not improve the growth rate of the economy. On the other hand, the governments in relatively rich countries have more incentive to misappropriate the money increasing the corruption level of the economy, although they may pursue growth-enhancing policies. Therefore, it hints towards the existence of a positive correlation between the 'good policies' adopted in utilization of the aid money and the level of corruption in the recipient countries. The paper also finds that more aid-flow to the poorer (richer) countries increase (decrease) their levels of corruption.

Keywords: Poverty, foreign aid, corruption, redistributive politics

JEL classifications: F53, O12, P48

1. Introduction

In recent times there has been a renewed interest in the literature on foreign aid. The papers like Mosley *et al.* (1987), Boone (1995) were skeptical about the efficacy of the foreign aid programs run by different countries as well as international agencies as they empirically showed "in all countries there is no significant correlation between aid and growth". Although it is not that the all aid flows are guided by the concern for raising the growth rate in the recipient countries[1] but Boone (1995) quotes an OECD (1992) report, which mentions 32% of the total aid flow was meant to be used

---

[1] See Alesina and Dollar (2000) for details.

THEORY AND PRACTICE OF FOREIGN AID
VOLUME 1   ISSN: 1574-8715
DOI: 10.1016/S1574-8715(06)01002-5

to improve economic infrastructure at the recipient countries. Boone (1995) also argued that the aid flow increased the size of the government in the recipient countries. This of course is demoralizing news for the donors as the aid fails to fulfill its apparent purpose. However, the empirical study done by Burnside and Dollar (2000) has provided a breather for the foreign aid programs. They argued empirically that the aid had been successful in raising growth rate in countries following 'good' policies. They pointed out, for the success of the aid program it is not that only the amount of aid matters, it is also important how efficiently they are utilized to generate the growth effect. That is why the 'good policies' of the recipient governments matter. This paper has been influential, as it has guided the behavior of the donors like the World Bank, DFID and the British IDA afterwards as these organizations picked up the suggestion of extending the aids selectively to the countries, which are poor and pursuing 'good policies'. Later, Collier and Dollar (2001, 2002) tried to use CPIA index[2] provided by the World Bank as an indicator of the countries with 'good policies'. So, the countries with poverty and good CPIA rank stand a better chance of receiving the foreign aid. However, the idea of linking poverty with 'good policies' pioneered by Burnside and Dollar (2000) faced criticisms from different corners.[3] Among these Dalgaard *et al.* (2004) points out the possible correlation between the two factors mentioned by Burnside and Dollar (2000) as both of them can be explained by some other common exogenous institutional factors. Their work takes the lead provided by the papers like Acemoglu *et al.* (2001) and Easterly and Levine (2003) exploring the possible links between the geographical factors and the emergence of institutions. It concludes that the climate is one of the factors, the effect of which is empirically significant to explain the efficiency of the aid allocation. In particular, it shows that aid has strong positive impact on growth outside the tropical region, however the impact is much smaller in the tropics.

In this paper, we suggest an alternative to the climatic factors. Here, we develop a theoretical framework to argue, in economies with democracy and widespread unemployment, poverty and 'bad policies' might go together leading to inefficient utilization of aid. In these economies, the aid is utilized in a way that helps the ruling government to win the election and stay in power. We call this 'redistributive politics'. When aid is given in these economies for improving the quality of infrastructure, there is a possibility that because of redistributive politics the money is spent in such a way that the quality of infrastructure suffers, failing to significantly influence the growth rate of the economy. We argue that more is the influence of redistributive politics, the poorer the country is.

---

[2] The CPIA index assesses the quality of a country's present policy and institutional framework in 20 different dimensions. The items are grouped into four categories: 'Economic Management', 'Structural Policies', 'Policies for Social Inclusion/Equity' and 'Public Sector Management and Institutions'. Each item has a 5% weight in overall rating.

[3] See for example Dalgaard *et al.* (2004), Easterly and Levine (2003), Easterly *et al.* (2004), Mosley *et al.* (2004).

Apparently this result is close to the findings of Boone (1995) as it also takes into account the influence of political factors at the receiving countries in aid utilization. Although it arrives at a similar conclusion that aid in poor recipient countries goes to increase the size of the government rather than lifting up the growth rate, it holds the 'elitist' regime, which maximizes the welfare of the fixed ruling coalition, responsible for the misutilization of aid. This is different from the spirit of our paper. In our paper we also accommodate for possibility of appropriation of aid by the ruling elite. We call it 'corruption'. Contrary to the results of Boone (1995) we point out that in the presence of redistributive politics, corruption and efficient utilization of aid can go together as we predict more corruption in richer recipient economies along with efficient utilization of aid.[4] Thus, this paper not only shows another possible correlation between poverty and some aspects of the CPIA index[5] explained by the redistributive politics, it also attempts to provide a theoretical prediction regarding the much-debated relation between corruption and aid.[6] It goes against the prevalent idea at the World Bank[7] that corruption leads to bad policies in utilization of aid. It suggests if aid is disbursed going by the 'good policies', the donors may end up by transferring the aid to a more corrupt country. The successful utilization of the aid-flow and the corruption at the receiving country can go hand in hand. Thereby, it provides a possible theoretical justification to the empirical finding of Alesina and Weder (2002) that there is no evidence that the foreign aid flows to the less corrupt countries. This paper tries to sound an alert that if the donors target indicators like 'good policies' and 'corruption' in disbursement of aid, they may end up discriminating against the relatively poor developing economies with lower growth rate, who are in the real need of the aid.

In the literature there have been conflicting claims about the direction in which higher disbursal of aid-flow affects the level of corruption of the recipient economy. On the one hand papers like Svensson (2000), Alesina and Weder (2002), etc., claim that more aid corrupts the recipient countries. On the other, Tavares (2003) claims that aid promotes honesty of the recipients. We attempt to resolve the issue in this paper. We show, in presence of redistributive politics, in the poorer economies more aid increases the level of corruption. However, in the richer economies, more aid reduces the level of corruption.

In the next section of the paper we develop the theoretical model and derive the results. In Section 3 we summarize the results and discuss the lessons we learn from this exercise regarding the aid-disbursement mechanism. The section following concludes.

---

[4] In this paper, we draw a clear distinction between the concepts of 'redistributive politics' and 'corruption'. The more of 'corruption' provides the ruling elite with the less scope of pursuing the 'redistributive politics' that helps winning the election. In contrast, in a closely related paper Lahiri and Raimondos-Moller (2004) assumes more 'corruption' in the form of the campaign contribution helps the ruling party in winning the election. It also considers an active donor and discusses the donor's choice about the size of the aid and the timing of its decision.

[5] See footnote 2.

[6] See Alesina and Weder (2002), Tavares (2003) for survey of the literature.

[7] See World Development Report (1997).

2. Model and results

We consider a developing country, which is a democracy with large-scale unemployment. It receives a monetary grant C from an international agency to spend on creation of infrastructure in sectors like transport, education, health, etc. to pursue its long-term development goal. Suppose the recipient country government, which is a democratically elected political party or coalition, is given freedom to choose the allocation of the grant under different heads of expenditure in the project. We assume there are two heads of expenditure. It can spend the money either to invest in purchasing capital or to employ unemployed people in unproductive jobs. As we denote I as the amount spent on capital and M as the amount spent for employing people, the budget constraint takes the following form: $I + M \leqslant C$. We draw from the standard public choice and political economy literature to argue that the government, or the ruling party, is partly benevolent and partly selfish[8]. It prefers spending the money both in purchasing more capital improving the quality of infrastructure as well as in creating employment that helps its probability of reelection. We assume that the capital-intensive project has far less employment potential than the direct employment generation policy. Since, if not spent in the stipulated period the money goes back to the donor without generating any of these benefits, the recipient country government decides to spend the entire amount of C and at the equilibrium the budget constraint gets satisfied with equality i.e. $I + M = C$. We assume, the government in the recipient country is corrupt and allows αC to be appropriated by the party members. Such an act of corruption proceeds in the following manner. First, the government announces decomposition between I and M. Then from each source α fraction is misappropriated. Hence, $(1 - \alpha)I$ and $(1 - \alpha)M$ are the actual amount of money being spent in purchasing capital and in creation of employment respectively. In aggregate, $\alpha I + \alpha(C - I) = \alpha C$ is the amount leaks out of the system due to corruption.

Redistributive politics in our framework works through employment generation. More employment means more political support and a greater probability of reelection. Note that the redistribution scheme run by the foreign aid money may work parallel to the standard schemes for redistribution available with any sovereign government such as the land reform program or the tax-transfer mechanisms. Sometimes the foreign aid relaxes the burden off the government in running other redistribution programs. There are some studies in the literature like Pack and Pack (1993), Swaroop *et al.* (2000) that point out this possibility. However, in this paper we assume the other programs do not exhaust the possibility of adopting further redistributive policies and the foreign aid program feeds well into the redistributive politics played by the recipient country government. Even if it substitutes other programs of the government to some extent, all the results of this paper go through. The government has the choice of spending a lot on capital i.e. choosing a high value of I and to raise the growth rate.

---

[8] Boone (1995) used similar specification of the government's objective function.

But, given the budget constraint the choice of higher I implies lower M i.e. the immediate employment generation potential is being sacrificed. In some situations this can have serious implication in terms of the reelection possibility of the political party[9] and it induces the ruling party to practice 'redistributive politics' by choosing higher value of M. The long run growth potential of the economy gets sacrificed in the process.

Before describing the government's objective function, let us define the function $p((1 - \alpha)I, \alpha C, n))$, which plays an important role in the subsequent discussion in this paper. In the argument of the function, the first term $(1 - \alpha)I$ denotes the amount spent in purchasing capital. We assume, $p_1 > 0$ i.e. implementation of a better quality project helps the reelection of the ruling party. The second term in the argument αC is the amount the ruling elite takes out of the system through corrupt activities for personal consumption. This definitely tarnishes the image of the government and reduces the probability of reelection. So, we assume $p_2 < 0$. The third term n represents the number of employment generated in the short run through the projects. The higher is the number of employment generated, the higher is the probability of reelection. This justifies our assumption $p_3 > 0$. In addition we assume, the usual argument of diminishing return holds for this function i.e. $p_{11} < 0$, $p_{22} < 0$ and $p_{33} < 0$. We assume the function to be additively separable i.e. $p_{ij} = 0$ for all $i \neq j$. We also assume for convenience, all the higher order derivatives of $p(\cdot)$ are zero. We use minimal degree of concavity in $p(\cdot)$ to drive home our point.

With such a structure in hand, we propose the following, possibly the simplest, objective function of a risk-neutral government.

$$\underset{\{I,M,\alpha\}}{\text{Max}} \quad \Omega = \theta(1 - \alpha)I + (1 - \theta)\big[\alpha C + p\big((1 - \alpha)I, \alpha C, n\big)v\big] \tag{1}$$

such that $I + M = C$, $I \geqslant 0$, $M \geqslant 0$ and $\alpha \in [0, 1]$ where $0 < \theta < 1$, the function $p(\cdot)$ have the properties described above. The government is partly selfish and partly benevolent. The weight the ruling party attaches to the social benevolence is θ and to the selfish endeavor is $(1 - \theta)$. Even if no other benefit is derived from the project, due to the government's social benevolence it derives a utility from the project. On the other hand, the second term represents its selfish benefits which has two components: the amount αC it takes out of the system through corrupt activities for personal consumption and the expected benefit $p(\cdot)v$ it derives through its reelection. In the term $p(\cdot)v$, v is a constant utility measure and $p(\cdot)$ is the probability function representing the probability of reelection. This assumes, if the ruling party fails to get reelected its utility reduces to zero. Observe also, the short-term employment generation through

---

[9] The higher value of I may promise employment in the future. However, we assume there is severe commitment problem on the part of the government, as no one believes in this promise. Typically the effects of a long run project unfold themselves gradually in the future with contraction of some of the sectors and expansion of some other sectors. Even if the overall expansionary effect dominates the contractionary effect, the common people suffer from the uncertainty about the future in the sense that they cannot see perfectly on which side they will be when the project will get implemented. See Fernandez and Rodrik (1991) for similar argument. See Robinson and Torvik (2004) for a treatment of the government's commitment problem.

projects affects the utility of the ruling government in no way other than improving its prospect of the probability of reelection.

Two points should be noted here. First, the political authority is concerned about the expected benefits from reelection and v is the summary of such benefits in the future. Second, we do not specify the concern of a median voter simply because the targeted pool of voters are identical.

Observe, the government spends the total amount of $(1 - \alpha)(C - I)$ for employing people in the projects. If n people find employment in the projects, per capita payment to the employees turns out to be $\frac{(1-\alpha)(C-I)}{R}$. Since R is the reservation payoff of the people getting employment through the project, the government in its choice of fund allocation to maximize Ω, must abide by the constraint:

$$\frac{(1 - \alpha)(C - I)}{n} \geqslant R \tag{2}$$

i.e. everyone has to be paid R at the minimum. Since $\frac{\partial p}{\partial n} > 0$ and $p_{ij} = 0$, constraint (2) must be binding.

Therefore,

$$n = \frac{(1 - \alpha)(C - I)}{R}. \tag{3}$$

Note that n is pushed to a level which is consistent with the typical laborer earning only the reservation pay off. One could make a provision for a pay off slightly greater than R and employment of fewer people. Hence, an additional trade-off can be introduced. We think that is unnecessary for the basic result we wish to highlight. Note that as the employment intensity of I is zero, increasing I will always have negative net employment effect given C as employment will be diverted away from the project.

As we describe the government's choice problem above, using Equation (3) the optimization exercise of the government in (1) can be rewritten as:

$$\text{Max}_{\{I, \alpha\}} \Omega = \theta(1 - \alpha)I$$

$$+ (1 - \theta)\left[\alpha C + p\left((1 - \alpha)I, \alpha C, \frac{(1 - \alpha)(C - I)}{R}\right)v\right] \tag{4}$$

such that $0 \leqslant I \leqslant C$ and $\alpha \in [0, 1]$.

Suppose, the interior solution to the problem (I^*, α^*) exists such that $0 < I < C$, $\alpha^* \in (0, 1)$. The first order condition for optimization implies at (I^*, α^*) the following equations hold:

$$\theta + (1 - \theta)p_1 v = \frac{(1 - \theta)p_3 v}{R}, \tag{5}$$

$$-I\left[\theta + (1 - \theta)p_1 v - \frac{(1 - \theta)p_3 v}{R}\right]$$

$$+ (1 - \theta)C + (1 - \theta)p_2 Cv - (1 - \theta)p_3 v\frac{C}{R} = 0. \tag{6}$$

Using Equation (5), Equation (6) can be rewritten as

$$1 + p_2 v = \frac{p_3 v}{R}. \tag{7}$$

We assume (5) and (7) yield permissible values of I and α. SOCs are satisfied with p_{11}, p_{22} and p_{33} being negative. We are interested in $\frac{dI}{dR}$ and $\frac{d\alpha}{dR}$ given (5) and (7).

Define the following

$$\frac{\partial^2 \Omega}{\partial I^2} = \Delta_{II}, \qquad \frac{\partial^2 \Omega}{\partial \alpha^2} = \Delta_{\alpha\alpha},$$

$$\frac{\partial^2 \Omega}{\partial \alpha \partial I} = \Delta_{I\alpha} \quad \text{and} \quad \frac{\partial^2 \Omega}{\partial I \partial \alpha} = \Delta_{\alpha I}.$$

Note that

$$\Delta_{I\alpha} = (1 - \theta)p_{11}(-I)v + \frac{(1 - \theta)v}{R}p_{33}\frac{(C - I)}{R}, \tag{8}$$

$$\Delta_{\alpha I} = \frac{p_{33}v}{R^2}(1 - \alpha) < 0. \tag{9}$$

Given I, if α is increased, marginal profitability from buying capital may go up or down because both p_1 and p_3 increase, leading to a possibility that the expenditure either on the purchase of capital or on the employment may go up. Given α, if I increases, the only effect to be considered is on p_3.

$$\frac{dI}{dR} = \frac{Z\Delta_{I\alpha} - \Delta_{\alpha\alpha}(1 - \theta)Z}{\Delta} \tag{10}$$

where $\Delta \equiv \Delta_{II}\Delta_{\alpha\alpha} - \Delta_{I\alpha}\Delta_{\alpha I} > 0$ for true maximum and

$$Z = \frac{p_3 v}{R^2} + p_{33}\frac{v(1 - \alpha)(C - I)}{R^3}. \tag{11}$$

Substituting for $\Delta_{\alpha\alpha}$ and $\Delta_{I\alpha}$ and simplifying, we get

$$\frac{dI}{dR} = \frac{-(1 - \theta)Z[p_{11}I + p_{22}C]v}{\Delta} > 0 \quad \text{if } Z > 0. \tag{12}$$

Let us look at the expression (10) and in particular at Z. Note that as R increases, n drops. Hence, for each unit of expenditure, less employment is generated. Therefore, given $p_3 > 0$, on the margin incentive to allocate for employment or incentive to go for redistribution led political return diminishes. Hence, instead of investing more in employment, more is allocated towards I. This is clear from LHS of (5) given p_3. But, there is another effect. As n decreases since $p_{33} < 0$, p_3 itself increases. Therefore, if one looks at (5), marginal cost of pursuing redistributive politics goes down. Hence, there are two offsetting effects reflected in Z. Also note that,

$$Z = \frac{v}{R^2}[p_3 + p_{33}n].$$

Observe, $Z > 0$ iff $p_3 + p_{33}n > 0$ or, $-\frac{\partial p_3}{\partial n}\frac{n}{p_3} < 1$. For $Z > 0$, which is necessary and sufficient for $\frac{dI}{dR} > 0$, p_3 must not be "too responsive" to changes in n. The elasticity of p_3 with respect to n (say ε_n) has to be less than 1.[10]

PROPOSITION 1. *If $\varepsilon_n < 1$, in presence of redistributive politics the richer countries will like to spend more in investing on capital intensive projects, which promotes growth of the economy. The poorer countries will like to adopt policies which generate more employment rather than growth.*

PROOF. See the discussion above.
What about $\frac{d\alpha}{dR}$?

$$\frac{d\alpha}{dR} = \frac{-\Delta_{II}Z + (1-\theta)(1-\beta)Z\Delta_{\alpha I}}{\Delta}$$

i.e. relatively poor region will have a low R and *ceteris paribus* higher n. This increases the "marginal cost" of corruption as redistributive politics seems to be a relatively efficient option reducing α and possibly I. However, lower R reduces I and increases α since $\Delta_{\alpha I} < 0$. These two effects counter each other. But calculating the magnitude of these effects reveals that

$$\frac{d\alpha}{dR} = \frac{-(1-\theta)(1-\alpha)p_{11}Zv}{\Delta} > 0. \qquad \square \tag{13}$$

PROPOSITION 2. *If $\varepsilon_n < 1$, degree of corruption α, will be greater in a relatively rich country.*

PROOF. See the discussion above. $\square$

Hence, the degree of corruption and expenditure on purchase of capital both are lower in a poorer region. It is also easy to check that

$$\frac{d[(1-\alpha)I]}{dR} = \frac{-(1-\theta)Zp_{22}Cv(1-\alpha)(1-\beta)}{\Delta} > 0. \tag{14}$$

In poorer countries with lower values of R the expenditure on capital, which induces growth potential, gets affected into different ways. There is a positive effect since the extent of leakage (α) is lower. There is a negative effect also since the ruling party chooses a lower amount of capital expenditure for the project. But Equation (14) suggests that the later effect dominates the former so that the net effect becomes negative. So, quality of investment in infrastructural projects through the use of the aid-money gets affected even with a fairly low degree of corruption. It is also straightforward

---

[10] For example, $p = bn + c\log n$ where $n > 1$ large, $b \leqslant \frac{1}{n} - \frac{1}{n^2}\log n$ and $c = \frac{1}{n}$ is a function that generates such a condition. It is easy to check that, $p_3 = b + \frac{c}{n}$ and $\frac{dp_3}{dn} = -\frac{c}{n^2}$ so that $\varepsilon_n = \frac{c}{n^2}\frac{n^2}{bn+c}$ which is less than 1.

to argue that even if the levels of corruption do not vary across the countries i.e. if p_{11} is negligible and $\frac{d\alpha}{dR} \approx 0$ (from Equation (13)), $[(1 - \alpha)I]$ can still be higher in the richer country simply because the scope of the redistributive politics is less there.

The results derived above makes a case where due to influence of redistributive politics, poverty and the 'bad policies' in the recipient country retarding growth go together. Therefore, if donor intends to raise the growth potential of the country receiving the aid and disburses the money going by the 'good' growth inducing policies adopted by the recipient, it may end up discriminating against the poorer countries who are really in the need of the aid. Also, there is no guarantee that the aid goes to the less corrupt countries since as we prove above the countries adopting 'good policies' are the countries which are relatively more corrupt.

Now, we look at the relation between the foreign aid and corruption. Does foreign aid corrupt? In present framework to answer this question we need to look at the sign of $\frac{d\alpha}{dC}$. If $\frac{d\alpha}{dC} > 0$, foreign aid promotes corruption at the recipient country. From Equation (5) and (7) it can be derived that

$$\frac{d\alpha}{dC} = \frac{-\frac{(1-\alpha)}{R^2}[\alpha p_{22} p_{33} - (1 - \alpha) p_{11} p_{33} + \alpha p_{11} p_{22} R^2]}{\Delta}. \tag{15}$$

Suppose, $f(R) = \alpha p_{22} p_{33} - (1 - \alpha) p_{11} p_{33} + \alpha p_{11} p_{22} R^2$. Since $\Delta > 0$, if $f(R) > 0$, from (15) it follows $\frac{d\alpha}{dC} < 0$. Similarly, if $f(R) < 0$, $\frac{d\alpha}{dC} > 0$ and if $f(R) = 0$, $\frac{d\alpha}{dC} = 0$.

Observe, since the derivatives of $p(\cdot)$ with order more than 2 are assumed to be zero, it can be derived: $f'(R) = \frac{d\alpha}{dR}[p_{22} p_{33} + p_{11} p_{33} + p_{11} p_{22} R^2] + 2\alpha p_{11} p_{22} R > 0$ as from Proposition 2 $\frac{d\alpha}{dR} > 0$ for all values of $R \geqslant 0$. For lower values of R, the ruling party has higher incentive to allocate more of the foreign aid money for the purpose of redistributive politics and to allocate less for corruption. The opposite happens for the higher values of R. Therefore, we can reasonably assume the implication of this is as $R \rightarrow 0$, $\alpha \approx 0$ and as $R \rightarrow \infty$, $\alpha \approx 1$. This in turn implies as $R \rightarrow 0$, $f(R) \approx (-p_{11} p_{33})$ and as $R \rightarrow \infty$, $f(R) \approx \infty$. Therefore, since $f(R)$ is continuous over $R \geqslant 0$, there exists a value of $R^* > 0$ such that $f(R) = 0$. It follows from the fact that $f'(R) > 0$, if $R < R^*$, $f(R) < 0$ and $\frac{d\alpha}{dC} > 0$; if $R > R^*$, $f(R) > 0$ and $\frac{d\alpha}{dC} < 0$. We note this result as the next proposition of the model as:

PROPOSITION 3. *In poorer countries with* $R < R^*$ *the aid increases corruption. In richer countries with* $R > R^*$ *it promotes honesty.*

PROOF. See the discussion above.   □

The above proposition attempts to resolve the ambiguity in the literature which arises from the opposite claims made by Svensson (2000), Alesina and Weder (2002) on the one hand and Tavares (2003) on the other. We claim that the result of Svensson, Alesina and Weder that the aid promotes corruption, holds only for the relatively poor

Sugata Marjit and Vivekananda Mukherjee

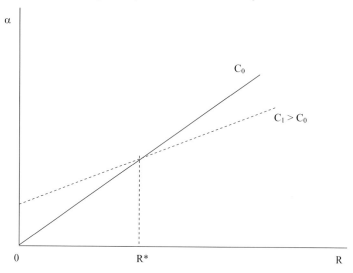

Fig. 1.   R: Reservation payoff; α: Extent of misappropriation.

recipients, whether the result of Tavares that the aid promotes honesty holds only for the relatively rich recipients. The intuition follows from Equations (5) and (7), the first order conditions for determination of (I^*, α^*) in a country. Observe, as more aid is disbursed, on the choice of the higher value of α both the marginal cost from redistributive politics and marginal benefit from increased corruption fall in a country, but in poorer countries the marginal cost falls at a higher rate than the marginal benefit. Therefore, the poorer countries choose a higher value of α. However, this leads to a higher choice of I too, which in turn suggests lowering the choice of α. Since the first effect dominates the second as more aid is disbursed the poorer countries end up by choosing a higher value of α. In the richer countries as more aid is disbursed, on the choice of the higher value of α both the marginal cost from redistributive politics and marginal benefit from increased corruption fall, but the marginal benefit falls at a higher rate than the marginal cost. Therefore, the richer countries choose a lower value of α. This leads to a lower choice of I, which in turn reinforces the choice of a lower value of α. The intuition is further clarified in Figure 1.

In Figure 1, to facilitate the exposition we have assumed a linear relationship between the values of R and α, in addition to the positive relationship which exists between them as we have already derived in Proposition 2. As the value of C changes the position of the graph changes. Proposition 3 suggests, in particular as the value of C rises the straightline showing the relationship between R and α becomes flatter and it pivots around R^*. Therefore as C rises the level of corruption of the rich rises and the poor falls. Although their levels of corruption converge to some extent, but due to Proposition 2 we know that the corruption level of the rich is higher than that of the poor.

3. Discussion and conclusions

The donors extending foreign aid to the developing countries usually have a different objective function than the government in the recipient countries. The governments in the poor economies with large-scale unemployment are induced to pursue redistributive politics, which is populist and helps them to win the election. The donors do not face this ground level reality in setting their objective. Therefore, even if they intend that the aid-money be spent on improving the quality of infrastructure that induces growth in the economy, eventually they end up increasing the unproductive work force. We prove in this paper, under certain condition this tendency is more intense in a poorer economy. We show, in a poorer economy it is not that the case that the corruption eats up foreign aid and fails to raise the growth rate, but it is the redistributive politics. In a richer economy we expect less of redistributive politics and more of corruption. But, in these economies corruption and the growth inducing 'good policies' go together. In the literature there had been conflicting claims about the direction in which higher disbursal of aid-flow affects the level of corruption of the recipient economy. We attempt to resolve the issue in this paper. We show, in the poorer economies, more aid increases the level of corruption. However, in the richer economies, more aid reduces the level of corruption.

What do we learn from this regarding the aid-disbursement strategy of the donors? First, the 'fungibility' of the aid money is more of a problem in large poorer countries. If the donors go by 'good policies at the recipient country' in disbursement of aid as suggested by Burnside and Dollar (2000), probably they can never reach these countries, where the aid is mostly needed. For these countries earmarking of the aid-budget by the donors and monitoring it strictly with a threat of withdrawal of the aid if exception is found may yield intended result. However, success of such a mechanism crucially depends on the proper information received about the utilization of the money in the recipient country, which is difficult to come by. Second, the non-government organizations (NGOs) holding similar objective as the donor may be entrusted to spend the money in these countries. This justifies the role of the NGOs in development projects at the large poorer countries. Third, the extent of corruption in utilization of the aid should not be an indicator for disbursement of foreign aid. This is because in the presence of redistributive politics the countries, which are expected to use the aid more efficiently, are likely to be more corrupt. Fourth, in disbursement of aid to relatively rich countries, the focus of the donors should not be in earmarking of the aid-budget like in the poorer countries, but it must be on the reduction of corruption in the utilization of the aid-money. Here, the NGOs may be used to raise the efficiency in utilization of the aid if the donor knows for sure the NGOs are less corrupt than the government. Fifth, disbursal of higher amount of aid may itself help reduction of corruption in the relatively affluent countries but may increase corruption in relatively poor countries.

Acknowledgement

The paper has received helpful comments from Sajal Lahiri. However, the usual disclaimer applies.

References

Acemoglu, D., Johnson, S., Robinson, J. (2001), The colonial origins of comparative development: an empirical investigation. *American Economic Review* 91, 1369–1401.

Alesina, A., Dollar, D. (2000), Who gives foreign aid to whom and why? *Journal of Economic Growth* 5, 33–63.

Alesina, A., Weder, B. (2002), Do corrupt governments receive less foreign aid? *American Economic Review* 92 (4), 1126–1137.

Boone, P. (1995), Politics and effectiveness of foreign aid. Centre for Economic Performance. *Discussion Paper*, No. 272, London School of Economics and Political Science.

Burnside, C., Dollar, D. (2000), Aid, policies and growth. *American Economic Review* 90, 847–868.

Collier, P., Dollar, D. (2001), Can the world cut poverty in half? How policy reform and effective aid can meet international development goals. *World Development* 29, 1787–1802.

Collier, P., Dollar, D. (2002), Aid allocation and poverty reduction. *European Economic Review* 45, 1470–1500.

Easterly, W., Levine, R. (2003), Tropics, germs and crops: how endowments influence economic development. *Journal of Monetary Economics* 50, 3–39.

Easterly, W., Levine, R., Roodman, D. (2004), Aid, policies and growth: comment. *American Economic Review* 94 (3), 774–780.

Dalgaard, C., Hansen, H., Tarp, F. (2004), On the empirics of foreign, aid and growth. *Economic Journal* 114, F191–F216.

Fernandez, R., Rodrik, D. (1991), Resistance to reform: status quo bias in the individual specific uncertainty. *American Economic Review* 81, 1146–1155.

Lahiri, S., Raimondos-Moller, P. (2004), Donor strategy under the fungibility of foreign aid. *Economics and Politics* 16 (2), 213–231.

Mosley, P., Hudson, J., Horrell, S. (1987), Aid, the public sector and the market in less developed countries. *Economic Journal* 97, 616–641.

Mosley, P., Hudson, J., Verschoor, A. (2004), Aid, poverty reduction and the 'New Conditinality'. *Economic Journal* 114, F217–F243.

Organization for Economic Cooperation and Development (1992), *Development Cooperation Report*. OECD, Paris.

Pack, H., Pack, J.R. (1993), The foreign aid and the question of fungibility. *Review of Economics and Statistics* 75 (2), 258–265.

Robinson, J.A., Torvik, R. (2004), White elephants. *Journal of Public Economics* 89, 197–200.

Svensson, J. (2000), Foreign aid and rent-seeking. *Journal of International Economics* 51, 437–461.

Swaroop, V., Jha, S., Rajkumar, A.S. (2000), Fiscal effects of foreign aid in a federal system of governance: the case of India. *Journal of Public Economics* 77, 307–330.

Tavares, J. (2003), Does foreign aid corrupt? *Economics Letters* 79, 99–106.

World Bank (1997), *The State in a Changing World, World Development Report 1997.* Oxford University Press, Washington, DC.

CHAPTER 3

Agglomeration and Aid

Steven Brakman[a], Harry Garretsen[b] and Charles Van Marrewijk[c]

[a]*University of Groningen, Department of Economics, PO Box 800, 9700 AV Groningen, The Netherlands*
E-mail address: s.brakman@rug.nl
[b]*Utrecht School of Economics, University of Utrecht, Vredenburg 138, 3511 BG Utrecht, The Netherlands*
E-mail address: h.garretsen@econ.uu.nl
[c]*Erasmus University Rotterdam, Department of Economics, H8-10, PO Box 1738,*
3000 DR Rotterdam, The Netherlands
E-mail address: vanmarrewijk@few.eur.nl

Abstract

We combine a key issue in development economics (explaining core-periphery patterns) for the first time with an analysis of unilateral transfers (foreign aid) using a New Economic Geography model. We show that (i) direct transfer paradoxes are not possible in a symmetric setting even if a bystander is present, (ii) the effects of foreign aid depend on the level of economic integration, (iii) aid only has a temporary effect (even if there is a bystander present) if the initial equilibrium is stable, and (iv) the recipient as well as the bystander benefits from foreign aid if the donor is large.

Keywords: International transfers, New Economic Geography, transfer paradoxes, bystander effects, welfare analysis

JEL classifications: E1, F1, F2, F3, O1, R1, R3

1. Introduction

The theory of international transfers has a long and interesting history. Without doubt the most famous discussion on this topic was the exchange in *The Economic Journal* between Keynes and Ohlin in 1929 (Keynes, 1929a, 1929b, 1929c; Ohlin, 1929a, 1929b). But much earlier other well-known economists like Hume, Smith, Ricardo, and Mill had already discussed the effects of international transfers. The early debates mostly revolved around war reparation payments in which the analysis of terms-of-trade effects or exchange rate effects dominated, see Brakman and Van Marrewijk (1998, 2007).

After the Keynes–Ohlin debate the focus of the modern literature on transfers soon moved to the welfare effects of a transfer. By means of a simple example Leontief

(1936) raised the possibility of transfer paradoxes (in which the donor gains and/or the recipient loses from the transfer). The main point of reference on this matter has been (and continues to be) Samuelson's (1947) assertion that Leontief's example requires unstable markets. More specifically, in a perfectly competitive, Walrasian stable, two-country world with two traded goods the donor's welfare falls and the recipient's welfare rises, see also Kemp (1964) and Mundell (1960). Samuelson's result, in general, does not hold if productive resources are transferred instead of purchasing power, if distortions are present in the system, if aid is tied, or if there are more than two countries. Transfer paradoxes are thus quite possible in more general settings, see e.g. Jones (1967, 1985), Ohyama (1974), Gale (1974), Chichilnisky (1980), Bhagwati *et al.* (1983), Kemp and Kojima (1985), Schweinberger (1990), Kemp (1995), Van Marrewijk and Michael (1998), Djajic *et al.* (1999), Lahiri *et al.* (2002), Kemp and Shimomura (2003), and Lahiri and Raimondos-Møller (2004).[1]

Given the recent surge in research in international economics on core-periphery structures, as initiated by the New Economic Geography (NEG) literature (also known as Geographical Economics), it is remarkable that an explicit analysis of aid in such a core-periphery context is lacking, particularly since Krugman (1993, 1995) partly found his inspiration for NEG in the development economics literature! With some exaggeration one might say that the largest problem in development economics is the persistence of global core-periphery patterns. In this chapter we address this gap in the literature and deal explicitly with aid or transfers in the context of a NEG model.[2]

Since the standard transfer literature emphasizes differences in preferences to generate terms of trade effects (and associated additional welfare effects) and the NEG model assumes identical preferences in the various countries, the reader might be inclined on the basis of Keynes's (1929a, p. 2) frequently quoted reasoning to conclude that:

> "If 1 pound is taken from you and given to me and I choose to increase my consumption of precisely the same goods as those of which you are compelled to diminish yours, there is no Transfer problem."

This conclusion would be wrong, however, for at least two reasons. First, despite the fact that there are identical preferences in the NEG model, the incorporation of transport costs creates price differences between the various goods. As the goods themselves are imperfect substitutes for one another, these price differences ensure that the phrase "I choose to increase my consumption of precisely the same goods as those of which you are compelled to diminish yours" does not hold (despite identical preferences). Terms of trade effects are therefore possible in our setting. In fact, as discussed

---

[1] See Brakman and Van Marrewijk (1998) for a survey of the transfer literature.

[2] The only study that addresses regional transfers is Baldwin *et al.* (2003). However, their focus is different as they analyze the effect of subsidies on the home market effect, and conclude, that *"the region that has the larger income or the region that is subsidized has an equilibrium share of industrial firms that is larger than its share of income or its relative subsidy. These biases are magnified by high levels of openness"* (p. 454). They then proceed by analyzing political issues to determine *"the equilibrium size and direction of subsidies"* (p. 454).

below, the mark-up pricing behaviour of individual firms ensures that these effects are directly related to changes in a country's wage rate. Second, the endogenous determination of the location of economic activity in the NEG model is influenced both by the direct income effects and the indirect price effects of a transfer. This dynamic NEG setting therefore allows us to fruitfully discuss a range of implications of international transfers on the existence and stability of core-periphery patterns hitherto not analyzed in the transfer literature. The emphasis in the discussion below will be on those new implications for the endogenous location of economic activity as well as on the welfare consequences of international transfers. We pay special attention to this analysis in the presence of a bystander – that is, a third country, because it is well-known from the literature on international transfers that an additional country might give rise to transfer paradoxes.

The paper is organized as follows. Section 2 briefly describes the core NEG model. Section 3 uses this model to study the consequences of foreign aid in a two-country setting. In accordance with most of the transfer literature but in contrast to most of the NEG literature, we extent our analysis to a three-country setting in Section 4. This is the smallest model that allows for a donor, a recipient and a bystander. Section 5 evaluates, summarizes, and concludes.

2. The model

We start with a brief review and explanation of the structure of the core NEG model as developed by Krugman (1991). The reader is referred to Brakman *et al.* (2001, Chapter 3) for a more detailed discussion. For our purposes this first model of the NEG literature suffices as other useful models (incorporating human capital and/or input linkages) essentially arrive at the same structure and conclusions (see Robert-Nicoud, 2004). After discussing generic demand and supply functions, we turn to the labour market, the introduction of various countries, and then equilibrium in the presence of interaction (transportation) costs.

2.1. Demand

Consider an economy consisting of two sectors, a numéraire sector (H), and a manufacturing (M) sector. For convenience one often refers to H as the agricultural sector. The most important characteristic of this sector is its immobility, i.e. the level of production is tied to a specific location. Every consumer in the economy has the same, nested Cobb–Douglas – CES preferences. Utility maximization of the first (Cobb–Douglas) part given in Equation (1) ensures that a share δ of income is spent on manufactured goods and the remainder $1 - \delta$ is spent on the H sector.

$$U = M^{\delta} H^{(1-\delta)}. \tag{1}$$

Manufactured goods are produced in many different varieties which are imperfect substitutes for one another as given in Equation (2). Sub-utility maximization of this second (CES) part gives the demand for a particular variety of manufactures j in Equation (3), where I is the exact price index of manufactures, ε is the price elasticity of demand, and Y is the level of total income (of which the share δ is spent on manufactures consumption).

$$M = \left(\sum_{i=1}^{n} c_i^{\rho} \right)^{1/\rho}, \tag{2}$$

$$c_j = p_j^{-\varepsilon} I^{\varepsilon-1} \delta Y; \quad \varepsilon \equiv 1/(1-\rho), \ I \equiv \left[\sum_{i=1}^{n} p_i^{1-\varepsilon} \right]^{1/(1-\varepsilon)}. \tag{3}$$

2.2. Manufacturing supply

Next, we turn to the supply side of the economy. Each variety i is produced under internal increasing returns to scale (by a single firm) using the cost function given in Equation (4), where the coefficients α and β describe the fixed and marginal input requirements per variety, respectively. Maximizing profits leads to the familiar mark-up pricing rule given in Equation (5). The manufacturing sector faces monopolistic competition, such that entry and exit of firms ensures that equilibrium profits are equal to zero, that is: $p_i x_i = W(\alpha + \beta x_i)$. Combining this with the mark-up pricing rule (Equation (5)) gives the break – even supply of a variety i, see Equation (6).

$$C(x_i) = W(\alpha + \beta x_i), \tag{4}$$

$$p_i(1 - 1/\varepsilon) = W\beta, \tag{5}$$

$$x_i = (\alpha/\beta)(\varepsilon - 1) \equiv x. \tag{6}$$

2.3. Labour market

There is only one factor of production, namely labour L (which can be normalized to 1).[3] The total amount of labour is given and fixed. The labour force is distributed over the manufacturing sector (share δ) and the numéraire sector (share $1-\delta$). Labour in the manufacturing sector is mobile over the various countries, as identified by a sub-index r for a total of R countries.[4] The distribution of the (mobile) manufacturing workers over the countries is represented by the share λ_r (so $\lambda_r \delta L$ mobile workers are located in country r) and the distribution of the immobile labor force is represented by a share ϕ_r (so $\phi_r(1-\delta)L$ immobile workers are located in country r). Obviously, we imposed the restrictions: $\lambda_r \geqslant 0$, $\phi_r \geqslant 0$, and $\sum_{r=1}^{R} \lambda_r = \sum_{r=1}^{R} \phi_r = 1$.

---

[3] As mentioned before, there are similar alternative NEG models with multiple factors of production.

[4] Again, as mentioned before, there are similar alternative NEG models (with input linkages) that do not require international labour mobility.

2.4. Equilibrium for a variety with transport costs

To allow for non-trivial location effects, we include interaction costs between different countries for the manufacturing sector. These costs include all kinds of social, psychological, cultural, physical, and policy-imposed (tariffs, quota's, etc.) obstacles to international interaction, but will be called transport cost for ease of reference. The transport costs are of the so-called iceberg type, that is if $T_{rs} \geqslant 1$ units of manufactures are shipped from country r to country s, only one unit of the good actually arrives in country s. We impose symmetry ($T_{rs} = T_{sr}$) and no internal trade costs ($T_{rr} = 1$).

Assume, for the sake of argument, that there are only two countries. Let p_{rs} be the price a producer located in country r charges in country s. Total demand for a variety produced in country 1 is the sum of the demand from country 1 (which is equal to $p_{11}^{-\varepsilon} I_1^{\varepsilon-1} \delta Y_1$, see Equation (3)) and the demand from country 2 (which is equal to $p_{12}^{-\varepsilon} I_2^{\varepsilon-1} \delta Y_2$). As the price elasticity of demand is the same in both countries the extent of the mark-up is the same. Since the marginal costs differ, however, the price charged locally by a firm located in country 1 is $p_{11} = W_1\beta/\rho$ (see Equation (5)), while the price charged in the other country (incorporating the transport costs) is $p_{12} = W_1 T_{12}\beta/\rho$. At this point it is useful to note that changes in a country's wage rate translate directly into changes in the terms-of-trade. Recalling that the break-even supply is given in Equation (6), we can now derive the market equilibrium condition for a variety produced in country 1 by adding the demand from countries 1 and 2 (note that country 2's demand must be multiplied by T_{12} to compensate for the part that melts away during transportation), substituting the prices charged in the different countries derived above, and equating this total demand to total supply, see Equation (7). Now note that, given the income levels and the price indices, we can explicitly solve this equation for W_1, the wage rate in country 1. Using the parameter normalization $L = 1$, $\beta = \rho$, $\alpha = \delta L/\varepsilon$ to simplify notation (see Brakman *et al.* (2001, Chapter 4) for an analysis and discussion of this normalization) and solving Equation (7) for the wage rate gives the general market equilibrium condition in Equation (8).

$$(\alpha/\beta)(\varepsilon - 1) = Y_1(W_1\beta/\rho)^{-\varepsilon} I_1^{\varepsilon-1} + Y_2(W_1\beta/\rho)^{-\varepsilon}(T_{12})^{1-\varepsilon} I_2^{\varepsilon-1}, \tag{7}$$

$$W_r = \left[\sum_{s=1}^{R} Y_s I_s^{\varepsilon-1} T_{rs}^{(1-\varepsilon)} \right]^{1/\varepsilon}, \quad r = 1, \ldots, R. \tag{8}$$

2.5. Short-run and long-run equilibrium

We are now in a position to briefly state and discuss the equations determining the short-run and long-run equilibrium in the core NEG model, see Equations (9)–(12). Equation (9) indicates that income in country i consists of two parts, namely income in the manufacturing sector $\lambda_i W_i \delta$ plus income in the numéraire sector $\phi_i(1 - \delta)$. In the remainder of the paper we use the symmetry assumption that $\phi_i = 1/2$ in the two-country case and $\phi_i = 1/3$ in the three-country case. Equation (10) gives the exact price-index of manufactures in each country. It is based on Equation (3) by substituting the number of varieties produced in each country and the relevant prices these producers charge in different countries, see Section 2.4. Equation (11) copies Equation (8) for convenience. Equations (9)–(11) together determine the short-run equilibrium, that is each country's income level, wage rate, and price index *given* the distribution of mobile production. Equation (12) defines the real wage rate of mobile workers in each country for this short-run equilibrium. It determines the redistribution of mobile activity from countries with low real wages to countries with high real wages until a long-run equilibrium is reached in which either the real wages are the same or all manufacturing activity is agglomerated in one country.

$$Y_i = \lambda_i W_i \delta + \phi_i (1 - \delta), \quad i = 1, \ldots, R, \tag{9}$$

$$I_r = \left[\sum_{s=1}^{R} \lambda_s W_s^{1-\varepsilon} T_{rs}^{1-\varepsilon} \right]^{1/(1-\varepsilon)}, \quad r = 1, \ldots, R, \tag{10}$$

$$W_s = \left[\sum_{r=1}^{R} Y_r T_{rs}^{1-\varepsilon} I_r^{\varepsilon-1} \right]^{1/\varepsilon}, \quad s = 1, \ldots, R, \tag{11}$$

$$w_s = W_s I_s^{-\delta}, \quad s = 1, \ldots, R. \tag{12}$$

3. Analyses of aid and agglomeration: the two-country case

The impact of foreign aid flows can now be introduced relatively easily in the model by subtracting aid A from the donor's income level and adding it to the recipient's income level. Without loss of generality we always take country 1 to be the donor and country 2 to be the recipient. We do not analyze the effects of taxes explicitly. So, who pays for the foreign aid? Implicitly we make one of two assumptions.

- All countries pay the same tax, and subsequently the proceeds are re-distributed to the recipient. This tax system reflects inter-country regional subsidies, or aid redistributed through a multi-national institution like the World Bank.
- Only the immobile labor force has to pay taxes. Such a system does not affect the decisions made by the footloose sector, which is central in NEG models. For these reasons we do not include the tax rate explicitly, as it would not change the essence of any of our conclusions and only clutter the analysis with an additional parameter.

3.1. Aid in the 2-country core model of geographical economics

Based on Equations (9)–(12) and incorporating foreign aid flows, the equations below determine the short-run equilibrium with foreign aid in the two-country case.

$$Y_1 = \delta \lambda_1 W_1 + (1 - \delta)/2 - A, \qquad Y_2 = \delta \lambda_2 W_2 + (1 - \delta)/2 + A, \tag{13}$$

$$I_1 = \left[\lambda_1 W_1^{1-\varepsilon} + \lambda_2 W_2^{1-\varepsilon} T^{1-\varepsilon} \right]^{1/(1-\varepsilon)},$$

$$I_2 = \left[\lambda_1 W_1^{1-\varepsilon} T^{1-\varepsilon} + \lambda_2 W_2^{1-\varepsilon} \right]^{1/(1-\varepsilon)}, \tag{14}$$

$$W_1 = \left[Y_1 I_1^{\varepsilon-1} + Y_2 T^{1-\varepsilon} I_2^{\varepsilon-1} \right]^{1/\varepsilon}, \qquad W_2 = \left[Y_1 T^{1-\varepsilon} I_1^{\varepsilon-1} + Y_2 I_2^{\varepsilon-1} \right]^{1/\varepsilon}, \quad (15)$$

$$w_1 = W_1 I_1^{-\delta}, \qquad w_2 = W_2 I_2^{-\delta}. \tag{16}$$

Equation (13) reflects the transfer from the donor to the recipient, the other equations are the two-country versions of (10)–(12). First, we investigate the marginal impact of foreign aid A, given by country 1 to country 2, around the spreading equilibrium ($\lambda_1 = \lambda_2 = 0.5$) evaluated at $A = 0$. In this set-up the spreading equilibrium in which the countries are identical in all respects is always a long-run equilibrium. Note, that at this spreading equilibrium Equations (13)–(15) hold for the following endogenous variables: $W_1 = W_2 = 1$, $Y_1 = Y_2 = 0.5$, and $I_1 = I_2 = [(1 + T^{1-\varepsilon})/2]^{1/(1-\varepsilon)}$.

We like to find out how a transfer affects this equilibrium. Following a similar procedure as developed by Fujita *et al.* (1999) to determine the breakpoint; we want to investigate changes in the spreading equilibrium if an infinitesimal transfer A is made from country 1 to country 2.[5] We will ignore all second order effects of induced changes (i.e. we use a linear approximation), such that we can write $dY = dY_1 = -dY_2$, $dW = dW_1 = -dW_2$, and similarly for the other variables. Differentiating Equation (13) and evaluating at the spreading equilibrium gives Equation (17). A similar procedure based on Equation (14) gives Equation (18).

$$dY = (\delta/2)\, dW - dA, \tag{17}$$

$$\frac{dI}{I} = \frac{I^{\varepsilon-1}(1 - T^{1-\varepsilon})}{2}\, dW. \tag{18}$$

To facilitate notation it is convenient to define $Z \equiv (1 - T^{1-\varepsilon})/(1 + T^{1-\varepsilon})$. Note, that Z is an index of trade barriers which ranges from 0 when there are no transport costs ($T = 1$) to 1 when transport costs are prohibitive ($T \to \infty$). With this notation we can rewrite Equation (18) at the spreading equilibrium as Equation (19). Finally, using this notation, differentiating Equations (15) and (16) and evaluating at the spreading equilibrium gives Equations (20) and (21).

$$\frac{dI}{I} = Z\, dW, \tag{19}$$

$$\varepsilon\, dW = 2Z\, dY + (\varepsilon - 1)Z\frac{dI}{I}, \tag{20}$$

$$I^\delta\, dw = dW - \delta\frac{dI}{I}. \tag{21}$$

System (19)–(21) gives us all the necessary information to calculate nominal wage changes and subsequently real wage changes. Substituting Equations (17) and (19) in Equation (20) and collecting terms gives Equation (22), expressing nominal wage changes in terms of parameters. As explained in Section 2, these changes in the wage rates translate into terms-of-trade effects through the mark-up pricing rule. Equation (22) shows, in particular, that on top of the direct income effect the donor is

---

[5] For the validity of this procedure see Baldwin (2001) and Ottaviano and Robert-Nicoud (2006).

affected by a negative term-of-trade effect and the recipient by a positive terms-of-trade effect. Evidently, this implies that if we substitute (22) in (17) the income level in country 1 falls and in country 2 rises, see Equation (23). Combining (19) and (22) gives the change of the price index following a transfer; the price index in country 1 falls and rises in country 2 (see Equation (24)), thus mitigating the impact effects of the wage rate changes for donor and recipient. Using Equations (19) and (21) we can nonetheless conclude, despite this price index effect, that the real wage rate in country 1 falls and in country 2 rises, see Equation (25). We summarize these findings in Proposition 1.

$$\frac{dW}{dA} = \frac{-2Z}{\varepsilon - \delta Z - (\varepsilon - 1)Z^2} < 0, \tag{22}$$

$$\frac{dY}{dA} = \frac{\delta}{2}\frac{dW}{dA} - 1 < 0, \tag{23}$$

$$\frac{dI}{dA} = IZ\frac{dW}{dA} < 0, \tag{24}$$

$$\frac{dw}{dA} = I^{-\delta}(1 - \delta Z)\frac{dW}{dA} < 0. \tag{25}$$

PROPOSITION 1. *The impact effects of an infinitesimal income transfer in the spreading equilibrium of the 2-country core model of geographical economics are:*

- *an increase in the wage rate for the recipient and a decrease of the wage rate for the donor (Equation (22)), that is (through the mark-up pricing rule) a negative (positive) terms-of-trade effect for the donor (recipient);*
- *an increase in the income level for the recipient and a decrease of the income level for the donor (Equation (23));*
- *an increase in the price index level for the recipient and a decrease in the price index level for the donor (Equation (24));*
- *an increase in the real wage rate for the recipient and a decrease in the real wage rate for the donor (Equation (25)).*

In contrast to most models in standard international transfer theory, see Brakman and van Marrewijk (1998), the core model of geographical economics is well suited to analyze the dynamic implications of foreign aid. Most of this dynamics is based on the simple, *ad hoc* assumption of a redistribution of manufacturing workers from countries with low real wages to countries with high real wages, see Equation (26). This is not only substantiated by extensive empirical literature, but can also be grounded in evolutionary game theory, see Weibull (1995), or justified in an endogenous growth framework, see Baldwin and Forslid (2000). Furthermore, Baldwin (2001) shows that this simple equation is consistent with forward looking behaviour. We restrict attention to the standard dynamics as given in Equation (26), where η indicates the speed of adjustment and $\bar{w}$ is the average real wage rate.

$$\frac{d\lambda_i}{\lambda_i} = \eta(w_i - \bar{w}), \quad \text{for } i = 1, 2; \quad \text{where } \bar{w} = \sum_i \lambda_i w_i. \tag{26}$$

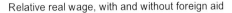

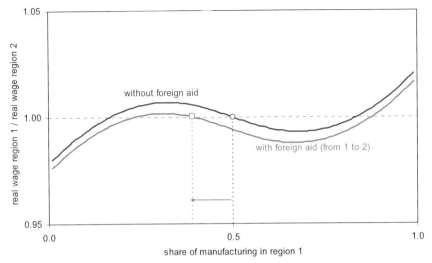

Parameters: $\delta = 0.4$; $\varepsilon = 5$; $T = 1.7$; $A = 0$ and $A = 0.01$.

Fig. 1.   *The dynamic impact of foreign aid (intermediate transport costs).*

Using a procedure similar to that used above to derive Equations (22)–(25), Fujita *et al.* (1999) show that the spreading equilibrium is locally stable if, and only if, the no-black-hole condition holds ($\rho > \delta$) and if the transport costs are large enough, more specifically if condition (27) holds.

$$Z \equiv \frac{(1 - T^{1-\varepsilon})}{(1 + T^{1-\varepsilon})} > \frac{\delta(1 + \rho)}{(\delta^2 + \rho)}. \tag{27}$$

This puts us in a position to determine the dynamics of foreign aid around the spreading equilibrium. First, write the relative real wage w_1/w_2 as a function, f say, of the distribution of the manufacturing workforce λ_1 and the amount of foreign aid A, conditional, of course, on the parameters of the model: $w_1/w_2 = f(\lambda_1, A)$. If condition (27) holds, we know that $f_\lambda'(0.5, 0) < 0$. Combining this with Proposition 1 (which established that $f_A'(0.5, 0) < 0$) and the dynamics of Equation (26) shows that the transfer of foreign aid around the spreading equilibrium leads to a reduction of manufacturing activity for the donor and an increase for the recipient.

Figure 1 illustrates the discussion above for the case of *intermediate* transport costs ($T = 1.7$). The figure depicts the real wage in country 1 relative to country 2 for all possible short-run equilibria (distributions of manufacturing workers). If the real wage in country 1 is higher than in country 2 workers will migrate from country 2 to country 1, and vice versa if the real wage is lower in country 1 than in country 2. As a consequence, there are three stable long-run equilibria in Figure 1, namely the spreading equilibrium and complete agglomeration in either country 1 or country 2. As a result of the transfer of foreign aid, the real wage falls for the donor and rises for the recipient around the spreading equilibrium, as can be seen by the downward shift of the short-run relative real wage curve, which causes an outflow of manufacturing activity from the donor to the recipient. There are two other cases to consider as well, see Brakman *et al.* (2001) for details. If transport costs are *large*, the spreading equilibrium is the only stable equilibrium and we arrive at a similar (local) conclusion as for the case of intermediate transport costs. If transport costs are *small*, however, the spreading equilibrium is unstable and the transfer of foreign aid leads to complete agglomeration of manufacturing activity in the recipient. Proposition 2 summarizes our discussion.

PROPOSITION 2. *The dynamic effect of an infinitesimal transfer of aid in the spreading equilibrium of the 2-country core model of geographical economics is*:

- *a small influx of manufacturing activity for the recipient and a small reduction for the donor if the spreading equilibrium is locally stable*;
- *complete agglomeration of manufacturing activity in the recipient if the spreading equilibrium is locally unstable.*

We can now discuss the extent to which foreign aid has temporary or permanent effects on agglomeration. First, look at Figure 1. The transfer of foreign aid shifts the short-run relative real wage curve down causing an increase of manufacturing activity for the recipient and a decrease for the donor. It is important to note that the downward shift, and therefore the impact on the distribution of manufacturing activity, only continues as long as country 1 continues to give foreign aid to country 2. Once country 1 ceases to provide foreign aid, the short-run relative real wage curve shifts back to its old position and the effect on the distribution of manufacturing activity is reversed. In this situation, the effects of the transfer of foreign aid are only *temporary* and conditional on the continuation of the flow of foreign aid. The situation is quite different in Figure 2, where the transfer of foreign aid also leads to a downward shift of the short-run relative real wage curve, which causes complete agglomeration of manufacturing activity in the recipient country. Again, once country 1 seizes to transfer foreign aid to country 2 the short-run relative real wage curve shifts back to its old position. This time, however, the consequences of the initial transfer are *permanent* as agglomeration in country 2 continues to be a stable equilibrium. Proposition 3 summarizes our discussion.

PROPOSITION 3. *The dynamic effects of an infinitesimal transfer of foreign aid in the spreading equilibrium of the 2-country core model of geographical economics are* temporary *if the spreading equilibrium is locally stable (i.e. stopping the flow of foreign aid reverses the economy to its original position). These dynamic effects are* permanent *if the spreading equilibrium is locally unstable (i.e. stopping the flow of foreign aid does not reverse the economy to its original position).*

In practice, Propositions 2 and 3 imply that the consequences of foreign aid are fundamentally different depending on the level of integration between donor and re-

Relative real wage, with and without foreign aid

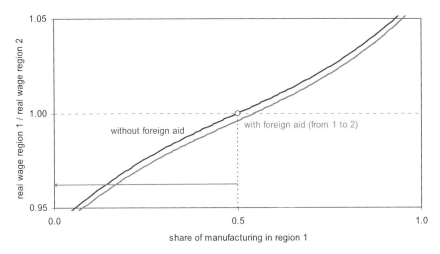

Parameters: $\delta = 0.4$; $\varepsilon = 5$; $T = 1.5$; $A = 0$ and $A = 0.01$.

Fig. 2. The dynamic impact of foreign aid (low transport costs).

cipient. If economic integration is high, that is if the level of transportation costs is low, aid can have dramatic, lasting effects on the distribution of economic activity. On the other hand, if the level of economic integration is low, that is transportation costs are high, the effects of foreign aid are temporary and the distribution of economic activity is only affected as long as the foreign aid flow continues. Empirical research indicates that even for the EU regions, which a priori presents an example of an highly integrated economy, the 'extent of agglomeration forces' is still quite small, indicating that the likelihood of only temporary effects of interregional transfers is high (Brakman *et al.*, 2006).

3.2. Complete agglomeration

In Section 3.1 we studied the consequences of aid in the spreading equilibrium. What happens if the donor and the recipient are not equal in size? The standard motivation for aid is a welfare difference between donor and recipient, where the donor is rich and the recipient is poor. In the NEG literature a limiting case is complete agglomeration: all footloose production takes place in the donor country (here, country 1). So, doing the analysis of aid in a NEG setting with complete agglomeration might be more relevant than taking the spreading equilibrium as our focal point. Equations (13)–(16) are again the starting point for our investigation. First, note that complete agglomeration in country 1 implies $\lambda_1 = 1$ and $\lambda_2 = 0$. Using this information shows that Equations (13)–(16) are solved for the following values of the endogenous variables:

$W_1 = I_1 = w_1 = 1$, $Y_1 = [(1 + \delta)/2] - A$, $Y_2 = [(1 - \delta)/2] + A$, and $I_2 = T$. The impact effects of a transfer are therefore straightforward.

PROPOSITION 4. *The impact effects of a transfer of aid in the agglomeration equilibrium of the 2-country core model of geographical economics are:*

- *no change in the wage rate of manufacturing workers or the price index for the donor and therefore no terms-of-trade effects;*
- *an increase in the income level for the recipient and a decrease of the income level for the donor.*

Since there are no manufacturing workers in the recipient it is not really appropriate to talk of their wage rate W_2, but we can calculate what this wage rate would have been by using Equation (15), see Equation (28). Similarly, we can calculate the implied real wage rate w_2 by using Equation (16), see Equation (29).

$$W_2 = \left[\left(\frac{1+\delta}{2} - A\right)T^{1-\varepsilon} + \left(\frac{1-\delta}{2} + A\right)T^{\varepsilon-1}\right]^{1/\varepsilon}, \tag{28}$$

$$w_2 = \left\{\left(\frac{1+\delta}{2} - A\right)T^{1-\varepsilon} + \left(\frac{1-\delta}{2} + A\right)T^{\varepsilon-1}\right\}^{1/\varepsilon} T^{-\delta}. \tag{29}$$

Noting that the real wage rate for mobile workers is equal to one in the donor country, it follows that it will be attractive for mobile workers to relocate from the donor country to the recipient once the implied real wage w_2 is larger than one. If that occurs, complete agglomeration of manufacturing activity in the donor country is no longer sustainable. Since this is equivalent to requiring w_2^ε larger than one, we can define the auxiliary function $g(T, A) \equiv w_2^\varepsilon$ as given in Equation (30).

$$g(T, A) \equiv \left(\frac{1+\delta}{2} - A\right)T^{-(\rho+\delta)\varepsilon} + \left(\frac{1-\delta}{2} + A\right)T^{(\rho-\delta)\varepsilon}, \tag{30}$$

(i) $g_T'(T, A) = \varepsilon\left\{-\left(\frac{1+\delta}{2} - A\right)(\rho + \delta)T^{-(\rho+\delta)\varepsilon-1}\right.$
$$\left. + \left(\frac{1-\delta}{2} + A\right)(\rho - \delta)T^{(\rho-\delta)\varepsilon-1}\right\},$$

(ii) $g(1, A) = 1$; $g_T'(1, A) = -\varepsilon[\delta(1 + \rho) - 2\rho A]$;
$$\lim_{T \to \infty} g(T, A) = \infty \text{ iff } \rho > \delta,$$

(iii) $g_A'(T, A) = T^{(\rho-\delta)\varepsilon} - T^{-(\rho+\delta)\varepsilon} > 0 \quad \text{if } T > 1.$

The main properties of function $g(T, A)$ are listed below Equation (30). We note that its value is one if there are no transport costs ($T = 1$), it is declining for sufficiently small transport costs and aid flows (as $g_T'(1, A) < 0$ provided $A < \delta(1 + \rho)/2\rho$), and its value is above one for sufficiently large transport costs (provided $\rho > \delta$, the

Sustain point with and without foreign aid

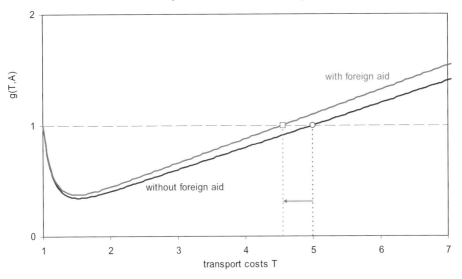

Parameters: $\delta = 0.6$; $\varepsilon = 5$; $A = 0$ and $A = 0.02$.

Fig. 3. Sustain point with and without foreign aid.

so-called no-black-hole condition). As illustrated in Figure 3, the agglomeration equilibrium is sustainable for sufficiently small transport costs (for T below a critical value such that $g(T, A) < 1$), but not for sufficiently large transport costs.

The impact of the transfer of foreign aid from the core to the periphery on the sustain point is illustrated in Figure 3, see also property (iii) of Equation (30). The flow of foreign aid increases the income level in the periphery, which makes it more attractive as a base for production. This shifts the $g(T, A)$ curve upwards as $g'_A(T, A) > 0$ for $T > 1$, leading to a shift to the left of the critical sustain point value, and thus to a smaller range of transport costs for which agglomeration of manufacturing activity is a sustainable equilibrium. Our findings are summarized in Propositions 5 and 6.

PROPOSITION 5. *The dynamic effect of a transfer of foreign aid in the agglomeration equilibrium of the 2-country core model of geographical economics is*:

- *no reallocation of manufacturing activity from core to periphery for sufficiently small foreign aid flows*;
- *a large reallocation of manufacturing activity from a core-periphery setting to an (asymmetric) spreading equilibrium or complete agglomeration in the recipient once the foreign aid flow exceeds a critical level.*

PROPOSITION 6. *If the transfer of foreign aid in the agglomeration equilibrium of the 2-country core model of geographical economics has a dynamic effect, then this effect is permanent (i.e. stopping the flow of foreign aid does not reverse the economy to its original position). More specifically, stopping the foreign aid flow will either lead to the spreading equilibrium (if the aid-induced economy is in its basin of attraction) or to complete agglomeration in the recipient country.*

4. The effects of a bystander: foreign aid in the 3-country model

The analysis of international transfers benefited enormously from examples that aimed to show under what circumstances transfer paradoxes might arise (see Brakman and Van Marrewijk, 1998, for a survey and discussion of these examples). Although not without some problems, the examples pointed out that if a bystander is present a transfer paradox might arise (the donor gains and/or the recipient looses from a transfer).[6] A general derivation was given by Bhagwati *et al.* (1983), who explicitly show that the presence of a bystander, which must actively be involved in international trade, is essential for paradoxes to arrive. A paradox may arise if the bystander's offer curve is inelastic (backward-bending) or if the bystander's export good is an inferior good for either the recipient or the donor. We therefore extend our analysis to include a third party, or 'bystander' that is not directly involved in the initial transfer. The set-up of this model is a straightforward extension of the two-country case analyzed above.[7]

$$Y_1 = \delta\lambda_1 W_1 + (1-\delta)/3 - A,$$
$$Y_2 = \delta\lambda_2 W_2 + (1-\delta)/3 + A,$$
$$Y_3 = \delta\lambda_3 W_3 + (1-\delta)/3, \tag{13'}$$

$$I_1 = \left[\lambda_1 W_1^{1-\varepsilon} + \lambda_2 W_2^{1-\varepsilon}T^{1-\varepsilon} + \lambda_3 W_3^{1-\varepsilon}T^{1-\varepsilon}\right]^{1/(1-\varepsilon)},$$
$$I_2 = \left[\lambda_1 W_1^{1-\varepsilon}T^{1-\varepsilon} + \lambda_2 W_2^{1-\varepsilon} + \lambda_3 W_3^{1-\varepsilon}T^{1-\varepsilon}\right]^{1/(1-\varepsilon)},$$
$$I_3 = \left[\lambda_1 W_1^{1-\varepsilon}T^{1-\varepsilon} + \lambda_2 W_2^{1-\varepsilon}T^{1-\varepsilon} + \lambda_3 W_3^{1-\varepsilon}\right]^{1/(1-\varepsilon)}, \tag{14'}$$

$$W_1 = \left[Y_1 I_1^{\varepsilon-1} + Y_2 T^{1-\varepsilon}I_2^{\varepsilon-1} + Y_3 T^{1-\varepsilon}I_3^{\varepsilon-1}\right]^{1/\varepsilon},$$
$$W_2 = \left[Y_1 T^{1-\varepsilon}I_1^{\varepsilon-1} + Y_2 I_2^{\varepsilon-1} + Y_3 T^{1-\varepsilon}I_3^{\varepsilon-1}\right]^{1/\varepsilon},$$
$$W_3 = \left[Y_1 T^{1-\varepsilon}I_1^{\varepsilon-1} + Y_2 T^{1-\varepsilon}I_2^{\varepsilon-1} + Y_3 I_3^{\varepsilon-1}\right]^{1/\varepsilon}, \tag{15'}$$

$$w_1 = W_1 I_1^{-\delta}, \qquad w_2 = W_2 I_2^{-\delta}, \qquad w_3 = W_3 I_3^{-\delta}. \tag{16'}$$

The distribution or geography of economic activity in this set-up can be depicted as an equilateral triangle, where the share of manufacturing production at the corners

---

[6] The reason for such paradoxes is that a transfer from country 1 to 2 affects the terms of trade. Because the bystander is also involved in international trade with countries 1 and 2, the price change also affects the value of the trade relations between countries 1 and 2 with respect to the bystander, thus influencing the total welfare change.

[7] Note that the position of the countries is symmetric relative to one another, that is the transport costs between countries 1 and 2 are equal to those between countries 1 and 3 and between 2 and 3.

represents complete agglomeration in one of the countries, see also the discussion of Figures 4 and 5 below. The great advantage of the depiction of space in our 3 country model as an equilateral triangle is that we can normalize distance and thereby ensure symmetry to the extent that transportation costs are the same between any pair of countries. Without this assumption the analysis below does not carry through, see also Brakman *et al.* (2006) on this issue.

4.1. The spreading equilibrium

We again investigate the marginal impact of foreign aid A, given by country 1 to country 2, around the spreading equilibrium ($\lambda_1 = \lambda_2 = \lambda_3 = 1/3$ and initially $A = 0$). At this spreading equilibrium equations (13')–(15') hold for the following endogenous variables: $W_1 = W_2 = W_3 = 1$, $Y_1 = Y_2 = Y_3 = 1/3$, and $I_1 = I_2 = I_3 = [(1+2T^{1-\varepsilon})/3]^{1/(1-\varepsilon)}$. We will ignore all second order effects of induced changes (i.e. we use a linear approximation), such that: $dY = dY_1 = -dY_2$, $dW = dW_1 = -dW_2$, and similarly for the other variables. Differentiating Equation (13') and evaluating at the spreading equilibrium gives Equation (17'). Similarly, differentiate Equation (14') and evaluate at the spreading equilibrium to get Equation (18').

$$dY = (\delta/3)\,dW - dA, \qquad dY_3 = (\delta/3)\,dW_3, \tag{17'}$$

$$\frac{dI}{I} = \frac{I^{\varepsilon-1}(1-T^{1-\varepsilon})}{3}\,dW + \frac{I^{\varepsilon-1}T^{1-\varepsilon}}{3}\,dW_3, \qquad \frac{dI_3}{I_3} = \frac{I^{\varepsilon-1}}{3}\,dW_3. \tag{18'}$$

Define $\bar{Z} \equiv (1 - T^{1-\varepsilon})/(1 + 2T^{1-\varepsilon})$, and note that $\bar{Z}$ is an adjusted index of trade barriers (for three countries instead of two) which ranges from 0 when there are no transport costs ($T = 1$) to 1 when transport costs are prohibitive ($T \to \infty$). With this notation we can rewrite Equation (18') at the spreading equilibrium as Equation (19'). Finally, by using this notation, differentiating Equations (15') and (16') and evaluating at the spreading equilibrium, we arrive at Equations (20') and (21').

$$\frac{dI}{I} = \bar{Z}\,dW + \frac{I^{\varepsilon-1}T^{1-\varepsilon}}{3}\,dW_3, \qquad \frac{dI_3}{I_3} = \frac{I^{\varepsilon-1}}{3}\,dW_3, \tag{19'}$$

$$\varepsilon\,dW = 3\bar{Z}\,dY + (\varepsilon - 1)\bar{Z}\frac{dI}{I} + T^{1-\varepsilon}I^{\varepsilon-1}\left(\frac{\varepsilon-1}{3}\frac{dI_3}{I_3} + dY_3\right),$$

$$\varepsilon\,dW_3 = I^{\varepsilon-1}\left(\frac{\varepsilon-1}{3}\frac{dI_3}{I_3} + dY_3\right), \tag{20'}$$

$$I^{\delta}\,dw = dW - \delta\frac{dI}{I}, \qquad I^{\delta}\,dw_3 = dW_3 - \delta\frac{dI_3}{I_3}. \tag{21'}$$

Investigating Equations (19')–(21') for country 3 quickly reveals that the first-order effect of the transfer for the bystander is no change at all: $dW_3 = dY_3 = dI_3 = dw_3 = 0$. This follows because from country 3's perspective any changes from the spreading equilibrium in a particular direction caused by country 1 are exactly compensated by opposite changes caused by country 2. Note that this effect would thus not holds if the transportation costs from the bystander to the donor would be different from those to the recipient. In any case, this symmetry assumption greatly simplifies the subsequent analysis for donor and recipient even if a bystander is present. Substituting the simplified Equations (17′) and (19′) in (20′) and collecting terms gives Equation (22′), determining what happens to the wage rate in country 1. From Equation (17′), it follows that the income level in country 1 falls and in country 2 rises (see Equation (23′)), while using Equation (19′) we see that the price index in country 1 falls and in country 2 rises (see Equation (24′)). Using Equations (17′) and (21′) we can nonetheless conclude, despite this price index effect, that the real wage rate in country 1 falls and in country 2 rises, see Equation (25′). Also note that the bystander exacerbates the wage rate effect (compare Equations (22) and (22′)) but mitigates the income effect (compare Equations (23) and (23′)). Our findings are summarized in Proposition 7.

$$\frac{dW}{dA} = \frac{-3\bar{Z}}{\varepsilon - \delta\bar{Z} - (\varepsilon - 1)\bar{Z}^2} < 0, \qquad \frac{dW_3}{dA} = 0, \tag{22'}$$

$$\frac{dY}{dA} = \frac{\delta}{3}\frac{dW}{dA} - 1 < 0, \qquad \frac{dY_3}{dA} = 0, \tag{23'}$$

$$\frac{dI}{dA} = I\bar{Z}\frac{dW}{dA} < 0, \qquad \frac{dI_3}{dA} = 0, \tag{24'}$$

$$\frac{dw}{dA} = I^{-\delta}(1 - \delta\bar{Z})\frac{dW}{dA} < 0, \qquad \frac{dw_3}{dA} = 0. \tag{25'}$$

PROPOSITION 7. *The impact effects of an infinitesimal transfer of aid in the spreading equilibrium of the 3-country core model of geographical economics are:*

- *an increase in the wage rate for the recipient, a decrease of the wage rate for the donor, and no effect for the bystander (Equation (22′)); that is (through the mark-up pricing rule) a negative (positive) terms-of-trade effect for the donor (recipient) and no net terms-of-trade effect for the bystander;*
- *an increase in the income level for the recipient, a decrease of the income level for the donor, and no effect for the bystander (Equation (23′));*
- *an increase in the price index level for the recipient, a decrease in the price index level for the donor, and no effect for the bystander (Equation (24′));*
- *an increase in the real wage rate for the recipient, a decrease in the real wage rate for the donor, and no effect for the bystander (Equation (25′)).*

Before we can briefly discuss the dynamic impact of foreign aid in a 3-country setting we have to extend the local stability condition (that is, the sustain point analysis) from a 2-country setting to a 3-country setting. Lemma 1 provides this condition. The proof of the lemma is delegated to Appendix A.

LEMMA 1. *The spreading equilibrium in the 3-country core model of geographical economics is locally stable if, and only if, the no-black-hole condition holds ($\rho > \delta$)*

and the transport costs are large enough, more specifically if condition (∗) *holds*:

$$\bar{Z} \equiv \frac{(1 - T^{1-\varepsilon})}{(1 + 2T^{1-\varepsilon})} > \frac{\delta(1 + \rho)}{(\delta^2 + \rho)}. \qquad (∗)$$

Based on this lemma, Proposition 8 below is the 3-country analogue to the first part of Proposition 2 in the 2-country setting, showing again that the recipient of foreign aid tends to attract economic activity at the expense of the donor if the spreading equilibrium is locally stable (that is if condition (∗) holds). Similarly, Proposition 9 is the 3-country analogue to Proposition 3 in the 2-country setting, arguing that the dynamic effects are temporary if the spreading equilibrium is locally stable.

PROPOSITION 8. *The dynamic effect of an infinitesimal transfer of aid for a locally stable spreading equilibrium of the 3-country core model of geographical economics is*:

- *a small influx of manufacturing activity for the recipient, a small reduction of manufacturing activity for the donor, and no effect for the bystander.*

PROPOSITION 9. *The dynamic effects of an infinitesimal transfer of foreign aid in the spreading equilibrium of the 3-country core model of geographical economics are* temporary *if the spreading equilibrium is locally stable (i.e. stopping the flow of foreign aid reverses the economy to its original position).*

4.2. Discrete transfers in an asymmetric setting

The analysis in Section 4.1 shows that, in contrast to the traditional analysis of infinitesimal or marginal transfers, the bystander has no additional influence on the donor or the recipient in our NEG setting (except for the multiplier effects). However, by explicitly calculating (numerically) discrete transfers in an asymmetric setting we can easily show that the effects for the bystander can be influential in our NEG model. This is illustrated in Figure 4, which shows the effects of a *discrete* transfer on the real wage rate of the bystander as a function of the distribution of the mobile labor force in a unit simplex. Figure 4 is a two-dimensional representation of the three-country model. If one gets closer to one of the corners this means that the country in question produces a larger share of total manufacturing output. We can distinguish three different areas in Figure 4: an area where the real wage increases, an area where it remains the same, and an area where it decreases. Figure 4 illustrates, therefore, that the effects of the transfer depend on the initial distribution of the footloose workers.

A closer investigation of Figure 4 reveals that in the area in which the donor (country 1) and the recipient (country 2) are similar in size (along the perpendicular line from the bystander's (country 3) corner) the effect on the real wage for the bystander is zero. If the donor and the bystander are relatively small compared to the recipient (in the north-east of the figure) the real wage rate declines, while if the donor and the

48 *Steven Brakman et al.*

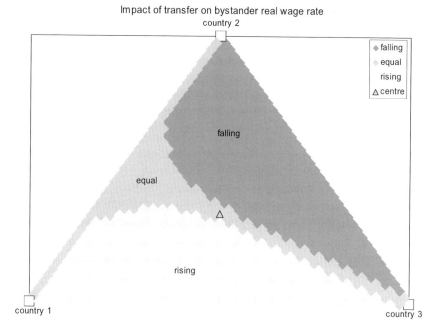

Parameters: $\delta = 0.4$; $\varepsilon = 5$; $T = 1.7$ and $A = 0.01$; "equal" is relative change smaller than 0.0001.

Fig. 4. Change in real wage rate of bystander (intermediate transport costs).

bystander are relative large compared to the recipient (in the south-west of the figure) the real wage increases.

The effects thus depend on whether or not the transfer is substantial for the recipient. For a small recipient a given transfer ($A = 0.01$) has a substantial effect on its income and real wage. Workers in the bystander country benefit because the 'extent of agglomeration forces' from the relatively large donor country become smaller, thus increasing the relative attractiveness for the bystander (note: the real wage rate always increases for the recipient and falls for the donor in Figure 4). Analogous reasoning holds for the north-east part of the figure, resulting in a decrease of the real wage rate for the bystander. This leads to the interesting conclusion that if aid is given to a particular recipient, other developing countries are also affected. Since we can safely assume that the income level of the donor is usually large compared to that of developing countries, Figure 4 indicates that the non-targeted bystander country usually benefits.

Figure 5 illustrates a similar exercise as Figure 4, but now for a *higher* level of transport costs ($T = 2$ instead of $T = 1.7$). Relative to Figure 4 two new areas appear in the north-western part of Figure 5. These new areas reflect the fact that for sufficiently high transport costs a transfer from a donor to a recipient that is similar in size reduces the attractiveness (real wage in the donor), making both re-location to the recipient

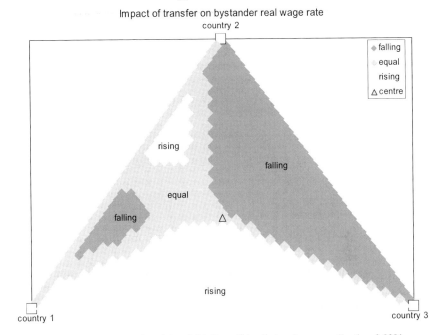

Impact of transfer on bystander real wage rate

Parameters: $\delta = 0.4$; $\varepsilon = 5$; $T = 2$ and $A = 0.01$; "equal" is relative change smaller than 0.0001.

Fig. 5. *Change in real wage rate of bystander (high transport costs).*

country and the bystander country more attractive, thus also increasing the bystander's real wage rate.

Note finally that when one starts from a spreading equilibrium in Figure 5 (the triangle $\triangle$ in the middle of the Figure), the real wage for the donor falls, increases for recipient and remains the same for the bystander (recall Proposition 7). In this case the 1st order dynamic effect in terms of Figure 5 is a move in the north-eastern direction which leads the economy to the area where the real wage for the bystander falls. The 2nd order dynamic effect after reallocation when we start from the spreading equilibrium is thus negative for the bystander.

5. Conclusions

The analysis of the economics of international transfers and foreign aid has tradition-ally been based on models characterized by perfect competition in which the location of economic activity is not an issue. It is, however, a stylized fact that economic ac-tivity is distributed unevenly across space, which calls for an analysis of the effects of transfers or aid using models allowing for core-periphery structures, where location matters and where, consequently, imperfect competition rules. It is for this reason that we think that new economic geography (NEG) models can be useful for the analysis of international transfers.

Using the core model of the NEG literature due to Krugman (1991), this chapter provides such an analysis. We first analyze the effects of foreign aid in a two-country world, and subsequently extend the analysis with a bystander country. In the standard literature on international transfers the presence of a bystander is essential for transfer paradoxes to arise. Our main findings can be summarized as follows (see the propositions for qualifications and details). First, transfer paradoxes are not possible even if a bystander is present. Second, the effects of foreign aid depend on the level of economic integration between donor and recipient. Third, if the equilibrium from which aid is given is stable, aid only has a temporary effect (even if a bystander is present). Fourth, if the donor is relatively large, not only the recipient but also the bystander benefits from foreign aid.

Acknowledgements

We would like to thank Sajal Lahiri for useful comments.

Appendix A. Stability around the spreading equilibrium in the 3-country model

We investigate the marginal impact of a movement of manufacturing workers from country 1 to country 2 around the spreading equilibrium ($\lambda_1 = \lambda_2 = \lambda_3 = 1/3$ and $A = 0$). Note that at this spreading equilibrium Equations (13')–(16') hold for the following endogenous variables: $W_1 = W_2 = W_3 = 1$, $Y_1 = Y_2 = Y_3 = 1/3$, and $I_1 = I_2 = I_3 = [(1 + 2T^{1-\varepsilon})/3]^{1/(1-\varepsilon)}$. We will ignore all second order effects of induced changes, such that we can write $dY = dY_1 = -dY_2$, $dW = dW_1 = -dW_2$, and similarly for the other variables. Differentiating Equation (13') and evaluating at the spreading equilibrium gives Equation (A.1). Similarly, differentiate Equation (14') and evaluate at the spreading equilibrium to get Equation (A.2).

$$dY = \delta\,d\lambda + (\delta/3)\,dW, \qquad dY_3 = (\delta/3)\,dW_3, \tag{A.1}$$

$$(1-\varepsilon)\frac{dI}{I} = I^{\varepsilon-1}\left(1 - T^{1-\varepsilon}\right)\left(\frac{1-\varepsilon}{3}\,dW + d\lambda\right) + \frac{(1-\varepsilon)I^{\varepsilon-1}T^{1-\varepsilon}}{3}\,dW_3,$$

$$\frac{dI_3}{I_3} = \frac{I^{\varepsilon-1}}{3}\,dW_3. \tag{A.2}$$

Define $\bar{Z} \equiv (1 - T^{1-\varepsilon})/(1 + 2T^{1-\varepsilon})$, and note that $\bar{Z}$ is an adjusted index of trade barriers (for three countries instead of two) which ranges from 0 when there are no transport costs ($T = 1$) to 1 when transport costs are prohibitive ($T \to \infty$). With this notation we can rewrite Equation (A.2) at the spreading equilibrium as Equation (A.3). Finally, using this notation, differentiating Equations (15') and (16') and evaluating at the spreading equilibrium gives Equations (A.4) and (A.5).

$$\frac{dI}{I} = \frac{3\bar{Z}}{1-\varepsilon}\,d\lambda + \bar{Z}\,dW + \frac{I^{\varepsilon-1}T^{1-\varepsilon}}{3}\,dW_3,$$

$$\frac{dI_3}{I_3} = \frac{I^{\varepsilon-1}}{3}\,dW_3, \tag{A.3}$$

$$\varepsilon\,dW = 3\bar{Z}\,dY + (\varepsilon - 1)\bar{Z}\frac{dI}{I} + T^{1-\varepsilon}I^{\varepsilon-1}\left(\frac{\varepsilon - 1}{3}\frac{dI_3}{I_3} + dY_3\right),$$

$$\varepsilon\,dW_3 = I^{\varepsilon-1}\left(\frac{\varepsilon - 1}{3}\frac{dI_3}{I_3} + dY_3\right), \tag{A.4}$$

$$I^{\delta}\,dw = dW - \delta\frac{dI}{I}, \qquad I^{\delta}\,dw_3 = dW_3 - \delta\frac{dI_3}{I_3}. \tag{A.5}$$

Investigating the equations for country 3 reveals that the first order effect of the migration flow is no change at all: $dW_3 = dY_3 = dI_3 = dw_3 = 0$. This follows because from country 3's perspective any change from the spreading equilibrium caused by country 1 are exactly compensated by opposite changes caused by country 2. Note that this effect only holds if the transportation costs from the bystander to the donor are the same as those to the recipient which greatly simplifies the subsequent analysis for countries 1 and 2 as:

$$\frac{dI}{I} = \frac{3\bar{Z}}{1-\varepsilon}\,d\lambda + \bar{Z}\,dW, \tag{A.3$'$}$$

$$\varepsilon\,dW = 3\bar{Z}\,dY + (\varepsilon - 1)\bar{Z}\frac{dI}{I}. \tag{A.4$'$}$$

Substituting (A.1) in (A.4$'$) and combining with (A.5) gives

$$\begin{bmatrix} 1 & -\bar{Z} \\ \bar{Z} & (\varepsilon - \delta\bar{Z})/(1-\varepsilon) \end{bmatrix}\begin{bmatrix} dI/I \\ dW \end{bmatrix} = \begin{bmatrix} 3\bar{Z}/(1-\varepsilon) \\ 3\delta\bar{Z}/(1-\varepsilon) \end{bmatrix}d\lambda, \tag{A.6}$$

$$\begin{bmatrix} dI/I \\ dW \end{bmatrix} = \frac{1}{\Delta}\begin{bmatrix} (\varepsilon - \delta\bar{Z})/(1-\varepsilon) & \bar{Z} \\ -\bar{Z} & 1 \end{bmatrix}\begin{bmatrix} 3\bar{Z}/(1-\varepsilon) \\ 3\delta\bar{Z}/(1-\varepsilon) \end{bmatrix}d\lambda, \tag{A.7}$$

where $\Delta \equiv ((1-\varepsilon)\bar{Z}^2 - \delta\bar{Z} + \varepsilon)/(1-\varepsilon)$, such that

$$\frac{dI}{I} = \frac{d\lambda}{\Delta}\frac{3\varepsilon\bar{Z}}{(1-\varepsilon)^2}(1 - \delta\bar{Z}), \qquad dW = \frac{d\lambda}{\Delta}\frac{3\bar{Z}}{(1-\varepsilon)}(\delta - \bar{Z}).$$

Finally, substituting in (A.5) gives the change in the real wage

$$\frac{dw}{d\lambda} = \frac{3\bar{Z}I^{-\delta}}{(\varepsilon - 1)}\left[\frac{\delta(2\varepsilon - 1) - \bar{Z}[\varepsilon(1 + \delta^2) - 1]}{\varepsilon - \delta\bar{Z} - (\varepsilon - 1)\bar{Z}^2}\right]$$

$$= \frac{3\bar{Z}I^{-\delta}(1 - \rho)}{\rho}\left[\frac{\delta(1 + \rho) - \bar{Z}(\delta^2 + \rho)}{1 - \delta\bar{Z}(1 - \rho) - \rho\bar{Z}^2}\right].$$

The second equality follows from the definition of ρ. The sign of the real wage change is then determined by the sign of the numerator of the expression in square brackets, which gives the expression in the text.

References

Baldwin, R. (2001), The core-periphery model with forward looking expectations. *Regional Science and Urban Economics* 31, 21–49.

Baldwin, R., Forslid, R. (2000), The core-periphery model and endogenous growth; stabilizing and destabilizing integration. *Economica* 67, 307–324.

Baldwin, R., Forslid, R., Martin, R., Ottaviano, G., Robert-Nicoud, F. (2003), *Economic Geography and Public Policy*. Princeton University Press, Princeton, NJ.

Bhagwati, J.N., Brecher, R.A., Hatta, T. (1983), The generalized theory of transfers and welfare: bilateral transfers in a multilateral world. *The American Economic Review* 73, 606–618.

Brakman, S., Van Marrewijk, C. (1998), *The Economics of International Transfers*. Cambridge University Press, Cambridge, UK.

Brakman, S., Garretsen, H., Van Marrewijk, C. (2001), *An Introduction to Geographical Economics*. Cambridge University Press, Cambridge, UK.

Brakman, S., Garretsen, H., Schramm, M. (2006), Putting new economic geography to the test: free-ness of trade and agglomeration in EU-regions. *Regional Science and Urban Economics* 36, 613–635.

Brakman, S., Van Marrewijk, C. (2007), Transfers, non-traded goods, and unemployment: an analysis of the Keynes–Ohlin debate. *History of Political Economy* 39, 121–143.

Chichilnisky, G. (1980), Basic goods, the effects of commodity transfers and the international economic order. *Journal of Development Economics* 7, 505–519.

Djajic, S., Lahiri, S., Raimondos-Møller, P. (1999), Foreign aid, domestic investment and welfare. *Economic Journal* 109, 698–707.

Fujita, M., Krugman, P.R., Venables, A.J. (1999), *The Spatial Economy; Cities, Regions, And International Trade*. MIT Press, Cambridge, MA.

Gale, D. (1974), Exchange equilibrium and coalitions: an example. *Journal of Mathematical Economics* 1, 63–66.

Jones, R.W. (1967), International capital movements and the theory of tariffs and trade. *Journal of International Economics* 5, 263–274.

Jones, R.W. (1985), Income effects and paradoxes in the theory of international trade. *The Economic Journal* 95, 330–344.

Kemp, M.C. (1964), *The Pure Theory of International Trade*. Prentice-Hall, Englewood Cliffs, NJ.

Kemp, M.C. (1995), *The Gains From Trade and The Gains from Aid*. Routledge, London.

Kemp, M.C., Kojima, S. (1985), Tied aid and the paradoxes of donor-enrichment and recipient-impoverishment. *International Economic Review* 26, 721–729.

Kemp, M.C., Shimomura, K. (2003), A theory of involuntary unrequited international transfers. *Journal of Political Economy* 111, 686–692.

Keynes, J.M. (1929a), The German transfer problem. *The Economic Journal* 39, 1–7.

Keynes, J.M. (1929b), The reparations problem: a discussion. II. A rejoinder. *The Economic Journal* 39, 179–182.

Keynes, J.M. (1929c), Mr. Keynes' views on the transfer problem. III. A reply. *The Economic Journal* 39, 404–408.

Krugman, P.R. (1991), Increasing returns and economic geography. *Journal of Political Economy* 99, 483–499.

Krugman, P.R., (1993), Toward a counter-counterrevolution in development theory. In: *Proceedings of The World Bank Annual Conference on Development Economics* 1992, pp. 15–38.

Krugman, P.R. (1995), *Development, Geography and Economic Theory*. MIT Press, Cambridge, MA.

Lahiri, S., Raimondos-Møller, P. (2004), Donor strategy under the fungibility of foreign aid. *Economics and Politics* 16, 213–231.

Lahiri, S., Raimondos-Møller, P., Wong, K.-Y., Woodland, A. (2002), Optimal foreign aid and tariffs. *Journal of Development Economics* 67, 79–99.

Leontief, W. (1936), A note on the pure theory of transfers. In: *Explorations in Economics: Notes and Essays Contributed in Honor of F.W. Taussig.* McGraw-Hill, New York, pp. 84–92.

Van Marrewijk, C., Michael, M.S. (1998), Tied to capital or untied foreign aid. *Review of Development Economics* 2, 61–75.

Mundell, R.A. (1960), The pure theory of international trade. *American Economic Review* 50, 67–110.

Ohlin, B. (1929a), The reparations problem: a discussion; transfer difficulties, real and imagined. *The Economic Journal* 39, 172–183.

Ohlin, B. (1929b), Mr. Keynes' views on the transfer problem. II. A rejoinder from Professor Ohlin. *The Economic Journal* 39, 400–404.

Ohyama, M. (1974), Tariffs and the transfer problem. *KEIO Economic Studies* 11, 29–45.

Ottaviano, G.I.P., Robert-Nicoud, F. (2006), The 'Genome' of NEG models with vertical linkages: a positive and normative synthesis. *Journal of Economic Geography* 6, 113–139.

Robert-Nicoud, F. (2004), The structure of simple 'New Economic Geography' models (or, on identical twins). *Journal of Economic Geography* 4, 1–34.

Samuelson, P.A. (1947), *Foundations of Economic Analysis*. Harvard University Press, Cambridge, MA.

Schweinberger, A.G. (1990), On the welfare effects of tied aid. *International Economic Review* 31, 457–462.

Weibull, J.W. (1995), *Evolutionary Game Theory*. MIT Press, Cambridge, MA.

CHAPTER 4

Does Foreign Aid Impede Foreign Investment?

Hamid Beladi[a] and Reza Oladi[b]

[a]*Department of Economics, University of Texas at San Antonio, 6900 North Loop,*
1604 West San Antonio, TX 78249-0633, USA
E-mail address: hamid.beladi@utsa.edu
[b]*Department of Economics, Utah State University, 3530 Old Main Hill, Logan, UT 84322-3530, USA*
E-mail address: oladi@econ.usu.edu

Abstract
This paper investigates the impact of foreign aid on foreign investment when foreign aid is used to finance a public consumption good. By formulating and analyzing a three-good general equilibrium model, we show that such foreign aid could crowd out foreign investment, given a factor intensity condition.

Keywords: Foreign aid, foreign investment

JEL classifications: F21, F35, H4

1. Introduction

The literature on income transfer goes as far back as Keynes (1929), where he argued that the German reparation payments after WWI had caused a decrease in its terms of trade, known as the orthodox view. Jones (1970) took the literature to a new direction and presented a number of cases where, in absence of trade barriers, an income transfer could result in an increase in donor's terms of trade and therefore pioneered an unorthodox and somewhat paradoxical view. His paper deals more with presumption and bias about the effects on the terms of trade of the transferring country than the actual effect. That is, the orthodox bias is that the terms of trade of the donor country is deteriorated following a transfer. Jones (1970) sets out to reverse that bias on the premise that "the real income loss represented by the transfer at initial prices may be mitigated by the 'secondary' effects of an improvement in the terms of trade".

The literature continues to this day and it has taken a number of different avenues. Jones (1975) reconsidered the effect of income transfer on terms of trade by assuming the existence of non-traded goods. Jones (1975) found that the different degrees of demand and supply disparities between countries is a prominent factor in determining the effects on a transferring country's terms of trade. As well, price sensitivity, both of

THEORY AND PRACTICE OF FOREIGN AID
VOLUME 1   ISSN: 1574-8715
DOI: 10.1016/S1574-8715(06)01004-9

demanders and producers, as a cause of trade strongly impacts terms of trade in a transfer where a non-traded good is present. Brecher and Bhagwati (1981), Bhagwati *et al.* (1983) and Srinivasan and Bhagwati (1984) indicated the conditions under which an income transfer would be immiserizing for the recipient country, thus establishing the welfare paradox. Brecher and Bhagwati (1981) made a clear distinction between foreign and national income in an economy where foreign ownership is present. When the national and aggregate incomes differ, the recipient country experiences a decrease in national welfare, which is contrary to the standard results. This immiserizing growth is also shown to occur in stable markets. Bhagwati *et al.* (1983) generalized these results by claiming that this paradox (immiserizing growth to the recipient of the transfer) can only occur with market stability if there are certain "distortions" in that economy. They set up a three-agent model, where two of the agents engage in a bilateral transfer, and the third outside agent is included in order to simulate a multilateral environment. After implementing the conditions of the immiserizing growth, though it appeared as if there were no distortions, in fact, the absence of optimal taxation existed as the said distortion. Hence, the generalization was established.

Kemp and Kojima (1985) and Schweinberger (1990), among others, investigated welfare paradox of an income transfer when such aid is tied. Kemp and Kojima (1985) verified that perverse outcomes occur in the presence of market stability when dealing with tied aid on the part of the recipient or donor. Unlike previous literature establishing the welfare paradox, their work is not reliant on an additional country or commodity. Schweinberger (1990) offered a slightly alternative model to Kemp and Kojima (1985). He claimed the effects of the tied aid puts constraint on the spending of the private sector's income. A surprising result of his model is that if aid is tied in the donor's export market, the donor paradox (enrichment of the donor) cannot occur. Beladi (1990) reexamines the welfare effects of international transfers in a two country general equilibrium model of trade in the presence of generalized unemployment. In this context he derives the necessary conditions for the occurrence of paradoxical as well as normal results on employment and welfare. Lahiri and Raimondos (1995) considered the welfare effects of aid tied to quantitative trade restrictions. They found that these quantitative distortions do not of themselves cause a transfer paradox because unlike price distortions, quotas alone do not bring distortions into other markets. In the case of quantitative trade restrictions, the transfer paradox only occurs with quota reform and only as a result of the welfare changes associated with that reform. Lahiri and Raimondos-Moller (1997) investigated foreign aid tied to tariff reforms. They presented conditions where Pareto-improvement occurs for the recipient and donor countries as well as the third outside country not involved in the transfer. By tying aid to changes in tariffs, they showed that theoretically, a certain level of welfare can be attained in the donor country, while the tariff reduction will not cause the recipient country's tariff revenue to decrease. Hatzipanayotou and Michael (1995) assumed that the recipient used foreign aid to finance a public consumption good, and they investigated the impact on terms of trade of both the recipient and donor. They also showed that the income transfer could be welfare enriching for the donor and welfare immiserizing for the recipient. In addition to this, they showed that a transfer can increase or decrease world welfare, thus improving or worsening the welfare of both countries. Yano and Nugent (1999) examined the impact of development aid on the welfare of a small open economy in presence of non-traded goods (as a significant amount of aid is spent on non-traded infrastructures) and demonstrated that welfare paradox can take place. They claimed that the expansion of non-traded sectors can outweigh the benefits of aid and therefore could result in welfare paradox. However, Choi (2004) indicated, in a set up with two factors two tradable goods and a non-traded good, the terms of trade for a small economy cannot be deteriorated. Thus he claimed that Yano and Nugent (1999) condition on non-traded good sector is not necessary.

More recently, Abe and Takarada (2005) attempted to resolve some of the issues surrounding the dispute between Kemp and Kojima (1985) and Schweinberger (1990). Their model of tied aid showed that when the households of the recipient country have knowledge of the transfers and have the ability to trade the purchased goods, no transfer paradoxes occur in the context of normal commodities. Kemp (2005) extended the theory of tied aid by creating a model that is compatible with non-tradable public consumption goods. He argued that with private consumption goods households can resell the aid on world markets, essentially "untying" the aid. The transfer paradox, in this context, still exists. Torsvik (2005) examined the implications of donor cooperation and mutual aid policy. He showed that donor cooperation is always beneficial when aid contracts are used. When contracts are not used, however, cooperation can harm the donor countries involved in the transfer. Alesina and Dollar (2000) studied the trends of foreign aid allocation. They find that political strategy plays a role as significant as the economic needs of the recipient countries in determining who gets what aid. The study reveals that all other things constant, democratic countries are granted more aid. And although politics strongly influence foreign aid allocation, the economies of recipient countries significantly stimulate foreign direct investments.

The purpose of the present paper is to raise an entirely different question: Does foreign aid crowd out foreign investment, given that the foreign aid is used by the recipient to finance a public consumption good? On the one hand, the recipient countries are often poor developing countries. On the other hand, the impact of foreign investment on economic development of such poor economies is indisputable. Therefore, it is imperative to investigate this question.

To answer our question, we consider a three-sector general equilibrium model with two tradable sectors (exportable and import competing) and a non-traded public consumption good sector. In this, our framework is closely related to Kemp (2005), Jones (1975) and Hatzipanayotou and Michael (1995).[1] As in Hatzipanayotou and Michael (1995), we assume that the recipient country uses foreign aid to finance the production of the public consumption good. We further assume that foreign investment takes place in the exportable sector. This last assumption (which is relaxed later in the paper) is compatible with the behavior of multinational corporations in less developed countries. As our result, we show that such foreign aid impedes foreign investment if

---

[1] See also Brecher and Diaz Alejandro (1977).

importable sector is more capital intensive than the public good sector. The reason is quite intuitive. An increase in foreign aid draws resources from the importable sector. As the capital intensity of importable sector is higher, some labor will also have to be moved from the exportable sector to the public good sector. This would reduce the marginal product of foreign capital, which in turn reduces foreign investment. Moreover, we investigate whether our result holds for an economy where foreign capital is used across the economy, implying that the domestic capital and the foreign capital are perfect substitute. We demonstrate that in fact a similar result holds and again factor intensity plays a crucial role.

In addition to being an appealing theoretical exercise, our paper has a vital policy implication. Accordingly, there might be a trade-off between foreign aid and foreign investment that policy makers should be aware of.

The rest of the paper is organized as follows. We present a model with foreign capital specificity in Section 2. Section 3 is allocated to the case where foreign capital is used across the economy, while Section 4 draws the concluding remarks.

2. Sector specific foreign investment

Assume a small open recipient economy producing three goods: an exportable, an import competing, and a non-traded public consumption good. The production technology for the exportable good is represented by the production function $x_e = F_e(L_e, K_f)$, where x_e, L_e, and K_f are the quantities of production of exportable, labor usage, and the foreign capital used by the exportable sector, respectively. We assume that foreign capital is only used by the exportable sector. This assumption is consistent with the observation that the multinational corporations are responsible for most of the foreign investments, which are targeted toward exports (we will relax this assumption in the next section). The production technology for the import competing sector is $x_i = F_i(L_i, K_i)$, where x_i is the production of import competing good, L_i and K_i are the labor and capital usage by this sector. The public good is produced privately and supplied to the public free of charge by the government. However, the government finances the production of this good through foreign aid. The production technology of the public good is represented by the production function $g = F(L_g, K_g)$, where g, L_g, K_g are the production of public good, labor used in the production of public good, and the domestic capital used by the public good sector, respectively. Finally, we assume all the neoclassical assumption regarding the above production functions, which exhibit constant returns to scale as well as diminishing marginal productivity.

We further assume that the markets for the tradable sectors are perfect competitive. Therefore, we have the following zero profit equilibrium conditions.

$$a_{Le}w + a_{Ke}r_f = p_e, \tag{1}$$
$$a_{Li}w + a_{Ki}r = p_i, \tag{2}$$

where a_{Lj}, a_{kj}, and p_j, $j = e, i$, are the unit labor cost, unit capital cost, and the price in sector j, respectively. Moreover, w, r_f, and r denote the wage rate, the return to foreign capital, and the return to domestic capital, respectively. Note also that the return to foreign capital and the prices of import competing and exportable goods are determined in the international markets and therefore they are fixed for our recipient economy.

As production of public consumption good is financed by the foreign aid, we have the following equilibrium condition for the public sector.

$$(a_{Lg}w + a_{Kg}r)g = T, \tag{3}$$

where a_{Lg} and a_{Kg} are the optimal unit labor and capital costs, respectively. T denotes foreign aid. The left-hand side of Equation (3) is the cost of public good.

The resource constraints are given by the following equations.

$$a_{Le}x_e + a_{Li}x_i + a_{Lg}g = L, \tag{4}$$

$$a_{Ke}x_e = K_f, \tag{5}$$

$$a_{Ki}x_i + a_{kg}g = K, \tag{6}$$

where L and K are the fixed endowments of labor and domestic capital, respectively. Equation (4) implies that labor is mobile across all three sectors. Equation (5) states that foreign capital is specific to the exportable sector, while Equation (6) indicates that domestic capital is mobile between the importable sector and the public sector. Equations (1)–(6) constitute our complete general equilibrium system with endogenous variables x_e, x_i, g, w, r, and K_f.

Now we answer the central question raised in this paper, assuming that foreign investment is specific to the exportable sector: What is the impact of foreign aid on foreign investment? By differentiating Equations (1)–(3), we obtain:

$$a_{Le}\hat{w} = 0, \tag{7}$$

$$a_{Li}\hat{w} + a_{Ki}\hat{r} = 0, \tag{8}$$

$$a_{Lg}\hat{w} + a_{Kg}\hat{r} + (a_{Lg}w + a_{Kg}r)g\hat{g} = T\hat{T}, \tag{9}$$

where circumflex denotes proportional changes. Equations (7)–(8) imply that $\hat{w} = \hat{r} = 0$. Using this and Equations (3) and (9), we conclude that:

$$\hat{g} = \hat{T}. \tag{10}$$

Now, by substituting Equation (5) into Equation (4) and then totally differentiating the resulting equation as well as Equation (6), we obtain:

$$\lambda_{Le}\hat{K}_f + \lambda_{Li}\hat{x}_i + \lambda_{Lg}\hat{g} = 0, \tag{11}$$

$$\lambda_{Ki}\hat{x}_i + \lambda_{Kg}\hat{g} = 0, \tag{12}$$

where λ_{Lj}, $j = e, i, g$, is the fraction of labor used in sector j and λ_{Kj}, $j = i, g$, is the fraction of domestic capital used by sector j. Note also that, in deriving Equations (11) and (12), we used the fact that unit factor costs do not change.

Finally, by solving Equations (11) and (12) and using Equation (10), we obtain:

$$L_e \hat{K}_f + L_g \left(\frac{k_i - k_g}{k_i} \right) \hat{T} = 0, \tag{13}$$

where $k_j = \frac{K_j}{L_j}$, $j = i, g$, is capital intensity in sector j. Thus, Equation (13) concludes the following proposition, which formally addresses the question we raised.

PROPOSITION 1. *Assume that foreign aid is used to finance a public consumption good and that foreign capital is specific to the exportable sector. Then, foreign aid impedes (encourages) foreign investment if the public sector is more (less) labor intensive than the import competing sector.*

This interesting result states that foreign aid could crowd out foreign investment depending on factor intensities in the import competing and the public sectors. The economic explanation behind this result is somewhat intuitive. An increase in foreign aid used to finance the production of a public consumption good would increase the production of public consumption good. This in turn results in movements of both capital and labor from the import competing sector to the public sector. Assuming that the import competing sector is more capital intensive than the public good sector, less labor for each unit of capital moves out of the import competing sector than required by the public sector. Thus, some labor must also move from the exportable sector to the public sector, resulting in a decrease in marginal productivity of capital in the exportable sector. As the return to foreign investment is fixed and determined internationally, due to the small country assumption, the level of foreign investment would fall. Now assume that the public sector is more capital intensive than the import competing sector. Then, as resources move out of the import competing sector, more units of labor for each unit of capital leave this sector than required by the public sector. As a result, some of these units of labor must move to the exportable sector, causing an increase in marginal productivity of foreign capital. This would result in an increase in the usage of foreign capital, leading to an increase in foreign investment.

3. Mobile capital

We next investigate whether the result of the preceding section will remain valid if we assume no distinction between domestic capital and foreign capital, i.e. we assume foreign investment takes place economy wide. To do so, we rewrite our model by assuming that the foreign capital is used in all three sectors. Equations (1)–(3) would then change to:

$$a_{Le}w + a_{Ke}r_f = p_e, \tag{14}$$

$$a_{Li}w + a_{Ki}r_f = p_i, \tag{15}$$

$$(a_{Lg}w + a_{Kg}r_f)g = T. \tag{16}$$

According to the above equilibrium conditions, as there is no distinction between domestic capital and foreign capital, the economy-wide rate of return to capital is the internationally determined rate of return. Therefore, such a rate of return is fixed for our recipient economy.[2]

Similarly, the resource constraints would change to:

$$a_{Le}x_e + a_{Li}x_i + a_{Lg}g = \bar{L}, \tag{17}$$

$$a_{ke}x_e + a_{Ki}x_i + a_{kg}g = \bar{K} + K_f. \tag{18}$$

Equation (18) indicates mobility of foreign capital, as well as domestic capital, across all three sectors of the economy. Our new complete economic system consists of Equations (14)–(18) with five endogenous variables x_e, x_i, g, w, and K_f. Recall that returns to capital is fixed in this system.

We now return to our question of whether foreign aid crowds out foreign investment within the context of this section. By differentiating Equation (14), we obtain Equation (7). Furthermore, we differentiate Equations (15) and (18) to obtain:

$$a_{Li}\hat{w} = 0, \tag{19}$$

$$a_{Lg}\hat{w} + (a_{Lg}w + a_{Kg}r)g\hat{g} = T\hat{T}. \tag{20}$$

Similar to the preceding section, we use Equations (7), (19), and (20) to derive Equation (10).

Next, we differentiate resource constraints, i.e. Equations (17) and (18), to get:

$$\lambda_{Le}\hat{x}_e + \lambda_{Li}\hat{x}_i + \lambda_{Lg}\hat{g} = 0, \tag{21}$$

$$\lambda_{Ke}\hat{x}_e + \lambda_{Ki}\hat{x}_i + \lambda_{Kg}\hat{g} = \hat{K}, \tag{22}$$

where $K = \bar{K} + K_f$. Note that, as the stock of domestic capital is fixed, $dK = dK_f$ implying that $\hat{K} = \frac{dK}{K} = \frac{dK_f}{K}$.

Finally, we use Equations (10), (21), and (22) to obtain:

$$dK_f = L_i(k_i - k_e)\hat{x}_i + L_g(k_g - k_e)\hat{T}. \tag{23}$$

We use Equation (23) to conclude the equivalence of Proposition 1. It states that the answer to our question depends on capital intensity ranking.

PROPOSITION 2. *Assume that foreign aid is used to finance a public consumption good and that foreign capital is used in all three sectors. Then, an increase in foreign aid decreases (increases) foreign investment if* $k_i > k_e > k_g$ ($k_g > k_e > k_i$).

Again, according to this proposition, foreign aid may crowd out foreign investment given the stated factor intensity ranking. Economic intuition is interesting. First, assume that the import competing sector is more capital intensive than the exportable

---

[2] It is worth noting that the system given by (14)–(16) is indeterminate if terms of trade is subject to change.

sector and that the capital intensity of exportable sector is greater than that of public good sector. Then, the expansion of the public good sector due to an increase in foreign aid will require movement of all factors from the tradable sectors to the public sector. On the one hand, as the import competing sector (and the exportable sector) is more capital intensive than the public good sector, the public sector needs less capital per unit of labor than released by the tradable sectors. On the other hand, the domestic capital is fixed while the foreign capital is variable. In conclusion, the economy as a whole will substitute domestic capital for foreign capital, resulting in a decrease in the use of foreign capital. Thus, foreign aid crowds out foreign investment. Now, let the public good sector be the most capital intensive sector, followed by the exportable sector. An increase in foreign aid expands the public sector at the expense of tradable sectors. However, as the public sector is the most capital intensive sector in the economy, this sector requires more capital for each unit of labor than moved out of the tradable sectors. To make up the difference, foreign capital moves in. Thus, under the stated factor intensity ranking, foreign aid encourages foreign investment.

4. Conclusion

Some of the foreign aid to developing economies is used to finance public consumption goods. On the other hand, foreign investment has played an increasingly important role in economic development of such economies. These stylized facts motivated us to question the impact foreign aid may have on foreign investment in recipient developing economies.

We used a three-good general equilibrium model to represent a recipient economy, assuming two traded goods and a non-traded public consumption good. First, we considered a case where foreign capital is used only in the exportable sector. We demonstrated that an increase in foreign aid, used to finance a public consumption good, would discourage foreign investment if the import competing sector is more capital intensive than the public good sector. Then, we examined whether our result is robust with regard to the assumption of sector specificity of foreign capital. To do this, we allowed perfect substitutability of foreign capital and domestic capital. We showed that foreign aid would cause a substitution of domestic capital for foreign capital, and thus a reduction of foreign capital usage, if the import competing sector is more capital intensive than the exportable sector and the exportable sector is more capital intensive than the public sector.

The possibility of crowding-out effect of foreign aid on foreign investment has a clear and imperative policy implication. Policy makers, specially in recipient developing economies, should be aware of such a possible trade-off.

This article opens an entirely new direction to the literature on foreign aid. In addition to its theoretical contribution and useful policy implication, our paper provides a foundation for empirical investigation of the impacts of foreign aid on foreign investment.

Acknowledgement

We are grateful to the volume editor for insightful comments on an earlier version of this paper. We are solely responsible for any possible remaining errors.

References

Abe, K., Takarada, Y. (2005), Tied aid and welfare. *Review of International Economics* 13, 964–972.

Alesina, A., Dollar, D. (2000), Who gives foreign aid to Whom and Why? *Journal of Economic Growth* 5, 33–63.

Beladi, H. (1990), Unemployment and immiserizing transfer. *Journal of Economics* (Zeitschrift für Nationalekonomie) 52, 253–265.

Bhagwati, J., Brecher, R., Hatta, T. (1983), The generalized theory of transfers and welfare: bilateral transfers in a multilateral world. *American Economic Review* 73, 606–618.

Brecher, R., Bhagwati, J. (1981), Foreign ownership and the theory of trade and welfare. *Journal of Political Economy* 89, 497–511.

Brecher, R., Diaz Alejandro, C.F. (1977), Tariffs, foreign capital and immiserizing growth. *Journal of International Economics* 7, 317–322.

Choi, E.K. (2004), Aid allocation and the transfer paradox in small open economies. *International Review of Economics and Finance* 13, 229–361.

Hatzipanayotou, P., Michael, M.S. (1995), Foreign aid and public goods. *Journal of Development Economics* 47, 455–467.

Jones, R. (1970), The transfer problem revisited. *Economica* 37, 178–184.

Jones, R. (1975), Presumption about the transfer problem. *Journal of International Economics* 5, 263–274.

Kemp, M.C. (2005), Aid tied to the donor's exports. *Pacific Economics Review* 10, 317–322.

Kemp, M.C., Kojima, S. (1985), Tied aid and the paradoxes of donor-enrichment and recipient-impoverishment. *International Economic Review* 26, 721–729.

Keynes, M. (1929), The German transfer problem. *Economic Journal* 39, 1–7.

Lahiri, S., Raimondos, P. (1995), Welfare effects of aid under quantitative trade restrictions. *Journal of International Economics* 39, 297–315.

Lahiri, S., Raimondos-Moller, P. (1997), On the tying of aid to tariff reform. *Journal of Development Economics* 54, 479–491.

Schweinberger, A. (1990), On the welfare effects of tied aid. *International Economic Review* 31, 457–462.

Srinivasan, T.N., Bhagwati, J. (1984), On transfer paradoxes and immiserizing growth. *Journal of Development Economics* 15, 111–115.

Torsvik, G. (2005), Foreign economic aid; should donors cooperate? *Journal of Development Economics* 77, 503–515.

Yano, M., Nugent, J.B. (1999), Aid, nontraded goods, and the transfer paradox in small countries. *American Economic Review* 89, 431–449.

CHAPTER 5

Infrastructure Aid, Deindustrialization and Urban Unemployment

Jai-Young Choi[a] and E. Kwan Choi[b,c]

[a]Department of Economics and Finance, Lamar University, Beaumont, TX 77710, USA
E-mail address: jai-young.choi@lamar.edu
[b]Department of Economics, Iowa State University, Ames, IA 50011, USA
E-mail address: kchoi@iastate.edu
[c]City University of Hong Kong, Hong Kong

Abstract
This paper investigates the role of infrastructure aid to developing countries beset with unemployment. Since unemployment persists in most developing countries with chronic foreign debts, the impact of infrastructure aid is analyzed using an extended Harris–Todaro model with two traded good sectors and a nontraded good sector. The paper delineates sufficient conditions under which infrastructure aid may lead to a Dutch disease effect.

Keywords: Infrastructure aid, deindustrialization, Harris–Todaro, Dutch disease, urban unemployment

JEL classifications: F21, O19, O41

1. Introduction

The role of infrastructure capital as an engine for growth has long been recognized by the world community. Developing countries lack infrastructure capital such as highways and clean water. Lack of infrastructure renders existing capital equipment inefficient and expedites wear and tear, while good infrastructure helps workers maintain their health and achieve peak efficiency. Accordingly, substantial infrastructure aid in both monetary and physical forms has been funneled constantly to the world's low-income countries since World War II. Despite the donors' good intentions, however, the aid has yielded varying results. Aid to some developing countries has been successful (e.g., aid to European countries by the Marshall Plan, and aid to Japan,[1]

---

[1] Japan received little aid during the Post-War era, except for a substantial injection of cash inflow as suppliers, which caused industrialization during the Korean War.

South Korea, and Taiwan), while development assistance to other countries has not (e.g., aid to sub-Saharan Africa). Even today many developing countries are asking high-income countries to forgive their debts while continuing to ask for more aid.[2]

Given this conflicting empirical evidence, it behooves aid researchers to investigate conditions under which immiserizing aid does not occur. A substantial body of literature exists that has investigated the impacts of aid to developing countries. Recently, a number of theoretical and empirical studies have suggested that through a "Dutch disease" like effect, aid actually may have undermined the growth of some low-income countries that received aid.[3] For instance, Younger (1992) noted that foreign aid produced a Dutch disease effect in Ghana, whereas Vos (1998) used a computable general equilibrium model to show that aid produced a strong Dutch disease effect in Pakistan. On the other hand, Nyoni (1998) showed that the flow of aid did not produce a Dutch disease effect in Tanzania. Nkusu (2004) showed that in the presence of unemployment currency appreciation may not occur, thereby removing the possibility of a Dutch disease effect altogether.

Among the theoretical works on the Dutch disease, two contributions are particularly noteworthy, those of Corden and Neary (1982), and Yano and Nugent (1999). Corden and Neary (1982) analyzed the effects of a resource boom in a two-good and two-factor model with sector-specific capital, and delineated the conditions under which the Dutch disease occurs. In their model, imports and exports are treated as a single traded good, and the prices of traded goods are constrained to move together. Further, the sector-specific capital and the results thereof make the model less interesting to policy makers of donor countries who are interested in long-run effects of aid.

Yano and Nugent (1999) have studied the Dutch disease effect in a 3×2 model with two traded goods and a nontraded good in the presence of full-employment. While the Yano–Nugent model represents an improvement vis-à-vis the Corden–Neary model, it does not capture two essential characteristics of low-income countries depicted in the celebrated Harris–Todaro (1970, HT henceforth) model: dual economic structure and chronic urban unemployment.

---

[2] The sub-Saharan countries in which aid distribution was not successful include Cameroon, Ethiopia, Ghana, Mozambique, Nigeria, and Zaire, among others.

[3] Developing a new source of growth (such as a new natural resource) can erode profits and production of other sectors. In particular, deindustrialization in the traded good sectors can occur as the new sector draws resources away from the traded-good sectors, and the nation's currency rises in value on foreign exchange markets. This problem has been called the "Dutch disease" after a situation that arose following the development of new natural gas fields under the North Sea. In this paper, we argue that a Dutch disease (or deindustrialization) in a sector occurs whenever the presence of a growth agent induces a contraction of the sector's output, not necessarily a contraction of the manufacturing sector. Empirical works on the Dutch disease include Benjamin *et al.* (1989), Younger (1992), Bandara (1995), Vos (1998), Nyoni (1998), Spatafora and Warner (1999), Adam and Bevan (2003), Stijns (2003), and Nkusu (2004), among many others. Theoretical studies on the Dutch disease include Corden and Neary (1982), Cassing and Warr (1985), Yano and Nugent (1999), and Choi (2004), among others.

The purpose of this paper is to fill the gap in the literature by investigating the effects of infrastructure aid on developing countries with urban unemployment. The primary focus is on the welfare effects of aid and the conditions under which deindustrialization occurs. We extend the HT model to include a nontraded good sector. The agricultural (exportable) sector is located in the rural region, and the manufacturing (importable) sector, as well as the nontraded good sector, are located in the urban region.[4] We retain the original HT hypothesis that urban unemployment exists due to the institutionally-set manufacturing wage and rural–urban labor migration occurs until the agricultural wage equals the expected manufacturing wage. Since workers are absorbed into the nontraded good sector in most developing countries,[5] we assume that (a) only workers in the urban manufacturing sector face the risk of unemployment, and (b) the expected wage in the manufacturing sector is equal to the wages in the agricultural and the nontraded good sectors.[6]

Several significant results emerge from the analysis. Infrastructure aid to a small open economy cannot be immiserizing, regardless of which sector receives the aid. The infrastructure aid to either one of the two trade good sectors causes an appreciation of the foreign exchange rate for the recipient country, but aid to the nontraded good industry results in a depreciation. The output effects of infrastructure aid to either of the traded sectors are indeterminate in general, i.e., infrastructure aid in one sector may increase or decrease its own output as well as the outputs of other sectors but infrastructure aid to the nontraded good sector necessarily increases its own output. The output effects of infrastructure aid depend on the ensuing changes in factor prices, unemployed–employed ratio, factor-intensity and factor abundance rankings, relative factor-saving effects of the aid, and the supply response of the nontraded good. These results may explain why the Dutch disease takes different forms in different developing countries as reported in the literature.

---

[4] In the original HT model there are three factors of production, labor, land, and capital. HT assumed that land is specific to agriculture, and capital is perfectly immobile between sectors. Corden and Findlay (1975) brought the HT model close to the neoclassical two sector model by incorporating intersectoral capital mobility. Several studies considered the existence of an informal sector in the urban area, including Todaro and Smith (2002).

[5] In many developing countries, the unemployed workers in the manufacturing sector are partially absorbed by low-paying jobs in the urban informal sector which usually produces nontraded goods, e.g., restaurant service, daily construction work, house keeping, private chauffer job, and various jobs in the underground economy. For this hypothesis on the nontraded good sector in the HT model, we are indebted to the useful conversation with Ali Khan (of Johns Hopkins University) during the Asian Pacific Journal of Economics and Accounting conference in Hong Kong during the summer of 2006.

[6] Since the wage in the nontraded good sector is flexible as in agriculture, we assume full employment also exists in the urban nontraded good sector.

2. *Assumptions and the basic properties of the model*

2.1. Assumptions

We employ a 3 × 2 HT type model with two traded goods and a nontraded good, and make the following assumptions:

(1) The government converts aid money into sector-specific infrastructure capital. Once the infrastructure capital is installed in a targeted sector, it reduces the production cost of the sector by saving the amount of resources required per unit of the sectoral output.[7]

(2) In the country receiving infrastructure aid, there are two regions and three sectors: the agriculture sector (Sector 1) in the rural region, and a manufacturing sector (Sector 2) and a nontraded good sector (Sector N) in the urban region. Each sector utilizes two factors of production (labor and capital).

(3) Full employment exists in the agricultural and the nontraded good sectors where the real wages are equal and flexible. However, unemployment exists in the urban manufacturing sector where the real wage (w_2) is institutionally set above the agricultural wage (w_1).

(4) Workers are free to enter any sector ex ante. Rural–urban labor migration occurs until the rural agricultural wage equals the expected manufacturing wage which is the probability of finding a job in the manufacturing sector ($L_2/(L_U + L_2)$) times w_2 where L_2 and L_U, respectively, denote the employed and the unemployed labor in the manufacturing sector.

When the labor market is in equilibrium, free entry ensures that the urban nontraded good sector pays the same wage as the rural sector, i.e., $w_N = w_1$, which is equal to the expected manufacturing wage, $w_2/(1 + \lambda)$, where $\lambda = L_U/L_2$ is the unemployed–employed ratio in the manufacturing sector.

(5) The recipient country is a price taker of the traded goods in the world market, and it exports the agricultural good and imports the manufactured good.

(6) Factor intensities of the goods are such that the manufactured good is the most capital intensive in both the physical and the value sense, and it is followed by the nontraded good and the agricultural good. Further, this factor intensity ranking does not change after the addition of infrastructure aid.[8]

---

[7] Infrastructure capital usually is considered as a public input. In the present study, we assume that the aid money is converted into sector-specific infrastructure capital (i.e., public input) for the targeted sector that does not directly benefit other sectors. This implies that infrastructure aid is tantamount to costless technological progress which updates the technology of the recipient sector. The effects of a general public input (that generates spillover benefits to other sectors) can be obtained by expanding the cost functions in Equation (1).

[8] For factor abundance-ranking, please see Section 4 (page 75).

2.2. Short-term, cost-saving effect of infrastructure aid

In the short run, factor prices are fixed and do not respond to a change in infrastructure capital. Let the input–output coefficients of the three sectors be

$$a_{ij} = a_{ij}(w_j, r, S_j), \quad i = L, K, \ j = 1, 2, N \tag{1}$$

where r and S_j respectively denote the rental rate and the infrastructure capital in the jth sector.

The unit cost of the jth good is denoted by

$$a_{Lj}(w_j, r, S_j)w_j + a_{Kj}(w_j, r, S_j)r = g_j(w_j, r, S_j), \quad j = 1, 2, N.$$

The unit-profit of the jth good is

$$\pi_j = p_j - g_j(w_j, r, S_j), \quad j = 1, 2, N.$$

While the factor prices remain unchanged in the short-run, infrastructure investment, whether it is labor- or capital-saving, lowers unit cost in the targeted sector,

$$\frac{\partial g_j}{\partial S_j} = \frac{\partial a_{Lj}}{\partial S_j} w_j + \frac{\partial a_{Kj}}{\partial S_j} r < 0,$$

and increases the unit-profit (π_i) of the sector,

$$\frac{\partial \pi_j}{\partial S_j} = -\frac{\partial g_j(w_j, r, S_j)}{\partial S_j} > 0, \quad j = 1, 2, N.$$

Thus, infrastructure investment in a sector makes it more competitive and in the short run causes the sector to expand. In the long run, since the local product and factor markets are competitive, whether infrastructure investment is targeted to improve the productivity in the agricultural, manufacturing, or nontraded good sector, it eventually causes a realignment of the factor prices.

2.3. Factor prices, urban unemployment and exchange rate in the long run

In the presence of competitive product and factor markets, average cost pricing prevails in the long run

$$a_{Lj}w_j + a_{Kj}r = p_j, \quad j = 1, 2, N. \tag{2}$$

Totally differentiating (2), we obtain

$$\theta_{Lj}\hat{w}_j + \theta_{Kj}\hat{r} = \hat{p}_j - (\theta_{Lj}\hat{a}_{Lj} + \theta_{Kj}\hat{a}_{Kj}), \quad j = 1, 2, N, \tag{3}$$

where a hat (^) denotes the rate of change. The input–output coefficients in (2) can be expressed as functions of the wage-rental ratio ($\omega_j = w/r$) and infrastructure capital. Totally differentiating $a_{ij} = a_{ij}(\omega, S_j)$ in (1), we get

$$\hat{a}_{ij} = b_{ij}^* - \delta_{ij}^* = \varepsilon_{ij\omega}\hat{\omega} - \varepsilon_{ijS}\hat{S}_j, \quad j = 1, 2, N, \tag{4}$$

where $b_{ij}^* = (1/a_{ij})(\partial a_{ij}/\partial \omega_j)\,d\omega_j$ is the change in input–output coefficient due to a change in wage–rental ratio, $\delta_{ij}^* = -(1/a_{ij})(\partial a_{ij}/\partial S_j)\,dS_j$ is the change in a_{ij} due to infrastructure investment into the jth sector, and ε_{ijk} is the elasticity of a_{ij} with respect to k ($i = L, K; j = 1, 2, N; k = \omega_j, S_j$).[9]

Define the elasticity of factor substitution of the jth sector as

$$\sigma_j = \frac{\hat{a}_{Kj} - \hat{a}_{Lj}}{\hat{w}_j - \hat{r}}, \tag{5}$$

where each σ_j is positive. Cost minimization implies

$$w_j a_{Lj} b_{Lj}^* + r a_{Kj} b_{Kj}^* = 0. \tag{6}$$

Dividing (6) by p_j, we obtain

$$\theta_{Lj} b_{Lj}^* + \theta_{Kj} b_{Kj}^* = 0. \tag{7}$$

Utilizing (4)–(7), we get

$$\hat{a}_{Lj} = -\theta_{Kj}\sigma_j(\hat{w}_j - \hat{r}) - \delta_{Lj}^*, \qquad \hat{a}_{Kj} = \theta_{Lj}\sigma_j(\hat{w}_j - \hat{r}) - \delta_{Kj}^*. \tag{8}$$

Using (8), (3) can be expressed as

$$\theta_{Lj}\hat{w}_j + \theta_{Kj}\hat{r} = \hat{p}_j + (\theta_{Lj}\delta_{Lj}^* + \theta_{Kj}\delta_{Kj}^*). \tag{9}$$

Since the developing country is a price taker, $\hat{p}_1 = \hat{p}_2 = 0$. Hence, (9) can be rewritten as

$$\theta_{L1}\hat{w}_1 + \theta_{K1}\hat{r} = T_1^*, \tag{9.1}$$

$$\theta_{L2}\hat{w}_2 + \theta_{K2}\hat{r} = T_2^*, \tag{9.2}$$

$$\theta_{LN}\hat{w}_N + \theta_{KN}\hat{r} = \hat{p}_N + T_N^*, \tag{9.3}$$

where $T_j^* = \theta_{Lj}\delta_{Lj}^* + \theta_{Kj}\delta_{Kj}^*$ represents the reduction in labor and capital costs per unit of the jth commodity owing to the infrastructure investment in the jth sector. Since the urban manufacturing wage is institutionally set ($\hat{w}_2 = 0$), there are two unknowns ($\hat{w}_1, \hat{r}$) in the two equations, (9.1) and (9.2). Thus, $\hat{w}_1$ and $\hat{r}$ are determined in the two equations. Since $\hat{w}_1 = \hat{w}_N$, $\hat{p}_N$ is determined in (9.3) as follows:

$$\hat{w}_1 = \frac{\theta_{K2}T_1^* - \theta_{K1}T_2^*}{\Delta}, \qquad \hat{r} = \frac{\theta_{L1}T_2^*}{\Delta},$$

$$\hat{p}_N = \frac{\theta_{LN}\theta_{K2}T_1^* + \theta_{L1}\theta_{LN}(r/w_1)(k_N - k_1)T_2^*}{\Delta} - T_N^*,$$

$$\hat{\alpha} = -\hat{w}_1 = \frac{\theta_{K1}T_2^* - \theta_{K2}T_1^*}{\Delta}, \tag{10}$$

where $\Delta = \theta_{L1}\theta_{K2} > 0$ and $\alpha = 1 + \lambda$. Note that $d\alpha = d\lambda$ and $\hat{\alpha} = d\lambda/(1 + \lambda)$ and that $\hat{\alpha} = -\hat{w}_1$ since $\alpha w_1 = w_2$.

---

[9] A similar mathematical procedure has been used by Batra (1973) and Choi and Yu (1987) in their analysis of the effects of technical progress.

2.3.1. Infrastructure aid to the agriculture sector

In the presence of infrastructure aid invested in the agriculture sector, $T_1^* > T_2^* = T_N^* = 0$. Thus, from (10), we obtain

$$\frac{\hat{w}_1}{T_1^*} = \frac{\theta_{K2}}{\Delta} > 0, \qquad \frac{\hat{r}}{T_1^*} = 0,$$

$$\frac{\hat{p}_N}{T_1^*} = \frac{\theta_{LN}\theta_{K2}}{\Delta} = \theta_{LN}\frac{\hat{w}_1}{T_1^*} > 0, \qquad \frac{\hat{\alpha}}{T_1^*} = -\frac{\theta_{K2}}{\Delta} < 0.$$

That is, infrastructure aid to the agriculture sector increases the agricultural wage and the price of the nontraded good and decreases the unemployed–employed ratio of the manufacturing sector, while leaving the rental rate unchanged. Note that $\hat{p}_N = \theta_{LN}\hat{w}_1$, i.e., the price of the nontraded good rises more slowly than the agricultural wage. Since the manufacturing wage is institutionally set ($\hat{w}_2 = 0$) and $T_2^* = T_N^* = 0$, the rental rate is determined in the manufacturing sector independently from the infrastructure aid to the agriculture sector (T_1^*) in Equation (9.2). Then in (9.1), the agricultural wage rises owing to the cost reduction (or the productivity increase) resulting from the infrastructure aid to the agriculture sector. While the terms of trade between the two traded goods are fixed at the world prices, the Corden and Neary (1982) real exchange rate (p_N/p_2)necessarily appreciates since $(\hat{p}_N/T_1^*) - (\hat{p}_2/T_1^*) = (\hat{p}_N/T_1^*) > 0$.

2.3.2. Infrastructure aid to the manufacturing sector

With infrastructure aid to the manufacturing sector, $T_2^* > T_1^* = T_N^* = 0$. Thus, from (10), we get

$$\frac{\hat{w}_1}{T_2^*} = -\frac{\theta_{K1}}{\Delta} < 0, \qquad \frac{\hat{r}}{T_2^*} = \frac{\theta_{L1}}{\Delta} > 0,$$

$$\frac{\hat{p}_N}{T_2^*} = \frac{\theta_{L1}\theta_{LN}(r/w_1)(k_N - k_1)T_2^*}{\Delta} > 0, \qquad \frac{\hat{\alpha}}{T_2^*} = \frac{\theta_{K1}}{\Delta} > 0.$$

Thus, infrastructure aid to the manufacturing sector lowers the agricultural wage, but raises the economy's rental rate and the unemployed–employed ratio of the manufacturing sector. Further, the aid raises the price of the nontraded good (since $k_N > k_1$ by assumption (6)), and the Corden and Neary (1982) real exchange rate (p_N/p_2) appreciates because $\hat{p}_N/T_2^* - \hat{p}_2/T_2^* = \hat{p}_N/T_2^* > 0$.

2.3.3. Infrastructure aid to the nontraded good sector

In the presence of infrastructure aid invested in the nontraded good sector, $T_N^* > T_2^* = T_1^* = 0$. Recall that in (9.1) and (9.2), the factor prices are uniquely determined by the international prices of the traded goods. Therefore, from (10), we obtain:

$$\frac{\hat{w}_1}{T_N^*} = 0, \qquad \frac{\hat{r}}{T_N^*} = 0,$$

$$\frac{\hat{p}_N}{T_N^*} = -1 < 0, \qquad \frac{\hat{\alpha}}{T_N^*} = 0.$$

While the infrastructure aid to the nontraded good sector does not affect the factor prices and the unemployed–employed ratio in the manufacturing sector, it lowers the price of the nontraded good (by the same proportion as the reduction in unit cost of the nontraded good owing to the infrastructure investment there), and depreciates the Corden and Neary (1982) real exchange rate. Now, the following proposition can be stated:

PROPOSITION 1.

(1) *Infrastructure aid to the agriculture sector, while not affecting the economy's rental rate, increases the agricultural wage and the price of the nontraded good, lowers the unemployed–employed ratio of the manufacturing sector, and causes an appreciation of the* Corden and Neary (1982) *real exchange rate;*

(2) *Infrastructure aid to the manufacturing sector lowers the agricultural wage, raises the economy's rental rate, the unemployed–employed ratio of the manufacturing sector and the price of the nontraded good if $k_N > k_1$, and causes an appreciation of the* Corden and Neary (1982) *real exchange rate;*

(3) *Infrastructure aid to the nontraded good sector does not affect the economy's factor prices and the unemployed–employed ratio in the manufacturing sector, while it lowers the price of the nontraded good and causes a depreciation of the* Corden and Neary (1982) *real exchange rate.*

3. Infrastructure aid, national income and welfare

Producer revenue, $R = p_1 Y_1 + p_2 Y_2 + p_N Y_N$, must be distributed to factor owners, either as labor or rental income. Thus, consumer income is

$$I = w_1 L_1 + w_2 L_2 + w_N L_N + rK$$
$$= w_1 L_1 + (1 + \lambda) w_1 L_2 + w_1 L_N + rK = w_1 L + rK. \tag{11}$$

Differentiating (11), we obtain

$$\hat{I} = \frac{\hat{w}_1 I - rK(\hat{w}_1 - \hat{r})}{I}. \tag{12}$$

Substituting the expressions for the effects of the infrastructure aid to the jth sector in 2.3.1–2.3.3, we derive

$$\frac{\hat{I}}{T_1^*} = \frac{\hat{w}_1 I - rK(\hat{w}_1 - \hat{r})}{T_1^* I} = \frac{\hat{w}_1(w_1 L)}{T_1^* I} > 0,$$

$$\frac{\hat{I}}{T_2^*} = \frac{\hat{w}_1 I - rK(\hat{w}_1 - \hat{r})}{T_2^* I} = \frac{\hat{w}_1 I}{T_2^* I} + \frac{rK}{T_2^* I \Delta} > 0,$$

$$\frac{\hat{I}}{T_N^*} = \frac{\hat{w}_1 I - rK(\hat{w}_1 - \hat{r})}{T_N^*} = 0. \tag{13}$$

Thus, infrastructure aid to either of the two traded good sectors increases national income. Developing countries are characterized by low wage and high capital rental. Infrastructure aid to the agriculture sector unambiguously raises both wage and national income. On the other hand, infrastructure aid to the manufacturing sector with a fixed wage raises national income, but tends to depress the wage level in other sectors, thereby lowering total labor income. Infrastructure investment in the nontraded good sector does not change the factor prices, and hence has no effect on national income. This implies that an investment of infrastructure aid in the agriculture sector unambiguously raises national income and helps the working class.

Consider the indirect utility written as:

$$V(p_1, p_2, p_N, I)$$
$$= U\big(X_1(p_1, p_2, p_N, I), X_2(p_1, p_2, p_N, I), X_2(p_1, p_2, p_N, I)\big). \tag{14}$$

The effects of infrastructure aid to either the exportable or importable sector on consumer welfare can be obtained by differentiating (14) with respect to S_j and holding the prices of traded goods constant. Using Roy's identity, $\partial V/\partial p_j = -(\partial V/\partial I)X_j$, we get

$$\frac{\partial V}{\partial S_j} = \frac{\partial V}{\partial p_N}\frac{\partial p_N}{\partial S_j} + \frac{\partial V}{\partial I}\frac{\partial I}{\partial S_j} = V_I\left(-X_N \frac{\partial p_N}{\partial S_j} + \frac{\partial I}{\partial S_j}\right).$$

Recall from (13) that aid to either the export or the import sector raises consumer income, whereas the aid to the nontraded good sector has no effect on it. For aid to the agriculture sector, we get from (2) $\frac{\partial p_N}{\partial S_1} = a_{LN}\frac{\partial w_1}{\partial S_1}$ and from (11) $\frac{\partial I}{\partial S_1} = L\frac{\partial w_1}{\partial S_1}$. Thus,

$$\frac{\partial V}{\partial S_1} = V_I(L - L_N)\frac{\partial w_1}{\partial S_1} > 0. \tag{15}$$

Aid to the agriculture sector raises not only the price of the nontraded good but also national income. It raises the flexible wage throughout the economy and the income effect more than offsets the price effect, and hence consumer welfare unambiguously rises.

Next, consider the effect of aid to the manufacturing sector. From (2), we get $\frac{\partial p_N}{\partial S_2} = a_{LN}\frac{\partial w_1}{\partial S_2} + a_{KN}\frac{\partial r}{\partial S_2}$ and from (11) $\frac{\partial I}{\partial S_2} = L\frac{\partial w_1}{\partial S_2} + K\frac{\partial r}{\partial S_2}$. Thus,

$$\frac{\partial V}{\partial S_2} = V_I\left(-X_N \frac{\partial p_N}{\partial S_2} + \frac{\partial I}{\partial S_2}\right) = V_I\left((L - L_N)\frac{\partial w_1}{\partial S_2} + (K - K_N)\frac{\partial r}{\partial S_2}\right)$$
$$= V_I \hat{S}_2 S_2 (w_1 L_T \hat{w}_1 + r K_T \hat{r}) > 0,$$

where $K_T = K - K_N = K_1 + K_2$ and $L_T = L - L_N = L_1 + L_2 + L_U$. Note that the bracketed term is

$$
w_1 L_T \hat{w} + r K_T \hat{r} = \frac{T_2^*}{\Delta}(-w_1 L_T \theta_{K1} + r K_T \theta_{L1})
$$

$$
= \frac{T_2^* w_1 L_T \theta_{L1}}{\Delta}\left(\frac{r K_T}{w_1 L_T} - \frac{\theta_{K1}}{\theta_{L1}} \right) > 0, \tag{16}
$$

since the traded sectors are more capital intensive than the agriculture sector. Therefore, the aid to the manufacturing sector raises not only the price of the nontraded good, but also national income. Despite the decline in the manufacturing wage, national income rises. Since the income effect more than offsets the price effect, consumer welfare unambiguously rises.

Recall that aid to the nontraded good sector only lowers the price of the nontraded good without affecting consumer income, $dI = L\, dw_1 + K\, dr = 0$. Differentiating (14) with respect to S_N and using Roy's identity, $\partial V/\partial p_N = -(\partial V/\partial I) X_N$, we get

$$
\frac{\partial V}{\partial p_N}\frac{\partial p_N}{\partial S_N} + \frac{\partial V}{\partial I}\frac{\partial I}{\partial S_N} = V_I\left(-X_N\frac{\partial p_N}{\partial S_N} + \frac{\partial I}{\partial S_N}\right) = V_I\left(-X_N\frac{\partial p_N}{\partial S_N}\right) > 0. \tag{17}
$$

Thus, infrastructure aid to the nontraded good sector unambiguously raises consumer welfare. Thus, we can state the following proposition:

PROPOSITION 2. *Infrastructure aid to a small open economy necessarily raises welfare, regardless of which sector receives the aid.*

This proposition indicates that despite the fixed wage in the urban manufacturing sector, no infrastructure aid to a small open economy can be immiserizing. Whether it is invested in agriculture, manufacturing or the nontraded good sector, infrastructure aid cannot cause immiserizing growth.

4. Sectoral outputs and deindustrialization

In the presence of infrastructure aid, optimal output of the ith sector can be written as $Y_j(p_1, p_2, w_2, L, K, S_j)$ for $j = 1, 2, N$. The employment conditions of labor and capital markets can be respectively rewritten as

$$
a_{L1}Y_1 + (1+\lambda)a_{L2}Y_2 + a_{LN}Y_N = L,
$$
$$
a_{K1}Y_1 + a_{K2}Y_2 + a_{KN}Y_N = K. \tag{18}
$$

Differentiating (18), we obtain

$$
\lambda_{L1}\hat{Y}_1 + \lambda_{L2}\hat{Y}_2 = \hat{L} - (\lambda_{L1}\hat{a}_{L1} + \alpha\lambda_{L2}\hat{a}_{L2} + \lambda_{LN}\hat{a}_{LN} + \alpha\lambda_{L2}\hat{\alpha} + \lambda_{LN}\hat{Y}_N),
$$
$$
\lambda_{K1}\hat{Y}_1 + \lambda_{K2}\hat{Y}_2 = \hat{K} - (\lambda_{K1}\hat{a}_{L1} + \lambda_{K2}\hat{a}_{K2} + \lambda_{KN}\hat{a}_{KN} + \lambda_{KN}\hat{Y}_N). \tag{19}
$$

Recalling that $\alpha = 1 + \lambda$ and $\hat{\alpha} = d\alpha/\alpha = d\lambda/(1 + \lambda)$, setting $\hat{L} = \hat{K} = 0$, and substituting (8) into (14), we obtain

$$\lambda_{L1}\hat{Y}_1 + \lambda_{L2}\hat{Y}_2 = \beta_L(\hat{w}_1 - \hat{r}) + T_L^* - \alpha\lambda_{L2}\theta_{K2}\sigma_2\hat{r} - \alpha\lambda_{L2}\hat{\alpha} - \lambda_{LN}\hat{Y}_N,$$
$$\lambda_{K1}\hat{Y}_1 + \lambda_{K2}\hat{Y}_2 = -\beta_K(\hat{w}_1 - \hat{r}) + T_K^* + \alpha\lambda_{K2}\theta_{L2}\sigma_2\hat{r} - \lambda_{KN}\hat{Y}_N, \qquad (20)$$

where

$$\beta_L = \lambda_{L1}\theta_{K1}\sigma_1 + \lambda_{LN}\theta_{KN}\sigma_N, \qquad \beta_K = \lambda_{K1}\theta_{L1}\sigma_1 + \lambda_{KN}\theta_{LN}\sigma_N,$$
$$T_L^* = \lambda_{L1}\delta_{L1}^* + \alpha\lambda_{L2}\delta_{L2}^* + \lambda_{LN}\delta_{LN}^*, \qquad T_K^* = \lambda_{K1}\delta_{K1}^* + \alpha\lambda_{K2}\delta_{K2}^* + \lambda_{KN}\delta_{KN}^*.$$

Note that β_i represents the change in the ith factor per unit of output that occurs in the agricultural and nontraded good sectors due to the change in wage-rental ratio (w_1/r), and T_i^* stands for the reduction in the requirement of the ith factor as the result of infrastructure investment in the three sectors $(i = L, K)$. Substituting (9.1)–(9.3) into (19), we obtain

$$\lambda_{L1}\hat{Y}_1 + \alpha\lambda_{L2}\hat{Y}_2 = AT_1^* - BT_2^* + T_L^* - \lambda_{LN}\hat{Y}_N,$$
$$\lambda_{K1}\hat{Y}_1 + \lambda_{K2}\hat{Y}_2 = -CT_1^* + DT_2^* + T_K^* - \lambda_{KN}\hat{Y}_N,$$

where

$$A = \theta_{K2}(\beta_L + \alpha\lambda_{L2}/\Delta) > 0,$$
$$B = (\beta_L + \alpha\lambda_{L2}\theta_{K2}\theta_{L1}\sigma_2 + \alpha\lambda_{L2}\theta_{K1})/\Delta > 0,$$
$$C = \beta_K\theta_{K2}/\Delta > 0, \qquad D = (\beta_K + \lambda_{K2}\theta_{L2}\theta_{L1}\sigma_2)/\Delta > 0. \qquad (21)$$

Solving (21) for $\hat{Y}_1$ and $\hat{Y}_2$, we get

$$\hat{Y}_1 = \frac{(A\lambda_{K2} + C\alpha\lambda_{L2})T_1^* - (B\lambda_{K2} + D\alpha\lambda_{L2})T_2^* + (\lambda_{K2}T_L^* - \alpha\lambda_{L2}T_K^*)}{|\lambda|}$$
$$- \frac{\lambda_{L2}\lambda_{LN}(L/K)(k_2 - \alpha k_N)\hat{Y}_N}{|\lambda|},$$
$$\hat{Y}_2 = \frac{-(C\lambda_{L1} + A\alpha\lambda_{K1})T_1^* + (B\lambda_{K1} + D\lambda_{L1})T_2^* - (\lambda_{K1}T_L^* - \lambda_{L1}T_K^*)}{|\lambda|}$$
$$- \frac{\lambda_{L1}\lambda_{LN}(L/K)(k_N - k_1)\hat{Y}_N}{|\lambda|}, \qquad (22)$$

where $|\lambda| = \lambda_{L1}\lambda_{K2} - \alpha\lambda_{K1}\lambda_{L2} = (L_1L_2/LK)(k_2 - \alpha k_1)$ is the determinant of λ_{ij} matrix $(i = L, K; j = 1, 2)$. Khan (1980) and Neary (1981) have shown that the HT model is stable if and only if $k_2 > \alpha k_1$. Neary (1981) stated that $k_2 > \alpha k_1$ implies that the manufacturing sector is capital-intensive relative to the agriculture sector. Subsequently, McCool (1982) noted that this condition implies that the manufacturing sector is capital-intensive relative to the agriculture sector in the value sense. Following Khan, Neary, and McCool, we will assume that manufacturing is the most capital-intensive sector in the physical and value senses, and it is followed by the nontraded good and the agricultural good (i.e., $k_2 > \alpha k_N < \alpha k_1$).

4.1. Infrastructure aid to agriculture and deindustrialization

In the presence of infrastructure aid in the agriculture sector, $\delta_{i1}^* > \delta_{i2}^* = \delta_{iN}^* = 0$ $(i = L, K)$, and $T_1^* > T_2^* = T_N^* = 0$. Furthermore, $T_L^* = \lambda_{L1}\delta_{L1}^*$ and $T_K^* = \lambda_{K1}\delta_{K1}^*$. Thus, the two equations in (22) reduce to

$$\hat{Y}_1 = \frac{(A\lambda_{K2} + C\alpha\lambda_{L2})T_1^*}{|\lambda|} + \frac{\lambda_{L1}\lambda_{L2}\delta_{L1}^*(L/K)(k_2 - \alpha k_1(\delta_{K1}^*/\delta_{L1}^*))}{|\lambda|}$$
$$- \frac{\lambda_{L2}\lambda_{LN}(L/K)(k_2 - \alpha k_N)\hat{Y}_N}{|\lambda|}, \tag{23}$$

$$\hat{Y}_2 = \frac{-(C\lambda_{L1} + A\lambda_{K1})T_1^*}{|\lambda|} - \frac{(\lambda_{K1}\lambda_{L1}\delta_{L1}^*(1 - \delta_{K1}^*/\delta_{L1}^*))}{|\lambda|}$$
$$- \frac{\lambda_{L1}\lambda_{LN}(L/K)(k_N - k_1)\hat{Y}_N}{|\lambda|}. \tag{24}$$

Equations (23) and (24) show that the effect of infrastructure aid to the agriculture sector on the output of each traded good has three components. In view of (20) and (21), it is not difficult to see that the first terms in the right-hand side of equations in (23) and (24) contain the output effects of infrastructure aid to the agriculture sector via both the changes in factor prices and the resulting factor substitution and the employment changes. To be specific, (a) The first term in (23), $(A\lambda_{K2} + C\alpha\lambda_{L2})T_1^*/|\lambda|$, represents the output effect on the agricultural output via the factor substitution and employment changes, and it is positive due to the Khan–Neary stability condition, $|\lambda| = k_2 - \alpha k_1 > 0$. (b) Similarly, the first term in (24), $-(C\lambda_{L1} + A\lambda_{K1})T_1^*/|\lambda|$, denotes the output effect on the manufacturing sector via the factor substitution and employment changes, and it is negative if the Khan–Neary stability condition is met.

Next, the second terms in the right-hand side of equations in (23) and (24) represent the secondary effects of infrastructure aid to the agriculture sector on the outputs of the traded goods via the reduction in labor and capital requirements per unit of the agricultural output. Specifically, (a) in the second term of (23), $\lambda_{L1}\lambda_{L2}\delta_{L1}^*(L/K)(k_2 - \alpha k_1(\delta_{K1}^*/\delta_{L1}^*))/|\lambda|$, the term in the bracket, $(k_2 - \alpha k_1(\delta_{K1}^*/\delta_{L1}^*))$ indicates the factor intensities of the two traded goods after the infrastructure aid to agriculture. For the system to remain stable after the infrastructure aid, $(k_2 - \alpha k_1(\delta_{K1}^*/\delta_{L1}^*)) > 0$. Here, three types of factor-saving infrastructure aid may be differentiated: (i) If the infrastructure aid is neutral in factor-saving ($\delta_{K1}^* = \delta_{L1}^*$), the second term reduces to δ_{L1}^*; (ii) If the infrastructure aid is a labor-saving type ($\delta_{K1}^* < \delta_{L1}^*$), the second term is greater than δ_{L1}^* and hence the secondary effect is strengthened vis-à-vis the neutral case; (iii) If the infrastructure aid is a capital-saving type ($\delta_{K1}^* > \delta_{L1}^*$), the second term is less than δ_{L1}^*, and hence the secondary effect is weakened vis-à-vis the neutral case. Next, (b) In the second term of (24), $-(\lambda_{K1}\lambda_{L1}\delta_{L1}^*(1 - \delta_{K1}^*/\delta_{L1}^*))/|\lambda|$, $\delta_{K1}^*/\delta_{L1}^*$ determines the sign of the secondary effect: (i) In the case of neutral factor-saving infrastructure aid (i.e., $\delta_{K1}^* = \delta_{L1}^*$), this secondary factor-saving effect on the manufacturing output vanishes; (ii) If the infrastructure aid is a labor-saving type ($\delta_{K1}^* < \delta_{L1}^*$), the second term is negative, and the secondary factor saving effect tends to lower the manufacturing output; and (iii) If the infrastructure aid is a capital-saving type ($\delta_{K1}^* > \delta_{L1}^*$), the second term is positive, and the secondary factor-saving effect tends to raise the manufacturing output.

Infrastructure aid necessarily changes the output of the nontraded good sector, and hence draws (releases) resources from (to) the agricultural and manufacturing sectors. These resource reallocation effects are captured in the third terms on the right-hand side of (23) and (24). Let $X_N(p_1, p_2, p_N, I)$ be the demand for the nontraded good. For the nontraded good, $X_N = Y_N$. As in Komiya (1967), the output of the nontraded good is determined by its demand. Since the prices of the traded goods are fixed,

$$\hat{Y}_N = \hat{X}_N = (\hat{X}_N/\hat{p}_N)\hat{p}_N + (\hat{X}_N/\hat{I})\hat{I}.$$

If the nontraded good is a normal good, then $\hat{X}_N/\hat{I} > 0$ and $\hat{X}_N/\hat{p}_N < 0$. It was shown in 2.3.1 that the infrastructure aid to the agriculture sector raises the unit cost of the nontraded good, i.e., $\hat{p}_N/T_1^* = (\theta_{LN}\theta_{K2})/\Delta > 0$. Thus, $(\hat{X}_N/\hat{p}_N)\hat{p}_N < 0$. Further, in (13), it has been shown that $\hat{I}/\hat{T}_1^* > 0$. Therefore, the income effect of infrastructure aid to the agriculture is necessarily positive, i.e., $(\hat{X}_N/\hat{I})\hat{I} > 0$. The net effect of infrastructure aid to the agriculture sector on the supply of the nontraded good depends on the relative magnitudes of the price and income effects.

Specifically, $\hat{Y}_N = \hat{X}_N \gtreqless 0$ if $(\hat{X}_N/\hat{I})\hat{I} \gtreqless |(\hat{X}_N/\hat{p}_N)\hat{p}_N|$.

Therefore, given $k_2 - \alpha k_N > 0$, the third term in (23), $-\lambda_{L2}\lambda_{LN}(L/K)(k_2 - \alpha k_N)\hat{Y}_N/|\lambda|$, is negative (positive) if $\hat{Y}_N > (<) 0$. That is, infrastructure aid to agriculture tends to lower (raise) the agricultural output via the expansion (contraction) of the nontraded good sector. (ii) Similarly, given $k_N > k_1$, the third term in (24), $-\lambda_{L1}\lambda_{LN}(L/K)(k_N - k_1)\hat{Y}_N/|\lambda|$, is negative (positive) if $\hat{Y}_N > (<) 0$. That is, infrastructure aid to the agriculture tends to lower (raise) the manufacturing output if it results in an expansion (a contraction) of the nontraded good sector.

It should be noted that the Findlay–Grubert (1959) and Corden and Findlay (1975) type of normal (or ultra-biased) output effect (respectively derived from the 2×2 Heckscher–Ohlin model and the 2×2 mobile-capital HT model) stipulates that growth in one sector increases its output and decreases the output of the other sector. Thus, we expect that in the present model, the normal growth-output effect occurs if the infrastructure investment in agriculture increases its output and decreases the manufacturing output. However, our analysis shows that in the present 3×2 HT model, the net effects of infrastructure aid to agriculture on the outputs of the traded goods depend on the signs and the relative magnitudes of the three component effects.

To be specific, if $\hat{Y}_N \leqslant 0$, the sum of the three component effects in (23) is clearly positive, and the infrastructure aid to the agriculture sector necessarily increases the agricultural output – thus, the normal result holds for the agricultural output. However, if $\hat{Y}_N > 0$ and the tertiary nontraded good effect is negative, then infrastructure aid to agriculture can increase or decrease the agricultural output. A contraction in the agriculture sector or deagriculturalization occurs ($\hat{Y}_1 < 0$) if $\hat{Y}_N > 0$ and

$$(A\lambda_{K2} + C\alpha\lambda_{L2})T_1^* + \lambda_{L1}\lambda_{L2}\delta_{L1}^*(L/K)\big(k_2 - \alpha k_1(\delta_{K1}^*/\delta_{L1}^*)\big)$$
$$< \big|\lambda_{L2}\lambda_{LN}(L/K)(k_2 - \alpha k_N)\hat{Y}_N\big|.$$

As for the effect on manufacturing output, the first component effect in (24) is negative, while the secondary and the tertiary effects can have any sign. The secondary effect is zero if the infrastructure aid is neutral in factor saving ($\delta_{K1}^* = \delta_{L1}^*$). However, the secondary effect is negative if the infrastructure aid is labor-saving ($\delta_{K1}^* < \delta_{L1}^*$), and it is positive if the infrastructure aid is capital-saving type ($\delta_{K1}^* > \delta_{L1}^*$). Since $k_N > k_1$, the tertiary nontraded good effect is negative (positive) if $\hat{Y}_N > (<)\,0$. Thus, the sum of the three component effects can have any sign. Sufficient conditions for the Dutch disease (or deindustrialization) to occur in the manufacturing sector are:

(i) Infrastructure aid to the agriculture sector is neutral in factor saving ($\delta_{K1}^* = \delta_{L1}^*$) or labor-saving ($\delta_{K1}^* < \delta_{L1}^*$), and the nontraded good sector expands ($\hat{Y}_N > 0$), or

(ii) infrastructure aid is the capital-saving type ($\delta_{K1}^* > \delta_{L1}^*$), $\hat{Y}_N > 0$, and

$$(A\lambda_{K1} + C\lambda_{L1})T_1^* + \big|\lambda_{L1}\lambda_{K1}\delta_{L1}^*(1 - \delta_{K1}^*/\delta_{L1}^*)\big|$$
$$< \big|\lambda_{L1}\lambda_{LN}(L/K)(k_N - k_1)\hat{Y}_N\big|, \quad \text{or}$$

(iii) infrastructure aid is the labor-saving type ($\delta_{K1}^* < \delta_{L1}^*$), $\hat{Y}_N < 0$, and

$$(A\lambda_{K1} + C\lambda_{L1})T_1^* + \big|\lambda_{L1}\lambda_{LN}(L/K)(k_N - k_1)\hat{Y}_N\big|$$
$$< \big|\lambda_{L1}\lambda_{K1}\delta_{L1}^*(1 - \delta_{K1}^*/\delta_{L1}^*)\big|.$$

4.2. Infrastructure aid to the manufacturing and deindustrialization

In the presence of infrastructure investment in the manufacturing sector, $\delta_{i2}^* > \delta_{i1}^* = \delta_{iN}^* = 0$ ($i = L, K$), and $T_2^* > T_1^* = T_N^* = 0$. Furthermore, $T_L^* = \alpha\lambda_{L2}\delta_{L2}^*$ and $T_K^* = \lambda_{K2}\delta_{K2}^*$. Thus, the two equations in (22) can be written as

$$\hat{Y}_1 = \frac{-(B\lambda_{K2} + D\alpha\lambda_{L2})T_2^*}{|\lambda|} + \frac{\alpha\lambda_{L2}\lambda_{K2}\delta_{L2}^*(1 - (\delta_{K2}^*/\delta_{L2}^*))}{|\lambda|}$$
$$- \frac{\lambda_{L2}\lambda_{LN}(L/K)(k_2 - \alpha k_N)\hat{Y}_N}{|\lambda|}, \tag{25}$$

$$\hat{Y}_2 = \frac{(B\lambda_{K1} + D\lambda_{L1})T_2^*}{|\lambda|} + \frac{\lambda_{L1}\lambda_{L2}\delta_{L2}^*(L/K)(k_2(\delta_{K2}^*/\delta_{L2}^*) - \alpha k_1)}{|\lambda|}$$
$$- \frac{\lambda_{L1}\lambda_{LN}(L/K)(k_N - k_1)\hat{Y}_N}{|\lambda|}. \tag{26}$$

The effect of infrastructure aid to the manufacturing sector on the output of each traded good consists of three component effects. In view of (19) and (20), the first terms in the right-hand side of equations in (25) and (26) contain the output effects of infrastructure aid to the manufacturing sector via both the changes in the factor prices and the resulting factor substitution, and the employment effect. To be specific, (a) The first term in (25), $-(B\lambda_{K2} + D\alpha\lambda_{L2})T_2^*/|\lambda|$, represents the output effect on the agricultural output via the factor substitution and employment effects, and it is negative. (b) Similarly, the first term in (26), $(B\lambda_{K1} + D\lambda_{L1})T_2^*/|\lambda|$, denotes the output effect on the manufacturing good via factor substitution and employment effects, and it is positive.

The second terms in the right-hand side of equations in (25) and (26) represent the effects of the infrastructure aid to the manufacturing sector on the outputs of the traded goods via the reduction in labor and capital requirements per unit of the manufacturing output. (a) In the second term in (25), $\alpha\lambda_{L2}\lambda_{K2}\delta_{L2}^*(1 - (\delta_{K2}^*/\delta_{L2}^*))/|\lambda|$, $\delta_{K2}^*/\delta_{L2}^*$ determines the sign of the secondary effect: (i) In the case of neutral factor-saving infrastructure aid (i.e., $\delta_{K2}^* = \delta_{L2}^*$), the secondary factor-saving effect on the agricultural output vanishes, (ii) If infrastructure aid is the labor-saving type (i.e., $\delta_{K2}^* < \delta_{L2}^*$), the second term is positive and the secondary effect tends to increase the agricultural output, and (iii) If infrastructure aid is the capital-saving type (i.e., $\delta_{K2}^* > \delta_{L2}^*$), the second term is negative and the secondary effect tends to decrease the agricultural output. (b) In the second term of (26), $\lambda_{L1}\lambda_{L2}\delta_{L2}^*(L/K)(k_2(\delta_{K2}^*/\delta_{L2}^*) - \alpha k_1)/|\lambda|$, $k_2(\delta_{K2}^*/\delta_{L2}^*) - \alpha k_1 > 0$ for the system to remain stable after the infrastructure aid. Again, three types of factor-saving infrastructure aid can be differentiated: (i) If the infrastructure aid is neutral in factor-saving ($\delta_{K2}^* = \delta_{L2}^*$), the second term is reduced to $\delta_{L2}^* > 0$; (ii) If infrastructure aid is labor-saving type ($\delta_{K2}^* < \delta_{L2}^*$), the second term is less than δ_{L2}^*, and hence the secondary effect is weakened vis-à-vis the neutral case; (iii) If infrastructure aid is the capital-saving type ($\delta_{K2}^* > \delta_{L2}^*$), the second term is greater than δ_{L2}^*, and the secondary effect is strengthened vis-à-vis the neutral case.

The third terms in the right-hand side of equations in (25) and (26) represent the effects of the infrastructure aid to the manufacturing sector on the outputs of the traded goods via the nontraded good effect. It has been shown in 2.3.2 that the infrastructure aid to the manufacturing sector raises the supply price of the nontraded good by raising the unit cost of the nontraded good, $\hat{p}_N/T_2^* = [\theta_{L1}\theta_{LN}(r/w_1)(k_N - k_1)T_2^*]/\Delta > 0$, and hence $(\hat{X}_N/\hat{p}_N)\hat{p}_N < 0$. Further in (13), it has been demonstrated that $\hat{I}/\hat{T}_2^* > 0$. Thus, $(\hat{X}_N/\hat{I})\hat{I} > 0$. The net effect of infrastructure aid to the manufacturing sector on the demand and output of the nontraded good depends on the relative magnitudes of the price effect and the growth-income effect. To be specific, $\hat{Y}_N = \hat{X}_N \gtrless 0$ if $(\hat{X}_N/\hat{I})\hat{I} \gtrless |(\hat{X}_N/\hat{p}_N)\hat{p}_N|$. Then, given $k_2 > \alpha k_N$, the third term in (25), $-\lambda_{L2}\lambda_{LN}(L/K)(k_2 - \alpha k_N)\hat{Y}_N/|\lambda|$, is negative (positive) if $\hat{Y}_N > (<)0$. That is, the infrastructure aid to the manufacturing sector tends to lower (raise) the agricultural output if it results in an expansion (a contraction) of the nontraded good sector. (b) Meanwhile, given $k_N > k_1$, the third term in (26), $-\lambda_{L1}\lambda_{LN}(L/K)(k_N - k_1)\hat{Y}_N/|\lambda|$, is clearly negative (positive) if $\hat{Y}_N > (<)0$. That is, infrastructure aid to the manufacturing sector tends to lower (raise) the manufacturing output via the expansion (contraction) of the nontraded good sector.

The foregoing analysis shows that in the present 3×2 HT model, the net effects of infrastructure aid to the manufacturing sector on the outputs of the traded goods depend on the signs and the relative magnitudes of the three component effects, and the

Findlay–Grubert (1959) and Corden and Findlay (1975) types of ultra-biased growth effect do not necessarily hold. As for the effect on agricultural output, the first component effect in (25) is always negative, while the secondary and the tertiary effects can have any sign. If the secondary effect is zero or negative (because $\delta^*_{K2} = \delta^*_{L2}$ or $\delta^*_{K2} > \delta^*_{L2}$) and the tertiary term is negative (because $\hat{Y}_N > 0$), then the sum of the three component effects is unambiguously negative. Thus, the agricultural output decreases. However, if the secondary and/or tertiary effects are positive because infrastructure aid is the labor-saving type ($\delta^*_{K2} < \delta^*_{L2}$) and/or $\hat{Y}_N < 0$, the effect on the agricultural output is indeterminate. Sufficient conditions for a contraction in agriculture ($\hat{Y}_1 < 0$) are

(i) $\delta^*_{K2} \geqslant \delta^*_{L2}$, and $\hat{Y}_N > 0$, or

(ii) $\delta^*_{K2} \geqslant \delta^*_{L2}$, and $\hat{Y}_N < 0$, and

$$\left| (B\lambda_{K2} + D\alpha\lambda_{L2})T^*_2 + \alpha\lambda_{L2}\lambda_{K2}\delta^*_{L2}\big[1 - (\delta^*_{K2}/\delta^*_{L2})\big] \right|$$
$$> \left| \lambda_{L2}\lambda_{LN}(L/K)(k_2 - \alpha k_N)\hat{Y}_N \right|, \quad \text{or}$$

(iii) $\delta^*_{K2} < \delta^*_{L2}$, and $\hat{Y}_N > 0$, and

$$\left| (B\lambda_{K2} + D\alpha\lambda_{L2})T^*_2 + \lambda_{L2}\lambda_{LN}(L/K)(k_2 - \alpha k_N)\hat{Y}_N \right|$$
$$> \left| \alpha\lambda_{L2}\lambda_{K2}\delta^*_{L2}\big[1 - (\delta^*_{K2}/\delta^*_{L2})\big] \right|, \quad \text{or}$$

(iv) $\delta^*_{K2} < \delta^*_{L2}$, and $\hat{Y}_N < 0$,

$$\left| (B\lambda_{K2} + D\alpha\lambda_{L2})T^*_2 \right|$$
$$> \left| \alpha\lambda_{L2}\lambda_{K2}\delta^*_{L2}\big[1 - (\delta^*_{K2}/\delta^*_{L2})\big] + \lambda_{L2}\lambda_{LN}(L/K)(k_2 - \alpha k_N)\hat{Y}_N \right|.$$

As for the effect on manufacturing output, the first and second component effects in (26) are positive, but the third component effect is positive (negative) if $\hat{Y}_N$ is negative (positive). Thus, the Dutch disease in the manufacturing sector occurs if $\hat{Y}_N > 0$ and the negative third component effect outweighs the sum of the positive first and second component effects. It requires the sufficient condition:

$$\hat{Y}_N > 0, \quad \text{and} \quad (B\lambda_{K1} + D\lambda_{L1})T^*_2 + \lambda_{L1}\lambda_{L2}\delta^*_{L2}(L/K)\big[k_2(\delta^*_{K2}/\delta^*_{L2}) - \alpha k_1\big]$$
$$< \left| \lambda_{L1}\lambda_{LN}(L/K)(k_N - k_1)\hat{Y}_N \right|.$$

4.3. Infrastructure aid to the nontraded good sector and deindustrialization

In the presence of infrastructure investment in the nontraded good sector, $\delta^*_{iN} > \delta^*_{i1} = \delta^*_{i2} = 0$ ($i = L, K$), and $T^*_N > T^*_1 = T^*_2 = 0$. Further, $T^*_L = \lambda_{LN}\delta^*_{LN}$ and $T^*_K = \lambda_{KN}\delta^*_{KN}$. Thus, the two equations in (22) can be written as

$$\hat{Y}_1 = \frac{\lambda_{L2}\lambda_{LN}\delta^*_{LN}(L/K)(k_2 - \alpha k_N(\delta^*_{KN}/\delta^*_{LN}))}{|\lambda|}$$
$$- \frac{\lambda_{L2}\lambda_{LN}(L/K)(k_2 - \alpha k_N)\hat{Y}_N}{|\lambda|}, \tag{27}$$

$$\hat{Y}_2 = \frac{\lambda_{L1}\lambda_{LN}\delta_{LN}^*(L/K)(k_N(\delta_{KN}^*/\delta_{LN}^*) - k_1)}{|\lambda|}$$

$$- \frac{\lambda_{L1}\lambda_{LN}(L/K)(k_N - k_1)\hat{Y}_N}{|\lambda|}. \tag{28}$$

As shown in 2.3.3, infrastructure aid to the nontraded sector does not affect the factor prices and the unemployed–employed ratio of the manufacturing sector. Thus, the output effects on the traded goods stemming from both the changes in the factor prices and the resulting factor substitution, and the employment effect (i.e., the first and second terms in equations in (22)) vanish. This leaves two component effects in (27) and (28). The first term in the right-hand side of (27) represents the output effect on the agricultural good via the reduction in labor and capital requirements per unit of the nontraded good, and it is positive since the manufacturing good remains capital-abundant relative to the nontraded good after the infrastructure aid, i.e., $k_2 > \alpha k_N(\delta_{KN}^*/\delta_{LN}^*)$. Similarly, the first term in the right-hand side of (28) denotes the output effects on the manufacturing good via the reduction in labor and capital requirements per unit of the nontraded good, and it is positive since the nontraded good remains capital-intensive relative to the agricultural good after the infrastructure aid (i.e., $k_N(\delta_{KN}^*/\delta_{LN}^*) > k_1$).[10]

The second terms in the right-hand side of equations in (27) and (28) represent the effects of infrastructure aid to the nontraded good sector on the outputs of the traded goods via the nontraded good effect. It was shown in 2.3.3 that infrastructure aid to the nontraded good sector lowers the price of the nontraded good ($\hat{p}_N/T_N^* = -1 < 0$). Thus, $(\hat{X}_N/\hat{p}_N)\hat{p}_N > 0$. Recall from (13) that infrastructure aid to the nontraded good sector does not affect national income, $\hat{I}/\hat{T}_N^* = 0$. Thus, $(\hat{X}_N/\hat{I})\hat{I} = 0$. The net effect of infrastructure aid to the nontraded good sector on the output of the nontraded good is unambiguously positive, i.e., $\hat{Y}_N = \hat{X}_N = (\hat{X}_N/\hat{p}_N)\hat{p}_N > 0$. It follows that the second term in (27) is negative since $k_2 > \alpha k_N$. That is, infrastructure aid to the nontraded good sector tends to decrease the agricultural output via an expansion of the nontraded good sector. Meanwhile, the second term in (28) is necessarily negative since $k_N > k_1$. That is, the infrastructure aid to the nontraded good sector tends to decrease the manufacturing output via an expansion of the nontraded good sector.

The net output effect of the infrastructure aid to the nontraded good sector on the output of each traded good is the sum of the two component effects. In (27), the first component effect is positive, while the second component effect is negative. Thus, the net effect of infrastructure aid to the nontraded good sector on the agricultural output may have any sign. The conditions for deagriculturalization are:

(i) $\lambda_{L2}\lambda_{LN}\delta_{LN}^*(L/K)\big[k_2 - \alpha k_N(\delta_{KN}^*/\delta_{LN}^*)\big] < \lambda_{L2}\lambda_{LN}(L/K)(k_2 - \alpha k_N)\hat{Y}_N.$

---

[10] If infrastructure aid to the nontraded good sector is the capital-saving type ($\delta_{KN}^* > \delta_{LN}^*$), the output effect on the agricultural (manufacturing) good is weaker (stronger) than the neutral case in factor saving. However, if infrastructure aid to the nontraded good sector is the labor-saving type ($\delta_{KN}^* < \delta_{LN}^*$), the output effect on the agricultural (manufacturing) good is stronger (weaker) than the neutral case in factor saving.

As for the net output effect on the manufacturing good, the first component effect in (28), $(1/|\lambda|)\lambda_{L1}\lambda_{LN}\delta_{LN}^*(L/K)[k_N(\delta_{KN}^*/\delta_{LN}^*) - k_1]$, is positive, while the second component effect, $-(1/|\lambda|)\lambda_{L1}\lambda_{LN}(L/K)(k_N - k_1)\hat{Y}_N$, is negative. Thus, the Dutch disease in the manufacturing sector or deindustrialization occurs when the second component effect outweighs the first component effect such that:

$$\lambda_{L1}\lambda_{LN}\delta_{LN}^*(L/K)\big[k_N(\delta_{KN}^*/\delta_{LN}^*) - k_1\big] < \lambda_{L1}\lambda_{LN}(L/K)(k_N - k_1)\hat{Y}_N.$$

That is, as in the case of the agricultural output, a Dutch disease or deindustrialization occurs if the infrastructure aid to the nontraded good sector results in a significant expansion of the nontraded good sector, and the negative effect on the manufacturing output outweighs the positive effect on the manufacturing output via the reduction in labor and capital requirement per unit of the nontraded good. The following proposition summarizes these results:

PROPOSITION 3. *Infrastructure aid to either the agriculture sector or the manufacturing sector may cause a Dutch disease in either industry. Infrastructure aid to the nontraded good sector necessarily increases its output, but may cause a Dutch disease in traded sectors.*

5. *Concluding remarks*

In this paper, we have explored the effects of infrastructure aid on a developing country in an extended 3×2 HT model of unemployment with two traded good sectors and a nontraded good sector. The analysis focused primarily on the welfare effects of infrastructure aid and the conditions for the Dutch disease. We obtained several significant results from the analysis. In particular, infrastructure aid to a small developing country cannot be immiserizing, regardless of which sector receives the aid. Further, infrastructure aid to either of the two traded good sectors causes an appreciation of the foreign exchange rate of the recipient country, while infrastructure aid to the nontraded good industry results in a depreciation. In general, the signs for the effects of infrastructure aid on the sectoral outputs are indeterminate, with an exception that infrastructure aid to the nontraded good sector necessarily increases its output. The generally indeterminate output effects occur because infrastructure aid creates component effects of varying signs on the sectoral outputs via changes in the factor prices and employment, the factor-intensity and factor-abundance rankings, the relative factor-saving effects of the aid, and the output response of the nontraded good to the aid. It is sufficient to mention here that these ambiguous output effects are consistent with the varying types of deindustrialization that have been reported by a number of studies on economic aid in the literature.

In closing, it should be noted that the present study, mainly theoretical in nature, reveals several positive aspects of infrastructure aid. The task of empirically identifying how each of the positive aspects actually works behind the economic stagnation and the different types of deindustrialization in the developing countries was not undertaken. This is a task we leave to future research in this area.

References

Adam, C.S., Bevan, D.L. (2003), Aid public expenditures and Dutch disease. *Centre for the Study of African Economies Working Paper*, No. 2003-02. University of Oxford, Oxford.

Bandara, J.S. (1995), The Dutch disease in a developing country: the case of foreign capital inflow to Sri Lanka. *Seoul Journal of Economics* 8, 311–329.

Batra, R.N. (1973), *Studies in the Pure Theory of International Trade*. St. Martin's, New York.

Benjamin, N.C., Devarajan, S., Weiner, R.J. (1989), The 'Dutch disease' in a developing country: oil reserves in Cameroon. *Journal of Development Economics* 30, 71–92.

Cassing, J.H., Warr, P.G. (1985), The distributional impact of a resource boom. *Journal of International Economics* 18, 301–319.

Choi, E.K. (2004), Aid allocation and the transfer paradox in small open economies. *International Review of Economics and Finance* 13, 245–251.

Choi, J.-Y., Yu, E.S.H. (1987), Technical progress and outputs under variable returns to scale. *Economica* 54, 249–253.

Corden, W.M., Findlay, R. (1975), Urban unemployment, intersectoral capital mobility, and development policy. *Economica* 62, 59–78.

Corden, W.M., Neary, J.P. (1982), Booming sector and de-industrialization in a small economy. *Economic Journal* 92, 825–848.

Findlay, R., Grubert, H. (1959), Factor intensities, technological progress and the terms of trade. *Oxford Economic Papers* 11, 111–121.

Harris, J.R., Todaro, M.P. (1970), Migration, unemployment and development, a two sector analysis. *American Economic Review* 60, 126–142.

Khan, A.M. (1980), Dynamic stability, wage subsidies, and generalized Harris–Todaro model. *Pakistan Development Review* 19, 1–14.

Komiya, R. (1967), Nontraded goods and the pure theory of international trade. *International Economic Review* 8, 132–152.

McCool, T. (1982), Wage subsidies, distortionary taxes in a mobile capital Harris–Todaro model. *Economica* 49, 69–80.

Neary, J.P. (1981), On the Harris–Todaro model with intersectoral capital mobility. *Economica* 48, 219–234.

Nkusu, M. (2004), Aid and the Dutch disease in low-income countries: informed diagnosis for prudent prognosis. *IMF Working Paper* 04/49. International Monetary Fund, Washington, DC.

Nyoni, T.S. (1998), Foreign aid and economic performance in Tanzania. *World Development* 26, 1235–1240.

Spatafora, N., Warner, A. (1999), Macroeconomic and sectoral effects of terms-of-trade shocks: The experience of the oil-exporting developing countries. *IMF Working Paper*, WP/99/134. International Monetary Fund, Washington, DC.

Stijns, J.-P. (2003), An empirical test of the dutch disease hypothesis using a gravity model of trade. *International Trade Working Paper*, No. 0305001. Washington University, St. Louis, Missouri.

Todaro, M.P., Smith, S.C. (2002), *Economic Development*. Addison–Wesley, Boston.

Vos, R. (1998), Aid flows and 'Dutch disease' in a general equilibrium framework in Pakistan. *Journal of Policy Modeling* 20, 77–109.

Yano, M., Nugent, J. (1999), Aid, nontraded goods, and the transfer paradox in small countries. *American Economic Review* 89, 431–449.

Younger, S.D. (1992), Aid and the Dutch disease: macroeconomic management when everybody loves you. *World Development* 20, 1587–1597.

CHAPTER 6

When Can Competition for Aid Reduce Pollution?

Nikos Tsakiris[a], Panos Hatzipanayotou[a,b], Michael S. Michael[b,c]

[a]Department of International and European Economic Studies,
Athens University of Economics and Business, 76, Patission Str., Athens 104 34, Greece
E-mail address: tsakiris@aueb.gr
[b]CESifo (Center for Economic Studies and the Ifo Institute of Economic Research), Germany
E-mail address: hatzip@aueb.gr
[c]Department of Economics, University of Cyprus, PO Box 20537 Nicosia, CY 1678, Cyprus
E-mail address: m.s.michael@ucy.ac.cy

Abstract

We examine the allocation of a pre-determined amount of aid from a donor to two recipient countries. The donor suffers from cross-border pollution resulting from production activities in the recipient countries. It is shown that the recipient with the higher fraction of aid allocated to public abatement and with the lower emission tax, receives a higher share of the aid when the donor allocates aid so as to maximize its own welfare. Competition for aid reduces cross-border pollution to the donor when recipients use the fraction of aid allocated to pollution abatement as a policy to divert aid from each other. But, it increases cross-border pollution when recipients use the emission tax to divert aid from each other.

Keywords: Competition for aid, cross-border pollution, pollution abatement

JEL classifications: Q28, F35, H41

1. Introduction

Growing levels of global pollution due to the intensification of global economic activity and the resulting cross-border pollution have become an important issue in current international negotiations, and in policy debates among various countries. Examples of such transboundary pollution are the acid rain, water pollution, and global warming.[1] When such negative international externalities are multidirectional i.e.,

---

[1] Grossman and Krueger (1995) examine the relationship between the scale of economic activity (i.e., growth) and environmental quality (e.g., water and air quality) for various types of pollutants. They find a monotonically decreasing relationship between per capita GDP and some pollutants, while some other

THEORY AND PRACTICE OF FOREIGN AID
VOLUME 1   ISSN: 1574-8715
DOI: 10.1016/S1574-8715(06)01006-2

cross-border pollution is generated by all countries, there is a strong incentive for policy co-ordination to reduce the environmental damage. However, in the case of unidirectional cross-border pollution i.e., when only some countries generate cross-border pollution while others do not, there is little or no incentive on the part of the polluting countries to unilaterally adopt measures of reducing the environmental damage (e.g., see (Baumol and Oates, 1994)). Moreover, in the case where the polluting countries are small developing economies, things become even more difficult given their inability to finance clean-up activities due to the severe economic constraints they are faced with. In such cases, developed countries and international organizations can use "carrot" policies, such as international transfers (foreign aid) to encourage developing economies to adopt measures of environmental protection. For example, the Danish Environmental Protection Agency provides environmental aid to Central and Eastern Europe to help safeguard natural resources and to reduce transboundary pollution from these countries. The Inter-American Development Bank (IDB), Japan's Overseas Economic Cooperation Fund (OECF), the European Commission, and the Global Environment Facility (GEF) provide extensive funding to developing economies for financing pollution abatement activities. A recent OECD (2003) study provides evidence of total environmentally-related assistance by donor to the EECCA region (Eastern Europe, Caucasus and Central Asia), for the period 1996–2001. According to this study, the European Union is the largest donor, having provided 17.7% of the total environmental assistance regarding the above period. The United States and Denmark are the next biggest donors, providing 17.3% and 12.2% of the total environmental assistance respectively, followed by Germany, United Kingdom, Sweden and Norway providing 9.1–5.9% of that assistance.

Another point of interest is that public sector pollution abatement activities seem to possess an important share to total pollution abatement and control expenditure. In relation to this point, Linster and Zegel (2003) report two revealing real world facts for the period 1990–2000. First, pollution abatement and control expenditures varied from 0.7 (Portugal in 1994) to 2.6% (Austria in 1998) of GDP per year. Second, for most countries, public expenditures for pollution abatement account for about 40–60% of the total pollution abatement and control expenditures.[2] Given these observations, it is important that both private and public abatement activities must be taken into account when we consider environmental policies.

Motivated by such stylized facts, we consider the issue of allocating international transfers or foreign aid,[3] in the presence of cross-border pollution, among asymmetric

pollutants display an inverted U-shaped with GDP per capita, with pollution increasing with income at low levels and decreasing with income at high levels. The inverse-U relationship between per capita income and pollution is known as Environmental Kuznets Curve (EKC). For recent literature reviews on empirical studies on the EKC see (Copeland and Taylor, 2003).

[2] For example, in 1994 the US government spent 0.3 percent of its GDP to abate air pollution which accounted for about 33 percent of the total expenditures on abating air pollution.

[3] Note that hereon we use the terms "international transfer" and "foreign aid" interchangeably.

recipient countries where pollution is simultaneously abated by their private and public sectors. Moreover, we examine the effectiveness of competition for aid policy as a track for reducing pollution.

For the purposes of our paper two strands of the international trade literature are of relevance. The first, relates to the links between foreign aid and environmental protection. The second refers to what is called "competition" for aid, when more than one country are the potential recipients of a fixed amount of foreign aid by a donor country.

Regarding the first strand of the literature, a number of studies have examined the interaction among foreign aid, pollution and welfare, under the existence or not of cross-border pollution. For example, in a trade model without cross-border pollution Chao and Yu (1999) examine the welfare effects of aid tied to pollution abatement in a pollution generating aid receiving country. On the other hand, in trade models with cross-border pollution, Copeland and Taylor (1995) consider a Ricardian set-up of a world economy consisting of two regions – North and South – each composed of many countries. Governments control pollution by pollution permits or quotas. They demonstrate, among other things, that untied income transfers may not have an impact on global pollution, and levels of national welfare. Turunen-Red and Woodland (2004), among others, examine a variety of Pareto-improving multilateral environmental reforms when compensating international lump-sum transfers are assumed. Naito (2003), in a two country model with transboundary pollution and without emission taxes, shows the possibility of Pareto-improving untied aid if the marginal propensity to consume in the donor country is sufficiently larger than in the recipient. Hatzipanay-otou *et al.* (2002), hereon HLM 02, show that even in the absence of international cooperation, cross-border pollution may reduce the total amount of pollution emission by inducing more foreign aid from the developed to developing countries.[4,5]

The literature on competition for aid is rather small, and it focuses on trade policy issues. Lahiri and Raimondos-Møller (1997), hereon LRM 97, examine the role of trade policy in the allocation of international income transfers. They demonstrate that the country with higher tariff receives a smaller share of aid and also that competition for aid induces recipient countries to reduce their optimal tariff rates.[6] Lahiri and Raimondos-Møller (2000) examine how lobbying by various ethnic groups in a

---

[4] Their model is one of two countries with foreign aid and cross-border pollution from the recipient to the donor country. Pollution in the latter country is simultaneously abated by the private and public sector, the latter financing its abatement activities through a fraction of aid received and emission tax revenue collected from the private sector.

[5] Schweinberger and Woodland (2005) in a model of tied aid, cross-border pollution and simultaneous provision of private and public pollution abatement investigate cases where tied foreign aid may not be effective in reducing pollution.

[6] They construct a three country, one donor and two recipients, model where the recipients first optimally choose their tariff rates, and afterwards the donor chooses the allocation of aid between them. Moreover, the donor country decides on the allocation of aid between the two recipients either by acting "selfishly" maximizing its own welfare, or by acting "altruistically" by maximizing the joint welfare of the two recipient countries.

donor country affects the allocation of international transfers to competing recipient countries.

Motivated by the stylized facts laid out in the introduction the objective of the present paper is to address the question of how environmental, rather than international trade, considerations can be the basis for the allocation of foreign aid between potentially recipient countries. In doing so, we synthesize and build upon the studies of the aforementioned international trade literature, i.e., HLM 02, and LRM 97 and 2000.

We construct a three country, one donor and two recipients, general equilibrium model, which combines environmental protection and competition for foreign aid. The donor is affected by production generated pollution in the two neighbouring recipient countries. The donor distributes a pre-determined (fixed) amount of aid between the two recipients. The latter countries control pollution through emission taxes and public pollution abatement which is funded by emission tax revenue and by a fraction of the aid received.[7,8] The donor, in deciding how to allocate aid between the two recipient countries, behaves "selfishly" i.e., it maximizes its own welfare. In this framework we derive the donor's Nash equilibrium fraction of aid allocated between the two recipients, and for each of the recipients we derive the Nash equilibrium emission tax rate and the fraction of aid allocated to pollution abatement.[9] Since the optimal allocation of aid is related to the emission tax rates and the proportion of aid allocated to public abatement activities in the recipient countries, it can be argued that it is likely that each recipient uses its environmental policies to divert aid from its rival recipient. This is what we call in the present paper, *competition for aid*. Our main results are as follows. Competition for aid reduces transboundary pollution from the recipient countries to the donor when recipients use the fraction of aid allocated to pollution abatement as a policy to divert aid from its rival recipient. However, competition for aid increases transboundary pollution transmitted to the donor when a recipient use the emission tax to divert aid from its rival.

---

[7] Brett and Keen (2000) report that in the US it is common for environmental taxes to be earmarked for specific environmentally related public expenditure, e.g., the financing of clean-up activities or of road construction and of public transport networks. Also, the OECD (2000) report of the Task Force for the implementation of the environmental action programmes for the Central and Eastern Europe, reports that the Kazakhstan's Law of Environmental Protection in 1999, stipulates that "... It should be prohibited to spend money from Environmental Protection Funds for purposes not connected with environmental protection ...". Revenues for these environmental funds are listed to come primarily from pollution charges, non-compliance fines and international assistance (aid) for environmental protection.

[8] The issue of public pollution abatement has also been considered, but in a completely different framework, by Chao and Yu (1999) and HLM 02.

[9] LRM 97 also presents a similar game structure in the context of trade liberalization. There the recipient countries take into account the donor's reaction to the tariff rates in the allocation of untied foreign aid and a terms of trade effect is the main mechanism which determines the allocation of foreign aid. Here, assuming all countries to be small open economies, cross-border pollution and the donor's reaction to environmental policies by the recipients determine the allocation of aid between them.

2. The model

We consider a three small open economies general equilibrium model – a donor developed country (indexed by a) and two recipients developing countries (indexed by β and γ respectively). In all three countries, a number of goods are produced using several primary factors of production, and are freely traded in the international markets at constant prices.[10] The endowments of the internationally immobile factors of production are fixed and factor markets are perfectly competitive. Pollution is generated as a by-product of production in the recipient countries and is transmitted to the developed country in the form of cross-border pollution. For analytical tractability two assumptions are made. First, no pollution is generated in the donor country, and second, the recipient countries suffer disutility only from their own pollution, i.e., there is no cross-border pollution between the two developing recipient countries. All countries suffer disutility from local or cross-border pollution. We first lay out the general equilibrium model of the recipient countries and then the model for the donor.

Pollution abatement in the recipient countries is simultaneously undertaken by private producers and the public sector. The private producers abate pollution in response to an emission tax, t^i, $i = \beta, \gamma$, imposed by the government. The public sector carries out an amount of abatement g^i, which is financed through emission tax revenue and a part of the foreign aid received. The private and the public sectors compete in factor markets on equal terms. The vector of total fixed factor endowments, V_i ($i = \beta, \gamma$) is decomposed into the part used by the private sector, V_i^p, and the part used for public abatement activities, V_i^g, i.e. $V_i = V_i^p + V_i^g$. The revenue function, $R^i(p, t, V^p)$, which is the country's maximum value of domestic production of private goods, is defined as

$$R^i\left(p, t^i, V_i^p\right) = \max_{x,z}\left\{ p'x^i - t^i z^i : (x, z) \in \Phi\left(V_i^p\right)\right\},$$

where p is the vector of constant world commodity prices; $\Phi(V_i^p)$ is a recipient country's aggregate technology set including both private production and pollution abatement technologies; and x^i and z^i are respectively the vector of net outputs and the amount of pollution emission. For simplicity we assume only one type of pollutant (z), which is generated only in one sector. For a given level of abatement carried out by the public sector g, the vector of factors used in the public sector V_i^g, is uniquely determined. Therefore, since the total endowments of all factors of production, V, is exogenously given, V_i^p is also uniquely determined for a given value of g^i. Moreover, since p does not vary in our analysis, for notational simplicity the revenue function can be written as $R^i(t^i, g^i)$. The $R^i(t^i, g^i)$ function is assumed strictly concave in

---

[10] It is well known that terms of trade effects are an integral part of the literature on foreign aid, since they can be the source of the so-called transfers paradox. Here, abstracting from such price effects is because, as we noted in the introduction, we want to highlight the role of environmental considerations in the international allocation of foreign aid.

g (i.e., R^i_{gg} is non-positive[11]), and it has the following properties (see (Abe, 1995)): $-R^i_g = -(\partial R^i/\partial g) = C^g_i(w)$, is the unit cost of public sector abatement and w is the vector of competitive factor returns.[12] It is also known (e.g., see (Copeland, 1994)) that:

$$z^i = -R^i_t(t^i, g^i). \tag{1}$$

The $R^i(t^i, g^i)$ function is assumed strictly convex in the emission tax rate (i.e., $R^i_{tt} > 0$), meaning that an increase in the emission tax rate lowers the amount of pollution by the private sector.

Taking into account both private and public sector pollution abatement, the net emission of pollution, r^i ($i = \beta, \gamma$), is defined as:

$$r^i = z^i - g^i = -R^i_t(t^i, g^i) - g^i. \tag{2}$$

The following assumption is maintained throughout the analysis.

ASSUMPTION. $R^i_{tg} > 0$.

In view of (1) we have $R^i_{tg} = -\partial z^i/\partial g^i$, and therefore this assumption states that the polluting good and public sector abatement activities are substitutes in production. Thus, an increase in the publicly provided pollution abatement reduces emission by the private sector.

As noted in the beginning of this section, we assume that the government of the recipient countries finances the cost of publicly provided pollution abatement (i.e., $g^i C^g_i = -g^i R^i_g(t^i, g^i)$) by the emission tax revenue (i.e., $t^i z^i = -t^i R^i_t(g^i, t^i)$) and by a fraction $0 < b^i \leqslant 1$ (where $i = \beta, \gamma$) of the foreign aid received. Regarding foreign aid we assume that in countries β and γ, respectively, an amount of $b^\beta f(\lambda T)$ and $b^\gamma f((1 - \lambda)T)$ of aid are allocated to financing public pollution abatement. The allocation parameter λ ($0 \leqslant \lambda \leqslant 1$) denotes the proportion of the aid allotted to country β (thus, a fraction $1 - \lambda$ is allocated to country γ).[13] In order to derive an interior solution in the international transfer problem, i.e., a solution in which both countries receive aid, some type of friction regarding its allocation needs to be introduced in the model. The friction introduced here is similar to that in LRM 97, where not all aid reaches its final destination. To formalize the wastage of aid we stipulate that the recipient countries β and γ receive only $f(\lambda T)$ and $f((1 - \lambda)T)$ amount, respectively, of the foreign aid. The f function is assumed to be increasing and concave, i.e., $f' > 0$ and $f'' < 0$. The remaining fraction of aid i.e., $(1 - b^i)$ is lump-sum distributed to

---

[11] Later on we relax this assumption and we examine the case where $R^i_{gg} = 0$. This assumption is compatible with a standard H–O framework where the number of goods equals or exceeds the number of factors of production, and where only commodity prices determine factor prices (see (Abe, 1992)).

[12] This result emerges from the cost minimization problem in the public sector.

[13] In the present context we do not require that the recipient countries provide matching funds for aid received.

local households in the recipient countries. Thus, each government's budget constraint can be written as:

$$b^\beta f(\lambda T) + t^\beta z^\beta = -g^\beta R_g^\beta\left(g^\beta, t^\beta\right), \quad \text{and} \tag{3}$$

$$b^\gamma f\left((1-\lambda)T\right) + t^\gamma z^\gamma = -g^\gamma R_g^\gamma\left(g^\gamma, t^\gamma\right). \tag{4}$$

Turning to the demand side in the recipient countries, the expenditure function $E^i(r^i, u^i)$ denotes the minimum expenditure required to achieve a level of utility u^i at the prevailing fixed world commodity prices, when the level of net pollution is r^i. The partial derivative of the expenditure function with respect to u, i.e., E_u^i is the reciprocal of marginal utility of income. Since pollution adversely affects household utility, the partial derivative of the expenditure function with respect to r^i (E_r^i), is positive and denotes the households' marginal willingness to pay for the reduction in pollution (e.g., see (Chao and Yu, 1999)). That is, a higher level of pollution requires a higher level of spending on private goods to mitigate its detrimental welfare effects in order to maintain a constant level of utility. The expenditure function is assumed to be strictly convex in r^i, i.e., $E_{rr}^i > 0$ implying that a higher level of net pollution raises the households' marginal willingness to pay for pollution abatement.

The budget constraint of each recipient country requires that private spending $E^i(r^i, u^i)$ must equal income from production of private goods ($R^i(g^i, t^i)$), plus income from publicly provided pollution abatement ($-g^i R_g^i(g^i, t^i)$) plus the fraction of aid distributed to domestic households in a lump-sum manner (i.e., $((1-b^\beta)f(\lambda T)$ and $(1-b^\gamma)f((1-\lambda)T))$). Using Equations (3) and (4), the budget constraints of the recipient countries can be written as:

$$E^\beta\left(u^\beta, r^\beta\right) = R^\beta\left(g^\beta, t^\beta\right) - g^\beta R_g^\beta\left(g^\beta, t^\beta\right) + \left(1-b^\beta\right)f(\lambda T), \quad \text{and} \tag{5}$$

$$E^\gamma\left(u^\gamma, r^\gamma\right) = R^\gamma\left(g^\gamma, t^\gamma\right) - g^\gamma R_g^\gamma\left(g^\gamma, t^\gamma\right) + \left(1-b^\gamma\right)f\left((1-\lambda)T\right). \tag{6}$$

As for the donor country, it allocates a pre-determined amount of aid T (in terms of the numeraire good) to the recipient countries. The donor country neither generates nor does it abate pollution. Utility in this country, however, is adversely affected by cross-border pollution originating in the recipient countries. Thus aggregate pollution affecting the donor country is defined as:

$$\rho = \theta^\beta r^\beta + \theta^\gamma r^\gamma, \tag{7}$$

where θ^i is the spill-over parameter from each recipient country. The donor country's income-expenditure identity requires that private spending, denoted by the expenditure function $E^\alpha(\rho, u^\alpha)$, must equal revenue from production of the private goods, R^α, minus the amount of foreign aid transferred to the recipient countries. That is,

$$E^\alpha\left(\rho, u^\alpha\right) = R^\alpha - T. \tag{8}$$

The properties of the $E^\alpha(\rho, u^\alpha)$ function follow those of the recipient countries. Since commodity prices are exogenous, and factors of production are inelastically supplied, and since there is no pollution and no private or public pollution abatement in the donor country, R^α is exogenous in our analysis.

Equations (2), (3), (4), (5), (6), (7) and (8) constitute a system of eight equations in terms of the eight unknowns, namely r^β, r^γ, ρ, g^β, g^γ, u^α, u^β and u^γ. The donor country's policy instrument is the aid allocating parameter (λ), while the policy instruments of each recipient country is the emission tax rate (t^i) and the fraction (b^i) of aid the local government allocates to financing the public sector pollution abatement. Appendix A lays out the complete comparative statics of the above system.

3. Pollution, welfare, and environmental policies

In this section we examine how the various policy instruments affect the levels of net pollution and welfare in the three countries. These results are to be used later on in the analysis.

3.1. Pollution, and environmental policies

The impact of the policy instruments on the levels of net pollution is obtained by differentiating Equations (2)–(4) to obtain:

$$dr^\beta = \Delta_\beta^{-1}\{-\left(1 + R_{tg}^\beta\right)b^\beta f'(\lambda T)T\,d\lambda - \left(1 + R_{tg}^\beta\right)f(\lambda T)\,db^\beta$$
$$+ \left[R_{tt}^\beta\left(t^\beta + R_g^\beta\right) - \left(1 + R_{tg}^\beta\right)\left(z^\beta + g^\beta R_{gt}^\beta\right) + R_{tt}^\beta g^\beta R_{gg}^\beta\right]dt^\beta\}, \tag{9}$$

$$dr^\gamma = \Delta_\gamma^{-1}\{\left(1 + R_{tg}^\gamma\right)b^\gamma f'((1-\lambda)T)T\,d\lambda - \left(1 + R_{tg}^\gamma\right)f((1-\lambda)T)\,db^\gamma$$
$$+ \left[R_{tt}^\gamma\left(t^\gamma + R_g^\gamma\right) - \left(1 + R_{tg}^\gamma\right)\left(z^\gamma + g^\gamma R_{gt}^\gamma\right) + R_{tt}^\gamma g^\gamma R_{gg}^\gamma\right]dt^\gamma\}, \tag{10}$$

where $\Delta_i = (t^i R_{tg}^i - R_g^i - g^i R_{gg}^i) > 0$, $i = \beta, \gamma$.

Equation (9) indicates that an increase in the fraction of aid allocated to pollution abatement (i.e., b^β), reduces the pollution level of each recipient country. This is because an increase in b^β raises the amount of funds used by the recipient countries for public abatement activities. A sufficient but not necessary condition for an increase in the emission tax rate (i.e., t^β) to reduce pollution in country β, is that the emission tax rate (t^β) is lower than the unit cost of public abatement $(-R_g^\beta)$. That is, if $t^\beta + R_g^\beta < 0$. Also, an increase in the share of foreign aid that each recipient country gets unambiguously reduces the pollution level of each recipient. A similar discussion holds for Equation (10). Note that since we assume constant commodity prices and the absence of cross-border pollution between the two recipient countries, changes in the policy instruments of the one do not affect directly the level of net pollution in the other.

Changes in gross pollution affecting the donor country are given as follows, after totally differentiating Equation (7):

$$d\rho = -\theta^\beta \Delta_\beta^{-1}\left(1 + R_{tg}^\beta\right)f(\lambda T)\,db^\beta$$
$$+ \theta^\beta \Delta_\beta^{-1}\left[R_{tt}^\beta\left(t^\beta + R_g^\beta\right) - \left(1 + R_{tg}^\beta\right)\left(z^\beta + g^\beta R_{gt}^\beta\right) + R_{tt}^\beta g^\beta R_{gg}^\beta\right]dt^\beta$$

$$- \theta^{\gamma} \Delta_{\gamma}^{-1} \left(1 + R_{tg}^{\gamma}\right) f\left((1 - \lambda)T\right) db^{\gamma}$$
$$+ \theta^{\gamma} \Delta_{\gamma}^{-1} \left[R_{tt}^{\gamma}\left(t^{\gamma} + R_g^{\gamma}\right) - \left(1 + R_{tg}^{\gamma}\right)\left(z^{\gamma} + g^{\gamma} R_{gt}^{\gamma}\right) + R_{tt}^{\gamma} g^{\gamma} R_{gg}^{\gamma} \right] dt^{\gamma}$$
$$- \left[\theta^{\beta} \Delta_{\beta}^{-1} \left(1 + R_{tg}^{\beta}\right) b^{\beta} f'(\lambda T) T - \theta^{\gamma} \Delta_{\gamma}^{-1} \left(1 + R_{tg}^{\gamma}\right) b^{\gamma} f'\left((1 - \lambda)T\right) T \right] d\lambda.$$

$$(11)$$

Equation (11) indicates that an increase in the fraction of aid allocated for public abatement activities b^i in either recipient reduces aggregate pollution in the donor. A higher emission tax rate t^i by a recipient reduces aggregate pollution affecting the donor country if the emission tax rate (t^i) is lower than the unit cost of public abatement $(-R_g^i)$ in that country. That is, as previously noted, if $t^i + R_g^i < 0$ (a sufficient but not necessary condition). The effect of increasing the fraction of aid λ allocated to country β, on the donor's aggregate pollution level is ambiguous, since on the one hand, an increase in λ *ceteris paribus* raises public pollution abatement in country β, and thus it reduces cross-border pollution from that country to the donor. On the other hand, however, the increase in the fraction λ reduces the fraction of aid allocated to country γ, thus it lowers public abatement in that country and raises cross-border pollution to the donor. Consequently, a sufficient condition for the increase in λ to reduce net pollution in the donor is that the induced decrease of cross-border pollution from country β outweighs the increase of cross-border pollution from country γ. In terms of the comparative statics of the model this sufficient condition is given as follows. Using Equation (11) and starting from equal shares of aid allocated to the two recipients (i.e., $\lambda = 1 - \lambda = \frac{1}{2}$), an increase of the fraction of aid received by β i.e., $d\lambda > 0$, decreases the donor's aggregate level of pollution if:

$$\frac{\theta^{\gamma}(t^{\beta} R_{tg}^{\beta} - R_g^{\beta} - g^{\beta} R_{gg}^{\beta})(1 + R_{tg}^{\gamma}) b^{\gamma}}{\theta^{\beta}(t^{\gamma} R_{tg}^{\gamma} - R_g^{\gamma} - g^{\gamma} R_{gg}^{\gamma})(1 + R_{tg}^{\beta}) b^{\beta}} < 1. \qquad (12)$$

A proof of this result is given in Appendix B. Intuitively, an increase in λ reduces pollution in country β and increases that in country γ. The net effect on cross-border pollution to the donor country depends on the parameters in the two recipient countries. To understand better the intuition of the above condition, we consider the case of symmetric recipient countries, in ways laid out below, in order to comment on the allocation of aid between them. Thus, the donor country who is interested in minimizing the inflow of pollution, allocates a higher fraction of aid to the country where:

(1) The fraction of foreign aid allocated to pollution abatement (i.e., b^i) is higher, when $t^{\beta} = t^{\gamma}, \theta^{\beta} = \theta^{\gamma}$, and $-g^{\beta} R_g^{\beta} = -g^{\gamma} R_g^{\gamma}$.
(2) The emission tax rate (i.e., t^i) is lower,[14] when $\theta^{\beta} = \theta^{\gamma}$, $-g^{\beta} R_g^{\beta} = -g^{\gamma} R_g^{\gamma}$, and $b^{\beta} = b^{\gamma}$.

---

[14] If the function f were linear, the country with the higher fraction (b^i) or lower emission tax (t^i) receives the entire aid.

(3) The degree of cross-border pollution (i.e., θ^i) is higher, when $t^\beta = t^\gamma$, $-g^\beta R_g^\beta = -g^\gamma R_g^\gamma$, and $b^\beta = b^\gamma$.

(4) The increase in total public pollution abatement expenditure due to a unit increase in public pollution abatement (i.e., $-R_g^i - g^i R_{gg}^i$) is lower, when $t^\beta = t^\gamma$, $\theta^\beta = \theta^\gamma$, $R_{tg}^\beta = R_{tg}^\gamma$, $b^\beta = b^\gamma$.

3.2. Welfare, and environmental policies

The effect of the policy instruments on national welfare levels in the three countries, is obtained by differentiating Equations (5), (6) and (8) as follows:

$$E_u^\alpha \, du^\alpha = A_\lambda d\lambda + A_{t^\beta} \, dt^\beta + A_{t^\gamma} \, dt^\gamma$$
$$+ A_{b^\beta} \, db^\beta + A_{b^\gamma} \, db^\gamma + A_{\theta^\beta} \, d\theta^\beta + A_{\theta^\gamma} \, d\theta^\gamma, \tag{13}$$

$$E_u^\beta \, du^\beta = B_\lambda \, d\lambda + B_{b^\beta} \, db^\beta + B_{t^\beta} \, dt^\beta, \tag{14}$$

$$E_u^\gamma \, du^\gamma = \Gamma_\lambda \, d\lambda + \Gamma_{b^\gamma} \, db^\gamma + \Gamma_{t^\gamma} \, dt^\gamma, \tag{15}$$

where the expressions and signs of the coefficients in the above equations are given in Appendix C.

Observing the coefficients of Equation (13) we note that changes in the utility of the donor are exclusively due to policy induced changes in cross-border pollution. The term A_λ indicates that an increase in the fraction λ of aid accruing to country (β), thus a reduction in the fraction $(1-\lambda)$ of aid to country (γ), raises the donor's welfare if the induced decrease in the level of pollution in the former country outweighs the increase in the level of pollution in the latter, thus resulting to a lower level of cross-border pollution affecting the donor. The terms A_{b^i} indicate that an increase in b^i unambiguously increases welfare in the donor country by reducing emission in the recipient countries and thus the level of cross-border pollution into the donor. Also, a sufficient but not necessary condition for an increase in t^i to increase welfare in the donor country, is that the emission tax rate (t^i) is lower than the unit cost of public abatement ($-R_g^i$). That is, if $t^i + R_g^i < 0$. The economic intuition behind the above results is as follows. With constant world commodity prices the donor country's welfare is affected only via changes in cross-border pollution. Thus the donor country prefers an allocation of aid that reduces its aggregate pollution level.

For the recipient countries, Equations (14) and (15), show that an increase in the fraction of foreign aid received, unambiguously improves welfare, since there is no co-financing of aid on the part of the recipient countries, i.e., $b^i \leqslant 1$. Aid unambiguously reduces the net emission level and it also increases income of the households, thus the terms B_λ and Γ_λ are positive in sign. An increase in the fraction of aid allocated to public abatement, i.e., b^i, has an ambiguous effect on the welfare of the recipient countries. On the one hand, a higher b^i unambiguously reduces net emission, which increases welfare, but on the other it reduces lump-sum transfers to the households which reduces welfare. An increase in the emission tax rate t^i has an ambiguous effect on welfare. On the one hand, it reduces pollution, but on the other, it moves resources away from the private sector to the public sector, thus, reducing private income and consumption.

4. The Nash equilibrium

Having examined the effects of the various policy instruments on pollution and welfare in the three countries, we now characterize the non-cooperative, Nash, equilibrium rates of these instruments.[15] We determine the Nash rates of the instruments b^i and t^i of the recipient countries and λ of the donor country. These results are of importance in the next section where we examine how competition for aid between the two recipient countries, affects the Nash equilibrium values of their emission tax rates and of the fraction of aid allocated to public pollution abatement.

The first order conditions for the case of a selfish donor are given by:

$$\Delta_\beta E_u^\beta \left(du^\beta / db^\beta \right) = B_{b^\beta} = 0, \tag{16}$$

$$\Delta_\beta E_u^\beta \left(du^\beta / dt^\beta \right) = B_{t^\beta} = 0, \tag{17}$$

$$\Delta_\gamma E_u^\gamma \left(du^\gamma / db^\gamma \right) = \Gamma_{b^\gamma} = 0, \tag{18}$$

$$\Delta_\gamma E_u^\gamma \left(du^\gamma / dt^\gamma \right) = \Gamma_{t^\gamma} = 0, \tag{19}$$

$$E_u^\alpha \left(du^\alpha / d\lambda \right) = A_\lambda = 0. \tag{20}$$

Equations (16)–(20) are solved simultaneously to obtain the Nash equilibrium values of the policy instruments in the three countries. From these equations, we obtain the following Nash equilibrium conditions:

$$t^\beta = E_r^\beta = -R_g^\beta, \tag{21}$$

$$t^\gamma = E_r^\gamma = -R_g^\gamma, \quad \text{and} \tag{22}$$

$$f'\left(\lambda^N T\right)\theta^\beta \left(\Delta_\beta^N\right)^{-1} b^\beta \left(1 + R_{tg}^\beta\right) = \theta^\gamma f'\left((1 - \lambda^N)T\right)\left(\Delta_\gamma^N\right)^{-1} b^\gamma \left(1 + R_{tg}^\gamma\right), \tag{23}$$

where $\Delta_i^N = [t^i (R_{tg}^i + 1) - g^i R_{gg}^i] > 0$. Hereon, the superscript N denotes the Nash equilibrium value of a variable.

Conditions (21) and (22) combine the Pigouvian rule for environmental taxation with the Samuelson rule for the optimal provision for public goods. The first equality in these conditions gives the Pigouvian rule, *viz.* the marginal willingness to pay for pollution abatement is equal to emission tax rate. The second equality of these equilibrium conditions gives the Samuelsonian rule, *viz.* the marginal willingness to pay for a public good is equal to the marginal cost of producing it. The Nash equilibrium pollution taxes (t_N^i) in the recipient countries are not Pareto efficient (optimal), since in choosing these values of their instruments they do not account for the spill over effects

---

[15] We assume that the recipient countries are free to choose the emission tax rate and how much of the aid it wants to allocate for public abatement of pollution. We assume that the donor cannot tie aid to pollution abatement, i.e., aid is perfectly fungible.

on the donor. Condition (23) equates the marginal benefit to the donor, due to lower cross-border pollution from country β, to the marginal cost, due to higher cross-border pollution from country γ, when the donor increases the fraction of aid λ allocated to country β at the expense of country γ.[16]

Making use of the above equilibrium conditions, the choice of the Nash equilibrium value of (λ^N) is stated in the following proposition.

PROPOSITION 1. *When the donor allocates a fixed amount of aid so as to maximize its own welfare, country β gets a higher proportion of the aid, under the following necessary and sufficient condition:*

$$\frac{f'(\lambda^N T)}{f'((1-\lambda^N)T)} = \frac{\theta^\gamma \Delta_\beta^N (1+R_{tg}^\gamma) b^\gamma}{\theta^\beta \Delta_\gamma^N (1+R_{tg}^\beta) b^\beta} < 1.$$

Consequently, it follows that $\lambda^N > \frac{1}{2}$ if the right-hand side of Equation (23) is less than unity.

Note that the above condition is the same as the condition (12), implying that the welfare of the donor is maximized when the inflow of cross-border pollution is minimized. This is so because in the present framework the total amount of aid allocated to the recipient countries is fixed, and there are no terms of trade effects among the three countries, or other international linkages e.g., international factor mobility. Thus, the only factor affecting the donor's welfare is cross-border pollution. The conditions under which the donor maximizes its welfare are the same as those in the discussion of Equation (12), stating the conditions under which aid minimizes the inflow of pollution into this country.

5. The competition for aid equilibrium

In this section we address the central question of this paper. That is "when can competition for aid reduce pollution?" Thus far it is shown that the allocation of aid depends on the relative magnitude of the emission tax rates and on the fraction of foreign aid allocated to pollution abatement in the two recipient countries. Based on this result, it can be argued that the recipient countries may want to use their environmental policy instruments in competing against each other for international transfers.

In this section we consider a two-stage game to analyze how competition for aid affects the Nash equilibrium emission tax and the fraction of aid allocated to pollution

---

[16] Differentiating Equations (3) and (4), the two recipient countries' government budget constraints, equilibrium condition (23) alternatively can be written as $\theta^\beta(1+R_{tg}^\beta)(\partial g^\beta/\partial \lambda) = -\theta^\gamma(1+R_{tg}^\gamma)(\partial g^\gamma/\partial \lambda)$, where $(\partial g^\beta/\partial \lambda) > 0$ and $(\partial g^\gamma/\partial \lambda) < 0$. That is, as λ increases, the marginal benefit (cost) to the donor country, due to lower (higher) cross-border pollution from country $\beta(\gamma)$ is due to higher (lower) public pollution abatement in the respective recipient country.

abatement, when the donor behaves selfishly in maximizing its own welfare. In the first stage each recipient country sets optimally either its emission tax rate (t^i) for a given value of the fraction of aid (b^i) allocated to public abatement, or vice versa. Then, in the second stage the donor decides on the allocation of aid between the two recipients. This we call the *"competition for aid equilibrium"* whose solution we compare to the one where the three countries act simultaneously. As commonly practiced, we solve the problem by a backward induction starting from the choice of λ by the donor in the second stage and then proceeding to the choice of the recipients' policy instruments in the first stage, taking into account the donor's reaction in this choice.[17,18]

5.1. The recipient countries set optimally their emission tax rate t^i

The reactions functions for the two recipient countries and for the donor can be derived respectively from Equations (14), (15) and (20). The recipient countries take into account the donor country's reaction when they determine their emission taxes.

Stage two: From Equation (20) we obtain the donor's reaction function as follows:

$$R_a: \lambda^* = \lambda^*(t^\beta, t^\gamma) \implies$$
$$f'(\lambda^N T)\theta^\beta \Delta_\beta^{-1} b^\beta (1 + R_{tg}^\beta) = \theta^\gamma f'((1 - \lambda^N)T)\Delta_\gamma^{-1} b^\gamma (1 + R_{tg}^\gamma) \qquad (24)$$

where λ^* denotes the optimal value of λ chosen by the donor in the competition for aid equilibrium. We examine how a change in the emission tax by each recipient country affects the allocation parameter. From Equation (20) we obtain:

$$\left(\frac{d\lambda^*}{dt^\beta}\right)_{reaction} = -\frac{A_{\lambda t^\beta}}{A_{\lambda\lambda}} < 0, \quad \text{and} \quad \left(\frac{d\lambda^*}{dt^\gamma}\right)_{reaction} = -\frac{A_{\lambda t^\gamma}}{A_{\lambda\lambda}} > 0, \qquad (25)$$

where as shown in Appendix D, $A_{\lambda t^\beta}$ is negative and $A_{\lambda t^\gamma}$ is positive. Also, $A_{\lambda\lambda}$ is negative.[19] The results in Equations (25) imply that a reduction in the emission tax rate in a recipient country increases the proportion of aid allotted to it. In other words, the donor allocates a higher proportion of aid to the country with the laxer environmental regulation, i.e., the lower emission tax rate, which emits more cross-border pollution to it.[20]

---

[17] We assume that all countries know the other countries' objective functions.

[18] Since the aim of the paper is to analyze the efficiency of competition for aid policy, the above scenario i.e., the decisions on environmental policies precede the allocation of aid, seems to be the appropriate one. Here, the alternative scenario, where the donor chooses aid in the first stage and then the recipient countries set their environmental policies, cannot address the issue of interest.

[19] Rearranging Equation (20) we get that $(du^\alpha/d\lambda) = (A_\lambda/E_u^\alpha)$. Since $(d^2 u^\alpha/d\lambda^2) = (A_{\lambda\lambda}/E_u^\alpha) < 0$, for maximizing welfare, we get $A_{\lambda\lambda} < 0$ since $E_u^\alpha > 0$.

[20] Within the Heckscher–Ohlin model it is known that $R_{gg}^i = 0$ (see footnote 10). In this case $A_{\lambda t^i} = 0$, thus, Equations (25) indicate that $(d\lambda^i/dt^i) = 0$, i.e., changes in the emission tax rates do not affect the allocation of the foreign aid.

Stage one: Making use of (14) and (15), we obtain the reaction functions of the recipient countries:

$$R^\beta: t^\beta\left(\lambda^*, t^i, b^i\right) \iff B_{t^\beta} + B_\lambda\left(\partial\lambda^*/\partial t^\beta\right) = 0, \tag{26}$$

$$R^\gamma: t^\gamma\left(\lambda^*, t^i, b^i\right) \iff \Gamma_{t^\gamma} + \Gamma_\lambda\left(\partial\lambda^*/\partial t^\gamma\right) = 0. \tag{27}$$

The second term in the above equations is the *competition for aid effect* (second stage effect) on the recipients' reaction functions. This effect, following the results of Equation (27), is negative for both countries. Recall from Appendix C that $B_\lambda > 0$ and $\Gamma_\lambda < 0$. Thus, competition for aid induces the recipient countries to choose an even lower emission tax rate compared to the inefficiently low emission tax rate in the Nash equilibrium, i.e., $t^i_C < t^i_N$, where t^i_N and t^i_C denote the equilibrium tax rates under Nash and competition for aid equilibrium, respectively.

PROPOSITION 2. *When the donor allocates aid so as to maximize its own welfare, competition for aid results in emission tax rates in the recipient countries that are lower relative to their Nash equilibrium tax rates, i.e., $t^i_N > t^i_C$. Thus, cross-border pollution in the donor is higher in the competition for aid relative to the Nash equilibrium.*

Intuitively, since the allocation of the aid depends on the levels of the emission taxes, it may be argued that the recipient countries can use the emission taxes strategically. In other words, since the donor country allocates a higher proportion of aid to the country with the lower emission tax rate, the recipient countries reduce the emission tax rates so as to obtain a higher fraction of a given amount of aid by the donor country. Therefore, competition for aid has a positive effect to the pollution level transmitted to the donor, since it reduces the emission taxes in both recipient countries. Another way of explaining this result is as follows: In the present context, *ceteris paribus*, the marginal benefit to the donor of a \$ of aid is higher in the recipient with the smaller emission tax rate and thus the higher level of pollution. Consequently, the donor allocates a higher fraction of aid to that country (see Equation (24)). Thus, competition for aid reduces the pollution taxes.

5.2. The recipient countries set optimally the fraction b^i of foreign aid allocated to pollution abatement

The reaction functions for the donor and the two recipient countries can be derived respectively from Equations (14), (15) and (20). The recipient countries take into account the donor country's reaction when they determine their fractions of aid allocated to public abatement.

Stage two: From Equation (20), we obtain the donor's reaction function as stated in Equation (24). We examine how a change in the fraction of aid allocated to pollution abatement by each recipient country affects the allocation parameter. From Equation (20) we obtain:

$$\left(\frac{d\lambda^*}{db^\beta}\right)_{\text{reaction}} = -\frac{A_{\lambda b^\beta}}{A_{\lambda\lambda}} > 0, \quad \text{and} \quad \left(\frac{d\lambda^*}{db^\gamma}\right)_{\text{reaction}} = -\frac{A_{\lambda b^\gamma}}{A_{\lambda\lambda}} < 0 \qquad (28)$$

where, as shown in Appendix D, $A_{\lambda b^\beta}$ is positive, $A_{\lambda b^\gamma}$ and $A_{\lambda\lambda}$ is each negative. The results in Equation (28) imply that an increase in the fraction of aid allocated to pollution abatement increases the proportion of aid going to it. The donor country rewards the country that allocates a higher fraction of foreign aid to the financing of public pollution abatement.[21]

Stage one: Making use of (14) and (15), we obtain the reaction functions of the recipient countries:

$$R^\beta: b^\beta\left(\lambda^*, b^i, t^i\right) \iff B_{b^\beta} + B_\lambda\left(\partial\lambda^*/\partial b^\beta\right) = 0, \qquad (29)$$

$$R^\gamma: b^\gamma\left(\lambda^*, b^i, t^i\right) \iff \Gamma_{b^\gamma} + \Gamma_\lambda\left(\partial\lambda^*/\partial b^\gamma\right) = 0. \qquad (30)$$

The second term in the above equations is the *competition for aid effect* in the recipients' reaction functions. This effect is positive for both countries. Thus, competition for aid induces both recipient countries to choose higher proportion of aid allocated to public abatement than the inefficiently low level in the Nash equilibrium, i.e., $b^i_C > b^i_N$.

PROPOSITION 3. *When the donor allocates aid so as to maximize its own welfare, competition for aid results in higher fractions of aid allocated to pollution abatement in the recipient countries, relative to the Nash equilibrium i.e., $b^i_C > b^i_N$. Thus, cross-border pollution in the donor is lower in the competition for aid relative to the Nash equilibrium.*

An intuition for this result can be as follows. Since aid is untied, from the viewpoint of the donor country, welfare is maximized when the recipient countries allocate the whole amount of aid received to public pollution abatement. Therefore, the donor country gives more aid to the country with the higher fraction of aid that goes for public pollution abatement (b^i). Therefore, the recipient countries in order to get more aid increase the proportion of aid that goes for pollution abatement. In this case, competition for aid has a negative effect to the pollution level transmitted to the donor, since it increases the fraction of aid allocated to public pollution abatement in both recipient countries. Another way of explaining this result is as follows: In the present context, *ceteris paribus*, the marginal benefit to the donor of a $ of aid is higher in the recip-

---

[21] Note that from the donor's point of view the optimal value of b^i is unity. Moreover, within the Heckscher–Ohlin framework changes in fraction of aid allocated to public abatement i.e., b^i affect the allocation of foreign aid in the same way as in the general case where $R^i_{gg} < 0$.

ient country who allocates a higher fraction of aid (b^i, $i = \beta, \gamma$) to public pollution abatement, and thus generates the lower level of pollution. Consequently, the donor allocates a higher fraction of aid to that country (see Equation (24)). Thus, competition for aid increases the fraction of aid allocated to public pollution abatement in the recipient countries.

6. Conclusion

This paper considers the allocation of a pre-determined amount of foreign aid among recipient countries. For this, we develop a one donor, two recipient countries general equilibrium model with cross-border pollution and private and public sector pollution abatement. The donor country chooses the proportion of aid allocated to each recipient, while the latter countries choose emission taxes and the fraction of aid allocated to the financing of public pollution abatement. In this context, we first derive the Nash allocation of a fixed amount of aid between the two recipients. In this equilibrium we demonstrate that the donor country allocates a higher fraction of aid to the country with, (i) the lower emission tax, or (ii) the higher cross-border pollution rate, or (iii) the higher fraction of aid going to public pollution abatement, or finally with (iv) the smaller increase in total expenditure on public pollution abatement when public pollution abatement increases by one unit. In all the cases above, we assume that the two recipient countries are symmetric in all other elements which affect the allocation of aid between them.

In the second part of the paper we develop a two stage or a competition for aid equilibrium where the two recipients compete against each other for foreign aid. Here, the central question of the analysis is whether such competition for aid can reduce pollution. We demonstrate that when the recipient countries compete for aid using the fraction of aid allocated to public abatement as their policy instrument, then, competition for aid encourages them to allocate a higher proportion of aid to public abatement. In this case, the donor enjoys a higher welfare relative to the Nash equilibrium due to lower levels of cross-border pollution. On the other hand, when the recipient countries compete for aid using the emission taxes as their policy instruments, then competition for aid leads them to reduce the emission tax rates. Now, the donor's welfare worsens relative to the Nash equilibrium due to higher levels of cross-border pollution.

Acknowledgements

The authors gratefully acknowledge the constructive comments by A. Woodland and other participants in the ETSG Annual Conference, September 2005, by S. Lahiri, A. Schweinberger and P. Koundouri. The usual disclaimer applies. N. Tsakiris acknowledges the financial support by the Greek Ministry of Education and the EU under the Irakleitos Research Fellowship Program.

Appendix A. The complete system of comparative statics

$$
\begin{bmatrix}
E_u^a & 0 & 0 & -E_\rho^a \theta^\beta (1+R_{tg}^\beta) & -E_\rho^a \theta^\gamma (1+R_{tg}^\gamma) \\
0 & E_u^\beta & 0 & -E_r^\beta (1+R_{tg}^\beta) - g^\beta R_{gg}^\beta & 0 \\
0 & 0 & E_u^\gamma & 0 & -E_r^\gamma (1+R_{tg}^\gamma) - g^\gamma R_{gg}^\gamma \\
0 & 0 & 0 & \Delta_\beta & 0 \\
0 & 0 & 0 & 0 & \Delta_\gamma
\end{bmatrix}
\begin{bmatrix}
du^a \\
du^\beta \\
du^\gamma \\
dg^\beta \\
dg^\gamma
\end{bmatrix}
$$

$$
= \begin{bmatrix}
\theta^\beta E_\rho^a R_{tt}^\beta \\
R_t^\beta - g^\beta R_{gt}^\beta + E_r^\beta R_{tt}^\beta \\
0 \\
-R_t^\beta + g^\beta R_{gt}^\beta - t^\beta R_{tt}^\beta \\
0
\end{bmatrix} dt^\beta
+ \begin{bmatrix}
\theta^\gamma E_\rho^a R_{tt}^\gamma \\
R_t^\gamma - g^\gamma R_{gt}^\gamma + E_r^\gamma R_{tt}^\gamma \\
0 \\
-R_t^\gamma + g^\gamma R_{gt}^\gamma - t^\gamma R_{tt}^\gamma \\
0
\end{bmatrix} dt^\gamma
$$

$$
+ \begin{bmatrix}
0 \\
T(1-b^\beta) f'(\lambda T) \\
-T(1-b^\gamma) f'((1-\lambda)T) \\
Tb^\beta f'(\lambda T) \\
-Tb^\gamma f'((1-\lambda)T)
\end{bmatrix} d\lambda
$$

$$
- \begin{bmatrix}
0 \\
-f(\lambda T) \\
0 \\
f(\lambda T) \\
0
\end{bmatrix} b^\beta
+ \begin{bmatrix}
0 \\
0 \\
-f((1-\lambda)T) \\
0 \\
f((1-\lambda)T)
\end{bmatrix} db^\gamma. \tag{A.1}
$$

The determinant of the right-hand side matrix of coefficients of the unknowns is $\Delta = E_u^a E_u^\beta E_u^\gamma \Delta_\beta \Delta_\gamma$ and it is positive.

Appendix B. Proof of Equation (12)

From Equation (11) we can write

$$
\begin{aligned}
\frac{dr}{d\lambda} &= -\left[\theta^\beta \Delta_\beta^{-1}(1+R_{tg}^\beta) b^\beta f'(\lambda T) T - \theta^\gamma \Delta_\gamma^{-1}(1+R_{tg}^\gamma) b^\gamma f'((1-\lambda)T) T\right] \\
&= -\left[\theta^\beta (1+R_{tg}^\beta) \frac{dg^\beta}{d\lambda} - \theta^\gamma (1+R_{tg}^\gamma) \frac{dg^\gamma}{d\lambda}\right]. \tag{B.1}
\end{aligned}
$$

Thus, starting from equal shares of aid to the two recipient countries, an increase in λ reduces net pollution in the donor country if:

$$
\left[\theta^\beta \Delta_\beta^{-1}(1+R_{tg}^\beta) b^\beta f'(\lambda T) T - \theta^\gamma \Delta_\gamma^{-1}(1+R_{tg}^\gamma) b^\gamma f'((1-\lambda)T) T\right]_{\lambda=\frac{1}{2}} > 0. \tag{B.2}
$$

After some algebraic manipulations, Equation (B.2) can be written as:

$$\left\{ f'\big((1-\lambda)T\big)\theta^\beta \Delta_\beta^{-1}\big(1+R_{tg}^\beta\big)b^\beta T \right.$$

$$\left. \times \left(\frac{f'(\lambda T)}{f'((1-\lambda)T)} - \frac{\theta^\gamma \Delta_\gamma^{-1}(1+R_{tg}^\gamma)b^\gamma T}{\theta^\beta \Delta_\beta^{-1}(1+R_{tg}^\beta)b^\beta T} \right) \right\}_{\lambda=\frac12} > 0. \tag{B.3}$$

Since the two countries are assumed to receive an equal share of aid, then $\{\frac{f'(\lambda T)}{f'((1-\lambda)T)}\}_{\lambda=\frac12} = 1$. Thus, the left-hand side expression in Equation (13) is positive if Equation (12) in the text holds.

Appendix C. Using Equations (9)–(11) we obtain the coefficients and signs of Equations (13)–(15)

$$A_\lambda = E_\rho^\alpha \theta^\beta \Delta_\beta^{-1}\big[\big(1+R_{tg}^\beta\big)b^\beta f'(\lambda T)T\big]$$
$$\quad - E_\rho^\alpha \theta^\gamma \Delta_\gamma^{-1}\big[\big(1+R_{tg}^\gamma\big)b^\gamma f'\big((1-\lambda)T\big)T\big]$$
$$\quad = -E_\rho^\alpha \theta^\beta \big(dr^\beta/d\lambda\big) - E_\rho^\alpha \theta^\gamma \big(dr^\gamma/d\lambda\big),$$

$$A_{t^\beta} = -E_\rho^\alpha \theta^\beta \Delta_\beta^{-1}\big[R_{tt}^\beta\big(t^\beta+R_g^\beta\big) - \big(1+R_{tg}^\beta\big)\big(z^\beta+g^\beta R_{gt}^\beta\big) + R_{tt}^\beta g^\beta R_{gg}^\beta\big]$$
$$\quad = -E_\rho^\alpha \theta^\beta \big(dr^\beta/dt^\beta\big),$$

$$A_{t^\gamma} = -E_\rho^\alpha \theta^\gamma \Delta_\gamma^{-1}\big[R_{tt}^\gamma\big(t^\gamma+R_g^\gamma\big) - \big(1+R_{tg}^\gamma\big)\big(z^\gamma+g^\gamma R_{gt}^\gamma\big) + R_{tt}^\gamma g^\gamma R_{gg}^\gamma\big]$$
$$\quad = -E_\rho^\alpha \theta^\gamma \big(dr^\gamma/dt^\gamma\big),$$

$$A_{b^\beta} = E_\rho^a \theta^\beta \Delta_\beta^{-1}\big(1+R_{tg}^\beta\big)f(\lambda T) = -E_\rho^a \theta^\beta \big(dr^\beta/db^\beta\big) > 0,$$

$$A_{b^\gamma} = E_\rho^a \theta^\gamma \Delta_\gamma^{-1}\big(1+R_{tg}^\gamma\big)f\big((1-\lambda)T\big) = -E_\rho^a \theta^\gamma \big(dr^\gamma/db^\gamma\big) > 0,$$

$$A_{\theta^\beta} = -E_u^\alpha r^\beta < 0, \quad \text{and} \quad A_{\theta^\gamma} = -E_u^\alpha r^\gamma < 0.$$

$$B_\lambda = f'(\lambda T)T\big\{(1-b^\beta) + \Delta_\beta^{-1}b^\beta\big[\big(1+R_{tg}^\beta\big)E_r^\beta - g^\beta R_{gg}^\beta\big]\big\}$$
$$\quad = -E_r^\beta\big(dr^\beta/d\lambda\big) + f'(\lambda T)T\big[(1-b^\beta) - \Delta_\beta^{-1}b^\beta g^\beta R_{gg}^\beta\big] > 0,$$

$$B_{b^\beta} = -f(\lambda T)\big\{1 - \Delta_\beta^{-1}\big[\big(1+R_{tg}^\beta\big)E_r^\beta - g^\beta R_{gg}^\beta\big]\big\}$$
$$\quad = -E_r^\beta\big(dr^\beta/db^\beta\big) - f(\lambda T)\big(1 - \Delta_\beta^{-1}g^\beta R_{gg}^\beta\big),$$

$$B_{t^\beta} = \Delta_\beta^{-1}\big\{-R_{tt}^\beta\big[g^\beta R_{gg}^\beta\big(E_r^\beta - t^\beta\big) + E_r^\beta\big(t^\beta+R_g^\beta\big)\big]$$
$$\quad + \big(z^\beta+g^\beta R_{gt}^\beta\big)\big[E_r^\beta\big(1+R_{tg}^\beta\big) + R_g^\beta - t^\beta R_{tg}^\beta\big]\big\}, \quad \text{or}$$

$$B_{t^\beta} = -E_r^\beta\big(dr^\beta/dt^\beta\big) + \Delta_\beta^{-1}\big[\big(z^\beta+g^\beta R_{gt}^\beta\big)\big(R_g^\beta - t^\beta R_{tg}^\beta\big) + R_{tt}^\beta g^\beta R_{gg}^\beta t^\beta\big],$$

$$\Gamma_\lambda = -f'\big((1-\lambda)T\big)T\big\{(1-b^\gamma) + \Delta_\gamma^{-1}b^\gamma\big[\big(1+R_{tg}^\gamma\big)E_r^\gamma - g^\gamma R_{gg}^\gamma\big]\big\}$$
$$\quad = -\Delta_\gamma E_r^\gamma\big(dr^\gamma/d\lambda\big) - f'\big((1-\lambda)T\big)T\big[(1-b^\gamma) - \Delta_\gamma^{-1}b^\gamma g^\gamma R_{gg}^\gamma\big] < 0,$$

$$\Gamma_{b^\gamma} = -f\big((1-\lambda)T\big)\big\{1 - \Delta_\gamma^{-1}\big[\big(1+R_{tg}^\gamma\big)E_r^\gamma - g^\gamma R_{gg}^\gamma\big]\big\}$$
$$\quad = -E_r^\gamma\big(dr^\gamma/db^\gamma\big) - f\big((1-\lambda)T\big)\big(1 - \Delta_\gamma^{-1}g^\gamma R_{gg}^\gamma\big),$$

$$\Gamma_{t^{\gamma}} = \Delta_{\gamma}^{-1}\big\{-R_{tt}^{\gamma}\big[g^{\gamma}R_{gg}^{\gamma}(E_r^{\gamma} - t^{\gamma}) + E_r^{\gamma}(t^{\gamma} + R_g^{\gamma})\big]$$
$$+ (z^{\gamma} + g^{\gamma}R_{gt}^{\gamma})\big[E_r^{\gamma}(1 + R_{tg}^{\gamma}) + R_g^{\gamma} - t^{\gamma}R_{tg}^{\gamma}\big]\big\}, \quad \text{or}$$
$$\Gamma_{t^{\gamma}} = -E_r^{\gamma}(dr^{\gamma}/dt^{\gamma}) + \Delta_{\gamma}^{-1}\big[(z^{\gamma} + g^{\gamma}R_{gt}^{\gamma})(R_g^{\gamma} - t^{\gamma}R_{tg}^{\gamma}) + R_{tt}^{\gamma}g^{\gamma}R_{gg}^{\gamma}t^{\gamma}\big].$$

Appendix D

$$A_{\lambda t^{\beta}} = \big(E_u^{\alpha}\big)^{-1}E_{\rho}^{\alpha}\theta^{\beta}f'(\lambda T)T\big(1 + R_{tg}^{\beta}\big)\left[\frac{2R_{gg}^{\beta}(dg^{\beta}/dt^{\beta})}{(\Delta_{\beta})^2}\right] < 0,$$

$$A_{\lambda t^{\gamma}} = -\big(E_u^{\alpha}\big)^{-1}E_{\rho}^{\alpha}\theta^{\gamma}f'((1 - \lambda)T)T\big(1 + R_{tg}^{\gamma}\big)\left[\frac{2R_{gg}^{\gamma}(dg^{\gamma}/dt^{\gamma})}{(\Delta_{\gamma})^2}\right] > 0.$$

Where we assume that the economy is on the upward-sloping part of the Laffer curve i.e., $(dg^i/dt^i) > 0$.

$$A_{\lambda b^{\beta}} = \big(E_u^{\alpha}\big)^{-1}E_{\rho}^{\alpha}\theta^{\beta}f'(\lambda T)T\big(1 + R_{tg}^{\beta}\big)$$
$$\times \left(\frac{(t^{\beta}R_{tg}^{\beta})^2 - 2R_g^{\beta}t^{\beta}R_{tg}^{\beta} + (R_g^{\beta})^2 + (g^{\beta}R_{gg}^{\beta})^2 - 2g^{\beta}R_{gg}^{\beta}t^{\beta}R_{tg}^{\beta} + 2R_{gg}^{\beta}t^{\beta}R_t^{\beta}}{(\Delta_{\beta})^3}\right) > 0,$$

$$A_{\lambda b^{\gamma}} = -\big(E_u^{\alpha}\big)^{-1}E_{\rho}^{\alpha}\theta^{\gamma}f'((1 - \lambda)T)T\big(1 + R_{tg}^{\gamma}\big)$$
$$\times \left(\frac{(t^{\gamma}R_{tg}^{\gamma})^2 - 2R_g^{\gamma}t^{\gamma}R_{tg}^{\gamma} + (R_g^{\gamma})^2 + (g^{\gamma}R_{gg}^{\gamma})^2 - 2g^{\gamma}R_{gg}^{\gamma}t^{\gamma}R_{tg}^{\gamma} + 2R_{gg}^{\gamma}t^{\gamma}R_t^{\gamma}}{(\Delta_{\gamma})^3}\right) < 0.$$

References

Abe, K. (1992), Tariff reform in a small open economy with public production. *International Economic Review* 33, 209–222.

Abe, K. (1995), The target rates of tariff and tax reform. *International Economic Review* 36, 875–885.

Baumol, W.J., Oates, W.E. (1994), *The Theory of Environmental Policy*. Cambridge University Press, Cambridge.

Brett, C., Keen, M. (2000), Political uncertainty and earmarking of environmental taxes. *Journal of Public Economics* 75, 315–340.

Chao, C., Yu, E. (1999), Foreign aid, the environment, and welfare. *Journal of Development Economics* 59, 553–564.

Copeland, B. (1994), International trade and the environment: Policy reform in a polluted small open economy. *Journal of Environmental Economics and Management* 26, 44–65.

Copeland, B., Taylor, M. (1995), Trade and transboundary pollution. *American Economic Review* 85, 716–737.

Copeland, B., Taylor, M. (2003), *Trade and the Environment, Theory and Evidence*. Princeton University Press, Princeton, NJ.

Grossman, G., Krueger, A. (1995), Economic growth and the environment. *Quarterly Journal of Economics* 110, 353–377.

Hatzipanayotou, P., Lahiri, S., Michael, M. (2002), Can cross-border pollution reduce pollution? *Canadian Journal of Economics* 35, 805–818.

Lahiri, S., Raimondos-Møller, P. (1997), Competition for aid and trade policy. *Journal of International Economics* 43, 369–385.

Lahiri, S., Raimondos-Møller, P. (2000), Lobbying by ethnic groups and aid allocation. *Economic Journal* 110, 62–79.

Linster, M., Zegel, F., (2003). Pollution abatement and control expenditure in OECD countries. *OECD Discussion Paper*, Paris.

Naito, T. (2003), Pareto-improving untied aid with environmental externalities. *Journal of Economics* 68, 161–169.

OECD (2000), Reforming environmental finance institutions in the Kazakhstan: conclusions and recommendations from the performance review of the Kazakhstan State environmental protection fund. *Report*, Paris.

OECD (2003), Trends in environmental expenditure and international commitments for the environment in Eastern Europe, Caucasus and Central Asia, 1996–2001. *Report*, Paris.

Schweinberger, A., Woodland, A. (2005), The short and long run effects of tied aid on pollution abatement, pollution and employment: a pilot model. *Discussion Paper*. Presented at the ETSG 7th Annual Meetings, Dublin.

Turunen-Red, A., Woodland, A. (2004), Multilateral reforms of trade and environmental policy. *Review of International Economics* 12, 321–336.

CHAPTER 7

Foreign Aid, International Migration and Welfare

Slobodan Djajić

The Graduate Institute of International Studies, 132 rue de Lausanne, CH-1211 Geneva, Switzerland
E-mail address: djajic@hei.unige.ch

Abstract

This paper examines the effects of foreign aid on emigration and welfare of the re-maining residents in an economy producing traded and non-traded goods. There are three distinct types of households: the rich, the poor, and the relatives of emigrants. Donor country's aid is provided to discourage the poor from emigrating. The extent to which it achieves this objective is shown to be an important factor determining the welfare implications of aid for every type of household residing in the economy. The paper also considers the impact of foreign aid on remittance flows and total foreign exchange earnings of the recipient country.

Keywords: Foreign aid, international migration, remittances

JEL classifications: F22, F35

1. Introduction

Suppose that foreign aid is provided by an advanced donor country only to the non-migrating poor households of a developing country. How does it affect their welfare, as well as the welfare of other households in the recipient country? How does it affect in-ternational migration and the flow of remittances? Does it have a positive or a negative impact on the overall foreign-exchange earnings of the recipient country? These are some of the key questions facing the developing economies that depend very heavily on both foreign aid and migrants' remittances as major sources of income and foreign exchange. From the point of view of the advanced donor countries, it is also important to understand the nature of the relationship among foreign aid, welfare, and migration flows, particularly at this time of heightened concern over unwanted immigration from the developing countries.[1]

---

[1] There exist very few theoretical studies on the links between foreign aid to households and international migration. The pioneering work of Gaytan-Fregoso and Lahiri (2000) examines the impact of aid on illegal

THEORY AND PRACTICE OF FOREIGN AID
VOLUME 1   ISSN: 1574-8715
DOI: 10.1016/S1574-8715(06)01007-4

The present study addresses these issues in the context of a simple model of foreign aid and international migration. The aid-receiving economy produces traded and non-traded goods with the aid of capital and labor. The model is therefore very similar to that originally employed by Rivera-Batiz (1982), and subsequently by Djajić (1986, 1998), Kirwan and Holden (1986), Quibria (1996), Rivera-Batiz (1986), and Tompson (1984), among others, in their study of the impact of emigration and remittances on the welfare of the source country. In the present version of this model, there are rich and poor households. Each household possesses one unit of labor, but the rich households own more capital than do the poor. Some of the workers from the poor households migrate to the advanced, donor country, participate in its relatively more lucrative labor market and send remittances back to their relatives in the recipient country. Others choose not to migrate.

If the donor country offers foreign aid in the form of income transfers to the poor household heads who do not migrate, will a flow of such transfers have a positive or negative impact on the welfare of the different types of households in the recipient country: the poor, the rich, and the remaining relatives of migrants working abroad? It is shown that the direct beneficiaries of aid do enjoy an improvement in welfare. The direct effect of aid on their income is found to outweigh any potential deterioration in their terms of trade in factor and commodity markets. The impact of the aid program on the welfare of other households depends, however, on the effectiveness of aid in discouraging emigration from the recipient country.

The remainder of the paper is organized as follows. Section 2 presents the model and examines the welfare implications of aid to non-migrating poor when international migration is taken to be exogenous. Section 3 conducts the same exercise in the more general setting where migration flows are responsive to the targeted aid transfers. Section 4 looks at the impact of aid on the stock of migrants, the implied remittance flows and total foreign-exchange earnings of the recipient country within a general-equilibrium framework of analysis. Finally, Section 5 summarizes the main results of the paper.

2. Foreign aid and welfare of the rich and the poor

Consider a world consisting of an advanced donor country and a less developed recipient country. The recipient country consists of $X + Y$ households which may be classified into two groups: the rich (Y) and the poor (X), each group being homogeneous. Every household is assumed to possess one unit of labor. The rich households, however, have k^y units of capital, while the poor own only k^x $(< k^y)$ units. The two groups interact with each other in both the factor and commodity markets. Two types

---

immigration, while the recent paper by Hatzipanayotou and Michael (2006) looks at the welfare implications of foreign aid designed to discourage migrants from coming to the donor country where they are eligible for social benefits.

of goods are produced, traded (T), which we take to be the numeraire, and an internationally non-traded good (N), whose price is given by P. Both goods are produced with the aid of capital and labor under perfect competition and constant returns to scale. We shall follow the convention of assuming that T is capital intensive in relation to N. For simplicity of exposition, we shall also assume that all households have identical, homothetic preferences.

Wages in the advanced, donor country, w^*, exceed the wages of the recipient country, w. While we assume that w^* is fixed, there is perfect wage flexibility and full employment of labor in the recipient country. Of the poor household heads, a number M are assumed to migrate to the donor country. They take the household's unit labor endowment abroad, while leaving their families and capital behind. As a result, there are M poor, migrant households living off their capital endowment and the flow of remittances, R, sent by the household head from abroad.[2] With the expenditure of each of these M households denoted by $E^M(P, U^M)$, the budget constraint, setting this group's total expenditure equal to its income, may be written as

$$ME^M\left(P, U^M\right) = M\left(R + rk^X\right), \tag{1}$$

where U^M is the level of welfare enjoyed by each migrant-dependent household and r is the rental rate on capital in the recipient country.

There are also $X - M$ poor families, whose household heads do not migrate, but supply their unit-labor endowment to the local market. These $X - M$ households thus enjoy a flow of income consisting of the recipient country's wage, w, the rental on their k^x units of capital, plus the flow of foreign aid, A, provided by the donor country to household heads who choose not to migrate. The budget constraint for this group of households is given by

$$(X - M)E^X\left(P, U^X\right) = (X - M)\left(w + rk^X + A\right), \tag{2}$$

where U^X is the level of welfare of each poor household whose head does not migrate. Similarly, for the Y rich households, whose welfare is measured by U^Y, labor plus capital income must be equal to expenditure

$$YE^Y\left(P, U^Y\right) = Y\left(w + rk^Y\right). \tag{3}$$

With the assumptions on the production side of the model outlined above, the maximized value of the economy's product can be simply represented by a standard revenue function $Q(P, K, L)$, where $K = Xk^X + Yk^Y$ and $L = X - M + Y$. The partial

---

[2] In relation to the works of Johnson (1967), Berry and Soligo (1969), and Bhagwati and Rodriguez (1975), Wong (1986) discusses the impact of emigration on welfare of the remaining residents in a one-good economy where emigrants leave behind some of their capital in the source country. While in the present model emigrants also leave their capital behind, there are two important distinctions with respect to the analytic framework: (i) in the present context (where the economy produces traded and non-traded goods rather than just one good) it matters whether the income from the capital owned by emigrants is consumed within the economy or abroad, and (ii) there are three rather than just two types of households in the present setting.

derivative of $Q(\cdot)$ with respect to P, $Q_P(P, Xk^X + Yk^Y, X - M + Y)$, represents the economy's supply of good N.

The market for non-traded goods is in equilibrium when total household demand for N is equal to the supply:

$$ME_P^M(P, U^M) + (X - M)E_P^X(P, U^X) + YE_P^Y(P, U^Y)$$
$$= Q_P(P, Xk^X + Yk^Y, X - M + Y), \tag{4}$$

where $E_P^i(P, U^i)$ is the compensated household demand function for good N of members of group i ($i = M, X, Y$). By Walras' Law, when the market for N clears, so does that for T.

By differentiating Equations (1)–(3), and noting that the reciprocity relationship implies

$$\partial w/\partial P = Q_{PL} \quad \text{and} \quad \partial r/\partial P = Q_{PK}, \tag{5}$$

we obtain

$$\left(E_P^M - Q_{PK}k^X\right)dP = dR - E_U^M \, dU^M, \tag{6}$$
$$\left(E_P^X - Q_{PK}k^X - Q_{PL}\right)dP = dA - E_U^X \, dU^X, \tag{7}$$
$$\left(E_P^Y - Q_{PK}k^Y - Q_{PL}\right)dP = -E_U^Y \, dU^Y, \tag{8}$$

where Q_{PK} and Q_{PL} represent the Rybczynski effects of a unit increase in capital and labor, respectively, on the economy's output of N. As good N is assumed to be labor intensive, $Q_{PK} < 0$ and $Q_{PL} > 0$. In Equations (6)–(8), E_P^i is what each household of type i contributes to the demand for good N and $Q_{PK}k^i + Q_{PL}$ is what it contributes to the supply (except for M households which do not have any labor in the local economy). We can then express the net purchases (or implicit trade) of each household in the market for good N by μ_i ($i = M, X, Y$).

$$\mu_M \equiv E_P^M - Q_{PK}k^X > 0, \tag{9}$$
$$\mu_X \equiv E_P^X - Q_{PK}k^X - Q_{PL} < 0, \tag{10}$$
$$\mu_Y \equiv E_P^Y - Q_{PK}k^Y - Q_{PL} \gtrless 0. \tag{11}$$

That $\mu_M > 0$ is obvious, because for migrant households consumption of N is positive while the contribution of their capital to the supply of N is negative (by the Rybczynski effect and the assumption that N is labor intensive). Of the remaining two groups, X and Y, it follows that at least one must be a net seller of N. If it is only one, it has to be X, because X has the same amount of labor as Y, but less capital. This implies that, in comparison with a Y household, each X household contributes more to the supply and less to the demand for N (due to lower income, assuming that $A < r(k^Y - k^X)$). Thus, we can be sure that $\mu_X < 0$, while μ_Y may be either positive or negative, depending on the parameters of the model and the magnitude of spending of emigrant-dependent households residing in the economy. The larger the total income and expenditure of M households relative to the total expenditure of the non-emigrant, rich and poor households, and the smaller the difference between k^Y and k^X, the more likely it is that the rich are also net sellers of N. In the discussion below, we shall refer to that case (i.e., $\mu_Y < 0$) as the one in which the rich and poor non-emigrants are "similar".

Using (9)–(11), Equations (6)–(8) can be written in a more compact form as

$$E_U^M \, dU^M = dR - \mu_M \, dP, \tag{12}$$

$$E_U^X \, dU^X = dA - \mu_X \, dP, \tag{13}$$

$$E_U^Y \, dU^Y = -\mu_Y \, dP, \tag{14}$$

showing that utility of each household depends on its terms of trade, while that of the M and X households also depends on remittances and aid, respectively.

We differentiate next Equation (4), the market-clearing condition for the non-traded good, to obtain $ME_{PP}^M \, dP + ME_{PU}^M \, dU^M + E_P^M \, dM + (X - M)E_{PP}^X \, dP + (X - M)E_{PU}^X \, dU^X - E_P^X \, dM + YE_{PP}^Y \, dP + YE_{PU}^Y \, dU^Y - Q_{PP} \, dP + Q_{PL} \, dM = 0$. This can simply be written as

$$\Sigma \, dP + ME_{PU}^M \, dU^M + (X - M)E_{PU}^X \, dU^X + YE_{PU}^Y \, dU^Y$$
$$= \left(E_P^X - E_P^M\right) dM - Q_{PL} \, dM \tag{15}$$

where $\Sigma \equiv ME_{PP}^M + (X - M)E_{PP}^X + YE_{PP}^Y - Q_{PP} < 0$ measures the responsiveness of the compensated excess demand for N to an increase in P. For the moment, let us assume that migration and remittances are not affected by the transfer of aid (i.e., we set $dR = dM = 0$ in Equations (12) and (15)). The assumption that M is constant will be subsequently relaxed in Section 3. The system of Equations (12)–(15) can now be solved for the effects of foreign aid to the non-migrating poor on the relative price of non-traded goods and the level of welfare of the three different types of households. We have

$$dP/dA = -(X - M)c^X/S > 0, \tag{16}$$

$$E_U^M \, dU^M/dA = \mu_M(X - M)c^X/S < 0, \tag{17}$$

$$E_U^X \, dU^X/dA = 1 + \mu_X(X - M)c^X/S > 0, \tag{18}$$

$$E_U^Y \, dU^Y/dA = \mu_Y(X - M)c^X/S \gtrless 0, \tag{19}$$

where $c^i = E_{PU}^i/E_U^i > 0$ is the marginal propensity of type i households ($i = M, X, Y$) to spend income on non-traded goods and $S = \Sigma - \mu_M Mc^M - \mu_X(X - M)c^X - \mu_Y Yc^Y$ is the slope of the uncompensated excess demand schedule for good N. Assuming Walrasian stability, $S < 0$. Thus a transfer of foreign aid to the non-migrating poor raises their expenditure and pushes up the price of non-traded goods in the recipient country. As stated in (16) this increase in price is positively related to the number of households benefiting from the transfer, $(X - M)$, and their marginal propensity to consume non-traded goods. It is inversely related to S, which measures the responsiveness of excess demand for N to a change in P.

In Equation (17), we see that this increase in P has a negative impact on the welfare of M households. They are net buyers of N, hence they suffer a welfare loss associated with a deterioration in their terms of trade. On the other hand, Equation (18) shows that aid benefits the non-migrating poor both directly, by the amount of the transfer, and indirectly through a terms of trade improvement. Unlike M households, the non-migrating poor are net sellers of N. The welfare of the rich, shown in (19), may either rise or fall, depending on whether they are net sellers or net buyers of N. As noted above μ_Y can be either positive or negative. If the rich are "similar" to the poor, $\mu_Y < 0$, hence the increase in P provides them with an improvement in the terms of trade. Alternatively, if $\mu_Y > 0$, the rich are made worse off, leaving only the aid-receiving poor with an improvement in welfare.

3. Aid and welfare with endogenous emigration

We consider next the more general case where the stock of migrants is affected by the flow of aid targeted at non-emigrants. It is natural to assume in the present context that the stock of migrants is directly related to the gap between what a poor, recipient-country worker can receive in the donor country, w^*, and what he receives at home, inclusive of the aid transfer. We may thus write

$$M = F(w^* - w - A). \tag{20}$$

In Section 2 above, M was exogenously given. In terms of Equation (20), the elasticity of M with respect to the income gap was assumed to be zero. In that case, an increase in aid raises w by causing expenditure on N and the price of N to increase. From Equation (16) and the reciprocity relationship, $\partial w / \partial P = Q_{PL}$, we can solve for the implied increase in w. That is,

$$dw/dA = -Q_{PL}(X - M)c^X/S > 0, \tag{21}$$

when the stock of migrants is exogenously given.

 Should any migrants return (or potential migrants be discouraged from emigrating) due to an increase in aid to the non-migrating poor, they would contribute to an increase in the supply of labor in the recipient country and an increase in the supply of N, relative to the demand, at any given P. This would at least dampen the expenditure-driven increase in P or, if the supply of labor in the local market increases sufficiently in response to the aid transfer, even cause P and w to decline. In equilibrium, the magnitude of the decline in w will depend on, among other parameters, the elasticity of M with respect to the income gap in Equation (20).

 If we consider the case opposite to that examined in Section 2 (i.e., the case of infinite elasticity, which we can think of as being one of "perfect" international labor mobility, where the cost of migration and family separation is zero), any increase in A would be accompanied by a return flow of emigrants to the point where w is reduced by as much as the increase in A. We then have $dw = -dA$, with M endogenously determined to clear the labor market at the new, lower w. In general, we would expect the elasticity of M with respect to the income differential to be less than infinite, but greater than zero. As a result of an endogenous response of M to an increase in aid to the non-migrating poor, we then have

$$dw = -\varphi\, dA, \quad \text{where } Q_{PL}(X - M)c^X/S \leqslant \varphi \leqslant 1. \tag{22}$$

We shall now examine, in this general case, the effects of an increase in aid to non-migrating poor on the welfare of the different households in the recipient country. In comparison with the case of an exogenously given M, we expect the welfare implications to be quite different. Instead of aid simply driving up the price of non-traded goods by causing an increase in expenditure of aid recipients, as in Section 2, it will have the opposite effect of reducing P if $\varphi > 0$. With the terms of trade possibly moving in the opposite direction, so may the level of welfare of any given household. Let us consider now the welfare consequences more explicitly.

Use of Equations (6)–(8) along with the reciprocity relationship and Equation (22) (which makes $dP = -\varphi\, dA/Q_{PL}$) yields,

$$-\left(E_P^M - Q_{PK}k^X\right)\varphi\, dA/Q_{PL} = dR - E_U^M\, dU^M, \tag{23}$$

$$-\left(E_P^X - Q_{PK}k^X - Q_{PL}\right)\varphi\, dA/Q_{PL} = dA - E_U^X\, dU^X, \tag{24}$$

$$-\left(E_P^Y - Q_{PK}k^Y - Q_{PL}\right)\varphi\, dA/Q_{PL} = -E_U^Y\, dU^Y. \tag{25}$$

If the remittance flow to each M household is constant (i.e., $dR = 0$), the effect of targeted aid on welfare of the three types of households can be written as

$$E_U^M\, dU^M = (\mu_M\varphi/Q_{PL})\, dA > 0, \tag{26}$$

$$E_U^X\, dU^X = (1 + \mu_X\varphi/Q_{PL})\, dA > 0, \tag{27}$$

$$E_U^Y\, dU^Y = (\mu_Y\varphi/Q_{PL})\, dA \gtrless 0. \tag{28}$$

Aid targeted at the non-migrating poor now benefits all poor households, regardless of whether they are of type X or M, provided that the stock of migrants is sufficiently responsive to a change in the international income differential to make $\varphi > 0$. For the M households, Equation (26) shows that in that case they benefit from an improvement in their terms of trade. This arises as aid brings about a reduction in migration and an increase in the supply of labor in the recipient country to generate a sufficient increase in the supply of non-traded goods so as to generate a decline in P. However, if the response of migration to targeted aid is weak (i.e., $\varphi < 0$), M households experience a deterioration of their terms of trade and a decline in welfare, which is qualitatively similar to what we have seen in Section 2.

The fate of the rich, shown in Equation (28) also hinges on their terms of trade. If $\varphi > 0$, the rich enjoy an improvement in their terms of trade and welfare when they are net buyers of N. Alternatively, if they are "similar" to the poor (i.e., net sellers of N), their welfare declines. Note that this result is precisely the opposite of that we obtained in Section 2 under the assumption that M is exogenously given or, more generally, whenever $\varphi < 0$. Responsiveness of migration flows to foreign aid is therefore of key interest not only to donor countries that host the immigrants or the poor who migrate, but it is also important to the rich of the recipient country who are indirectly affected by migration through a change in their terms of trade.

Turning to the effect of aid on the welfare of the direct beneficiaries, the poor who do not migrate, we note that the total effect in Equation (27) consists of the direct effect dA, plus the indirect (terms-of-trade) effect $(\mu_X \varphi / Q_{PL}) \, dA$. Since $\mu_X < 0$, the indirect effect is negative when $\varphi > 0$, but positive, as in Section 2, when $\varphi < 0$. It can be easily shown, however, that targeted aid does in fact benefit the non-migrating poor for the entire range of φ. In the event that $\varphi < 0$, (27) is necessarily positive as $\mu_X < 0$. To see that (27) is also positive when $0 \leqslant \varphi \leqslant 1$, we can write $E_U^X \, dU^X = (E_P^X - Q_{PK} k^X)(\varphi / Q_{PL}) \, dA + (1 - \varphi) \, dA$. This expression is unambiguously positive as $(E_P^X - Q_{PK} k^X) > 0$. Thus the targeted non-emigrant poor always gain from foreign aid, although the magnitude of their welfare gain is inversely related to φ, as can be seen in (27). The reason is that the greater the value of φ, the lower the value of P and the lower the welfare of net sellers of N.

An interesting question is whether M or X households benefit more from this aid program. We have already seen that the M households experience a decline in welfare when $\varphi < 0$, but gain if $\varphi > 0$. Moreover, in (26), the magnitude of the welfare gain can be seen to increase in φ. Thus, if it is possible for the M households to gain more from aid than the direct beneficiaries, it would clearly be the case when $\varphi = 1$. By comparing (26) and (27) for $\varphi = 1$, we find that M households benefit more than the X households if $\mu_M > Q_{PL} + \mu_X$, which is simply $E_P^M > E_P^X$. In other words, if income and expenditure of a typical M household exceeds that of an X household. Anecdotal evidence on the expenditure pattern of M households in countries of emigration would suggest that this is in fact the case. We cannot therefore rule out the possibility that the M households may benefit more from aid than the aid recipients themselves.

The intuition behind this result is simple to grasp in the case of $\varphi = 1$. The wage earnings of X households decline in that case by as much as the increase in aid, so the only sources of potential welfare gain for them is from an increase in rental on capital and a decline in the cost of purchasing N. The income gain from an increase in rental on capital is identical to that enjoyed by the M households, as both X and M families own exactly k^X units of capital. What is left to compare is the benefit of being able to purchase good N at a lower price. Thus, in the extreme case of $\varphi = 1$, if the M households have higher income and expenditure on good N, they benefit more from the aid program than the X households that receive the aid.

4. Aid, emigration, and foreign exchange earnings

To determine the endogenous response of the stock of migrants to an increase in targeted aid, we start with Equation (15) and use $dP = -(\varphi / Q_{PL}) \, dA$ along with Equations (26)–(28) to obtain

$$-(\Sigma \varphi / Q_{PL}) \, dA + M c^M (\mu_M \varphi / Q_{PL}) \, dA$$
$$+ (X - M) c^X (1 + \mu_X \varphi / Q_{PL}) \, dA + Y c^Y (\mu_Y \varphi / Q_{PL}) \, dA$$
$$= (E_P^X - E_P^M) \, dM - Q_{PL} \, dM. \tag{27}$$

The left-hand side of this expression is simply the excess demand for N caused (directly and indirectly through a change in P) by the transfer of aid, while the right-hand side shows the excess supply of N generated by the change in the stock of migrants. This expression can be simplified to yield the change in M in response to an increase in targeted aid as

$$dM/dA = \left[(S\varphi/Q_{PL}) - (X - M)c^X\right]/\left[\left(E_P^M - E_P^X\right) + Q_{PL}\right] < 0. \qquad (27')$$

So the stock of migrants diminishes in response to an increase in aid, except for the extreme case, treated in Section 2, where M is constant and $\varphi = Q_{PL}(X - M)c^X/S$. The decrease in M is larger, the greater the sensitivity (φ) of migration to the international income differential, the greater the sensitivity (S) of excess demand for N to a change in P, the greater the number of households $(X - M)$ receiving aid, the greater their propensity (c^X) to consume good N, the smaller the difference between the M and X households in terms of income and hence expenditure on N, and the smaller the Rybczynski effect of a change in the economy's supply of labor on the output of N.

Let us now denote by E the economy's total foreign exchange inflow that can be attributed to aid and remittances.

$$E = (X - M)A + RM. \qquad (28)$$

Assuming that R is constant,[3] the change in this inflow in response to an increase in aid is given by

$$dE/dA = (X - M) + (R - A)\,dM/dA. \qquad (29)$$

With the aid of $(27')$, we can write (29) as

$$dE/dA = (X - M)$$
$$+ (R - A)\left[(S\varphi/Q_{PL}) - (X - M)c^X\right]/\left[\left(E_P^M - E_P^X\right) + Q_{PL}\right]. \qquad (30)$$

In general, this expression may be either positive or negative, depending on the values of the model's parameters. What we can show, however, is that for a relatively weak response of migration to the aid program, $dE/dA > 0$. Let us consider the case in which M declines in response to aid just sufficiently to prevent w and P from rising (i.e., $\varphi = 0$). An increase in E occurs in that case provided that

$$(X - M)\left[\left(E_P^M - E_P^X\right) + Q_{PL}\right] + \left[(R - A)(X - M)c^X\right] > 0. \qquad (31)$$

It can be shown that this inequality is indeed satisfied. With all types of households sharing identical, homothetic preferences, $(E_P^M - E_P^X) = (R - w - A)c^X$, so that (31) can be written as $(X - M)(Q_{PL} - wc^X) > 0$. Let $\eta = Q_{PL}(P/w)$ be the Stolper–Samuelson elasticity of w with respect to P. Since $\eta > 1$ (the magnification

---

[3] In the context of a different model, Gaytan-Fregoso and Lahiri (2000) go a step further to endogenize the flow of remittances enjoyed by each emigrant household.

effect) and $Pc^X < 1$ (assuming that both goods are normal), it follows that dE/dA is necessarily positive for $\varphi = 0$.

The value of E may, however, decline in response to an increase in A for a sufficiently large value of φ. We can solve (30) for the critical value of φ, call it φ^*, such that E remains unchanged following an increase in A.

$$\varphi^* = -(X - M)(w/PS)(\eta - Pc^X)Q_{PL}/(R - A) > 0. \tag{32}$$

For any $\varphi > \varphi^*$, an increase in targeted aid will reduce the combined flow of aid and remittances to the recipient country. The impact of reduced migration on the flow of remittances is then larger than the increase in the flow of aid. Alternatively, if $\varphi < \varphi^*$, the total inflow of foreign exchange is boosted by the increase in aid.

This critical value is obviously an increasing function of the number $(X - M)$ of direct beneficiaries of aid, but a decreasing function of the gap between R and A. Also note that it is a decreasing function of S, and of any other parameter we have seen in (27'), except for φ, which contributes to a larger decline in M for any given increase in aid. The important point is that foreign aid targeted at reducing migration will not necessarily reduce the flow of foreign exchange into the recipient country. It will bring about a reduction in E only if migration is sufficiently responsive to the aid program so that $\varphi > \varphi^* > 0$. As we have already seen in Section 3, however, in that case the aid program is unambiguously beneficial to the poor of the recipient country, regardless of whether they are migrant or non-migrant households. Perhaps that should be the overriding criterion in the evaluation of any aid program.

5. Concluding remarks

The present study examines the implications of providing foreign aid to the poor household heads of a developing country who do not migrate to the donor country. Such an aid program can be seen as being designed to encourage potential migrants to remain at home. In a setting of this type, a number of interesting questions emerge. First, how do such targeted aid transfers affect the welfare of the poor, both the families that stay at home and those whose household head works abroad, making the family ineligible for the transfer? What is the effect on the welfare of the rich? How does aid affect international migration, remittance flows and the economy's overall foreign-exchange inflows?

The analysis of these issues is conducted within a general-equilibrium framework under alternative assumptions with respect to the sensitivity of migration flows to the targeted aid program. When this sensitivity is low, the aid transfer to the non-migrating poor households is found to have a positive effect on their welfare, while lowering the welfare of the emigrant-dependent households. Welfare of the rich can move in either direction, depending on how much capital they own relative to the poor and on other parameters of the model.

Alternatively, if the sensitivity of migration to targeted aid is high, all poor households are found to benefit from the aid transfers. The welfare of the rich can move, once again, in either direction, although the criteria for welfare improvement is now the reverse of what it was in the case of low sensitivity of migration to the aid program. The paper ends with the analysis of the impact of aid on the stock of migrants and remittance flows. While targeted aid is found to have a negative impact on the stock of migrants and remittances, the effect on the overall inflow of foreign exchange, including aid and remittances can be positive, even if migration drops sufficiently to lower the wages of the recipient country.

References

Berry, R.A., Soligo, R. (1969), Some welfare aspects of international migration. *Journal of Political Economy* 77, 778–794.

Bhagwati, J.N., Rodriguez, C.A. (1975), Welfare-theoretical analysis of the brain drain. *Journal of Development Economics* 2, 195–221.

Djajić, S. (1986), International migration, remittances and welfare in a dependent economy. *Journal of Development Economics* 21, 229–234.

Djajić, S. (1998), Emigration and welfare in an economy with foreign capital. *Journal of Development Economics* 56, 433–445.

Johnson, H.G. (1967), Some economic aspects of the brain drain. *The Pakistan Development Review* 7, 379–411.

Kirwan, F., Holden, D. (1986), Emigrants' remittances, non-traded goods and economic welfare. *Journal of Economic Studies* 13, 52–58.

Gaytan-Fregoso, H., Lahiri, S. (2000), Foreign aid and illegal immigration. *Journal of Development Economics* 63, 515–527.

Hatzipanayotou, P., Michael, M.S. (2006), Migration, tied foreign aid and the welfare state. Paper presented at the WIDER Conference on Aid: Principles, Policies and Performance, June 16–17, 2006.

Quibria, M.G. (1996), International migration, remittances and income distribution in the source country. *Bulletin of Economic Research* 48, 29–46.

Rivera-Batiz, F. (1982), International migration, non-traded goods and economic welfare in the source country. *Journal of Development Economics* 11, 81–90.

Rivera-Batiz, F. (1986), International migration, remittances and economic welfare in the source country. *Journal of Economic Studies* 13, 3–19.

Tompson, H. (1984), International migration, non-traded goods and economic welfare in the source country: a comment. *Journal of Development Economics* 16, 321–324.

Wong, K.-Y. (1986), The economic analysis of international migration: A generalization. *Canadian Journal of Economics* 19, 357–362.

CHAPTER 8

The Hope for Hysteresis in Foreign Aid

Gil S. Epstein[a,b,c] and Ira N. Gang[b,c,d]

[a]*Department of Economics, Bar-Ilan University, 52900 Ramat-Gan, Israel*
E-mail address: epsteig@mail.biu.ac.il
url: http://faculty.biu.ac.il/~epsteig
[b]*IZA, Bonn, Germany*
[c]*CReAM, London, UK*
[d]*Department of Economics, Rutgers University, 75 Hamilton St, New Brunswick, NJ 08901-1248, USA*
E-mail address: gang@economics.rutgers.edu
url: http://econweb.rutgers.edu/gang/

Abstract

We argue that a purpose of foreign aid is to whet the appetite of the recipient to bring about a long term commitment to what the donor perceives as a need, but the recipient may rank lower down on his list of undertakings, or may be sufficiently resource constrained as to be unable to start the project. In other words, we explore the implications and conditions for success of a donor trying to affect long-term recipient policy by creating path dependence. Once the project is established, aid can be removed without reversing the process that has been set in motion.

Keywords: Foreign aid, governance, decentralization, rent seeking

JEL classifications: O10, O19, F35, O11, C23, O47, E21, E22

1. Introduction

The literature on foreign aid is replete with theories and empirical evidence on appropriate aid policies and strategies: the evaluation of the success or failure of aid, the implications of aid for donors and recipients, corruption, fungibility, equity and efficiency, intermediate short-term analysis and micro- and macro-economic outcomes, among others. Here we investigate how a donor can utilize the "stickiness" of aid policy to achieve its policy goals.

When a donor engages in a particular development/aid project, it may be argued – and casually is argued – that the purpose of the aid is to whet the appetite of the recipient in order to bring about a long term commitment to what the donor perceives as a need, but which the recipient may rank lower down on his list of undertakings or may be sufficiently resource constrained as to be unable to start the project. The question

THEORY AND PRACTICE OF FOREIGN AID
VOLUME 1 ISSN: 1574-8715
DOI: 10.1016/S1574-8715(06)01008-6

that the donor faces is what is needed to get the project implemented, how without making a permanent commitment.

We consider the situation in which a donor wishes to support a project in a certain country. The donor possesses a notion of his ideal (unconstrained) investment necessary to have the best outcome; however he also faces costs that must be taken into consideration when determining the optimal (constrained) investment in the project at hand. We develop a two-period model in which the donor invests in a project only during the first period and the recipient country invests only during the second period. Ideal total investment in the project may differ for the donor and the recipient. Knowing this, the donor calculates his optimal investment in the project for the first period.

Our argument borrows from the discussion of hysteresis in the economic history literature. Hysteresis, or path dependence, expresses the long term consequences of earlier, perhaps arbitrary, decisions. Under "policy hysteresis" a temporary policy can have permanent effects. Once the project is established, it is not readily reversible. Here we explore the behavior of donors and recipients when donors explicitly want to initiate a program that will continue after they stop funding it.

We rely on notions of foreign aid and its effects and implications developed in the fiscal federalism literature on aid. A major concern of this literature is the stickiness of foreign aid – whether or not aid effectively goes to where the donor intended it to go. A finding of this literature is that aid does "stick" in the sense that aid inflows cause increases in development expenditures – while aid may be fungible, it is not completely so (Heller, 1975; Gang and Khan, 1990, 1999; Khan and Hoshino, 1992; Pack and Pack, 1993; Iqbal, 1997; Feyzioglu *et al.*, 1998; World Bank, 1998; Ahmed, 1998; McGillivray and Ahmed, 1999; McGillivray, 2000; McGillivray and Morrissey, 2001; Hagen, 2006).

We proceed by building the structure of the model, highlighting the insights it provides along the way.

2. The model

2.1. The donor

Consider a donor country (or NGO) that wishes to help a recipient country by supporting a certain project in the recipient. The donor possesses a notion of the ideal (unconstrained) investment necessary to have the best outcome for the recipient country and aims to provide the recipient the best possible project it can under its limitations and as close to the ideal level as possible. The ideal level, I, is assumed to be a continuous variable defined on the interval $(0, \bar{I})$. As the donor moves closer to the ideal point, I, the donor's utility increases as the donor is more successful in attaining its goal. However, in reality the donor may not always be able to create a project at the ideal level, I, and may choose to create a project at level x which is lower than his ideal level. One could think of situations where the ideal level may be lower than the actual because of different restrictions. To simplify we assume that the actual level is always lower than the ideal level. Therefore, the utility of the donor depends on the difference between the ideal level, I, and the actual investment level x, $(I - x)$.

The donor's payoff is given as,

$$U_1 = \begin{cases} -\frac{(I-x)^2}{w} - ax & \text{for } I > x, \\ -aI & \text{for } I = x, \end{cases} \qquad (1)$$

where I is the ideal project level that the donor thinks the recipient country needs, x is the actual level chosen by the donor, and a is the cost of one unit of the investment in the project – the marginal cost of production. w represents the recipient country's wealth. To simplify we assume constant marginal cost for the donor. This payoff function assumes that as the donor invests at a level closer to his ideal point, his utility increases. If the donor invests at a level that is equal to the ideal level, $I = x$, then the utility will equal to the costs of the project, aI. Of course the donor will not invest at a level which is higher than his ideal level. The main idea here is the wealthier the recipient, the less the donor cares about the project and thus loses less when there are deviations from his ideal project level.

The donor chooses the actual level of investment in the project, x, so as to maximize his payoff, U. The first order condition determining optimal investment is,

$$\frac{\partial U_1}{\partial x} = 2\frac{(I - x)}{w} - a \quad \text{for } I > x. \qquad (2)$$

Solving the first order conditions[1] we obtain that the optimal level of investment by the donor equals,

$$x_1^* = I - \frac{aw}{2} > 0. \qquad (3)$$

In order for $x > 0$, a or w cannot be too big. If w is high, the donor does not care too much about the recipient. Moreover, if a is high, the cost of investing is very high. Thus the benefit (which is a negative function of w) has to be higher then the cost (which is a direct function of a)!

As we can see, the project's optimal level of donor investment has the following properties,

$$\frac{\partial x_1^*}{\partial I} > 0, \qquad \frac{\partial x_1^*}{\partial a} < 0, \qquad \frac{\partial x_1^*}{\partial w} < 0. \qquad (4)$$

Namely,

(1) *The higher the donor's ideal level, the more it will invest in the recipient country;*
(2) *As the investment costs increase, the investment level decreases;*
(3) *The donor invests fewer resources in wealthier than in less-wealthy countries.*

---

[1] Second order conditions are ensured: $\frac{\partial^2 U_1}{\partial x^2} = -2\frac{1}{w} < 0$ for $I > x$.

Given the optimal investment level, we calculate the optimal payoff of the donor investing x^* resources in the project by substituting into (1),

$$U_1^* = \frac{a^2 w}{4} - aI < 0. \tag{5}$$

As we can see, the optimal payoff of the donor has the following properties:

$$\frac{\partial U_1^*}{\partial I} < 0, \qquad \frac{\partial U_1^*}{\partial a} = \frac{aw}{2} - I < 0, \qquad \frac{\partial U_1^*}{\partial w} > 0, \tag{6}$$

$\frac{\partial U_1^*}{\partial a} < 0$ since $x^* = I - \frac{aw}{2} > 0$.

In other words,

(1) *As the ideal level of the donor increases, his payoff decreases*;
(2) *As investment costs increase, the payoff decreases*;
(3) *As the wealth of the recipient country increases, the payoff increases.*

2.2. The recipient country

Let us now consider the recipient country. Assume that the recipient has a similar type of payoff function as the donor. The ideal project level for the recipient is given by J and the actual level invested by the recipient is given by y. The recipient country faces marginal cost, b, in creating the project. Notice that investment by the recipient is to create the project; latter we will describe it as continuing the project that the donor started.

The payoff function of the recipient country is assumed to equal,

$$V = \begin{cases} -\frac{(J-y)^2}{w} - by & \text{for } J > y, \\ -bJ & \text{for } J = y. \end{cases} \tag{7}$$

If the recipient country could choose its optimal investment in the project than it would choose a level that equals,[2]

$$y^* = J - \frac{bw}{2} > 0, \tag{8}$$

with an optimal payoff at a level,

$$V^* = \frac{b^2 w}{4} - aJ < 0. \tag{9}$$

This, of course, is parallel to investment by the donor represented by Equations (3) and (5) and has the same type of comparative statics conclusions as presented above.

---

[2] The first order conditions, $\frac{\partial V}{\partial y} = 0$ and the second order conditions are ensured.

2.3. Two-period model

We assume a two-period model where in the first period the donor invests in the project and in the second period the recipient country continues the investment by itself. Assume that the recipient country will be continuing the project after the donor finishes its investment. The recipient country will, of course, start from the point where the donor finished. When deciding on its optimal investment the donor takes into account the fact that the recipient will continue this project. We assume that the donor knows both the recipient's behavior with respect to the continuation of investment in this project and its ideal investment, J. Of course, it may well be the case that the ideal level of the project for the donor, I, is not identical to the ideal level of the recipient country, J. However, the donor knows how the recipient country will react to each level of investment by the donor. This is a Stackelberg type of game where the donor takes into account how his investment will affect the recipient, while the recipient only takes as given what the donor has invested and thus determines its optimal investment level in the project in the second period.

The donor may or may not care about what happens after it leaves the project, i.e., whether or not the recipient continues to invest. To simplify, assume that the level of investment by the donor is strictly lower than the ideal level, $x < I$. We assume that the payoff of the donor is given as,

$$U_2 = \alpha \left(-\frac{(I-x)^2}{w} - ax \right) + (1-\alpha) \left(-\frac{(I-x-y)^2}{w} - by \right)$$

$$\text{for } I > x, \tag{10}$$

where $0 \leqslant \alpha \leqslant 1$ is the weight the donor puts on the utility from the first period. If $\alpha = 1$ then the donor only values the benefits from the investment in the project at the time that he is involved in its investment and after he leaves the project he does not care anymore about it. If $\alpha = 0$, the donor cares only about the long run affects of the project. If $\alpha = \frac{1}{2}$, the donor put identical weights on both periods and have an equal benefit from the time he invests and the time that the recipient country continues to invest in the project. As α ($0 \leqslant \alpha \leqslant 1$) increases, the weight the donor puts on the first period (during which he invests in the project) increases at the cost of a decrease in the weight placed on the second period (when the donor is no longer connected to the project).

We also assume that the donor, when taking into consideration the second period, calculates the payoff around its own ideal level, I. This is the level the donor thinks the project should be and is not necessarily the ideal level, J, of the recipient. Of course, he will also take into consideration the ideal level of the recipient country in terms of the recipient country's reactions to his investment. Moreover, the donor takes into consideration that in the second period, an investment of x has already been carried out; thus the distance to achieve the ideal level is $I - x$. This is in comparison to the case of the first period when they are starting from scratch.

The donor knows that the recipient country will choose an optimal level as given by (8) that maximizes the recipient's payoff in the second period. However, the donor also knows that the starting point for the recipient is not J, but the investment level of the donor x^*. Moreover, we assume that the cost of investing in the project by the recipient is a function of the fact that the donor has already invested in the first period. In other words, if the recipient country believes its ideal level is J and the donor has already invested x, then the gap is now $J - x$, since the recipient country is receiving an already started project. The payoff function of the recipient will no longer be the one described in be (7) and will instead equal,

$$V = \begin{cases} -\frac{((J-x)-y)^2}{w} - by & \text{for } J - x > y, \\ -b(J-x) & \text{for } J - x = y. \end{cases} \tag{7'}$$

We assume that the marginal cost of investing in the project by the recipient country equals b and is also a function of the investment level of the donor. It may well be that the marginal cost in the second period is lower than the marginal cost in the first period, $b < a$. In this case the investment by the donor decreases the marginal costs of the recipient country. The reason for this is that the donor has started the work and has undertaken the high cost elements of the project and what is left for the recipient are the lower cost investment items. If $b > a$, the donor has invested in the lower costs elements of the project – the easier part of the project – leaving the harder part for the recipient to complete. If $b = a$, then the donor has no effect on the costs of production for the recipient in the second period.

Therefore, the optimal investment of the recipient country in the second period, y, equals,

$$y^* = (J - x) - \frac{bw}{2}. \tag{11}$$

In light of (11) let us now rewrite the payoff of the donor taking into account (7') and the two-periods of investment,

$$U_2 = \alpha \left(-\frac{(I-x)^2}{w} - ax \right) + (1-\alpha) \left(-\frac{(I-y^*(x))^2}{w} - by^*(x) \right). \tag{12}$$

Plugging into (12) the ideal level of investment of the recipient (11) which is a function of the investment of the donor from the first period, we obtain that the payoff function of the donor over the two time periods for $I > x$ and $y^* \geqslant 0$ equals,

$$U_2 = \alpha \left(-\frac{(I-x)^2}{w} - ax \right)$$
$$+ (1-\alpha) \left(-\frac{((I-x) - ((J-x) - \frac{bw}{2}))^2}{w} - b \left((J-x) - \frac{bw}{2} \right) \right). \tag{12'}$$

The donor maximizes his payoff as stated in (12') by determining his optimal investment in the project, x. The first order conditions satisfy

$$\frac{\partial U_2}{\partial x} = b(1-\alpha) - \frac{\alpha(-2I + aw + 2x)}{w}. \tag{13}$$

Solving the first order condition, $\frac{\partial U_2}{\partial x} = 0$, we obtain[3]

$$x_2^* = \frac{1}{2}\left(2I + \left(-a + \left(-1 + \frac{1}{\alpha}\right)b\right)w\right). \tag{14}$$

As we discuss below, we are assuming that the investment level of the recipient country is positive, $y^* > 0$. This optimal investment by the donor may generate a negative investment by the recipient country. For the case where the investment is "negative" we will have to rewrite the donor's payoff function. For now we assume that the investment in the second period is positive.

Let us now consider the effects of changes in the different variables on the level of investment in this case. It can be verified that,

$$\frac{\partial x_2^*}{\partial a} < 0; \qquad \frac{\partial x_2^*}{\partial \alpha} < 0; \qquad \frac{\partial x_2^*}{\partial b} = -\frac{1}{2}\left(\frac{\alpha - 1}{\alpha}\right)w \geqslant 0, \tag{15}$$

and

$$\frac{\partial x_2^*}{\partial w} = \frac{1}{2}\left(-a + \frac{(1 - \alpha)}{\alpha}b\right).$$

In other words:

(1) *An increase in donor's investment cost decreases investment in the first period;*
(2) *Increasing the weight the donor sets on the first period, the period in which it invests in the recipient country (a decrease in the effect of future benefits from the investment for the donor), decreases the donor's investment in the first period;*
(3) *An increase in the cost of investment for the recipient (in the second period) increases the donor's investment;*
(4) *An increase in the wealth of the recipient, w, has an ambiguous affect on donor's investment. The main reason for this result is that the wealth affects utility via the cost structure. The ambiguity is a function of three parameters: the weight the donor places on the present time, α, and the costs of production in the first period, a, and the second period, b. The sign of $\frac{\partial x_2^*}{\partial w}$ rests on the sign of $((1 - \alpha)b - \alpha a)$. Namely if the donor sets the same weight on both periods, $\alpha = (1 - \alpha) = \frac{1}{2}$, then if the costs in the second period are higher than the first period, $b > a$, the donor increases his investment. And if the costs in the first period are higher, $b < a$, the donor decreases his investment. If the costs are identical, a change in wealth has no effect. In general, not only do costs matter, but also the weight the donor assigns to each period. Therefore, the weighted cost (the cost times the weight assigned to the period) determines whether the donor increases or decreases investment.*

---

[3] Second order condition holds: $\frac{\partial^2 U_2}{\partial x^2} = -\frac{2\alpha}{w} < 0$.

2.4. The recipient country's investment

In the light of the donor's optimal investment let us now consider the recipient's optimal investment. The optimal investment by the recipient country is given by (11), $y^* = (J - x) - \frac{bw}{2}$, where this is a function of the donor's optimal investment. Given the donor's optimal investment level as shown in Equation (14), we may calculate the optimal level invested by the recipient,

$$y^* = J - I + \frac{(a\alpha - b)w}{2\alpha}. \tag{16}$$

As we can see from (16), the recipient's optimal investment level depends on several parameters: the ideal level of the recipient country, J, the ideal level of investment of the donor, I, and the difference in the ideal levels of the donor and the recipient country, $J - I$. It also depends on the weight the donor sets on the effect investment has on the present (and future) period, as well as on the cost of investment during both periods, a and b, and on the wealth of the recipient country, w.

Let us first discuss the ideal levels of the different groups. We examine three cases:

(1) the ideal levels of the donor and the recipient are identical ($J = I$);
(2) the ideal level of the recipient country is higher than that of the donor, $J > I$;
(3) the ideal level of the recipient country is lower than that of the donor, $J < I$.

2.5. Case I: Ideal levels equal, $I = J$

In this case the donor and the recipient see eye-to-eye with regard to the ideal level of investment in the project. Both think the ideal level should be the same. From (16) it is clear that the recipient's investment equals $y^* = \frac{(a\alpha - b)w}{2\alpha}$. Therefore, the recipient country invests in the project in the second period only if y^* as presented above is positive. Namely, $\frac{(a\alpha - b)w}{2\alpha} > 0$. Therefore, the sign of the investment of the recipient in the second period rests on the sign of $a\alpha - b$. If $a\alpha > b$, then either the cost of investment in the second period is sufficiently larger than that of the second period, or the weight assigned for the first period is sufficiently large. If the cost of investment is identical, $a = b$, then the recipient country will not invest in the second period. Moreover, in order for the recipient country to invest in the second period the difference between the costs of investment in both periods has to be sufficiently large. In other words, it must hold that $\alpha > \frac{b}{a}$. Thus, the ratio of the costs of investment in the second period relative to the first period, $\frac{b}{a}$, has to be lower than the time preference of the donor, α. Thus:

In the case where the donor's and recipient's ideal investment levels are identical

(1) *and the cost of investment in both periods are the same, then the recipient country will not invest in the second period;*
(2) *in order for the recipient country to be willing to invest in the second period it must be the case that the cost of investment in the second period is sufficiently lower than that of the first period.*

2.6. Case II: Donor's ideal levels are smaller than of the recipient country, $I < J$

In this case the ideal level of the donor is lower than the ideal level that of the recipient. In other words the recipient thinks that the importance of the project is greater than what the donor thinks. In this case, the recipient wants the project much more than the donor is willing to give. Since $I < J$, the investment of the recipient country may well be positive even if the cost of production (investment) in the second period is high, $\alpha < \frac{b}{a}$. Even so, if the costs of the investment in the two-periods are not identical, it may be that the recipient country will not invest in the second period. However, the difference between the costs of investment so that the recipient country will invest in the second period depends on the difference between the ideal levels of investment.

In the case where the recipient country has a higher ideal level than the donor, the recipient wants a higher level project than the donor thinks it needs and, thus, there is a higher chance of continuing the investment in the second period after the donor finishes its funding.

2.7. Case III: Donor's ideal level is higher than that of the recipient, $J < I$

This is the case where the donor values the project more than the recipient country. In other words, the donor thinks that the project is more important than the recipient and therefore the donor believes that this project should have a higher investment level, while the recipient is not so enthusiastic. This may well be because the recipient has other projects in which it wishes to invest. It is clear that in this case the cost of production will mainly fall on the donor rather than on the recipient. From (16) we see that in order for the investment level of the recipient to be positive, it must be that $\frac{(a\alpha - b)w}{2\alpha}$ is "sufficiently" positive. Namely, the costs of production in the second period must be sufficiently low so that the donor will not invest too much in the first period, as a result of high investment costs, and thus it will be worthwhile for the recipient to invest in the second period (see analysis above for the case of differences in investment costs). The main reason why the recipient will invest even though the donor invested with a higher ideal level is that when the donor makes its investment, it takes into account what its own ideal level is even during the second period (I) and not the recipient's ideal level (J). Thus:

In the case that the ideal level of investment in the project is higher for the donor than the recipient country, in order for the recipient country to invest in the second period, the cost of production most be sufficiently lower in the second period than in the first period.

2.8. Donor's investment and recipient country's investments cost

As we have seen above, a major element in our discussion is the cost of investment in the second period. As a result of an investment by the donor in the first period the cost of production may decrease in the second period. This has an effect on the willingness of the recipient to invest in the project in the second period. In this setup the cost of investment may decrease as a result of the investment during the first period. It may well be that $b < a$, the investment by the donor decreases the marginal costs of the recipient country. The reason for this is that the donor has started the work and has made high cost investments, so what is left for the recipient is lower cost investments. If $b > a$, the donor invests in the lower cost elements – the easier part of the project – and the recipient now has the harder part of the project to complete. If $b = a$ then the donor has no affect on the costs of production of the recipient country.

In a more general model we could have that the marginal cost of investment in the second period is a continuous function of investment by the donor in the first period. This may well cause the donor to increase its investment in the first period to create the circumstance for the recipient country to invest in the second period.

2.9. Comparing the levels of investment, x_1^* and x_2^*

2.9.1. The recipient country's investment is positive

Let us first concentrate on the case where the optimal level of investment by the recipient country is positive, $y^* > 0$. The difference between the two levels of investment, the first that does not take into consideration the investment in the second period and the second that takes into consideration of the investment of the recipient country in the second period. Comparing (3) and (14) we obtain that,

$$x_1^* - x_2^* = \frac{(\alpha - 1)}{2\alpha} bw \tag{17}$$

In other words:

(1) *as the weight assigned to the first period, α, increases, the difference between the two investment decreases;*
(2) *as the cost of investment by the recipient country is higher, the difference between the investments increases;*
(3) *as the recipient country is wealthier, the difference between the two investments increases.*

2.9.2. The cost of investment in the second period and investment in the first period

The effect of the cost of investment in the second period is a very important component in the decision making.

As this cost decreases then the differences between the investments is smaller since the investment in the first itself has created a decrease in cost which enables the recipient country to invest. In the case where the costs do not decrease, then the donor takes a bigger proportion of investment on itself.

2.9.3. No investment by the recipient country, $y^* = 0$

Let us now look at the case where from the calculations above we find that the "optimal" investment level by the recipient country is negative. Note than in the second period there will be no investment by the recipient country and the utility generated in the second period will only be a function of the ideal level of the donor and its investment in the first period. In such a case the recipient country will not invest in the second period and thus the payoff of the donor will no longer be as presented (12). Of course, for the first period nothing will change. The main change is the benefit from the second period. Here the donor will obtain a benefit only from his own investment in the first period as there will be no investments in the second period by the recipient. Therefore, the payoff function of the donor over the two-periods will equal

$$U_2 = \alpha\left(-\frac{(I-x)^2}{w} - ax\right) + (1-\alpha)\left(-\frac{(I-x)^2}{w}\right), \tag{18}$$

which equals

$$U_2 = -\frac{(I-x)^2}{w} - a\alpha x. \tag{18'}$$

The donor will maximize U_2 with respect to x and calculate its optimal investment level. It is clear that if $\alpha < 1$ then this is the same type of problem when the donor does not take into consideration the second period, however, with lower investment costs, $a\alpha < a$.

The optimal investment thus equals,

$$x_2^* = I - \frac{a\alpha w}{2} > x_1^*. \tag{19}$$

Therefore, we obtain the same type of results as before with regard to the relationship between the different variables determining the optimal investment level. The difference between the two investment levels will thus equal

$$x_1^* - x_2^* = \frac{(\alpha-1)}{2}aw. \tag{20}$$

The results here are very similar to the case where y^* is positive. The difference between the investments will decrease with the weight assigned to the first period, α. The difference will now be a function of the costs of the first period, a, and not those of the second period, b, since the investment in the first period does not have an affect on the cost of investment in the second period.

3. Conclusion

In the last few years it has become popular to discuss economic development in terms of developing the proper set of institutions – including the legal framework and social conventions (for example, Epstein and Gang, 2006a, 2006b). International aid was brought into this discussion in terms of its influence on institutional development and its impact on growth and other indicators of development. While not universally embraced, a stylized fact of development policy became that good governance is a necessary pre-requisite for aid to be effective in terms of raising a nation's rate of growth.

We suggest another yardstick for measuring the success of aid policy, one that is unfortunately more difficult to measure than growth and whose impact may be more difficult to pin down. Yet is may be as important. In Case III, in a quite straightforward way the donor wants to direct the course of development. For example, aid may be given to a country to develop the oil extraction industry, conditional on most of the revenue from that industry going to the poor. The donor wants things for the recipient country and without the donor the recipient would not have invested so much since they have other priorities.

What we are arguing is that an important aspect of donor activity is its desire to influence recipient policy over the long haul. It tries to do this by creating path dependence; providing a desirable role for hysteresis in its foreign aid policy. Once the project is established, aid can be removed without reversing the process that has been set in motion. Quite simply, the donor wants its project to stick. We place a formal structure on this; highlighting the major considerations in implementing and evaluating this type of policy.

References

Ahmed, A. (1998), Aid and fiscal behaviour in developing Asia. In: Alauddin, M., Hossan, S. (Eds.), *Development, Governance and Environment in South Asia: Special Focus on Bangladesh*. Macmillan, London.

Epstein, G.S., Gang, I.N. (2006a), Contests, NGOs and decentralizing aid. *Review of Development Economics* 10 (2), 285–296.

Epstein, G.S., Gang, I.N. (2006b). Decentralizing aid with interested parties. *WIDER Research Paper* 2006/06, http://www.wider.unu.edu. Last accessed June 21, 2006.

Feyzioglu, T., Swaroop, V., Zhu, M. (1998), A panel data analysis of the fungibility of foreign aid. *World Bank Economic Review* 12 (1), 29–58.

Gang, I.N., Khan, H.A. (1990), Foreign aid, taxes, and public investment. *Journal of Development Economics* 34 (1–2), 355–369.

Gang, I.N., Khan, H.A. (1999), Foreign aid and fiscal behaviour in a bounded rationality model: Different policy regimes. *Empirical Economics* 24 (1), 121–134.

Hagen, R.J. (2006), Buying influence: aid fungibility in a strategic perspective. *Review of Development Economics* 10 (2), 267–284.

Heller, P.S. (1975), A model of public fiscal behaviour in developing countries: aid, investment and taxation. *American Economic Review* 65 (3), 429–445.

Iqbal, Z. (1997), Foreign aid and the public sector: a model of fiscal behaviour in Pakistan. *Pakistan Development Review* 36 (2), 115–129.

Khan, H.A., Hoshino, E. (1992), Impact of foreign aid on the fiscal behaviour of LDC governments. *World Development* 20 (10), 1481–1488.

McGillivray, M. (2000), Aid and public sector fiscal behaviour in developing countries. *Review of Development Economics* 4 (2), 156–163.

McGillivray, M., Ahmed, A. (1999), Aid, adjustment and public sector fiscal behaviour in the Philippines. *Journal of the Asia – Pacific Economy* 4 (2), 381–391.

McGillivray, M., Morrissey, O. (2001), Aid illusion and public sector fiscal behaviour. *Journal of Development Studies* 37 (6), 118–136.

Pack, H., Pack, J.R. (1993), Foreign aid and the question of fungibility. *Review of Economics and Statistics* 75 (2), 258–265.

World Bank (1998), *Assessing Aid. What Works, What Doesn't, and Why.* Oxford University Press, New York.

CHAPTER 9

A Pareto-Improving Foreign Aid in a Dynamic North–South Model

Koji Shimomura[†]

Research Institute for Economics and Business Administration, Kobe University,
2-1 Rokkodai-cho, Nada, Kobe 657-8501, Japan

Abstract
Constructing a simple dynamic North–South model in which factors of production are internationally immobile and there is no international credit market, it is possible that a persistent and unilateral foreign aid makes both North and South better off. We also show that the Pareto-improving transfer involves local indeterminacy.

JEL classifications: D90, F11, F43, O40, O41

1. Introduction

How does international transfer of income affect the welfare levels of donor and recipient countries? This problem has been paid much attention to since Paul Samuelson (1947) claimed that a transfer impoverishes the donor country, but enriches the recipient country in a perfectly competitive, two-good, two-country and Walrasian-stable trading world. Samuelson's result has been extended in many directions, for example, to a many-commodity case, to take into account public goods, non-traded goods, costly administration of foreign aid, tied aid, lobbying and rent-seeking, and so on.[1] It is also well known, under the name of "transfer paradox", that a transfer can make the recipient country worse off and the donor better off, when there is a bystander country.[2]

While the literature on international transfer is very large, the theoretical possibility of a Pareto-improving foreign aid in the sense that both the donor and recipient countries are better off has been pursued by a small number of researchers. See, among

---

[†] Sadly, Professor Koji Shimomura passed away on February 24, 2007 when this volume was at the production stage, after a courageous battle with ill health. We shall miss him greatly.
[1] Kemp and Abe (1994), McDougall (1965), Jones (1975, 1985), Kemp and Wong (1993), Kemp and Kojima (1985), Ohyama (1974), and Kemp and Shimomura (1991) are a part of the contributions.
[2] One of the recent excellent survey on transfer paradox is in Brakman and van Marrewijk (1998).

THEORY AND PRACTICE OF FOREIGN AID
VOLUME 1   ISSN: 1574-8715
DOI: 10.1016/S1574-8715(06)01009-8

others, Lahiri and Raimondos-Møller (1995), Lahiri *et al.* (2002), Galor and Polemar-chakis (1987) and Ono (2007). The first two papers are static. The former assumes quantitative trade distortions, while the latter distortions are based on the tiedness of foreign aid to the recipient's trade policies. The third and fourth papers are dynamic. The distortions in the third one comes from the inherent inefficiency of overlapping generation models, and the existence of Keynesian unemployment plays an important role in the fourth paper.

Needless to say, a Pareto-improving international transfer would be impossible in a competitive general equilibrium model without contradicting the First Fundamental Theorem. Thus, those contributions have made clear which distortions may make a Pareto-improving foreign aid possible. The purpose of this paper is to show that if there is neither international factor movements nor international borrowing and lend-ing markets and if domestic equilibrium interest rates differ among countries, so are the rates of marginal substitution between the home and foreign households along a dynamic general equilibrium path. It immediately follows that the trading world on the dynamic general equilibrium path is Pareto-suboptimal, in which case the static fundamental theorem is insufficient to exclude a Pareto-improving transfer.

This paper is not the first to discuss the possibility of a Pareto-improving transfer based on the lack of international lending and borrowing. Constructing a simple two-period and two-country model, Djajić *et al.* (1999) derived a sufficient condition for a Pareto-improving transfer.

The Djajić–Lahiri–Raimondos-Møller paper is certainly an important contribution to the dynamic theory of foreign aid. However, they focused on a two-period case where no transfer is assumed at period two. They have not discussed whether the donor country is kept receiving a transfer permanently or the two countries change their role as the donor or recipient countries. The present paper, on the other hand, assumes a dynamic two-country model with an infinite time horizon to show that under certain conditions on technologies and preferences there is an unilateral and persistent foreign aid from one country to the other which can make both countries better off. That is, there is a case such that foreign aid works as an coordinating device.

A Pareto-improving international transfer may not be just an object of theoretical curiosity. Why a country is willing to make a foreign aid which is harmful to her people is an issue that is sometimes discussed in developed countries. For example, Japan has made a large amount of foreign aid to many countries including the People's Republic of China for a long time. Some conservative political leaders and the media in Japan now reveal some resentment to the PRC which has never acknowledged the persistent foreign aid from Japan. If we find a theoretical possibility of a foreign aid that makes both Japan and China better off, it may play some marginal role to mitigate such public resentment.

Transfer paradox has a parallel problem. If the benevolent government of the re-cipient country knows that an international transfer makes her people worse off, it is rational for the government to refuse the implementation of the transfer. So, if the re-sult in this paper is correct, we can claim, without assuming any distortional factors other than the lack of an international competitive credit market, that foreign aid is an economic policy from the viewpoint of both donor and recipient countries which is rational to the extent that the dynamic general equilibrium concept is realistic.

Section 2 sets up the North–South model. Section 3 characterizes the steady state. Section 4 presents two main results. One of them is that, like Nishimura and Shimomura (2006), the aforementioned assumption which is often made in trade theory makes local indeterminacy theoretically possible. The other is that, under certain conditions on production technologies and preferences, there is a self-fulfilling expectation under which a persistent foreign aid makes both North and South better off along a dynamic general equilibrium path with the persistent foreign aid. Section 5 suggests a couple of future research agenda beyond the present study.

2. The model

Let us set up the dynamic North–South model. Most assumptions concerning both production and consumption sides of the model are standard in trade theory. There are two countries, North and South, and two tradable goods, Good 1 and Good 2. Good 1 is a pure consumption good and Good 2 is a consumable capital which serves as the numeraire. One can interpret Good 1 as an agricultural product while Good 2 as a manufacturing one.

In North, both goods can be produced by standard constant-returns-to-scale technologies that are described by increasing, quasi-concave and linearly homogeneous production functions. Factors of production are labor and capital. We assume away factor-intensity reversal between them. Following the Oniki and Uzawa (1965) tradition in dynamic trade models, we assume that while newly produced Good 2 is tradable, the existing capital and labor are internationally immobile.[3] Moreover, we assume away an international credit market, while there is a competitive credit market in each country. The supply of labor in each country is constant over time.

We assume that production technologies available in North and South are internationally different. South can only produce Good 1 by primitive technologies in the sense that the good is produced by using labor only. It seems to me that, unfortunately enough, those assumptions are realistic in many underdeveloped countries even in the contemporary world.

Let us denote the felicity function of the representative household in North by $u(c_1, c_2)$. We assume that it is twice-differentiable, increasing, and strictly concave in the consumption of Good 1 and Good 2, c_1 and c_2. The dynamic optimization problem to be solved by the North representative household can be formulated as follows.

$$U^N = \max_{c_1, c_2} \int_0^\infty u(c_1, c_2) \exp[-\rho t]\, dt$$

sub. to $\dot{k} = wl + rk - \delta k - pc_1 - c_2$, $k(0) > 0$ given, (1)

---

[3] Note that the assumption is standard in dynamic trade models.

where k and l are the stocks of capital and labor owned by the North household, respectively, p the price of Good 1 in terms of Good 2, w the wage rate, r the rental rate. ρ and δ are the positive and constant rates of time preference and capital depreciation.

Under incomplete specialization, w and r are the functions of p.[4] We shall focus on the case in which both goods are produced in North.

Associated with problem (1) is the Hamiltonian

$$H = u(c_1, c_2) + \lambda\big[w(p)l + \big(r(p) - \delta\big)k - pc_1 - c_2\big]. \tag{2}$$

The necessary conditions for optimality are

$$\frac{\partial H}{\partial c_1} = u_1(c_1, c_2) - \lambda p = 0, \tag{3}$$

$$\frac{\partial H}{\partial c_2} = u_2(c_1, c_2) - \lambda = 0, \tag{4}$$

$$\dot{\lambda} = \lambda\big[\rho + \delta - r(p)\big], \tag{5}$$

$$\dot{k} = w(p)l + \big(r(p) - \delta\big)k - pc_1 - c_2 \tag{6}$$

and the transversality condition

$$\lim_{t \to \infty} k(t)\lambda(t)\exp[-\rho t] = 0, \tag{7}$$

where $u_i(c_1, c_2)$ denotes the partial derivative of the felicity function with respect to c_i, $i = 1, 2$.

Let us turn to South. The welfare of the representative household there is

$$\int_0^\infty u^*(c_1^*, c_2^*)\exp[-\rho^* t]\,dt, \tag{8}$$

where $\rho^* > 0$ is the rate of time preference. Since there is no capital accumulation and production is completely specialized to Good 1 by using labor alone, the total wage income is equal to pY_1^*, where Y_1^* is the maximum output of Good 1 in South, which is assumed to be constant over time.

For simplicity, we assume that the South felicity function is quasi-linear,

$$u^*(c_1^*, c_2^*) = v(c_1^*) + c_2^*$$

---

[4] Let $\Lambda_i(w, r)$, $i = 1, 2$, be the unit cost function of good i. If production is incompletely specialized in North, we have the price = unit-cost condition for both goods:

$$p = \Lambda_1(w, r),$$

$$1 = \Lambda_2(w, r).$$

Solving for w and r, we have the solution $(w(p), r(p))$.

where $v(\cdot)$ is assumed to be increasing and strictly concave, $v' > 0$ and $v'' < 0$. Then, the dynamic optimization problem the South household faces is

$$U^S = \max_{c_1^*, c_2^*} \int_0^\infty u^*(c_1^*, c_2^*) \exp[-\rho^* t]\, dt$$

subject to

$$\dot{A}^* = r^* A + p Y_1^* - p c_1^* - c_2^*,$$

where A^* is the net credit owned by the South household and r^* is the rate of interest in the South. We assume away an international credit market, and at each point in time we have the market-clearing condition in the South domestic credit market, $A^* = 0$ and $r^* = \rho^*$. Therefore, the static budget constraint condition

$$0 = p Y_1^* - p c_1^* - c_2^*$$

always holds. It follows from the quasi-linear felicity function that the demand for Good 1 is the function of p alone, $c_1^* = D_1(p)$, where $D_1(\cdot)$ is the inverse function of $v'(\cdot)$, and the demand function for Good 2 is

$$D_2(p) \equiv p Y_1^* - p D_1(p).$$

Then, the welfare level of the South representative household is

$$U^S = \int_0^\infty \left[v\big(D_1(p)\big) + p Y_1^* - p D_1(p) \right] \exp[-\rho^* t]\, dt.$$

Finally, the world market-clearing condition for Good 1 is

$$0 = \big(w'(p)l + r'(p)k - c_1\big) - \big(D_1(p) - Y_1^*\big), \tag{9}$$

where we use the duality property such that the partial derivative of the GNP function, $w(p)l + r(p)k$, with respect to p is the supply of Good 1.

Our dynamic general equilibrium model of North–South trade consists of five equations, (3)–(6), and (9) with the transversality condition (7). The endogenous variables are c_1, c_2, k, λ and p.

3. The steady state

3.1. A general model

The steady state is defined as a dynamic general equilibrium path along which all variables are constant over time. Denote the steady-state values by $(c_1^e, c_2^e, \lambda^e, p^e, k^e)$. They satisfy the steady-state conditions as follows.

$$0 = u_1\big(c_1^e, c_2^e\big) - \lambda^e p^e, \tag{10}$$
$$0 = u_2\big(c_1^e, c_2^e\big) - \lambda^e, \tag{11}$$
$$0 = \rho + \delta - r\big(p^e\big), \tag{12}$$

$$0 = w(p^e)l + (r(p^e) - \delta)k^e - p^e c_1^e - c_2^e, \tag{13}$$

$$0 = (w'(p^e)l + r'(p^e)k^e - c_1^e) - (D_1(p^e) - Y_1^*). \tag{14}$$

Let us check under what conditions $(c_1^e, c_2^e, \lambda^e, p^e, k^e)$ uniquely exists. First, from (12), the steady-state price, say p^e, is uniquely determined for a given $\rho + \delta > 0$. Second, combining (10) and (11), we obtain

$$p^e = \frac{u_1(c_1^e, c_2^e)}{u_2(c_1^e, c_2^e)}, \tag{15}$$

which is one of the most familiar conditions in economics. On the other hand, from (12) and (13) we obtain "the budget constraint"

$$w(p^e)l + \rho k^e = p^e c_1^e + c_2^e. \tag{16}$$

Combining (15) and (16), we obtain "the static demand function" for Good 1, $\tilde{c}_1(p^e, w(p^e)l + \rho k^e)$.

See Figure 1(a). GH is the graph of $c_1 = \tilde{c}_1(p^e, w(p^e)l + \rho k)$ when Good 1 is a normal good. Thus, the slope should be positive. On the other hand, the straight line DF is the supply of Good 1 under the assumption that Good 1 is more labor-intensive than Good 2. Due to the Stolper–Samuelson theorem, $r'(p^e)$ is negative. Since South exports Good 1, k^e is determined so that the distance AB is equal to $Y_1^* - D_1(p^e)$.

Figure 1(a) assumes that both goods are "normal". If Good 1 is an "inferior" good in North, the graph of the demand function is negatively sloped as is depicted in Figure 1(b). Since Good 1 is a pure consumption good like grains, Figure 1(b) may be more realistic than Figure 1(a).

ASSUMPTION 1. There exists a unique steady state.

3.2. A specific case

Let us show a specific case of our model for which we have a unique steady state. First, we specify the North felicity function as

$$u(c_1, c_2) = \alpha(c_1 + c_2) - \frac{\beta}{2}\{(c_1)^2 + (c_2)^2\} - \gamma c_1 c_2, \tag{17}$$

where $\alpha > 0, \beta > 0, \gamma > 0$, and $\beta > \gamma$, and the South felicity function as

$$u^*(c_1^*, c_2^*) = \alpha^* c_1^* - \frac{1}{2}\beta^*(c_1^*)^2 + c_2^*, \tag{18}$$

where $\alpha^* > 0$ and $\beta^* > 0$. The North production technologies are assumed to be Leontief in the sense that a_{lj} (respectively a_{kj}) units of labor (respectively capital services) are needed in order to produce Good j, $j = 1, 2$ and the coefficients are all constant. Following Nishimura and Shimomura (2006), we further specify them as

$$a_{k1} = 0, \qquad a_{l1} = a > 0, \qquad a_{k2} = a_{l2} = 1. \tag{19}$$

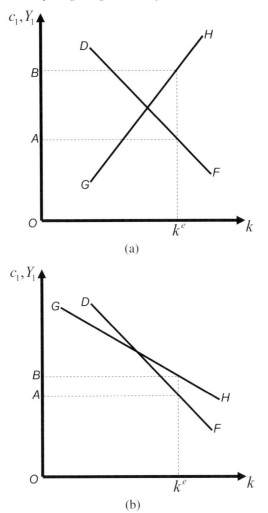

Fig. 1. (a) *Good 1 is normal and labor-intensive:* *GH:* $c_1 = \tilde{c}_1(p^e, \rho k + w(p^e)l)$; *DF:* $Y_1 = r'(p^e)k + w'(p^e)l$; *AB:* $Y_1^* - D_1(p^e)$. (b) *Good 1 is inferior and labor-intensive:* *GH:* $c_1 = \tilde{c}_1(p^e, \rho k + w(p^e)l)$; *DF:* $Y_1 = r'(p^e)k + w'(p^e)l$; *AB:* $Y_1^* - D_1(p^e)$.

Under those specifications, we can explicitly solve (10) and (11) for c_1^e, c_2^e and $D_1(p^e)$ as follows.

$$c_1(p^e, \lambda^e) = \frac{\alpha}{\beta + \gamma} - \frac{\lambda^e(p^e \beta - \gamma)}{\beta^2 - \gamma^2},$$

$$c_2\left(p^e, \lambda^e\right) = \frac{\alpha}{\beta + \gamma} - \frac{\lambda^e(\beta - p^e\gamma)}{\beta^2 - \gamma^2},$$

$$D_1\left(p^e\right) = \frac{\alpha^*}{\beta^*} - \frac{p^e}{\beta^*}.$$

Since $r(p) = (a - p)/a$ and $w(p) = p/a$, (12) is specified as

$$\rho + \delta = 1 - \frac{p^e}{a}$$

or

$$p^e = a(1 - \rho - \delta),$$

which is positive if $\rho + \delta < 1$.

Next, let us consider (13) and (14). They are specified as

$$0 = \frac{p^e}{a}l + \rho k^e - \frac{\alpha(p^e + 1)}{\beta + \gamma} + \frac{\lambda^e\{\beta(p^e)^2 - 2\gamma p^e + \beta\}}{\beta^2 - \gamma^2} \qquad (20)$$

and

$$0 = \frac{1}{a}\left(l - k^e\right) - \frac{\alpha}{\beta + \gamma} + \frac{\lambda^e(\beta p^e - \gamma)}{\beta^2 - \gamma^2} - \left(\frac{\alpha^*}{\beta^*} - \frac{1}{\beta^*}p^e\right) + Y_1^*. \qquad (21)$$

We shall obtain k^e and λ^e that satisfy (20) and (21). First, notice that the system can rewritten as

$$\rho k^e + \left[\frac{\beta}{\beta^2 - \gamma^2} + h^1\left(p^e\right)\right]\lambda^e = -\frac{p^e}{a}l + \frac{\alpha}{\beta + \gamma} + h^2\left(p^e\right),$$

$$\frac{1}{a}k^e + \left[\frac{\gamma}{\beta^2 - \gamma^2} + h^3\left(p^e\right)\right]\lambda^e = \frac{l}{a} - \frac{\alpha}{\beta + \gamma} - \frac{\alpha^*}{\beta^*} + Y_1^* + h^4\left(p^e\right),$$

where $h^j\left(p^e\right)$, $j = 1, \ldots, 4$, are continuous functions of p^e which satisfy $h^j(0) = 0$. If

$$\frac{\rho\gamma}{\beta^2 - \gamma^2} - \frac{\beta}{a(\beta^2 - \gamma^2)} = \frac{a\rho\gamma - \beta}{a(\beta^2 - \gamma^2)} > 0$$

or

$$a\rho\gamma - \beta > 0, \qquad (22)$$

then the above system has a unique solution (k^e, λ^e). Particularly, if

$$l = \tilde{l} \equiv \left\{\frac{1}{\rho}\left[\frac{\alpha}{\beta + \gamma} + h^2\left(p^e\right)\right] + a\left[\frac{\alpha}{\beta + \gamma} + \frac{\alpha^*}{\beta^*} - Y_1^* - h^4\left(p^e\right)\right]\right\}\frac{\rho}{\rho + \frac{p^e}{a}},$$

then the unique solution is

$$k^e = \frac{1}{\rho}\left[-\frac{p^e}{a}l + \frac{\alpha}{\beta + \gamma} + h^2\left(p^e\right)\right] > 0 \quad \text{for a small } p^e > 0, \text{ and } \lambda^e = 0.$$

Note also that if

$$\frac{\alpha}{\beta + \gamma} + \frac{\alpha^*}{\beta^*} - Y_1^* > 0, \tag{23}$$

then $l - k^e > 0$ for a small $p^e > 0$. Totally differentiating the system with respect to k^e, λ^e and l, we have

$$\frac{d\lambda^e}{dl} = \frac{\rho + \frac{p^e}{a}}{\frac{a\rho\gamma - \beta}{\beta^2 - \gamma^2} + h^5(p^e)},$$

where $h^5(p^e)$ is a continuous function of p^e with the property $h^5(0) = 0$. Therefore, $d\lambda^e/dl > 0$ for a small $p^e > 0$, and if $l = \tilde{l} + \varepsilon$ where ε is positive but very small, λ^e is also positive but very small.

Note that we can make $p^e = a(1 - \rho - \delta)$ positive but arbitrarily small by approaching δ to $1 - \rho$ from below.

Now let us examine other steady-state values. When λ^e and p^e is close to zero, under our specification of technologies,

$$Y_1^e = \frac{1}{a}(l - k^e) \doteq \frac{\alpha}{\beta + \gamma} + \frac{\alpha^*}{\beta^*} - Y_1^* > 0$$

and

$$Y_2^e = k^e > 0.$$

Therefore, both goods are produced at the steady state in North. With respect to consumption, when λ^e and p^e is close to zero,

$$c_1^e \doteq c_2^e \doteq \frac{\alpha}{\beta + \gamma} > 0,$$

$$D_1 \doteq \frac{\alpha^*}{\beta^*} > 0 \quad \text{and} \quad \frac{D_2}{p^e} = Y_1^* - \frac{\alpha^*}{\beta^*} + \frac{p^e}{\beta^*} \doteq Y_1^* - \frac{\alpha^*}{\beta^*}.$$

Thus, if

$$Y_1^* - \frac{\alpha^*}{\beta^*} > 0, \tag{24}$$

$D_2 > 0.$

PROPOSITION 1. *Suppose (22)–(24) hold. If δ is smaller than but sufficiently close to $1 - \rho > 0$, and if ε is positive but very close to zero, then there exists a unique steady state in which North produces both goods.*

PROOF. What is left to prove is that it is impossible for North to be completely specialized to the production of Good 2 at a steady state. Suppose that the complete specialization is established. The world market-clearing condition for Good 1 is

$$\frac{\alpha}{\beta + \gamma} - \frac{\bar{\lambda}(\beta\bar{p} - \gamma)}{\beta^2 - \gamma^2} + \frac{\alpha^*}{\beta^*} - \frac{\bar{p}}{\beta^*} - Y_1^* = 0.$$

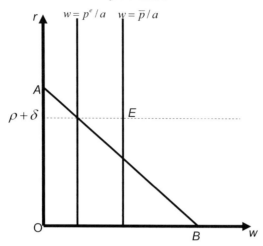

Fig. 2. *(price) = (average cost) lines AB: $1 = r + w$ [note that North has to be completely specialized to the production of Good 1 at point E, NOT Good 2].*

Would it be possible for $\bar{p}$ to be very small? Suppose that $\bar{p} \doteqdot 0$. Then, the market-clearing condition means

$$\frac{\alpha}{\beta + \gamma} + \frac{\alpha^*}{\beta^*} - Y_1^* \doteqdot \frac{-\bar{\lambda}\gamma}{\beta^2 - \gamma^2} < 0,$$

which contradicts (23). Therefore, $\bar{p}$ cannot be very small. Thus we can make p^e smaller than $\bar{p}$. However, in that case the North factor prices is determined at point E in Figure 2, in which North has to be specialized to the production of Good 1, a contradiction. □

4. Indeterminacy and a Pareto-improving foreign aid

Let us show two results here. First, we obtain local indeterminacy in the case described in Figure 1(b). Second, we show that when local indeterminacy takes place and under some conditions on preferences and technologies, a persistent aid from North to South makes both countries better off.

Let us define the Pareto-improving foreign aid. Suppose that the world economy was in the steady state until time zero. Denote the discount sums of utilities of the North and South households in the steady state by

$$\bar{U}^N = \int_0^\infty u(\bar{c}_1, \bar{c}_2) \exp[-\rho t]\, dt,$$

$$\bar{U}^S = \int_0^\infty u^*(\bar{c}_1^*, \bar{c}_2^*) \exp[-\rho^* t]\, dt,$$

respectively. If there is no aid from North to South, these welfare levels must hold even after time zero. Now, suppose that North makes a small and constant amount of transfer, say T, to South permanently from time zero on. Denoting the equilibrium levels of the North and South discounted sums of utility after time zero by U_T^N and U_T^S, we say that the foreign aid is Pareto-improving if $U_T^N > \bar{U}^N$ and $U_T^S > \bar{U}^S$.

4.1. Indeterminacy

4.1.1. A general model

First of all, let us check the stability properties of the present model. More specifically, in this subsection we show under what conditions local indeterminacy is established in the present model. Solving (3) and (4) for c_1 and c_2 and denoting the solutions by $c_1(p, \lambda)$ and $c_2(p, \lambda)$, we can describe the main part of the present model as follows:

$$\dot{k} = w(p)l + \big(r(p) - \delta\big)k - pc_1(p, \lambda) - c_2(p, \lambda), \tag{25}$$

$$\dot{\lambda} = \lambda\big[\rho + \delta - r(p)\big], \tag{26}$$

$$0 = \big(w'(p)l + r'(p)k - c_1(p, \lambda)\big) - \big(D_1(p) - Y_1^*\big). \tag{27}$$

Before pursuing the main business of this subsection, let us derive some properties of the "demand functions", $c_1(p, \lambda)$ and $c_2(p, \lambda)$. Totally differentiating (3) and (4) with respect to c_1, c_2, p and λ, we derive

$$\begin{bmatrix} u_{11} & u_{12} \\ u_{21} & u_{22} \end{bmatrix} \begin{bmatrix} dc_1 \\ dc_2 \end{bmatrix} = \begin{bmatrix} p^e \\ 1 \end{bmatrix} d\lambda + \begin{bmatrix} \lambda^e \\ 0 \end{bmatrix} dp,$$

where $u_{ij} \equiv (\partial^2 u)/(\partial c_j \partial c_i)$, $i, j = 1, 2$. The assumed strict concavity of the felicity function implies that the determinant of the coefficient matrix, say J, is positive and therefore invertible. Thus, inverting the coefficient matrix, we obtain

$$c_1^\lambda\big(p^e, \lambda^e\big) \equiv \frac{\partial c_1}{\partial \lambda} = \frac{1}{J}\big(u_{22}p^e - u_{12}\big),$$

$$c_2^\lambda\big(p^e, \lambda^e\big) \equiv \frac{\partial c_2}{\partial \lambda} = \frac{1}{J}\big(u_{11} - u_{12}p^e\big),$$

$$c_1^p\big(p^e, \lambda^e\big) \equiv \frac{\partial c_1}{\partial p} = \frac{1}{J}\lambda^e u_{22} < 0,$$

$$c_2^p\big(p^e, \lambda^e\big) \equiv \frac{\partial c_2}{\partial p} = \frac{-1}{J}\lambda^e u_{12}.$$

Inspecting the partial derivatives, we find the preliminary results which we shall use later.

LEMMA. (i) $p^e c_1^\lambda + c_2^\lambda < 0$. (ii) $\lambda^e c_1^\lambda = p^e c_1^p + c_2^p$. (iii) $\mathrm{sign}[p^e c_1^p + c_2^p] = \mathrm{sign}[u_{22}p^e - u_{12}]$. *Since* $u_{22} < 0$, (ii) *and* (iii) *imply that* c_1^λ *is positive only if* $u_{12} < 0$.

Now, let us return to our main business. Solving (27) for p, substituting it to the other two equations (25) and (26), we have

$$\dot{x}_k = \left\{\rho - \frac{r'(p^e)}{\Delta}(z - \lambda^e c_1^\lambda)\right\}x_k - \left\{(p^e c_1^\lambda + c_2^\lambda) - \frac{c_1^\lambda}{\Delta}(z - \lambda^e c_1^\lambda)\right\}x_\lambda, \qquad (28)$$

$$\dot{x}_\lambda = \frac{-\lambda^e r'(p^e)}{\Delta}[-r'(p^e)x_k + c_1^\lambda x_\lambda], \qquad (29)$$

where $x_k \equiv k - k^e, x_\lambda \equiv \lambda - \lambda^e,$

$$z \equiv D_1(p^e) - Y_1^* < 0$$

and

$$\Delta \equiv w''(p^e)l + r''(p^e)k^e - c_1^p(p^e, \lambda^e) - D_1'(p^e).$$

Letting $x_p \equiv p - p^e$, we see

$$x_p = \frac{1}{\Delta}[c_1^\lambda x_\lambda - r'(p^e)x_k]. \qquad (30)$$

Now, we can obtain the characteristic equation from (28) and (29).

$$\Gamma(x) \equiv \begin{vmatrix} x - \{\rho - \frac{r'(p^e)}{\Delta}(z - \lambda^e c_1^\lambda)\} & (p^e c_1^\lambda + c_2^\lambda) - \frac{c_1^\lambda}{\Delta}(z - \lambda^e c_1^\lambda) \\ -\frac{\lambda^e (r'(p^e))^2}{\Delta} & x + \frac{\lambda^e r'(p^e)c_1^\lambda}{\Delta} \end{vmatrix}$$

$$= x^2 + \left(\frac{r'(p^e)z}{\Delta} - \rho\right)x - \frac{\lambda^e r'(p^e)}{\Delta}\{\rho c_1^\lambda - r'(p^e)(p^e c_1^\lambda + c_2^\lambda)\}$$

$$= 0. \qquad (31)$$

We shall make the following assumptions.

ASSUMPTION 2 *(the static Walrasian stability condition).* $\Delta > 0$.

ASSUMPTION 3. The pure consumption good (Good 1) is more labor-intensive than the consumable capital (Good 2).

Assumption 2 is traditional in the static literature on international transfers. Assumption 3 seems to be realistic. It follows from the Stolper–Samuelson theorem that $r'(p^e) < 0$.

Since South exports Good 1, i.e., $z < 0$, the two assumptions together imply that $r'(p^e)z/\Delta$ is positive. We immediately derive the first main result from (31).

PROPOSITION 2. *Local indeterminacy holds if*

$$\frac{r'(p^e)z}{\Delta} - \rho > 0 \qquad (32)$$

and

$$\rho c_1^\lambda - r'(p^e)(p^e c_1^\lambda + c_2^\lambda) > 0. \qquad (33)$$

REMARK. Local indeterminacy requires that c_1^λ is positive. It is clear that $c_1^\lambda > 0$ means that Good 1 is an inferior good.

Let us draw the phase diagram under the assumption $c_1^\lambda > 0$. It is clear from (29) that

$$\left. \frac{d\lambda}{dk} \right|_{\dot\lambda=0} = \frac{r'(p^e)}{c_1^\lambda} < 0. \tag{34}$$

See Figure 3, in which the $\dot\lambda = 0$ line is AEB. Since $c_1^\lambda > 0$, $\dot\lambda$ is positive (respectively negative) above (respectively below) AEB. On the other hand, from (28) the slope of the $\dot k = 0$ line is

$$\left. \frac{d\lambda}{dk} \right|_{\dot k=0} = \frac{\{\rho - \frac{r'(p^e)}{\Delta}(z - \lambda^e c_1^\lambda)\}}{\{(p^e c_1^\lambda + c_2^\lambda) - \frac{c_1^\lambda}{\Delta}(z - \lambda^e c_1^\lambda)\}}. \tag{35}$$

The subtraction of (34) from (35) yields

$$\left. \frac{d\lambda}{dk} \right|_{\dot k=0} - \left. \frac{d\lambda}{dk} \right|_{\dot\lambda=0} = \frac{\rho c_1^\lambda - r'(p^e)(p^e c_1^\lambda + c_2^\lambda)}{\{(p^e c_1^\lambda + c_2^\lambda) - \frac{c_1^\lambda}{\Delta}(z - \lambda^e c_1^\lambda)\}c_1^\lambda}. \tag{36}$$

Due to (33), the numerator of (36) is positive. Moreover, since (33) implies that $(p^e c_1^\lambda + c_2^\lambda) > (\rho c_1^\lambda / r'(p^e))$, we see that

$$\left(p^e c_1^\lambda + c_2^\lambda\right) - \frac{c_1^\lambda}{\Delta}\left(z - \lambda^e c_1^\lambda\right) > \frac{\rho c_1^\lambda}{r'(p^e)} - \frac{c_1^\lambda}{\Delta}\left(z - \lambda^e c_1^\lambda\right)$$

$$= -\frac{c_1^\lambda}{r'(p^e)}\left(\frac{r'(p^e)z}{\Delta} - \rho\right) + \frac{\lambda^e (c_1^\lambda)^2}{\Delta}, \tag{37}$$

which is positive, because of (32). Therefore, $(d\lambda/dk)|_{\dot k=0} > (d\lambda/dk)|_{\dot\lambda=0}$.

Based on the foregoing argument, we can depict the phase diagram like in Figure 3, where the $\dot k = 0$ curve is negatively sloped. Since

$$\dot x_k = \left\{\rho - \frac{r'(p^e)}{\Delta}(z - \lambda^e c_1^\lambda)\right\}x_k - \left\{(p^e c_1^\lambda + c_2^\lambda) - \frac{c_1^\lambda}{\Delta}(z - \lambda^e c_1^\lambda)\right\}x_\lambda$$

$$= \left\{\rho x_k - \left(p^e c_1^\lambda + c_2^\lambda\right)x_\lambda\right\} - \frac{(z - \lambda^e c_1^\lambda)}{\Delta}\left(r'(p^e)x_k - c_1^\lambda x_\lambda\right)$$

$$= \rho x_k - \left(p^e c_1^\lambda + c_2^\lambda\right)x_\lambda$$

along AB, $\dot k$ is positive (respectively negative) below (respectively above) CD. Therefore, we can depict arrows like in Figure 3. For a historically given capital stock $k(0)$, as long as an initial co-state variable $\lambda(0)$ is chosen in such a way that $(k(0), \lambda(0))$ is in a neighborhood of the steady state, the solution to the dynamic system (25)–(27) converges to the steady state. Thus, there is a continuum of equilibrium paths converging to the steady state.

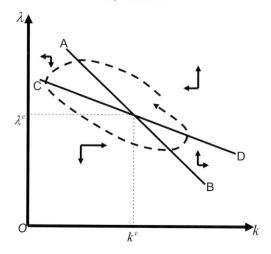

Fig. 3.   The phase diagram in the case of indeterminacy.

4.1.2. A specific case

Let us consider the specification discussed in Section 3.2. When p^e and λ^e are sufficiently close to zero,

$$\Delta \doteq \frac{1}{\beta^*} > 0$$

and

$$z \doteq \frac{\alpha^*}{\beta^*} - Y_1^* < 0.$$

Therefore, (32) is satisfied if

$$\frac{r'(p^e)z}{\Delta} - \rho \doteq \frac{1}{a}(\beta^* Y_1^* - \alpha^*) - \rho > 0,$$

which holds if a is sufficiently small. Next,

$$\rho c_1^\lambda - r'\left(p^e\right)\left(p^e c_1^\lambda + c_2^\lambda\right) \doteq \frac{1}{\beta^2 - \gamma^2}\left[\rho\gamma - \frac{\beta}{a}\right],$$

which is positive under (22). Finally, it is clear that the specification concerning technologies implies that Good 1 is more labor intensive. Therefore, it satisfies Assumption 3, and we have indeterminacy for the specific model.

4.2. A Pareto-improving foreign aid

4.2.1. A general model

Now, let us introduce foreign aid into the present model. We assume that (i) before time zero the world economy is in the steady state and (ii) North starts transferring T

units of income for ever after time zero. The present model becomes

$$\dot{k} = w(p)l + \big(r(p) - \delta\big)k - pc_1(p, \lambda) - c_2(p, \lambda) - T,$$
$$\dot{\lambda} = \lambda\big[\rho + \delta - r(p)\big],$$
$$0 = \big(w'(p)l + r'(p)k - c_1(p, \lambda)\big) - \big(D_1(p) - Y_1^*\big).$$

Let us consider the system of variational equations whose coefficients are evaluated at the pre-transfer steady state. Let $k_T \equiv \partial k/\partial T$, $\lambda_T \equiv \partial\lambda/\partial T$, and $p_T \equiv \partial p/\partial T$. The system of variational equations is

$$\dot{k}_T = \left[\rho - \frac{r'(p^e)(z - \lambda^e c_1^\lambda)}{\Delta}\right]k_T - \left[(p^e c_1^\lambda + c_2^\lambda) - \frac{c_1^\lambda}{\Delta}(z - \lambda^e c_1^\lambda)\right]\lambda_T - 1, \quad (38)$$

$$\dot{\lambda}_T = \frac{-\lambda^e r'(p^e)}{\Delta}\big[-r'(p^e)k_T + c_1^\lambda \lambda_T\big] = -\lambda^e r'(p^e)p_T. \quad (39)$$

See Figure 4, which is the phase diagram of the pair of variations (k_T, λ_T). Apparently, the intersection of the $\dot{k}_T = 0$ line and the $\dot{\lambda}_T = 0$ line is a stable stationary state of the system of variational equations. As is shown in the figure,

$$\bar{k}_T \equiv k_T(\infty) = \frac{c_1^\lambda}{\rho c_1^\lambda - r'(p^e)(p^e c_1^\lambda + c_2^\lambda)} > 0$$

and

$$\bar{\lambda}_T \equiv \lambda_T(\infty) = \frac{r'(p^e)}{\rho c_1^\lambda - r'(p^e)(p^e c_1^\lambda + c_2^\lambda)} < 0.$$

Since k is the state variable, $k_T(0)$ must be zero. Thus, Figure 4 tells us that if $\lambda_T(0) < 0$ and $|\lambda_T(0)| < \overline{OS}$, for any $t > 0$, $\lambda_T(t) < 0$.

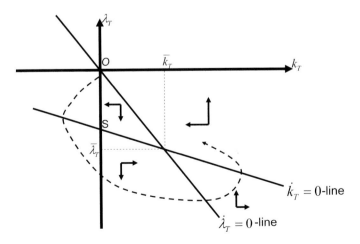

Fig. 4.   *The phase diagram of variations.*

Having the foregoing results in mind, let us calculate the effect of a small foreign aid on the welfare of North, i.e., the donor country.

$$
\frac{\partial U^N}{\partial T}\bigg|_{T=0} = \int_0^\infty \frac{\partial}{\partial T} u\big(c_1(p,\lambda), c_2(p,\lambda)\big) \exp(-\rho t)\, dt
$$
$$
= \int_0^\infty \big[\{u_1\big(c_1^e, c_2^e\big)c_1^p + u_2\big(c_1^e, c_2^e\big)c_2^p\} p_T
$$
$$
+ \{u_1\big(c_1^e, c_2^e\big)c_1^\lambda + u_2\big(c_1^e, c_2^e\big)c_2^\lambda\}\lambda_T\big] \exp(-\rho t)\, dt.
$$

Applying (3) and (4), we continue,

$$
= \int_0^\infty \big[\big(\lambda^e p^e c_1^p + \lambda^e c_2^p\big) p_T + \big(\lambda^e p^e c_1^\lambda + \lambda^e c_2^\lambda\big)\lambda_T\big] \exp(-\rho t)\, dt
$$
$$
= \lambda^e \big(p^e c_1^p + c_2^p\big)\int_0^\infty p_T \exp(-\rho t)\, dt + \lambda^e \big(p^e c_1^\lambda + c_2^\lambda\big)\int_0^\infty \lambda_T \exp(-\rho t)\, dt
$$
$$
= \lambda^e \bigg[\lambda^e c_1^\lambda \int_0^\infty p_T \exp(-\rho t)\, dt + \big(p^e c_1^\lambda + c_2^\lambda\big)\int_0^\infty \lambda_T \exp(-\rho t)\, dt\bigg]. \quad (40)
$$

4.2.2. A specific case

Let us examine whether (40) is positive in the specified model discussed in Sections 3.2 and 4.1.2. Using (39), we can rewrite (40) as

$$
\lambda^e \bigg[\lambda^e c_1^\lambda \int_0^\infty \frac{\lambda_T}{-\lambda^e r'(p^e)} \exp(-\rho t)\, dt + \big(p^e c_1^\lambda + c_2^\lambda\big)\int_0^\infty \lambda_T \exp(-\rho t)\, dt\bigg]
$$
$$
= \lambda^e \bigg[-\frac{c_1^\lambda}{r'(p^e)} \int_0^\infty \lambda_T \exp(-\rho t)\, dt + \big(p^e c_1^\lambda + c_2^\lambda\big)\int_0^\infty \lambda_T \exp(-\rho t)\, dt\bigg]. \quad (41)
$$

We can show that as λ^e approaches 0, so does $\int_0^\infty \lambda_T \exp(-\rho t)\, dt$.[5] Hence, for a sufficiently small $\lambda^e > 0$,

$$
\text{sign}\bigg[-\frac{c_1^\lambda}{r'(p^e)} \int_0^\infty \lambda_T \exp(-\rho t)\, dt + \big(p^e c_1^\lambda + c_2^\lambda\big)\int_0^\infty \lambda_T \exp(-\rho t)\, dt\bigg]
$$
$$
\doteq \text{sign}\bigg[\big(p^e c_1^\lambda + c_2^\lambda\big)\int_0^\infty \lambda_T \exp(-\rho t)\, dt\bigg]. \quad (42)
$$

If $\lambda_T(0)$ is chosen to be between 0 and point S in Figure 4 so that $\lambda_T(t)$ is always negative. Therefore $\int_0^\infty \lambda_T \exp(-\rho t)\, dt < 0$. It follows from $\big(p^e c_1^\lambda + c_2^\lambda\big) < 0$ that

---

[5] See Appendix A.

(42) is positive, which implies that (40), i.e.,

$$\frac{\partial U^N}{\partial T}\bigg|_{T=0} > 0.$$

Finally, since p returns to the pre-transfer steady-state level p^e in the long run, the welfare level of South has to rise due to the income effect as long as ρ^* is sufficiently small. Therefore both North and South have to be better off due to the permanent foreign aid.

THEOREM. *There is a dynamic general equilibrium model such that a self-fulfilling expectation makes possible an equilibrium path along which a persistent foreign aid makes both North and South better off.*

5. Concluding remarks

In this paper, we showed that a Pareto-improving foreign aid is possible in a plausible dynamic North–South model in which South is completely specialized to the production of an agricultural good and exports it to North. The South production technology is more primitive than North in the sense that it does not use capital as its input.

We have focused on the case of infinite time horizon which is a standard assumption in dynamic general equilibrium models. One may wonder if we can derive the same Pareto-improving result in a finite horizon.[6] It is one of my next research agenda to answer this question.

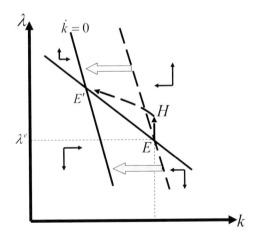

Fig. 5. *The phase diagram in the case of determinacy* [note that along the post-transfer stable arm (the broken curve HE′) λ is always larger than the pre-transfer level λ^e].

---

[6] I am grateful to Henry Wan Jr for suggesting me to study the case of finite horizon after this paper.

We have a conjecture such that the Pareto-improving foreign aid is closely related to indeterminacy. Consider a case in which the steady state is saddlepoint-stable, which is the case if the $\dot{k} = 0$ curve is steeper than the $\dot{\lambda} = 0$ curve. See Figure 5. As a result of a persistent foreign aid, the $\dot{k} = 0$ curve has to shift to the left. Then, at time zero, $\lambda(0)$ jumps from E to H, and then converges to the new steady state E'. Therefore, along the transition, $\lambda(t)$ is always larger than the pre-transfer level, which means that λ_T is always positive. Thus, considering the argument in the last section, it is plausible to have $(\partial U^N/\partial T)|_{T=0} < 0$. It is also one of my next research agenda to prove it strictly.

Acknowledgements

An early version of this paper was presented at 2004 Taipei International Conference on Growth and Development in Global Perspective, Academia Sinica, Taipei. I am grateful to M.J. Crucini, Kazumichi Iwasa, Sajal Lahiri, Albert Schweinberger, and Henry Wan Jr for their valuable comments and suggestions.

Appendix A. As $\lambda^e \to 0$, $\int_0^\infty \dot{\lambda}_T(t)e^{-\rho t}\,dt \to 0$

Let us prove that as $\lambda^e \to 0$, $\int_0^\infty \dot{\lambda}_T(t)e^{-\rho t}\,dt \to 0$. First, for brevity, let us define

$$b(\lambda^e) \equiv \frac{r'(p^e)}{\Delta}(z - \lambda^e c_1^\lambda) - \rho, \tag{A.1}$$

$$\eta(\lambda^e) \equiv \frac{c_1^\lambda}{\Delta}(z - \lambda^e c_1^\lambda) - (p^e c_1^\lambda + c_2^\lambda), \tag{A.2}$$

$$\theta(\lambda^e) \equiv \frac{(r'(p^e))^2}{\Delta}, \tag{A.3}$$

$$\varsigma(\lambda^e) \equiv \frac{-r'(p^e)c_1^\lambda}{\Delta}. \tag{A.4}$$

Since

$$\Delta \equiv -c_1^p(p^e, \lambda^e) - D_1'(p^e)$$
$$= \frac{\beta \lambda^e}{\beta^2 - \gamma^2} + \frac{1}{\beta^*}$$

and

$$z \equiv D_1(p^e) - Y_1^*$$
$$= \frac{\alpha^*}{\beta^*} - \frac{p^e}{\beta^*} - Y_1^*,$$

Δ does depend on λ^e, while z does on p^e. Then,

$$\dot{k}_T = \left\{ \rho - \frac{r'(p^e)}{\Delta}(z - \lambda^e c_1^\lambda) \right\} k_T - \left\{ (p^e c_1^\lambda + c_2^\lambda) - \frac{c_1^\lambda}{\Delta}(z - \lambda^e c_1^\lambda) \right\} \lambda_T - 1,$$

$$\dot{\lambda}_T = \frac{-\lambda^e r'(p^e)}{\Delta}\left[-r'(p^e)k_T + c_1^\lambda \lambda_T \right] = -\lambda^e r'(p^e) p_T$$

can be rewritten as

$$\dot{k}_T = -b(\lambda^e)k_T + \eta(\lambda^e)\lambda_T - 1, \tag{A.5}$$

$$\dot{\lambda}_T = \lambda^e \theta(\lambda^e)k_T + \lambda^e \varsigma(\lambda^e)\lambda_T = -\lambda^e r'(p^e) p_T. \tag{A.6}$$

Note that when p^e is very small, as $\lambda^e \to 0$,

$$b(\lambda^e) \to b(0) \equiv \frac{\beta^*}{a}\left(Y_1^* + \frac{p^e}{\beta^*} - \frac{\alpha^*}{\beta^*} \right) - \rho \doteq \frac{\beta^*}{a}\left(Y_1^* - \frac{\alpha^*}{\beta^*} \right) - \rho > 0,$$

$$\eta(\lambda^e) \to \eta(0) \equiv \frac{-(\beta p^e - \gamma)\beta^* z}{(\beta^2 - \gamma^2)} - (p^e c_1^\lambda + c_2^\lambda)$$

$$\doteq \frac{\gamma \beta^*}{(\beta^2 - \gamma^2)}\left(\frac{\alpha^*}{\beta^*} - Y_1^* \right) + \frac{\beta}{(\beta^2 - \gamma^2)} < 0,$$

$$\theta(\lambda^e) \to \theta(0) \equiv \frac{\beta^*}{a^2},$$

$$\varsigma(\lambda^e) \to \varsigma(0) \equiv \frac{-\beta^*(\beta p^e - \gamma)}{a(\beta^2 - \gamma^2)} \doteq \frac{\gamma \beta^*}{a(\beta^2 - \gamma^2)}.$$

Let us solve (A.5) and (A.6). Substituting $k_T = A_k e^{xt}$ and $\lambda_T = A_\lambda e^{xt}$ into

$$\dot{k}_T = -b(\lambda^e)k_T + \eta(\lambda^e)\lambda_T,$$

$$\dot{\lambda}_T = \lambda^e \theta(\lambda^e)k_T + \lambda^e \varsigma(\lambda^e)\lambda_T,$$

we derive

$$\begin{bmatrix} x + b(\lambda^e) & -\eta(\lambda^e) \\ -\lambda^e \theta(\lambda^e) & x - \lambda^e \varsigma(\lambda^e) \end{bmatrix} \begin{bmatrix} A_k \\ A_\lambda \end{bmatrix} = \begin{bmatrix} 0 \\ 0 \end{bmatrix}. \tag{A.7}$$

Let us denote the roots of the characteristic equation

$$\det \begin{bmatrix} x + b(\lambda^e) & -\eta(\lambda^e) \\ -\lambda^e \theta(\lambda^e) & x - \lambda^e \varsigma(\lambda^e) \end{bmatrix} = 0$$

by $x_1(\lambda^e)$ and $x_2(\lambda^e)$. We know that as $\lambda^e \to 0$,

$$x_1(\lambda^e) \to -b(0) < 0 \quad \text{and} \quad x_2(\lambda^e) \to 0.$$

If λ_e is positive and close to 0, both of the two roots are negative real numbers.

Now let us follow the standard way of deriving the solution. We have

$$(x_1(\lambda^e) + b(\lambda^e))A_k^1 - \eta(\lambda^e)A_\lambda^1 = 0,$$
$$(x_2(\lambda^e) + b(\lambda^e))A_k^2 - \eta(\lambda^e)A_\lambda^2 = 0$$

or

$$A_\lambda^1 = \frac{x_1(\lambda^e) + b(\lambda^e)}{\eta(\lambda^e)}A_k^1,$$

$$A_\lambda^2 = \frac{x_2(\lambda^e) + b(\lambda^e)}{\eta(\lambda^e)}A_k^2.$$

Using these equations, we obtain the solution

$$k_T = A_k^1 e^{x_1(\lambda^e)t} + A_k^2 e^{x_2(\lambda^e)t} + \bar{k}_T, \tag{A.8}$$

$$\lambda_T = \frac{x_1(\lambda^e) + b(\lambda^e)}{\eta(\lambda^e)}A_k^1 e^{x_1(\lambda^e)t} + \frac{x_2(\lambda^e) + b(\lambda^e)}{\eta(\lambda^e)}A_k^2 e^{x_2(\lambda^e)t} + \bar{\lambda}_T, \tag{A.9}$$

where

$$\bar{k}_T = \frac{-\varsigma(\lambda^e)}{b(\lambda^e)\varsigma(\lambda^e) + \eta(\lambda^e)\theta(\lambda^e)} \doteq \frac{-\varsigma(0)}{b(0)\varsigma(0) + \eta(0)\theta(0)}$$

$$= \frac{a\gamma}{a\rho\gamma - \beta} > 0,$$

$$\bar{\lambda}_T = \frac{\theta(\lambda^e)}{b(\lambda^e)\varsigma(\lambda^e) + \eta(\lambda^e)\theta(\lambda^e)} \doteq \frac{\theta(0)}{b(0)\varsigma(0) + \eta(0)\theta(0)}$$

$$= -\frac{(\beta^2 - \gamma^2)}{a\rho\gamma - \beta} < 0.$$

Now, using the initial conditions,

$$-\bar{k}_T = A_k^1 + A_k^2,$$

$$\lambda_T(0) - \bar{\lambda}_T = \frac{x_1(\lambda^e) + b(\lambda^e)}{\eta(\lambda^e)}A_k^1 + \frac{x_2(\lambda^e) + b(\lambda^e)}{\eta(\lambda^e)}A_k^2,$$

we derive

$$A_k^1 = \frac{\eta(\lambda^e)}{x_2(\lambda^e) - x_1(\lambda^e)} \begin{vmatrix} -\bar{k}_T & 1 \\ \lambda_T(0) - \bar{\lambda}_T & \frac{x_2(\lambda^e) + b(\lambda^e)}{\eta(\lambda^e)} \end{vmatrix}$$

$$= \frac{-\eta(\lambda^e)}{x_2(\lambda^e) - x_1(\lambda^e)} \left[\frac{\bar{k}_T(x_2(\lambda^e) + b(\lambda^e))}{\eta(\lambda^e)} + \lambda_T(0) - \bar{\lambda}_T \right],$$

$$A_k^2 = \frac{\eta(\lambda^e)}{x_2(\lambda^e) - x_1(\lambda^e)} \begin{vmatrix} 1 & -\bar{k}_T \\ \frac{x_1(\lambda^e) + b(\lambda^e)}{\eta(\lambda^e)} & \lambda_T(0) - \bar{\lambda}_T \end{vmatrix}$$

$$= \frac{\eta(\lambda^e)}{x_2(\lambda^e) - x_1(\lambda^e)} \left[\lambda_T(0) - \bar{\lambda}_T + \frac{\bar{k}_T(x_1(\lambda^e) + b(\lambda^e))}{\eta(\lambda^e)} \right].$$

Therefore, we now obtain

$$
\begin{aligned}
\lambda_T =\ & \frac{x_1(\lambda^e) + b(\lambda^e)}{\eta(\lambda^e)} \frac{(-\eta(\lambda^e))}{x_2(\lambda^e) - x_1(\lambda^e)} \\
& \times \left[\frac{\bar{k}_T(x_2(\lambda^e) + b(\lambda^e))}{\eta(\lambda^e)} + \lambda_T(0) - \bar{\lambda}_T \right] e^{x_1(\lambda^e)t} \\
& + \frac{x_2(\lambda^e) + b(\lambda^e)}{\eta(\lambda^e)} \frac{\eta(\lambda^e)}{x_2(\lambda^e) - x_1(\lambda^e)} \\
& \times \left[\lambda_T(0) - \bar{\lambda}_T + \frac{\bar{k}_T(x_1(\lambda^e) + b(\lambda^e))}{\eta(\lambda^e)} \right] e^{x_2(\lambda^e)t} + \bar{\lambda}_T.
\end{aligned}
$$

Differentiate λ_T with respect to time. We have

$$
\begin{aligned}
\dot{\lambda}_T =\ & \frac{x_1(\lambda^e)(x_1(\lambda^e) + b(\lambda^e))}{\eta(\lambda^e)} \frac{(-\eta(\lambda^e))}{x_2(\lambda^e) - x_1(\lambda^e)} \\
& \times \left[\frac{\bar{k}_T(x_2(\lambda^e) + b(\lambda^e))}{\eta(\lambda^e)} + \lambda_T(0) - \bar{\lambda}_T \right] e^{x_1(\lambda^e)t} \\
& + \frac{x_2(\lambda^e)(x_2(\lambda^e) + b(\lambda^e))}{\eta(\lambda^e)} \frac{\eta(\lambda^e)}{x_2(\lambda^e) - x_1(\lambda^e)} \\
& \times \left[\lambda_T(0) - \bar{\lambda}_T + \frac{\bar{k}_T(x_1(\lambda^e) + b(\lambda^e))}{\eta(\lambda^e)} \right] e^{x_2(\lambda^e)t}.
\end{aligned}
$$

Therefore,

$$
\begin{aligned}
\int_0^\infty \dot{\lambda}_T(t) e^{-\rho t}\, dt =\ & \frac{x_1(\lambda^e)(x_1(\lambda^e) + b(\lambda^e))}{\eta(\lambda^e)} \frac{(-\eta(\lambda^e))}{x_2(\lambda^e) - x_1(\lambda^e)} \\
& \times \left[\frac{\bar{k}_T(x_2(\lambda^e) + b(\lambda^e))}{\eta(\lambda^e)} + \lambda_T(0) - \bar{\lambda}_T \right] \int_0^\infty e^{[x_1(\lambda^e)-\rho]t}\, dt \\
& + \frac{x_2(\lambda^e)(x_2(\lambda^e) + b(\lambda^e))}{\eta(\lambda^e)} \frac{\eta(\lambda^e)}{x_2(\lambda^e) - x_1(\lambda^e)} \\
& \times \left[\lambda_T(0) - \bar{\lambda}_T + \frac{\bar{k}_T(x_1(\lambda^e) + b(\lambda^e))}{\eta(\lambda^e)} \right] \int_0^\infty e^{[x_2(\lambda^e)-\rho]t}\, dt \\
=\ & \frac{x_1(\lambda^e)(x_1(\lambda^e) + b(\lambda^e))}{\eta(\lambda^e)} \frac{(-\eta(\lambda^e))}{x_2(\lambda^e) - x_1(\lambda^e)} \\
& \times \left[\frac{\bar{k}_T(x_2(\lambda^e) + b(\lambda^e))}{\eta(\lambda^e)} + \lambda_T(0) - \bar{\lambda}_T \right] \frac{1}{\rho - x_1(\lambda^e)} \\
& + \frac{x_2(\lambda^e)(x_2(\lambda^e) + b(\lambda^e))}{\eta(\lambda^e)} \frac{\eta(\lambda^e)}{x_2(\lambda^e) - x_1(\lambda^e)} \\
& \times \left[\lambda_T(0) - \bar{\lambda}_T + \frac{\bar{k}_T(x_1(\lambda^e) + b(\lambda^e))}{\eta(\lambda^e)} \right] \frac{1}{\rho - x_2(\lambda^e)}.
\end{aligned}
$$

As $\lambda^e \to 0$, $x_1(\lambda^e) \to -b(0)$, and $x_2(\lambda^e) \to 0$. Therefore,

$$\left[x_2(\lambda^e) - x_1(\lambda^e)\right] \to b(0) \doteq \frac{\beta^*}{a}\left(Y_1^* - \frac{\alpha^*}{\beta^*}\right) - \rho > 0,$$

$$\rho - x_1(\lambda^e) \to \rho + b(0) > 0,$$

$$\rho - x_2(\lambda^e) \to \rho.$$

Finally, $\eta(\lambda^e) \to \eta(0) \doteq \frac{\gamma\beta^*}{(\beta^2-\gamma^2)}(\frac{\alpha^*}{\beta^*} - Y_1^*) + \frac{\beta}{(\beta^2-\gamma^2)} < 0$. Therefore, as $\lambda^e \to 0$,

$$\int_0^\infty \dot{\lambda}_T(t)e^{-\rho t}\, dt \to 0,$$

as was to be proved.

References

Brakman, S., van Marrewijk, C. (1998), The Economics of International Transfers. Cambridge University Press, Cambridge.

Djajić, S., Lahiri, S., Raimondos-Møller, P. (1999), Foreign aid, domestic investment and welfare. *Economic Journal* 109, 698–707.

Galor, O., Polemarchakis, H.M. (1987), Intertemporal equilibrium and the transfer paradox. *The Review of Economic Studies* 54, 147–156.

Jones, R. (1975), Presumption and the transfer problem. *Journal of International Economics* 5, 263–274.

Jones, R. (1985), Income effects and paradoxes in the theory of international trade. *Economic Journal* 95, 330–344.

Kemp, M.C., Abe, K. (1994), The transfer problem in a context of public goods. *Economics Letters* 5, 223–226.

Kemp, M.C., Kojima, S. (1985), Tied aid and the paradoxes of donor-enrichment and recipient-impoverishment. *International Economic Review* 26, 721–729.

Kemp, M.C., Shimomura, K. (1991), "Trade" or "aid"? In: Takayama, A., Ohyama, M., Ohta, H. (Eds.), *Trade, Policy, and International Adjustments*. Academic Press, San Diego, pp. 19–35.

Kemp, M.C., Wong, K.-y. (1993), Paradoxes associated with the administration of foreign aid. *Journal of Development Economics* 42, 197–204.

Lahiri, S., Raimondos-Møller, P. (1995), Welfare effects of aid under quantitative trade restrictions. *Journal of International Economics* 39, 297–315.

Lahiri, S., Raimondos-Møller, P., Wong, K.-y., Woodland, A.D. (2002), Optimal foreign aid and tariffs. *Journal of Development Economics* 67, 79–99.

McDougall, I. (1965), Non-traded goods and the transfer problem. *The Review of Economic Studies* 32, 67–84.

Nishimura, K., Shimomura, K. (2006), Indeterminacy in a two-country dynamic model. *Economic Theory* 29, 307–324.

Ohyama, M. (1974), Tariffs and the transfer problem. *Keio Economic Studies* 11, 29–45.

Oniki, H., Uzawa, H. (1965), Patterns of trade and investment in a dynamic model of international trade. *The Review of Economic Studies* 32, 15–38.

Ono, Y. (2007), International transfer in the presence of unemployment. In: Lahiri, S. (Ed.), *Theory and Practice of Foreign Aid*. In: Frontiers of Economics and Globalization, vol. 1. Elsevier, Amsterdam (Chapter 10 of this volume).

Samuelson, P. (1947), *Foundations of Economic Analysis*. Harvard University Press, Cambridge, MA.

CHAPTER 10

International Transfer under Stagnation

Yoshiyasu Ono[*]

Institute of Social and Economic Research, Osaka University,
6-1, Mihogaoka, Ibaraki, Osaka 567-0047, Japan
E-mail address: ono@iser.osaka-u.ac.jp

Abstract

Using a two-country two-commodity dynamic optimization model that gives rise to a liquidity trap, this paper investigates the effect of an international transfer on consumption and employment in the donor and recipient countries. It shows that a transfer from a country with unemployment to a country with full employment raises both countries' consumption. It deteriorates the donor's current account and hence depreciates its currency, which improves the international competitiveness of its products. Thus, employment and consumption increases in the country. It in turn improves the terms of trade for the recipient country, which benefits it since it maintains full employment.

Keywords: International transfer, persistent unemployment, exchange rate, liquidity trap

JEL classifications: F41, F42, F35

1. Introduction

An international transfer is usually considered to benefit the recipient country and harm the donor one in a pure economic sense. Thus, an aid is usually taken as an altruistic policy, a political/security investment or a compensation for trade liberalization at a financial cost.[1] A donor country tends to reduce foreign aid as it stagnates because of the government budget deficit, as is the case of Japan.

However, it is sometimes said by policy makers that the transfer may also benefit the donor country from its demand creation effect on the recipient country. An

---

[*] I am indebted to Shinsuke Ikeda and Sajal Lahiri for their very helpful comments and suggestions. This research is financially supported by the Grants-in-Aid for Scientific Research, JSPS, Japan.

[1] See Maizels and Nissanke (1984) for an empirical analysis on the underlying principles of aid allocation and the balance of motivations between the needs of recipient countries and the interests of donor countries.

THEORY AND PRACTICE OF FOREIGN AID
VOLUME 1   ISSN: 1574-8715
DOI: 10.1016/S1574-8715(06)01010-4

example was the Marshall Plan proposed by the US Secretary of State George C. Marshall in 1947, probably one of the most important aid program in the history. After World War II supply capacities of European countries deadly suffered from the war and the USA offered up to $20 billion for relief. The US government believed that it not only helped European countries but also benefited the US economy by creating European demand for US commodities. In fact, in the website called "Information USA" they write: "The Marshall Plan, it should be noted, benefited the American economy as well. The money would be used to buy goods from the United States, and they had to be shipped across the Atlantic on American merchant vessels."[2] Such a spirit was taken over by the Independent Commission on International Development Issues, a panel lead by former German Chancellor Willy Brandt in the early 1980s (Brandt Commission, 1980, 1983). It focused on the North–South problem and stressed the importance of foreign aid from North to South by saying that it would benefit the donors as well as the recipients through not only stabilizing political/security situations but also creating import demand and expanding employment in North.

As stated above, it is quite natural that a transfer raises the recipient country's demand for the products of the donor country. However, this does not necessarily benefit the donor country since the recipient's demand increase simply reflects the initial transfer of the purchasing power that was given up by people in the donor country. In fact, in a standard setting with Walrasian stability and no distortions it has been found that a transfer benefits the recipient country and harms the donor country since Samuelson (1947) discussed the possibility of the transfer paradox mentioned by Leontief (1936).[3] If a paradox arises, it does through an excessive change in the terms of trade that dominates the income redistribution owing to the transfer.

In order to generate such a paradoxical case theorists either consider the case where Walrasian stability is invalid or introduce some distortions to their models. In a dynamic setting Epstein (1987) and Yano (1993) point out the possibility of a transfer paradox by focusing on the difference between Walrasian stability and saddle-point stability. Along this line Gombi and Ikeda (2003) incorporate habit formation in a two-country dynamic model and show the paradox to arise under the saddle-point stability. Fries (1983) obtains the paradox by assuming production uncertainty and no asset trade while Galor and Polemarchakis (1987) finds the paradox on a non-efficient path in an overlapping generations framework. There are also some studies that explore the possibility of Pareto-superior aid. In a static model it arises when the aid is tied to either relaxation of a quantitative restriction (Lahiri and Raimondos-Møller, 1995) or a tariff reform (Lahiri and Raimondos-Møller, 1997). Without international borrowing and lending it also arises in a two-period setting (Djajic *et al.*, 1999) and in

---

[2] See http://usinfo.state.gov/usa/infousa/facts/democrac/57.htm for this statement.
[3] See Bhagwati *et al.* (1983, 1985) for a general analysis of the transfer paradox with distortions in static two-country and three-country frameworks.

an infinite-time setting (Shimomura, 2007). However, none of them treats the case of unemployment.

This paper focuses on the case of unemployment. In the presence of unemployment an increase in the recipient country's import owing to a transfer may cause the donor country to expand employment and hence increase total production. Thus, the transfer paradox may arise through an increase in the donor country's income rather than a change in the terms of trade. Moreover, if the recipient country then faces full employment, receiving a transfer benefits it. Thus, a transfer from a country with unemployment to a country with full unemployment may benefit both the donor and recipient countries. The Marshall Plan may in fact have brought net benefits to not only European countries but also the USA through an employment creating effect of the European demand increase.

When treating macroeconomic fluctuations in an open economy context, the new open economy macroeconomic models, e.g., Obstfeld and Rogoff (1995), Christiano *et al.* (1997), Hau (2000), and Betts and Devereux (2000a, 2000b), are widely utilized.[4] Using a period analysis with monopolistic competition and nominal price/wage stickiness they assume that prices/wages can be modified only at the beginning of each period, and examine the effects of various policies that are executed in the middle of the period. In this setup unemployment arises only in the period and full employment recovers in the next period and thereafter. Thus, they cannot deal with persistent unemployment.

To show a transfer paradox that may arise in the presence of persistent unemployment, this paper uses a two-country dynamic model that accommodates persistent unemployment, presented by Ono (2006).[5] In this framework Walrasian sluggish adjustment of nominal wages is assumed, and nevertheless a transfer paradox is found to arise. For example, a transfer from a country with unemployment to a country with full employment benefits both countries. Moreover, if both countries face unemployment, a transfer benefits the donor country and harms the recipient country.

In what follows the basic structure of the model is presented in Section 2. Section 3 describes three kinds of steady states; full employment in both countries, full employment in a country and unemployment in the other, and unemployment in both countries, and shows conditions under which each case arises. Furthermore, the effect of a transfer is examined in each case. It is generally found that a transfer from a country with unemployment benefits itself whereas a transfer from a country with full employment harms itself. Some concluding remarks are made in Section 4.

---

[4] See Lane (2001) for an extensive survey on the new open economy macroeconomics.

[5] In a closed economy setting Ono (1994, 2001) presents a dynamic optimization monetary model that accommodates persistent unemployment. Ono (2006) extends it to an international context and shows that fiscal spending raises employment and consumption in the country since it leads to a currency depreciation, which in turn decreases employment and consumption in the other country.

2. The model

There are two countries, the home and the foreign country. They produce different commodities: the home country's product is called commodity 1 and the other's is called commodity 2. Each production technology is assumed to be linear-homogeneous,

$$y_1 = \theta_1 l, \qquad y_2^* = \theta_2 l^*, \tag{1}$$

where y_1 and y_2^* are each country's output, l and l^* labor input, and θ_1 and θ_2 constant input–output coefficients.

Households of the two countries consume both commodities. The instantaneous utility of the representative household in each country is

$$u(c_1, c_2) + v(m), \qquad u^*(c_1^*, c_2^*) + v^*(m^*),$$

where c_i is the home country's consumption of commodity i ($i = 1, 2$) and * represents the foreign country's variables. Money utility functions $v(m)$ and $v^*(m^*)$ satisfy the following properties:[6]

$$v'(m) > 0, \quad v''(m) < 0, \quad \lim_{m \to 0} v'(m)m > 0,$$

$$v^{*\prime}(m^*) > 0, \quad v^{*\prime\prime}(m^*) < 0, \quad \lim_{m^* \to 0} v^{*\prime}(m^*)m^* > 0. \tag{2}$$

Consumption utility functions $u(c_1, c_2)$ and $u^*(c_1^*, c_2^*)$ are assumed to have the same functional form:

$$u(c_1, c_2) = (1/\sigma) \ln\left(\kappa_1 c_1^\sigma + \kappa_2 c_2^\sigma\right),$$

$$u^*(c_1^*, c_2^*) = (1/\sigma) \ln\left(\kappa_1 c_1^{*\sigma} + \kappa_2 c_2^{*\sigma}\right).$$

Under this utility function general price levels P and P^* in the two countries are given by functions of only the nominal prices of the two commodities. They are

$$P = 1/\left[\kappa_1^{1/(1-\sigma)} P_1^{-\sigma/(1-\sigma)} + \kappa_2^{1/(1-\sigma)} (\varepsilon P_2^*)^{-\sigma/(1-\sigma)}\right]^{(1-\sigma)/\sigma},$$

$$P^* = 1/\left[\kappa_1^{1/(1-\sigma)} (P_1/\varepsilon)^{-\sigma/(1-\sigma)} + \kappa_2^{1/(1-\sigma)} (P_2^*)^{-\sigma/(1-\sigma)}\right]^{(1-\sigma)/\sigma}, \tag{3}$$

where P_1 and P_2^* are respectively the nominal prices of the two commodities and ε is the nominal exchange rate. From (3), real commodity prices p_1 and p_2 are

$$p_1(\omega)(\equiv P_1/P) = \left[\kappa_1^{1/(1-\sigma)} + \kappa_2^{1/(1-\sigma)} \omega^{-\sigma/(1-\sigma)}\right]^{(1-\sigma)/\sigma},$$

$$p_2(\omega)(\equiv P_2^*/P^*) = \omega p_1(\omega) = \left[\kappa_1^{1/(1-\sigma)} \omega^{\sigma/(1-\sigma)} + \kappa_2^{1/(1-\sigma)}\right]^{(1-\sigma)/\sigma}, \tag{4}$$

---

[6] The last property of $v(m)$ and that of $v^*(m^*)$ in (2) are imposed to rule out hyper-inflationary paths, as in the standard money-in-utility model (see Blanchard and Fischer, 1989, pp. 241–243).

where ω is the relative commodity price:

$$\omega = \varepsilon P_2^* / P_1.$$

Since $P^* = P/\varepsilon$ from (3), inflation rates $\pi \, (= \dot{P}/P)$ and $\pi^* \, (= \dot{P}^*/P^*)$ satisfy

$$\pi - \dot{\varepsilon}/\varepsilon = \pi^*.$$

This equation and the no-arbitrage condition of financial assets:

$$R + \dot{\varepsilon}/\varepsilon = R^*$$

yield

$$r = R - \pi = R^* - \pi^*,$$

i.e., the real interest rate is internationally the same.

Each household holds two kinds of assets, the currency of his (or her) own country m or m^* and international interest-bearing assets b or b^*, where b and b^* are assumed to be homogeneous real bonds. The currency of the other country is not held by a household since it yields neither interest nor utility. Therefore, his (or her) asset constraint is

$$a = b + m, \qquad a^* = b^* + m^*, \tag{5}$$

all measured in real terms. Since real interest rate r is internationally the same, as stated above, the flow budget equation is

$$\dot{a} = ra + wx - c - Rm, \qquad \dot{a}^* = ra^* + w^*x^* - c^* - R^*m^*, \tag{6}$$

where w and w^* are real wages and x and x^* are actual labor supplies.[7] Each household's labor endowment is normalized to unity, but x (or x^*) may not necessarily be unity since unemployment may arise. They are

$$x = \min(1, l), \qquad x^* = \min(1, l^*).$$

The households maximize

$$U = \int_0^\infty \big(u(c_1, c_2) + v(m) \big) \exp(-\rho t) \, dt,$$

$$U^* = \int_0^\infty \big(u^*(c_1^*, c_2^*) + v^*(m^*) \big) \exp(-\rho t) \, dt,$$

---

[7] The nominal flow budget equation is

$$\dot{A} = Wx + RPb - Pc,$$

where $A \, (= Pa)$ represents nominal total assets. Equation (6) is derived from this equation and (5).

subject to (5) and (6), where both households have the same subjective discount rate ρ. The first-order intratemporal optimal conditions are

$$p_1(\omega)c_1 = \delta(\omega)c, \qquad p_2(\omega)c_2 = [1 - \delta(\omega)]c,$$
$$p_1(\omega)c_1^* = \delta(\omega)c^*, \qquad p_2(\omega)c_2^* = [1 - \delta(\omega)]c^*, \qquad (7)$$

where c and c^* represent each household's consumption expenditure and $\delta(\omega)$ is the expenditure share of commodity 1 that satisfies

$$\delta(\omega) = \kappa_1^{1/(1-\sigma)} / \left[\kappa_1^{1/(1-\sigma)} + \kappa_2^{1/(1-\sigma)} \omega^{-\sigma/(1-\sigma)} \right]$$
$$= 1 + p_1'(\omega)\omega/p_1(\omega) = p_2'(\omega)\omega/p_2(\omega),$$
$$1 > \delta(\omega) > 0, \quad \delta'(\omega) = [\sigma/(1-\sigma)][\delta(1-\delta)/\omega] > 0. \qquad (8)$$

The Euler equations are

$$\rho + \dot{c}/c + \pi = R = v'(m)c, \qquad \rho + \dot{c}^*/c^* + \pi^* = R^* = v^{*\prime}(m^*)c^*, \qquad (9)$$

and the transversality conditions are

$$\lim_{t \to \infty} \lambda(t)a(t) \exp(-\rho t) = 0, \qquad \lim_{t \to \infty} \lambda^*(t)a^*(t) \exp(-\rho t) = 0, \qquad (10)$$

where λ and λ^* are the co-state variables of a and a^* respectively.

Since the markets of each money and the international asset perfectly adjust, in the money markets:

$$M/P = m, \qquad M^*/P^* = m^*, \qquad (11)$$

and in the international asset market:

$$b + b^* = 0. \qquad (12)$$

Adjustments of the internationally integrated commodity markets are also perfect, and hence from (7)

$$\theta_1 x = c_1 + c_1^* = \delta(\omega)(c + c^*)/p_1(\omega),$$
$$\theta_2 x^* = c_2 + c_2^* = [1 - \delta(\omega)](c + c^*)/p_2(\omega). \qquad (13)$$

In contrast, the labor market is internationally segmented and nominal wage adjustment in each country is sluggish so that unemployment may exist. Nominal wages W $(= Pw)$ and W^* $(= P^*w^*)$ adjust in a sluggish manner, depending on the respective excess demand rate:[8]

$$\dot{W}/W = \alpha(l - 1), \qquad \dot{W}^*/W^* = \alpha^*(l^* - 1). \qquad (14)$$

---

[8] This assumption is imposed in order to allow disequilibrium to occur in the labor market; otherwise the possibility of unemployment is intrinsically avoided. Note that under this assumption the possibility of full employment in steady state is not eliminated. In fact, the next section obtains the full employment steady state under this assumption. See van der Ploeg (1993) for the same type of sluggish price adjustment.

Under the linear technology represented by (1), if $\theta_1 P_1 > W$, then $l = \infty$ and thus W immediately increases to $\theta_1 P_1$ even under the sluggish wage adjustment in (14). If $\theta_1 P_1 < W$, then $l = 0$ and hence commodity supply is zero, causing P_1 to jump upward so that $\theta_1 P_1 = W$ owing to perfect adjustment of the commodity market. Thereafter, l takes the level under which the commodity market equilibrium obtains and P_1 and W in parallel follow (14) in which actual labor supply x replaces l. The movements of P_2^* and W^* analogously obtain. Therefore, at any point in time

$$p_1\theta_1 = w(= W/P), \qquad p_2\theta_2 = w^*(= W^*/P^*),$$
$$\dot{P}_1/P_1 = \dot{W}/W = \alpha(x-1), \qquad \dot{P}_2^*/P_2^* = \dot{W}^*/W^* = \alpha^*(x^*-1). \tag{15}$$

From (15) and the definition of $\delta(\omega)$ given in (8), inflation rates π and π^* are

$$\pi = \alpha(x-1) + [1-\delta(\omega)]\dot{\omega}/\omega, \qquad \pi^* = \alpha^*(x^*-1) - \delta(\omega)\dot{\omega}/\omega. \tag{16}$$

Equations (5), (6), (11) and the first two equations of (15) yield the foreign-asset dynamics:

$$\dot{b} = rb + p_1\theta_1 x - c, \qquad \dot{b}^* = rb^* + p_2\theta_2 x^* - c^*. \tag{17}$$

Obviously, the two equations imply each other under (12) and (13).

3. International transfer

This section obtains the steady state conditions with full employment and those with unemployment, and examines the effect of an international transfer on employment and consumption in the recipient and donor countries. Whether full employment is realized or not, in the steady state c stays constant and each country's current account is balanced. Therefore, from (9) and (17),

$$c = \rho b + p_1\theta_1 x, \qquad c^* = -\rho b + p_2\theta_2 x^*. \tag{18}$$

3.1. Full employment in both countries

First, the case of full employment in the two countries is considered as a benchmark. In this case,

$$x = 1, \qquad x^* = 1,$$

and then from (18)

$$c = \rho b + p_1\theta_1, \qquad c^* = -\rho b + p_2\theta_2.$$

Therefore, from (8) and (13) ω, c and c^* are

$$\omega = (\kappa_2/\kappa_1)(\theta_1/\theta_2)^{1-\sigma},$$
$$c = \kappa_1\theta_1^\sigma[\kappa_1\theta_1^\sigma + \kappa_2\theta_2^\sigma]^{(1-\sigma)/\sigma} + \rho b,$$
$$c^* = \kappa_2\theta_2^\sigma[\kappa_1\theta_1^\sigma + \kappa_2\theta_2^\sigma]^{(1-\sigma)/\sigma} - \rho b. \tag{19}$$

From (19) it is found that a reduction in b reduces c and increases c^*. Thus, a transfer from a country to the other naturally harms the donor country and benefits the receipient country. The transfer paradox does not arise in this case.

From (9) and (19), in this state real balances m and m^* must satisfy

$$v'(m)\{\kappa_1\theta_1^\sigma[\kappa_1\theta_1^\sigma + \kappa_2\theta_2^\sigma]^{(1-\sigma)/\sigma} + \rho b\} = \rho,$$
$$v^{*\prime}(m^*)\{\kappa_2\theta_2^\sigma[\kappa_1\theta_1^\sigma + \kappa_2\theta_2^\sigma]^{(1-\sigma)/\sigma} - \rho b\} = \rho. \tag{20}$$

3.2. Transfer from a country with unemployment to a country with full employment

A liquidity trap is introduced into the present model and the possibility of unemployment in the steady state is examined. Equation (9) gives liquidity demand functions in the two countries:

$$R = v'(m)c, \qquad R^* = v^{*\prime}(m^*)c^*.$$

From (2), R (or R^*) is found to be negatively related to m (or m^*). A liquidity trap arises if $v'(m)$ (or $v^{*\prime}(m^*)$) has a positive lower bound:[9]

$$v'(\infty) = \beta > 0, \qquad v^{*\prime}(\infty) = \beta^* > 0. \tag{21}$$

In this case R (or R^*) decreasingly approaches a positive constant given by βc (or $\beta^* c^*$) and stays there as m (or m^*) increases (see Figure 1).

In the presence of the liquidity trap the solutions of m and m^* that satisfy (20) may not exist. The condition under which m (or m^*) does not exist is

$$\rho b \geqslant \rho/\beta - \kappa_1\theta_1^\sigma(\kappa_1\theta_1^\sigma + \kappa_2\theta_2^\sigma)^{(1-\sigma)/\sigma} \iff m \text{ does not exist.}$$
$$\rho b \leqslant \kappa_2\theta_2^\sigma(\kappa_1\theta_1^\sigma + \kappa_2\theta_2^\sigma)^{(1-\sigma)/\sigma} - \rho/\beta^* \iff m^* \text{ does not exist.} \tag{22}$$

Therefore, in the steady state the home country faces unemployment and the foreign country realizes full employment if b satisfies

$$\rho b \geqslant \min(\rho/\beta - \kappa_1\theta_1^\sigma(\kappa_1\theta_1^\sigma + \kappa_2\theta_2^\sigma)^{(1-\sigma)/\sigma},$$
$$\kappa_2\theta_2^\sigma(\kappa_1\theta_1^\sigma + \kappa_2\theta_2^\sigma)^{(1-\sigma)/\sigma} - \rho/\beta^*).$$

It implies that a country with great foreign assets tends to face unemployment since it has to consume so much above interest earnings from abroad that demand becomes

---

[9] This property is empirically shown by Ono (1994, Chapter 3), and more extensively by Ono *et al.* (2004) using both a parametric and a non-parametric approach. Theoretically, this property obtains in Veblen's framework (1899) where households care about 'status'. For example, if $v(m)$ is replaced by $v(m - \bar{m})$, where $\bar{m}$ implies the social average of m, $v'(m - \bar{m})$ stays to be fixed at $v'(0)$ as m expands since m always equals $\bar{m}$ in the present setting. By regarding this value to be β, the following argument is valid. See Clark and Oswald (1998) for an extensive survey on the 'status' literature.

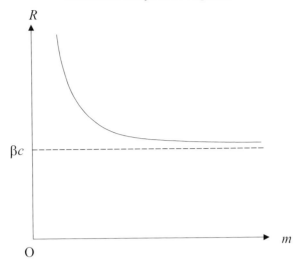

Fig. 1. Money demand with a liquidity trap.

large enough to support full employment. It is easier for a country with great debts to realize full employment since people have to work enough to pay interests to the foreign country in addition to its own consumption expenditure.

In this asymmetric steady state[10] x and x^* satisfy

$$x < 1, \qquad x^* = 1.$$

Then, from (9), (13), (16) and (18),

$$R = \beta c = \rho + \alpha(x - 1),$$
$$0 < \theta_1 x = \theta_2(\kappa_1\omega/\kappa_2)^{1/(1-\sigma)} < \theta_1, \tag{23}$$

which give c and x as functions of ω. From (23),

$$dx/d\omega > 0, \qquad dc/dx > 0. \tag{24}$$

It implies that a deterioration in the terms of trade raises the employment rate and hence stimulates consumption in the country that faces unemployment. Note that c and x are both represented by functions of only ω. Finally, ω is determined so that it satisfies (17). Substituting c and x derived from (23) into the first equation of (17) yields

$$\dot{b} = \rho b - (\rho - \alpha)/\beta$$
$$+ p_2(\omega)\theta_2(\kappa_1/\kappa_2)^{1/(1-\sigma)}\omega^{\sigma/(1-\sigma)}\left[1 - \alpha/\left(\beta p_1(\omega)\theta_1\right)\right] = 0. \tag{25}$$

---

[10] The stability is analyzed in Appendix A.

Once ω is thus determined, the steady state levels of c and x are determined by (23). Furthermore, c^* is determined by the first equation of (18) in which $x^* = 1$:

$$c^* = -\rho b + p_2(\omega)\theta_2. \tag{26}$$

From (4) and (26),

$$\partial c^*/\partial \omega > 0, \qquad \partial c^*/\partial b < 0, \tag{27}$$

i.e., a rise in ω or a decrease in b (or equivalently an increase in b^*) benefits the foreign country. It implies a standard property: a country that realizes full employment benefits from an improvement in its terms of trade or an increase in its foreign assets. Note that the effects on consumption and employment of an improvement in the terms of trade are quite opposite to those of the country with unemployment, as shown by (24).

Given the above properties, the effects of a change in b on consumption in the two countries are examined. From (25),

$$\partial \dot{b}/\partial b = \rho > 0.$$

Therefore, if the following property:[11]

The Marshall–Lerner condition: $\partial \dot{b}/\partial \omega > 0$,

is valid, then

$$d\omega/db < 0,$$

i.e., an increase in a country's foreign asset holding lowers the relative price of the foreign product. Therefore, (24) and (27) imply

$$dx/db < 0, \qquad dc/db < 0; \qquad dc^*/db < 0.$$

Formally,

PROPOSITION 1. *Suppose that a country faces unemployment and that the other realizes full employment. If the Marshall–Lerner condition is valid, a transfer from the country with unemployment to the country with full employment increases employment and consumption in not only the recipient country but also the donor country.*

The proposition is intuitively explained as follows. If a country transfers some wealth to the other country so that its foreign asset holding decreases, its current account deteriorates, causing its currency to depreciate and hence the relative price of its product to be lower. The price reduction benefits the donor country if it faces unemployment since it expands world demand for its product and thus increases employment and consumption. Furthermore, if the recipient country realizes full employment, the transfer makes it richer through an increase in its foreign asset holding and

---

[11] Sufficient conditions for this property to be valid are discussed in Appendix A.

an improvement in the terms of trade. Thus, if the donor country faces unemployment and the recipient country realizes full employment, a transfer increases consumption in both countries.

3.3. Stagnation in both countries

If both conditions in (22) hold and hence

$$\kappa_2\theta_2^\sigma \left(\kappa_1\theta_1^\sigma + \kappa_2\theta_2^\sigma\right)^{(1-\sigma)/\sigma} - \rho/\beta^*$$
$$\geq \rho b \geq \rho/\beta - \kappa_1\theta_1^\sigma \left(\kappa_1\theta_1^\sigma + \kappa_2\theta_2^\sigma\right)^{(1-\sigma)/\sigma} \tag{28}$$

the two countries face a shortage of demand, causing unemployment to arise. This case exists if

$$\left(\kappa_1\theta_1^\sigma + \kappa_2\theta_2^\sigma\right)^{1/\sigma} \geq \rho/\beta + \rho/\beta^*. \tag{29}$$

This is the case where both countries' liquidity preference and productivity are large – i.e., the world supply capacity exceeds the world demand capability.

Note that from (20) the steady state in which both countries realize full employment is possible only if

$$\rho/\beta - \kappa_1\theta_1^\sigma \left(\kappa_1\theta_1^\sigma + \kappa_2\theta_2^\sigma\right)^{(1-\sigma)/\sigma} \geq \rho b \geq \kappa_2\theta_2^\sigma \left(\kappa_1\theta_1^\sigma + \kappa_2\theta_2^\sigma\right)^{(1-\sigma)/\sigma} - \rho/\beta^*,$$

implying that under (29) the steady state with full employment in both countries never obtains. Thus, if there is b under which the steady state with unemployment in both countries obtains, the steady state with full employment in both countries never arises.

In the steady state with unemployment in both countries prices and wages to continue to decline in both countries, making $v'(m)$ and $v^{*'}(m^*)$ converge to β and β^* respectively, as assumed in (21). Therefore, from (9) and (16) in which c, c^* and ω stay constant, c, c^*, x and x^* satisfy

$$\beta c = \rho + \alpha(x - 1), \qquad x = \delta(\omega)(c + c^*)/\left[p_1(\omega)\theta_1\right],$$
$$\beta^* c^* = \rho + \alpha^*(x^* - 1), \qquad x^* = \left[1 - \delta(\omega)\right](c + c^*)/\left[p_2(\omega)\theta_2\right]. \tag{30}$$

From (18) and (30), x and x^* are given by

$$x = x(\omega, b) \equiv (\rho - \alpha - \beta\rho b)/\left[\beta p_1(\omega)\theta_1 - \alpha\right],$$
$$x^* = x^*(\omega, b) \equiv (\rho - \alpha^* + \beta^*\rho b)/\left[\beta^* p_2(\omega)\theta_2 - \alpha^*\right].$$

In order to satisfy (i) an increase in c^* (or c) raises c (or c^*), and (ii) x (or x^*) is between 1 and 0 when $b = 0$, in (30), the following conditions must hold.[12]

$$\beta p_1\theta_1 > \rho > \alpha, \qquad \beta^* p_2\theta_2 > \rho > \alpha^*. \tag{31}$$

---

[12] This steady state is the same as presented by Ono (2006). He shows that these conditions are required for the dynamic stability to hold.

From (4), (30) and (31),

$$\partial x(\omega, b)/\partial \omega > 0, \qquad \partial x(\omega, b)/\partial b < 0, \qquad \partial c/\partial \omega > 0, \qquad \partial c/\partial b < 0,$$
$$\partial x^*(\omega, b)/\partial \omega < 0, \qquad \partial x^*(\omega, b)/\partial b > 0, \qquad \partial c^*/\partial \omega < 0, \qquad \partial x^*/\partial \omega > 0. \tag{32}$$

Substituting c and x that satisfy (30) into (17) yields

$$\dot{b} = \rho b + \{[(\rho - \alpha^*)\delta(\omega)/\beta^*][1 - \alpha/(\beta p_1(\omega)\theta_1)]$$
$$- [(\rho - \alpha)(1 - \delta(\omega))/\beta][1 - \alpha^*/(\beta^* p_2(\omega)\theta_2)]\}/A, \tag{33}$$

where

$$A = 1 - \alpha\delta(\omega)/[\beta p_1(\omega)\theta_1] - \alpha^*[1 - \delta(\omega)]/[\beta^* p_2(\omega)\theta_2] > 0.$$

Relative price ω is determined so that $\dot{b} = 0$. Once ω obtains, from (30) c, x, c^* and x^* are determined.

Since $\partial\dot{b}/\partial b = \rho > 0$ from (33), under the Marshall–Lerner condition:

$$\partial\dot{b}/\partial\omega > 0, \tag{34}$$

it is satisfied that

$$d\omega/db < 0. \tag{35}$$

Therefore, an increase in the foreign asset improves the current account and thus raises the value of its own currency, causing the relative price of the foreign commodity to decrease. Furthermore, if the country faces unemployment, it harms the competitiveness of its products and hence worsens unemployment, as represented in (32). It lowers consumption. In fact, from (32) and (35),

$$dx/db < 0, \qquad dc/db < 0, \qquad dx^*/db > 0, \qquad dc^*/db > 0.$$

These properties are summarized as follows:

PROPOSITION 2. *If unemployment exists in both countries and the Marshall–Lerner condition holds, a country's transfer to the other improves employment and increases consumption in the donor country. It in turn decreases employment and consumption in the recipient country.*

Thus, it is beneficial for a country with unemployment to transfer its foreign assets to the other country whether the recipient country realizes full employment or not. However, it is harmful for a country with full employment to transfer its foreign asset to the other.

4. Conclusion

In a standard two-country setting with full employment an international transfer mostly benefits the recipient country but harms the donor country. It is because the donor country reduces, and the recipient country raises, wealth through the transfer. In the presence of unemployment in the donor country, however, there is a room for it to expand national income through an increase in employment. Therefore, if the transfer stimulates employment, both countries may benefit from it. This paper examines this property and finds that a transfer from a country with unemployment to a country with full employment increases consumption in both countries.

The mechanism is the following. An asset transfer deteriorates the donor country's current account, causing its currency to depreciate and hence the price of its products to decline. Therefore, it enlarges world demand for the products and thus expands employment in the donor country. If the increase in employment equals the increase in interest payments to the recipient country, the donor country suffers no net loss: people in the donor country work more exactly to cover the additional interest payment. In this case, however, employment is larger than the level before the transfer, causing the deflation rate to be smaller. Therefore, consumption as well as employment is stimulated, which benefits the donor country.

This property provides a somewhat paradoxical implication of foreign aid. Developing countries are poor because of smaller productivity whereas developed countries may stagnate because of a demand shortage. In such a case a transfer from a developed country to a developing country benefits not only the recipient country by an increase in its wealth but also the donor country by an increase in its employment. Therefore, it is better for them to increase foreign aid so that the recipient countries' demand for the donors' products stimulates the donors' business activities especially when they face serious unemployment. In reality, however, developed countries tend to reduce foreign aid in such a case.

Appendix A. Stability and the Marshall–Lerner condition

Stability: Since the local stability of the dynamics around the steady state with unemployment in both countries is analyzed by Ono (2006), this appendix focuses on the stability around the asymmetric steady state, where $v'(m) = \beta$. From (9), (14), (16) and the time differentiation of (11),

$$\dot{\omega} = \left\{ \left[\beta - v^{*\prime}(m^*)\gamma \right] c - \alpha(x-1) + \alpha^*(x^*-1) \right\} \omega,$$
$$\dot{c} = \left\{ \delta(\omega) \left[\beta c - \alpha(x-1) - \rho \right] + \left[1 - \delta(\omega) \right] \left[v^{*\prime}(m^*)\gamma c - \alpha^*(x^*-1) - \rho \right] \right\} c,$$
$$\dot{m}^* = \left\{ \delta(\omega) \left\{ \left[\beta - v^{*\prime}(m^*)\gamma \right] c - \alpha(x-1) \right\} - \left[1 - \delta(\omega) \right] \alpha^*(x^*-1) \right\} m^*,$$

where x and x^* are given by (13) and $\gamma = c^*/c$, which is constant over time. The steady state is given by (23). Thus, the characteristic equation in the neighborhood of the steady state is

$$\begin{vmatrix} -[\alpha/(1-\sigma)][\alpha x + \delta(\alpha^* - \alpha x)] - \lambda & (\alpha^* - \alpha)\omega/c & -v^{*\prime\prime}\gamma c\omega \\ [\delta(1-\delta)/(1-\sigma)](\alpha^* - \alpha x)c/\omega & [\rho - \delta\alpha - (1-\delta)\alpha^*] - \lambda & (1-\delta)v^{*\prime\prime}\gamma c^2 \\ [\delta(1-\delta)/(1-\sigma)](\alpha^* - \alpha x)m^*/\omega & -[\delta\alpha + (1-\delta)\alpha^*]m^*/c & -\delta v^{*\prime\prime}\gamma cm^* - \lambda \end{vmatrix}$$
$$= 0,$$

where λ is a characteristic root. This equation reduces to

$$\lambda^3 + A_2\lambda^2 + A_1\lambda + A_0 = 0,$$

where

$$\begin{aligned} A_2 &= -(\lambda_1 + \lambda_2 + \lambda_3) \\ &= -\rho + \big(\delta\alpha + (1-\delta)\alpha^*\big) + \delta v^{*\prime\prime}(m^*)m^*\gamma c + \big[\alpha x(1-\delta) + \alpha^*\delta\big]/(1-\sigma), \\ A_1 &= -v^{*\prime\prime}(m^*)m^*\gamma c\{\delta\rho - \big[\delta\alpha + (1-\delta)\alpha^* + \delta\alpha^*/(1-\sigma)\big]\} \\ &\quad - \big[(1-\delta)\alpha x(\rho - \alpha^*) + \delta\alpha^*(\rho - \alpha)\big]/(1-\sigma), \\ A_0 &= -\lambda_1\lambda_2\lambda_3 = -\alpha^* v^{*\prime\prime}(m^*)m^*\gamma c\{\delta\rho - \alpha\big[\delta + x(1-\delta)\big]\}/(1-\sigma). \end{aligned}$$

Note that λ_1, λ_2 and λ_3 are the three solutions of λ. Therefore, if

$$\alpha \ll \rho, \tag{A.1}$$

then $A_0 > 0$ and $A_2 < 0$, implying that the real parts of the three solutions of λ must be two positive numbers and a negative number. Since c and ω are jumpable while m^* is not, the equilibrium path is saddle-stable for a given γ.

Note that none of the dynamic equations of c, ω and m^* depends on b. The dynamic equation of b is

$$\dot{b} = rb + p_1\theta_1 x - c,$$

where $\partial\dot{b}/\partial b = \rho > 0$ in the neighborhood of the steady state. Therefore, the dynamics of b is unstable and hence γ is chosen so that $\dot{b}$ eventually becomes zero.

The Marshall–Lerner condition: The validity of the Marshall–Lerner condition is examined in the case where the donor country faces unemployment and the other realizes full employment and in the case where both countries face unemployment.

First, in the asymmetric case from (8) and (25) one obtains

$$\begin{aligned} \partial\dot{b}/\partial\omega &= \big[\theta_2/(\beta\theta_1)\big](\kappa_1/\kappa_2)^{1/(1-\sigma)}\omega^{\sigma/(1-\sigma)} \\ &\quad \times \{[1 - (1-\sigma)(1-\delta)]\beta p_1(\omega)\theta_1 - \alpha\}/(1-\sigma). \end{aligned}$$

Therefore, if (31) is valid (i.e., $\beta p_1(\omega)\theta_1 - \alpha > 0$) and σ is close to 1, the Marshall–Lerner condition holds.

Since the second property of (23) implies

$$\omega < (\kappa_2/\kappa_1)(\theta_1/\theta_2)^{1-\sigma},$$

and $p_1(\omega)$ is given by (4), $\beta p_1(\omega)\theta_1 - \alpha$ is positive if

$$\beta\kappa_1\theta_1^\sigma\big(\kappa_1\theta_1^\sigma + \kappa_2\theta_2^\sigma\big)^{(1-\sigma)/\sigma} - \alpha > 0. \tag{A.2}$$

From the first property of (22), full employment cannot be reached when b equals zero if

$$\rho \leqslant \beta \kappa_1 \theta_1^\sigma \left(\kappa_1 \theta_1^\sigma + \kappa_2 \theta_2^\sigma\right)^{(1-\sigma)/\sigma}.$$

Note that this implies (A.2) when (A.1) is valid.

Next, in the case of unemployment in both countries the home country's current account is obtained by substituting x and c that satisfy (30) into the first equation of (17). It is

$$\dot{b} = \rho b + \left\{ \frac{(\rho - \alpha^*)\delta(\omega)}{\beta^*}\left(1 - \frac{\alpha}{\beta p_1(\omega)\theta_1}\right) \right. $$
$$\left. - \frac{(\rho - \alpha)[1 - \delta(\omega)]}{\beta}\left(1 - \frac{\alpha^*}{\beta^* p_2(\omega)\theta_2}\right)\right\}/A,$$

from which

$$\partial \dot{b}/\partial\omega = \left\{\left[\sigma - \alpha/(\beta p_1 \theta_1)\right](\rho - \alpha^*)/\beta^* + \left[\sigma - \alpha^*/(\beta^* p_2 \theta_2)\right](\rho - \alpha)/\beta\right\}$$
$$\times \delta(1 - \delta)/\left[(1 - \sigma)A\right] + (dA/d\omega)\rho b/A.$$

From (31), as long as b is small, $\partial \dot{b}/\partial\omega > 0$ if σ is close to 1.

In sum, in both cases the Marshall–Lerner condition is valid if (31) is valid and σ is close to 1.

References

Betts, C., Devereux, M.B. (2000a), Exchange rate dynamics in a model of pricing-to-market. *Journal of International Economics* 50, 215–244.

Betts, C., Devereux, M.B. (2000b), International monetary policy coordination and competitive depreciation: a reevaluation. *Journal of Money, Credit, and Banking* 32, 722–745.

Bhagwati, J.N., Brecher, R.A., Hatta, T. (1983), The generalized theory of transfers and welfare: bilateral transfers in a multilateral world. *American Economic Review* 73, 606–618.

Bhagwati, J.N., Brecher, R.A., Hatta, T. (1985), The generalized theory of transfers and welfare: exogenous (policy-imposed) and endogenous (transfer-induced) distortions. *Quarterly Journal of Economics* 100, 697–714.

Blanchard, O.J., Fischer, S. (1989), *Lectures on Macroeconomics*. MIT Press, Cambridge, MA.

Brandt Commission (1980), *North–South: A Programme for Survival*. Pan Books, London.

Brandt Commission (1983), *Common Crisis North–South: Cooperation for World Recovery*. MIT Press, Cambridge, MA.

Christiano, L.J., Eichenbaum, M., Evance, C.L. (1997), Sticky prices and limited participation models of money: a comparison. *European Economic Review* 41, 1201–1249.

Clark, A.E., Oswald, A.J. (1998), Comparison-concave utility and following behaviour in social and economic setting. *Journal of Public Economic* 70, 133–155.

Djajic, S., Lahiri, S., Raimondos-Møller, P. (1999), Foreign aid, domestic investment and welfare. *Economic Journal* 109, 698–707.

Epstein, L.G. (1987), A simple dynamic general equilibrium model. *Journal of Economic Theory* 41, 68–95.

Fries, T. (1983), The possibility of an immiserizing transfer under uncertainty. *Journal of International Economics* 15, 297–311.

Galor, O., Polemarchakis, H.M. (1987), Intertemporal equilibrium and the transfer paradox. *Review of Economic Studies* 54, 147–156.

Gombi, I., Ikeda, S. (2003), Habit formation and the transfer paradox. *Japanese Economic Review* 54, 361–380.

Hau, H. (2000), Exchange rate determination: the role of factor price rigidities and nontradeables. *Journal of International Economics* 50, 421–447.

Lahiri, S., Raimondos-Møller, P. (1995), Welfare effects of aid under quantitative trade restrictions. *Journal of International Economics* 39, 297–315.

Lahiri, S., Raimondos-Møller, P. (1997), On the tying of aid to tariff reform. *Journal of Development Economics* 54, 479–491.

Lane, P.R. (2001), The new open economy macroeconomics: a survey. *Journal of International Economics* 54, 235–266.

Leontief, W. (1936), Note on the pure theory of capital transfer. In: Taussig, F.W. (Ed.), *Explorations in Economics: Notes and Essays Contributed in Honor of F.W. Taussig*. McGraw-Hill, New York, 84–91.

Maizels, A., Nissanke, M.K. (1984), Motivations for aid to developing countries. *World Development* 12, 879–900.

Obstfeld, M., Rogoff, K. (1995), Exchange rate dynamics redux. *Journal of Political Economy* 103, 624–660.

Ono, Y. (1994), *Money, Interest, and Stagnation*. Oxford University Press, Oxford.

Ono, Y. (2001), A reinterpretation of Chapter 17 of Keynes's *General Theory*: effective demand shortage under dynamic optimization. *International Economic Review* 42, 207–236.

Ono, Y. (2006), International asymmetry in business activity and appreciation of a stagnant country's currency. *Japanese Economic Review* 57, 101–120.

Ono, Y., Ogawa, K., Yoshida, A. (2004), Liquidity trap and persistent unemployment with dynamic optimizing agents: empirical evidence. *Japanese Economic Review* 55, 356–371.

van der Ploeg, F. (1993), Channels of international policy transmission. *Journal of International Economics* 34, 245–267.

Samuelson, P.A. (1947), *Foundations of Economic Analysis*. Harvard University Press, Cambridge, MA.

Shimomura, K. (2007), A Pareto-improving foreign aid in a dynamic North–South model. In: Lahiri, S. (Ed.), *Theory and Practice of Foreign Aid*. In: Frontiers of Economics and Globalization, vol. 1. Elsevier, Amsterdam (Chapter 9 of this volume).

Veblen, T. (1899), *The Theory of the Leisure Class*, 1934 edition. Modern Library, New York.

Yano, M. (1993), Welfare aspects of the transfer problem. *Journal of International Economics* 15, 277–289.

CHAPTER 11

A Dynamic Analysis of Tied Aid

Chi-Chur Chao[a,b], Bharat R. Hazari[c], Jean-Pierre Laffargue[d] and Eden S.H. Yu[c]

[a]*Department of Economics, Chinese University of Hong Kong, Shatin, Hong Kong*
E-mail address: ccchao@cuhk.edu.hk
[b]*Department of Economics, Oregon State University, Corvallis, OR 97330, USA*
[c]*Department of Economics & Finance, City University of Hong Kong, Kowloon, Hong Kong*
E-mail address: bhazari@gmail.com; efedenyu@cityu.edu.hk
[d]*CEPREMAP, PSE and University of Paris I, 48 Boulevard Jourdan, 75014 Paris, France*
E-mail address: jean-pierre.laffargue@wanadoo.fr

Abstract

In this paper we examine the impact of tied aid on capital accumulation and welfare in the presence of a quota on imports. Using a simulation model we establish that tied aid can lower the relative domestic price of the manufactured good and therefore reduce the stock of capital. In the presence of a strong production externality from capital accumulation and high tying ratio, tied aid may immiserize the recipient country.

Keywords: Tied aid, quotas, capital, welfare

JEL classifications: F11, F35

1. Introduction

Ever since the famous debate between Keynes (1929) and Ohlin (1929), movements in the terms of trade and its impact on welfare have been a central issue in the study of the transfer problem. Keynes claimed that aid can alter the donor's terms of trade and therefore welfare. Ohlin questioned this line of reasoning. If aid can result in the terms of trade to favour the donor country, a paradoxical result, donor enrichment and recipient impoverishment, given by Leontief (1936) may arise. However, assuming market stability, Samuelson (1952) showed that the welfare of the donor decreases while the welfare of the recipient increases, regardless of the direction of shift in the terms of trade (which may be induced, for example, by a transfer). Later research nevertheless established that the transfer paradox can still happen in a stable economy with either more than two countries or in the presence of distortions.[1] Subsequently,

---

[1] See Bhagwati *et al.* (1983) for discussions.

THEORY AND PRACTICE OF FOREIGN AID
VOLUME 1   ISSN: 1574-8715
DOI: 10.1016/S1574-8715(06)01011-6

the research on international transfers has been focused to find specific distortions that can cause transfer paradox.

Bhagwati *et al.* (1985) classify distortions into exogenous and (transfer-induced) endogenous distortions. The literature related to exogenous distortions includes Bhagwati (1971) on distortions and welfare, Brecher and Bhagwati (1982) on a production externality, Brecher (1974) and Beladi (1990) on unemployment, and Choi and Yu (1987) on variable returns to scale. In addition, exogenous distortions may arise from government policy interventions. For example, tariffs distort the importable sector of the economy (Martin (1977)). In this setting, as shown by Ohyama (1974), Jones (1985) and Yano and Nugent (1999), transfers can lower the recipient's welfare because it aggravates the tariff distortion in the importable sector.

As far as endogenous distortions induced by transfers are concerned, there exist two lines of thought that have been considered: rent-seeking and tied aid. The former activity may be unproductive, as pointed out by Bhagwati and Srinivasan (1980), and therefore aid may be wasted, while the latter imposes a restriction on usage of aid, reducing the flexibility in the recipient country. For example, Kemp and Kojima (1985) and Schweinberger (1990) discuss the case of tying aid to consumption. This forced expenditure pattern can be immiserizing for the recipient country. Recently, Lahiri and Raimondos (1995) consider aid tied to purchases of the importable good, which is under a quota restriction. Although aid in this form mitigates the trade distortion, the paradox of donor enrichment and recipient impoverishment may still arise. Chao and Yu (2001) extend their tied-aid model to a dynamic setting by focusing on the impact of tied aid on capital accumulation.[2] Although tied aid brings a direct gain, it also causes a decline in the stock of capital. The welfare effect of tied aid depends on the direct gain of aid and the induced loss of capital decumulation; therefore the overall effect is ambiguous in a dynamic setting.

The purpose of this paper is to employ a simulation method to investigate the welfare implication of aid tied to a purchase of quota-restricted imports in a dynamic economy. To highlight the role played by capital accumulation, a production externality arising from the capital stock is explicitly incorporated in the production function. This externality was first considered by Arrow (1962) in a growth framework, in which knowledge creation is a side product of investment. Essentially, each firm's knowledge is a public good so that firm can have free access to it. Romer (1986, 1989) extended this insight to model endogenous growth. Barro and Sala-i-Martin (2003) provide a comprehensive survey of this literature.[3] We will show that accumulation of capital is positively related to the price of the quota-restricted foreign good. Aid tied for purchasing the foreign good can lower its relative price and hence capital accumulation in the economy, if the tying ratio is substantial. This suggests that to avoid the fall in the capital stock, tightening import quota (i.e., zero quota) is optimal when a large capital

---

[2] Brock (1996) considers the effect of un-tied aid on capital accumulation in a dynamic framework.

[3] This production externality arising from the capital stock is employed, for example, in Liu and Turnovsky (2005).

externality is present. Thus, tied aid for relaxing quota may immiserize the recipient country. On the contrary, the optimal level of import quota is large when the capital externality is low. In this case, tied aid that relaxes the quota restriction can be welfare improving if the initial level of quota is set too low.

The paper is organized as follows. Section 2 provides a discrete-time dynamic model of trade and foreign aid. Section 3 uses a simulation method to examine optimal quota structures under various capital externalities and its welfare implications of tied aid. Section 4 provides conclusions.

2. The model

Consider a two-country model and each country produces two goods: an agricultural good X and a manufactured good Y. The home country exports good X and imports good Y. There are no restrictions on the exports of good X but a quota Q is imposed by the home country on the imports of good Y. This quota restriction limits the exports of good Y by the foreign country.[4] It is also assumed that the home country receives an aid, denoted by T, from the foreign country. To increase the exports beyond the quota level, the foreign country requires the home country to use τ portion of the aid to purchase more good Y. Total supply of good Y in the domestic economy therefore consists of domestic production, import quota and tied-aid purchase (i.e., $Y + Q + \tau T$). This form of tying aid to imports was first discussed in Lahiri and Raimondos (1995) in a static model. This paper extends their model to a dynamic analysis with capital accumulation.

2.1. Firms

The domestic firms produce goods X and Y by using labour (L_i) and capital (K_i). Total capital (K_{-1}) is inherited from the past and it can be allocated freely between sectors at the beginning of the period, i.e., $K_{-1} = K_X + K_Y$. As expressed in Romer (1986, 1989), total capital serves as a proxy for knowledge in the economy, and it yields a positive externality to the production of the manufactured good Y. The production functions are specified in the Cobb–Douglas form:

$$X = A_X L_X^{\alpha_1} K_X^{\alpha_2}, \tag{1}$$

$$Y = A_Y K_{-1}^{\beta_3} L_y^{\beta_1} K_y^{\beta_2}, \tag{2}$$

where $A_X > 0$, $A_Y > 0$, $\alpha_i > 0$, $\beta_i > 0$, for $i = 1, 2$, and $\alpha_1 + \alpha_2 < 1$ and $\beta_1 + \beta_2 < 1$ are respectively the total shares of labour and capital income in production of goods X and Y. It is assumed that $\beta_2 > \alpha_2$, i.e., the manufactured-good sector is capital intensive relative to the agricultural-good sector. It is noted that $\beta_3 \geqslant 0$,

---

[4] See Falvey (1988) for detail.

capturing the externalities from total capital to the global productivity of factors in the manufactured-good sector. The presence of this externality also highlights the role of capital accumulation in the dynamic model.

Let good X be the numeraire, and the domestic relative price of the manufactured good Y is denoted by p. The goods and factor markets are assumed to be perfectly competitive. Given the relative price p, wage rate w and the externality from K_{-1}, the production sectors choose L_i and K_i to maximize the returns on capital, i.e., Max $X + pY - w(L_X + L_Y)$, subject to (1) and (2). For a given state variable K_{-1}, the optimal conditions with respect to L_i and K_i are:

$$\alpha_1 A_X (K_X/L_X)^{\alpha_2} L_X^{\alpha_1+\alpha_2-1} = \beta_1 p A_Y K_{-1}^{\beta_3} (K_Y/L_Y)^{\beta_2} L_Y^{\beta_1+\beta_2-1} = w, \tag{3}$$

$$\alpha_2 A_X (L_X/K_X)^{\alpha_1} K_X^{\alpha_1+\alpha_2-1} = \beta_2 p A_Y K_{-1}^{\beta_3} (L_Y/K_Y)^{\beta_1} K_Y^{\beta_1+\beta_2-1} = r, \tag{4}$$

where r denotes the domestic rental rate on capital. From Equations (3) and (4), the factor price frontiers are described by

$$\left(\frac{w}{\alpha_1}\right)^{1-\alpha_2} \left(\frac{r}{\alpha_2}\right)^{\alpha_2} L_X^{(1-\alpha_1-\alpha_2)} = A_X, \tag{5}$$

$$\left(\frac{w}{\beta_1}\right)^{1-\beta_2} \left(\frac{r}{\beta_2}\right)^{\beta_2} L_Y^{(1-\beta_1-\beta_2)} = A_Y K_{-1}^{\beta_3} p. \tag{6}$$

Note that $L_X + L_Y = L$, which shows the endowment of labour. Due to the flexible wage rate, labour is fully utilized in the economy. We assume that there is no growth of the labour force in the economy.

2.2. Goods market equilibrium

Domestic households consume goods X and Y, denoted by C_X and C_Y. By the Walras' law, we need to consider the market of good Y only. In the dynamic model, the manufactured good Y is used not only for consumption (C_Y) but also for capital investment ($K - K_{-1}$). The market equilibrium condition for good Y requires the equality between its demand and supply:

$$C_Y + (K - K_{-1}) = Y + Q + \tau T. \tag{7}$$

As mentioned earlier, T is the aid received in terms of good Y and τ is the tying ratio for purchasing the quota-restricted good. Note that by letting the world price of good Y be p^*, the value of the aid is p^*T to the home economy. Thus, tied purchase of good Y is τT described in Equation (7).

2.3. Households

Households set their consumption plan over time by maximizing their intertemporal utility subject to the budget constraint. The current utility function of households is chosen as: $U(C) = C^{(1-\lambda)}/(1 - \lambda)$, where $C = [b^{1/(1+\sigma)} C_X^{\sigma/(1+\sigma)} +$

$\bar{b}^{1/(1+\sigma)}C_Y^{\sigma/(1+\sigma)}]^{(1+1/\sigma)}$ represents their total consumption. It is noted that σ is the elasticity of substitution between goods with $1 + \sigma \geqslant 0$. Here, $b \in [0, 1]$ and $\bar{b} = 1 - b$ capture the relative preferences for each good, and $\lambda > 0$ expresses the inverse of the intertemporal rate of substitution. The intertemporal utility of consumers is thus specified as: $W = \sum_{t=0}^{\infty}(1 - \rho)^t U(C)$, where $0 < \rho < 1$ is the subjective discount rate of households.

As for revenues, domestic households receive factor income from production and aid from the foreign country. Since each firm operates under decreasing returns to scale with respect to its production factors, it earns a rent. Total rent, $R = X + PY - (wL + rK_{-1})$, is assumed to be distributed to households (who own the firms). We assume that when households make their saving/investment decision, they do not internalize the positive effect of the capital externality in each manufacturing firm. Additionally, there are quota rents accrue to the domestic government, which are assumed to be returned to domestic households in a lump-sum fashion. The budget constraint of the households is: $C_X + pC_Y + p(K - K_{-1}) = wL + rK_{-1} + R + (p - p^*)(Q + \tau T) + p^*T$, where $p > p^*$ due to the quota restriction of the imports of good Y. Denoting μ as the Lagrange multiplier, the optimality conditions of the households' program for C_X, C_Y and K are:

$$b^{1/(1+\sigma)}C^{1/\sigma}C_X^{-1/(1+\sigma)} = \mu, \tag{8}$$

$$b^{1/(1+\sigma)}C^{1/\sigma}C_Y^{-1/(1+\sigma)} = \mu p, \tag{9}$$

$$\mu - \mu_{+1}(1 + r_{+1}) = 0. \tag{10}$$

Combining Equations (8) and (9), the relationship between the good price and consumption is derived as: $bC_Y/\bar{b}C_Y = p^{-(1+\sigma)}$. This gives total consumption: $C = (C_X/b)(b + \bar{b}p^{-\sigma})^{(1+\sigma)/\sigma}$. Substituting C into Equation (8) and then using Equation (10), the evolution of capital in terms of its rate of return is governed by

$$1 + r_{+1} = \frac{1}{1 - \rho}\left(\frac{C_X}{C_{X,+1}}\right)^{-\lambda}\frac{(b + \bar{b}p^{-\sigma})^{(1+1/\sigma)(1-\lambda)-1}}{(b + \bar{b}p_{+1}^{-\sigma})^{(1+1/\sigma)(1-\lambda)-1}}. \tag{11}$$

In steady state, $C_X = C_{X,+1}$ and $p = p_{+1}$, we have: $1 + r = 1/(1 - \rho)$. Hence, the rate of return on capital is approximately equal to the rate of time preference.

It is worthwhile to note the direct impact of aid on the domestic price of good Y in the steady state. Aid tied to purchase the importable good increases the supply of good Y by τ in Equation (7) for each unit of T. On the demand side, tied aid raises revenue by $p^* + \tau(p - p^*)$ expressed in the budget constraint, thereby increasing the demand for good Y: $\partial C_Y/\partial T = [p^* + \tau(p - p^*)](U_{XY} - pU_{XX})/\Delta$, where $\Delta > 0$.[5] With the given specification of U, we have: $\partial C_Y/\partial T = [p^* + \tau(p - p^*)]C_Y/(C_X + pC_Y)$.

---

[5] This can be derived by maximizing steady-state utility $U = U(C_X, C_Y)$, subject to the budget constraint: $C_X + pC_Y = I$, where $I = wL + rK + R + (p - p^*)(Q + \tau T) + p^*T$. Solving the optimal conditions, we obtain: $\partial C_Y/\partial I = (U_{XY} - pU_{XX})/\Delta$, where $\Delta = 2pU_{XY} - p^2U_{XX} - U_{YY} > 0$. Note that $\partial I/\partial T = p^* + \tau(p - p^*)$.

Consequently, the domestic price of good Y rises (falls) if the demand effect is larger (smaller) than the supply effect [i.e., $\partial C_Y/\partial T > (<)\,\tau$ or $p^* C_Y/C_X > (<)\,\tau/(1-\tau)$]. The change in the domestic price of good Y plays a crucial role in affecting capital accumulation in Equation (7) and hence welfare in the economy as a whole.

3. Simulations

3.1. Reference steady state

On the basis of the above theoretical analysis, it is instructive to conduct simulations. At the outset, we calibrate the reference steady state. Initial values for sectoral outputs, goods price and total labour employment are chosen as: $X = 0.5$, $Y = 1$, $p = 1$ and $L = 10$,[6] and parameters are specified as: $\alpha_1 = 0.60$, $\alpha_2 = 0.10$, $\beta_1 = 0.40$, $\beta_2 = 0.40$, $\beta_3 = 0.50$, $\rho = 0.05$, $\sigma = -0.50$ and $\lambda = 0.50$. The initial amount of foreign aid is set as: $T = 0.01$, and the tying ratio is absent (i.e., $\tau = 0$). We also assume that the quota on imports represents 20% of domestic output of the importable good ($Q = 0.2Y$), and that the world price of the importable good is equal to 90% of its domestic price ($p^* = 0.9p$).

Using Equations (1)–(11) in the steady state, we compute the endogenous variables: $C_X = 0.329$, $C_Y = 1.2$, $K = 8.55$, $K_X = 0.95$, $K_Y = 7.6$, $L_X = 4.2857$, $L_Y = 5.7143$, $w = 0.07$, $r = 0.0526$, $U = 2.473$ and $W = 49.4611$. In addition, we compute the direct effect of aid on the demand for good X: $\partial C_Y/\partial T = 0.706$. The eigenvalues in the neighbourhood of the reference steady state are equal to 0.4354 and 1.087. The local condition of existence and uniqueness are satisfied. As we will compare sums of discounted utilities when the convergence speed to the steady state may be slow, we simulated the model over 500 periods.[7]

3.2. Optimal quota

We first look for the optimal quota by starting from the reference steady state and then by fixing the quota at different levels. For each new value of the quota, the economy will progressively adjust to this new quota and converge to a new steady state. We will compute the value of the sum of discounted utilities of households and look for the quota that maximizes this sum. It should be noted that, in the reference steady state, the quota is equal to 20% of the reference value of the output of good Y.

---

[6] The important assumptions for the calibration are the relative sizes of both sectors and the difference between the domestic and the foreign price of the importable good. The amounts of import quota and foreign aid are also crucial.

[7] The model was simulated and its eigenvalues computed with the software Dynare, which was run under MATLAB. Dynare was developed by Michel Juillard, and can be downloaded from the website: http://www.cepremap.cnrs.fr/dynare.

(1) Consider the case when the externality coefficient β_3 is 0.5. Then the optimal quota is zero (i.e., $Q^o = 0$), suggesting no imports of good Y. When the level of quota is tightened to this level, the domestic price of the importable good Y immediately rises and then it decreases at a slow rate and converges to a value lower than its initial value ($p = 0.974$). This reduces the consumption of the importable good but raises total capital over time until $K = 11.5051$. Consequently, current utility falls as a function of tightening the quota, and it then smoothly increases and converges to a value higher than its reference value ($U = 2.7196$). The result of a zero optimal quota is due to the high degree of the capital externality. It requires a high price of good Y for accumulation of more capital. Zero quotas on imports serve this purpose. Under this condition, tied aid for importing good Y may induce a negative impact on welfare of the economy.

(2) As the capital externality gets smaller, the optimal quota becomes positive. We illustrate this point by considering the case that $\beta_3 = 0.10$.[8] The domestic price of good Y increases sharply when a lower quota is set. Then, it decreases at a slow rate and converges to a value higher than its initial value. Capital increases smoothly and converges to a higher value. Current utility decreases, then increases at a slow rate to a value higher than its reference value. The optimal quota is then equal to 17% of the reference value of the output of good Y (i.e., $Q^o = 0.17Y$). It is lower than the reference quota ($Q = 0.2Y$). So, tied aid for loosening the quota restriction may mitigate the direct gain of the aid to the economy.

(3) As for the case in which the capital externality is absent ($\beta_3 = 0$), the optimal quota becomes large and is around 0.24 time the output of good Y in the reference state ($Q^o = 0.24Y$). This is the best approximation of free trade that we can reach under the assumption of a permanent change to a constant quota. Of course, free trade is the optimal trade policy in the absence of externality. If we relax the quota by increasing it from its reference value, capital will smoothly decrease over time and converge to a lower value because the importable good is more capital intensive than the exportable good. The domestic price of imported good immediately decreases by a big amount, then it increases at a slow rate and converge to a value lower than its initial value. Current utility increases at the time of the change of policy, then smoothly decreases and converges to value lower than its reference value.

In summary, the optimal level of quota is inversely related to the degree of capital externalities. In particular, no imports are optimal when the externality is high, whereas free trade is the first-best policy for the small open economy without the cap-

---

[8] Changing the value of parameter β_3 does not alter the reference steady state, which is the initial state of the economy just before the change in the value of the quota.

ital externality. The latter result echoes the traditional wisdom on free trade for the small open economy.

3.3. Tied aid

In this section, we turn to the welfare effect of tied aid. For the following experiments, we raise the amount of T from 0.01 to 0.02 and then examine its welfare implications under various capital externalities.

(1) When the capital externality is large ($\beta_3 = 0.50$), we obtain the following changes in welfare for different values of the tying ratio in Table 1.

When aid increases without tie, capital will smoothly increase over time and converge to a higher value. The domestic price of imported good immediately increases, then it decreases at a slow rate and converge to a value lower than its initial value. Current utility decreases at the time of the change, then smoothly increases and converges to a value higher than its reference value.

These results are exactly opposite to those reached under a relaxation of the quota. Note that 0.7665 is the long run value of $\partial C_Y / \partial T$. When $\tau < 0.7665$, the effect of the increase of aid is stronger than the effect of the relaxation of the quota, and we get the same dynamics as when there aid is not tied. When $\tau > 0.7665$, the effect of the relaxation of the quota dominates the effect of the increase in aid. So, the domestic prices of the importable good and fixed capital have dynamics opposite to the previous one. When $\tau = 0.7665$, fixed capital and the price of imports remain the same. Current utility immediately increases to its higher level. Aid increases welfare, but the relaxation of the quota decreases it. For $\tau < 2.25$, the first effect dominates. However, for $\tau > 2.25$, an increase in tied aid decreases consumers' welfare. Of course, the more tied the aid, the lower the increase in welfare (or the stronger its decrease). The threshold on τ, after which tied aid decreases the welfare of the recipient country, decreases with the magnitude of the externality. For instance for $\beta_3 = 1$, the threshold is equal to 1.501.

(2) When the externality is in the intermediate range ($\beta_3 = 0.10$), the optimal quota is positive ($Q^o = 0.17Y$) but it is lower than the reference quota ($Q = 0.2Y$).

Table 1. *Large externality ($\beta_3 = 0.5$)*

τ	Increase in welfare
0	0.2368
0.7665	0.1577
1	0.1333
1.5	0.0806
2	0.0270
2.25	0
2.5	−0.0273

Table 2.   Medium externality ($\beta_3 = 0.1$)

τ	Increase in welfare
0	0.1632
0.7039	0.1582
1	0.1556

Table 3.   No externality ($\beta_3 = 0$)

τ	Increase in welfare
0	0.1443
0.7030	0.1567
1	0.1614

So, we expect to find results similar to those of the previous case, but with a slower decrease of welfare when the tying ratio τ increases. The following result in Table 2 confirms this conjecture.

(3) Finally, in the absence of externalities ($\beta_3 = 0$), the free-trade level of imports is optimal. Tied aid for relaxing the initial quota mitigates the distortion on imports of good Y. Thus, welfare of consumers increases with the larger tying ratios. Table 3 provides the result on the change in welfare.

In the case when there is no tie, or more generally when $\tau < 0.703$, capital will smoothly increase over time when aid increases and converge to a higher value. The domestic price of imported good immediately increases, and then it decreases at a slow rate and converges to a value higher than its initial value. Current utility decreases at the time of the change, then smoothly increases and converges to a value higher than its reference value.

From the above experiments, we can conclude that for a small open economy with a quota restriction on imports, tied aid for importing more manufactured good can lower its domestic price and hence reduce the capital stock in a dynamic model. However, tied aid unambiguously improves welfare since the direct gain from the aid always outweighs the loss of capital if any.

4. Concluding remarks

Using a dynamic simulation model, we have examined the welfare effect of tied aid for a small open economy with a quota restriction on imports. The economy considered receives aid which is tied to purchase the importable good from the donor country. To highlight the effect of capital accumulation, we have added an externality from total capital into the production of the manufacturing sector. Capital accumulation is positively related to the price of the capital-intensive importable good. Our simulation results show that if the tie of aid is substantial, aid can lower this good price and thus reduce capital accumulation. When the capital externality is large, the optimal quota is zero. In this case, tied aid for relaxing quota will lower capital accumulation if the tying ratio is large enough. However, this capital decumulation effect is not large enough to outweigh the direct gain from aid. It is only for very high values of the tying ratio that tied aid will immiserize the recipient country. Further, when the capital externality is low, the optimal quota is large. Tied aid that relaxes the quota is always welfare improving.

Acknowledgements

We would like to thank Sajal Lahiri for helpful suggestions. This paper was written when Jean-Pierre Laffargue was visiting at the City University of Hong Kong in April 2006. The work described in this paper was supported by a grant from the Research Grants Council of the Hong Kong Special Administrative Region, China (Project No. CUHK4603/05H).

References

Arrow, K.J. (1962), The economic implications of learning by doing. *Review of Economics Studies* 29, 155–173.

Barro, R.J., Sala-i-Martin, X. (2003), *Economic Growth*. MIT Press, Cambridge, MA.

Beladi, H. (1990), Unemployment and immiserizing transfer. *Journal of Economics* 52, 253–265.

Bhagwati, J.N. (1971), The generalized theory of distortions and welfare. In: Bhagwati, J.N., Jones, R.W., Mundell, R.A., Vanek, J. (Eds.), *Trade, Balance of Payments, and Growth: Papers in International Economics in Honor of C.P. Kindleberger*. North-Holland, Amsterdam, pp. 69–90.

Bhagwati, J.N., Srinivasan, T.N. (1980), Revenue seeking: a generalization of the theory of tariffs. *Journal of Political Economy* 88, 1069–1087.

Bhagwati, J.N., Brecher, R., Hatta, T. (1983), The generalized theory of transfers and welfare: bilateral transfers in a multilateral world. *American Economic Review* 73, 606–618.

Bhagwati, J.N., Brecher, R., Hatta, T. (1985), The general theory of transfers and welfare: exogenous (policy-imposed) and endogenous (transfer-induced) distortions. *Quarterly Journal of Economics* 100, 697–714.

Brecher, R.A. (1974), Minimum wage rates and the pure theory of international trade. *Quarterly Journal of Economics* 88, 98–116.

Brecher, R.A., Bhagwati, J.N. (1982), Immiserizing transfers from abroad. *Journal of International Economics* 13, 353–364.

Brock, P.L. (1996), International transfers, the relative price of non-traded goods, and the current account. *Canadian Journal of Economics* 29, 163–180.

Chao, C.C., Yu, E.S.H. (2001), Import quotas, tied aid, capital accumulation, and welfare. *Canadian Journal of Economics* 34, 661–676.

Choi, J.Y., Yu, E.S.H. (1987), Immiserizing transfer under variable returns to scale. *Canadian Journal of Economics* 20, 634–645.

Falvey, R.E. (1988), Tariffs, quotas and piecemeal policy reform. *Journal of International Economics* 25, 177–183.

Jones, R.W. (1985), Income effects and paradoxes in the theory of international trade. *Economic Journal* 95, 330–344.

Kemp, M.C., Kojima, S. (1985), Tied aid and the paradoxes of donor-enrichment and recipient-impoverishment. *International Economic Review* 26, 721–729.

Keynes, J.M. (1929), The German transfer problem. *Economic Journal* 39, 1–7.

Lahiri, S., Raimondos, P. (1995), Welfare effects of aid under quantitative trade restrictions. *Journal of International Economics* 39, 297–315.

Leontief, W. (1936), Note on the pure theory of capital transfer. In: *Explorations in Economics: Notes and Essays Contributed in Honor of F.W. Taussig*. McGraw-Hill, New York.

Liu, W.F., Turnovsky, S.J. (2005), Consumption externalities, production externalities, and long-run macroeconomic efficiency. *Journal of Public Economics* 89, 1097–1129.

Martin, R. (1977), Immiserizing growth for a tariff-distorted small economy. *Journal of International Economics* 7, 323–328.

Ohlin, B. (1929), The German transfer problem: a discussion. *Economic Journal* 39, 172–182.

Ohyama, M. (1974), Tariffs and transfer problem. *Keio Economic Studies* 11, 29–45.

Romer, P.M. (1986), Increasing return and long run growth. *Journal of Political Economy* 94, 1002–1037.

Romer, P.M. (1989), Capital accumulation in the theory of long-run growth. In: Barro, R.J. (Ed.), *Modern Business Cycle Theory*. Harvard University Press, Cambridge, pp. 51–127.

Samuelson, P.A. (1952), The transfer problem and transport costs: the terms of trade when impediments are absent. *Economic Journal* 62, 278–304.

Schweinberger, A.G. (1990), On the welfare effects of tied aid. *International Economic Review* 31, 457–462.

Yano, M., Nugent, J.B. (1999), Aid, nontraded goods, and the transfer paradox in small countries. *American Economic Review* 89, 431–449.

PART II

Methodological and Empirical Studies on Aid

CHAPTER 12

Evaluating Aid Impact: Approaches and Findings

Howard White

Institute of Development Studies, University of Sussex, Falmer, Sussex BN1 9RE, UK
E-mail address: h.white@ids.ac.uk

Abstract
There is a substantial literature evaluating the impact of aid at the macroeconomic level using cross-country regressions. However, despite econometric advances in recent years, there remain many flaws in this approach. Similar problems beset cross-country analysis of the impact of aid on poverty indicators. More reliable estimates of the poverty impact of aid come from project-level analyses from which can be built up a picture of aid impact at the country level. This paper presents the findings from three such studies carried out by the Independent Evaluation Group of the World Bank.

Keywords: Economic development, government programs

JEL classifications: O1, I38

1. Introduction

Since the 1990s there has been a growing consensus that the primary aim for aid is poverty reduction. The World Bank aspires to 'a world free of poverty' and the UK Department for International Development has a goal of 'eliminating world poverty'. So, how effective is aid in reducing poverty?

Given the importance attached to poverty reduction, the poverty-reducing effects of aid are not well documented. This is not a new statement, but one which recurs throughout discussions of aid; Mosley (1987) called the lack of attention to poverty impact 'a disgrace' and the title of the 2006 Evaluation Gap Working Group report 'When will we ever learn?' points to the gap in our knowledge on account of a lack of impact studies. By impact studies they mean, as do I, studies which conduct a counterfactual analysis of the situation with versus without aid.

However, the current emphasis on results-based management has strengthened recent calls to build up a stronger portfolio of evaluative evidence. This paper considers approaches to examining the impact of aid, which ultimately means how it affects poverty. It is a somewhat personal account, since this topic has been the focus of my own work over the last 15 years. The paper begins, as did I, with macroeconomic approaches to examining the aid-poverty link, which mainly focus on the aid-growth relationship. Such approaches, notably cross-country regressions, are largely discounted as being able to tell us that much about aid and poverty. What is proposed instead is a core of micro-level impact evaluations, buttressed by other evaluation tools.

2. Macroeconomic approaches

Most analysis of aid at the macroeconomic level is concerned with the link between aid and growth. In such an approach the poverty-reducing effects of aid come through the growth channel: aid increases growth which reduces poverty, with a poverty-growth elasticity somewhere in the range -0.5 to -2.[1] In their analysis of how aid should be allocated to maximize its poverty-reducing impact, Collier and Dollar (2001, 2002) explicitly assume the aid-poverty-growth channel to be the only aid-induced route to poverty reduction.[2]

Hence the very considerable literature examining the relationship between aid and growth is our starting point. We turn later to the small literature examining aid-poverty linkages at a macro-level by other means. The aid-growth literature may be divided into three generations. The first generation presented simple correlations and simple regressions. A negative relationship was often found, though it was widely recognized that 'reverse causation' might be at work, i.e. poorly performing poor countries got more aid. For example, assistance to drought and conflict affected countries would certainly help drive such a negative correlation. The second generation of literature applied single equation multivariate analysis. Results were published both for and against growth, though those saying aid had no impact (e.g. Mosley *et al.*, 1987) seemed to have the louder voice. But, whilst this approach was an improvement, a number of problems remained. I listed a range of issues in a number of papers published in the 1990s (White 1992a, 1992b, 1998: Chapter 2, and White and Luttik, 1994), which may be summarized as:

(1) Omitted variable bias: A large number of variables have been used in growth equations. Levine and Renelt (1992) reported that over 50 variables had found to be significantly correlated with growth, but few of these results were robust, i.e. the coefficient was no longer significant once other variables were included. But later work by Sala-i-Martin in his papers 'I just ran two million regressions' and 'I just ran four million regressions' (Sala-i-Martin, 1997a, 1997b) found a wider range of variables to be significant, though many variables often included in growth

---

[1] The large range for poverty elasticities reflects the facts that: (1) elasticities do indeed vary across countries, with a greater poverty impact of aid in countries with lower inequality, and (2) there are two approaches to calculating the elasticity: cross country regressions, and the slope of the cumulative distribution of income or expenditure from household survey data, the latter yielding larger estimates.

[2] Earlier versions of the paper used infant mortality as a dependent variable, but this analysis was dropped in the published versions.

equations were still found not to be robust. None of these studies thought aid sufficiently important to be included. There are two conclusions from this literature. First, a comprehensive specification of the growth equation is required, but such a specification means that aid will likely prove insignificant. But, both papers find investment to be a robust determinant of growth, and Sala-i-Martin also finds human capital (health and education) to be robust. Hence if aid positively affects these intermediate variables, then it can be concluded to affect growth. It is also clear that models which include aid on the right-hand side along with investment or human capital are ruling out major channels through which aid might affect growth and so under-estimating its effects.

(2) Single-equation estimation of a simultaneous relationship: there are two issues here. One, just touched upon, is that aid may affect some of the variables included on the right-hand side, so only a partial effect is being estimated. Second, aid itself may be a function of these variables, donors giving aid to more disadvantaged countries. The model underlying the empirical specification was rarely spelled out so it was not clear what the author thought about these issues, nor what they thought the estimate aid-growth coefficient meant.

(3) Parameter instability: the aid-growth coefficient varies across time and space, and according to the type of aid. Averaging across all of these is not likely to yield a very meaningful result.

On account of these problems I concluded that the cross-country literature had not yielded useful information about the macro-impact of aid and that the more promising approach would be detailed country-level case studies focusing on intermediate variables (investment, public spending etc.). The study *Does Aid Work?* (Cassen *et al.*, 1986) had come to somewhat similar conclusions. Two books (White, 1998 and White and Dijkstra, 2003) do just that, documenting in particular that aid does increase investment and public expenditure and that fears about aid-induced inflation (Dutch disease) are generally over-stated.

This advice, and the alternative approach, was universally ignored and there has been a flourishing of cross-country aid-growth regressions since that time, constituting a third generation.[3] Major innovations in this literature have been (1) instrumenting for aid to allow for simultaneity, (2) introducing an interactive aid-policy term, and (3) varying the aid measure. Have these changes increased the robustness of the results?

Some of the new papers adopted a World Bank – proposed measure of Effective Development Assistance. But these changes in the aid measure were unnecessary and incorrect. The correct measure to use to measure the growth impact is the net inflow in the time period under-consideration. Further adjusting for future repayments is in effect to double-count these repayments. However, the issue assumed less importance

---

[3] Including one of my own more commonly cited papers, Lensink and White (2001). In our defence, the main point of that paper was to show that *if* there are negative returns to aid, then the threshold at which these negative returns set in is considerably higher than that being claimed in the influential Burnside and Dollar (2000) paper (an updated version is Burnside and Dollar, 2004).

once aid was instrumented, as it now routinely is, to account for simultaneity. Whilst doing do is an undoubted improvement, it does not solve the problem that aid's total impact is not being captured if other aid-affected variables remain on the right-hand side of the equation.

The most controversial change has been the aid-policy interaction term, with Burnside and Dollar (2000, 2004) arguing that aid has a larger impact the 'better' policies are.[4] However, most the literature concerned with this effect finds that aid *does* have a significant positive impact independent of policies, that policies themselves are often insignificant, and the aid policy term less important than found by Burnside and Dollar (e.g. Easterly *et al.*, 2004; Hansen and Tarp, 2000 and 2001, and Lensink and White, 2001). Moreover, as argued in Lensink and White (2000), the aid-policy interactive term can also be taken to mean that policy reforms only work when funded by aid. I would say that the experience of well-funded reform (e.g. Ghana in the 1980s and Sri Lanka in the late 1970s) compared to badly funded reform (e.g. Malawi in the 1980s and Zambia in the 1990s, which had negative net transfers in many years despite large gross aid flows) bears this out (see also White, 1999a).

The innovations in the third-generation have thus addressed some, but not all, of the problems in the cross-country regression approach. The problem of parameter instability is partially addressed by use of panel data sets (allowing the coefficient to vary across time and space, though still with some level of aggregation). A few papers distinguish different types of aid, and these papers are more likely to find that aid has a positive impact on growth. For example, the paper of Clemens *et al.* (2004) uses only that aid intended to be growth-increasing, finding a rate of return of 13 percent. Hence the conclusion that can be drawn from the latest generation in this literature is that aid does promote growth and hence poverty reduction. But this is not a very satisfactory finding as, even if one can turn a blind eye to the methodological difficulties in the approach, it certainly neglects many ways in which aid can reduce poverty.

A major component of the 'new poverty agenda' is the recognition of the multidimensional nature of poverty. That is, poverty is not lack only lack of income (income-poverty), but deprivation in other aspects too – at least health and education, and others would extend this to empowerment. These factors are only imperfectly correlated with income, and, as argued in successive *Human Development Reports* can be improved independently of income. Moreover, it is often aid-supported interventions which will be responsible for these income-independent moves in health and education outcomes.

The defence for focusing on the aid-growth link is that sustainable improvements in social outcomes require a good growth record. This statement is correct, but does not in fact support the case for neglecting other channels of aid impact. In fact countries that have gone for a growth-centric approach, and neglected social development, and in the end achieved neither economic nor social development (Ranis *et al.*, 2000 and

---

[4] The finding is sometimes incorrectly stated as aid alone having no impact. This is incorrect, since aid has a positive impact on growth over all observed values of the policy index.

White, 1999b). On the other hand, countries which have laid a good base of human capital have managed to shift to high growth performance; this is at least part of the story behind the East Asian success stories, including the most recent cases of China and Vietnam. Hence looking at aid's impact on aggregate poverty needs to consider how aid has affected other social outcomes.

A small number of papers have regressed social outcomes such as the infant mortality rate on aid (and other variables), also examining the indirect channel of aid's impact on social spending (e.g. Gomanee *et al.*, 2004, Mosley *et al.*, 2004 and Masud and Yontcheva, 2005). As with the growth literature, the evidence is mixed. But the same arguments apply against this approach as were made against aid-growth cross-country regressions. A more fruitful approach would be to see how aid affects intermediate variables, such as the health (e.g. immunization rates) and education outputs (e.g. trained teachers and textbook availability), and to do this through country case studies rather than cross-country regression analysis. Unfortunately, the literature of quantitatively rigorous country or program level assessments of aid impact is rather thin. As one aid official commented despairingly after listening to a series of academic papers on aid at a conference at WIDER in Helsinki: we need to get these academics away from their computers and into the field so they can understand how aid actually works. My own experience of doing field-level evaluation for a number of agencies has forced me to the same conclusion.

This section concludes with just one comment from that experience. The evaluations I conducted in the 1990s were mostly of macroeconomic assistance. Hence we were concerned to examine aid's impact on macro-aggregates such as public spending. The accounting-based approach I developed (White, 1998),[5] took as its starting point, as should any macro-approach, the construction of a consistent macro-data set in which aid flows were clearly identified. This task had to be done using national data to get the required degree of disaggregation, and highlighted the fact that aid data were amongst the most dubious of a host of dubious data. For example, the amount of aid which was off versus on budget was rarely known and varied from year to year, but was of critical importance in analyzing aid's fiscal effects. Very detailed work was required to construct the accounts under these circumstances. The official DAC aid data, the standard source for cross-country work, were of no use whatsoever, and bore little relation to national sources on aid flows. Not only were cross-country regressions blandly washing away the intricacies of how aid may affect growth (and so by implication poverty), they were not even using the right data.

3. Microeconomic analysis: methodological issues

By microeconomic analysis I mean evaluation of the impact of specific projects, programs or policies. The results agenda has increased attention on impact evaluation,

---

[5] This approach was strongly influenced by the 'Money and Finance' project led by Valpy Fitzgerald, Karl Jansen and Rob Vos at the Institute of Social Studies in The Hague, where I was also working at that time.

and there is a lively debate on how it should be done. As noted in the introduction, the statement that we know surprisingly little about aid's poverty impact is not a new one. It has been repeated most recently by the Evaluation Gap Working Group (2006) which calls for more independent evaluation. A similar call is made in Easterly (2006) critique of aid.

My involvement in project-level evaluations has been with the World Bank's Independent Evaluation Group (IEG, formerly the Operations Evaluation Department). For the last four years I have been responsible for IEG's program of impact evaluations. This program was started just at a time when interest in impact evaluation was growing, as was the debate as to how it should be done. IEG's program has taken a particular stand, promoting rigorous, but well-contextualized and policy relevant evaluations. These debates are reviewed first, followed by presentation of some results.

There has been growing support for the use of randomized impact evaluation designs as a way of overcoming selection bias.[6] This is first explained, and then the limitations of the approach identified.

It is usually the case that project beneficiaries have been selected in some way, including self selection. This selection process means that beneficiaries are *not* a random sample of the population, so that the comparison group should also not be a random sample of the population as a whole, but rather drawn from a population with the same characteristics as those chosen for the intervention. If project selection is based on observable characteristics then this problem can be handled in a straightforward manner. But it is often argued that unobservables play a role, and if these unobservables are correlated with project outcomes then obtaining unbiased estimates of project impact becomes more problematic.

Two examples illustrate this point:

(1) Small businesses which have benefited from a microcredit scheme are shown to have experienced higher profits than comparable enterprises (similar locations and market access) which did not apply to the scheme. But beneficiaries from the scheme are selected through the screening of applications. Entrepreneurs who make the effort to go through the application process, and whose business plans are sound enough to warrant financing, may anyhow have done better than those who could not be bothered to apply in the first place or whose plans were deemed too weak to be financed.

(2) Many community-driven projects such as social funds rely on communities to take the lead in applying for support to undertake community projects, such as rehabilitating the school or building a health clinic. The benefits of such community-driven projects are claimed to include higher social capital. Beneficiary communities are self-selecting, and it would not be at all surprising if those which have higher levels of social capital to start with are more likely to apply. Comparing social capital at the end of the intervention between treatment and comparison

---

[6] For a longer discussion see World Bank (2006).

communities, and attributing the difference to the intervention, would clearly be mistaken and produce an over-estimate of project impact.

These problems make the attraction of random allocation clear. If the treatment group is chosen at random then a random sample drawn from the sample population is a valid comparison group, and will remain so provided contamination can be avoided. This approach does not mean that targeting is not possible. The random allocation may be to a subgroup of the total population, e.g. from the poorest districts.

Experimental design requires that the eligible population be identified and then a random sample of that population be 'treated', i.e. included in the project. For example, only 200 schools are chosen at random to be included in the project out of the 1,200 schools in 10 project districts. The untreated (or a random sample of the untreated) are a valid comparison group since there should be no systematic difference between their characteristics and those of the treatment group. It is in this case that the comparison group can properly go by the name of the control group, since the experimental approach implies that the evaluator controls the environment to ensure that the control does not become contaminated.

Examples of when a randomized approach might be appropriate are for:[7]

• Pilot projects, which are by definition limited in size and do not treat the whole eventual target population. An example was a program by an Indian NGO to put a untrained second (female) teacher in the classrooms, mainly to address the problem of school closures because of teacher absenteeism: 42 eligible schools were identified, with the program implemented in half of the 42 which were chosen at random. Closures in the program schools were 24 percent compared to 39 percent in the control. Girls' attendance rose 50 percent. However, test scores were not affected. The program was not scaled up as it was decided to not be cost effective. The best know example of a randomized trial in a developing country is the Mexican conditional cash transfer scheme, PROGRESA. In the pilot phase 506 communities were selected, half of which got the program. The impact evaluation findings of better health and higher enrolments helped make the case of scaling up the program.

• Phased or expanding programs: random selection of the treated into the first phase, with those to be treated in the second phase acting as the control group. In Kenya a deworming program was implemented in 75 randomly selected schools. Including spillover effects (on account of reduced transmission of diseases) years of schooling rose by an average of 0.15 years per treatment.

• Program-induced randomization occurs where a budget limit means that beneficiaries are chosen on a random (lottery) basis. An example is school placement in Chicago: parents can apply for a different school than the nearest one, but only a randomly chosen sub-sample get their choice. Whilst those getting their choice do better in school than do children who did not apply to move, they actually do worse than unsuccessful lottery applicants (i.e. the positive impact with the naïve control

---

[7] The examples here are taken from Duflo (2004).

is picking up positive parental influences, but actually getting placed elsewhere is bad possibly because of the disruption). In Columbia school vouchers for private education were allocated on a random basis.

There are misconceptions about the randomized approach, so that it is held to be wholly inappropriate in a development setting. This is not so, and it has been success-fully applied in several cases. Indeed, several of the claimed problems of a randomized approach are common to all impact evaluations. First, randomization is no more ex-pensive than any other survey-based impact evaluation. Second, experimental design requires that beneficiaries are chosen at random from the eligible population, e.g. slum residents; there is no requirement at all that the population as a whole be considered for treatment. In the case of the school improvement project mentioned in the previous paragraph, a measure of targeting can still be achieved by selecting poor districts as the project districts. Third, allocating benefits to only a subset of potential beneficiaries is a result of the project budget constraint, not the decision to randomize. Hence there is nothing morally reprehensible about the decision to keep an untreated group – the same is true with any comparison group. Equally, the desire to keep an uncontaminated comparison is just as true as any impact study with a baseline. Finally, a randomized design need not necessarily imply a black box approach (see below), though this has indeed often been so in practice.

However, there *are* limits to the applicability of randomization in development eval-uation. The first is that the evaluation design may perforce be *ex post*, so that the opportunity to randomize has long since passed. Second, the term 'treatment group' reflects the medical antecedents of the randomized approach. The medical analogy is apt since discrete, homogeneous interventions – like taking a pill – are most amenable to a randomized approach. Where the nature of the intervention varies, then either multiple comparisons are required or an alternative needed which recognizes this heterogeneity. Many development interventions are complex in design, so that a ran-domized evaluation design may be appropriate for at best a subset of the intervention. Third, the experiment implies that the evaluator maintains control. This may not be possible. Those selected for the intervention may not want to take part, so selectivity bias comes back in. Or those not selected may lobby for inclusion, or for a compara-ble intervention, and so become contaminated. Or randomization may just prove to be a political non-starter. Other programs intend to be comprehensive in scope, such as attaining universal primary education, or support to heavily-indebted countries under the Highly Indebted Poor Country (HIPC) initiative, under which all heavily indebted low-income countries qualified for assistance. And projects working with a small num-ber of entities, such as institutional development activities, cannot use a randomized approach.

Hence, experimental methods are in practice only applicable to a narrow range of the interventions supported by most aid agencies. Where they are applicable then they should be used, certainly more so than is done at present. Project managers need be made aware from the outset of the implications of randomization for program design. The evaluation design should incorporate study components of a qualitative nature and be sure to collect data across the log frame. Where experimental approaches are not applicable then the evaluator need turn to one of the alternatives discussed below.

The main alternatives are:

(1) *The pipeline approach* takes as the comparison group individuals, households or communities which have been selected to participate in the project, but not yet done so. In principle, there is therefore no selectivity bias, but this assumes that there has been no change in selection criteria, *and* that all applicants were not ranked and then the project 'worked down' the list. If the latter is the case then the approach ensures a bias rather than avoids it.

(2) *Natural experiments*: Sometimes a control group occurs 'naturally'. A well-known example is from Israel in which legislation dictates a maximum class size of 30, so that any class reaching 31 has to be divided into two smaller classes. This policy provides a natural experiment for the analysis of class size on student learning

(3) *Propensity score matching*: Selection may be based on a set of characteristics rather than just one. Hence the comparison group need be matched on all these characteristics. This may seem a rather difficult task. But it can be managed through a technique called propensity score matching (PSM). Once the control is identified then project impact can be estimated using single or double difference estimates. PSM identifies a group of individuals, households or firms with the same observable characteristics as those participating in the project. It does this by estimating a statistical model of the probability of participating (propensity to participate) using a regression model with participation as the zero-one dependent variable, and a set of observable characteristics, which must be unaffected by the intervention, as the explanatory variables. The theory underlying this procedure is that matching on a linear combination of X characteristics in this way is an unbiased estimate of the result from matching individually on each of the X characteristics – something that would prove impossible to do in practice. The coefficients are used to calculate a propensity score, and participants matched with non-participants based on having similar propensity scores. In practice there are a range of ways of performing this matching, with the most common being to match each participant with their five 'nearest neighbor' non-participants (i.e. the five non-participants with the closest propensity score). The difference in the mean outcome from the two groups is taken as project impact.

(4) *Regression-based approach*: Impact measurement by comparing project and comparison areas tells us nothing about the channels through which the project has its impact. The intervention is left as a black box. Regressions can help open the black box through a two, or more, stage process. Impact can be examined by modeling the determinants of the outcome of interest. This approach can draw on well-established literatures modeling those outcomes. Amongst the explanatory variables will be factors which are affected by the intervention. Knowing how much an explanatory variable has changed as a result of the intervention (which may be determined by examining double differences for that indicator, or itself be subject to regression analysis) allows calculation of the project effect via that

particular channel. The project may have its effect not only by changing the quantity of a factor but its productivity. Regression analysis can readily accommodate this possibility by allowing the coefficient on the variable to vary before and after the intervention. The contribution of the changes in quantity and productivity can be calculated separately (a procedure known as the Oaxaca decomposition). When using the regression-based approach two points need be borne in mind. First, there have been important developments in micro-level statistical analysis in recent years, so the evaluator need be familiar with 'the state of the art' in their particular area in order to retain credibility. Second, the regression based approach may not remove the problem of selection bias. But it can do so if selection is based on observables, provided data are available on these observables and the selection process is correctly modeled. Hence it is very important that the evaluator be very aware of who benefits from the intervention. There are a variety of statistical approaches which can be used to eliminate the selectivity bias.

Being technically rigorous is only part of the story: to be most useful the evaluation needs to be policy relevant. To do this it must not be a black box. Black box impact evaluations give a verdict on outcomes (impact or not), but do not look inside the workings of the project to understand this result. This is unfortunately all too common. One of the managers of a multi-million dollar evaluation of a currently favored approach confessed to me that the study said nothing about how these projects could be improved. Rather less abashed was the leader of a million dollar evaluation of a nutrition program in Central America who, when asked about policy conclusions, replied that they were none of her business. The best way to open the black box is to use a theory-based approach which examines all the links in the causal chain from inputs to outcomes (see Carvalho and White, 2004, for an exposition of the approach, examples are given below).

4. Aid and poverty: evidence from case studies

4.1. Case study 1: Basic education in Ghana

In 1986 the Government of Ghana embarked on an ambitious program of educational reform, shortening the length of pre-University education from 17 to 12 years, reducing subsidies at the secondary and tertiary levels, increasing the school day and taking steps to eliminate unqualified teachers from schools. These reforms were supported by four World Bank aid programs – the Education Sector Adjustment Credits I and II, Primary School Development Project and the Basic Education Sector Improvement Project.

There was no clearly defined 'project' for this study, rather support to the sub-sector through four large operations. The four projects had supported a range of activities, from rehabilitating school buildings to assisting in the formation of community-based school management committees. To identify the impact of these various activities a regression-based approach was adopted which analyzed the determinants of school attainment (years of schooling) and achievement (learning outcomes, i.e. test scores). For some of these determinants – notably books and buildings – the contribution of the World Bank to better learning outcomes could then be quantified. The methodology thus adopted a theory-based approach to identify the channels through which a diverse range of interventions were having their impact.

The first major finding from the IEG study (World Bank, 2004) concerned the factual.[8] Contrary to official statistics, enrolments in basic education have been rising steadily over the period. This discrepancy was readily explained: in the official statistics, both the numerator and denominator were wrong. The numerator was wrong as it relied on the administrative data from the school census, which had incomplete coverage of the public sector and did not cover the rapidly growing private sector. A constant mark up was made to allow for private sector enrolments, but the IEG analysis showed that had gone up fourfold (from 5 to 20% of total enrolments) over the 15 years. The denominator was based on the 1984 census with an assumed rate of growth which turned out to be too high once the 2000 census became available, thus under-estimating enrolment growth.

More strikingly still, learning outcomes have improved markedly: 15 years ago nearly two-thirds (63 percent) of those who had completed grades 3–6 were, using the English test as a guide, illiterate. By 2003 this figure had fallen to 19 percent. The finding of improved learning outcomes flies in the face of qualitative data from many, though not all, 'key informant' interviews. But such key informants display a middle class bias which persists against the reforms which were essentially populist in nature.

Also striking are the improvements in school quality revealed by the school-level data: For example: (1) In 1988, less than half of schools could use all their classrooms when it was raining, but in 2003 over two-thirds can do so; (2) Fifteen years ago over two-thirds of primary schools reported occasional shortages of chalk, only one in 20 do so today, with 86 percent saying there is always enough; and (3) The percentage of primary schools having at least one English textbook per pupil has risen from 21 percent in 1988 to 72 percent today and for math books in Junior Secondary School (JSS) these figures are 13 and 71 percent, respectively.

School quality has improved across the country, in poor and non-poor communities alike. But there is a growing disparity within the public school sector. Increased

---

[8] In 1988/1989 Ghana Statistical Service (GSS) undertook the second round of the Ghana Living Standards Survey (GLSS 2). Half of the 170 areas surveyed around the country were chosen at random to have an additional education module, which administered math and English tests to all those aged 9–55 years with at least three years of schooling and surveyed schools in the enumeration areas. Working with both GSS and the Ministry of Education, Youth and Sport (MOEYS), IEG resurveyed these same 85 communities and their schools in 2003, applying the same survey instruments as previously. In the interests of comparability, the same questions were kept, although additional ones were added pertaining to school management, as were two whole new questionnaires – a teacher questionnaire for five teachers at each school and a local language test in addition to the math and English tests. The study thus had a possibly unique data set – not only could children's test scores be linked to both household and school characteristics, but this could be done in a panel of communities over a fifteen year period. The test scores are directly comparable since exactly the same tests were used in 2003 as had been applied fifteen years earlier.

reliance on community and district financing has meant that schools in relatively prosperous areas continue to enjoy better facilities than do those in less well off communities.

The IEG study argues that Ghana has been a case of a quality-led quantity expansion in basic education. The education system was in crisis in the seventies; school quality was declining and absolute enrolments falling. But by 2000, over 90 percent of Ghanaians aged 15 and above had attended school compared to 75 percent 20 years earlier. In addition, drop-out rates have fallen, so completion rates have risen: by 2003, 92 percent of those entering grade 1 complete Junior Secondary School (grade 9). Gender disparities have been virtually eliminated in basic enrolments. Primary enrolments have risen in both disadvantaged areas and amongst the lowest income groups. The differential between both the poorest areas and other parts of the country, and between enrolments of the poor and non-poor, have been narrowed but are still present.

Statistical analysis of the survey results showed the importance of building school infrastructure on enrolments. Building a school, and so reducing children's travel time, has a major impact on enrolments. While the majority of children live within 20 minutes of school, some 20 percent do not and school building has increased enrolments among these groups. In one area surveyed, average travel time to the nearest school was cut from nearly an hour to less than 15 minutes with enrolments increasing from 10 to 80 percent. In two other areas average travel time was reduced by nearly 30 minutes and enrolments increased by over 20 percent. Rehabilitating classrooms so that they can be used when it is raining also positively affects enrolments. Complete rehabilitation can increase enrolments by as much as one third. Across the country as a whole, the changes in infrastructure quantity and quality have accounted for a 4 percent increase in enrolments between 1988 and 2003, about one third of the increase over that period. The World Bank has been the main source of finance for these improvements. Before the first World Bank program communities were responsible for building their own schools. The resulting structures collapsed after a few years. The Bank has financed 8,000 school pavilions around the country, providing more permanent structures for the school which can better withstand the weather.

Learning outcomes depend significantly on school quality, including textbook supply. Bank-financed textbook provision accounts for around one quarter of the observed improvement in test scores. But other major school-level determinants of achievement such as teaching methods and supervision of teachers by the head teacher and circuit supervisor have not been affected by the Bank's interventions. The Bank has not been heavily involved in teacher training and plans to extend in-service training have not been realized. Support to "hardware" has been shown to have made a substantial positive contribution to both attainment and achievement. But when satisfactory levels of inputs are reached – which is still far from the case for the many relatively deprived schools – future improvements could come from focusing on what happens in the classroom. However, the Bank's one main effort to change incentives – providing head teacher housing under the Primary School Development Project in return for the head teacher signing a contract on school management practices – was not a great success. Others, notably DFID and USAID, have made better progress in this direction but with limited coverage.

The policy context, meaning government commitment, was an important factor in making the Bank's contributions work. The government was committed to improving the quality of live in rural areas, through the provision of roads, electricity and schools, as a way of building a political base. Hence there was a desire to make it work. Party loyalists were placed in key positions to keep the reform on track, the army used to distribute textbooks in support of the new curriculum in the early 1990s to make sure they reached schools on time, and efforts made to post teachers to new schools and make sure that they received their pay on time. Teachers also benefited from the large civil service salary increase in the run up to the 1992 election.

Better education leads to better welfare outcomes. Existing studies on Ghana show how education reduces fertility and mortality. Analysis of IEG's survey data shows that education improves nutritional outcomes, with this effect being particularly strong for children of women living in poorer households. Regression analysis shows there is no economic return to primary and JSS education (i.e. average earnings are not higher to children who have attended primary and JSS compared to children who have not), but there is a return to cognitive achievement. Children who attain higher test scores as a result of attending school can expect to enjoy higher income; but children who learn little in school will not reap any economic benefit.

The major policy finding from the study relates to the appropriate balance between hard and software in support for education. The latter is now stressed. But the study highlights the importance of hardware: books and buildings. It was also of course important that teachers were in their classrooms: government's own commitment (borne out of a desire to build political support in rural areas) helped ensure this happened.

In the many countries and regions in which educational facilities are inadequate then hardware provision is a necessary step in increasing enrolments and improving learning outcomes. The USAID project in Ghana encourages teachers to arrange children's desks in groups rather than rows – but many of the poorer schools do not have desks. In the words of one teacher, "I'd like to hang posters on my walls but I don't have posters. In fact, as you can see, I don't have any walls".

These same concerns underlie a second policy implication. Central government finances teacher's salaries and little else for basic education. Other resources come from donors, districts or the communities themselves. There is thus a real danger of poorer communities falling behind, as they lack both resources and the connections to access external resources. The reality of this finding was reinforced by both qualitative data – field trips to the best and worst performing schools in a single district in the same day – and the quantitative data, which show the poorer performance of children in these disadvantaged schools. Hence children of poorer communities are left behind and account for the remaining illiterate primary graduates which should be a pressing policy concern.

The study highlighted other areas of concern. First amongst these is low teacher morale, manifested through increased absenteeism. Second is the growing importance of the private sector, which now accounts for 20 percent of primary enrolments com-

pared to 5 percent 15 years earlier. This is a sector which has had limited government
involvement and none from the Bank.

4.2. Case study 2: Meeting the health MDGs in Bangladesh

Bangladesh began the 1970s as a new country in a dire situation. The ravages of war
and famine meant that the prospects for development appeared bleak. Social indicators
were among the worst in the world. Women could expect to have on average seven
children during their child-bearing years, but two of those would die before reaching
their fifth birthday. Three-quarters of all children were malnourished.

Thirty years on the situation has changed drastically. The total fertility rate has
fallen from seven to less than three, and under-five mortality from over 250 per 1,000
live births to around 80 by 2004 (Figure 1). The World Bank's (IEG's) reworking of the
DHS data contested the widely-held view that fertility decline had reached a plateau
in the 1990s. These rates of progress mean that Bangladesh is on track to meet the
Millennium Development Goals. Malnutrition remains high but has begun to decline
in the last decade.

IEG's study (World Bank, 2005) of the factors behind this success utilized existing
data sets. The analysis drew on both cross-country data, from a variety of sources, and
national data mainly from the Demographic Health Surveys of 1992/1993, 1996/1997
and 1999/2000. Multivariate analysis of the determinants of health and nutrition outcomes was carried out. This approached allowed the identification of interventions in a
range of sectors which had affected health outcomes. While it was possible to carry out
cost-effectiveness analysis, a full theory-based approach could not be applied because
of the absence of process indicators.

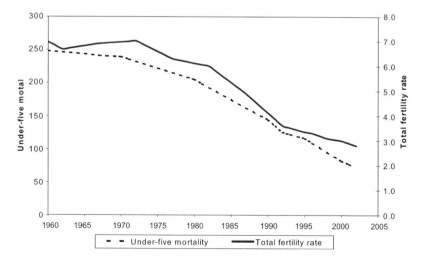

Fig. 1.   Both fertility and under-five mortality have fallen.

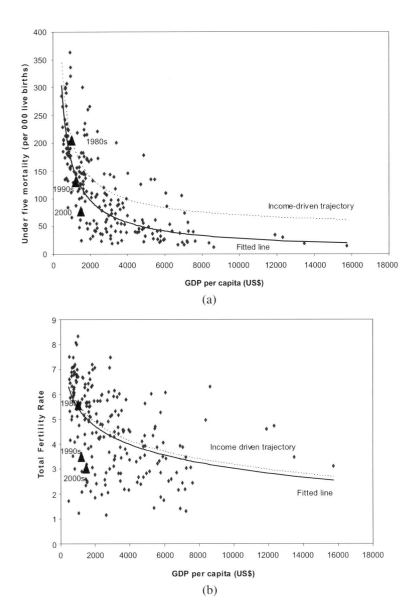

(a)

(b)

Note: See discussion in text for explanation.

Fig. 2.   Bangladesh's improvement in social outcomes is greater than can be explained by economic growth alone. (a) Under-five mortality; (b) Total fertility rate.

Howard White

**Table 1.   *Growth in GNP per capita accounts for at most one-third of the reduction
             in mortality. . . and less than a fifth of lower fertility***

	1980 actual	2000 actual	2000 income-based estimate	Percent reduction explained by income
Under-five mortality	205.0	77.5	163.1	32.9
Total fertility rate	5.6	3.0	5.2	16.0

Source: calculated from data used for Figure 2.

Economic growth is usually seen as a critical factor in reducing poverty in its various dimensions. Bangladesh is no exception to this point, and the country's respectable growth record has indeed played a part in the country's improved social outcomes. But it is not the whole story. Figure 2 shows under-five mortality and fertility plotted against income per capita for a cross-section of 78 countries at different points in time. Each data point represents the decade averages of income and the social outcome shown, using values from the 1970s to the current decade, so that there are up to four observations for each country.

The solid line in each figure is the average relationship between income and the social outcome (that is "the fitted line"). In the 1980s Bangladesh (indicated by the triangular data points, each labeled by its decade) lay above the average for under-five mortality and fertility, meaning that those indicators were worse than should be expected for a country at its income level. If these indicators had improved following the internationally-established relationship with income then subsequent observations for Bangladesh would have laid along the dashed line. But in fact these later observations lie below the fitted line, showing that Bangladesh now does better than expected for a country at its income level. This finding suggests that there have been important, non-income-related, factors behind the improvement in mortality and fertility in Bangladesh.

The numbers behind these graphs provide an upper estimate of the extent to which growth in GDP per capita has contributed to improved social outcomes in Bangladesh (Table 1). For example, under-five mortality was 205 per 1,000 live births in the 1980s. Income growth alone would have reduced it to 163 by 2000, but by then the actual rate was 78. Hence at most just under one-third of the improvement comes from higher average income. For fertility the share of income is even less, explaining at most 16 percent of the observed reduction.

The question of what then explains the additional reduction was analyzed through multivariate analysis of both cross-country and household data. The results revealed the following regarding selected interventions:

- Immunization coverage was at less than 2 percent in the early 1980s, but grew in the latter part of the decade (largely with the support of UNICEF and WHO, but later also other donors including the World Bank) so that by 1990 close to half of all children were fully vaccinated in their first 12 months. Immunization has averted over 2 million child deaths in the last two decades, at a cost of between $100 and $300 per life saved.

- The World Bank financed the training of approximately 14,000 traditional birth attendants (TBAs) until the late nineties, at which point training TBAs was abandoned following a shift in international opinion toward a policy of all births being attended by Skilled Birth Attendants. However, the evidence presented in this report shows that training TBAs saved infant lives, at a cost of $220–800 per death averted.
- Female secondary schooling expanded rapidly in the 1990s, especially in rural areas partly as a result of the stipend paid to all female students in grades 6–10 in rural areas supported by Norwegian aid, the Asian Development Bank, the World Bank and government. Amongst the benefits of the increase in female secondary schooling are lower infant and child mortality, at a cost of $1,080–5,400 per death averted.
- Rural electrification, supported through three World Bank programs in the 1980s and 1990s, reduces mortality through income effects, improving health services, making water sterilization easier and improving access to health information, especially from TV. Taking these various channels into account means that children in households receiving electrification have an under-five mortality rate 25 per 1,000 lower than that of children in non-electrified households.

The IEG study had the following policy implications: (1) Publicly-provided services, with external support, were an efficacious and cost-effective means of improving health outcomes; (2) Interventions from several sectors improved health outcomes. But this multi-sectoral causation did not mean that interventions had to be delivered in a multi-sectoral manner (a common claim in relation to the MDGs resulting in unnecessarily complex design); and (3) Local evidence needs to be taken into account in making resource allocation decisions. The training of TBAs was abandoned in Bangladesh following international fashion, but local evidence shows it to have been effective in reducing infant mortality.

4.3. Case study 3: Agricultural extension services in Kenya

The Training and Visit (T&V) system of agricultural extension sought to strengthen links between research and extension, and get these results to farmers through frequent visits by extension workers to farmers – at least monthly and often more frequently. The approach was widely adopted in the 1980s, with much World Bank support. However it began to attract critics. It was known to be costly and there was scant evidence of any impact on agricultural productivity. The IEG study (World Bank, 2000) entered this debate in order to provide such evidence for the case of Kenya. A theory-based approach was adopted so that the study considered a set of intermediate indicators as well as the impact on final outcomes.

The study suggested that agricultural extension has a potentially important role to play: the data showed that farmers who were aware of improved practices usually put them into effect. This suggests that lack of knowledge was indeed a constraint. But the Bank's two National Extension Projects (NEP I and II) were not seen as having alleviated that constraint and so had no discernible impact on production.[9]

The use of the theory-based approach revealed several places in which the causal chain had broken down, so that the interventions were not functioning as planned. First, for much of the project, there was little if any link from research to extension, so that there were no new messages for extension workers to take to farmers. Hence when workers did visit farmers on a monthly basis both sides viewed these meetings as rather repetitive. By the time NEP II was started the main messages being delivered by extension services, regarding maize production, had already been adopted by virtually all farmers, so there was no scope for further benefits without some innovation in the information being conveyed.

But in fact less than one-tenth (7 percent) of contact farmers were visited on a monthly basis. This fact reflected the failure of the institutional development aspect of NEP I and II. Most extension workers continued to operate in the same way as they had before the project, hence the project can be expected to have had little impact on farming practices. The failure of ID was partly a failure of incentives but also a result of the changing fiscal climate. Government resources were shrinking so the extension service became increasingly reliant on donor finance, most of which went to pay salaries so there was little left over to support intensive delivery of extension services. This situation meant that the project was not sustainable. And although farmers were indeed willing to pay for extension services, it was nowhere near what they were actually costing under this system.

The report pointed clearly to changes which needed to be made. In its current form extension services were having little impact and so by definition were inefficient. However, impacts were discernible for poorer areas: extension services had played a role in allowing less productive areas to catch up. But delivery had been concentrated in the more productive areas where they had least impact! The IEG study thus recommended a re-targeting to poorer areas. It also pointed out that messages had to be better tailored to the needs of farmers, rather than a uniform package being delivered to all farmers. One way to achieve this was to become less top down and more responsive to farmer demands. Finally, the rate of innovation did not support such an intensive delivery system: a leaner extension service with broader coverage would be more efficient.

4.4. Case study 4: Weak impact from a nutrition program in Bangladesh

The Bangladesh Integrated Nutrition Program (BINP) was launched in 1995 with the objective of 'reducing malnutrition to the extent that it ceases to be a health problem'. The intervention was based on growth monitoring, food supplementation and nutritional counseling, with an emphasis on the latter. Community Nutrition Promoters (CNPs) were recruited in each community at a ratio of one CNP for every 1,000

---

[9] The study exploited the availability of panel data to conduct a fixed effects multivariate analysis.

population in some areas and every 1,500 in others. CNPs, recruited from women with children, and a minimum 8 years of education, were responsible for implementation of most project activities at the community level, in collaboration with the Women's Group; they worked under the supervision of the Community Nutrition Organizer (CNO, each of whom was responsible for 10 CNPs).

The key assumption behind CNBC is that "bad practices" are responsible for malnutrition in Bangladesh. This point of view was strongly argued in the BINP appraisal document: "behaviors related to feeding of young children have at least as much (if not more) to do with the serious problem of malnutrition in Bangladesh as poverty and the resultant household food insecurity do" (World Bank, 1995: 4). Therefore changing bad practice to good will bring about nutritional improvements. There are a number of steps in the causal chain behind this approach:

(1) The right people (those making decisions regarding under-nourished children) are targeted with nutritional messages;
(2) These people participate in project activities, and so are exposed to these messages;
(3) Exposure leads to acquisition of the desired knowledge;
(4) Acquisition of the knowledge leads to its adoption (i.e., a change in practice);
(5) The new practices make a substantial impact on nutritional outcomes.

Supplementary feeding was provided to malnourished children and pregnant women. For this program to work:

(1) The target groups have to enrol in the program;
(2) The criteria are correctly applied in selecting those to receive supplementary feeding;
(3) Those selected for supplementary feeding attend sessions to receive the food;
(4) There is no leakage (e.g., selling of food supplements or giving food to other family members), or substitution (reducing other food intake);
(5) The food is of sufficient quantity and quality to have a noticeable impact on nutritional status (and, in the case of pregnant women, to be of sufficient magnitude to have an appreciable impact on birth weight).

Various studies have found somewhat different results with respect to the impact of BINP. But most these studies had problems of an inadequate comparison group. The IEG study (World Bank, 2005) tackled this problem by constructing a comparison from a national nutrition survey dataset using propensity score matching. This analysis found positive impacts on both WAZ and HAZ at midterm and endline, with the effect on WAZ being the larger of the two. But the impact found is very small: the project is found to have reduced malnutrition by less than 2 percent. This is far less than planned, and indicates a low level of cost effectiveness. Simulations suggest that simply buying food and giving it away to families with children would have reduced malnutrition by the same amount for half the cost, even allowing for administration costs and higher leakage of such a scheme. This weak impact is readily explained once the weak links in the causal chain are exposed (Table 2).

Table 2.   Links in the BINP causal chain

Assumption	Children	Mothers
Attend growth monitoring sessions	Over 90 percent of children attend GM sessions.	Over 70 percent participate in monitoring pregnancy weight gain.
Targeting criteria correctly applied; participants stay in program to receive food	Nearly two-thirds of eligible children not fed (reasons: do not attend GM in first place, wrong application of targeting criteria, drop out of feeding).	60 percent of eligible women not receiving supplementary feeding.
Acquire knowledge and put it into practice	One-third of mothers of children receiving supplementary feeding do not receive nutritional *counselling*. There is a knowledge practice gap (see mothers).	There is a knowledge practice gap, driven by material resource or time constraints.
No leakage or substitution	One quarter of children fed at home, increasing possibility of both leakage and substitution.	One-third admit sharing food, and there is substitution for those who do not. At most 40 percent of eligible women receive full supplementation.
Feeding and nutritional advice have an impact on nutritional status	Supplementary feeding has a positive impact on child nutritional status, especially for the most malnourished children. There is only weak evidence of any impact from nutritional *counselling*.	Pregnancy weight gain is too little to have a notable impact on low birth weight, except for most malnourished mothers. Moreover, mother's pre-pregnancy nutritional status is more important than pregnancy weight gain. Consequently, birth weight gains are slight, though greater for children of severely malnourished mothers. Eating more during pregnancy is the main channel for both pregnancy weight gain and higher birth weight.

First, there was a problem in the implementation of counselling, which was targeted at mothers, whereas fathers and mothers-in-law are also part of the decision making process regarding child health and nutrition. There were also targeting problems in the provision of supplementary feeding, and evidence that it substituted for existing food rather than being additional to it. Moreover, many women receiving food said they had not received the nutritional counselling, which was central to the project design. A major of success, however, was that those who did receive counselling acquired the desired knowledge regarding better nutritional practices. Unfortunately, there was a large 'knowledge-practice' gap, whereby mothers saying they were aware of a particular practice failed to actually do it. Finally, some of the changes could be expected to have, anyhow, a low impact.

5. Conclusion: the macro–micro-paradox revisited

Concluding that there was at best a zero link between aid and growth, Mosley (1987) posed the 'macro–micro-paradox'. That is, how can we reconcile the large number of positive project-level evaluations with the lack of aid impact at the aggregate level. A number of reasons have been offered for this, including that the project-level evaluations are wrong, partly because of the apparently well-known biases which exist on evaluators to come to positive findings. Such an explanation betrays a lack of experience with carrying out evaluations, and even with the contents of the large number of highly critical evaluation studies. Whilst of course some operational staff may want 'a good report', it is just as likely that there are pressures to expose what staff see as shortcomings of the program. But the evaluator is meant to be independent of these pressures from both sides, and I have certainly never felt constrained in what I write in evaluation reports. The paradox is far more likely explained by the many shortcomings in the cross-country macro-approach.

Project-level studies provide ample evidence of the ways in which aid has worked to help the poor. There are of course examples also of aid not working – and even where it does work there are improvements to be made. Since actual fieldwork delivers useful policy lessons to help aid work better research resources should be directed to this end. Fulfilling aid's mission of eliminating global poverty will only be possible if researchers move off the side lines and get involved with aid as it actually works.

References

Burnside, C., Dollar, D. (2000), Aid, policies, and growth. *American Economic Review* 90, 847–868.

Burnside, C., Dollar, D. (2004), Aid, policies, and growth: revisiting the evidence. *Policy Research Working Paper* 3251, World Bank, Washington, DC.

Carvalho, S., White, H. (2004), Theory-based evaluation: the case of social funds. *American Journal of Evaluation* 25, 141–160.

Cassen, R., et al. (1986), *Does Aid Work?* Clarendon Press, Oxford.

Clemens, M., Radelet, S., Bhavnani, R. (2004), Counting chickens when they hatch: the short-term effect of aid on growth. *Center for Global Development Working Paper* #44, Center for Global Development, Washington, DC.

Collier, P., Dollar, D. (2001), Can the world cut poverty in half? How policy reform and effective aid can meet the international development goals. *World Development* 29, 1787–1802.

Collier, P., Dollar, D. (2002), Aid allocation and poverty reduction. *European Economic Review* 46, 1475–1500.

Duflo, E. (2004), Scaling Up and Evaluation. Paper for World Bank Annual Bank Conference on Development Economics, Bangalore, India.

Easterly, W. (2006), *The White Man's Burden: Why Aid Does so Much Harm and so Little Good*. Penguin Press, New York.

Easterly, W., Levine, R., Roodman, D. (2004), Aid, policies, and growth: comment. *American Economic Review* 94, 774–780.

Evaluation Working Group (2006), *When Will We Ever Learn? Improving Lives Through Impact Evaluation*. Center for Global Development, Washington, DC.

Gomanee, K., Morrissey, O., Mosley, P., Verschoor, A. (2004), *Aid, government expenditure and aggregate welfare*, CREDIT, University of Nottingham, Nottingham, mimeo.

Hansen, H., Tarp, F. (2000), Aid effectiveness disputed. *Journal of International Development* 12, 375–398.

Hansen, H., Tarp, F. (2001), Aid and growth regressions. *Journal of Development Economics* 64, 545–568.

Lensink, R., White, H. (2000), Assessing aid: a manifesto for aid in the 21st century? *Oxford Development Studies* 28.

Lensink, R., White, H. (2001), Are there negative returns to aid? *Journal of Development Studies* 37, 42–65.

Levine, R., Renelt, D. (1992), A sensitivity analysis of cross-country growth regressions. *American Economic Review* 82, 942–963.

Masud, N., Yontcheva, B. (2005), Does foreign aid reduce poverty? Empirical evidence from nongovernmental and bilateral aid. *IMF Working Paper* 05/10. World Bank, Washington, DC.

Mosley, P. (1987), *Overseas Aid: Its Defense and Reform*. Wheatsheaf, Brighton.

Mosley, P., Hudson, J., Horrell, S. (1987), Aid, the public sector and the market in developing countries. *Economic Journal* 97, 616–642.

Mosley, P., Hudson, J., Verschoor, A. (2004), Aid, poverty reduction and the new conditionality. *The Economic Journal* 114, F217–F243.

Ranis, G., Stewart, F., Ramirez, A. (2000), Economic growth and human development. *World Development* 28, 197–219.

Sala-I-Martin, X. (1997a), I just ran two million regressions. *American Economic Review* 87, 178–183.

Sala-i-Martin, X. (1997b), *I just ran four million regressions*. Columbia University, mimeo.

White, H. (1992a), The macroeconomic impact of development aid: a critical survey. *Journal of Development Studies* 21, 163–240.

White, H. (1992b), What do we know about aid's macroeconomic impact? An overview of the aid effectiveness debate? *Journal of International Development* 4, 121–137.

White, H. (Ed.) (1998), *Aid and Macroeconomic Performance*. McMillan, Basingstoke.

White, H. (1999a), Aid and economic reform. In: Kayizzi-Mugerwa, S. (Ed.), *The African Economy: Policy, Institutions and the Future*. Routledge, London.

White, H. (1999b), Global poverty reduction: are we heading in the right direction? *Journal of International Development* 11, 503–519.

White, H., Dijkstra, G. (2003), *Program Aid and Development*. Routledge, London.

White, H., Luttik, J. (1994), The countrywide effects of aid. *Policy Research Working Paper* 1337, World Bank, Washington, DC.

World Bank (1995), *Staff Appraisal Report. Bangladesh Integrated Nutrition Project*. Population and Human Resources Division, Washington, DC.

World Bank (2000), *Agricultural Extension: The Kenya Experience*. World Bank, Washington, DC.

World Bank (2004), *Books, Buildings and Learning Outcomes: An Impact Evaluation of World Bank Support to Basic Education in Ghana*. World Bank, Washington, DC.

World Bank (2005), *Maintaining Momentum to 2015? An Impact Evaluation of External Support to Maternal and Child Health and Nutrition in Bangladesh*. World Bank, Washington, DC.

World Bank (2006), *Impact Evaluation: The Experience of the Independent Evaluation Group of the World Bank*. World Bank, Washington, DC.

CHAPTER 13

Scaling Up of Foreign Aid and the Emerging New Agenda

George Mavrotas

World Institute for Development Economics Research, United Nations University (UNU-WIDER),
Katajanokanlaituri 6 B, FIN-00160 Helsinki, Finland
E-mail address: mavrotas@wider.unu.edu

Abstract

The paper discusses various important issues of development aid in the context of the emerging new landscape for Official Development Assistance (ODA) and in particular how aid effectiveness issues are now perceived in a world of scaled-up aid. The paper also discusses the overall nexus between aid, growth and domestic policies in aid-recipient countries by reflecting on the relevant ongoing debate in this area. A substantial part of the paper is devoted to the discussion of the central issues involved in development aid, particularly in connection with recent calls in the international development community for scaling-up aid so that the *Millennium Development Goals* can be attained, as well as the challenging new policy agenda in this regard.

Keywords: Foreign aid, scaling up ODA, aid effectiveness, Millennium Development Goals

JEL classifications: F35

1. Introductory remarks

Does aid work? Robert Cassen and Associates in the well-known study published under the same title in 1986 argued quite rightly that 'much of the public discussion of aid has been distorted by prejudice, ideology and selective glimpses of parts of the evidence' and that ... 'most aid does succeed in terms of its own objectives and obtains a reasonable rate of return; but a significant proportion does not'. Twenty years after the publication of the above seminal study, aid issues are still dominated by politics and ideology in many cases; yet, the overall context in which development aid is now perceived and assessed is dramatically different. Indeed, the last two decades witnessed various important changes in the landscape of foreign aid

THEORY AND PRACTICE OF FOREIGN AID
VOLUME 1   ISSN: 1574-8715
DOI: 10.1016/S1574-8715(06)01013-X

which eventually pushed the aid agenda to new interesting directions. In the early 1990s, following the collapse of the former Soviet Union and the end of the Cold War many observers predicted the 'end of history' for aid on the assumption that a crucial motive for aid giving that dominated the pre-1990 period, namely political and strategic motives of the donor community, would loose its importance in the aftermath of the Cold War. Nevertheless, recent years have witnessed a revived interest in aid issues and at the same time numerous studies of aid have emerged, some of them quite influential in policy circles. The above dramatic change in the aid arena was mainly the outcome of a number of important events in recent years. A major development in this area was the publication in 1996 of the OECD-DAC report entitled *Shaping the 21st Century: The Contribution of Development Cooperation* which was quite instrumental in generating the new momentum on aid, since, by setting new priorities for aid, it marked the increasingly widespread adoption of the *International Development Targets* and particularly the commitment to halve absolute poverty by 2015 as an important element in the rethinking of development aid, thus laying the foundations for the emergence of the *Millennium of Development Goals* later on.

Following the publication of the OECD-DAC Report on Development Assistance another important development in the aid scene in recent years was the World Bank study *Assessing Aid* that was published in 1998. Even though many of the empirical findings of the above study remain controversial, this report seems to have been the most influential aid study in shaping both the policy debate and the research focus since the publication of *Does Aid Work?* by Robert Cassen and Associates. A major contribution of *Assessing Aid* to the vast literature on aid is that it mobilized a new and still growing literature on the crucial nexus between policies in aid-recipient countries, aid and growth.

At the political level, the momentum was built, however, with the UN Conference on *Financing for Development* held in Monterrey in March 2002 and the widespread consensus among bilateral donors and multilateral agencies regarding the need to meet the Millennium Development Goals (MDGs) by 2015. The consensus reached in Monterrey was a major step forward in revamping the aid agenda since there is now widespread agreement that more aid is required to meet the MDGs but at the same time improving dramatically aid effectiveness, mobilizing domestic resources and exploring new sources of development finance beyond aid, are all crucial factors. Obviously mobilizing political will as well as building public support for further increases in aid becomes now the central objective following the important developments in Monterrey. But at the same time the international community is trying to explore other possible sources of funding beyond aid in view of the fact that substantial time may be needed for donors to double aid – see Figure 1 regarding recent progress with ODA increases from DAC countries and predictions for further increases up to 2010. In this regard various proposals have been debated recently. They include the widely discussed British proposal on the *International Finance Facility* aiming to 'frontload' aid through a securitization process in international capital markets so that

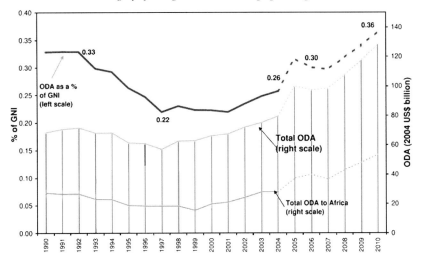

Source: OECD-DAC, *Development Cooperation Report*, 2005. www.oecd.org/dac/stats/dac/dcrannex.

Fig. 1. *Net Official Development Assistance from OECD-DAC countries during the period 1990–2004 and DAC projections up to 2010.*

MDGs can be attained,[1] the US' *Millennium Challenge Account*[2] which grants aid to those recipients that democratize their society and adhere to sound economic policies, the recent French initiative to increase French aid to sub-Saharan Africa by 50 percent so that to accelerate progress regarding the MDGs, the UN Millennium Project Report (2005) and the Report of the Commission for Africa (2005) which call for a new aid policy with much larger donations of aid in the aftermath of the Monterrey consensus. Donor initiatives aiming at the improvement of the whole coordination effort in the donor community have also emerged. The most important ones include the *Declaration on Aid Harmonization* by aid donors in Rome in February 2003 and the *Paris Declaration on Aid Effectiveness* in March 2005 which emphasized that donors should move fast towards aid coordination to accelerate progress with aid effectiveness and MDG attainment. Taken together, these altruistic initiatives seem to indicate that strategic donor behaviour where donors use their influence through foreign aid relations to achieve their own goals has declined. However, as argued quite convincingly by Burnell (2004), issues related to strategic donor behaviour and *realpolitik* have not lost completely importance in recent years, although it would be also fair to say that aid is now more developmental and more pro-poor as compared to the allocation of foreign assistance during the Cold War.

---

[1] See Mavrotas (2004) and Mosley (2004) for a detailed discussion and Lin and Mavrotas (2004) for a simulation exercise based on a theoretical model on IFF.

[2] See Clemens and Radelet (2003) for a critical assessment of the above initiative.

In what follows I discuss various important issues of development aid against the emerging new background for Official Development Assistance (ODA) and in particular how aid effectiveness issues are now perceived in this new setting for aid. The rest of the paper is structured as follows. In Section 2, I discuss the link between development aid and domestic policies in aid-recipient countries by reflecting on the relevant debate in this area whereas in Section 3, I focus on the key issues involved in development aid particularly in connection with recent calls in the international development community for scaling up aid so that the MDGs can be attained. Section 4 concludes the paper by reflecting on the emerging new agenda for foreign aid.

2. Aid effectiveness and the role of domestic policies: consensus or an ongoing debate?

For almost half a century numerous empirical studies have tried to address in various ways the impact of aid on growth in aid-recipient countries and thus shed light on the crucial aid effectiveness issue. For many years the empirical literature on the effectiveness of aid remained inconclusive partly due to lack of good data on aid but also partly due to inappropriate econometrics and simplistic empirical specifications employed in most of the empirical studies.[3] However, important changes in the aid arena in recent years,[4] revived *inter alia* the interest in aid effectiveness issues. Needless to say, current discussion (and debate) on how progress with the MDGs can be made has generated additional interest in aid effectiveness issues. As already mentioned, one of these changes is related to the focus of the research and policy aid community in recent years on the impact of domestic policies in recipient countries on the overall aid-growth nexus. In this regard, the turning point in the aid-growth empirics was the Burnside and Dollar (2000) seminal paper published in the *American Economic Review* in 2000 (and in fact its earlier version published as a World Bank Working Paper in 1997 by the same authors as a background paper for the World Bank study *Assessing Aid* (1998)) – see Burnside and Dollar (1997). One of the key conclusions of the Burnside and Dollar (2000) paper was that aid works better in countries with sound policy regimes, i.e. that "... aid has a positive impact on growth in developing countries with good fiscal, monetary, and trade policies but has little effect in the presence of poor policies", Burnside and Dollar (2000, p. 847).

The above study has been very influential among donor agencies since it provided the donor community with a policy criterion for allocating aid, namely that aid should be allocated on a selective basis to those countries that have adopted good policies in

---

[3] It is clearly beyond the scope of the present paper to review the vast literature of the aid-growth empirics. Tarp (2000), Beynon (2002, 2003), Dalgaard *et al.* (2004), Collier and Dollar (2004), Addison *et al.* (2005a, 2005b) and Radelet (2006) provide recent assessments of the aid effectiveness literature; see also Mosley (1987), White (1992) and Cassen (1994) on earlier reviews of the literature.

[4] Burnell (2004) provides a fascinating discussion of the changing landscape of aid in the 1990s; see also Addison *et al.* (2005a).

view of the central finding of the study that aid works only in a good policy environment.[5] At the same time, the study has mobilized a relatively large and still growing empirical literature in recent years trying to delve deeper into the aid-policies-growth nexus emphasized in the Burnside and Dollar paper. Most of these studies have questioned the validity of the empirical results (and thus the policy lessons emerging from the Burnside and Dollar study) on many grounds such as inappropriate econometrics, problematic definition of the 'policy' variable, inappropriate specification of the empirical model, endogeneity issues etc.[6] In a recent critique of the Burnside and Dollar paper, Easterly *et al.* (2004), by adding 4 more years (1994–1997) to the original Burnside and Dollar dataset convincingly show that the Burnside–Dollar finding regarding the aid-policy interaction is not robust to the use of this additional data thus casting serious doubts on the policy implications emanating from the Burnside and Dollar study. Another study which drew attention recently is Rajan and Subramanian (2005a). The authors examine the effects of aid on growth using cross-sectional and panel data (over the period 1960–2000) and after correcting for the bias that aid typically goes to poorer countries or to countries after poor performance. They report little robust evidence according to which aid affects positively or negatively growth. They cannot find evidence that aid works better in better policy regimes and geographical environments. They conclude that the findings do not imply that aid cannot be beneficial in the future but rather that the international aid architecture needs to be re-examined. More recently, Antipin and Mavrotas (2006) take a fresh look at the aid-growth empirics by adding a new methodological dimension in the Burnside and Dollar paper and the overall aid effectiveness literature. By using three different data sets (including the one used in the Burnside and Dollar paper) and Bayesian instrumental variable methods, they tested the robustness of the central finding of the Burnside and Dollar paper related to the aid and policy interaction coefficient. In doing so, they applied Bayesian instrumental variable techniques to find the most probable parameter values in the growth equation. Similarly to the approach adopted in Easterly *et al.* (2004) they did not deviate from the Burnside and Dollar specification since their primary focus was to test the central empirical finding of the Burnside and Dollar paper without employing a different specification. They also test for the exogeneity of the instrumental variables used. It was found that the problematic interaction term of aid and policy is not statistically significant in the model even with the heteroscedastic-consistent estimator, and most importantly, its marginal effect on real per capita GDP growth is substantially smaller than in the Burnside and Dollar (2000) paper. This obviously raises important questions regarding the robustness of the Burnside and Dollar findings and the validity of the crucial policy implications emerging from the above study.

---

[5] See Collier and Dollar (2001, 2002), Beynon (2002, 2003), McGillivray (2003), Munro (2005), Isopi and Mavrotas (2006) and Amprou *et al.* (2006) on the aid selectivity issue.

[6] See Hansen and Tarp (2000, 2001), Dalgaard and Hansen (2001), Lensink and White (2001), Guillaumont and Chauvet (2001) and more recently Dayton-Johnson and Hoddinot (2003), Denkabe (2004), Chauvet and Guillaumont (2004), Dalgaard *et al.* (2004) and Ram (2004).

3. Scaling up foreign aid: challenge or opportunity?

As already stressed, recent calls to increase substantial foreign aid to make substantial progress with the MDGs generated a new interest among researchers and policy makers regarding the macroeconomic implications of such a "big-push" approach. At the same time, there exists an ongoing debate whether additional aid could be absorbed effectively, while issues related to diminishing returns to aid, the possible adverse effects of increased aid flows on real exchange rates in aid-recipients, possible crowding-out effects of new forms of development finance and debt relief and policy coherence among the various sources of finance in connection with the overall effort to make progress with the MDGs have been under scrutiny recently. In what follows I reflect on some of these issues as well as the emerging new agenda for development aid.

3.1. Absorbing large amounts of aid

As already mentioned, recent years have witnessed a number of new initiatives in the area of development assistance and development finance in general in response to the need to increase substantial capital flows to developing countries so that the internationally agreed MDGs can be achieved. A central issue seems to be the capacity of the aid-recipients to absorb such large amounts of development assistance and whether the right institutional mechanisms are in place to facilitate the absorption of additional aid. Relevant studies include Berg *et al.* (2006), de Renzio (2005), Gupta *et al.* (2005), Addison *et al.* (2005a, 2005b), Heller (2005), Gomanee *et al.* (2005), Addison and Mavrotas (2004), Foster (2003) and Heller and Gupta (2002) among others. In this regard I want to stress that *aid absorption* should be distinguished from *aid effectiveness* in the relevant discourse. Even if we assume high levels of absorption in the countries concerned the effectiveness of aid flows cannot be guaranteed since the latter concerns the overall impact of aid on the macroeconomy, a rather complicated process as the vast aid effectiveness literature seems to suggest.[7] It has been argued that if aid donors were to meet the ODA target of 0.7 percent of donor country GNP, aid flows would increase to about US$175 billion. This, obviously, would help substantially with the progress made to achieve the MDGs, but at the same time it would pose a number of serious challenges for aid-recipient countries at both the micro and macro level (Heller and Gupta, 2002). More precisely, doubling for example aid would face diminishing marginal rates of return but this could become a serious problem at very high aid-to-GDP ratios. By using a wide array of estimators Dalgaard and Hansen (2006) report evidence according to which the average aggregate gross rate return on "aid investments" falls in a 20–30 percent range which is equivalent to the return on investments

---

[7] In recent IMF work on this topic, absorption is defined as the widening of the current account deficit (excluding aid) due to increased aid and it measures the extent to which aid engenders a real resource transfer through higher imports or through a reduction in the domestic resources devoted to producing exports. Along these lines, absorption is distinguished from spending i.e. the widening of the fiscal deficit (excluding aid) accompanying an aid increase (see Berg *et al.*, 2006).

funded by other sources than aid. At the same time, there is no evidence that countries which receive high levels of aid have performed poorly. Some of recent success stories in Africa clearly show how large amounts of aid can yield substantial rates of return: Uganda received more than 20 percent of aid as share of GDP in the early 1990s but managed to register high growth rates above 7 percent, reducing at the same time poverty (mainly through the *Poverty Eradication Action Fund*) by 20 percent. Mozambique, with a 50 percent aid-to-GDP ratio in the 1990s, achieved high growth rates, reaching 12 percent in 1998. Recipients with high aid levels (above 20 percent of income), most of them in Africa, increased on average their per capita GDP by 1.3 percent per year over the period 1995–2000 (World Bank, 2003). Needless to say, the past has also taught us many useful lessons from countries failing to take advantage of large aid inflows and these lessons should be borne in mind in the current debate about the implications of a "big-push" approach for development aid. Furthermore, these trends alone cannot suggest a robust conclusion regarding the impact of aid on growth (and the overall effectiveness of development aid) in the region since the aid-growth relationship can be affected by a number of factors which are not captured by the simple aid-growth empirics. This issue has been discussed recently by Gomanee *et al.* (2005), in the context of the impact of aid on growth in a group of 25 sub-Saharan African countries over the period 1970–1997, who highlighted the importance of domestic investment as a crucial transmission mechanism in the aid-growth nexus. In a very recent study, Guillaumont and Guillaumont (2006) quite rightly conclude that the big push and absorptive capacity approaches cannot be reconciled without a reform on the aid architecture associated with recent calls for scaling up aid. This also echoes Maxwell (2002) who suggests that it would be a missed opportunity to increase aid without considering the apparatus for delivering such large amounts of money. Bourguignon and Sundberg (2007) look at the issue of building absorptive capacity to meet the MDGs by addressing absorptive capacity in low-income countries from both a theoretical and empirical perspective. They also present a framework for undertaking country specific analysis, which relates the macroeconomic environment and economic growth on the one hand, and sector-specific micro-constraints affecting implementation of the social MDGs on the other.

3.2. Dealing with volatile and unpredictable aid flows in an world of scaled-up aid

The new research agenda on aid and the MDGs generated *inter alia* an interest in a crucial issue namely the volatility of aid flows. Indeed, managing aid volatility, and in particular the unpredictability of aid flows, is of crucial importance for the attainment of the MDGs.[8] There is now a substantial body of evidence that aid volatility is bad for economic growth (Lensink and Morrissey, 2000; Bulíř and Hamann, 2001). The negative impact of aid volatility on growth is robust across different country groups and

---

[8] Very recently, aid volatility issues have also been discussed within the context of aid to *difficult partnership countries* (Levin and Dollar, 2005).

different specifications in the growth equation. Indeed, average aid flows are found to have a significant positive effect on economic growth only after conditioning on the negative impact of volatility. Pallage and Robe (2001) report evidence according to which aid flows are highly volatile over time (on average, two to three times as volatile as the recipient's output) and overwhelmingly pro-cyclical. Obviously, identifying and dealing with this uncertainty is a priority for development planning and the achievement of the MDGs. The issue of aid volatility and aid predictability has also been raised recently within the context of the British proposal for the International Finance Facility in view of its focus on less volatile and predictable aid flows.

Bulíř and Hamann (2003), by using data covering 72 countries over the period 1975–1997 focus on a comparative analysis of the volatility of aid flows and the volatility of domestic revenue in aid recipients, rather than on the volatility of aid inflows *per se*. They found that aid flows are more volatile than domestic fiscal revenues and tend also to be pro-cyclical, and that there are much larger prediction errors in programme assistance than in project aid, and a stronger tendency to over-estimation. They also find that fiscal planners are highly uncertain of aid receipts, the information content of aid commitments being either very small or statistically insignificant. More recently, Fielding and Mavrotas (2005a, 2005b), examined aid volatility using data for 66 aid recipients over the period 1973–2002 by also disaggregating total aid inflows into sector and programme aid. They found that *inter alia* the institutional quality of the aid recipient affects the stability of sector aid but not that of programme assistance, and that macroeconomic stability affects the stability of both kinds of aid, as does the extent to which a country relies on a small number of individual donors. Their results point to the importance of disaggregating aid when modelling the unpredictability of aid inflows. This has important policy implications with respect to progress towards achievement of the MDGs: modelling a single aid aggregate can mask underlying heterogeneity in the determinants of the unpredictability of different types of aid. This is particularly important for aid recipient governments who are attempting to manage aid unpredictability by some combination of adjustment to tax and spending plans, adjustment of foreign exchange reserves or domestic non-monetary financing (Bulíř and Lane, 2002; Foster, 2003). For these countries, improved forecasting of both short-term and medium-term aid is vital, although in the latter case informal indications from donors are also likely to be important. Finally, Hudson and Mosley (2006), by revisiting the Bulir and Hamann's analysis of aid volatility argue that there are problems with both the data and the methodology employed in the above study. Similarly to Fielding and Mavrotas (2005a, 2005b) they disaggregate aid by aid donor and type and construct an empirical model which seeks to explore the causes and effects of aid volatility.

3.3. Potential Dutch-disease effects and increased aid

Dutch disease type issues associated with large amounts of foreign aid is not a new topic in the voluminous literature of aid effectiveness. Early studies include Younger (1992), Vos (1998) and Kasekende and Atingi-Ego (1999) among others. The issue has also been discussed in the past in connection with the potential undesirable effects on the real exchange rate of a windfall emanating from a commodity boom. The Dutch disease issue has attracted new interest by researchers and policymakers alike recently in connection with the scaling up scenarios of foreign aid – see Heller (2005) for an excellent discussion and Gupta *et al.* (2005) and Killick and Foster (2007) for recent assessments with regard to sub-Saharan Africa.

It may well be argued that large and sustained aid flows may cause some appreciation of the nominal and real exchange rates in recipient countries. Indeed, since most aid is provided to governments whose expenditure is mainly on non-tradeables such as public services, there is clearly a likelihood of short-run Dutch disease effects. In this case aid may have two effects: a distortionary effect on price incentives to producing tradeables and a direct positive income effect. Obviously, the final outcome will be determined by how the economy responds to the distortion. However, in case substantial aid flows are supported by appropriate economic policies in recipient countries, the net gains to higher sustained levels of aid remain strongly positive and donors should therefore continue to make these resources available to recipient countries pursuing sound macroeconomic policies on this front (DFID, 2002). In practice, there is little evidence that countries receiving high volumes of aid in the 1990s have, when accompanied by appropriate macropolicy, experienced negative effects on their tradable sector (see also Adam, 2001 for a discussion). Very recently, however, Rajan and Subramanian (2005b), in a comprehensive study on the topic using both cross-country and within-variation econometric methodology found that foreign aid have systematic adverse effects on an aid-recipient country's competitiveness as reflected in a decline in the share of labour intensive and tradeable industries in the manufacturing sector. They argue that these effects emanate from the real exchange rate appreciation which is caused by aid. It has been argued, however, that Dutch disease issues might not be a reason for concern if the additional aid flows are channeled to public infrastructure projects which in turn can improve the productivity of the private sector in the countries concerned (Adam, 2005; Adam and Bevan, 2004). Needless to say, in a world of scaled-up aid Dutch disease effects are most likely to occur in the case of countries with already high levels of aid inflows. These countries are expected to experience large macroeconomic effects including possible negative effects on relative prices. Thus, it would be premature at this stage to discount completely Dutch disease as potential negative effect of scaling up aid (see (Killick and Foster, 2007) for a comprehensive discussion).

3.4. Fiscal management of increased aid

Scaling up aid may pose serious policy challenges to many aid recipients regarding the fiscal management of large amounts of aid flows (as will be the case on the overall macroeconomic management front).[9] The issue regarding the impact of aid on tax effort and savings behaviour in the aid-recipient country is certainly not a new one and

---

[9] See Heller (2005).

the seminal contribution in the subject dates back to 1970 when Keith Griffin argued (Griffin, 1970) in his well-known *domestic savings displacement hypothesis* that aid may reduce savings in countries receiving aid and that aid flows may be also responsible for a relaxation of the tax effort in the countries concerned. The above hypothesis has been extensively discussed and tested in the aid effectiveness literature for many years.[10] The impact of aid on the fiscal sector attracted a revived interest by researchers and policymakers alike in the 1990s with the emergence of a new theoretical and empirical literature known as the 'fiscal response literature'[11] building on the seminal paper by Heller (1975).[12] A separate strand of this literature deals with the fungibility issue, namely that the aid-recipient government may reduce its own resources from the sector which receives aid and channel them to other sectors of the budget.[13]

In a scaling-up aid scenario, obviously a crucial issue will be the successful coordination of the objectives of fiscal policy with the exchange rate and monetary policies pursued by the central bank in aid-recipient countries receiving large amounts of aid inflows (Heller *et al.*, 2006). Heller *et al.* (2006) in a recent study argue that the following factors will determine the final outcome in this case:

- The government's decision on how much to spend of the aid inflows and the composition of that spending.
- How much aid will not be spent but rather used to build up reserves.
- The government's behaviour regarding financing expenditure programmes when aid is also volatile.
- And finally, how the additional aid flows will be used.

Of course, it has to be borne in mind that at the end of the day donors may prove less generous than anticipated and/or we may witness a substantial increase not of aggregate aid but rather an increase in certain types of development cooperation. This will inevitably determine the extent to which fiscal and macroeconomic management in aid-recipients will be affected.

3.5. Aid heterogeneity and scaling up: does it make a difference?

Another major shortcoming of much of the aid literature is the neglect of the heterogeneous character of aid inflows. It has been correctly argued that aid is heterogeneous and each of its components exerts different macroeconomic effects on the aid-recipient economy (Cassen, 1986). The use of a single figure for aid, a typical feature of the aid

---

[10] White (1992) provides a comprehensive discussion of the early literature on the subject.
[11] The term is attributed to White (1992).
[12] See McGillivray and Morrissey (2004) for a recent review of this literature.
[13] Empirical studies in the area of fungibility include Pack and Pack (1990, 1993), Khilji and Zampelli (1991) and Feyzioglu *et al.* (1998); see also White (1998) for a detailed discussion.

effectiveness literature,[14] cannot capture this aid heterogeneity, thus leading to aggregation bias in the empirical 'evidence' reported (Cassen, 1994; White, 1998; Mavrotas, 2002a, 2002b, 2005a; Clemens *et al.*, 2004 and Mavrotas and Ouattara 2006a, 2006b). But why is this the case? Firstly, because of different conditions relating to each type of aid in different countries e.g. the state of aid co-ordination may vary among aid recipients for the various aid modalities, there is an extra reason to expect different effects of aid among aid-recipients; the *ceteris paribus* assumptions of the aid-growth empirics may be disturbed by such considerations. Secondly, within an endogenous fiscal response framework,[15] if the aid-recipient government attaches different utility to each category of aid, using a single figure of aid would lead to aggregation bias in the results and conclusions reached. Last but not least, aid heterogeneity might not be an issue if there is evidence that the composition of aid has remained the same over time in countries receiving aid. However, if the proportions are changing, as they are, and changing in different degrees for different countries, this will definitely affect the econometric results.

Of relevance to the aid heterogeneity issue is the ongoing debate regarding the advantages of the General Budget Support (GBS) over other types of assistance, in particular project aid. It needs to be stressed that aid provided through GBS is disbursed through the financial management system of the aid-recipient government and thus it assumes an overall understanding and agreement on the government's development strategy. This basically implies that both donors and recipient monitor implementation of the agreed development strategy as a whole and not just the use of the aid inflows. In this regard, GBS are expected to have a number of advantages such as improved donor coordination and harmonization, lower transaction costs as compared to other forms of aid, alignment with partner country systems and policies, more predictable aid flows and enhanced effectiveness of the state and public administration (see IDD and Associates, 2006; Cordella and Dell'Ariccia, 2003; Eifert and Gelb, 2005 and Gupta *et al.*, 2006 for a discussion).

In this context, looking at aid effectiveness from a different angle i.e. by examining the impact of the various aid modalities on macroeconomic variables in aid-recipients can provide us with further insights on *how aid really works* in countries receiving aid. This is obviously becoming a central issue in a scaling up aid scenario, particularly under the rather reasonable assumption that the coming years may witness a substantial increase not necessarily in aggregate aid, but rather in specific forms of assistance.

3.6. The two faces of Janus: foreign aid and the role of institutions

Institutions in aid-recipient countries have of course an important role to play in aid effectiveness enhancement, of crucial importance for the ongoing discussion and debate regarding progress that needs to be made with the MDGs. At one extreme, aid

---

[14] Exceptions are Levy (1987), Mavrotas (2002a, 2002b, 2005a), Clemens *et al.* (2004), Ouattara (2005), Rajan and Subramanian (2005a) and Mavrotas and Ouattara (2006a, 2006b).

[15] This means that aid is endogenized in the government utility function.

may contribute to a virtuous circle of economic growth and poverty reduction through fostering desirable policy change, building effective institutions, and relieving constraints on funds for investment, leveraging in private resources. Arguably India is in this category but also Uganda. At the other extreme, aid may contribute to a vicious circle where the provision of external finance serves to delay policy reforms, undermine the effectiveness of institutions, and contribute to conflict over the distribution of economic rents. Somalia in the 1970s & 1980s is an example where aid undermined institutions and governance.[16] Aid has also been conceived of as an instrument for achieving "capacity building" so as to develop institutional arrangements conducive for growth. On the other hand, the phenomenon of "aid dependence", of particular relevance to many aid dependent economies in Africa, has been conceptualized as aid-induced institutional decline in the model developed by Azam *et al.* (1999). Along the above lines, exploring further the channels through which aid serves to strengthen the policy & institutional framework (e.g. by enabling improvements in savings, investment, public sector management and growth), but also examining the circumstances under which aid may undermine policy & institutions is crucial. There are in practice also complex interactions between policy, institutions and public expenditure. For example, successful institutional development is likely to increase the positive impact of public expenditure on the growth process (Jones and Shaw, 2001).[17]

Needless to say, political economy aspects of aid giving are relevant to the overall nexus between aid and institutions. Political economy issues are of growing importance in recent years in view of the new focus on aid following the Monterrey consensus in 2002 and the need to increase substantial aid flows so progress can be made with the MDGs. Work in this area is mostly related to governance issues in the aid apparatus both in terms of donors and recipients. It is fair to argue, however, that a rigorous analysis of donor incentives and of the overall interaction of interest based donor and recipient policies has been largely neglected in the voluminous aid literature. On the important issue of the political economy of aid see a recent Special Issue edited by Sajal Lahiri and Katharina Michaelowa in the *Review of Development Economics* in 2006 and the papers therein, in particular regarding the role of institutions within aid agencies and the conflicting objectives adopted in many cases, the delivery mechanisms involved and the incentives which may affect the overall assessment of the various aid modalities adopted by donors (Lahiri and Michaelowa, 2006).[18]

---

[16] See Kayizzi-Mugerwa (2003) for an excellent discussion of issues related to institutional development in Africa.

[17] See also Fozzard and Foster (2004).

[18] It is also important to stress that the theoretical literature on foreign aid has generally ignored the multilateral system and the channels through which the donor behaviour may affect multilateral institutions (Kanbur, 2003). Obviously important political economy issues may arise in this case. Part of the theoretical aid literature has tried to illuminate the overall balance between bilateral and multilateral aid by trying to explore the nature of the game between recipients and donors. See for example Murshed and Sen (1995), Azam and Laffont (2003), Murshed (2004) and Milner (2006).

3.7. Aid, FDI and other sources of development finance: policy coherence issues

As already mentioned in the introductory remarks of this chapter, aid has increased substantially following the Monterrey consensus and many donors are currently mobilizing their efforts towards further aid increases. This, however, will take time as Figure 2 seems to suggest since only a few donors have already managed to reach the 0.7 UN target, with the remaining group of donors expected to reach the target (at least on the basis of the commitments made in Monterrey and at the G8 Summit in Gleneagles in July 2005) in the coming years. However, time is of the essence in connection with the need to make rapid progress with the MDGs, thus other sources of development finance beyond aid need also to be considered. Recent proposals on new sources of financing include the use of Global Funds, the US Millennium Challenge Account, the British proposal for an International Finance Facility, and proposals for global taxation, a Global Premium Bond, the expansion of SDRs, but also ways to encourage the flow of private finance (FDI, portfolio flows and remittances) – for a comprehensive discussion of most of the above proposals see a recent UNU-WIDER major study, conducted in collaboration with UN-DESA, on "Innovative Sources for Development Finance", and directed by Sir Anthony Atkinson (Atkinson, 2004). In this regard, some proposals have been extensively discussed in the literature (e.g. Tobin tax) while others are entirely or relatively new (e.g. IFF, Global Premium Bond), some of these proposals require a high level of international unanimity, some can be introduced by a sub-set of countries or individual countries ('flexible geometry'), while

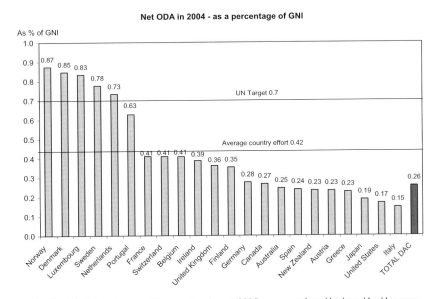

Source: OECD-DAC, *Development Cooperation Report*, 2005. www.oecd.org/dac/stats/dac/dcrannex.

Fig. 2.   Net Official Development Assistance in 2004 as a percentage of GNI.

still others can be purely private initiatives (Atkinson, 2004). It is also important to stress that there is a *distinct risk of crowding out* in some of the proposals (the *additionality issue*) i.e. that new sources of finance or existing sources other than aid (e.g. FDI) may crowd-out development aid.

A related issue is the overall relationship between FDI and foreign aid. Although more aid is important, aid cannot deliver the kinds of benefits, particularly in knowledge transfer that FDI promises. In this regard, FDI can play a very positive role in helping to achieve the MDGs by their target date of 2015. With only a decade to go, employment growth will have to be very fast indeed to achieve the ambitious target of halving global income poverty and this requires a considerable acceleration in investment, by both domestic and foreign companies (see Addison *et al.* 2006 for a detailed discussion). Further to this, the potentially 'catalyzing' effect of aid on FDI is frequently mentioned as a rationale for giving aid to low-income countries, although the empirical evidence associated with this line of argument is not conclusive (see Rodrik, 1995; Bird and Rowlands, 1997 and Ratha, 2001). Harms and Lutz (2006) test the above hypothesis regarding the aid-FDI nexus by using panel data covering a large number of developing and emerging economies over the 1990s and by also controlling for the institutional environment in the countries concerned. They found that the marginal effect of aid flows on FDI is close to zero, and that, (surprisingly) the effect is strictly positive for countries in which the private sector faces a substantial regulatory burden.

Other forms of development finance related to domestic resource mobilization should also be considered within the context of the MDG financing. Domestic resource mobilization broadly defined to include not only saving mobilization and (domestic) private investment recovery, but also the building of inclusive financial sectors and the improvement of financial access in developing countries has a substantial potential which if materialized can help significantly towards the achievement of the MDGs. Domestic resource mobilization has also the additional advantage of engaging local communities directly in the overall development financing process. Furthermore, financial sector development can enhance saving mobilization and domestic investment for pro-poor growth. The issue is becoming of crucial importance in view of the overall low savings rates of many developing economies in recent years and the fact that a substantial number of developing countries have undertaken a series of financial reforms recently to improve economic performance (Mavrotas, 2005b).

Needless to say, coordinating the various sources of development finance, which are currently being mobilized in connection with the MDGs, poses a serious challenge for the international development community. This is basically an issue of *policy coherence* which is expected to draw a lot of attention in academic and policy circles in a world of increased aid and development finance. At the same time, though, it is bound to remain a central issue in the whole effort to coordinate the various resource flows channeled to the developing world. As has been argued recently by Cogneau and Lambert (2006), 'if aid is to remain targeted to the poorest of the poor a change will need to occur. Rather than the selective aid policies pursued today – which are neither effective nor fair – the introduction of the notion of equality of opportunity between countries would be a better means of maintaining the compensatory function of public development aid'.

Finally, of relevance to the policy coherence issue and the need for enhanced coordination is the issue of delivery mechanisms of additional aid flows (and other forms of development finance) which has been the subject of a debate recently, in particular as far as sub-Saharan Africa is concerned. The recently-released UNCTAD report on *Economic Development in Africa 2006: Doubling Aid: Making the 'Big Push' Work* (UNCTAD, 2006) clearly stressed that the additional aid flows should be released in predictable amounts over a long-term period, should be more focused on enabling African economies to produce a broader range of goods and create more jobs and should be channeled to those countries' general budgets so that their legislatures can best decide how to spend it. In this context, according to the Report, the current chaotic system in which too many agencies are pushing too many development projects that sometimes compete to each other, often don't match recipients' development goals and are costly to administer will be replaced by a new aid architecture more capable of delivering efficiently the additional aid flows to the region. This can be done, UNCTAD argues, by revisiting the idea of a *UN funding window*.

4. Concluding remarks

The above discussion clearly suggests that a new agenda in the area of foreign aid has emerged with important challenges, but also opportunities, for both the donor and recipient communities.

- Making substantial effort to reduce the volatility of aid flows and increase their predictability can clearly affect the progress we can make in achieving the MDGs. In this regard, improving aid coordination by moving fast towards the implementation of the *Paris Declaration on Aid Effectiveness* would be an important step forward.
- But also crucial is the key-challenge on how to bring about the major changes to donor *modus operandi* that would enable the emerging conclusions about aid effectiveness to be reflected in foreign aid practice. *This is a challenge for restructuring the aid apparatus, a challenge for revamping the current aid architecture substantially*. In this regard, Cohen *et al.* (2006) by looking at the grants vis-à-vis loans debate argue that the traditional paradigm of ODA should be re-examined and the various aid instruments need to further develop.
- Examining more carefully the various channels through which different forms of aid may affect the macroeconomy of aid recipients is also vital for making aid work better in a world of scaled-up aid.
- Targeting aid sectors more efficiently seems to be the key. Dreher *et al.* (2006) analyze the aid portfolio of various bilateral and multilateral donors to test whether they have prioritized aid in connection with the MDGs. They found that donors differ not only in terms of their overall generocity and the general poverty orientation of aid but also in the extent to which their sectoral aid allocation is conducive to achieving more specific MDGs. They conclude that aid targeting issues are also relevant and

that unless the targeting of aid is improved scaling up aid will not have the desired effects.

- Delving deeper into the channels and the mechanisms through which the impact of aid operates in countries emerging from conflict is also crucial for broad-based post-conflict recovery. The role of aid in conflict-affected countries (both those at war and those attempting 'post-conflict' reconstruction) is highly controversial, and equally there is no clear understanding of how aid might contribute to preventing conflict from breaking out or escalating, and how different types of aid influence outcomes (Addison, 2000, Demekas *et al.*, 2002, Picciotto, 2004, Addison and McGillivray, 2004). Provided that resources are available following the end of the conflict, rebuilding shattered infrastructure is a rather straightforward task. The real challenge, however, is how to transform institutions and policies since in many cases these favour one social group over another. The focus, therefore, should be on transformation, rather than reconstruction for broad-based recovery in conflict-affected countries. This is more challenging task for aid than simple reconstruction (Addison, 2003b).[19]
- Finally, while it is also important for the development community to explore new sources of finance to make substantial progress with the MDGs, increasing aid should be prioritized since aid remains a vital source of finance for many developing countries particularly in sub-Saharan Africa. Obviously, crowding-out issues are of relevance in this case since some of the proposals currently being debated may crowd out existing sources of finance such as ODA. It is, thus, central for donors to honour the commitments made at Monterrey regarding substantial increases in aid flows up to 2015.
- At the same time, it is imperative for aid recipients to undertake a major effort to use these additional flows most efficiently by moving fast with the implementation of appropriate reforms on the governance front.

It will be only after all this is taken into consideration that we most possibly have plenty of reasons to be more optimistic about the future of this important source of development finance and its great potential to affect people's lives in the developing world.

References

Adam, C. (2001), *Uganda: exchange rate management, monetary policy and aid*. Bank of Uganda and University of Oxford, mimeo.

Adam, C. (2005), Exogenous inflows and real exchange rates: theoretical quirk or empirical reality? Prepared from the Seminar on Foreign Aid and Macroeconomic

---

[19] And related to the previous point, in many conflicts it is essential to get involved in poverty reduction projects before a peace deal is achieved since it would help to achieve a broad-based post-conflict recovery (Addison, 2003a; de Sousa, 2003).

Management, organized by the IMF Institute and the African Department, 14–15 March.

Adam, C., Bevan, D. (2004), Aid and the supply side: public investment, export performance and Dutch disease in low income countries. *Discussion Paper*, No. 201, University of Oxford.

Addison, T. (2000), Aid and conflict. In: Tarp, F. (Ed.), *Foreign Aid and Development: Lessons Learnt and Directions for the Future*. In: Routledge Studies in Development Economics, vol. 17.

Addison, T. (Ed.) (2003a), *From Conflict to Recovery in Africa*. Oxford University Press, Oxford.

Addison, T. (2003b), Africa's recovery from conflict: making peace work for the poor. *UNU-WIDER Policy Brief*, No. 6, World Institute for Development Economics Research of the United Nations University, Helsinki.

Addison, T., Mavrotas, G. (2004), Development aid to Africa: issues, challenges and agendas. Paper presented at the UNU-TICAD III Experts' Group Workshop, March 2004, United Nations Center, Tokyo.

Addison, T., McGillivray, M. (2004), Aid to conflict-affected countries: lessons for donors. Paper presented at the Global Policy Workshop on *Security and Development*, Global Development Network Fifth Annual Development Conference, *Understanding Reform*, January 24–30, New Delhi.

Addison, T., Mavrotas, G., McGillivray, M. (2005a), Aid, debt relief and new sources of finance for meeting the millennium development goals. *Journal of International Affairs* 58, 113–127.

Addison, T., Mavrotas, G., McGillivray, M. (2005b), Aid to Africa: an unfinished agenda. *Journal of International Development* 17, 989–1001.

Addison, T., Guha-Khasnobis, B., Mavrotas, G. (2006), FDI to developing countries: the unfinished agenda. *World Economy* 29, 1–8.

Amprou, J., Guillaumont, P., Guillaumont, S.J. (2006), Aid selectivity according to augmented criteria. Paper presented at the WIDER Development Conference on *Aid: Principles, Policies and Performance*, WIDER Helsinki, 16–17 June.

Antipin, J.-E., Mavrotas, G. (2006), On the empirics of aid and growth: a fresh look. *WIDER Research Paper*, No. 5, Helsinki.

Atkinson, A.B. (Ed.) (2004), *New Sources for Development Finance*. Oxford University Press for UNU-WIDER, Oxford.

Azam, J.-P., Laffont, J.-J. (2003), Contracting for aid. *Journal of Development Economics* 70, 25–58.

Azam, J.-P., Devarajan, S., O'Connell, S.A. (1999), Aid dependence reconsidered. *Working Paper*, Centre for the Study of African Economies, Oxford, 99-5.

Berg, A., Hussain, M., Aiyar, S., Roache, S., Mirzoev, T., Mahone, A. (2006), The macroeconomics of managing increased aid inflows: experiences of low-income countries and policy implications. Paper presented at the WIDER Development Conference on *Aid: Principles, Policies and Performance*, WIDER Helsinki, 16–17 June.

Beynon, J. (2002), Policy implications for aid allocations of recent research on aid effectiveness and selectivity. In: Arvin, B.M. (Ed.), *New Perspectives on Foreign Aid and Economic Development*. Praeger, Westport, Connecticut.

Beynon, J. (2003), Poverty efficient aid allocations: collier/dollar revisited. *Economic and Statistics Analysis Unit Working Paper*, Overseas Development Institute, London, (2).

Bird, G., Rowlands, D. (1997), The catalytic effect of lending by the international financial institutions. *World Economy* 20, 967–991.

Bourguignon, F., Sundberg, M. (2007), Absorptive capacity and achieving the millennium development goals. In: Mavrotas, G., Shorrocks, A. (Eds.), *Advancing Development: Core Themes in Global Economics*. Palgrave Macmillan.

Bulíř, A., Hamann, J. (2001), How volatile and unpredictable are aid flows and what are the policy implications? *IMF Working Paper* 01/167, International Monetary Fund, Washington, DC.

Bulíř, A., Hamann, J. (2003), Aid volatility: an empirical assessment. *IMF Staff Papers* 50, 65–89.

Bulíř, A., Lane, T. (2002), Aid and fiscal management. *IMF Working Paper* 02/112, International Monetary Fund, Washington, DC.

Burnell, P. (2004), Foreign aid resurgent: new spirit or old hangover. *Research Paper*, No. 2004/44, World Institute for Development Economics Research, Helsinki.

Burnside, C., Dollar, D. (1997), Aid, policies and growth. *Policy Research Working Paper*, World Bank, Washington, DC (1777).

Burnside, C., Dollar, D. (2000), Aid, policies and growth. *American Economic Review* 90, 847–868.

Cassen, R. (1986), *Does Aid Work?* Oxford University Press, Oxford.

Cassen, R. (1994), *Does Aid Work?* second ed. Oxford University Press, Oxford.

Chauvet, L., Guillaumont, P. (2004), *Aid effectiveness in an unstable environment*. CERDI, mimeo.

Clemens, M., Radelet, S. (2003), The millennium challenge account: how much is too much, how long is long enough? *Working Paper*, No. 23, Center for Global Development, Washington, DC.

Clemens, M., Radelet, S., Bhavnani, R. (2004), Counting chickens when they hatch: the short-term effect of aid on growth. *Working Paper*, No. 44, Center for Global Development, Washington, DC.

Cogneau, D., Lambert, S. (2006), *Aid and Coherence of OECD Country Policies*. Policy Insights, vol. 24. OECD Development Centre, Paris.

Cohen, D., Jacquet, P., Reisen, H. (2006), Beyond 'Grants versus Loans': how to use ODA and debt for development. Paper presented at the WIDER Development Conference on *Aid: Principles, Policies and Performance*, WIDER Helsinki, 16–17 June.

Collier, P., Dollar, D. (2001), Can the world cut poverty in half? How policy reform and effective aid can meet international development goals? *World Development* 29, 1787–1802.

Collier, P., Dollar, D. (2002), Aid allocation and poverty reduction. *European Economic Review* 45, 1470–1500.

Collier, P., Dollar, D. (2004), Development effectiveness: what have we learnt? *Economic Journal* 114, F244–F271.

Commission for Africa Report (2005), *Our common interest: report of the commission for Africa*, March.

Cordella, T., Dell'Ariccia, G. (2003), Budget support versus project aid: a theoretical appraisal. *IMF Working Papers* 03/88, International Monetary Fund, Washington, DC.

Dalgaard, C.-J., Hansen, H. (2001), On aid, growth and good policies. *Journal of Development Studies* 37, 17–41.

Dalgaard, C.-J., Hansen, H. (2006), The return to foreign aid. Paper presented at the WIDER Development Conference on *Aid: Principles, Policies and Performance*, WIDER Helsinki, 16–17 June.

Dalgaard, C.-J., Hansen, H., Tarp, F. (2004), On the empirics of foreign aid and growth. *Economic Journal* 114, F191–F216.

Dayton-Johnson, J., Hoddinot, J. (2003), Aid, policies and growth redux. Unpublished manuscript.

Demekas, D.G., McHugh, J.E., Kosma, T. (2002), The economics of post conflict aid. *Working Paper*, No. 02/198, International Monetary Fund.

Denkabe, P. (2004), Policy, aid, and growth: a threshold hypothesis. *Journal of African Finance and Economic Development* 6, 1–21.

DFID (2002), The macroeconomic effects of aid. *Policy Paper by the Department for International Development*, London, December.

Dreher, A., Nunnenkamp, P., Thiele, R., (2006), Sectoral aid priorities: are donors really doing their best to achieve the millennium development goals? Paper presented at the WIDER Development Conference on *Aid: Principles, Policies and Performance*, WIDER Helsinki, 16–17 June.

de Renzio, P. (2005), Can more aid be spent in Africa? In: *ODI Opinions*. Overseas Development Institute, London.

de Sousa, C. (2003), Rebuilding rural livelihoods and social capital in Mozambique. In: Addison, T. (Ed.), *From Conflict to Recovery in Africa*. Oxford University Press for UNU-WIDER, Oxford.

Easterly, W., Levine, R., Roodman, D. (2004), New data, new doubts: a comment on Burnside and Dollar's 'Aid, polices and growth (2000)'. *American Economic Review* 94 (2).

Eifert, B., Gelb, A. (2005), Improving the dynamics of aid: toward more predictable budget support. *World Bank Policy Research Working Paper* 3732.

Feyzioglu, T., Swaroop, V., Zhu, M. (1998), A panel data analysis of the fungibility of aid. *World Bank Economic Review* 12 (1).

Fielding, D., Mavrotas, G. (2005a), The volatility of aid. *WIDER Discussion Paper*, World Institute for Development Economics Research (2005/06).

Fielding, D., Mavrotas, G. (2005b), On the volatility of foreign aid: further evidence. Paper presented at the UNU-WIDER Project Meeting *"Development Aid: A Fresh Look"*, September 2005, Helsinki.

Foster, M. (2003), The case for increased aid. *Report to the Department for International Development* (DfID), London.

Fozzard, A., Foster, M. (2004), Changing approaches to public expenditure management in low-income aid dependent countries. In: Addison, T., Roe, A. (Eds.), *Fiscal Policy for Development, Poverty Reconstruction and Growth*. Palgrave Macmillan.

Gomanee, K., Girma, S., Morrissey, O. (2005), Aid and growth in sub-Saharan Africa: accounting for transmission mechanisms. *Journal of International Development* 17, 1055–1075.

Griffin, K. (1970), Foreign capital, domestic savings and economics development. *Bulletin of the Oxford University Institute of Economics and Statistics* 32, 99–112.

Gupta, S., Powell, R., Yang, Y. (2005), The macroeconomic challenges of scaling up aid to Africa. *IMF Working Paper* 05/179.

Gupta, S., Pattilo, C., Wagh, S. (2006), Are donor countries giving more or less aid? *Review of Development Economics* 10, 535–552.

Guillaumont, P., Chauvet, L. (2001), Aid and performance: a reassessment. *Journal of Development Studies* 37, 66–87.

Guillaumont, P., Guillaumont, S.J. (2006), Big push versus absorptive capacity: how to reconcile the two approaches. Paper presented at the WIDER Development Conference on *Aid: Principles, Policies and Performance*, WIDER Helsinki, 16–17 June.

Hansen, H., Tarp, F. (2000), Aid effectiveness disputed. *Journal of International Development* 12, 375–398.

Hansen, H., Tarp, F. (2001), Aid and growth regressions. *Journal of Development Economics* 64, 547–570.

Harms, P., Lutz, M. (2006), Aid, governance and private foreign investment: some puzzling findings for the 1990s. *Economic Journal* 116, 773–790.

Heller, P.S. (1975), A model of public fiscal behaviour in developing countries; aid, investment and taxation. *American Economic Review* 65, 429–445.

Heller, P.S. (2005), Pity the finance minister: issues in managing a substantial scaling up of aid flows. *IMF Working Paper* 05/180.

Heller, P., Gupta, S. (2002), More aid – making it work for the poor. *World Economics* 3, 131–146.

Heller, P.S., Katz, M., Debrun, X., Thomas, T., Koranchelian, T., Adenauer, I. (2006), Making fiscal space happen! Managing fiscal policy in a world of scaled-up aid. *WIDER Research Paper*, No. 125, World Institute for Development Economics Research.

Hudson, J., Mosley, P. (2006), Aid volatility, policy and development. Paper presented at the WIDER Development Conference on *Aid: Principles, Policies and Performance*, WIDER Helsinki, 16–17 June.

IDD and Associates (2006), *Evaluation of General Budget Support: Synthesis Report*. International Development Department, University of Birmingham, May.

Isopi, A., Mavrotas, G. (2006), Aid allocation and aid effectiveness: an empirical analysis. *WIDER Research Paper*, No. 07, Helsinki.

Jones, S., Shaw, U. (2001), Development effectiveness and assessment issues. *Contribution to Working Paper on Development Effectiveness*, Department for International Development (DFID), UK.

Kanbur, R. (2003), The economics of international aid. In: Kolm, C., Mercier-Ythier, J. (Eds.), *Handbook on The Economics of Giving, Reciprocity and Altruism*. North-Holland, Serge.

Kasekende, L.A., Atingi-Ego, M. (1999), Uganda's experience with aid. *Journal of African Economies* 8, 617–649.

Kayizzi-Mugerwa, S. (Ed.) (2003), *Reforming Africa's Institutions: Ownership, Incentives and Capabilities*. United Nations University Press, Tokyo.

Khilji, N., Zampelli, E. (1991), The fungibility of US assistance to developing countries and the impacts on recipient expenditures: a case study of Pakistan. *World Development* 19, 1095–1106.

Killick, T., Foster, M. (2007), The macroeconomics of doubling aid to Africa and the centrality of the supply side. *Development Policy Review*, in press.

Lahiri, S., Michaelowa, K. (2006), The political economy of aid. *Review of Development Economics* 10 (2), 177–344 (special issue).

Lensink, R., Morrissey, O. (2000), Aid instability as a measure of uncertainty and the positive impact of aid on growth. *Journal of Development Studies* 36, 31–49.

Lensink, R., White, H. (2001), Are there negative returns to aid. *Journal of Development Studies* 37, 42–65.

Levin, V., Dollar, D. (2005), The forgotten states: aid volumes and volatility in difficult partnership countries. Paper prepared for DAC Learning and Advisory Process on Difficult Partnerships.

Levy, V. (1987), Anticipated development assistance, temporary relief aid, and consumption behaviour of low-income countries. *Economic Journal* 97, 446–458.

Lin, T., Mavrotas, G. (2004), A contract perspective on the international finance facility. *WIDER Research Paper*, World Institute for Development Economics Research, Helsinki (2004/60).

Mavrotas, G. (2002a), Foreign aid and fiscal response: does aid disaggregation matter? *Weltwirtschaftliches Archiv* (Review of World Economics) 138, 534–559.

Mavrotas, G. (2002b), Aid and growth in India: some evidence from disaggregated aid data. *South Asia Economic Journal* 3, 19–49.

Mavrotas, G. (2004), The international finance facility. In: Atkinson, A.B. (Ed.), *New Sources of Development Finance*. Oxford University Press for UNU-WIDER, Oxford.

Mavrotas, G. (2005a), Aid heterogeneity: looking at aid effectiveness from a different angle. *Journal of International Development* 17, 1019–1036.

Mavrotas, G. (2005b), Savings and financial sector development: assessing the evidence. In: Green, C., Kirkpatrick, C., Murinde, V. (Eds.), *Finance and Development: Surveys of Theory, Evidence and Policy*. Edward Elgar.

Mavrotas, G., Ouattara, B. (2006a), Public fiscal behaviour and aid heterogeneity in aid-recipient economies. *Journal of Developing Areas* 39, 1–15.

Mavrotas, G., Ouattara, B. (2006b), Aid disaggregation, endogenous aid and the public sector in aid-recipient economies. *Review of Development Economics* 10, 432–449.

Maxwell, S. (2002), More aid? Yes – and use it to reshape aid architecture. In: *ODI Opinions*. ODI, London.

McGillivray, M. (2003), Aid effectiveness and selectivity: integrating multiple objectives in aid allocations. Paper presented at the Joint OECD DAC/Development Centre Aid Seminar. OECD Headquarters, Paris.

McGillivray, M., Morrissey, O. (2004), The fiscal effects of aid. In: Addison, T., Roe, A. (Eds.), *Fiscal Policy for Development: Poverty, Reconstruction and Growth*. Palgrave Macmillan, Basingstoke.

Milner, H. (2006), Why multilateralism? Foreign aid and principal-agent problems. Paper presented at the WIDER Development Conference on *Aid: Principles, Policies and Performance*, WIDER Helsinki, 16–17 June.

Mosley, P. (1987), *Overseas Aid: Its Defense and Reform*. Wheatsheaf Press.

Mosley, P. (2004), The international finance facility: Can it deliver? Policy arena. *Journal of International Development* 16, 863–895.

Munro, L. (2005), Focus–Pocus? Thinking critically about whether aid organizations should do fewer things in fewer countries. *Development and Change* 36, 425–447.

Murshed, S.M. (2004), Strategic interaction and donor policy determination. *International Review of Economics and Finance* 13, 311–323.

Murshed, S.M., Sen, S. (1995), Aid conditionality and military expenditure reduction in developing countries: models of asymmetric information. *Economic Journal* 105, 498–509.

Ouattara, B. (2005), A new database on project and programme aid disbursement and its application the savings displacement hypothesis. *Discussion Paper*, No. 0501, Department of Economics, The University of Manchester.

Pack, H., Pack, J.R. (1990), Is foreign aid fungible? The case of Indonesia. *Economic Journal* 100, 188–194.

Pack, H., Pack, J.R. (1993), Foreign aid and the question of fungibility. *Review of Economics and Statistics* 75, 258–265.

Pallage, S., Robe, M. (2001), Foreign aid and the business cycle. *Review of International Economics* 9, 636–667.

Picciotto, R. (2004), Towards a comprehensive security and development framework. Paper presented at the Global Policy Project Workshop on *Security and Development*, Global Development Network, New Delhi, 25–26 January.

Radelet, S. (2006), A primer on foreign aid. *Working Paper*, No. 92, Center for Global Development, Washington, DC.

Rajan, R., Subramanian, A. (2005a), Aid and growth: what does the cross-country evidence really show? *IMF Working Paper* 05/127.

Rajan, R., Subramanian, A. (2005b), What undermines aid's impact on growth? *IMF Working Paper* 05/126.

Ram, R. (2004), Recipient country's 'policies' and the effect of foreign aid on economic growth in developing countries: additional evidence. *Journal of International Development* 16, 201–211.

Ratha, D. (2001), *Complementarity between multilateral lending and private flows to developing countries: some empirical results*. World Bank, mimeo.

Rodrik, D. (1995), Why is there multilateral lending? In: Bruno, M., Pleskovic, B. (Eds.), *Annual World Bank Conference on Development Economics*, pp. 167–205.

Tarp (Ed.) (2000), *Foreign Aid and Development: Lessons Learnt and Directions for the Future*. Studies in Development Economics, vol. 17. Routledge, London.

UN Millennium Project (2005), *Investing in Development: A Practical Plan to Achieve the Millennium Development Goals*. United Nations, New York.

UNCTAD (2006), *Economic Development in Africa: Doubling Aid: Making the "Big Push" Work*. UNCTAD, Geneva.

Vos, R. (1998), Aid flows and Dutch disease in a general equilibrium framework for Pakistan. *Journal of Policy Modelling* 20, 77–109.

White, H. (1992), The macroeconomic impact of development aid: a critical survey. *Journal of Development Studies* 28, 163–240.

White, H. (1998), *Aid and Macroeconomic Performance: Theory, Empirical Evidence and Four Country Cases*. Macmillan, London.

World Bank (1998), *Assessing Aid: What Works, What Doesn't and Why*. Oxford University Press, Oxford.

World Bank (2003), *Global Development Finance 2003*. Washington, DC.

Younger, S. (1992), Aid and the Dutch disease: macroeconomic management when everybody loves you. *World Development* 20, 1587–1597.

CHAPTER 14

Aid and Development: The Mozambican Case

Channing Arndt[a], Sam Jones[b] and Finn Tarp[c]

[a]*Purdue University and National Directorate of Studies and Policy Analysis,*
Ministry of Planning and Development, Av. Ahmed Sekou Touré n° 21, 7° Andar, Maputo, Mozambique
E-mail address: channingarndt@gmail.com
[b]*National Directorate of Studies and Policy Analysis, Ministry of Planning and Development,*
Av. Ahmed Sekou Touré n° 21, 7° Andar, Maputo, Mozambique
E-mail address: esamjones@gmail.com
[c]*Department of Economics, University of Copenhagen, Studiestræde 6, DK-1455 Copenhagen K, Denmark*
E-mail address: Finn.Tarp@econ.ku.dk

Abstract

We consider the relationship between external aid and development in Mozambique from 1980–2004, identifying the specific mechanisms through which aid has influenced the developmental trajectory of the country. We undertake both a growth accounting analysis and review the intended and unintended effects of aid at the micro-level. Sustained aid flows to Mozambique, in conflict and post-conflict periods, have made an unambiguous, positive contribution to rapid growth since 1992. However, proliferation of donors and aid-supported interventions has burdened local administration, indicating a need for deeper domestic government accountability. To sustain growth, Mozambique must maximize benefits from natural resources while promoting constructive international market integration.

Keywords: Mozambique, foreign aid, development

JEL classifications: F35, O10, O55

1. Introduction

Over the past 25 years Mozambique has been one of the most aid dependent countries in the world, receiving aid in the order of 40% of national income each year for the past decade. The mix of ideologies through which Mozambique has traveled since Independence is astounding. Colonialism, idealism, socialism, war fuelled by racism, economic collapse and stout liberalism, finally gave way to growth and economic recovery from 1992 (Tarp *et al.*, 2002). Mozambique therefore provides a useful case to deepen our understanding of the potential role of aid in furthering economic development. In this chapter we focus on Mozambique and ask:

THEORY AND PRACTICE OF FOREIGN AID
VOLUME 1   ISSN: 1574-8715
DOI: 10.1016/S1574-8715(06)01014-1

- Can aid be linked to growth and developmental outcomes in the past?
- What are the specific channels through which aid has impacted on outcomes?
- What do we learn about the general role of aid in development from reflecting on the Mozambican experience?
- What are the challenges to continued growth and development that might restrict Mozambique from fully benefiting from future aid flows?

The relevance of a detailed case study of Mozambique is highlighted by the ongoing controversy over aid. This is typified by the contrast between the skeptical position of Easterly (2006) and more optimistic advocates such as Sachs (2005), who argues that a doubling of global aid flows is a moral obligation of rich nations that will send 'forth mighty currents of hope' leading to 'the end of poverty'. While the view that aid works in promoting growth and development has gained ground in recent years, see Tarp (2006), a number of disagreements remain evident. These include: (i) the necessary and sufficient conditions for aid to have a positive contribution on the development process; (ii) how economic policy and deeper structural characteristics interact with the efficiency of foreign aid; and (iii) the impact of the institutional framework through which aid is channeled. A general aim of this paper is to provide a country-specific study of aid and growth in one of the most aid dependent countries in the world with a view to shedding further light on these concerns.

The chapter is structured as follows: after this introduction, we provide a brief literature background and lay out our methodology. We then discuss trends at an aggregate level starting with a historical overview (Section 3.1), moving onto a quantitative growth accounting exercise (Section 3.3). Sections 4 and 5 document evidence at the micro-level, looking at specific intended and unintended aid effects across a variety of channels, including aid management. We return in Section 6 to the international aid-growth debate, considering the past and future challenges for the country; Section 7 concludes.

2. Methodology

2.1. Aid and growth in the literature

The methodological difficulties in connecting external aid and developmental outcomes echo problems found in the earlier literature on the evaluation of stabilization and structural adjustment programs.[1] To be able to measure the effect of aid, the researcher ideally should be able to compare the value of a chosen final-outcome indicator in two strictly independent situations: with and without aid. To establish the 'true' measure of aid impact, one needs to fully account for all other intermediate influences that have affected our final outcome.[2] Alternatively, if a group of countries

---

[1] See Mosley *et al.* (1991) for the various methodologies applied.
[2] This includes choosing the length of individual time units and an appropriate overall time horizon, which are by no means simple choices.

is compared (with and without aid) the analyst needs to account for the impact on the chosen indicator of the other differences between the units of observation, as in a controlled experiment. This challenge of establishing an appropriate counterfactual is generic to the social sciences and is further confounded in this case by the extended time periods under analysis as well as difficulties in measuring our choice variables. Furthermore, given the substantial 'distance' separating the independent (input) and dependent (final outcome) variables, their theoretical relationship is indefinite generating the potential for large specification errors in any evaluation.

Given these methodological difficulties, it is unsurprising that the question whether aid works or not has been approached from numerous perspectives.[3] As a point of departure, however, it is relevant to stress that there is widespread agreement that aid has often been successful at the microeconomic level. This is evident from project evaluations undertaken by the Independent Evaluation Group of the World Bank who report an average rate of return of 22 per cent for the period 1993–2002. This is supported in numerous surveys including, for example, Mosley (1987) and Cassen and Associates (1994). Thus, few dispute that aid interventions have helped to improve social outcomes in, for example, the areas of health and appropriate technology. Even so, Mosley's (1987) celebrated micro–macro-paradox suggested that while aid seems to be effective at the microeconomic level, identifying any positive impact of aid at the macroeconomic level appeared harder, or even impossible, at least in cross-country econometric work. While, at the time it was formulated this perspective resounded with a general atmosphere of aid fatigue, the 'iron law of regressions', in the terminology of Hausman (2001), has received less attention as an explanation for this paradox. Once we try to explain a 'dirty' dependent variable (i.e., growth) with noisy data and weak proxies for variables such as institutions, regression results are biased towards zero. What Mosley and many after him have struggled with is how to control for the diverse and changing circumstances under which aid has been implemented.

Recent econometric work in this area emphasizes endogeneities and non-linearity in the aid-growth relationship, as set out in Dalgaard *et al.* (2004) as well as the various studies listed in Clemens *et al.* (2004). In our assessment, this research suggests at least two broad conclusions. First, the way in which data are dealt with is critically important for the results drawn – methodological choices matter. Second, the impact of aid on growth is not the same across aid recipients. There are differences in aid efficiency from country to country; and it remains unclear what drives these differences. In particular, the role of 'deep' structural characteristics in affecting how aid impacts on growth is not yet fully understood. At the same time, while the single most common results of recent empirical aid-growth studies is that aid has a positive impact on per capita growth, aid is by no means a panacea for growth and poverty reduction. Cross-country econometrics has brought us this far, and will proceed, but there is a clear need for country case studies to provide deeper insight into the changing role of the numerous potential channels connecting the independent and dependent variables.

---

[3] See Hansen and Tarp (2000). The reader may also wish to consult Cassen and Associates (1994) for a useful literature survey with a broad scope. Other references include World Bank (1998b) and Tarp (2000).

2.2. Methodological approach

The rest of this chapter examines the Mozambican aid-growth experience, providing a country-level perspective from which to reflect on some of the current debates surrounding aid effectiveness. Rather than assuming, *ex-ante*, any fixed relationship between aid and developmental outcomes, we divide the analysis between aggregate (macro-) and sectoral (micro-) evidence. As noted above, for a macro–micro-paradox to hold at the country-level we would expect to find only project-level evidence of growth returns to aid. To review the aggregate trends, we not only review descriptive evidence of trends in net aid and social outcome indicators, but also undertake a careful growth accounting exercise. As we shall see for Mozambique, it is precisely because the volume of aid has been so large in relative economic terms that it is possible to identify positive growth effects at the aggregate level.

The growth accounting also directs attention to a number of specific sectors. Thus, the micro-level analysis undertakes a careful review of the intended and unintended effects of aid across different sectors in historical perspective. Distinguishing between intended and unintended effects focuses discussion on the balance between growth-enhancing effects of aid, on the one hand, and the negative growth-retarding effects on the other. This intends to capture the multiplicity of channels through which aid can affect outcomes, as well as their shifting importance over time. While the choice of intended and unintended effects cannot be comprehensive and is to some extent subjective, both the sectoral composition of aid disbursements and the explicit policies adopted by donor agencies over time provides a clear guide to the intended effects. Relevant unintended effects can be drawn from the wide-ranging aid-growth theoretical and empirical literature (e.g., Kanbur, 2003), as well as secondary analytical sources for the country.

2.3. Aid fungibility

Before considering the connection between aid and outcomes, we must address the critique that aid is fungible. This refers to the idea that public funds from different sources may be interchangeable, making it impossible to postulate any direct connection between specific public expenditure outcomes (development) and specific sources of financing (external aid). Fungibility proponents hold that external aid does not alter the hypothetical portfolio of government spending before aid, meaning that aid really only finances whatever the government chooses (see Devarajan and Swaroop, 1998; World Bank, 1998b).

Standard definitions of aid fungibility focus on the expenditure portfolio, arguing that external assistance replaces local financing permitting the latter to be used for lower priority spending either within the aid-receiving sector or elsewhere. This critique is not highly relevant to Mozambique given the sheer volume of aid relative to local revenue. Most analyses of fungibility in fact recognize that where donor inflows are substantial compared to other sources of financing, aid is at best *partially* fungible

(Berg, 2002: 21). As documented in Section 3.2, for almost 20 years net external aid has made up over 50% of government spending being equal in value to and essentially financing the entire government investment budget. A further weakness of the fungibility criticism for Mozambique is the existence of large off-budget flows, also discussed below. These flows are not coordinated at an aggregate, government-wide level and it is frequently the case that the government as a whole and even the relevant sectors do not have complete information as regards the size or objectives of external funding. Together these factors necessarily limit the extent to which aid can be described as fungible with other sources of funding.

An alternative perspective on fungibility relates to the revenue side, arguing that external assistance substitutes for local sources of government income that would have been raised in the absence of external sources (see for example Adam and O'Connell, 1999). This argument also struggles in the face of the extremely large volumes of aid inflows. The total replacement of external aid by internal revenues would have demanded a doubling of internal revenue from an average of 12.1 to 26.8% of GDP during the post-civil war period. Given that cross-country evidence broadly supports a positive association between per capita income and the tax-to-GDP ratio (as per Wagner's Law), a tax take of this size would be a clear outlier among the group of low income countries to which Mozambique belongs.

There is also a more subtle argument that internal revenue growth has been suppressed by the availability of external funds, the hypothesis being that there would have been more effective reform and/or efficiency gains in revenue collection in the absence of external assistance. The data demonstrates that internal revenue growth has only matched GDP growth in the post-civil war era, leading to a relatively stable tax-to-GDP ratio at around 12% for the period and relatively consistent failures to meet tax-to-GDP ratio growth targets. Whether this can be attributed uniquely to the effect of external assistance is uncertain in the absence of a solid counterfactual. Nevertheless, evidence for large increases in discretionary tax exemptions alongside high rates of fiscal evasion, estimated at a rate of 36% of recorded imports (Van Dunem, 2006), point to a greater degree of flexibility in the implementation and/or reform of fiscal policy than may otherwise have been the case without large aid inflows. These institutional issues are discussed in Sections 5.4 and 5.5, but the point remains that high aid intensity in Mozambique allows us to disregard any strong criticisms of aid fungibility in this case.

3. Aggregate trends in aid and growth

3.1. Historical context

A relevant starting point for an overview of the modern history of Mozambique is the period of economic expansion under Portuguese colonial rule in the early 1960s until 1973. During this period the Mozambican economy was structured mainly as a service economy to neighboring states, integrated into a regional economy dominated by South African industrial capital through the provision of transport services and migrant labor. Together these sources accounted for the majority of foreign exchange earnings.

The 1960s had witnessed the emergence of the first unified nationalist movement, FRELIMO (*Frente de Libertação de Moçambique*), focusing initially on sporadic guerrilla warfare in the northern provinces of Mozambique from their base in Tanzania. Military operations gradually expanded through to the 1970s but the situation changed dramatically with a *coup d'etat* in Portugal in 1974, in part a reaction to the economic and political fallout of its activities in Africa. Negotiations of a cease-fire and terms of Independence were quickly organized; however, the intention of organizing a smooth transfer of power to FRELIMO was not altogether successful and ended in the rapid departure of over 200,000 Portuguese settlers. This exodus was accompanied by the (illegal) export of assets as well as numerous acts of economic sabotage, particularly against fixed capital assets.

The first few years of Independence were marked by a movement toward socialist central planning and nationalization of productive means including factories and farms abandoned by the Portuguese. In certain respects this orientation represented a pragmatic response to a complex of conditions including the absence of a local managerial class, the virtual collapse of the pre-Independence economy, the power of industrial capital directed by racist regimes in South Africa and Rhodesia, and the historical alignment of Portugal on the Western side of the Cold War divide. The objective of state-planned accumulation concentrated primarily on the development of a modern agricultural sector through mechanized collective and state farming accompanied by social investments.

In stark contrast to the projected rapid rates of economic growth contained in central plans, history records serious economic decline in the 1973–1992 period. Clearly economic policy was challenged by the chaotic socio-economic environment. Largely on account of the dearth of skilled locals, development policy and targets often relied on the advice of a broad range of foreign experts from Eastern-bloc countries as well as UN advisors. The presence of foreigners throughout the government and economy was pervasive – by the early 1980s over 20,000 foreigners were employed across sectors, often in senior positions (Pinto, 1985). The agricultural sector, for example, was supported by Bulgarians and East Germans dominated the central planning functions (O'Meara, 1991; Arndt *et al.*, 2000a).

The developmental challenge was exacerbated by three factors. First, following the departure of the Portuguese, the rural–urban exchange economy on which rural cash crop production depended almost totally collapsed. Second, in response to its neighbor's Independence, South Africa diverted cargo away from Mozambican ports and severely cutback its use of Mozambican migrant workers. From 1976, Mozambique also participated in the international sanctions applied to Rhodesia, leading to further reductions in export revenue (Hall and Young, 1997). Third, the early Independence period was scarred by a succession of natural disasters affecting agricultural production and transport infrastructure.[4] These shocks occurred alongside an increase in demands for imports to support investment and military requirements. The result was a severe deterioration in the current account balance from a deficit of US$115 million in 1973 to a deficit of US$423 million in 1980 (IMF, 2001: 33).

The emergence of civil war from the early 1980s until 1992 was decisive in undermining economic growth. Again, regional dynamics played a central role as the main resistance movement RENAMO (*Resistência Nacional de Moçambique*) was established under a Rhodesian initiative to weaken the Mozambican government and permit a more effective counter-insurgency against Zimbabwean fighters based in Mozambique. From 1976 military insurgency within Mozambique was dominated by Rhodesian interests although RENAMO soon started to make its own strikes against infrastructure targets, becoming an increasing drain on the government. Despite Zimbabwean Independence, achieved in 1980, the South African military quickly replaced Rhodesian support for RENAMO leading to a further escalation of insurgency with the explicit objectives of destabilization and destruction of economic assets.

By the mid-1980s the economic situation of the country was desperate. Lack of foreign exchange, a shortage of inputs, irregular power supplies and transportation constraints had led to a 50% fall in industrial production by 1986 compared to 1981 (Arndt *et al.*, 2000a: 302). Control of the money supply largely had been lost due to the perceived necessity to keep the economy afloat and maintain minimum functioning of state-controlled firms (Hanlon, 2001). In the context of wide-ranging price controls this generated extensive repressed inflation and a severely overvalued exchange rate, both of which contributed to the rapid expansion of parallel markets. Despite having been a net external creditor at Independence, the combination of ambitious investment projects, military spending and the contraction of export earnings meant that the debt stock ballooned to over US$2.4 billion by 1984, requiring an annual debt service equal to approximately 10% of GDP. In addition, ongoing crisis in agricultural production related to the war and abnormal climatic conditions, internal rural–urban migration and the failure of collective farms provoked an increasing reliance on external food assistance.

Without resources to confront the crisis, external financing became vital not least to service debt obligations and purchase food imports. Soviet-bloc allies were, however, reluctant to increase their financial assistance, and already in the early 1980s Samora Machel began more decisively to look to Western countries for economic support.[5] The West used this crisis-born opportunity to nudge Mozambique toward a more neutral international stance via provision of developmental aid (Pinto, 1985).

---

[4] In 1977 the Incomati and Limpopo rivers flooded followed by the Zambezi in 1978, causing over US$90 million in damage alone. In 1980 a severe and prolonged drought started and it lasted until 1983 affecting over 1.5 million people (Hall and Young, 1997). Further floods occurred in 1984–1985 and two other severe droughts in 1986–1987 and 1991–1992 respectively. Thus, 12 of the 18 years from 1975 to 1992 were in some way affected by climatic abnormality.

[5] Both the UN and some bilateral donors such as Sweden already had large numbers of advisors in Mozambique from the late 1970s.

Market-based economic reforms were introduced slowly and with more vigor following the death of Samora Machel in a plane crash in 1986. The first of many Paris
Club debt rescheduling agreements was reached in 1984, membership of the Bretton
Woods institutions in 1986, and in 1987 the formal adoption of a structural-adjustment
Economic Rehabilitation Programme (ERP). The latter contained the usual range of
depreciation, price liberalization and structural reform commitments in exchange for
further debt rescheduling and acutely necessary external financing, including US$330
million in emergency assistance raised by the United Nations.

By the late 1980s the dynamics of the civil war were changing. Although RE-
NAMO had continued to disrupt the countryside, the increasing market-orientation
of FRELIMO and the thawing of the Cold War undermined the rationale for continued destabilization. Also, by this point in the conflict both factions were exhausted
(Rupiya, 1998). In March 1989, in response to the growing emergency caused by
insufficient agricultural production and with over seven million Mozambicans facing starvation, RENAMO announced a temporary ceasefire to facilitate relief efforts.
Peace talks began in Rome in 1990 and continued sporadically through to October
1992 with the signing of a General Peace Agreement. Before the end of 1992, US$400
million was raised in humanitarian and reconstruction assistance and a United Nations

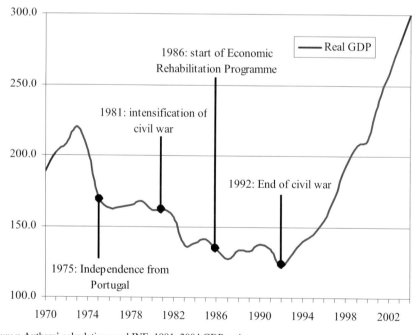

Source: Authors' calculations and INE, 1991–2004 GDP series.

***Fig. 1. Mozambique real GDP 1970–2004, in billions of Meticais (constant 1980
prices).***

Operation (ONUMOZ) was formally established with a broad mandate. The movement from peace to stability, culminating in general elections in October 1994, was broadly successful. This testifies not only to the genuine desire for peace among all parties and the relatively well-coordinated efforts of donors, but also to Mozambique's acute level of dependence on external finance by this time (Jett, 2002).

Since 1994, Mozambique has maintained a positive developmental momentum, moving from immediate post-war 'emergency' to longer-term reconstruction, poverty reduction and economic growth. As shown in Figure 1, economic growth since 1993 has been rapid. A sectoral breakdown indicates that growth has been supported by robust recovery of the agricultural sector, with manufactures, transport and communications also playing major roles. Growth also has been boosted by a small number of large enclave-type foreign investments but even excluding their impact, annual real growth is estimated to have averaged 6.5% for the period 1992–2004, against 7.8% on aggregate.

3.2. Foreign aid

An analysis of the impact of foreign aid demands understanding of its changing role and composition. This is problematic due to the extremely varied types of external aid as well as weaknesses in the available data, a problem not unique to Mozambique but of particular magnitude given the aggregate economic intensity of external finance. We define external aid broadly, covering all forms of external financing towards Mozambique including grants, credits, aid-in-kind, technical assistance and debt relief. In addition we recognize the need to distinguish between gross and net aid flows due to the impact of foreign debt repayments which reduce the effective aid available for real expenditures.

Table 1 summarizes the Mozambican aid data from three principal sources – the Central Bank's Balance of Payments (BOP) statistics, the government fiscal accounts, and the OECD Development Assistance Committee (DAC) database covering both the aid commitments and disbursements made to Mozambique from its members. In principle, these sources should tally, however the obvious discrepancies highlight the fact that no source is either complete or bias-free. The DAC figures are considerably higher than those of the BOP for most periods. This is largely because the DAC data gives a more complete and accurate treatment of certain types of aid, such as aid-in-kind and technical assistance, that may not be correctly valued or even captured by domestic sources, especially where the full value of the flows does not enter the beneficiary country. Even so, the DAC data only covers financing made by its contributing members, a group which does not include all donors to Mozambique. This is shown by the relatively low DAC figures for the 1980–1989 years when substantial external financing originated from Soviet-bloc countries; this issue is also relevant today as "new donors" such as the People's Republic of China are beginning to make relatively large amounts of financing available to selected developing countries.

An advantage of using government statistics is that, theoretically, they should capture all aid flows including those from non-DAC participants. The gap between the

Table 1.   *External aid estimates, annual averages for each period, in US$ millions*

	1980–1984	1985–1989	1990–1994	1995–1999	2000–2004	1980–2004
Gross aid, excl. debt relief						
DAC commitments	170.8	623.4	837.3	655.7	1,078.1	673.1
DAC disbursements	199.3	635.7	1,178.5	899.6	1,054.6	793.5
BOP	600.0	549.5	710.8	591.4	696.2	629.6
Net aid, before debt service						
DAC disbursements	198.1	617.8	1,095.0	817.4	950.5	735.8
BOP	512.8	789.8	940.1	794.1	921.7	791.7
Net aid, after debt service						
BOP	458.5	651.2	787.6	646.2	825.3	673.8
Government budget execution	233.2	326.1	392.3	420.7	621.9	398.8
Net debt stock	1,208.0	3,014.6	4,105.4	4,641.5	2,984.0	3,190.7
GDP (nominal)	5,004.6	3,492.7	2,388.2	3,013.4	4,349.6	3,328.7

Source: OECD DAC database; Banco de Moçambique (for BOP); INE (2005) for government budget; and authors' estimates.
Notes: Net aid for DAC data is taken as their given net aid figure (which is net of loan repayments) and we subtract debt relief grants; for BOP net aid is calculated according to IMF (2005) being the value of the current account deficit (before debt service charges) minus private financing to the capital account and changes in net reserves; GDP is calculated in nominal terms using the average annual US$/MZM exchange rate.

DAC and BOP data, however, as well as the much more substantial gap between the BOP figures and the government's fiscal accounts estimate for net aid after debt service, indicates the existence of substantial aid flows not captured by domestic sources. These refer to off-budget aid funds which are negotiated and managed directly between individual donors and sector ministries, falling partially or fully outside the compass of central government information systems (see World Bank, 2001a). Whilst in principle these amounts should enter the aggregate BOP statistics, both data collection weaknesses and the existence of various non-financial aid flows, such as pre-paid imports, mean this is not assured and, even if captured, they may not be correctly classified. Alternative information confirms that the BOP figures are not comprehensive – selective disbursement figures stated in Ernst & Young Mozambique (2006) for 2005, for example, suggest that the 17 principal donors to Mozambique who account for around 90% of total aid, disbursed US$1,015.2 million in total aid of which US$908.7 was made to the Mozambican government. In contrast, the preliminary BOP estimate for total gross aid in 2005 is US$811.8 million, indicating that around 20% of total aid and/or at least 10% of aid to the government is not adequately captured by government sources.

Both the DAC and BOP series indicate substantial short-term volatility of aid flows, not least due to changing humanitarian needs. Even so, and despite disagreement as to absolute aid levels, some broad trends can be identified. The early 1980s were associated with a very rapid increase in both the net debt burden and repayment obligations,

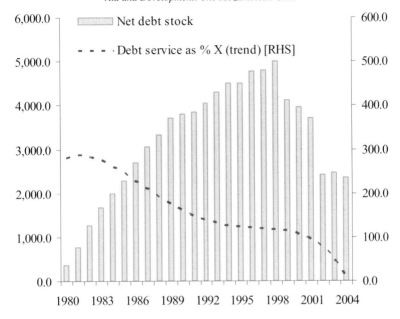

Source: Banco de Moçambique and authors' estimates.

Fig. 2. ***Net debt stock in US$ millions (LHS) and debt service as percent of exports***
(RHS).

such that by the late 1980s over 50% of gross aid was being used to pay debt obligations. While the advent of IMF and World Bank supported programs allowed some
debt renegotiation, the trend level of aid in the 1990s was broadly stable. As shown in
Figure 2, only since the late 1990s do we note a marked reduction in total annual debt
repayments. This has occurred under the HIPC, enhanced HIPC and Paris Club programs to which Mozambique has been party and, therefore has considerably reduced
the gap between net aid before and after debt service.[6]

Table 1 also quantifies the relative economic weight or intensity of external assistance. Whatever definition of aid one takes, the relative resource increment from
external aid has been consistently high in terms of GDP. Gross aid including debt relief grants from the DAC data has averaged over 40% of GNI per capita since 1985,
with a peak of 93.2% in 1992. The considerable weight of aid in the economy is stark
in relation to external trade. Figure 3 clearly shows that net aid has been the dominant
source of foreign exchange to support goods imports throughout the period. Indeed,
the increase in net aid from 1984 was associated with a higher level of imports both

---

[6] Note for the rest of the chapter, and unless stated otherwise, we use the BOP measure of net aid as it
best captures movements in effective aid available to the government and is consistent with other balance
of payments items.

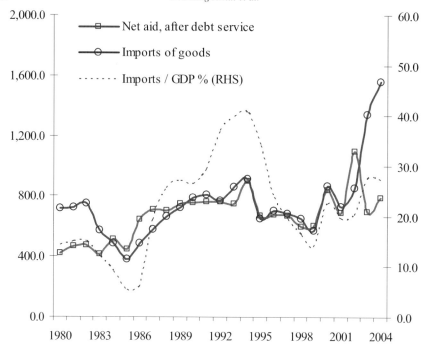

Source: Banco de Moçambique, balance of payments (BOP) series.

Notes: For the definition of net aid see notes to Table 1.

Fig. 3.   Net aid and imports of goods to Mozambique in US$ millions, 1980–2004.

in absolute terms and in relation to GDP, indicating that the initiation of structural adjustment enabled a relaxation of foreign exchange shortages which had developed by the early 1980s. External aid also has played a critical long-term role in support of government expenditure. Since the mid-1980s, external financing has been equivalent to over 100% of government investment and approximately 50% of total government expenditure. Recalling that these government figures exclude off-budget expenditures financed from external sources, the true weight of external finance in total government expenditure including off-budgets is likely to be higher at around 60%.

Although the DAC data on aid commitments may be biased as to the final level of disbursement, it provides a consistent indication of the relative priority given to different sectors. Employing the conceptual distinction between humanitarian, late- and early-impact external aid made by Clemens *et al.* (2004), we find the composition of funds has changed very substantially with the shift from conflict to peace (see Table 2).[7] As to be expected, during the civil war period, the majority of aid went to

---

[7] Early-impact aid refers to aid which is more likely to have a growth-enhancing effect in the short-run; this included general budget support given its contribution to the balance of payments. Late-impact aid

Table 2. **OECD DAC commitments to Mozambique by funding objective, annual**
average weight in percent per period

	1980–1984	1985–1989	1990–1994	1995–1999	2000–2004	change %
Humanitarian funding	37.7	33.3	15.5	12.7	9.3	−75
Early impact funding:	42.3	53.0	45.1	40.9	46.7	10
Infrastructure	15.3	21.3	20.4	16.2	17.6	15
Agriculture	23.6	15.0	9.0	9.2	4.3	−82
Private sector	3.4	10.2	5.8	2.4	6.1	79
General budget support	0.1	6.5	10.0	13.0	18.7	36,718
Later impact funding:	20.0	13.7	39.4	46.5	43.9	120
Social sectors	8.7	7.0	19.2	27.7	25.9	199
Government and civil society	0.0	0.0	4.7	8.6	11.3	–
Others	11.3	6.7	15.6	10.1	6.7	−41

Source: OECD DAC database (see: www.oecd.org/dac/).
Notes: Classification between humanitarian, early- and late-impact funding is the authors'; humanitarian
funding covers disaster relief, food security and commodity assistance.

humanitarian relief as well as some early-impact funding; since 1992 there has been
a trend switch from humanitarian funding into later impact funding. For example, assistance to social sectors has risen from an average of 7% of total aid for the five year
period 1985–1989 to 25.9% in 2000–2004. Also noticeable is the long-term stability of
assistance to early-impact funding, particularly infrastructure. These recent trends are
confirmed from government budget execution figures. In 2003, for example, over 70%
of externally-financed expenditure was affected to education, health and infrastructure. Finally, alongside recent growth in late-impact aid we notice a broadening of the
scope of aid. This is exemplified by the trend growth in funding to the arguably more
complex areas of 'government and civil society' from zero in the 1980s to over 11%
of total aid in 2000–2004.

The final aspect of trends in external assistance concerns aid modalities. Two main
changes are evident from the data. First, there has been a considerable shift away from
credit towards grant-based financing consistent with Mozambique's increasing alignment with the Bretton Woods institutions and concern with debt sustainability. According to the BOP series, grants now comprise around 70% of gross aid inflows compared
to less than 20% in the early 1980s. Second, an increasing portion of aid is not tied
to specific projects but rather is 'programmatic', being disbursed to common funding pools managed at either a sector or government-wide level. These instruments are
intended to promote greater government ownership as well as enhance the efficiency
and coordination of government expenditure. While direct budget support began in the

refers to all other aid, excluding that for humanitarian or immediate relief purposes, that is likely to have
a longer-term impact on economic growth and/or developmental outcomes. See Clemens *et al.* (2004) for
a detailed description of the categorization they apply; however it should be noted that here we follow the
spirit rather than the detail of their categorization.

early 1990s under the guise of support to the balance of payments, more coordinated funding mechanisms have gained political and financial weight principally in the last five years; these instruments now represent around 40% of gross aid in the government budget. The move toward more coordinated funding, however, is not consistent across donors but rather coexists with a continued reliance on project financing. For example, while the Netherlands provides around 74% of its aid to Mozambique through these coordinated modes, the USA only gives 15% and Japan 0% (USAID, 2004). Even for the 17 principal direct budget support donors, the weight of project aid in their total disbursements to the government actually has increased from 36.9% in 2004 to a projected estimate of 42.3% in 2006, representing an absolute increase of US$78 million (Ernst & Young Mozambique, 2006).

Lastly, and consistent with these trends, we note a trend increase in the sheer number of donors active in the country. According to DAC statistics there were 16 multilateral and bilateral donors providing external assistance to Mozambique in 1987, increasing to 29 by 2004. The 2005 government budget identifies over 107 different organizations providing external funding to the public sector which is likely to be an underestimate given the existence of off-budget flows. This is not to mention the large number of international NGOs operating in the country for which official statistics are lacking but are considered to number well over 150.

3.3. Growth accounting evidence

A first step towards uncovering the sources of economic growth in Mozambique can be made through a growth accounting exercise.[8] The technique is widely applied and need not be presented from first principles (see Barro, 1998). It is useful to note, however, that results across the literature show that once we account for the quality or productivity of factor inputs entering the aggregate production function, the relative contribution of residual total factor productivity (TFP) to growth typically falls. This is fitting for Mozambique as, in response to the neglectful legacy of Portuguese colonial rule which left approximately 93% of the population illiterate at Independence (UNDP, 2000; UNESCO, 2000; MPF and MINED, 2003), the newly Independent government prioritized a massive expansion of literacy programs and primary schooling (UNDP, 2000; Buendía Gómez, 1999). This expansion, albeit constrained by civil war, achieved considerable advances and has continued since 1992, indicating the need to reflect changes in human capital quality in our estimation.

Mindful of these issues, the methodology we adopt follows Young's (1994) application of a transcendental logarithmic (translog) production function and associated factor input indices to East Asian growth. A distinct advantage of this specification, compared to a more rudimentary Cobb–Douglas formulation, is that it imposes no constraints on variations in factor shares over time. Moreover, the approach is highly

---

[8] This section draws on Jones's (2006) background paper to this study in which a detailed presentation of the methodology and results can be found.

flexible, permitting the development of disaggregated factor indices and measurement of the individual contribution of sub-factor components to aggregate output growth. Our estimation procedure makes extensive use of this feature, disaggregating human capital (labor) into six categories reflecting differences in location (rural/urban) and completed level of education. We also split fixed capital into private and public sector components.

A few methodological aspects of the accounting exercise should be highlighted. First, estimates of the human capital stock bring together data from a variety of sources including population censuses, household surveys and education enrolment figures. The estimation approach follows standard techniques found in the literature (e.g., Barro and Lee, 1993; Nehru *et al.*, 1995; Ahuja and Filmer, 1995), but in the absence of certain data series we incorporate information contained in education transition matrices estimated by Arndt and Muzima (2004) for Mozambique, as well as graduation probabilities implicit in the data. Secondly, we use the 2002/2003 nationally representative household consumption survey to estimate the share of each labor sub-category in total payments to labor.[9] Education-level consumption premiums required to calculate these shares are taken from a Mincerian-type regression in which consumption is regressed on a measure of education and a vector of control variables.[10] We assume these consumption premiums are stable over time; a proposition broadly confirmed by 1996/1997 household survey data as well the observation that socialist wage and price controls are likely to have dampened wage differentials during the early period.

Thirdly, to estimate the split between public and private capital stock we separately calculate the aggregate and government fixed capital stocks for the period via the perpetual inventory method. This allows us to treat the private sector stock as a residual and we take the respective sub-factor shares as simple weights of public and private fixed capital in aggregate capital. A further feature of this exercise is application of varying depreciation rates over time in order to reflect the impact of civil war. We estimate the overall public capital depreciation rate peaked during the height of the war at around 13%, falling to a more typical level of 5% in the post-war period. Finally, we also allow the aggregate factor shares, which represent the relative contribution of each factor to total product, to vary over the estimation period. While it is common to fix these shares, rapid changes both during and after the civil war, undermine the validity of this assumption. This is confirmed by social accounting matrices developed for the post-war period which suggest that the fixed capital share of total factor income has fallen from approximately 40% in 1995, to 30% in 2002 (see Arndt *et al.*, 1998, 2000b; Tarp *et al.*, 2002). Thus, in order to capture the changing pattern of labor and factor accumulation during the period, we allow the labor and factor shares to move according to relative scarcities.

---

[9] Suitable wage data is neither available on a time series basis nor relevant as only a minority of the active workforce comes under the formal sector. Thus we presume consumption data provides a more reliable basis for inter-household welfare comparisons (Ravallion, 1992; MPF *et al.*, 1998).

[10] Note the estimation results, detailed in Jones (2006), are highly comparable to those from similar regressions on the same survey data estimated in Maximiano *et al.* (2005) and Fox *et al.* (2005).

Table 3.   *Growth accounting results, annual average growth (in log form) by period and contribution to GDP growth (% Y)*

	Real GDP Y	TFP A	Fixed capital		Human capital		
			Govmt.	Private	Unskilled	Primary	Secondary
1981–2004	2.6	0.3	0.5	0.7	0.1	0.2	0.7
% Y	100.0	10.6	20.4	28.3	5.8	8.6	26.4
1993–2004	7.5	2.6	1.0	2.5	0.0	0.3	1.0
% Y	100.0	34.6	13.5	33.6	0.6	4.1	13.7
1993–1998	7.6	3.4	1.0	2.1	0.4	0.2	0.5
% Y	100.0	44.8	12.9	28.3	5.1	2.3	6.6
1999–2004	7.4	1.8	1.0	2.9	−0.3	0.4	1.6
% Y	100.0	24.0	14.1	39.1	−4.1	5.9	21.1

Source: Jones (2006).
Note: *Government* fixed capital refers to the public sector fixed capital stock including public infrastructure; *private* fixed capital refers to that of the private sector. *Unskilled* human capital refers to economically active persons without any school qualification; *primary* refers to workers whose maximum level of completed education is at the primary level; *secondary* refers to workers with a secondary school qualification or above.

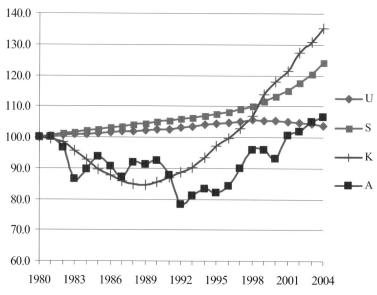

Source: Jones (2006).
Notes: *A* – residual TFP; *U* – uneducated labour; *S* – skilled labour comprising primary and secondary school graduates; *K* – fixed capital stock including both public and private sector components.

Fig. 4.   *Trends in translog indices derives from growth accounting results (1980 = 100).*

Table 3 summarizes the findings, also presented graphically in Figure 4 which indexes trends in the explanatory variables based on log growth rates. As can be seen, the civil war period is associated with substantial falls in both the aggregate capital stock (K) and the TFP index (A), despite slow gains in uneducated (U) and skilled (S) labor stocks, the latter comprising workers with primary schooling or above. The civil war and post-war periods are starkly different, the latter showing particularly strong gains in the capital and skilled labor stocks as well as trend recovery in the TFP residual to slightly above its 1980 level.

Three main results shed light on the relationship between aid and growth. First there have been strong returns to education at the level of aggregate output. For the period as a whole (1981–2004), pure educational improvements account for 15.5% of observed growth; however, this result should be treated with caution as it is due in part to the gradual improvement in education levels during the civil war period in contrast to aggregate output decline. The post-war phase is more appropriate for analysis and shows a rising contribution of education to growth, consistent with known improvements in both enrolment and efficiency rates (MPF and MINED, 2003). The 13.9% estimated contribution of education to overall growth for 1999–2004 is a relatively high rate for a developing country in cross-country terms (see Benito-Spinetto and Moll, 2005: 48–49). This contribution is also reflected in the changing structure of the workforce – in particular we note weak expansion of unskilled labor since the civil war and even a negative contribution (−4.1%) of this category from 1999–2004. The latter result simply indicates that with better coverage of primary education, the number of workers without any education has started to fall in absolute terms. As a corollary, gains due to education are increasingly attributable to better educated, urban-based workers. This can be seen from the breakdown of human capital growth between skilled and unskilled labor in Table 3. Moreover, drawing on the more detailed tables in Jones (2006) we find that the contribution to growth from the skilled workforce during the post-war period has been strongly and increasingly driven by secondary-level education (in both urban and rural areas). This points to the relevance of matching education policy to changes in economic structure and the possibility of key trade-offs between the wholesale expansion of education at all levels in all areas against targeted interventions aimed at more specific population segments.

Second, at an aggregate level it appears incontrovertible that the recovery and continued expansion of the fixed capital stock has been a foundation of post-war growth. Indeed, as with skilled human capital, growth here has played a larger role in later as compared to earlier post-war phases – for 1993–1998 capital accumulation explains 41.2% of growth rising to 53.1% for 1999–2004. The breakdown of capital growth between the government and private sectors also points to an interesting trend; while the accumulation of private sector capital has remained dominant in aggregate terms, government sector investment played a larger relative role in the immediate post-war period. This may be indicative of a degree of crowding-in of private sector investment, at least in a post-conflict setting, as well as the critical function of public infrastructure reconstruction for the reestablishment of markets and reduction of transaction costs.

We have already established (Section 3.2) that public investment has been funded, in its entirety, by aid inflows both prior to and after the civil war.

Third, growth in what might be considered TFP or technical advancement has been moderate but consistent since 1992. For the post-war period TFP growth explains a reasonable 34.6% of growth, consistent with the realization of peace, the return of dislocated populations, the reestablishment of internal markets and progress towards macroeconomic stability. This suggests a robust recovery of the production possibilities frontier that had been weakened by civil war. Two results, however, would indicate that these rates of TFP growth may not be guaranteed for the future. In the later post-war phase the growth contribution of TFP fell compared to the early post-war phase, a sign of a slowing rate of improvement. Second, in the long-view since 1980 the aggregate change in TFP has not been impressive, explaining only 10.6% of growth. Of course, changes in the TFP term capture more than just technology and this result is consistent with the effects of civil war and a succession of natural disasters from 1980 to 1992; in fact all the large falls shown in the TFP index in Figure 1 (1982–1983; 1991–1992; 2000) exactly correspond to natural disasters. Even so, these short-term fluctuations in TFP growth highlight the continued vulnerability of the economy to production shocks caused by climatic disturbances.

3.4. Trends in socio-economic indicators

Before reviewing the sectoral evidence, we should address the question whether these aggregate trends are reflected in final developmental outcomes. In fact, rapid economic growth of the post-war period has been accompanied by robust improvements across a wide range of socio-economic indicators. These support the authenticity of the growth record and show that it has had a relatively broad-based, impact at the household level. The headline achievement has been a reduction in the poverty headcount index from 69.4% in 1996/1997 to 54.1% in 2002/2003 based on nationally representative household survey data (MPF, 2004). Recent poverty estimates, consistent with these surveys and based on preliminary data from a national employment survey, confirms a continued decline in the poverty headcount to around 50% of the population in 2005 (Mathiassen and Øvensen, 2006). Agricultural income surveys for similar periods confirm the trend increase in household incomes (MPF, 2004). For example, while the household surveys indicate a 22% improvement in the poverty headcount index for the period 1996/97 to 2002/03, agricultural income surveys suggest a 27% average increase in agricultural production incomes for the same period.

A summary review of health, education and other socio-economic indicators also demonstrates a broadly consistent pattern of improvements in the post-war period. Table 4 shows infant and child mortality rates have dropped rapidly and particularly since 1997, corresponding to the first nationally representative health survey. Vaccine coverage and malnutrition indicators also show good progress. Advances in the education profile of the population already have been presented (also see Section 4.2). Progress on these aggregate level indicators is not simply the product of large improvements

Table 4. Summary of socio-economic indicators

	1997	2003
Health:		
Infant mortality rate (per 1000 births)	147.0	124.0
Child mortality rate (per 1000 1–5 year olds)	219.0	178.0
Vaccine coverage (% 1–2 year olds)	47.3	63.3
Acute malnutrition (% children aged 12–24 months)	12.8	6.9
Education:		
Gross schooling rate, EP1 (%)	74.7	98.3
Gross schooling rate, EP2 (%)	19.3	43.5
Adults with EP1 or EP2 completed (%)	20.3	26.5
Adults with ES1 or above completed (%)	2.6	4.8
Working population without schooling (millions)	5.9	5.7
Various:		
Access to collective transport (% rural population)	22.3	41.7
Access to a market (% rural population)	25.7	42.5
Access to protected water source (% population)	23.2	39.2
Radio ownership (% population)	28.9	45.5

Source: IDS 1997, 2003; IAF 1996/1997, 2002/2003; INE (2005); Jones (2006); Ibraimo (2005).

Notes: EP1 and EP2 refer to the first and second stages of primary school; ES1 refers to the first stage of secondary school.

for a minority of the population; rather, as Ibraimo (2005) documents, the regional coefficient of variation for a wide range of socio-economic indicators has fallen, indicating a reduction in regional disparities. Even so, regional GDP estimates made by UNDP (2001: 25) denote continuing large provincial differences, the bulk of economic production being concentrated in only a few regions and particularly the South.

This progress is indicative of a positive developmental trend over the last decade compared to the civil war period; but this does not mean that there are no grounds for concern. Obviously, these post-war advances are relative to the extremely deficient levels of economic production and provision of public services occasioned by the combined effects of colonialism, rapid Independence and civil war. In comparative perspective, Mozambique remains one of the poorest countries in the world, ranking 168 out of 177 countries on the human development index and with a relatively low life expectancy at birth of 41.9 years compared to 43.6 in 1980 (INE, 2005) and an average of 46.1 for sub-Saharan Africa as a whole (UNDP, 2005). In part this fall in life expectancy is attributable to growth in the HIV/AIDS prevalence rate, currently situated at around 16.2% of the adult population (see Ministério de Saude, 2005), over double the 7.3% average for sub-Saharan Africa (UNDP, 2005).

In addition to these issues, Mozambique faces very considerable economic challenges. Whilst inequality does not appear to have risen substantially between the first and second household surveys (see James *et al.*, 2005), the risk of unequal access to the benefits of growth remains a concern. Moreover, exports outside of certain large industrial projects only cover around a third of imports (excluding these mega-projects) and have remained broadly stable at around 7% of GDP since the end of the civil war. As such, additional sustainable sources of foreign exchange must be developed over the long-term to replace external assistance.

4. Aid and intended outcomes

4.1. Macroeconomic policy

The promotion of 'good macroeconomic policy' is clearly important, and the pursuit of longer-term macroeconomic stability and sustainability has been a principal motivation behind donor macroeconomic support such as stabilization and structural adjustment lending. While there is no single, commonly-agreed definition of what constitutes good macroeconomic policy, there is a broad consensus that it refers to helping to ensure a reasonably stable and predictable macroeconomic environment. There are two main paths where we find a relationship between external aid and macroeconomic policy. First, technical assistance and policy advice can support the government and Central Bank in their management of the economy. Going further, external agencies may make financial assistance conditional on certain policy and/or structural reforms. Second, external financing through balance of payments support and debt relief can help avoid sudden crises as well as support a more sustainable overall macroeconomic balance consistent with economic development.

Mozambique's achievement of enhanced macroeconomic stability in the post-war era is well documented (see for example Tarp and Lau, 1996; Arndt *et al.*, 2000a; World Bank, 2001b). Although the acceptance of IMF and World Bank programs in the later 1980s did not engender immediate stabilization, trends in a range of indicators show robust gradual improvements through to now. For example, very large reductions have been achieved in the black-market exchange rate premium from over 3000% in 1985 to below 10% in 1995. The rate of inflation, around 50% per year during the mid-1980s, has fallen to an average of 13% in the five years to 2004. Improvements in debt sustainability have been discussed above (also Figure 2), and show that the ratio of debt service to exports has fallen rapidly from its peak in the early 1980s with a further downward spurt in the most recent period reflecting the impact of debt relief and higher economic (export) growth. Mozambique's international reserves have grown steadily from a nadir of negative US$357 million in 1983 to positive US$961 million in 2004. These indicators therefore show consistent movement throughout the 1990s toward a more robust macroeconomic environment compared to the civil war period. Finally, the robust upturn of the residual TFP term found in the growth accounting exercise underlines a clear improvement in the overall macroeconomic environment in the post-war era.

The critical role of external assistance in these trends has been unambiguous from the point of view of supporting the external balance. Relatively high levels of aid inflows have supported the current account deficit and provided crucial foreign exchange necessary for consumer and investment inputs. World Bank (2001b: 20) estimates that from 1987 to 1999 over 65% of all foreign exchange available to Mozambique came through foreign assistance. Debt rescheduling and forgiveness also have brought Mozambique into a much more sustainable long term debt position enabling, as noted previously, a trend increase in net aid available to the government to support development expenditures. However, it should not be overlooked that the country continues to rely on such inflows, permitting the government to run a relatively large current account deficit of nearly US$800 million before transfers in 2004, higher in absolute terms than the deficit in 1986. Therefore, comprehensive external sustainability, where all foreign currency needs are generated from internal resources, does not appear to be a feasible policy objective in the short- or medium-terms.

A couple of issues remain controversial, namely the extent to which policy changes have contributed to macroeconomic performance and the influence of external agencies over domestic policy formulation. The 1987 economic rehabilitation program was oriented at both stabilization and structural change. Measures included tighter fiscal and monetary policy, price and trade liberalization as well as extensive privatization and institutional reforms to promote fiscal/monetary control and permit the allocation of resources within the economy according to market principles. Of course, not all of these reforms were attempted at once and there is a general consensus that, despite a slow start, more rapid progress has been achieved since the mid-1990s with the end of civil war, demobilization and relocation of internal refugees (World Bank, 2001b). For example, a privatization program was initiated in 1989, but achieved limited progress until after the war in the mid-1990s; by 1994 only 5% of the gross value of industrial output had been transferred to private hands rising to 37% by mid-1996 (World Bank, 1995).

Fiscal reforms commenced immediately driven by falls in real tax revenue in the early 1980s. In 1987 a framework law was passed allowing a switch in tax policy to allow a greater role for indirect taxation (Byiers, 2005). Financial sector reform began in 1992 with the separation of the commercial and core central banking functions of the *Banco de Moçambique* followed by privatization of the two major commercial banks, completed in 1997. These reforms have been essential in asserting greater independence of the central bank, enabling it to concentrate on its core task of macroeconomic management. The monthly CPI data shows this very clearly – control over inflation was achieved exactly when the privatization of the commercial banks was finalized. Budgetary and public sector reforms have occurred since the late 1990s, comprising reform of the tax and customs administrations among numerous other initiatives. Whilst these reforms are still ongoing it remains clear they have reduced economic distortions and provided a much improved basis for macroeconomic management.

The available evidence suggests that external donors have been instrumental in these policy developments. *A priori*, the extent of Mozambique's reliance on external finance simply would not have been compatible with any substantial policy divergence between the government and the donor community. Arndt *et al.* (2000a: 303) documentation of the structural adjustment period confirm that the influence of donors and particularly the World Bank and IMF was 'massive' – many of the new economic policies were drafted from Washington and external assistance was made conditional on

256 *Channing Arndt et al.*

their implementation. The government openly recognized the depth of this influence. At a conference in the early 1990s the President referred to the degree of independent policy maneuverability, remarking: "We are totally dependent on inputs from outside. If they are not forthcoming in the correct manner it is of no use." (quoted in Saul, 1991: 106). According to Hanlon (2002), the 'grip' of the IMF over fiscal policy was so acute in the early 1990s that bilateral donors made a public complaint over an IMF-imposed fiscal cap on public investment.

The 'joint review' process instituted under a memorandum of understanding signed by the government and direct budget support donors (GRM & PAPs, 2004) illustrates the depth to which the policy environment in Mozambique continues to be influenced by external, donor agencies. The latest annual review of government performance, (regarding 2005), involved the evaluation of government policy, reforms and implementation across twenty four working groups each comprising representatives from the government, donors and civil society (PAP Secretariat, 2006). The process lasted for well over one month, demanding substantial government resources.

4.2. Social service provision

As already shown, a major donor objective has been to support the provision of social services, their growing weight in total aid being evident from the aid commitments data (Table 2). Establishing a clear link, however, between public spending on social services and final outcomes is notoriously difficult due to exogenous variables that influence these outcomes. While this is particularly acute in the area of health (Heltberg *et al.*, 2001), education outcomes are moderately easier to relate back to spending as the achievement of a school qualification simply cannot occur without schools and teachers. Furthermore, it is recognized that education levels represent a robust proxy indicator for a variety of determining variables (Caldwell and Caldwell, 1985). Education tends to improve one's capacity to recognize and act upon hygiene and sanitation problems as well as to take better advantage of economic opportunities. We therefore treat the education sector in greater detail than the health sector.

In order to trace the impact of external assistance through to final education and health outcomes, two intended or direct outcomes of public expenditure are of immediate interest – namely, the expansion of services to the target population and improvements in the efficiency or quality of these services. Included in the first dimension are equity considerations, such as reaching previously under-represented sections of the population. The relevance of the second aspect should not be understated – better quality services ensure expenditure is translated more effectively into final outcomes. These issues form the core of standard public expenditure reviews, a number of which have been undertaken for Mozambique by external agencies and which we use to substantiate the analysis.

Sections 3.1 and 3.4 have noted improvements in the education system and the educational profile of the population since 1980. In the post-war period alone (1992–2004) the number of students matriculating in the primary school system (EP1 and

Table 5. Summary of education indicators, 1992 and 2004

	Primary		Secondary		All		
	1992	2004	1992	2004	1992	2004	% Δ
Pupils ('000s)	1,296	3,556	46	290	1,342	3,846	187
Schools	3,556	9,489	48	170	3,604	9,659	168
Teachers	24,323	60,020	2,881	9,729	27,204	69,749	156
Trained teachers (% total)	67	59	92	62	69	59	−15
Pupils per teacher	53	59	16	30	49	55	12
Pupils per school	364	375	948	1,706	372	398	7
Government spending (mil. US$)	–	–	–	–	117.6	253.0	115.1
External funding (% of total)	–	–	–	–	53.8	37.4	−30.4

Source: Ministry of Education.

EP2) increased by 174% while matriculations to the secondary system (ES1 and ES2) increased by 537%. There can be little doubt that the increase in students and consequent output from the system has been driven by an expansion of access to schooling made possible by public spending increases supported by external funds. The expansion of the public network of schools since 1992 is shown in Table 5; on average, each year around 500 new schools have been constructed and 3,500 new teachers recruited.

Historical data on public spending on education is not available on a consistent basis and is complicated by off-budget resources and expenditures. However, a compilation of estimates from various sources, also in Table 5, indicates total spending on education has doubled since 1992 to US$253 million in 2004 of which, on average, almost 50% has derived from external sources. Growth in both internal and external funding has enabled total education spending to remain relatively stable as a percentage of GDP, averaging 4.7% for the period. At an aggregate level, therefore, the outcome of a substantially expanded education system and improved educational profile of the population, which in turn has been linked to economic growth via the growth accounting exercise, can be associated with increased public spending. *Ceteris paribus*, the magnitude of this expansion would not have been possible without external financial support.

Despite these improvements, a deeper analysis of trends in the education sector reveals a number of emerging difficulties. First, the enrolment profile shows a strong bias in access towards primary levels with low coverage at the secondary level. This is associated with low net and gross enrolment rates beyond the first primary school cycle (EP1). In 2004, for example, the number of pupils entering the two secondary levels was equivalent to 8% of pupils in the primary system (up from 3.5% in 1992). UNESCO (2005) statistics suggest Mozambique's net enrolment rate for levels EP2 to ES2 (ISCED levels 2 and 3) is 12% against a 30% regional average in 2002/2003. There are two implications of this prioritization of primary schooling. First, there is a notable increase in pressure within the system as graduates from EP1 and EP2 frequently find they cannot continue their education. In 2005 alone, vacancies in the secondary system were 70,000 short of the number of pupils completing primary education (PAPs Secretariat, 2006).

Second, and related to the above problem of diminishing access at higher levels, the expansion of the education system has not been accompanied by similar efficiency gains, as discussed in detail by World Bank (2003a, 2003b).[11] High repetition and desistance rates at all scholastic levels result in high average costs per graduating student and are one indication of a low quality of education services. Although the survival rate to the last grade in EP1, for example, has increased from 34.0% in 1993 to 42.9% in 2003, it remains the case that the majority of students starting EP1 will not conclude this level. Put another way, it takes an average of 21 input resource years to produce one primary school graduate (EP1 and EP2) compared to only 10 years in Zambia (World Bank, 2003b) or seven years in theory. These inefficiencies continue through the system such that on average 212 resource years are required for a student to reach the final year of secondary school. The relatively high burden of central administration costs and high absolute school construction costs (also noted in the aforementioned World Bank studies) further undermine the overall efficiency of the sector.

A third worrying tendency is the deterioration of pupil–teacher ratios that has accompanied the expansion in pupil numbers. Between 1992 and 2004 the ratio deteriorated by 11.2% at the primary level (EP1 and EP2) and by 88.7% at the secondary level, the latter figure reinforcing the higher priority given to primary education. In 2002/2003 according to UNESCO (2005) the primary school (EP1) pupil–teacher ratio was 67, only exceeded in sub-Saharan Africa by Chad with 68. From the point of view of quality, it is widely recognized that a teacher–pupil ratio above 45 can severely reduce effectiveness. Aggravating this development is an increasing use of unqualified teachers, which again is most notable at the secondary level where 38% of all teachers were unqualified in 2004 against only 7.5% in 1992.[12] These teachers have been employed to reduce pressure (enable expansion) within the system in the apparent absence of a sufficient output of qualified teachers from training institutes possibly as well as in reaction to the higher costs of hiring qualified teachers. These points indicate, therefore, that while external aid has unambiguously supported quantitative expansion, the quality of education has remained at best stable if not fallen.

Tendencies in the health sector also indicate the existence of quality concerns despite significant progress in widening access to services. The historical importance of

---

[11] This is not to say there have been no efficiency gains; Arndt and Muzima (2004) and MPF and MINED (2003) observe gradual improvements in transition rates through the post-war period.

[12] The definition of unqualified in Ministry of Education data captures those teachers who do not possess one of the recognized teaching qualifications and/or do not have a qualification from a higher (tertiary) education institution. Note that in 2004 the majority (50%) of all qualified teachers held a CFPP (*Centro de Formação de Professores Primários*) qualification for which the minimum entry requirement is completion of primary school cycle EP2. As a result, one cannot assume that even all qualified primary teachers hold a secondary school level qualification.

external funds and therefore their contribution to progress in the health sector is, as in the education sector, undeniable. Following expansion of external assistance to the sector in the late 1980s, aid consistently has financed around 60–70% of total spending against only 9% in 1983 (MPF and MISAU, 2004). Since the end of the civil war, external and internal funds have grown at similar rates, permitting total health care spending to rapidly increase in real terms from an estimated US$5.0 per capita in 1997 to US$10.7 in 2002 (World Bank, 2003b). External funding also has financed around 80% of all capital investment such that the construction and rehabilitation of health service infrastructure, a major priority in the 1990s, has been due in large part to this funding. The real expansion in health services is patent from the available delivery statistics. For example, the number of public health centers grew from 161 in 1994 to 683 in 2004; the total number of beds provided by the public health service grew from around 9,000 in 1994 to over 17,000 in 2004 (INE, 2005). The number of pre-natal consultations has doubled and vaccine coverage has expanded very significantly (see Table 4).

This expansion of access contrasts with efficiency and equity concerns in the sector. In particular, analyses point to continued sizeable inequalities in service delivery outputs and weak incentives for staff to provide more efficient, better quality services. Maputo City, for example, receives around four times the average funding per person and has over three times the average number of beds per person (data for 1999 in World Bank, 2002). In response to staff incentive problems, real expenditure growth has enabled large increases in remuneration but this has not been matched by improvements in personnel productivity. Between 1997 and 2000, for example, real staff expenditure increased by 94% while services delivered per staff member only increased by 7% (World Bank, 2003b). In comparative terms, salaries remain low in the sector which can be linked to evidence of various quality- and equity-harming activities. These include staff pursuing secondary income generating activities, the diversion of funds from goods and services into personnel compensation, and the non-application of fee-wavers and/or over-charging for certain users (World Bank, 2003b). Such difficulties are compounded by large caseloads and concomitant pressure on medical staff; in 2002, for example, there were approximately 43,584 inhabitants per doctor in Mozambique against an average of 21,970 in sub-Saharan Africa. Lastly, poor staff pay and conditions create weaker incentives for both technical and administrative staff to work in remote or under-served provinces, aggravating equity considerations. In turn, these under-staffed locations can face absorptive capacity difficulties due to greater technical constraints. World Bank (2002), for example, identifies that the most poorly serviced province, Zambézia, also tends to have the lowest budget execution rates while the better served provinces, with higher staff-population ratios, show generally higher and more consistent rates.

Evidence from the two sectors discussed here thus demonstrates that external aid has had a very positive impact on service delivery expansion. This has been reflected in the positive trend in social development indicators as well as the strong contribution of education in the growth accounting. It is not evident, however, that improvements in the quality of services have been achieved by nearly the same extent. These issues reinforce the point that the efficiency and equity of public expenditure should not be obscured by a focus on quantitative expansion alone. Rather, there is a risk that where the former is neglected not only the realization of the latter may become increasingly difficult but also the impact of expenditure on final outcomes is undermined. In terms of the impact on growth, lowering the quality of education may lower the salary-premium associated with educational attainment.

4.3. Public infrastructure development

The positive relationship between household well-being and access to public infrastructure has been observed consistently across the literature. From the point of view of intended outcomes, the objective of external aid towards the provision of public infrastructure is to enhance access to these public goods in the most effective, equitable and sustainable manner possible. With respect to Mozambique, we have noted that one of the government's priorities since the end of the civil war has been the rebuilding and expansion of public infrastructure, including water, energy and communications networks. The fundamental contribution of both government and private investment to post-war economic growth has been highlighted in the growth accounting exercise. It is relevant therefore to consider the role of external aid in this sector.

Due to space limitations, rather than consider all aspects of public infrastructure we focus exclusively on the roads sector. This is apposite not only because the network registered substantial damage during the war. It is also crucial to trade and production in a sparsely populated and geographically diverse country such as Mozambique. Indeed, the road network is the principal means of transport in the country, representing over 60% of the value added of the transport and communications sector (INE). We also recall that prior to Independence, Mozambique served as a key provider of transport services to neighboring countries, indicating the considerable economic potential of the sector.

The available statistics indicate that since 1992 very substantial progress has been made in rehabilitating and upgrading the classified road network. At the end of the war only 10% of roads were in good/fair condition and 50% were impassable.[13] By 2002, 56% of the road network had been restored to good/fair condition and only 8% were impassable. Routine maintenance had been expanded to cover over 10,000 km of the network per year against less than 4,000 km in 1994. These improvements are reflected by large increases in real traffic volumes; road cargo traffic, for example, increased by over 650% from 1993–2002 and passenger traffic increased by over 100%. Tertiary and unclassified roads have also benefited from substantial rehabilitation, indicating that developmental efforts have not focused exclusively on arteries linking the main urban centers. Over 6,000 km of these rural feeder roads have been rehabilitated, mainly in more remote provinces, principally using labor intensive techniques with a local workforce. According to World Bank (2003b) over 40 of these labor-intensive

---

[13] Unless otherwise stated, the statistics in this section are taken from Herman (2003).

brigades are operative in 10 provinces and these programs have provided employment to over 40,000 people (UNDP, 2002).

The direct, developmental impact of these trends is apparent at both an aggregate and microeconomic level. At the household level, both government and donors have stated repeatedly that access to transport is a central determinant of rural production and overall household well-being (e.g., World Bank, 2001b). Survey evidence confirms that rehabilitation of the road network has made a robust contribution to poverty reduction to date. According to household survey data in Table 4, the percentage of the population with access to markets and collective transport almost doubled between 1997 and 2003. Estimates by Herman (2003) combining road density and poverty data suggest there is a negative correlation between access to roads and poverty. Nhate and Simler (2002) find that districts with a higher incidence of poverty tend to be served, if at all, by roads in a poor condition; conversely, districts with access to better roads appear to show lower poverty levels. Qualitative analyses of poverty reinforce the very close connection between access to transport and well-being (Mate *et al.*, 2005).

Comparative agricultural income survey data (for 1996 and 2002) indicate substantial gains from activities logically and necessarily linked to better access to transport and market-based opportunities. Three findings can be highlighted here. First, with respect to income from crop production, there has been a substantial diversification in the number of crops produced per household increasing from an average of 4.7 to 7.9 between the two survey dates. Second, increases in net income per person over the period have derived principally from wage employment (47%) and non-crop household production (39%). Within the latter category we notice that resource extraction activities such as wood cutting and charcoal production, often requiring transport for movement on a large scale, registered the most rapid growth, particularly in terms of the number of households engaged in this activity. Third, the surveys register a large jump from 7% to 23% of households owning a bicycle. All of these trends are consistent with gains from improved access to markets and reduced transport costs made possible through road network rehabilitation.

Finally, from a macroeconomic standpoint, the sectors encompassing transport, communications and commercial activities, whose performance depends on the road network, have contributed strongly to aggregate economic growth in the post-war period. Government statistics estimate that the weight of these sectors in real GDP has remained around 30% for the entire 1992–2004 period, adding on average around 2 percentage points to annual real GDP growth, equivalent to 20% of aggregate growth for the period. Thus micro- and macro-economic evidence provides consistent support for the hypothesis that improvements in public infrastructure have enabled significant welfare gains from increased trade and access to markets and other public services.

The considerable influence of external assistance over the institutional and financial development of the roads sector is clear. As suggested in Section 3.2, support to public infrastructure consistently has been one of the main priorities of aggregate external aid to the country. Donors have been active in the sector since at least 1981 (UNDP; 2002), although the main phase of expansion of external support has occurred since 1992. Data collected by Herman (2003) and World Bank (2003b) show that during the period 1996–2002 donors have financed approximately 75% of all expenditure in the roads sector. While the majority of this financing has been towards rehabilitation, with the government covering less than 10% of such costs, donors have also supported recurrent maintenance and administration expenditures. For 2003 and 2004, the government accounts (*Conta Geral do Estado*) suggest donor funding was equal to at least 60% of total expenditure in the sector. This figure is an underestimate as it *excludes* the indirect contribution of external funding via general budget support classified as internal investment.

In terms of the structure of external funding, the World Bank has been the lead agency since 1992 and has come to dominate both policy-development and analysis in the sector, evident from the substantial strategy and institutional changes that the Bank has made integral to its programs. For example, the 1989 government transport strategy prioritized links to neighboring countries. In contrast, the actual strategy executed since 1992 has been oriented more toward improving access routes within the country (World Bank, 1998a). World Bank emphasis on the use of private contractors has been reflected by an increasing use of competitive tendering as well as moves towards the privatization of parastatal publics works companies (Herman, 2003). More recently in April 1999, the government undertook significant institutional reform, consistent with donor preferences, establishing the National Roads Administration (*Administração Nacional de Estadas, ANE*) as an autonomous body. However, according to the World Bank this reform did not go far enough and a second generation of deeper reforms to clarify and separate responsibilities within ANE has been called for (Herman, 2003).

Despite observed achievements, the sector has been marred by difficulties in achieving maintenance targets caused principally by uneven and inadequate government financial contributions to the sector as well as institutional weaknesses (Herman, 2003). During the 1990s this led to the build-up of a massive backlog in maintenance requirements and consequently an increase in the length of the network needing rehabilitation (World Bank, 2003b). For example, through 1994 to 1999 periodic maintenance only covered an average of 434 km per year against a target of over 3,000 km generating a backlog of over 16,000 km. In response to these internal funding difficulties, the current World Bank roads program envisages donors funding a substantial portion of maintenance expenditures, decreasing over time. Recent reforms to both the Road Fund and its financial arrangements would appear to place the sector on a more sustainable future footing (PAP Secretariat, 2006) although the success of this will depend on future government capacity and commitment.

From the growth accounting results we recall that government investment has made a considerable impact on economic growth. Within government investment, which we have seen is dependent on external funding, the roads sector represents one of the major expenditure items. The above overview thus confirms the deep influence, both financial and institutional, of external agencies over road sector development throughout the post-war period. The positive effect of external aid on growth through the financing of much-needed public infrastructure appears quite distinct in this case.

4.4. Agricultural production

The importance of the agricultural sector to growth and poverty reduction is well established. Indeed, "it is difficult to conceive of large scale reductions in poverty without agricultural sector growth" (GRM, 2006: 18). This observation stems from basic structural features of the Mozambican economy. Nearly 70% of the population is rural and more than 90% of economically active people in rural areas point to agriculture as their principal occupation. Moreover, poverty rates are higher in rural versus urban areas.

Agriculture is also central to concerns related to gender and gender equity. Women are much more likely than men to cite agriculture as their primary occupation. In addition, women compose a larger share of the rural population than men. Overall, while employment in non-agricultural sectors is an important route out of poverty, the shear volume of employment in the agricultural sector implies that agricultural sector growth is a condition sine qua non for large scale reductions in poverty at least through the medium term.

Finally, agriculture is important because fundamental growth prospects in the sector are good. As pointed out by Coughlin (2006), Mozambique possesses both a long coastline and vast tracts of virgin arable land. Numerous rivers traverse the country on their way to the ocean opening possibilities for irrigation on both large and small scales. As a result, agriculture and agricultural processing are regarded in the Mozambican PRSP as leading sectors for economic development.

Since 1992, performance of the agricultural sector, in terms of trend, has been relatively good. As highlighted in Section 3.4, agricultural income surveys indicate growth in real income per adult equivalent between 1996 and 2002 of 65% using the mean and 30% using the median. The same survey also indicates: (i) strong diversification in terms of number of crops grown; (ii) an increase in mean area cropped per household; (iii) diversification in household income sources with increases in the relative importance of livestock, wage, and small business income; and (iv) improvements in indicators of sophistication of production, such as use of animal traction, chemical fertilizer, manure, and irrigation. While conflicting estimates emerge from different sources, the official data confirm agricultural production gains at about 25–30 percent for the same period. This is largely in line with income and consumption gains (as well as other welfare indicators such as health and assets). In addition, the growth in the number of crops planted indicates a relative shift in effort away from major crops and towards other crops, particularly higher value horticultural crops, over the period 1996–2002.

A large portion of donor-funded activities in the agricultural sector are carried out under the overall framework of the PROAGRI program channeled through the Ministry of Agriculture. However, specific project-assistance to the Ministry and a diverse set of NGO operations remain. Donor support accounts for some 80% of total spending in the sector. This corresponds to about 5% of total government spending, equivalent to less than 2% of GDP. As such, this falls short of the commitment to allocate 10% of total government spending to agriculture as made by African heads of state and government at the African Union summit in Mozambique in 2003. These figures are broadly consistent with the weight of agriculture in DAC donor commitments (Table 2) which suggest that support to agriculture has fallen from 9% of donor funds in 1990–1991 to 4.3% in 2000–2004. Thus, while flows have been important in absolute terms they have been below stated commitments in relative terms. Moreover, it should be recognized that the challenges of the agricultural sector are extremely large given the dispersed family-farm and technologically underdeveloped nature of agricultural production in Mozambique.

Allocation of funds within the sector appears to be unbalanced. For example, in 2006, agricultural research accounts for only about 10% of the total resource allocation of the Ministry (GRM, 2006) and extension amounts to 5%. Ministry insiders describe the effective allocation to research as considerably less than 10%. In contrast, general and administrative expenses budgeted for 2006, at 38% of the budget, are more than twice the allocation to research and extension combined.

Assessing the impact of foreign aid to agriculture is complicated. While gains in school enrolments or vaccination coverage rates are quite easily attributable to the Ministries of Education and Health respectively, gains in agricultural production and rural income stem from a wide variety of sources, many of which are entirely unrelated to the activities of the Ministry of Agriculture. Such possible sources include favorable climate outcomes, improved marketing infrastructure such as roads, higher literacy rates amongst the population, improved health, and a general snapback from depressed conditions post war. In short, demonstrating impact of external funding to the agricultural sector is far more difficult than in many of the social sectors.

The complexities of the endeavor, combined with data constraints, which are gradually receding, have contributed to the relative dearth of solid impact evaluation of agricultural sector spending. World Bank (2005), for example, presents an attempt to link extension programs of both the government and NGOs with key variables such as agricultural production/income and poverty. Unfortunately, substantial methodological concerns means that their broadly positive conclusions appear to be overstated both in terms of magnitude and robustness.

Failure to document impact of programs in the agricultural sector does not necessarily imply an absence of impact. There could be impact and no documentation. Certainly, the Ministry of Agriculture does have some tangible successes to point to. For example, agricultural statistics have improved from an effectively non-existent base in 1992 (though ample room for continued improvement remains). A detailed market information system now makes available price information via publication and radio broadcast on a wide scale. In addition, farmers, particularly better-off farmers, report using this price information in their marketing decisions (Walker *et al.*, 2004). Contract growing schemes in cotton and tobacco have experienced some success in producing for export and in introducing purchased inputs into the production process. With the current high world prices for sugar, the decision to place high border protection on sugar in order to maintain a domestic sugar price sufficient to attract investment looks, at the moment, positively clairvoyant. Finally, a small number of improved

agricultural technologies have been disseminated on a reasonably wide scale (Coughlin, 2006).

Nevertheless, despite these changes it is clear that the strategically important research and extension activities of the Ministry remain very weak. Arguably, research and extension should be the fundamental core of government support to the sector. Instead, we note that these activities are repeatedly described as under-funded with a concomitant failure to generate and disseminate technologies adapted to local circumstances that are capable of broad impact (Coughlin, 2006; Eicher, 2004; Gemo *et al.*, 2005). Some orders of magnitude are instructive. As shown in Table 5, the Ministry of Education employed nearly 70,000 teachers in 2004 with the number of teachers growing continuously since 1992. The Ministry of Agriculture, on the other hand, employed 708 extension agents in 2004 with the number of extension agents essentially constant since 1999 (MADER, 2004). The extension system is evidently a very long way from providing national coverage, and there is no positive growth trend.

In our overall assessment, it would appear that, while donor support to agriculture has been forthcoming, there is a perplexing lack of attention to what appear to be priority needs, and donor support has not been sufficiently consistent. A case in point is the fluctuating attention paid to agricultural research and extension. Only recently does one find renewed emphasis on this area within the donor community. In sum, it is difficult to establish the contribution of donor support/government activity to the increased agricultural production and rural incomes observed over the past decade. Donor support has contributed to increased institutional capacity within the Ministry of Agriculture; however, considerable challenges remain, particularly in agricultural research and extension, before these gains are consolidated into a system that catalyzes sustained agricultural growth.

5. Aid and unintended outcomes

5.1. Currency effects

The salient debate concerning the relationship between capital inflows and exchange rates concerns the extent to which these inflows may lead to unintended distortions of the nominal and/or real exchange rates of the recipient country. For the purpose of this section we undertake a review of two main issues, namely the impact of external assistance on the level and volatility of the exchange. We focus here on shorter-term effects and cover in Section 5.2 the longer-term structural effects and deeper potential influence on the private sector of aid flows.

The existence of 'Dutch disease' is frequently cited as a potentially damaging effect of increased aid inflows (Adam, 2005; IMF, 2005). The fundamental concept here is that a sustained increase in capital inflows can lead to a re-allocation of productive incentives within the economy away from the production of tradables (exports and domestically produced import substitutes) and towards non-tradables (goods and services produced and consumed domestically). The mechanism through which this occurs is an increase in the price of the latter goods *relative* to the former through increased

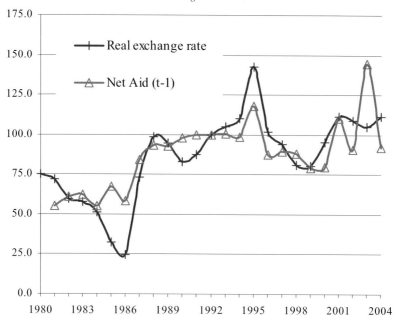

Source: Banco de Moçambique, INE, IMF and authors' calculations.

Notes: Real exchange rate is calculated in standard empirical fashion as the nominal rate multiplied by the ratio of world to domestic prices; world prices are taken as a selected basket of world commodity prices from IMF commodity price statistics and domestic prices are represented by the official consumer price index. For net aid see notes to Table 1; $t-1$ indicates a one period lag used to capture transmission effects.

Fig. 5.   *Real exchange rate and net aid (lagged one period) indices, 1980–2004.*

domestic spending occasioned by the capital inflow. The shift in prices squeezes the profit margins of exporters, makes imports relatively cheaper and therefore can lead to a relative contraction of exporting industries as seen in the Netherlands after the discovery of natural gas giving the phenomenon its name. While this is the theory, the empirical reality is often ambiguous (Adam, 2005), not least due to difficulties in estimating accurately the real exchange rate defined as the ratio of the prices of tradables to non-tradables. In the context of Mozambique, distinguishing the unique exchange rate impact of foreign aid from changes in macroeconomic policy and structural reforms is far from easy. Nevertheless, it is possible to uncover some tentative conclusions for the relationship between aid and the real exchange rate in Mozambique for the period 1980–2004.

Figure 5 plots the real exchange rate against a lagged (one period) index of net aid. The two variables indicate a strong positive association whereby increases in aid are associated with a real depreciation, confirmed by a Spearman's Rho statistic of 55%. This allows us to reject the null hypothesis at the 1% level that the two variables are independent. While there is little doubt that aid inflows have affected resource allocation (see Section 5.2), these trends suggest that Mozambique is not a patient showing standard Dutch Disease symptoms. This is undoubtedly related to the fact that aid inflows have been transmitted quickly through to movements in the current account deficit via imports. This is shown by the relationship between the level of imports and net aid shown in Figure 3; the two variables not only are equal in value but also track one another so closely that a change in net aid in one year is associated with an equivalent change in imports *in the same year*. The IMF (2005) analysis of the increase in net aid to Mozambique in the early 2000s supports this conclusion.

To be sure, the above analysis does not mean that aid inflows have had no interaction with the real exchange rate. More recently, the annual and intra-annual volatility of both nominal and real exchange rates has been a dominant concern. Volatility can generate substantial negative effects for exporters; even temporary real movements (overshooting) can generate long-term effects where fixed investments are made in response to these changes (Adam, 2005). Alternatively, ongoing volatility can reduce investment in the tradables sector due to perceptions of elevated currency risk and weak government credibility and/or capacity to maintain currency stability. In 2004, for example, the nominal rate with the US$ appreciated by 21% followed by a 28% depreciation the following year, with much greater shifts between peaks and troughs. Monthly changes are also often large – between October and December 2005 the nominal rate appreciated 10% despite a 7% rise in consumer prices for the same period indicating an even larger real appreciation.

While it is not possible to prove conclusively that these variations can be connected directly to aid inflows in the absence of data on the timing of aid flows, the evidence is highly suggestive. Recall that foreign aid financed on average 90% of the current account deficit (1980–2004). Furthermore, aid inflows typically are volatile, lumpy and do not arrive according to a schedule known by the Central Bank. This generates liquidity management challenges and can contribute toward exchange rate volatility in a thin market. Broadly, evidence indicates that even direct budget support, which ought to be the 'most' predictable, does not always arrive as planned. Analysis of actual against planned quarterly disbursements for 2003 to 2005 shows a preponderance to disburse in the first half of the year less direct budget support than pledged followed by more than pledged in the second. Ernst & Young Mozambique (2006) also find that despite improvements in the predictability of budget support, 30% of budget support donors did not disburse according to schedule in 2005 and over 20% did not meet the deadline to pre-advise the government their intended disbursement schedule. The point here is that external aid generates substantial foreign exchange management challenges, particularly where aid is one of the principal sources of currency and there is no necessary coincidence in the timing of supply and demand of such funds. It is highly likely that the extent of these challenges have exacerbated real and nominal exchange rate volatility.

5.2. Structural distortions

As noted above, empirical analysis of 'Dutch Disease' tends to focus on appreciation of the real exchange rate as measured by the nominal exchange rate deflated by the ratio of world and domestic prices. However an analysis of these effects does not necessarily capture the full impact on long-term productive incentives associated with aid inflows. Aid has certainly affected resource allocation evidenced by the relative amount of resources going into the public sector. The basic issue, therefore, is the extent to which aid has undermined the potential development of the domestic private sector via a misalignment of the real exchange rate compared to its hypothetical position under long-run external balance.[14]

Perhaps the best way to pose this question is to consider the principal constraints to growth in the post-war period. We submit that the complete lack of a domestic entrepreneurial class, high levels of illiteracy, highly deficient public infrastructure and lack of penetration into international markets have been fundamental impediments. None of these can be attributed to aid. Thus, it is unhelpful to suggest that aid would have been more productive had it been allocated, for example, towards labor-intensive manufacturing such as textiles production. One can of course point to specific areas where aid could have been spent more efficiently, as evident in the discussion of other sections of this paper, but this does not subtract from the principal argument here. However, these reflections relate to the past and one should carefully scrutinize the validity of this approach as a guide to the future, discussed in Section 6.

A final observation is that while one might speculate about how aid could have been directed more pointedly to private sector development in the past this cannot be perceived as a specific critique of aid to Mozambique, i.e. aid failure. Instead this has been inherent, first, to the statist approach to development characteristic before 1980 and, second, to the neo-liberal paradigm where prices were the exclusive key to unlock private sector growth. More targeted approaches to private sector development involving aid is a more recent phenomenon.

5.3. Fiscal imbalances

The analysis of the education sector, and to a lesser extent the health sector, has made clear that quantitative expansion in access may not always be matched by improvements, or even maintenance of existing low-levels of quality. The pertinent issue is whether these trends directly relate to the structure of funding and, specifically, cumulative pressure on recurrent budgets *caused* by (aid-financed) investment expenditures. Certainly in the education sector the skew in the enrolment profile towards the first level of primary schooling matches a historical skew in expenditure from both internal and external sources. Throughout the 1990s, primary education has represented at least 60% of total education spending; in 1998, for example, 44% of expenditure, excluding related administrative costs, went to EP1 compared to 12% for EP2 and only 9% for the entire secondary system (World Bank, 2003a: 30). According to MPF and MINED (2003) the weight of external funding has been slightly more heavily in favor

---

[14] See Rajan and Subramanian (2005) for elaboration.

of primary schooling, being in line with the influential view that (universal) access to primary schooling should be a key priority for low income countries. Whether or not this external consensus has *driven* the allocation of education funds in Mozambique is impossible to judge, although the fit between this consensus and the evident needs of Mozambique clearly has facilitated the flow of external funds to the sector.

Of more significance, however, is that external funds have predominantly financed the construction of schools rather than ongoing staff or maintenance requirements. This is in line with the well-known preference of donors to fund capital investment as opposed to recurrent costs. In 2000, for example, 65% of all capital expenditures in the public education sector were funded by donors as against 15% of recurrent costs (World Bank, 2003b: 50). Investment has been a priority in the sector with some estimates suggesting up to a third of all education spending may have been on school construction during the 1990s (World Bank, 2003a: 37). Deterioration of both the pupil–teacher and the qualified teacher ratios would indicate that recurrent funding, from internal sources, has not been able to keep pace with the investment-led expansion in access. This is not only due to an insufficiency of internal tax receipts nor is this because education has received a relatively low proportion of internal funds. Macroeconomic stability has obliged fiscal caution, particularly in the domain of public sector salaries. As part of the IMF program with Mozambique there has been an implicit cap on total government salary expenditure at less than 8% of GDP.

A further challenge, as discussed by the World Bank (2003b), relates to the relatively high salaries and unequal pay structure of qualified teachers, seen as an impediment to growth of the teacher stock particularly beyond EP1 level. A consequent recommendation has been a reduction in these salaries. This would diminish incentives to enter the teaching profession, running counter to the need to attract substantially more teachers in the context of a relatively small stock of working adults holding a secondary level qualification and growing private sector demand. The point is that continued rapid expansion of the education sector, particularly at the primary level, may not be compatible with fiscal and macroeconomic objectives or with labor market dynamics.

In common with the education sector, pressures on recurrent expenditure in the health sector also appear to result from the prioritization of expanded coverage of services through health infrastructure expansion. This agenda is certainly shared, if not driven, by external partners and has led to a weight of investment in total spending of around 15%–20% (1997–2000), deemed to be excessive for a low income country (MPF and MISAU, 2004).[15] Indeed, the same review of health sector spending concludes that, "... investments have been made with little reflection and concern for

---

[15] This view, however, is not encountered consistently across Ministry of Health documents. A 2001 study of funding sources argued that investment rates were unacceptably low in the sector and recommended the development of an investment plan and creation of a new common investment fund. In contrast, according to MPF and MISAU (2004: 73), in 2002 the Ministry produced a preliminary investment plan explicitly *limiting* new investments precisely due to their recurrent cost implications.

their impact on future recurrent costs." (2004: 18; authors' translation). Despite recent evidence of tighter control of investment and a greater willingness of donors to support recurrent costs, the 2005 ministerial sector plan estimates that the weight of investment remains around 18% (MISAU, 2005).

The above discussion has established a connection between the scaling-up of the provision of public goods, made possible through external support, and longer-term recurrent funding challenges. The message is that the customary focus of external aid on meeting sector-specific goals can generate unintended fiscal imbalances at least at an aggregate level. In turn, funding shortages or delays associated with these imbalances can undermine the quality and effectiveness of service delivery.

5.4. Policy and planning implications

Fiscal imbalances often are a symptom of planning weaknesses at either the aggregate or sector levels. The former is encountered where funding requirements identified (agreed) at the sector-level are not compatible with aggregate budget demands and/or public financial management capacities. In other words, sector- and aggregate-level expectations may be disconnected. Planning incoherence is found within a sector where the dynamic, long-term impacts of policy interventions simply are not considered fully by the sector itself. Two common features of external funding can contribute to planning difficulties at the sector level. First, informational and institutional fragmentation can occur when a sector receives funds from various sources earmarked for distinct activities. This is aggravated when funding inflows are not synchronized with sector plans and/or when they make specific reporting and accounting demands. Second, the different policy priorities of funding agencies *within* a given sector can generate inconsistencies in the pursued objectives. Together these effects can act against both coordinated policymaking and the more equitable distribution of resources.

A case in point here is the health sector which, due to its very high reliance on external funding, embraces a large number of funding agencies each with specific preferences and working procedures. A problematic relationship between external assistance and policy coordination was identified as early as 1995 when the Health Sector Recovery Program was initiated (see World Bank, 2002). MPF and MISAU (2004) and World Bank (2002, 2003b) continue to make similar observations, also noting substantial inefficiencies in resource management connected with the coordination of external aid. Although common funding instruments are now significant in the sector, the majority (60%) of external funding according to the 2006 sector plan continues to arrive in the form of projects over which the central ministry has varying levels of control and information. Despite progress, the ministry plan for 2005 remarks that external investment funds are unpredictable and poorly integrated with wider sector planning mechanisms (MISAU, 2005: 14). Cabral *et al.* (2005) detailed review of resources in the sector confirms that a unified, single annual resource planning exercise still does not take place.

In the education sector, we have noted that the long-term fiscal implications of investment activities have not been considered in detail, either by the sector or more generally by the government. In the minimum, it would appear that donors have been complicit with this trend – sector plans and donor reviews often fail to stress the considerable fiscal challenges presented by current education targets. Weakness in sectoral planning was highlighted recently in negotiations with the IMF for the preparation of the 2006 budget. Reflecting legitimate budget concerns, the IMF expressed skepticism concerning the very large number of new recruits requested by the education sector as these were not supported by robust planning documents or longer-term resource projections.[16] Even at an aggregate level, the 2005 joint donor-government review (PAP Secretariat, 2006: 14) fails to place the recognized resource needs of the sector within its wider (non-sectoral) fiscal context. These challenges may also have been exacerbated by a lack of coordination or even competition among donors. For example, a Nordic review of the PRSP processes criticizes Washington-based World Bank staff for pushing the Fast-track for Education initiative outside the sector working-group approach (Scanteam, 2003). Thus there are elements of weak planning at both the sector and aggregate levels in this case.

The case of the roads sector demonstrates the simple existence of a disconnection between sector- and macro-level planning. Here the government, in agreement with the World Bank, made clear multi-annual pre-commitments regarding its financial contribution to the sector and consequent maintenance targets. While donor-funded rehabilitation works were completed largely as planned, inadequate and uneven government transfers to the Road Fund from internal revenue resulted in a 'massive failure' of periodic maintenance (Herman, 2003). Why the government did not transfer sufficient funds (to the extent that the Road Fund often received substantially less than the value of raised fuel taxes) appears mainly to have been due to the precedence of aggregate fiscal and macroeconomic targets imposed by the Ministry of Planning and Finance (World Bank, 2003b: 14). The point here is that as external aid has dynamic long-term fiscal implications, the effective scaling-up of aid interventions demands considerable coordinated planning both within and across these sectors.

Planning incoherence at an aggregate level can also be associated with external funding. A principal driver behind this is the elevated importance and autonomy of government sectors in comparison to central (coordinating) ministries, an unintended effect of external assistance being targeted specifically and often disbursed directly to the sectors. Where external assistance is substantial (as in the case of Mozambique) central planning instruments, including the government budget can be undermined and become of limited importance for individual sectors. The most obvious example of this is found in the historical importance of off-budget flows already discussed. In the health sector alone, estimates for 2002 and 2003 suggest that over 20% of funds forecast as being available to the sector were not inscribed in the government budget, over 50% of executed funds did not pass through the central treasury, and over 40% of received funds were not reflected in government execution accounts (Cabral

---

[16] The education ministry initially requested funding to permit the recruitment of 11,500 new staff; the final budget, nonetheless, projected the recruitment of only 4,715 new teachers (PAPs Secretariat, 2006).

et al., 2005). Although there are certain internal revenues also considered off-budget, the vast majority of such flows come from external sources. A result is a lack of information at the central government level concerning the volume and allocation of funds even where sectors are aware of this data. The quality of aggregate fiscal projections and planning is thus undermined, further weakening incentives for sectors to participate fully in government-wide planning exercises. Furthermore, such participation is associated with high transaction costs as well as the downside risk that internal government funding will be reduced if planning ministries are aware of the true volume of finance available to the sector (Cabral *et al.*, 2005; Hodges and Tibana, 2005).

In sum, the historical tendency of channeling external funding directly towards sectors, bypassing central review and management, has contributed both to weak central planning capacities and poorly coordinated policy interventions (World Bank, 2003b: 33–34). The gradual movement towards pooled funding (program) instruments in Mozambique since the mid-1990s has been, in part, a response to these unintended negative effects. While we acknowledge these instruments have been helpful, a number of reservations can be made as to their effective contribution to sectoral and aggregate planning. First, it has been stressed that pooled mechanisms are growing *alongside* rather than replacing traditional project-based instruments. As the former tend to place much greater demands on individual ministries in terms of time and capacity (Pavignani and Hauck, 2002), clear progress in reducing the overall transaction costs associated with external aid are not yet obvious. Killick's (2005: 47–50) review of the status and benefits of sector program instruments confirms this. Second, with expansion of sectoral pooled instruments rather than general budget support alone, aid to Mozambique continues to have a very strong sectoral focus. As a result, information sharing and aggregate coordination remains weak, recognized explicitly in the 2005 government-donor review (PAP Secretariat, 2006: 21). Third, and particularly at the sector level, pooling instruments have been developed on an *ad hoc* basis with little interaction between sectors or with central planning functions. This further exacerbates the sectoral dimension of aid flows. Lastly, coordination at all levels is being undermined by the emergence of large, (multi)-sectoral funds such as the Millennium Challenge Account (MCA) which often are not linked to pooled instruments or sector plans. Thus, recent changes in funding modalities are not uniform and have yet to yield distinct improvements in the quality of sector or aggregate planning; it would be misleading, therefore, to view the expansion of new instruments as a panacea.

5.5. Corruption and institutional effects

The discussions in previous sections indicate a two-way relationship between external aid and the institutional framework. We have noted that the relatively rapid movement away from socialist central planning and the implementation of wide-ranging reforms necessitated substantial adaptation of the institutional framework, itself. Some of the resulting institutional changes, such as the independence of the Central Bank and reduction of government interference in the market, undeniably have had a long-term beneficial economic impact. At the same time, we have argued that the tendency to channel funding towards individual sectors, often through projects, has contributed to institutional fragmentation and planning weaknesses.

Analysis of the relationship between public sector corruption and external aid provides a concrete example of the historical interweaving of aid and institutional development in Mozambique. Various analysts (e.g., Mosse, 2004; Hanlon, 2002) contrast the evidence of extremely low levels of corruption during the immediate post-Independence socialist era against examples of low and high-level corruption throughout the public sector in modern Mozambique. The latter was exemplified by the murders in 2000 and 2001, and subsequent judicial inertia, of the investigative journalist Carlos Cardoso and the temporary administrator of a crisis-ridden commercial bank, António Siba Siba Macuácua. Both investigated the connections of senior political figures to substantial bank frauds in the 1990s. More recently, the admission that corruption now has a deep hold was unmistakable during the Presidential campaign of 2004 in which the victor and current President, Armando Guebuza, criticized an entrenched culture of neglect and license (*"espírito de deixar andar"*) within the public sector.

The issue here is not whether corruption exists or has intensified, but rather what relation these perceptible trends have had with external aid. Of course the extent to which one can hold external agencies responsible for the emergence of public sector corruption ultimately is a matter of historical opinion. A useful perspective, however, comes from recognizing, first, that Mozambican public life has had to be 'reinvented' (Pitcher, 2003) under the rapid transformation from a socialist to a market-led orientation and, second, that this has taken place without corresponding changes to the composition or structure of the ruling elite. As in many other contexts, where domestic actors superficially have limited room for maneuver in face of a strong external agenda, it is often the case that this agenda is accepted but also, at a deeper level, reconfigured and adapted to suit domestic needs. In the Mozambican case after the end of civil war, the need to maintain political stability and reward influential military personnel clearly interacted with opportunities presented by market-reforms (privatization) and inflows of external funds. An observed result of this interaction has been both the politicization and immature development of those public institutions which might promote accountability and transparency in the use of public funds, a feature of the political landscape that Mosse (2004) considers has been strategic for reproduction of elites.

Of further interest is the extent to which external agencies have understood and/or attempted to redress these negative institutional dynamics associated with external aid. Certainly the recent donor emphasis on public financial management and justice reforms represents recognition of deficiencies in these areas that may be aggravated by external funds. Evaluations of past interventions have noted that insufficient attention has been given to institutional strengthening such as the development of internal checks and balances through internal audit and an independent judiciary. For example, an independent evaluation of the EC's support of post-war rehabilitation argues that the program was "... biased towards physical rather than institutional rehabilitation." (APT Consult, 1999: 50). A former head of the World Bank's office in Mozambique, who served during the epoch of rapid privatization and policy reform, has also commented that both the Bank and the government neglected certain political and institutional challenges in the 'rush' to achieve concrete results (Pomerantz, 2005). Despite these admissions, the staggering number of donor-supported endeavors to which the government either has committed or is required to respond continues to generate uneven and often unmanageable institutional pressures in an environment of well-known coordination difficulties and human capacity constraints (Sulemane and Kayizzi-Mugerwa, 2001; Hodges and Tibana, 2005).

6. Mozambique in the current debate

6.1. Reflecting on the past

The above analysis of the intended and unintended consequences of aid in Mozambique provides grounds to reflect on a number of current debates concerning the impact and effectiveness of external assistance. Clearly, the extent to which one can extrapolate from the specific case of Mozambique to general trends in external assistance is limited – an advantage of cross-country analysis is in providing some kind of credible counterfactual (Tarp, 2006). At the same time, the cross-country evidence has been inconclusive in identifying when and why external assistance has a positive effect on both macro- and micro-developmental outcomes. While the case of Mozambique may represent an outlier in aid-growth regressions, its importance lies in contributing to a better understanding of the processes that generate the considerable observed variance in the relationship between aid and growth both over time and across countries.

Focusing on the general impact of aid on growth, we should address the possible critique that Mozambican growth has been independent of external aid. Certainly, 'natural' post-war recuperation has been important. This is so via the return of internally displaced peoples to rural areas and improved incentives for private investment, but even here external aid has played a pivotal role. The majority of commentators, such as Vines (1998), argue that financial incentives for peace, including aid pledges and direct payments to the warring parties, were vital to secure the final peace accord. Democratic elections in 1994, 1999 and 2004 have also been heavily financed by external agencies. In addition, we have shown that external resource transfers have been the primary source of foreign exchange, providing a direct contribution to economic stability. The nature of this stabilizing aid effect has been to nudge the economy back toward its production possibilities frontier, easing restrictions on factor productivity related to political and economic instability. While this may promote short-term growth, it does not necessarily augment the long-term equilibrium level of productivity. For Mozambique this possibility is implied by the observed declining growth rate of TFP in later as compared to earlier past-war phases. The growth response to external aid therefore is unlikely to be constant but rather will be partly a function of the recipient country's distance from its theoretical production possibilities frontier and the marginal effect of aid in support of economic and political stability.

Table 6. *Classification of each year according to growth rate and developmental aid ratio, 1980–2004*

		Developmental aid ratio (d)		Total
		Below $\bar{d}$	Above $\bar{d}$	
Growth rate (g)	Below $\bar{g}$	10	2	12
	Above $\bar{g}$	2	11	13
	Total	12	13	25

[Chi squared statistic = 11.5; $p = 0.00068$]
Source: Authors' calculations.
Notes: Categories show counts of years in which variables are observed below or above their period averages. Growth rate refers to real GDP growth; the developmental aid ratio refers to the percentage of aid in total aid that can be classified as having a developmental (as opposed to humanitarian) objective in the spirit of Clemens *et al.* (2004).

In addition, we can identify more direct long-term growth effects via external financing of government investment. The most immediate and quantified example of this is found for Mozambique in the expansion of education, which has seen substantial progress since 1992. While the growth impact of investment in roads and health infrastructure has not been quantified in a similar fashion, it is reasonable to conclude that the direct contributions to economic growth of government and private sector investment in the post-war period, whose shares in actual growth represented 13.5% and 33.6% respectively, would have been substantially reduced in the absence of such external finance. Most obviously, growth in commerce, tourism and construction has been strongly supported by government investment in public infrastructure financed by external aid.

These findings substantiate the argument that the potential growth-response of the economy to aid is highly variable, in terms of both its level *and* timing, depending critically on the composition of the aid portfolio and its correspondence with actual developmental needs. Returning to the example of education, the observed growth effect attributable to graduates from the secondary school education system cannot be derived solely from aid-financed investments in the past four years – the period typically examined in aid-growth regressions. Rather, the impact of education is, necessarily, a cumulative process where expansion of the primary and secondary systems over many years provides the basis for lagged population-level economic effects. Thus, in our case, it is sustained investment in education during the war and afterwards that is now yielding aggregate economic benefits. In contrast, infrastructure investment is likely to have had a much more immediate impact, illustrated by the jump in the percentage of the population with access to markets between 1997 and 2003 (Table 4).

This evidence would seem to support the existence of virtuous and vicious aid-growth episodes characterized by an interaction between the quality and credibility of growth on the one hand and the composition (and quality) of the aid portfolio on the other. A vicious episode may emerge where prolonged or repeated humanitarian crises stimulate high inflows of humanitarian aid. The effect of any growth-oriented aid in these episodes is, at best, likely to be undermined by the effects of the crisis and, at worst, can generate highly perverse institutional incentives that act to prolong the crisis (e.g., Bolongaita, 2004). Where sustained growth is not a credible political objective, we may find low growth alongside considerable (humanitarian) aid inflows. More virtuous episodes are generated from improved conditions which stimulate domestic support for a more growth-conducive environment as well as a shift to more developmental types of aid. The Mozambican experience represents a shift from a vicious to a virtuous episode, marked by the end of civil war and the emergence of sustained growth supported by external aid. Table 6, classifies each year for the period 1980–2004 by whether growth was above/below the mean and whether the percentage of developmental aid in total aid was above/below the period mean. While there is an obvious positive association, our argument is not that this is a simple causal relationship but rather there is a strong mutual interaction between both the quality of aid and the quality of economic growth

Related to the question of aid composition is the existence of diminishing returns which, in cross-country aid-growth regressions, refers to falling marginal returns to increases in the volume of external aid represented by a quadratic aid term. In Mozambique, evidence for diminishing returns comes from the fiscal pressures generated by externally financed investments in public and social infrastructure. It is evident that the rate of return from such investments, reflected in rates of poverty reduction or economic growth, was particularly high in the early post-war period due to the very low base from which they were made. However, our analysis suggests these rates are unlikely to be sustained due to difficulties in meeting recurrent costs without prejudicing the quality of public goods offered. The existence of fiscal constraints indicates that as the economy tends towards its maximum (fiscal) capacity to absorb aid, the average rate of return on aid inflows is likely to fall. In these cases we would expect to find a growing focus on improving the productivity of aid through, *inter alia*, institutional strengthening. To some extent this is found in Mozambique. There is now a growing emphasis on later-impact governance reforms.

Turning to the aid-policy relationship, the discussion of Section 5 and the arguments of this section challenge the simplistic notion that aid can only be effective in a good policy environment. In opposition to a substantial portion of the literature which treats policy and public institutions as being independent of external aid, we argue that the nature and structure of external funding both responds to and shapes the institutional framework over time, especially where aid volumes are high. As in Mozambique, aid can be instrumental in promoting a 'better' policy/institutional environment which in turn supports future growth. However, even where the quality of the policy environment is high, the average rate of return to aid is likely to be lower when there are substantial constraints on absorptive capacity.

On the other hand, and despite Easterly's (2005) suggestion that 'the best plan is no plan' with regard to external aid, the Mozambique case suggests that external aid has the potential to induce perverse institutional developments which undermine long-term growth prospects. The effective capacity of the current aid system to address and correct for such effects, however, is likely to be limited by the structure of incentives facing both donors and the government. These create entrenched support for frag-mented and poorly coordinated aid flows. For donors there are considerable incentives to free-ride on information sharing, planning and coordination activities. This is not only because they are costly and time-consuming activities but also because they have an externality of providing public benefits for other donors. This engenders a classic first-mover problem, restricting the extent to which any single donor is willing to in-vest in these areas. At the same time, and in part due to the domestic political pressures facing donor agencies, there are strong incentives to fund activities which yield more concrete, immediate results that can be shown to a demanding principal (de Renzio *et al.*, 2005). Of course, while the extent of this collective action problem is difficult to determine in the aggregate, this issue has at least arisen in specific instances. Since 2004, for example, the Millennium Challenge Account (MCA) has been a heavy de-mander of government capacity with no contributions to local capacity to date and no identifiable plans for capacity building in the future. The MCA emphasizes concrete and identifiable results *for MCA funded programs* to the exclusion of any other criteria. Political pressure from the United States Congress is frequently referred to explicitly by MCA staff as a major driver behind their behavior.

On the government side one also encounters substantial incentives that support dis-persed and uncoordinated access to external aid. As has been noted extensively for Mozambique and elsewhere (e.g., Killick, 2005; MPF and MISAU, 2004), external funds often provide private benefits for civil servants in the form of salary increments and opportunities for training, travel and consultancies. Moreover, confronted by the financial weight, capacity and political influence of donor agencies, there remains a perception that attempts to limit (or direct) external aid inflows will yield few benefits and only high political and technical costs. These incentives combine with a legacy of long-term dependence on external aid and reliance on foreign experts (Pitcher, 2003). As a result, political space to discuss the potential negative consequences of external aid and how it might be better managed is limited, shown by the continued absence of an external aid policy despite explicit appeals from donors for the government to move in this direction.

A wider dimension to this discussion thus relates to the impact of external aid on political institutions and the state-citizen relationship. As has been discussed by Moss *et al.* (2006) among others, external aid can weaken government accountability to the public either via a reduced need to develop an effective and efficient tax ad-ministration system or due to a greater orientation towards (better organized) external donors. The analysis presented in Section 2.3 supports the hypothesis that political attention to internal revenue generation probably has been affected by the availability of external finance. Hodges and Tibana (2005) go further, arguing that the quality and public relevance of core political processes, such as the government budget, have been weakened by the government's reliance on external funding. Certainly one observes a split in political accountability to the public, via democratic institutions on the one hand, and the donors via extra-democratic processes on the other. Despite the move to common funding instruments such as budget support, these are not associated with a reduced level of donor influence. Rather, more coordinated approaches to government evaluation, associated with common funding instruments, increases the financial risk to the government of any change in donor sentiment. They also provide an enhanced (more effective) platform for donors to influence the broad policy priorities and reform choices of the government. Thus, given historical factors and the continued capacity deficiencies in Mozambique, the political challenge remains how to strengthen incentives in support of genuine domestic policy leadership and a commitment to the learning-by-doing of developmental policy.

Finally, cross-country analyses often highlight the effect of (exogenous) structural economic factors and the effectiveness of external aid. Numerous such factors have been identified ranging from climatic conditions (e.g., Sachs, 2003), natural resources, the amount of land in the tropics (Dalgaard *et al.*, 2004) and past colonial experiences (Acemoglu *et al.*, 2000). From a country case-study perspective it is not possible to evaluate the relative influence of these fixed factors due to the absence of a counter-factual. However, the argument here is that factors which shape the evolution of political and economic institutions have a critical role in explaining past and present aid performance. Historical experiences such as the interaction between local and colonial political practices as well as the impact of natural resources on political development are relevant. It is these highly endogenous political economy variables that remain at the heart of a 'deep' understanding of the variance and evolution in returns to aid in any given setting over time.

6.2. Looking ahead

In spite of achievements since 1992, in which aid has played a critical role, there is no room for complacency as regards Mozambique's future. The country remains one of the poorest in the world, and the economy is characterized by, at best, an incipient private business sector. The population is mainly rural, depending on peasant agriculture and highly vulnerable to climatic vagaries. Aside from the contribution of a few industrial mega-projects, there is limited penetration into world markets and imports are heavily financed by external aid. Despite substantial progress in the expansion of public infrastructure and social services, coverage of these public goods remains limited.

There is a need to be alert to the possibility that high rates of return to aid in the past do not provide a guarantee that aid will be productive in the future. First, there is increasing evidence that absorptive constraints are starting to bind, especially in the social sectors where internal resources to cover recurrent expenditure may not expand in line with investment plans. Consequently, the management of expectations concerning what external aid can realistically achieve is critical. The strategic prioritization and allocation of aid both across and within sectors will become a key challenge. For example, in the education sector it may well be the case that increased attention to technical and higher-levels of education will now yield higher returns.

Second, continued returns to aid depend on addressing the institutional effects of heavy aid inflows. Shifting domestic incentives towards critical assessment of aid and its impact with a view to informing genuine domestic policy formation stands out as a major issue. While government will obviously have to deal with the donor community, it is fundamental that accountability and transparency vis-à-vis the Mozambican public is deepened. Both government and the donor community should take a pro-active stance in this regard. This implies a need for new thinking about donor-recipient institutional relationships. It should be recognized that providing foreign aid involves implicit contracts and donors should be alert to the possibility of using this as a lever for increased government awareness and action. At the same time, government should insist that domestic institutions and frameworks of internal control are used and further developed as the basis for aid evaluation and impact analysis. The same goes for the internal planning and policy analysis where the donors must allow the government to increasingly assume the real substantive coordinating and 'leading' role rather than the somewhat empty formalism sometimes seen. While much can be said in favor of budget support, this has also led to a much deeper level of donor intrusiveness which is unlikely to lead to effective government leadership and institutional development over time. If budget support (and other forms of aid) is to be effective in the future, well functioning and capable domestic systems must be nurtured and seen as a key priority on both the government and donor side of the aid relationship. There is a plethora of ways in which foreign aid can further this objective, including the judicious use of experienced technical assistance on the side of government. It will in many cases demand that donors refrain from intervening in more detailed planning and implementation. This is not without risks but is also fundamental to ensure sustained real development. It would be detrimental if the government is left with the impression that the real hard choices and risks inherent in the development process are borne by the donors rather than themselves.

Third, as already alluded, part of the development of an effective development-oriented government will involve the deepening of its relationship with the Mozambican public. At present we have seen that accountability is often stronger vis-à-vis the donor community leaving parliamentary scrutiny as an 'add-on' with limited real content. Broad-based democracy requires concerted action that goes beyond the holding of regular elections. The nurturing of effective checks and balances on government activity will represent an important element in enhancing the credibility of democratic processes. In this government and donors should be pro-active.

Mozambique is a low income country but it does possess significant growth potential based on its own resources and geographic features – including several thousand kilometers of coastline, plenty of agricultural land and some mineral deposits. In addition, while its regional location close to South Africa represents a challenge, there are substantial opportunities such as access to investment capital and transport networks that might work in Mozambique's favor. In this context, it is meaningful to insist on formulating a forward-looking economic growth strategy, supported by foreign aid, as the basis for overcoming poverty and underdevelopment. This includes not only improvements in the general business environment, as aptly set out in recent government planning documents, but also strategic interventions geared towards infrastructure upgrading and the penetration of selected export markets. While short-run economic impacts from export trade are unlikely to be significant, the longer-term potential from successful integration into world markets is substantial.

We have no presumption of being able to predict in which markets Mozambique has dynamic comparative advantage. However, we reiterate that Mozambique is no basket case. Important elements to a growth strategy include recognition of the potential gains from significantly improving both port and transport infrastructure and resource management, including a boost to agricultural research and productivity. A vital part of this would be to establish an integrated policy package that addresses the nexus between public revenue, trade, and industrial policy. What this implies for the future of aid is not that social sectors can be ignored; but it does highlight: (i) the potential importance of constructive engagement and partnerships with the government in these investment-demanding areas which are bound to be associated with an element of economic risk; and (ii) the strategic importance of strengthening domestic capacity for economic policy analysis and formulation.

Finally, one should consider the implications of substantial increases in foreign aid which are currently on the international agenda. These are particularly relevant for Mozambique which is correctly perceived as a 'good performer' where returns to aid have been high in the past. Scaling-up is, however, associated with both risks and opportunities, which must be evaluated with equal care. Concerns about 'Dutch Disease' would of course intensify with more aid. Does this mean that Mozambique should refrain from engaging in negotiation about scaling-up? We believe the answer is no; but the above reflections on the institutional effects of foreign aid become even more important. Consequently, a purely incremental approach to the allocation of additional foreign aid is not prudent. Mozambique should not shrink from programs that are intensive in imports. Scaling-up might consider initiatives such as: (i) an all-out attack on malaria with a view to its eradication; (ii) a significantly improved, high-quality North-South road; and (iii) specific regional development initiatives facilitating economic transformation and development, in line with Dupraz *et al.* (2006) and GRM (2006).

7. Conclusion

Mozambique is a success story in terms of growth and poverty reduction since 1992. We have demonstrated that aid has played a fundamental role in making this possible. Without sustained aid at a high level Mozambique would not have been able to: (i) establish peace so smoothly; (ii) manage the challenge of post-war stabilization; or (iii) carry out widespread reconstruction. As a result, Mozambique now is in a much stronger position than at Independence. Based on the growth accounting carried out in this paper, we conclude that aid-financed government investment in public goods (particularly public infrastructures, education and health) has been a fundamental channel through which aid has contributed to development outcomes. Intended outcomes of aid have been largely achieved. Agriculture appears to be an important exception where the potential contribution of aid to agricultural transformation and development is yet to materialize.

Common criticisms that aid generates 'Dutch Disease' and leads to structural distortions do not appear relevant in the Mozambique experience up until now. Even so, aid has not been without problems. The historical trend of channeling external funding directly towards sectors, bypassing central review and management, has contributed to poorly coordinated policy interventions and fiscal imbalances. The staggering number of donor-supported programs continues to generate uneven and often unmanageable institutional pressures.

A general lesson from this study is that sustained aid can be a critical precondition for developmental success. Foreign aid must adapt to the changing nature of the developmental challenge ranging from humanitarian relief, the establishment of peace, macroeconomic stabilization and further-on to reconstruction and genuine development. The response to aid will differ in these circumstances but it is critical to maintain a consistent focus on the benefits accruing from virtuous as opposed to vicious aid-growth episodes. Two important caveats apply. First, aid cannot turn history but can provide much needed resources for investment and capacity building. Second, aid is bound to have institutional effects which, if not addressed carefully, can eventually threaten to undermine the overall aid effort. From this perspective, aid and institutional development should be addressed together, at least when aid flows are of a significant size. Moreover, careful attention to diminishing returns and absorptive capacity is essential.

Looking ahead, we have noted that the contribution of aid to TFP growth may be declining. This suggests that past success is no guarantee of future progress. In this context, a coherent nexus of efficient revenue, trade and industrial policies should be put in place within the framework of a dynamic and forward-looking growth strategy. Aid can help in this regard through technical assistance in strengthening domestic policy analysis and formulation. Moreover, the developmental perspective needs to shift from incremental to more strategic productivity-enhancing measures. This includes improvements in the general business environment and actions geared towards infrastructure upgrading and the penetration of selected export markets. This should be done without overstretching the necessary balance between the capacity and roles of the government and private sector.

A final dimension which merits substantive attention is the desirability of shifting overall responsibility and coordination towards domestic institutions. The aid relationship should be perceived as a contract with mutual obligations. Donors should provide resources and focus on overall implementation and performance, as opposed to more detailed (and intrusive) aid management. In addition, when requested they should provide high quality technical support that simultaneously relieves current capacity constraints and enhances local capacity over time. To government falls the task of setting overall priorities, managing implementation and carrying out evaluation. Integral to this is ensuring the effective use of technical support. The PRSP process makes strides in this direction but represents only a first step. Ultimately, government needs to be primarily accountable to the Mozambican public. These institutional challenges will determine the future success or failure of aid and development in Mozambique.

Acknowledgements

The authors are grateful for support from UNICEF for this project. General support for capacity building within the National Directorate of Studies and Policy Analysis of the Ministry of Planning and Development from the development cooperation programs of Denmark, Sweden, and Switzerland is also gratefully acknowledged.

References

Acemoglu, D., Johnson, S., Robinson, J.A. (2000), The colonial origins of comparative development: an empirical investigation. *NBER Working Paper*, No. 7771, National Bureau of Economic Research, Cambridge, MA.

Adam, C. (2005), Exogenous inflows and real exchange rates: theoretical quirk or empirical reality? In: *International Monetary Fund Seminar on Foreign Aid and Macroeconomic Management*, Maputo, March 14–15.

Adam, C., O'Connell, S. (1999), Aid, taxation and development in sub-Saharan Africa. *Economics and Politics* 11 (3), 225–253.

Ahuja, V., Filmer, D. (1995), Educational attainments in developing countries: new estimates and projections disaggregated by gender. *Policy Research Working Paper Series* 1489, The World Bank.

APT Consult (1999), *Evaluation of the Rehabilitation Programme in Mozambique*. London, UK.

Arndt, C., Muzima, J. (2004), Estimating efficiency trends in education: a minimum cross entropy approach with application to Mozambique. *National Directorate of Studies and Policy Analysis Discussion Papers*, No. 2E, Ministry of Planning and Development, Republic of Mozambique.

Arndt, C., Cruz, A., Jensen, H.T., Robinson, S., Tarp, F. (1998), Social accounting matrices for Mozambique: 1994–95. *Trade and Macroeconomics Division Discussion Paper*, No. 28, IFPRI, Washington, DC.

Arndt, C., Jensen, H.T., Tarp, F. (2000a), Stabilization and structural adjustment in Mozambique: an appraisal. *Journal of International Development* 12 (3), 299–323.

Arndt, C., Jensen, H.T., Tarp, F. (2000b), Structural characteristics of the economy of Mozambique: a SAM based analysis. *Review of Development Economics* 4 (3), 292–306.

Barro, R.J. (1998), Notes on growth accounting. *NBER Working Paper*, No. 6654.

Barro, R.J., Lee, W.J. (1993), International comparisons of educational attainment. *Journal of Monetary Economics* 32 (3), 363–394.

Benito-Spinetto, M., Moll, P. (2005), *Background Paper: Macroeconomic Developments, Economic Growth and Consequences for Poverty*. World Bank, Maputo, Mozambique.

Berg, E. (2002), Increasing the effectiveness of aid: a critique of some current views. Paper Prepared for Expert Group Meeting, Department of Economic and Social Affairs, United Nations.

Bolongaita, E. (2004), Controlling corruption in post-conflict countries. *Kroc Institute Occasional Paper*, No. 26 (2). Joan B. Kroc Institute for International Peace Studies, University of Notre Dame.

Buendía Gómez , M. (1999), *Educação Moçambicana. História de um processo: 1962–1984*. Livraria Universitária – UEM, Maputo.

Byiers, B. (2005), Tax reforms & revenue performance in Mozambique since independence. *DNEAP Working Paper*, No. 12E, Direcção Nacional de Estudos e Análise de Políticas, Ministério de Planificação e Desenvolvimento, República de Moçambique.

Cabral , L., Cumbi , A., Vinyals , L., Dista , S. (2005), *Estudo sobre os "off-budgets" no sector de Saúde. Relatório Final*. Ministério das Finanças, Ministério de Saúde e Ministério da Planificação e Desenvolvimento, República de Moçambique.

Caldwell, J., Caldwell, P. (1985), Education and literacy as factors in health. In: Halstead, S.B., Walsh, J., Warren, K.S. (Eds.), *Good Health at Low Cost*. Rockefeller Foundation, New York, pp. 181–185.

Cassen, R., Associates (1994), *Does Aid Work?* Clarendon Press, Oxford.

Clemens, M., Radelet, S., Bhavnani, R. (2004), Counting chickens when they hatch: The short-term effect of aid on growth. *Working Paper*, No. 44, Center for Global Development, Washington, DC.

Coughlin, P. (2006), Agricultural intensification in Mozambique: infrastructure, policy and institutional framework. EconPolicy Research Group Lda, Maputo. Presented at Hotel VIP, Maputo, 12 September 2006.

Dalgaard, C.-J., Hansen, H., Tarp, F. (2004), On the empirics of foreign aid and growth. *Economic Journal* 114, F191–F216.

de Renzio, P., Booth, D., Rogerson, A., Curran, Z. (2005), Incentives for harmonization and alignment in aid agencies. *ODI Working Paper*, No. 248, London.

Devarajan, S., Swaroop, V. (1998), *The Implications of Foreign Aid Fungibility for Development Assistance*. Development Research Group, World Bank, Washington, DC.

Dupraz, J., Handley, G., Wills, O. (2006), *Childhood Poverty in Mozambique: a Situation and Trends Analysis*. UNICEF, Maputo, Moçambique.

Easterly, W. (2005), *How to Assess the Need for Aid: The Answer: Don't Ask*. New York University, Department of Economics.

Easterly, W. (2006), *The White Man's Burden: Why the West's Efforts to Aid the Rest Have Done so Much Ill and so Little Good*. Penguin Press, New York.

Eicher, C. (2004), Mozambique: building African models of agricultural extension. In: Riveira, W., Alex, G. (Eds.), *National Strategy and Reform Process: Case Studies of International Initiatives, vol. 5 of Extension Reform for Rural Development (Discussion Paper, No. 12)*. Agriculture and Rural Development Department, World Bank, Washington, DC.

Ernst & Young Mozambique (2006), *Review of the PAPs' Performance in 2005 and PAPs' PAF matrix Targets for 2006*, mimeo.

Fox, L., Bardasi, E., Van den Broeck, K. (2005), *Poverty in Mozambique: Unraveling Changes and Determinants*. Africa Region Working Paper Series, vol. 87. World Bank, Washington, DC.

Gemo, H., Eicher, C., Teclemanrian, S. (2005), *Mozambique's Experience in Building a National Extension System*. Michigan State University Press, East Lansing.

Governo da República de Moçambique (GRM) e Parceiros para Apoio Programático (PAPs) (2004), *Memorando de Entendimento*. Maputo, Moçambique.

Governo da República de Moçambique (GRM) (2006), *Segundo Plano de Acção para a Redução da Pobreza Absoluta (PARPA II)*. Second draft. Maputo, Moçambique.

Hall, M., Young, T. (1997), *Confronting Leviathan; Mozambique since Independence*. Hurst & Company, London.

Hanlon, J. (2001), Matando a galinha dos ovos de ouro. *Metical*, Nos. 1073–1084, Maputo, Moçambique.

Hanlon, J. (2002), Are donors to Mozambique promoting corruption? Paper submitted to the Conference 'Towards a New Political Economy of Development', Sheffield 3–4 July.

Hansen, H., Tarp, F. (2000), Aid effectiveness disputed. *Journal of International Development* 12 (3), 375–398.

Hausman, J. (2001), Mismeasured variables in econometric analysis: problems from the right and problems from the left. *The Journal of Economic Perspectives* 15, 57–67.

Heltberg, R., Simler, K., Tarp, F. (2001), Public spending and poverty in Mozambique, *WIDER Discussion Paper*, No. 2001/63.

Herman, L. (2003), *Mozambique PER: Background Paper on Roads*. World Bank, Maputo, Mozambique.

Hodges, T., Tibana, R. (2005), *The Political Economy of the Budget Process in Mozambique*. Oxford Policy Management, Principia, Lisbon.

Ibraimo, M. (2005), Evolução das Disparidades no Bem-Estar dos Agregados Familiares e o Acesso a Bens e Serviços, 1997 e 2003. *DNEAP Working Paper*, No. 14P. Direcção Nacional de Estudos e Análise de Políticas, Ministério de Planificação e Desenvolvimento, República de Moçambique.

Instituto Nacional de Estatística (INE) (2005), *30 Anos de Independência Nacional: Um Retrato Estatístico*. Maputo, Moçambique.

International Monetary Fund (IMF) (2001), Republic of Mozambique: selected issues and statistical appendix. *IMF Country Report*, No. 01/25.

International Monetary Fund (IMF) (2005), *The Macroeconomics of Managing Increased Aid Inflows: Experiences of Low-Income Countries and Policy Implications*. Policy Development and Review Department, Washington, DC.

James, R., Arndt, C., Simler, K. (2005), Has economic growth in Mozambique been pro-poor? *DNEAP Working Paper*, No. 8E, Direcção Nacional de Estudos e Análise de Políticas, Ministério de Planificação e Desenvolvimento, República de Moçambique.

Jett, D. (2002), Lessons unlearned – or why Mozambique's successful peacekeeping operation might not be replicated elsewhere. *Journal of Humanitarian Assistance*, http://www.jha.ac/Ref/aar008.htm (document posted: 20 January 2002).

Jones, S. (2006), Growth accounting for Mozambique (1980–2004). *DNEAP Working Paper*, No. 22E, Direcção Nacional de Estudos e Análise de Políticas, Ministério de Planificação e Desenvolvimento, República de Moçambique.

Kanbur, R. (2003), The economics of international aid. *Working Paper*, No. 39. Department of Applied Economics and Management, Cornell University, New York.

Killick T. (2005), Perfect partners? The performance of programme aid partners in Mozambique, 2004. Report commissioned by the Programme Aid Partners to Mozambique.

MADER (2004), *Strategy Document: PROAGRI II*. MADER, Maputo.

Mate, A., das Neves Tembe, J., Arnaldo, C., Zonjo, J., Adalima, J., Gune, E. (2005), Estudo Qualitativo Sobre A Pobreza: Casos das províncias de Inhambane e Sofala. *DNEAP Working Paper*, No. 23P, Direcção Nacional de Estudos e Análise de Políticas, Ministério de Planificação e Desenvolvimento, República de Moçambique.

Mathiassen, A., Øvensen, G. (2006), Mission report from a short-term mission on a model for predicting poverty. *Unpublished Preliminary Report*, INE and Statistics, Norway.

Maximiano, N., Arndt, C., Simler, K.R. (2005), Qual foi a dinâmica dos determinantes da pobreza em Moçambique? *Directorate of Studies and Policy Analysis Discussion Papers*, No. 11P, Ministério de Planificação e Desenvolvimento, Moçambique.

Ministério do Plano e Finanças (MPF) e Ministério da Educação (MINED) (2003), *A despesa pública com a educação em Moçambique*. Maputo, Moçambique.

Ministério do Plano e Finanças (MPF), Universidade Eduardo Mondlane e Instituto Internacional de Pesquisa em Políticas Alimentares (1998), *Pobreza e Bem-Estar em Moçambique: Primeira Avaliação Nacional (1996–97)*. Maputo, Moçambique.

Ministério do Plano e Finanças (MPF), Universidade Eduardo Mondlane, Instituto Internacional de Pesquisa em Políticas Alimentares e Universidade de Purdue (2004), *Pobreza e Bem-Estar em Moçambique: Segunda Avaliação Nacional*, Maputo, Moçambique.

MISAU (2005), *Plano Operacional 2005*. Ministério de Saúde, Maputo, Moçambique.

Mosley, P. (1987), *Overseas Aid: Its Defence and Reform*. Wheatsheaf Books, Brighton.

Mosley, P., Toye, J., Harrigan, J. (1991), *Aid and Power: The World Bank and Policy-Based Lending Analysis and Policy Proposals*. Routledge, London.

Moss, T., Pettersson, G., van de Walle, N. (2006), An aid-institutions paradox? A review essay on aid dependency and state building in sub-Saharan Africa. *Working Paper*, No. 74, Center for Global Development, Washington, DC.

Mosse, M. (2004), *Corrupção em Moçambique: Alguns elementos para debate*, mimeo.

Nehru, V., Swanson, E., Dubey, A. (1995), A new database on human capital stock in developing and industrial countries: sources, methodology and results. *Journal of Development Economics* 46 (2), 379–401.

Nhate, V., Simler, K. (2002), *Mapeamento da Pobreza em Moçambique: Desagregação das Estimativas da Pobreza e Desigualdade aos Níveis de Distrito e Posto Administrativo*. Ministério do Plano e Finanças, Maputo, Moçambique.

O'Meara, D. (1991), The collapse of Mozambican socialism. *Transformation* 14, 82–103.

PAPs Secretariat (2006), *Aide-Mémoire of the Joint Review of 2005*. Governo da República de Moçambique (GRM) e Parceiros para Apoio Programático (PAPs), Maputo, Mozambique.

Pavignani, E., Hauck, V. (2002), Pooling of technical assistance in the context of aid management reform: the Mozambique case study. *ECDPM Discussion Paper*, No. 39, ECDPM, Maastricht.

Pinto, J. (1985), The White House's confusing signals on Mozambique. *Backgrounder*, No. 455, The Heritage Foundation.

Pitcher, M.A. (2003), *Transforming Mozambique: The Politics of Privatization, 1975–2000*. Cambridge University Press, Cambridge.

Pomerantz, P. (2005), A little luck and a lot of trust aid relationships and reform in Southern Africa. In: Gill, S., Pugatch, T. (Eds.), *At the Frontlines of Development: Reflections from the World Bank*. World Bank, Washington, DC.

Rajan, R., Subramanian, A. (2005), What undermines aid's impact on growth? *NBER Working Paper*, No. 11657, National Bureau of Economic Research, Cambridge, MA.

Ravallion, M. (1992), Poverty comparisons. *Living Standard Measurement Study Working Paper*, No. 88, World Bank, Washington, DC.

Rupiya, M. (1998), Historical context: war and peace in Mozambique. In: Armon, J., Hendrickson, D., Vines, A. (Eds.), *The Mozambican Peace Process in Perspective*. In: Accord: An International Review of Peace Initiatives, Issue 3. Conciliation Resources, London.

Sachs, J. (2003), Institutions don't rule: direct effects of geography on per capita income. *NBER Working Paper*, No. 9490, National Bureau of Economic Research. Cambridge, MA.

Sachs, J. (2005), *The End of Poverty: Economic Possibilities for Our Time*. Penguin Press, New York.

Saul, J.S. (1991), Mozambique: the failure of socialism? *Transformation* 14, 104–110.

Scanteam (2003), World Bank and IMF Follow-Up to PRSP: The case of Mozambique. Study commissioned by the Embassies of the Nordic Countries in Mozambique.

Sulemane, J., Kayizzi-Mugerwa, S. (2001), The Mozambican civil service incentives, reforms and performance. *WIDER Discussion Paper*, No. 2001/85.

Tarp, F. (Ed.) (2000), *Foreign Aid and Development: Lessons Learnt and Guidelines for the Future*. Routledge, London and New York.

Tarp, F. (2006), Aid and development. *Swedish Economic Policy Review* 13 (2), 9–61.

Tarp, F., Lau, M.I., (1996), Mozambique: Macroeconomic performance and critical development issues. *Development Economics Research Group Working Paper*, No. 2, University of Copenhagen.

Tarp, F., Arndt, C., Jensen, H.T., Robinson, S., Heltberg, R. (2002), Facing the development challenge in Mozambique. *IFPRI Research Report*, No. 126, Washington, DC.

UNESCO (2000), *Education for All: The Year 2000 Assessment Report of Mozambique*, www2.unesco.org/wef/countryreports/mozambique/contents.html.

UNESCO (2005), *Global Education Digest 2005: Comparing Education Statistics Across the World*. UNESCO Institute for Statistics, Montreal.

United Nations Development Program (UNDP) (2000), *National Human Development Report*. Maputo, Mozambique.

United Nations Development Program (UNDP) (2001), *National Human Development Report*. Maputo, Mozambique.

UNDP (2002), Re-opening Mozambique: lessons learned from the Feeder Road Programme. *United Nations Development Programme*, Maputo, Mozambique.

UNDP (2005), International cooperation at a crossroads: aid, trade and security in an unequal world. *Human Development Report* 2005, United Nations Development Programme.

United States Agency for International Development (USAID) (2004), General budget support: an alternative assistance approach. Mozambique Country Case Study. *PPC Evaluation Working Paper*, No. 18, USAID Bureau for Policy and Program Coordination.

Van Dunem, J.E. (2006), Confronting the issue of the elasticity of customs evasion in Mozambique. *An Empirical Study*. Ninth Annual Conference on Global Economic Analysis, Addis Ababa, Ethiopia, June 2006.

Vines, A. (1998), The business of peace: 'Tiny' Rowland, financial incentives and the Mozambican settlement. In: Armon, J., Hendrickson, D., Vines, A. (Eds.), *The Mozambican Peace Process in Perspective*. In: Accord: An International Review of Peace Initiatives, Issue 3. Conciliation Resources, London.

Walker, T., Tschirley, D., Low, J., Pequenino Tanque, J., Boughton, D., Payongayong, E., Weber, M. (2004), *Determinants of Rural Income in Mozambique in 2001–2002*, mimeo.

World Bank (1995), Mozambique: impediments to industrial sector recovery. *Southern Africa Department Report*, No. 13752-MOZ.

World Bank (1998a), *Rebuilding the Mozambique Economy: Assessment of a Development Partnership*. Washington, DC.

World Bank (1998b), *Assessing Aid: What Works, What Doesn't and Why*. Oxford University Press.

World Bank (2001a), Mozambique public expenditure management review. *Report*, No. 22985-MOZ, Maputo, Mozambique.

World Bank (2001b), Mozambique country economic memorandum: growth prospects and reform agenda. *Report*, No. 20601-MZ, Maputo, Mozambique.

World Bank (2002), Improving health for the poor in Mozambique: the fight continues. *Africa Region Human Development Working Paper Series*.

World Bank (2003a), Cost and financing of education opportunities and obstacles for expanding and improving education in Mozambique. *Africa Region Human Development Working Paper Series*, Washington, DC.

World Bank (2003b), Mozambique public expenditure review. Phase 2: Sectoral expenditures. *Report*, No. 25969-MZ, Maputo, Mozambique.

World Bank (2005), *Impacts of Extension Services in Rural Mozambique*. Environ-
    ment, Rural and Social Development Department, World Bank, Washington, DC.
Young, A. (1994), The Tyranny of numbers: confronting statistical realities of the East
    Asia growth experience. *NBER Working Paper*, No. 4680, mimeo.

CHAPTER 15

Aid and Economic Development in Africa

Arne Bigsten

Department of Economics, School of Business, Economics, and Law, Göteborg University,
Box 640, SE 405 30 Göteborg, Sweden
E-mail address: arne.bigsten@economics.gu.se

Abstract

The question discussed in this paper is whether foreign aid can help accelerate growth in African countries. The paper reviews growth determinants and growth constraints in Africa and discusses how aid can help relieve the constraints. Issues covered are the choice of aid modalities, donor coordination, conditionality, and international integration. A key question addressed is how aid should be organized not to overburden the recipient system and to provide incentives for policy makers to perform. The paper also touches upon the need for international trade reforms and public goods investments.

Keywords: Aid, development, Africa

JEL classifications: F35, O19

1. Introduction

The dramatic economic divergence in the world economy started with the industrial revolution in the 18th century. The dominance of the West and its off-shoots increased at least until the mid-20th century, but since then its dominance has declined (Maddison, 2001). During the last few decades large parts of the world including the two most populous countries, China and India, have taken off and are growing faster than the industrial countries. The only major region of the world that has continued to slip further behind is sub-Saharan Africa. Poverty in Africa increased in the 1980s and 1990s, while it declined in the rest of the World (Chen and Ravallion, 2004). The main reason for the dismal result of poverty reduction efforts is poor growth. In a famous paper (Easterly and Levine, 1997) referred to the African experience as the "African growth tragedy". However, from 1995 Africa has seen positive per capita income growth and 2003–2005 per capita incomes in Africa grew 1.7, 2.6, and 3.5 percent respectively in the wake of the commodity boom. This is the best growth period for three decades, although it is uneven across countries. Still, average per capita incomes in Sub-Saharan Africa were about the same in 2005 as they were in mid-1970s.The question we discuss in this paper is whether foreign aid can help sustain and even accelerate this positive growth in the countries seeing improvements and whether it can help the laggard countries to improve the growth performance.

The next section reviews some aspects of the growth literature to identify the factors that determine the growth outcomes for nations, and after that we look at the Africa-specific experience. Against this background we then discuss what aid can do to relieve the constraints that hold back growth in Africa.

2. What determines growth?

There are several schools of thought on long-term economic development that can provide insights into what is needed for Africa to take off. Classical growth theory focuses on investment, technological change, and the diffusion of technology. New institutional economics argues that countries must have appropriate institutions in place to be able to take advantage of new technologies. New economic geography focuses on location and introduces distance into trade models to explain how growth spreads.

Both neoclassical growth theory in the Solow tradition and endogenous growth theory regard technological change as the main force of long-term growth. While Solow type models predict income convergence across countries, divergence is possible in endogenous growth models. In endogenous growth theory knowledge accumulation can either be a deliberate process of knowledge production or be the result of learning by doing. Externalities or spillovers from knowledge are central to endogenous growth theory (Grossman and Helpman 1991, 1995). The literature on technology gaps suggests that growth depends on the distance to the technological frontier, and that the ability of e.g. African countries to apply the technology will depend on their absorptive capacity and technological congruence (Abramowitz, 1994).

That investment and technological progress are necessary for growth is clear, but the question then is why growth outcomes have been so dramatically different in different parts of the world. There is a vast literature estimating reduced form regressions, where per capita incomes or growth of countries are regressed directly on various proxies for institutional quality including the political institutions. The estimated coefficients for the institutional variables measuring the security of property rights and constraints on the executive are generally highly significant (Hall and Jones, 1999; Acemoglu *et al.*, 2001, 2002, 2003). It thus seems clear that the capacity to absorb and effectively implement new technology depends on domestic factors such as social capabilities, human capital, and institutions. These are then the "deeper" determinants of growth than investment.

So what hinders poor countries from effective implementation of best practice policies and institutions? Institutionalists believe that the character of institutions and incentives is highly path dependent (North, 1990). The argument here is that network-externalities and vested interests hold back change, as do informal constraints in customs and traditions, which are hard to change through policy reforms. Elites may be reluctant to support policy reforms that give secure property rights if it makes it possible for competing elites to emerge. The incumbent elite may choose to block certain investments for fear of losing political power if an independent economic elite evolves.

Crafts and Venables (2002) argue that the world is not an even playing-field, and that the chances of joining the growth club are unevenly distributed. East and South-East Asia is the most recent major region to make its income level converge towards that of the "rich club", while take-off has generally not happened in Africa. The World Bank (1993) explanation of the East-Asian miracle is that good institutions and policy paved the way for investment and productivity growth. Development-oriented states managed to create institutions that could lower transaction costs, and they also pursued increasingly outward-oriented policies. That the emergence of a growth-supporting institutional structure is important seems unquestionable, but we know that there have been many attempts at institutional reform that have not delivered the goods (Easterly, 2001; Taylor, 2002). Why have they worked in some instances but seldom in Africa? What can aid do for institutional and policy reform?

Crafts and Venables further argue that most growth studies so far have underestimated the role of geography. They emphasize that size and distance are important determinants of development, and that agglomeration benefits dominate the process. In their approach the issue of transaction costs across space is crucial. These costs depend on geography, but they may be altered by technological change as well as policy interventions. Crafts and Venables emphasize the need to allow for changes in the costs of transport and for the importance of economies of scale. The theory as set out by Krugman and Venables (1995) aims to explain both agglomeration and dispersion of production. The starting point is that investment in a country is determined by a combination of internal factors and factors characterizing the relationship to other countries. The domestic factors are factor endowments, skills, technology and social infrastructure. The international factors are access to world product markets and to suppliers of intermediate goods, factors or production, and knowledge. Distance is here an important constraint. One may note that even technology flows are highly distance sensitive (Venables, 2001; Keller, 2002).

Inward orientation has in many studies been identified as having a negative effect on growth.[1] Redding and Venables (2001) estimate a model, which allows for access costs, and it turns out that these can explain most of the variation across countries in manufacturing wages. The picture thus seems rather bleak for Africa, where access costs generally are high. Also Redding and Schott (2003) are pessimistic about the long term prospects of the "periphery". However, we may note that the Asia-pacific

---

[1] There is an abundance of work showing that openness to trade and economic growth is related (Edwards, 1998). This has been criticized on the grounds that it has been hard to decide on the direction of causality (Rodriguez and Rodrik, 2000), but recent studies have shown fairly convincingly that there is a causal effect from trade to growth (Frankel and Romer, 1999; Irwin and Terviö, 2002) and that trade liberalization supports growth. Bigsten *et al.* (2004) show that there is learning from exporting in African manufacturing. See also survey of Africa evidence by Collier and Gunning (1999).

managed to reach economic take-off and get into a virtuous circle where access costs fell as the global centre of activity moved closer and closer to the region and thus access costs were reduced. When wage gaps become large enough and transactions costs fall there will be relocation of production from the centre towards parts of the periphery. The main point in Krugman and Venables (1995) model is that convergence will not be uniform. Even if all poor countries were to get their institutions in order, they would still not all take off at the same time. Economic expansion will occur sequentially in different parts of the periphery. The question of interest here is when Africa's turn will come.

International capital flows can be important ingredients in a growth process. Real capital flows are in a way a substitute for trade flows, and there is a broad consensus that they generally help increase the welfare of the recipient country. However, there is not as yet general agreement about the balance of benefits versus costs of financial liberalization (Obstfeld, 1998). There is evidence that financial integration in general has beneficial effects on growth, but the results for LDCs are mixed (Eichengreen, 2001; Agenor, 2002). The communications revolution has meant that distance matters less, but the distance friction in financial transactions still remains surprisingly high. Financial flows have largely bypassed Africa, and the increasing concentration of aid to Africa can be seen as a response to this.

So what do we conclude from this brief discussion? Our starting point is that factor accumulation and technological change are necessary for growth. But what are their determinants? Our literature review suggests that flows and impact of investment and technology depend on existing social capabilities, institutions, and human capital. Societies with good organization in terms of economic, social and political institutions which protect private property prosper. At the same time we know that organization and institutions of society are hard to change, and particularly so for an outside agent such as an aid donor. We have also noted that the costs of economic interaction across distance affect the geographical distribution of economic activity. Thus, economic activity depends on internal capacity, but we must also take account of relationship with other countries. To take off African countries need access to world markets and to external suppliers of goods, factors, and knowledge.

3. African growth constraints

In the early cross-country regressions on growth there was often an African dummy that was significantly negative. In recent work, however, this has generally been eliminated by the inclusion of relevant explanatory variables. Africa seems to grow more or less in the same fashion as other regions, but it rates poorly on many of the variables that determine growth (Hoeffler, 2002). Factors that are found to be robust explanations of Africa's poor growth are "expensive investment goods, low levels of education, poor health, adverse geography, closed economies, too much public expenditure and too many military conflicts" (Artadi and Sala-i-Martin, 2003: 1; Tsangarides, 2005). This type of research thus identifies constraints that matter specifically in Africa and which then could be targeted by donors trying to help Africa grow.

There is also a recent literature focusing not directly on the long-run growth patterns, but on growth accelerations and the extent to which these can be sustained (Hausmann *et al.*, 2004). Using this approach on African countries Pattillo *et al.* (2005) find that growth tends to accelerate when policies and institutions improve. Growth episodes that are sustained for a decade or more are characterized by growth in trade and investment, low debt and democratic institutions. There is a strong link from institutional quality, policy stance and growth accelerations. Hausmann *et al.* found that economic liberalization and democratization were associated with sustained accelerations, while the effect of positive terms of trade shocks were not sustained. In conclusion Pattillo *et al.* note that key factors supporting growth accelerations are trade, investment, productivity, policy, and sound institutions. Pattillo *et al.* (2005: 31) find that growth in SSA would increase by 1.7 percentage points if the continent achieved the average world quality of institutions. They do not find any consistent association between geography or resource availability and growth episodes, though. They also find that the link between changes in political institutions and economic institutions is weak inn SSA.

The most ambitious study trying to explain variations in African economic growth has been undertaken by the African Economic Research Consortium (O'Connell, 2004b; Collier and O'Connell, 2004). The project has attempted to identify the growth opportunities and constraints and to explain the success or failure of countries in seizing the opportunities. The study characterizes opportunities for growth along two dimensions. The first dimension divides countries into three geographical categories, namely coastal countries, landlocked countries, and resource rich countries (irrespective of location). The second dimension is the degree of polarization in the society, from not polarized to moderately polarized and highly polarized countries. This study thus fits nicely into the structure identified above, where institutions and geography were identified as key factors.

After having defined the opportunities, the study goes on to investigate how domestic governments have shaped the growth environment in the various countries covered. Four different types of anti-growth syndromes are identified from the case studies. First, there is the regulatory syndrome which refers to excessive government interventions in markets. Second, there is the redistributive syndrome, where efficiency-reducing resource transfers play a dominant role in government policy. Third, there is the intertemporal syndrome, which redistributes resources from the future to the present via for example looting by the elite or unsustainable government spending booms generally followed by sharp adjustments. Fourth, there is the state breakdown syndrome, that is civil wars or severe political instability. Finally, there are also some countries that are characterized as syndrome-free. The empirical analysis shows that an absence of syndromes increases the growth rate by almost 2 percent per year.

When looking globally at the performance of landlocked countries, Collier and O'Connell (2004) find strong evidence that resource-scarce landlocked economies have dramatically worse opportunities for growth, and that there are two basic mechanisms behind this. First, being landlocked implies high constraints on market access, which has the effect that manufactures are precluded from significant entry into the global market. Second, without high-value resources, landlocked countries are wholly dependent upon agriculture. There is no example of any such a third world country experiencing rapid growth during the period of 1960–2000. The issue of geography is thus very important in the African context.

O'Connell notes that growth accelerations in Africa often have tended to evaporate. One reason is that growth in the early stages of the acceleration is not real. For example, most of the government component of GDP is measured at cost, and thus increases with the growth of government wages. Since government wages often exceed the opportunity cost of government workers, the resulting increase in measured real GDP is partly illusory. If the government expansion proves unsustainable, it is generally hard for the government to lay off workers, and instead other types of expenditures will be cut with negative supply side effects. Overspending booms are therefore often followed by economic decline.

The main conclusion of the AERC study is that African growth has faltered due to dysfunctional political-economic configurations or syndromes. Africa's poor growth performance is not the product of a uniform phenomenon but due to the interaction of different syndromes with different effects in different countries with different opportunities.

An alternative characterization of the African growth problem is due to Jeffrey Sachs (Sachs *et al.*, 2004), who argues that Africa is caught in a poverty trap and that therefore small changes are not enough. He argues that African countries will not be able to break out of the poverty trap unless large-scale foreign assistance is injected into the system. What is needed is an investment strategy alongside international changes in policies and governance structures.

Sachs does not accept the view that the poor African performance is due to poor governance. He argues that this is in itself an effect of poverty, and that poor countries are poorly governed because of lack of resources and skills. He argues that African countries are not more badly governed than other poor countries, but that there is a poverty trap. Savings are needed to cover replacement investment, investment to compensate for population growth, and finally investment to increase the capital stock. Since savings in Africa are low, the continent tends to get stuck in a low level of equilibrium. This is a classical argument from the early writings in development economics. What is needed, according to Sachs, is a big push of investment to get the economy to the point at which it can converge to the high level equilibrium. Sachs identifies three reasons for the poverty trap. First, savings are too low, since people are too poor to save enough. Second, they have many children. Third, capital has a threshold level below which it is not productive. Investments are lumpy. Savings are therefore not enough to increase the capital stock. At the macroeconomic level poverty-trap models suggests that African countries need to attain a threshold income level and that they then would take off.

Critics of Sachs have pointed out that in a conventional growth model countries experiencing a large negative shock should grow quickly once conditions change for the better, whereas in the poverty trap model they would stagnate. If financial resources were the binding constraint, African countries that have enjoyed persistent commodity booms should have leveraged those into an exit from the trap. They have systematically failed to do so, for example because of distributional struggles. The simple poverty trap story is thus debatable, but it is still reasonable to argue that a certain constellation of factors including certain investment levels are required to establish a process of self-sustaining growth.

Sachs agrees that the impact of geographical and bio-physical conditions need to be taken into account. Transport costs are very high in Africa, since most of the population lacks access to waterways. Poor transport infrastructure means that producers cannot compete in the world market, at least not if imported inputs are required in production.[2] Sachs also notes that the continent is dry and sparsely populated, and the land is hardly irrigated at all and there is little fertilizer use. The health situation in Africa is worse than anywhere else, and life expectancy is low. Malaria is a huge problem, and recently also AIDS has emerged as an enormous burden. Sachs' conclusion is that what is needed for Africa is a large injection of foreign aid to finance national investment programmes based on domestic Poverty Reduction Strategies. Sachs *et al.*, provide a programme to improve the preconditions for growth. The interventions focus on agriculture, health and education. A platform needs to be built in agriculture and human development.

What are the problems of this strategy? The starting point of the discussion was that Africa faces larger challenges than other regions. The demand on policy makers is larger than in other regions at the same time as there is a serious governance problem. In recent years African economies have changed many of their policies in a sensible direction, but the problem of revamping the administrative machinery is a task of a much larger order. Implementation is a key problem in Africa. There are several studies that suggest that the main problem in Africa is not investment levels but returns to investment.[3] The main question concerning large aid injections is therefore how the new or expanded programmes are to be managed. How can one reach a situation where governments have incentives and possibilities to deliver efficient administration? Tight foreign control by donors in the form of policy conditionality has generally not worked well.

Sachs *et al.* assume constant state of the art efficiency in service delivery, or that absorptive capacity is not a problem. In a critical comment on Sachs *et al.* O'Connell (2004a) argues that they have underplayed both the uncertainties in his prescription and the constraints on an effective scaling up of aid. The innovation of the Sachs paper is that it advocates a massive and externally funded scaling up of country public service delivery. But the central thrust of the recent literature on African development has been to dismiss capital fundamentalism as a viable interpretation of Africa's way forward! Pritchett and Woolcock (2004) point out that many of the MDG services are

---

[2] Hulten (1996) finds that about a quarter of the difference in growth between SSA and East Asia can be explained by differences in the effective use of infrastructure.

[3] Dollar and Easterly (1999) estimated that Zambian income levels would have been with normal rates of returns on investments undertaken since independence. The difference is enormous!

both transaction intensive and discretionary. Unlike many macroeconomic reforms, the delivery of many health and education services requires the collaboration of multiple individuals who make highly discretionary choices in an environment where many key actions are unobservable. Such services cannot be delivered by a few politically protected technocrats. They are subject to deep incentive problems. The empirical link from spending on health and education to outcomes is notoriously weak (World Bank, 2004c). The question about governance is not whether it is good relative to income levels, but whether it is good enough in absolute terms to avoid sharply diminishing returns or even outright deterioration when managing a massive scaling up of public services. O'Connell believes there is a large scope for scaling up donor activity in the broad area of science-intensive regional public goods, including basic research in health and agriculture. He also believes in bolder efforts at debt relief.

4. The evolution of aid strategies

The character of aid to Africa has been influenced by both geopolitics and our thinking about development. Geopolitically the post World War II period can be dived into the cold war period and the post cold war period, where the ambition to contain the power of the Eastern Bloc influenced donor practices until the fall of the Berlin Wall. With regard to development thinking the view was initially that the main constraint on development was capital accumulation, and the role of aid thus was to supplement domestic savings. It was also argued that there were market failures and externalities that government and planners needed to deal with, and infant industries that had to be protected. In the 1970s it was felt that trickle-down to the poor from general growth was not efficient, and the basic needs came into focus. The idea was that poverty reduction efforts should focus on agriculture and social sectors such as education and health. In the beginning of the 1980s LDCs were badly hit by the debt crisis and global macroeconomic imbalances. The policy focus shifted to domestic policy failures and the achievement of macroeconomic balance came into focus. The continued use of discrete investment projects to channel aid became problematic, and adjustment loans and debt relief became more important.

Partly as a result of the critique of the results of the market based policies there was in the 1990s a shift back towards a policy emphasizing poverty reduction as the ultimate objective of development and there was increasing support for specific interventions to achieve this goal. The current situation is one where some elements of all earlier phases are present. There is no return to a belief in extensive state intervention and inward oriented policies, but the important role of the government is recognized. There is furthermore a strong emphasis on its accountability. Macro policy is still important but there is a renewed emphasis on the need for specific interventions to help the poor. The role of institutions is considered to be crucial in determining the outcome of policies.

The current aims of development efforts agreed by the international community were set out in the Millennium Development Goals to be reached by 2015. The key

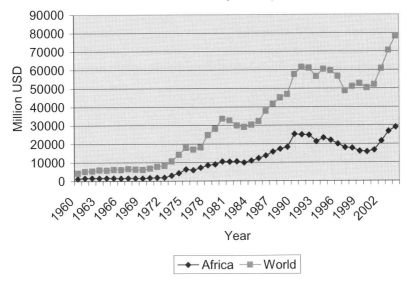

Source: OECD (2006): International development statistics, geographical distribution of financial flows.

Fig. 1.** **Total ODA net to all developing countries and to Africa 1960–2004 (million USD).

is poverty reduction alongside a series of social goals. The impact of a certain rate of growth on poverty will vary by the degree of initial inequality, so when choosing development strategy in a certain country one needs to take the starting position into account. Changing the distribution is more important in better off and highly unequal societies, while growth is relatively more important for poverty reduction in countries with low average incomes and low inequality.[4] In the case of Africa income levels are mostly so low that growth will be essential for almost all countries for them to reach the MDG of halving poverty (Bigsten and Shimeles, 2007).

The volume of aid to Africa (and the rest of the world) increased until the early 1990s (see Figure 1), but in the aftermath of the end of the Cold War and due to a certain aid fatigue there was decline in aid flows in the 1990s. Since the beginning of the millennium, however, there has been a renewed increase in aid flows and the

---

[4] Traditionally economists have been concerned about the risk that egalitarian policies will be detrimental to growth. For example, it was assumed that the rich were the savers, and that shifting incomes towards the poor would reduce the national savings rate. This is certainly a concern, but there are also factors that work in the opposite direction. The most widely cited example relate to the credit market. If there are credit market failures, particularly the poor will lack access to credit, which will mean that large segments of the population may fail to realize their economic potential. It has also been argued that inequality increases the risk for macroeconomic instability and makes it less likely that the government can undertake reforms that require cooperation and social trust. The econometric evidence on all these issues is somewhat mixed, but there is in any case no longer a consensus that equality hampers growth.

major donors have made huge commitments for the future. At the Gleneagles summit in 2005 the G8 leaders promised an increase in aid to Africa by \$25 billion per year by 2010. Whether this promise will be realized may be questioned, but we still can expect a major increase in aid to Africa. The central question today is how this can be effectively used.

5. *The growth constraints and aid*

So far we have reviewed the literature on growth in Africa and described the change in emphasis in aid strategies. We have noted that growth in Africa has generally been poor. There has been an academic controversy about the nature of the relationship between aid and growth, but there seems to emerge a picture that aid has had a positive but limited impact on African growth (Tarp, 2006; Collier, 2006). Still, as a starting point for our discussion of future aid strategies we need to acknowledge that aid will not be the key determinant of African growth, but it may facilitate the growth process by helping to relieve some constraints. We have also noted that there are considerable differences across countries in the types of constraints they face. This also needs to be considered when aid strategies for individual countries are chosen.

Let us first summarize the growth constraints we have identified and then discuss how aid strategies should be defined to address these:

(1) On a basic level growth is determined by factor accumulation and technological progress. Capital accumulation is important for growth, and this can be either domestically or externally financed. Savings rates in Africa are modest compared to those in the fast-growing countries in Asia. International private investment flows have come to dominate external resource flows to regions outside Africa, but this has not happened in Africa. Aid can have a certain role as a source of investment capital, but the bulk of investment resources will have to come from internal or external private sources. Therefore the more important role of aid is to help create an environment where private investors want to invest.

Technological improvements in Africa have so far largely come with the importation of investment goods, so the ability to finance imports will continue to be important for technological development. Domestic FoU and improvements in the ability to absorb new technologies are also important dimensions, where aid can help.

Absorptive capacity and growth generally depends fundamentally on human capital accumulation, and this is one of the key areas that are focused for example in the UN Big Push initiative. That human capital is important is beyond question, but the question is how aid is to be related to this need. Traditionally donors have intervened directly through educational projects or programmes. Is this the best way to channel money?

(2) What happens to the primary determinants of growth just discussed depends on the deeper determinants, that is institutions and policies. These have been identified as the key determinants of growth in Africa, and the impact of aid on those is

therefore of crucial importance.[5] When aid strategy is chosen one must therefore consider how it can best help improve institutions and policies, which can pave the way for increased investment and productivity growth. What happens to institutions and policies in turn depends on what happens in the political arena, and the impact of aid there will also have to be considered by donors. If there is no serious domestic constituency for reform it will be hard to bring about sustained improvements in institutions and policy.

(3) We also noted that agglomeration and transaction costs are very important growth constraints, and in particular in the land-locked countries which are quite numerous in Africa. Attempts to facilitate the access of African countries to markets are crucially important if they are to be able to benefit from the globalization. This does not only imply support for investments in Africa to improve infrastructure, but even more so the liberalization of trade with Africa. A successful completion of the Doha Round would have meant a lot to Africa. The structure of the financial relations with the industrial countries also needs to be considered.

(4) Finally, even further removed but potentially as important are investments in regional public goods that are important for growth. International investments in research efforts to deal with the HIV/AIDS and other health issues would be of great importance, as would agricultural research aiming at developing new and better varieties and methods of production suited to Africa. This is an area where donor investments are no hampered by the poor absorptive capacity of the countries that will benefit.

After grouping important growth constraints in these four groups, we need to deepen our discussion about what aid can do. Aid represents a transfer of resources. The donor choice of the amount to transfer will not be discussed further. The issue here is instead how the money allocated can be used most effectively to deal with the growth constraints identified. There are several dimensions that may be considered in such a discussion, for example whether aid should be given to production sectors, social sectors, infrastructure, or institutions, be given in the form of project aid, programme aid, budget support or debt reduction, what form of conditionality if any should be applied, and finally whether aid should be given via multilateral, bilateral, or NGO channels. The rest of the paper seeks to answer some of these questions and to define what the important donor choices are.

During the 1980s and 1990s African countries undertook reforms of economic policies within the framework of the structural adjustment programmes, but the results in terms of growth were rather meagre. We would argue that the policy choices in Africa now are reasonably good, but that many countries have been unable to implement these policies in an effective way. How the implementation works in turn depends on

---

[5] Collier (2006) notes that particularly the resource-rich countries have large and often corrupt government sectors, since they earn sizeable resource rents which accrue to the government. The key for this group is to improve the efficiency by which they spend public money, through knowledge transfers and governance conditionality trying to make the government more accountable to its citizens.

the institutional structure and how the political process works. If donors jointly decide to increase resource transfers to Africa as suggested by the UN (2005) and the Commission for Africa (2005), the demands on recipient country policy makers will become even larger at the same time there are already serious aid absorption and governance problems.[6] The concern about large aid injections is therefore how new or expanded programmes are to be managed.[7] How can one reach a situation where governments have possibilities and incentives to deliver efficient administration? Tight foreign control by donors via conditionality has generally not worked well. When it comes to the analysis of aid impacts it is therefore important to consider how the donor-recipient relationship is organized and affects institutions and implementation.

6. In search of an aid strategy for Africa

For a developing country to grow it needs a balanced portfolio of investments in production on the one hand and in social sectors, infrastructure, and institutions that support production activities on the other. The balance between these different sectors should be something that the recipient government is best suited to decide upon, since there is a need to take account of local conditions and constraints. Given that there is substantial fungibility in government budgets it will furthermore be hard for donors to use project and programme support to bring about a balance that differs significantly from that desired by the recipient government.

It may be more feasible for donors to impose conditions on the structure of government expenditures when providing budget support. Within the PRGF framework there are certain limits as to how low the shares of different poverty oriented expenditures can be if the country is to receive the aid transfers. To the extent that such restrictions shift resources from expenditures that are less relevant for growth such as military expenditures, they can have a positive growth impact. Donor restrictions on such an aggregate level are also less costly in terms of transaction costs than those associated with project packages. Still, generally donor driven sector allocation of aid is unlikely to be of major importance for growth outcomes. What matters is that there is a government in place that implements policies and builds institutions for the provision of public services and for support of private investment and technological development.

---

[6] As a spin-off of the recent literature on aid effectiveness some empirical estimates have emerged that indirectly measures the administrative constraints. Hansen and Tarp (2001) found that aid has a positive effect on growth also in bad policy environments, but they also identified an absorption problem. They found that the positive effect of aid inflows ceases when aid is about 25 percent of GDP.

[7] Pritchett and Woolcock (2004) point out that many of the MDG-services are both transaction intensive and discretionary. Unlike many macroeconomic reforms, the delivery of many health and education services requires the collaboration of multiple individuals who make highly discretionary choices in an environment where many key actions are unobservable. Such services cannot be delivered by a few politically protected technocrats. They are subject to deep incentive problems. The empirical link from spending on health and education to outcomes is notoriously weak (World Bank, 2004a).

If one accepts that the choice of sector into which to channel aid is best decided by the recipient, the other dimensions mentioned above remain crucial from a donor perspective. The important strategic choices for the donors then concern issues such as aid modality, donor coordination, and conditions associated with the aid. It is thus not a question about the final uses of aid. The ultimate goal of aid must be to build a domestically controlled system that eventually can function without donor interventions. It has always been possible for donors to create project "islands" that work well as long as they themselves are in charge, but the real test is what happens once they transfer the projects to local control and financing. Often the projects that have been under strict donor control are then found to be unsustainable (Bigsten *et al.*, 1994a, 1994b). The need to develop locally controlled and managed institutions is acknowledged by donors, whose strategy now is to enhance recipient "ownership" of development and aid programmes.

The ambition now is that bilateral as well as multilateral aid shall be integrated into the government budget. This is a key feature of the new aid modality introduced by the IFIs, the Poverty Reduction and Growth Facility (PRGF). The aim of the PRGF facility is to give the governments more policy space, and there has been some increased flexibility in the stance of the IMF. It now interprets fiscal targets more flexibly and is more willing to overlook breaches of macroeconomic targets if there is good performance on social priority expenditures. There has been some reduction in the extent of conditionality within the programmes, but in the end the reduction of conditions that donors will be willing to accept is going to depend on whether the government is able to put transparent reporting systems in place. Although the new initiative with policy making based on the PRS system is geared to increase ownership, the work done by the recipient government is still de facto largely oriented towards satisfying the demands of the donors. The IFIs have evaluated the implementation of the PRGF in several countries (IMF-IEO, 2004; World Bank, 2004b) and found that so far the changes have been limited. African economies suffer from lack of implementation capacity, and this tends to become an even more acute problem when aid increases rapidly.

The mechanisms for aid delivery are very important for how it is used and how effectively. Recipients of aid still have to deal with dozens of official donors and NGOs and hundreds of separate projects and programmes. Knack and Rahman (2004) note that there are both short-term transaction costs in the form of waste of resources, but there are also long-term costs due to donor practices that undermine the quality of governance. Tarp concludes from his review of the aid literature that "the institutional set up for bilateral aid deliveries remains complex, uncoordinated and overburdened with many diverse tasks and aims, and calls for reform of the un have become common" (Tarp, 2005: 8). The recent efforts of the OECD (2003, 2005) have focused on reducing transaction costs by harmonizing operational policies and procedures, such as standardizing reporting and monitoring systems, and establishing a web site to disseminate information on completed and country planned analytical work. So far the impact of those initiatives has been limited, since individual donors still hold on to their own goals and their own procedures.

The conclusion that has been drawn on the basis of the analyses done on the donor policies of the 1980s and 1990s is that effective and sustained reforms in these areas will not be realized unless the recipient country government owns and are committed to their own development programmes. The dilemma is that no donor is likely to give aid without being concerned about its results. So can one find some aid format that provides a reasonable compromise between the control needs of recipients on the one hand and the donors on the other? The aspects that we will discuss next are donor coordination, aid modalities, and conditionality.

7. Donor coordination and aid modalities

The aid relationship affects the efficiency with which aid resources, and other resources for that matter, are used. Lack of donor coordination leads to increased administrative complications and costs and possibly contradictory behavioral incentives. The donors are in principle aware of the importance of donor coordination and have recently issued two declarations[8] on issues such as harmonization, alignment, untying and coordination (Bigsten, 2006a).

The donor coordination problem is that they have a common interest in development at the same time as they have separate goals. So the first problem is to find a way to aggregate donor preferences and aid doctrines? They may reflect different views on what matters for development, but they typically also reflect different national interests. How hard it is to coordinate donors will depend on how similar their preferences are. In reality it has been hard to achieve donor coordination, since each donor has his own agenda and aid policies, and is often pursuing his own goals even if they are in conflict with those of the recipient government or those of other donors. There are political constraints at home and administrative and accounting practices to adhere to. Donors are faced with a complicated collective action problem, but it is important to overcome if the recipient is to be able to build a more capable state. Donors are also faced with a free rider problem, since some donors may try to claim more than their due share of credits for successful interventions (Torsvik, 2005).

International donor coordination at its most general level takes the form of large international meetings. These meetings result in agreements on some general principles by which donor government can be measured and also possibly held accountable. The Millennium Summit in September 2000 is a recent example of a general conference where world leaders agreed on certain common targets, the Millennium Development Goals, for the development efforts until 2015. Now the MDGs are accepted as a frame for development policy in most countries, and this in itself means that the aid of different donors will be coordinated to some extent by accepting the same goals. Earlier the structural adjustment programmes filled a similar function.

---

[8] The Rome Declaration (OECD, 2003) and the Paris Declaration (OECD, 2005).

At the recipient country level there are often groups with donors and the recipient government that try to coordinate activities. This focuses on country specific development problems can take the form of Roundtables or Consultative Group meetings, which can be held within the country itself or abroad (Disch, 1999). Here both policies and fund raising issues are discussed. They may deal with the coordination of policies, budgets and implementation for whole development programmes or sectoral programmes. There are also many governments that have established local aid coordination bodies, usually chaired by the Ministry of Finance or the Central Bank.

From the 1980s there have been attempts to at least introduce donor coordination at the at sector level, known as sector wide approaches (SWAPs), where donors agree to pool resources within some specific sector such as health. Pooling schemes such as sector-wide programmes can be seen as a step in the direction of budget support, but the transactions costs in negotiating those programmes have often been high (OECD, 2003). The trend towards budget support could in principle help to some extent to enhance ownership, but "if budget support is coupled with more complex management requirements and demands by donors for deeper reform and better reporting, transactions cost may change very little, and the main benefit may come in the form of strengthening government systems" (OECD, 2003). Disch (1999) actually found that it is easier to reach agreements among donors on policies (at least in principle), while it is harder to do so with regard to procedures and practices.

Donor accountability for development results could be enhanced by the appointment of a lead donor, who would have an enhanced reputational stake in the country's development outcome. Alternatively donors could specialize by sector or channel their own aid to a specific sector through another agency. There have been some initiatives along these lines, but so far not much has happened. The importance for individual donors of a global presence weighs more heavily than efficiency considerations.

So far bilateral donors have been rather unwilling to give up too much of their autonomy. It may therefore in the short term be realistic to take some modest first steps to make the handling of aid inflows easier for the recipient governments. Such an approach was proposed by the Commission for Africa (2005: 364). It suggested, as an interim solution, that donors should mutually recognize each other's procedures. This has worked within the European Union, where the members have accepted each others procedures as valid without requiring harmonization around a specific procedure (Bigsten, 2006b). In this case it would mean that donors would work from each others reports and thereby reduce the reporting burden of the recipient countries.

An early international initiative to tackle the coordination problem was the setting up of multilateral aid institutions. The UNDP was originally set up as an agency that would coordinate donors, but its real impact has been rather limited. The multilateral institutions were created to channel aid resources in a coordinated fashion to poor countries, but donor countries have been reluctant to give up control of the use of the bulk of their aid money. European countries nowadays channel a sizeable part of their aid through the EU, which therefore can be seen as a coordinating agency. Donors also coordinate their handling of the debt problems of LDCs through the Paris Club.

Kanbur notes with regard to the multilateral initiatives: "One of the strongest arguments in favor of moving in the direction of multilateralism was to reduce the influence of vested interest in each donor country. The idea is that when faced with a demand from a domestic constituency to skew away from a generally accepted development doctrine, the government could use the fact of an international agreement as a check. In effect, through multilateral agreements they would tie their own hands. But what if the domestic constituencies could lobby their government to in turn lobby the multilateral agency? This clearly happens." (Kanbur, 2003: 20). The industrial countries do channel a certain amounts of their aid through the multilateral institutions, but this is still a much smaller amount then what goes through bilateral channels.

Since multilateral institutions have not been able to attract the bulk of donor resources, other alternative coordination ideas to achieve coordination have been proposed. Kanbur *et al.* (1999) have introduced the idea of a common pool described as follows: "The objectives are (i) to reduce day-to-day interference in the management of the aid program, (ii) reduce fragmentation within and across projects and policies, (iii) improve "ownership" of the development strategy by the domestic political economy of the recipient country, and (iv) still give donors the right to modulate their funding based on recipient characteristics. The concept works as follows. Aid flows support the overall program of the government rather than this or that project. After a period of dialogue, with the donors but more importantly with its own population, the government puts forward an overall program of expenditures, with alternative scenarios based on different levels of aid flows. The donors look at this, and put into a common pool resources that will finance the overall program along with domestic and other resources. At no time is a particular part of the program identified with a particular donor. All aspects of aid are folded into this structure." This is an attractive idea.

In a recent paper Ranis (2006) presents a new version of the common pool idea (in the form of a new window with some multilateral organization such as UNDP). He also accepts the conclusion that ownership is essential for effective aid. His idea is that recipient countries shall draw up their own development plans and then on the basis of those apply for money from the new facility. The recipients are also expected to provide their own targets, or what he refers to as self-conditionality. It is then up to the donors to accept the application for aid or not. The donors will thus have a much more passive banker-like role. The recipients can use the money to buy technical assistance if they so choose. Technical assistance can then for example be geared towards institution building.

The common pool idea in some form seems to be an attractive solution to the coordination problem. If it is adopted the next question that needs to be discussed is on what conditions the resources are to be made available.

8. *What form of conditionality?*

The structural adjustment loans were associated with policy conditionality, and the various forms of debt cancellation have also been associated with conditionality. There has been a very extensive debate about the effectiveness of this. Killick (1999) concluded that conditionality did not work because donors could not agree to impose the sanctions that they had threatened to impose. This is referred to as the Samaritan's Dilemma, that is there is a moral problem withholding aid from poor people that you want to help which will be hurt in the short term (Svensson, 2003). Conditionality as practiced by the donors during this period was ineffective in bringing about sustained policy changes, if these were not in line with those really desired by domestic policy makers.[9]

Still, the result of the structural adjustment era was that most countries shifted to more market oriented policies and the distortions of the earlier period were reduced (Bigsten *et al.*, 2001). Initially the growth outcomes were very poor, but from 1995 there have at least been some improvement in African per capita incomes. Still, the results have been such that it seems reasonable to shift the focus from the policies themselves towards the structures and institutions that implement them. We would argue that the African development problem now is not primarily one of policy choice but one of policy implementation.

Collier (2006) notes that corrupt elites tend to benefit from a dysfunctional government. Policy conditionality is one option to deal with this problem, but it did not work very well in the past. The alternative is governance conditionality aimed at weakening the dominance of the governing elite. This is more hopeful, since it is more legitimate. Democracy has two important dimensions, electoral competition and checks and balances. Particularly resource rich countries need democracy to avoid elite capture of rents, but it needs checks and balances to prevent that the elections are converted into corrupt patronage games which is financed by the resource rents. One needs system scrutiny to achieve honesty and other systems to achieve efficiency. Since scrutiny is a public good it is subject to collective action problems, and donors could here help organize citizens. They could probably also stimulate peer group evaluations (Bigsten and Durevall, 2003).

The process of scrutiny has a severe agency problem. To reduce this, donors could help improve information for the principals, build the capacity to analyze it, and to promote incentives for agents to perform. Once a system is there the donors have an important role to play be insisting that rewards and penalties are built in and are implemented. Audit systems and parliamentary scrutiny are key areas of intervention. Collier (2006) thus wants to see a shift from policy conditionality to governance conditionality. The former undermined accountability to citizens, while the latter would reinforce it. A good system would be common to all donors, predictable and agreed.

Governance conditionality seems like an attractive option, but again it may be too radical a step for the donors to rely on that alone. Therefore it may be more realistic to

---

[9] Explanations as to why conditionality has not worked have been sought within the principal-agent framework, where the donor is the principal and the recipient the agent. Here the donor will only transfer resources if it improves his objective function. The donor can demand that the recipient undertakes certain actions. These can possibly make the recipient better off and then also the donor if he values the welfare of the recipient.

propose the introduction of governance conditionality combined with a modicum of the more flexible form of conditionality proposed by Ranis.

9. International integration

The G8 Africa Action Plan and the Blair Commission have promised dramatically increased aid flows to Africa as well as new initiatives to write off debt. Still, the Doha-Round would have been even more important if it had been possible to end it successfully. There is considerable evidence suggesting that trade is more important to growth in Africa than anywhere else (Bigsten *et al.*, 2004). Trade reform is one way to reduce the economic distance to the global market.

Much of the changes that are needed to reduce distance frictions in Africa are in the realm of domestic policy makers. What is required is on the one hand improved transport infrastructure and on the other hand, improvement in the other aspects of infrastructure that are important for trade such as the financial system and customs. Here much remains to be done before Africa becomes a serious contender for location of production that is outsourced from the industrial countries. Wage levels are relatively low, but not generally low compared to the levels in e.g. China. And in relation to productivity levels the competitive situation looks even worse. Moreover, for production to be outsourced to Africa competitive unit costs of production will not do the trick, unless African producer can guarantee both quality and timely deliveries. The latter is a major problem if the products are part of a production chain or if it needs to reach the final market in time for planned campaigns.

The need and scope for an export-drive is largest in the resource-scarce coastal economies. What is needed is an environment that is conducive to new exporters and aid should be geared to support critical export infrastructure and providing guarantees against expropriation. One type of donor intervention that one could envisage which would not suffer from the incentive problems discussed above would be to set up regular development banks independent of the government. These could be financed by aid money, but then be run on a more or less commercial basis. They could possibly specialize in financing related to international trade and help link up African firms to the international market. With donor guarantees they would be able to take somewhat larger risks than regular private banks, but the ambition should be to be commercially viable. These banks could possibly facilitate outsourcing to Africa of low-cost production segments, which is where Africa potentially would have its comparative advantages. Such a bank geared to help entrepreneurs could also have an indirect positive effect by making it possible for this group to increase in size and power, and they would then in turn be a force to reckon with for the government.

10. Concluding remarks

In this paper we first identified the most binding growth constraints in African economies to be poor institutions and policies. When it comes to the limited growth impact of aid in Africa we have argued that this has been related to poor implementation of institutional and policy reforms, and the insight from this debate is that the old form of conditionality has not worked. The "ownership" discussion is relevant and sustained institutional and effective and sustained policy improvements require governments to be committed to their own policies. The key challenge therefore is to find effective ways of channelling resources into the development programmes that the recipient believes in (and that donors also believe in since they will not channel money into programmes that they do not themselves believe in). We then discussed how aid should be designed to help relieve those constraints in an effective way. We have not focused directly on the actual formulation of national development strategies, but rather discussed efficient ways to injecting aid into the system.

The key question that we have discussed is how aid should be organized not to overburden the recipient system and to provide incentives for policy makers to perform. For reforms to be sustained there must be incentives for policy makers to do so. The external incentives to produce good results will be supported by a system where the chances of receiving aid form a common pool really depends on whether one has delivered good policies and institutional improvements during the earlier phases of development.

We have also noted that apart from interventions going through the government, there is a range of international efforts that need to be done within the areas of trade reform and public goods investments. And we also noted that there are interventions that can be done independently over the government, although these have not been the focus in this paper.

References

Abramowitz, M. (1994), Catch-up and convergence in the postwar growth boom and after. In: Baumol, W.J.R., Nelson, R., Wolf, E.N. (Eds.), *Convergence of Productivity – Cross-National Studies and Historical Evidence*. Oxford University Press, Oxford.

Acemoglu, D., Johnson, S., Robinson, J.A. (2001), The colonial origins of comparative development: an empirical investigation. *American Economic Review* 91 (5), 1369–1401.

Acemoglu, D., Johnson, S., Robinson, J.A. (2002), Reversal of fortune: geography and institutions in the making of the modern world income distribution. *Quarterly Journal of Economics* 117 (4), 1231–1294.

Acemoglu, D., Johnson, S., Robinson, J.A. (2003), An African success story: Botswana. In: Rodrik, D. (Ed.), *In Search of Prosperity: Analytic Narratives on Economic Growth*. Princeton University Press, Princeton, NJ.

Agenor, P.-R. (2002), Does globalisation hurt the poor? *Policy Research Working Paper* 2922. World Bank, Washington, DC.

Artadi, E., Sala-i-Martin, X. (2003), The economic tragedy of the XXth century: growth in Africa. *NBER Working Paper*, No. 9865. Cambridge, MA.

Bigsten, A. (2006a), Coordination et utilisations des aides. *Revue d'Economie du Developpement* 2, 77–103.

Bigsten, A. (2006b), *EU Development Policy: A report for the project The European Union in the Global Economy.* Bruegel, Brussels, mimeo.

Bigsten, A., Durevall, D. (2003), Globalisation and policy effects in Africa. *The World Economy* 26 (8), 1119–1136.

Bigsten, A., Shimeles, A. (2007), Can Africa reduce poverty by half by 2015? *Development Policy Review* 25 (2), 147–166.

Bigsten, A., Adam, C., Collier, P., O'Connell, S., Julin, E. (1994a), *Evaluation of Swedish Development Co-Operation with Tanzania: A Report for the Secretariat for Analysis of Swedish Development Assistance. Ds 1994:113.* SASDA, Stockholm.

Bigsten, A., Adam, C., Andersson, P., Collier, P., O'Connell, S. (1994b), *Evaluation of Swedish Development Co-Operation with Zambia: A Report for the Secretariat for Analysis of Swedish Development Assistance. Ds 1994:114.* SASDA, Stockholm.

Bigsten, A., Mutalemwa, D., Tsikata, Y., Wangwe, S. (2001), Aid and reform in Tanzania. In: Devarajan, S., Dollar, D., Holmgren, T. (Eds.), *Aid and Reform in Africa.* World Bank, Washington, DC.

Bigsten, A., Collier, P., Dercon, S., Fafchamps, M., Gauthier, B., Gunning, J.W., Oduro, A., Oostendorp, R., Pattillo, C., Söderbom, M., Teal, F., Zeufack, A. (2004), Do African firms learn from exporting? *Journal of Development Studies* 40 (3), 115–171.

Chen, S., Ravallion, M. (2004), How has the world's poorest fared since the early 1980s? *World Bank Research Observer* 19 (2), 141–169.

Collier, P. (2006), Africa: an agenda for decisive change. *Swedish Economic Policy Review* 13 (2), 169–198.

Collier, P., Gunning, J. (1999), Explaining African economic performance. *Journal of Economic Literature* 37 (1), 64–111.

Collier, P., O'Connell, S. (2004), Opportunities, syndromes and episodes, draft of chapter 2 in *Explaining African Economic Growth.* Cambridge University Press, in press.

Commission for Africa (2005), *Our Common Interest: Report of the Commission for Africa.* London.

Crafts, N., Venables, A. (2002), Globalization in history: a geographical perspective. *Discussion Paper*, 3079. Centre for Economic Policy Research, London School of Economics.

Disch, A. (1999), Aid coordination and aid effectiveness. *Evaluation Report* 8.99, Norwegian Ministry of Foreign Affairs, Oslo.

Dollar, D., Easterly, W. (1999), The search for the key: aid, investment, and policies in Africa. *Policy Research Working Paper*, No. 2070. World Bank, Washington, DC.

Easterly, W. (2001), The lost decades: developing countries' stagnation in spite of policy reform 1980–1998. *Journal of Economic Growth* 6 (2), 135–157.

Easterly, W., Levine, R. (1997), Africa's growth tragedy: politics and ethnic diversity. *Quarterly Journal of Economics* 112, 1230–1250.

Edwards, S. (1998), Openness, productivity and growth: what do we really know? *Economic Journal* 108, 383–398.

Eichengreen, B. (2001), Capital account liberalization: what do cross-country studies tell us? *World Bank Economic Review* 15 (3), 341–365.

Frankel, J., Romer, D. (1999), Does trade cause growth? *American Economic Review* 89, 379–399.

Grossman, G.M., Helpman, E. (1991), *Innovation and Growth in the Global Economy.* MIT Press, Cambridge, MA.

Grossman, G.M., Helpman, E. (1995), Technology and trade. In: Grossman, G.M., Rogoff, K. (Eds.), *Handbook of International Economics,* vol. 3. North-Holland, Amsterdam.

Hall, R.E., Jones, C.I. (1999), Why do some countries produce so much more output per worker than others. *Quarterly Journal of Economics* 114 (1), 83–116.

Hansen, H., Tarp, F. (2001), Aid and growth regressions. *Journal of Development Economics* 64, 547–570.

Hausmann, R., Pritchett, L., Rodrik, D. (2004), Growth accelerations. *NBER Working Paper,* No. 10566, Cambridge, MA.

Hoeffler, A.E. (2002), The augmented slow model and the African growth debate. *Oxford Bulletin of Economics and Statistics* 64, 135–158.

Hulten, C.R. (1996), Infrastructure capital and economic growth: How well you use it may be more important than how much you have. *NBER Working Paper,* No. 5847, Cambridge, MA.

IMF Independent Evaluation Office (2004), *Evaluation of the IMF's role in poverty reduction strategy papers and the poverty reduction and growth facility.* Washington, DC.

Irwin, D.A., Terviö, M. (2002), Does trade raise income? Evidence from the twentieth century. *Journal of International Economics* 58, 1–18.

Kanbur, R. (2003), The economics of international aid. In: Christophe-Kolm, S., Mercier-Ythier, J. (Eds.), *Handbook on "The Economics of Giving, Reciprocity, and Altruism".* North-Holland, Amsterdam.

Kanbur, R., Sandler, T., Morrison, K. (1999), *The Future of Development Assistance: Common Pools and International Public Goods.* Johns Hopkins University Press, Baltimore.

Keller, W. (2002), Geographic location and international technology diffusion. *American Economic Review* 92 (1), 120–142.

Killick, T. (1999), *Aid and the Political Economy of Policy Change.* Routledge with ODI, London and New York.

Knack, A., Rahman, A. (2004), Donor fragmentation and bureaucratic quality in aid recipients. *Background Paper to World Development Report,* 2004, World Bank, Washington, DC.

Krugman, P., Venables, A.V. (1995), Globalisation and inequality of nations. *Quarterly Journal of Economics* 110, 857–880.

Maddison, A. (2001), *The World Economy. A Millennial Approach.* OECD, Paris.

North, D.C. (1990), *Institutions, Institutional Change and Economic Performance.* Cambridge University Press, Cambridge.

Obstfeld, M. (1998), The global capital market: benefactor or menace? *Journal of Economic Perspectives* 12, 9–30.

O'Connell, S. (2004a), Ending Africa's poverty trop: comments. *Brookings Papers on Economic Activity* 1, 223–230.

O'Connell, S. (2004b), Explaining African economic growth: emerging lessons from the growth project. Paper presented at the biannual AERC workshop, Nairobi.

OECD (2003), *Harmonizing Donor Practices for Effective Aid Delivery*. OECD, Paris.

OECD (2005), *Paris Declaration on Aid Effectiveness. Ownership, Harmonisation, Alignment, Results, and Mutual Accountability*. OECD, Paris.

OECD (2006), *International Development Statistics*. Netversion.

Pattillo, C., Gupta, S., Carey, K. (2005), Sustaining growth accelerations and pro-poor growth in Africa. *IMF Working Paper* WP/05/195, IMF, Washington, DC.

Pritchett, L., Woolcock, M. (2004), Solutions when the solution is the problem: arraying the disarray in development. *World Development* 32 (2), 191–212.

Ranis, G. (2006), Toward the enhanced effectiveness of foreign aid. *Discussion Paper*, No. 938, Economic Growth Center, Yale University, New Haven, CT.

Redding, S., Schott, P.K. (2003), Distance, skill deepening and development: will peripheral countries ever get rich? *NBER Working Paper* 9447, Cambridge, MA.

Rodriguez, F., Rodrik, D. (2000), *Trade policy and economic growth: a sceptics guide to the cross-national evidence*. University of Maryland and Harvard University, mimeo.

Sachs, J., McArthur, J.W., Schmidt-Traub, G., Kruk, M., Bahadur, C., Faye, M., McCord, G. (2004), Ending Africa's poverty trap. *Brookings Papers on Economic Activity* 1, 117–240.

Svensson, J. (2003), Why conditional aid does not work and what can be done about it. *Journal of Development Economics* 70 (2), 381–402.

Tarp, F. (2005), *Foreign Aid*. Department of Economics, Copenhagen University, mimeo.

Tarp, F. (2006), Aid and development. *Swedish Economic Policy Review* 13 (2), 9–62.

Taylor, A.M. (2002), Globalization, trade and development: some lessons from history. *NBER Working Paper* 9326, Cambridge, MA.

Torsvik, G. (2005), Foreign economic aid: should donors cooperate? *Journal of Development Economics* 77, 503–515.

Tsangarides, C.G. (2005), Growth empirics under model uncertainty: is Africa different? *IMF Working Paper* 05/18, IMF, Washington, DC.

UN (2005), *Investing in Development: A Practical Plan to Achieve the Millennium Development Goals*. New York.

Venables, A. (2001). Geography and international inequalities: the impact of new technologies. Paper prepared for World Bank Annual Bank Conference on Development Economics, World Bank, Washington, DC.

World Bank (1993), *The East Asian Miracle: Growth and Public Policy*. Oxford University Press, Oxford.

World Bank (2004a), *Rwanda: Country Assistance Evaluation*. Operations Evaluation Department, Washington, DC.

World Bank (2004b), *The Poverty Reduction Strategy Initiative. An Independent Evaluation of the World Bank's Support Through 2003*. Washington, DC.

Worl Bank (2004c), *World Development Report 2004*. Washington, DC.

CHAPTER 16

Aid and Growth in Kenya: A Time Series Approach

Oliver Morrissey[a], Daniel M'Amanja[b] and Tim Lloyd[a]

[a]School of Economics, Sir Clive Granger Building, University of Nottingham,
University Park, Nottingham NG7 2RD, England, UK
E-mail addresses: oliver.morissey@nottingham.ac.uk; tim.lloyd@nottingham.ac.uk
[b]Economics Department, Central Bank of Kenya, PO Box 60000, Nairobi, Kenya
E-mail address: Amanjadm@centralbank.go.ke

Abstract

There is now a large, if rather contentious and inconclusive, cross-country empirical literature on the effectiveness of aid in contributing to economic growth. Surprisingly, perhaps, there are very few country studies of aid effectiveness, and none of which we are aware that adopt a time series econometric approach to analyzing the impact of aid on growth. This chapter is an attempt to fill that gap, through a study of Kenya over the period 1964–2002. The core hypothesis underlying our approach is that aid does not have a direct effect on growth, but can have indirect effects through mediating channels. Given the requirements of time series techniques, we focus on two channels for the aid-growth relationship, one through effects on government fiscal relationship (as aid finances public spending) and another through effects on investment (as aid finances public investment). The analysis is no more than indicative but suggests a number of reasons why aid has not been effective in Kenya: reliance on aid loans to finance unanticipated budget deficits, low productivity of public investment and adverse effects of government behavior on private investment. Addressing these deficiencies is necessary if Kenya is to be enabled to utilize aid to improve its poor economic performance.

Keywords: Aid, fiscal aggregates, investment, growth, Kenya

JEL classifications: F35, O23, O55

1. Introduction

The issue of aid effectiveness, assessing if aid contributes to economic growth, has attracted considerable attention within the past ten years due to the publication of

THEORY AND PRACTICE OF FOREIGN AID
VOLUME 1   ISSN: 1574-8715
DOI: 10.1016/S1574-8715(06)01016-5

a number of empirical papers based on cross-country regressions. Despite decades of receiving billions of dollars in aid, most poor countries, especially those in sub-Saharan Africa (SSA), have failed to sustain even modest rates of real per capita economic growth. This would appear to suggest that that aid has failed, in the sense that it has not contributed to growth, at least for recipient countries in general. Alternatively, it may be that aid has been insufficient in itself to counter inherent characteristics of poor countries that impair growth. These characteristics include adverse natural (geographic) features, weak institutions and poor government, and an unfavorable economic structure (e.g. dependence on primary commodity exports). In other words, it may be the case that aid has supported a better growth performance than would have otherwise prevailed, but this performance has nevertheless been poor.

There is now a large empirical literature investigating the effectiveness of aid, almost all studies testing if the coefficient on aid is positive and significant in a cross-country panel growth regression. There is a moderately clear division in the literature (see Morrissey, 2006). The World Bank (1998), Burnside and Dollar (2000) and studies adopting a similar approach argue that aid is ineffective: aid only has a significant positive impact on growth if the government implements 'good' policies, and the policy reform conditions associated with aid are not effective at ensuring good policies are chosen. Studies adopting different empirical approaches tend to find evidence that aid is effective. Hansen and Tarp (2001), Dalgaard *et al.* (2004) amongst others, find that aid itself has a significant positive effect on growth that is independent of policy. A number of factors help to explain why results differ, especially differences in the sample, specification and econometric technique used in each study. It is also true that results tend to be sensitive to how aid is measured: studies that exclude types of aid that are unlikely to have any medium-term impact on growth (e.g. technical assistance), to derive a measure that captures the short-term impact of aid on growth (Clemens *et al.*, 2004), tend to find a significant positive coefficient on aid, even for SSA (Gomanee *et al.*, 2005).

As countries are heterogeneous and many factors promote and constrain growth, acting in different ways across countries, it is not surprising that it is difficult to explain cross-country variations in growth, hence results vary. Recent contributions to the cross-country literature have been reviewed and reassessed in Roodman (2004), and are not considered in any detail here. The cross-country evidence seems to suggest that aid does contribute to growth, but the effect is quite small and is influenced by, if not conditional on, other (country-specific) factors, which may include policy.

However, cross-country studies only highlight what appears to be important in general or on average; analytical country studies are needed to understand the growth process, and which factors were most important, in individual countries (e.g. Rodrik, 2003). This paper is in the latter tradition, but employs a multivariate time series estimation approach to investigate some of the determinants of economic growth in a single, small open developing country. Specifically, we aim to investigate the effects of foreign aid, fiscal aggregates and investment on growth in Kenya since the 1960s. Whilst a country-specific approach allows one to address issues, for the country, that are not addressed adequately in cross-country studies and avoids some of the problems in cross-country approaches, it raises many new problems. First, the empirical spec-ification appropriate for cross-country studies is not readily applicable to time series country analysis. Many of the factors that explain cross-country variations in growth may not be helpful to explain variations over time within a country, either because annual data are unavailable or because the variables tend to change very slowly over time (e.g. institutions and governance). Second, the econometric concerns in time se-ries analysis are different, specifically whether or not variables are non-stationary and cointegrated. Third, and related, the length of time for which data are available is typ-ically very short for the techniques being used. One implication is that the power and size of tests tends to be low, and another is that it is desirable to restrict the number of variables included to as few as can be justified.

Notwithstanding these difficulties, we adopt the technique of vector autoregressive (VAR) modeling to assess if investment, aid and trade (imports) have had significant effects on growth in Kenya over the past four decades. Data constraints prohibit in-cluding all potential variables in a single cointegrating vector (given the relatively short time series, a VAR including more than four variables is unlikely to yield robust estimates). Furthermore, it is desirable to use the minimally cointegrating vector, i.e. to find the cointegrating relationship that includes as few of the variables that eco-nomic theory suggests should be significant. Consequently, we estimate two separate relationships: the effect of aid on growth mediated by fiscal aggregates (as most aid goes to the government and therefore affects budgetary behavior) and the effect medi-ated by investment (as aid finances investment, and capital accumulation is a driver of growth).

The paper is organized as follows. Section 2 provides a brief overview of some rel-evant literature on growth in developing countries, concentrating on the relationships and variables of interest here, and outlines the general specification of the empiri-cal models. Our analytical starting point is that aid does not affect growth directly, so it is important to identify indirect channels through which aid can affect growth. Section 3 presents the analysis of the 'fiscal channel' for the aid-growth relationship, while Section 4 considers the 'investment channel'. Both sections discuss the data and theoretical basis for the specification before presenting results for the long-run (cointe-grating) relationships and for the short-run (dynamic) model. Conclusions and policy implications are in Section 5.

2. *The modelling approach*

Theory suggests that the major direct effect of aid on growth is through effects on (public) investment. In simple terms, aid finances the provision of public goods and these are required to establish the platform for private sector development. Studies that explicitly allow for this effect through investment tend to find a positive impact of aid on growth, even for SSA (Lensink and Morrissey, 2000; Gomanee *et al.*, 2005). As the aid is mostly given to the government and directed at public investment, this suggests a *fiscal channel*: aid influences the level and allocation of government recur-rent and investment spending, and may also influence tax effort and borrowing (the fiscal effects of aid, see (McGillivray and Morrissey, 2004)), and the resulting fiscal aggregates impact on growth. However, not all aid is intended for investment, not all investment is financed by aid, and public investment can have effects on private investment. This suggests one should also consider the *investment channel*: aid influences public investment which in turn has effects on private investment, and the interaction impacts on growth.

In theory, foreign aid could relax any or all of three constraints on investment (Bacha, 1990). The savings constraint arises if, as is likely in low-income countries, domestic savings are insufficient to meet (public) investment requirements; aid (foreign savings) relaxes the constraint. The foreign exchange constraint arises because investment requires imported capital goods and the 'free' foreign exchange available from export earnings may be insufficient; as aid is in the form of foreign exchange, it permits a higher level of (capital) imports. The fiscal constraint captures the possibility that government behavior affects private savings and public investment can affect private investment; aid, by financing public investment and reducing the need to raise seignorage revenue to finance a deficit, can relax this constraint. If foreign aid is used to relax these constraints it is expected to be positively correlated with investment and growth (Hjertholm *et al.*, 2000). Gomanee *et al.* (2005) show that aid has a beneficial impact on growth in sub-Saharan African countries through financing public investment, although the impact on growth is small because productivity is low. Of course, aid may not have these beneficial effects (which in effect is what we can test), or may have other adverse effects (which we may be able to infer, but do not test).

Other important determinants of growth (positively or negatively) include human capital, technological advancement, government consumption expenditure, taxes, population growth, inflation, measures of rule of law, governance and democracy. In a single country study, the time series approach cannot incorporate all these factors; some are not measured annually, some change very slowly over time (and would thus be poor at explaining annual growth which can vary significantly) and there is simply a limit to the number of variables that can feasibly be included. Hence the focus of this paper on only a sub-set of factors; within the large literature on growth determinants, we focus on foreign aid, investment, and imports.

The analysis is based on a vector autoregressive (VAR) approach, which for our purposes offers several advantages over single equation approaches. These advantages include the ability to deal with several endogenous variables and cointegrating vectors, the ability to test for weak exogeneity and parameter restrictions, and to handle both $I(1)$ and $I(0)$ variables in one system. Of equal importance, the VAR approach does not require the imposition of structural relationships; essentially, one estimates reduced forms. The VAR approach is data based and little economic theory is imposed directly: although the structure is atheoretical, economic theory is invoked to select the appropriate normalization and to interpret the results. The VAR approach assumes all variables in the system are potentially endogenous, so each variable is explained by its own lags and lagged values of the other variables. We start with a vector autoregressive (VAR) model of the form:

$$x_t = \Phi_1 x_{t-1} + \Phi_2 x_{t-2} + \cdots + \Phi_k x_{t-k} + \mu + \varepsilon_t \tag{1}$$

where x_t is an $n \times 1$ vector of variables under study, Φ_i, $i = 1, 2, \ldots, k$ is an $n \times n$ matrix of parameters, μ a vector of deterministic components and $\varepsilon_t \sim iid(0, \Sigma)$. According to Granger's representation theorem, when there is cointegration, the VAR model given in (1) can be reformulated into a vector error correction model (VECM) that incorporates short- and long-run dynamics, and takes the following form:

$$\Delta x_t = \mu + \Gamma_i \Delta x_{t-1} + \Gamma_2 \Delta x_{t-2} + \cdots + \Gamma_{k-1} \Delta x_{t-k-1} + \Pi x_{t-k} + \varepsilon_t \qquad (2)$$

where Δx_t is a vector of growth rates, $\Gamma_j = -[I - \sum_{i=1}^{j} \Phi_i]$ is an $n \times n$ matrix containing information on short run adjustments of changes in x_t, $\Pi = -[I - \sum_{i=1}^{k} \Phi_i]$ is an $n \times n$ impact matrix of parameters containing information on long-run adjustments, μ is a vector of constants, ε_t is $n \times 1$ vector of white noise errors, and I is an identity matrix (details on the method can be found in (Favero, 2001; Harris, 1995; Johansen and Juselius, 1992)). All variables used in the analysis, except output (in per capita terms) are expressed as shares in GDP before taking their logs. The data is taken from the *Kenya Economic Survey* (Republic of Kenya, various issues), checked against or supplemented from Ryan (2002).

3. Aid, fiscal policy and growth

The literature on the fiscal impact of aid (McGillivray and Morrissey, 2004) demonstrates that one is essentially estimating a form of simultaneous relationship. In the traditional approach, a reduced form equation is estimated. In using the VAR approach, this reduced form representation is achieved by assuming one cointegrating vector linking the fiscal variables, using theory to guide any restrictions in interpreting the VAR (see Osei *et al.*, 2005). This approach restricts attention to the fiscal variables only; therefore one cointegrating vector is justified. Our analysis for Kenya goes a step further, in also considering the additional link to growth. This suggests the possibility of more than one cointegrating vector, as in principal one has a simultaneous equation system with one relationship between the fiscal variables, and then a relationship between the fiscal variables and growth.

There are established growth models that explicitly incorporate government activity (Barro and Sala-i-Martin, 1995). The basic model assumes that government services are productive public goods and government's influence on growth is via two channels: the negative effect of taxation on incentives and the positive effect of public services on the private sector. The prediction of theory is that productive government expenditures and non-distortionary taxation are positively associated with economic growth, whereas unproductive government expenditures and distortionary taxation correlate negatively with economic growth (Barro, 1990). In practice, it is difficult to separate productive and unproductive spending and identify which taxes are relatively distortionary, so empirical evidence is mixed (Barro, 1990; Levine and Renelt, 1992; Easterly and Rebelo, 1993). M'Amanja and Morrissey (2005) provide a detailed analysis of this issue for Kenya, and find no evidence that any taxes had adverse effects on growth; investment spending had a positive effect whereas only some recurrent spending appeared to have an adverse impact. This suggests that it is acceptable not to disaggregate tax revenue in our analysis. Although it may be desirable to disaggregate spending, the need to limit the number of variables included in the VAR prevents us from doing this (public investment is identified separately in Section 4).

We employ an empirical approach that allows and tests for the possibility of more than one cointegrating vector, and follow the cointegrating VAR methodology of Johansen and Juselius (1990). The theoretical concerns outlined above facilitate the interpretation of more than one cointegrating vector if that is what we find, although they only provide guidance to the specification of each vector. As is well known, many variables impact on growth and we are only considering a sub-set of variables. Consequently, although our 'fiscal representation' is complete (the budget variables are all included, omitting borrowing to avoid estimating an identity), the growth equation is incomplete (in the sense that our model does not capture all the relevant determinants of growth). This is an inevitable limitation of single country time series analysis of growth. However, our concern is not with identifying the determinants of growth, rather it is with identifying the fiscal impact of aid and how this relates to growth.

The analysis is based on five variables (full details on the analysis can be found in M'Amanja *et al.*, 2005): total government expenditure (*TEXP*), total tax revenue (*TAX*), output is real per capita income (*Yp*) and there are two measures of foreign aid, external grants (*GRANT*) and net external loans (*LOAN*). On average, the level of total government expenditure excluding debt repayments for the period 1964–2002 is 25% of GDP while tax revenue accounts for 21% of GDP on average. Grants and loans constitute only about 1% and 2% of GDP respectively as a period average. This is much lower than what is reported in donor aid statistics. We use the Kenyan data because this is the data upon which financial and economic planning is based by Kenyan policy makers (i.e. as revealed by the government's own budget data), it allows us to distinguish grants and loans, and much of the aid reported by donors does not actually go to the government (much technical assistance, for example, is not even spent in Kenya). Figure 1 shows the trend of the fiscal and aid variables for Kenya for the period 1964–2002.

It is evident that expenditure and revenue have been moving together over the period up to the early 1990s. Although the relationship appears different during the 1992–2002 period, tests revealed no evidence of structural breaks. Aid loans appear more volatile than grants. Such volatility is symptomatic of the unstable relationship between donors and the government, in which the government backtracks on agreed donor conditions whenever the economy peaks only to go back to donors when the economy begins to wobble. This 'cycling' with donors has characterized the Kenyan economy since the advent of structural adjustment programs in early 1980s, and is likely to diminish the effectiveness of aid.

Following Osei *et al.* (2005) we start by formulating a general VAR model of the relationship between fiscal aggregates, aid and economic growth. All variables are found to be non-stationary so we test for cointegration in a multivariate framework using

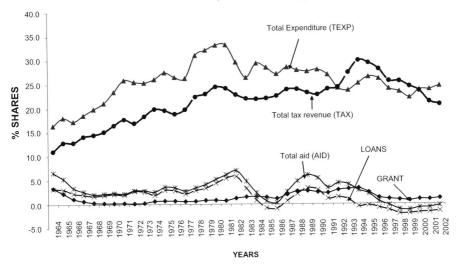

Fig. 1.   Trends in fiscal aggregates and aid, 1964–2002.

the Johansen (1988) maximum likelihood procedure (for details see M'Amanja *et al.*, 2005). The results allow us to accept that there are two cointegrating relationships (see Appendix A). Milesi-Ferretti and Roubini (1995) argue that where the government is free to borrow, taxes may have zero long-run effect on growth; the government effect on long-run growth is through expenditure, and taxes have no or a marginal impact, as M'Amanja and Morrissey (2005) found for Kenya. For the growth relation in the first cointegrating vector, we therefore normalize on output and put a zero restriction on tax revenue. For the fiscal relation represented by the second cointegrating vector, we may exclude output as our interest is to investigate the relationship between aid, taxes and expenditure. In this case, normalization is on aid loans and a zero restriction is imposed on output.

The results for the just-identified model are reported in Table 1. Aid loans exhibit a negative correlation with output in the long-run, although expenditure and aid grants have significant positive effects. We conjecture that the government seeks aid loans in the face of a fiscal deficit, so this is consistent with observing a negative effect of deficits on long-run income. The results for the fiscal vector support the conjecture as expenditure has a positive effect on loans while tax revenue has a negative effect. Furthermore, the coefficient on *TEXP* is much higher than that on *TAX*, implying that the responsiveness of loans to spending is greater than the responsiveness to tax revenue. Aid grants have an insignificant relationship with aid loans.

This model is supported by the variable exclusion tests in Table 2. The exclusion tests strongly reject the null of non-significance of variables except that of aid grants which appeared insignificant in both the output and fiscal vectors, although the *t*-test suggests that the aid grants coefficient is significant in the output vector. Exclusion and *t*-test statistics indicate that expenditure, tax revenue and foreign loans are significant

Table 1. Long-run estimates for the fiscal model

Variable	Output vector		Fiscal vector	
	Coefficient	t-stat	Coefficient	t-stat
Output *(Yp)*	–	–		
Expenditure *(TEXP)*	0.39	6.15	3.98	7.92
Revenue *(TAX)*			−2.29	−5.95
Aid grants *(GRANT)*	0.02	2.19	−0.04	−0.45
Aid loans *(LOAN)*	−0.10	−6.40	–	–

Note: The output vector is normalized on Yp and excludes *TAX*; the fiscal vector is normalized on *LOANS* and excludes Yp.

Table 2. Long-run exclusion tests for the fiscal model

	H_0: Coefficient is zero ($\beta_i = 0$)			
Variable	Output vector		Fiscal vector	
	$\chi^2(1)$	P-value	$\chi^2(1)$	P-value
Output *(Yp)*	–	–		
Expenditure *(TEXP)*	3.2178	0.0728	8.7308	0.0031
Revenue *(TAX)*			6.3044	0.0428
Aid grants *(GRANT)*	0.9708	0.3245	0.0818	0.7749
Aid loans *(LOAN)*	2.6950	0.1007	–	–

Note: The P-values indicate the level at which the null hypothesis that β_i is zero can be rejected. Both expenditure and loans (at 10% significant level) appear important in the output vector whilst expenditure and tax revenue are significant in the fiscal vector.

in the cointegrating relations. Given the theoretical importance of our variables in explaining growth, we include all four variables in the long-run relationships.

The positive sign of the coefficient implies that government spending contributes to growth in the long-run. No distinction is made between investment and recurrent expenditure. However, as the former is a far lower share of spending than the latter, the presumption must be that recurrent spending contributes to per capita output (or, at least, does not retard growth). It is also worth noting that tests justify excluding tax from the long-run output model, implying that taxes have no negative impact on per capita income.

The results for aid are less clear, as they depend on the measure used. Grants appear beneficial, as they have a positive effect on income (output). As grants do not generate future interest payments, they are not associated with increased spending. The weak significance of grants may reflect their low value throughout the study period. The results suggest that loans are sought to finance an 'unanticipated' fiscal deficit, and are therefore negatively associated with output. If tax revenue is lower than expected and/or spending is higher than planned, loans are required. There is an inverse rela-

Table 3. Parsimonious short-run fiscal model

Variable	Equation (1) (DYp)	Equation (2) (DTEXP)	Equation (3) (DTAX)	Equation (4) (DGRANT)	Equation (5) (DLOAN)
CONSTANT	−1.54	−0.002	0.002	−14.53	−1.82
	(−4.76)	(−0.19)	(0.22)	(−3.24)	(6.08)
DYp_{t-1}	–	0.72	0.74	–	2.25
	–	(1.90)	(2.52)	–	(2.38)
$DTEXP_{t-1}$	–	–	−0.38	−3.15	−1.21
	–	–	(−2.85)	(−3.80)	(−2.32)
$DTAX_{t-1}$	0.14	0.28	0.53	3.05	2.78
	(2.57)	(1.65)	(3.36)	(3.27)	(4.39)
$DGRANT_{t-1}$	−0.03	–	–	–	–
	(−3.18)	–	–	–	–
$DLOANT_{t-1}$	0.03	–	–	0.48	0.51
	(2.65)	–	–	(2.76)	(4.78)
$ECM1_{t-1}$	−0.36	–	–	2.95	–
	(−4.78)	–	–	(2.78)	–
$ECM2_{t-1}$	0.02	–	–	−0.62	−0.39
	(2.60)	–	–	(−5.39)	(−5.95)

Note: t-statistics in parentheses (significant values in bold). Further over-identifying restrictions on the model were rejected by the likelihood ratio test and relevant diagnostics are satisfactory.

tionship between aid loans and grants, so a short-fall in grant income also appears to encourage increased loans. M'Amanja *et al.* (2005) corroborate these results with impulse response analysis of shocks in aid loans on fiscal variables. There is a rise in output in the first three years of the shock in loans but output falls thereafter. In contrast, shocks in grants have an overall positive effect on per capita output.

To capture the short-run dynamics of the model, a VECM was formulated based on the identified long-run relationships. Error correction terms, $ECM1_{t-1}$ and $ECM2_{t-1}$, from the two cointegrating relations are included to capture the speed of adjustment to a disturbance in the long-run equilibrium in respective vectors. The presence of cointegrating relationships in the long-run model implies that all terms in the VECM are stationary and therefore conventional t-statistics can be used to evaluate the model. Results of the parsimonious short-run model are in Table 3.

Tax revenue and external loans appear to have, in the short-run, beneficial effects on growth, but past grants have a negative effect, which is surprising. The negative effect of grants may reflect adverse effects of donor conditions which require the government to provide 'counterpart' spending to match grants. Given budgetary constraints this matching spending may lead to a need for increased domestic borrowing. The positive effect of tax revenue is consistent with the argument that taxes themselves have no adverse (distortionary) effects and finance beneficial spending (M'Amanja and Morrissey, 2005). External loans appear to be beneficial in the short-run, perhaps because they accommodate excess spending (finance a deficit). The error correction term possesses the appropriate sign and is significant.

In the expenditure equation, only income and to a lesser extent tax revenue appear to be significant, both of which have positive association with expenditure. The result is consistent with our interpretation of the long-run: it is when tax revenue is insufficient to fund expenditure that aid is required. The results for the tax equation are not easily interpreted for expenditure. Contrary to expectation, expenditure has a negative correlation with growth of tax revenue. It could be the case that it is only current expenditure that has a positive association with growth of current tax revenue (i.e. increasing revenue permits increases in spending, which is allocated to recurrent expenditure), and not past expenditure.

In the equation for grants, changes in expenditure have an inverse relation with growth of grants, suggesting that donors reduce grants in the light of increased government spending. Conversely, changes in tax revenue have a positive association with growth of grants, suggesting that grants in Kenya are associated with increased tax effort. There is also a positive relationship between loans and grants reflecting the possibility that aid is given in 'packages' comprising grants and loans. In the equation for loans, growth of lagged income, expenditure, tax revenue and loans are all significant determinants of growth of loans. The positive relationship between income and loans can be interpreted to mean that growth permits taking new loans. Similarly, if tax revenue is rising the ability to service loans is stronger. The negative coefficient on lagged spending suggests cyclical behavior: loans are taken to meet a deficit, then subsequently loans are lower (thus, when expenditure increases the deficit requires a loan and subsequently new loans are lower). The positive coefficient on lagged loans suggests that loans are disbursed over more than one year. The error correction term from the fiscal relation possesses the right sign and is significant, implying cointegration and also justifies our choice of loans for normalization.

4. Aid, investment and growth

To address the 'investment channel' we again estimate a VAR model containing five variables (for full details see M'Amanja and Morrissey, 2006): real per capita income (Yp), private investment ($PINV$), government investment ($GINV$), foreign aid ($LOAN$), and imports of goods and services (IMP). Private and public investment are included to test if the latter influences the former (positively or negatively). Aid is included as it is an important source of financing for public investment; in this case we use only loans as grants can be excluded from the output relationship (Table 2). Imports are included as the trade variable to capture the need for imported investment goods and embodied technological transfer through imported inputs (and financing the foreign exchange constraint suggests that imports are the relevant trade variable). While this obviously omits factors that are important for growth, and even some that may be important for investment and growth (e.g. monetary policy), provided the variables included in the system are cointegrated they do form a long-run equilibrium relationship so we can draw some inferences.

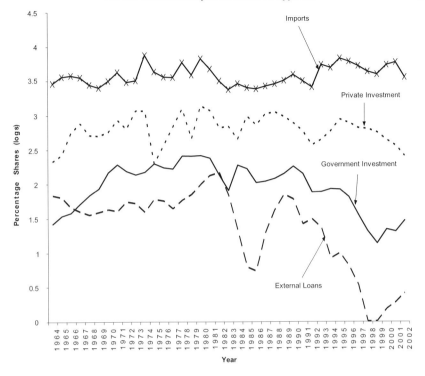

Fig. 2. Trends of imports, private and public investment, 1964–2002.

In terms of estimating the VAR, there is a possibility of two cointegrating vectors, an investment relationship and an output (growth) relationship. Gomanee *et al.* (2005) argue that the effect of aid on growth is via its effect on investment, and that the two relationships should be separated in estimation. The 'aid-growth models' in Mosley *et al.* (1987), Burnside and Dollar (2000) and Hansen and Tarp (2001) also implicitly separate effects of aid on investment from effects of investment on growth, even if their estimation does not make the distinction. This suggests two cointegrating vectors, so the Johansen and Juselius (1992) methodology is employed in identifying these vectors. The results allow us to accept that there are two cointegrating relationships (see Appendix B). In essence, one cointegrating vector captures the behavioral equation for investment, while the second represents the reduced form growth equation. Trends of shares of imports, private and public investment are shown in Figure 2.

Tests support treating all variables as non-stationary and selecting two lags as the optimal lag length for the VAR model. There was evidence of outliers (or breaks) in the import series and, following the method of Hendry and Juselius (2001), we introduce a dummy in 1973/1974 to capture the impact brought about by the 1973 oil shock, and the concomitant policy pronouncements such as the tightening of financial and trade controls (Ryan, 2002). Such events tend to have both short-term and long-

324   *Oliver Morrissey et al.*

Table 4. *Long-run estimates for the investment model*

Variable	Output vector		Investment vector	
	Coefficient	*t*-stat	Coefficient	*t*-stat
Output *(Yp)*	–	–		
Private Invest *(PINV)*	0.56	11.23	–	–
Public Invest *(GINV)*	0.30	3.78	−0.35	−2.38
Imports *(IMP)*	0.44	2.89	−0.78	−2.75
Aid loans *(LOAN)*	−0.22	−4.65	0.27	2.84

Note: The output vector is normalized on *Yp* and excludes the shift dummy in estimation; the investment vector is normalized on *PINV* and excludes *Yp* (but a shift dummy is used to estimate the vector). All variables are found to be significant in the estimated long-run relationship.

term effects on the economy and are modeled to allow both the permanent mean shift and a permanent blip in the system. To do this, we introduce a mean-shift dummy $(Ds74_t)$ taking the value zero between 1964 and 1973 and one from 1974 to 2002 (i.e. $Ds74_t = 1$ for $t = 1974$–2002, 0 otherwise) such that its first difference becomes an impulse dummy. The shift dummy is restricted to lie in the cointegrating space whilst its first difference enters the model unrestrictedly and therefore only appears in the short-run. With these modifications, we can write the VECM as:

$$\Delta x_t = \mu + \Gamma_1 \Delta x_{t-1} + \Gamma_2 \Delta x_{t-2} + \cdots + \Gamma_{k-1} \Delta x_{t-k-1}$$
$$+ \Pi x_{t-k} + \psi_s \Delta Ds74_t + \varepsilon_t \tag{3}$$

We imposed two normalizations and two parameter restrictions to exactly identify the model (full details are in M'Amanja and Morrissey, 2006). In the first cointegrating vector, which we took to represent the reduced form output relation, we normalized on output and put a zero restriction on the mean shift dummy. In the second vector, which describes the investment relationship, normalization was on private investment and a zero restriction on output. Table 4 provides parameter estimates for the two identified long-run relations.

Both types of investment exhibit a positive relationship with real per capita output in Kenya, and this appears to be stronger for private investment; a 10% increase in private investment leads to about 5.6% increase in output while a similar increase in government investment leads to a 3.0% increase. This suggests, as might be expected, that private investment is more productive. The negative association between aid and growth may be due to our use of aid loans and is consistent with the results in Section 3. Imports appear to play a positive role in the growth process, presumably by providing capital goods and the necessary intermediate inputs for firms. This suggests that imports have supported technology transfer and domestic investment. The output equation is error correcting: any deviation from the long-run equilibrium is corrected by about 27% in each subsequent period. The relatively low speed of adjustment may be due to structural rigidities in the economy.

The second vector is normalized on private investment. Government investment and imports are negatively related to private investment while aid loans have a significant positive correlation with private investment. These results suggest that government investment crowds out private investment, a matter of concern as public investment is less productive. Some possible reasons for this include the fact that it is likely that public investment competes for available resources, or could be producing output that substitutes for rather than complements private investment. In addition, there is a possibility that deficit financing, which has been a common feature of Kenya's fiscal management since the mid 1970s, leads to crowding out of private investment via its pressure on interest rates. This is consistent with the finding that aid loans have a negative association with income but a positive association with private investment (as they relax the deficit financing constraint). The negative correlation between imports and private investment is somewhat surprising. A possible explanation for this is that certain components of imports could be competing with domestic production. Excessive protection of domestic industries for nearly three decades of independence created uncompetitive industries and therefore when foreign trade was liberalized, most of the domestic firms were ill prepared for the ensuing external competition.

Our finding on the relationship between public and private investment contrasts with that of Matin and Wasow (1992). Over the period 1968–1988 covered in their study, they found a strong positive association between private and public investment. However, we believe our results are plausible on two counts: first, we cover a longer period (1964–2002) and take into account dynamic and system-wide interactions among variables, and second it could be true that government investment was more productive before the 1990s than after. Perhaps our study is capturing the strong negative effect of unproductive public investment since the 1990s, a period when there was also net repayment of aid loans. Foreign aid loans are positively related to private investment. Because aid loans go to the government, it can be argued that these loans finance government expenditures that have a direct beneficial effect on private investment, such as transport and communication systems and other infrastructure, but do not require domestic financing (through domestic borrowing or taxes). The negative correlation between public and private investment suggests that it is the (domestic) financing of public investment that has a crowding-out effect. Foreign resources ease the government budget constraint and reduce the need for government to borrow from the domestic credit market, in turn releasing funds to the private sector. Similarly, reduction of government domestic borrowing due to availability of external aid alleviates pressure on domestic interest rates.

A vector error correction model (VECM) was estimated starting with a general over-parameterized model, depicted in Equation (3), then subjected to a systematic reduction and testing process until a robust parsimonious model was obtained. This is reported in Table 5.

In the output equation, the growth rate of real per capita output depends positively on changes in past private investment and aid loans. It can be argued that the positive sign on loans means that in the short-run, aid is a less distortionary way of financing a deficit. The other variables do not seem to matter for growth in the short run. The re-

Table 5. *Parsimonious short-run (VECM) investment model*

Variable	Equation (1) (DYp)	Equation (2) (DPINV)	Equation (3) (DGINV)	Equation (4) (DLOAN)	Equation (5) (DIMPO)
Constant	1.96	10.10	6.61	14.27	−5.86
	(5.95)	**(3.64)**	**(2.41)**	**(3.26)**	**(−3.56)**
$DPINV_t$	–	–	−0.25	−0.18	0.35
	–	–	**(−2.00)**	(−0.91)	**(3.76)**
$DPINV_{t-1}$	0.04	−0.16	0.13	–	0.10
	(2.44)	(−1.03)	(0.99)	–	(1.06)
$GPINV_t$	−0.03	−0.33	–	–	0.27
	(−1.10)	(−1.52)	–	–	**(2.19)**
$DLOAN_t$	−0.02	−0.17	–	–	0.19
	(−1.20)	(−1.18)	–	–	**(2.45)**
$DLOAN_{t-1}$	0.04	0.13	0.15	0.61	−0.13
	(2.82)	(1.04)	(1.59)	**(4.37)**	**(−1.83)**
$DIMPO_t$	0.03	0.99	0.49	0.81	–
	(0.80)	**(3.76)**	**(2.76)**	**(2.58)**	–
$DIMPO_{t-1}$	–	–	0.41	−0.39	–
	–	–	**(2.09)**	(−1.28)	–
$DDs74$	−0.03	−0.30	–	−0.51	0.38
	(−1.22)	**(−1.59)**	–	**(−2.30)**	**(4.15)**
$DDs74_{-1}$	−0.02	−0.53	–	–	0.10
	(−0.81)	**(−2.87)**	–	–	(0.79)
$ECT1_{t-1}$	−0.39	−1.94	−0.91	−3.53	1.36
	(−4.89)	**(−2.93)**	(−1.62)	**(−3.86)**	**(3.72)**
$ECT2_{t-1}$	−0.22	−1.16	−0.87	−1.42	0.61
	(−6.30)	**(−3.92)**	**(−2.78)**	**(−2.88)**	**(3.29)**

Notes: Standard t-statistics in parentheses; figures in bold mean the coefficient is significant (at least at 10% level). Further over-identifying restrictions on the model were rejected by the likelihood ratio test and relevant diagnostics are satisfactory.

sults are consistent with the long-run finding that private investment is more productive than public investment (which has no short-run impact, perhaps because it finances projects with a long gestation period). The growth rate of private investment in the short-run depends positively on imports and negatively on the 1974 oil crisis impulse dummy. Perhaps what the positive import coefficient is showing is that in the short-run they serve as capital goods or intermediate inputs but in the long-run additional imports represent increased competition with domestic production. Furthermore, it could be the case that as the economy expands imports of consumables increase relative to imports of inputs, which hurts private investment. As for the dummy variable, our results confirm what would be expected in the short-run when there is a negative shock to the economy: an adverse effect on private investment and by implication on economic growth.

In the government investment equation, our results reveal a negative influence of private investment, which further underlines the negative correlation between the two types of investments. A possible interpretation is that when private investment is rising the government sees less need to expand investment. Current imports have a strong positive relationship with government investment. None of the other variables except the error and the constant terms appear to be significant in determining public investment.

Turning to the aid equation, our results suggest that changes in current imports and past foreign aid have a positive influence on growth of loans. Regarding the former, donors may be 'rewarding' increased demand for imports (from donors). Regarding the latter, it suggests that the greater the ability of a country to absorb foreign resources, the greater the likelihood that it would attract more aid. Investment – public and private – does not seem to be an important factor influencing growth of foreign aid in the short run. Growth of imports in the short run depend positively on changes in the current level of private and government investment, foreign aid as well as the 1974 dummy. As previously argued, most imports are needed as capital goods or intermediate inputs for both private and public investment. Thus the positive relationship between these two variables and imports confirm the theoretical expectation. Similarly, foreign aid is required to meet foreign exchange requirements for imports which explains the positive relationship. If the dummy captures the effect of the oil crisis, we would expect a negative relationship with imports because the effect of the 1973–1974 oil shock was to raise the prices of imported goods. One way to interpret the positive sign is to assume the dummy is capturing the increase in the value (cost) of imports. Matin and Wasow (1992) and Glenday and Ryan (2003) identify foreign exchange constraints as the main constraint on growth of imports in Kenya, especially the poor performance of imports over the 1983–1993 period. It is possible that the negative constant term is capturing, amongst other factors, policy interventions that constrained imports.

5. *Conclusion: has aid failed in Kenya?*

We have employed time series econometric techniques to investigate the relationships between fiscal aggregates, investment, aid and growth in Kenya. The results lend support to our broad hypothesis that aid does not impact on growth directly but through 'mediating variables', in our case fiscal variables and investment. Notwithstanding the limitations of multivariate time series analysis, our results suggest the presence of (at least) two channels, fiscal and investment, for aid to impact on growth. Furthermore, the results indicate that the effect of aid depends on the type of aid. Grants appear to contribute to growth by financing public spending in a non-distortionary manner. However, the positive impact is very weak, perhaps because grants have been relatively small. Aid loans, on the other hand, appear negatively associated with growth. Our inference is that this is because loans are sought to finance unanticipated deficits, and it is these deficits rather than adverse effects of aid that reduce growth (income).

There are a number of related findings. Government spending appears to have beneficial effects on growth in Kenya, whereas tax revenue is neutral. There is no evidence of the distortions associated with raising taxes having a direct negative influence on growth, but taxes may have an indirect positive effect through financing government expenditure. These results support the findings of M'Amanja and Morrissey (2005) who distinguish distortionary and non-distortionary taxes and productive and unproductive expenditures. Another important finding is that private investment appears significantly more productive than public investment, but is to some extent crowded out by public investment.

We draw three implications for policy in Kenya. First, the evidence suggests that government spending in its totality has contributed to per capita income and growth in Kenya. It cannot be presumed that this is an effect of government investment only, as the variable used was total spending, and investment is a relatively small share. A policy recommendation is that there is a need to re-examine the composition of government expenditure with a view to assessing the contribution of its components to efficiency and re-directing it to growth promoting activities. Furthermore, there is no evidence that the distortions associated with domestic taxes have retarded growth, suggesting that the tax system is not inefficient.

Second, there is a need to actively encourage private investment, as it appears significantly more productive than public investment, through measures such as mobilization of domestic savings and creation of a stable macroeconomic environment. This has implications for fiscal policy as there is a suggestion in our results that deficits encourage borrowing and public investment financed by domestic borrowing tends to crowd-out private investment. This is one issue that warrants further investigation. Aid is not irrelevant here: if aid is used to finance public spending, or foreign borrowing substitutes for domestic deficit financing, the possible crowding-out effect could be reduced. Furthermore, access to imported investment and intermediate goods seems to be important for private investment, and aid can play a role in relaxing foreign exchange constraints in financing imports.

Third, there are implications for the form of aid. In Kenya, it appears that expenditure and tax revenues are in effect beyond the direct control of government (i.e. they are difficult to adjust in the short-run), so aid loans is the instrument they adjust to meet fiscal deficits. The results suggest that the government takes out aid loans when there is a deficit to finance, and consequently aid loans are negatively associated with growth. Aid grants, on the other hand, are positively associated with growth; even if the grants are used to fund a deficit, they incur no future repayment obligations and therefore do not retard long-run income. In general, aid loans have been used largely as a borrowing instrument to substitute for tax effort. This undermines the effectiveness of aid in promoting growth. Aid to Kenya could be more effective if given in the form of grants, and associated with fiscal discipline.

Our results are no more than indicative as the analysis is somewhat limited, but do illustrate the rather complex relationships underlying effects of aid on growth, and as such go further than cross-country empirical studies. It is not only the case that the effects of aid are not direct, but also that an apparent adverse association between aid and growth may be due to mediating factors. For example, aid loans have a negative association with income not because the loans themselves reduce growth but because loans are sought when deficits are high, and high deficits (and the resulting debt burden) have an adverse impact. Similarly, the weak association between grants and growth is not a direct effect of grants, but rather arises because they finance government spending that contributes to income and/or means that deficits are lower than would otherwise be the case. Furthermore, implicit in our analysis is the observation that expected grant revenue is known in advance, and thus facilitates budget planning, whereas aid loans are an outcome of a budget 'failure' – the deficit is, for whatever reason, higher than planned.

Kenya is an example of an aid recipient that has experienced a poor growth record, but this is not evidence that aid has failed. In part, the weak positive contribution of aid reflects the relatively low level of grants to Kenya, as grants have the greatest positive effect through the fiscal channel. The observation that aid as recorded in the Kenyan budget is very low relative to what donors say they allocate to Kenya (the measure used in cross-country studies) also suggests that a large of share of aid allocated to Kenya is not directly spent in Kenya (although some may be donor projects that do not appear in the budget). The weak contribution to growth also reflects the evidence that the productivity of public investment (financed at least in part by aid) is low and tends to crowd-out private investment. To increase aid effectiveness in Kenya, more aid in the form of grants and increasing the productivity of investment, especially incentives to the private sector, appear necessary.

Appendix A. Cointegration tests for the fiscal model

Table A. Test statistics for cointegrating rank for the fiscal model

Rank	Null	Alt.	λ_{Trace} [Prob]	λ_{Trace} (T-nm)	Null	Alt.	λ_{Max} [Prob]	λ_{Max} (T-nm)
0	$r = 0$	$r \geqslant 1$	86.67[0.001]**	63.24[0.149]	$r = 0$	$r = 1$	38.15[0.011]*	27.84[0.228]
1	$r \leqslant 1$	$r \geqslant 2$	48.52[0.042]*	35.40[0.432]	$r \leqslant 1$	$r = 2$	24.14[0.131]	17.61[0.539]
2	$r \leqslant 2$	$r \geqslant 3$	24.38[0.191]*	17.79[0.591]	$r \leqslant 2$	$r = 3$	13.06[0.461]	9.53[0.787]
3	$r \leqslant 3$	$r \geqslant 4$	11.32[0.196]	8.26[0.446]	$r \leqslant 3$	$r = 4$	7.46[0.445]	5.45[0.688]
4	$r \leqslant 4$	$r = 5$	3.85[0.050]*	2.81[0.094]	$r \leqslant 4$	$r = 5$	3.85[0.050]*	2.81[0.094]

Note: Results of the trace and max tests are conflicting (both adjusted for small sample size and the unadjusted). The trace unadjusted test indicates at least two cointegrating vectors, but the max test at least one cointegrating vector. There is need to evoke other criteria for determining the number of cointegrating vectors (see M'Amanja *et al.*, 2005). A visual inspection of the plots of the cointegrating vectors reveals a stationary relation for the output vector, borderline cases for the expenditure and aid vectors, and a non-stationary vector for tax revenue. Economic theory allows possibility of two long-run relations describing the output-expenditure equilibrium and the fiscal relation. This theoretical expectation largely agrees with the outcome of the trace test and plots of cointegrating vectors. Consequently, we assume two cointegrating relationships for subsequent analysis.

Appendix B. Cointegration tests for the investment model

Table B. Test statistics for cointegrating rank for investment model

Rank	Null	Alt.	λ_{Trace} [Prob]	λ_{Trace} (T-nm)	Null	Alt.	λ_{Max} [Prob]	λ_{Max} (T-nm)
0	$r=0$	$r \geqslant 1$	101.38[0.000]**	73.98[0.021]*	$r=0$	$r=1$	37.40[0.015]*	27.29[0.256]
1	$r \leqslant 1$	$r \geqslant 2$	63.98[0.001]**	46.69[0.063]	$r \leqslant 1$	$r=2$	32.58[0.008]**	23.77[0.145]
2	$r \leqslant 2$	$r \geqslant 3$	31.40[0.032]*	22.92[0.258]	$r \leqslant 2$	$r=3$	20.79[0.054]	15.17[0.289]
3	$r \leqslant 3$	$r \geqslant 4$	10.61[0.240]	7.75[0.192]	$r \leqslant 3$	$r=4$	10.25[0.200]	7.48[0.443]
4	$r \leqslant 4$	$r=5$	0.37[0.543]	0.27[0.603]	$r \leqslant 4$	$r=5$	0.37[0.199]	0.27[0.603]

Note: The trace test (both adjusted for small sample size and the unadjusted) show at least two cointegration vectors. However, the critical values used by the econometric programme do not take into account inclusion of dummy variables which alters conventional critical values. It can be argued however that inclusion of one dummy may not alter significantly the critical values and therefore we may in fact assume two cointegrating vectors (see M'Amanja and Morrissey, 2006).

References

Bacha, E. (1990), A three-gap model of foreign transfers and the GDP growth rate in developing countries. *Journal of Development Economics* 32, 279–296.

Barro, R.J. (1990), Government spending in a simple model of endogenous growth. *Journal of Political Economy* 98, 103–125.

Barro, R.J., Sala-I-Martin, X. (1995), *Economic Growth*. McGraw-Hill, New York.

Burnside, C., Dollar, D. (2000), Aid, policies, and growth. *American Economic Review* 90, 847–868.

Clemens, M., Radelet, S., Bhavnani, R. (2004), Counting chickens when they hatch: the short-term effect of aid on growth. *CGD Working Paper Number* 44 (July). Centre for Global Development, Washington, DC.

Dalgaard, C., Hansen, H., Tarp, F. (2004), On the empirics of foreign aid and growth. *The Economic Journal* 114, F191–F216.

Easterly, W., Rebelo, S. (1993), Fiscal policy and economic growth: an empirical investigation. *Journal of Monetary Economics* 32, 417–458.

Favero, C. (2001), *Applied Macroeconometrics*. Oxford University Press, Oxford.

Glenday, G., Ryan, T. (2003), Trade liberalisation and economic growth in Kenya. In: Kimenyi, M.S., Mbaku, J.M., Mwaniki, N. (Eds.), *Restarting and Sustaining Economic Growth and Development in Africa: the Case of Kenya*. Ashgate, Aldershot.

Gomanee, K., Girma, S., Morrissey, O. (2005), Aid and growth in sub-Saharan Africa: accounting for transmission mechanisms. *Journal of International Development* 17, 1055–1076.

Hansen, H., Tarp, F. (2001), Aid and growth regressions. *Journal of Development Economics* 64, 547–570.

Harris, R. (1995), *Using Cointegration Analysis in Economic Modelling*. Prentice-Hall, New Jersey.

Hendry, D.F., Juselius, K. (2001), Explaining cointegration analysis: Part II. *The Energy Journal* 22, 75–120.

Hjertholm, P., Laursen, J., White, H. (2000), Foreign aid and the macroeconomy. In: Tarp, F. (Ed.), *Foreign Aid and Development*. Routledge, London, pp. 351–371 (Chapter 15).

Johansen, S. (1988), Statistical analysis of cointegrating vectors. *Journal of Economic Dynamics and Control* 12, 231–254.

Johansen, S., Juselius, K. (1990), Maximum likelihood estimation and inference on cointegration – with application to the demand for money. *Oxford Bulletin of Economics and Statistics* 52, 169–211.

Johansen, S., Juselius, K. (1992), Testing structural hypothesis in a multivariate cointegration analysis of the PPP for UK. *Journal of Econometrics* 53, 211–244.

Lensink, R., Morrissey, O. (2000), Aid instability as a measure of uncertainty and the positive impact of aid on growth. *Journal of Development Studies* 36, 31–49.

Levine, R., Renelt, D. (1992), A sensitivity analysis of cross-country regressions. *American Economic Review* 82, 942–963.

McGillivray, M., Morrissey, O. (2004), Fiscal effects of aid. In: Addison, T., Roe, A. (Eds.), *Fiscal Policy for Development*. Palgrave/WIDER, Basingstoke, pp. 72–96.

M'Amanja, D., Morrissey, O. (2005), Fiscal policy and economic growth in Kenya. School of Economics, University of Nottingham: *CREDIT Research Paper* 05/06 (under Research Papers at http://www.nottingham.ac.uk/econmics/credit).

M'Amanja, D., Morrissey, O. (2006), Foreign aid, investment and growth in Kenya: a time series analysis. School of Economics, University of Nottingham: *CREDIT Research Paper* 06/04 http://www.nottingham.ac.uk/econmics/credit.

M'Amanja, D., Lloyd, T. Morrissey, O. (2005) Fiscal aggregates, aid and growth in Kenya: a vector autoregressive (VAR) analysis. School of Economics, University of Nottingham: *CREDIT Research Paper* 05/07 (under Research Papers at http://www.nottingham.ac.uk/econmics/credit).

Matin, K., Wasow, B. (1992), Adjustment and private investment in Kenya. *World Bank Policy Research Working Papers WPS* 878, The World Bank, Washington, DC.

Milesi-Ferretti, G., Roubini, N. (1995), Growth effects of income and consumption taxes: positive and normative analysis. *NBER Working Paper Series WP* 5317.

Morrissey, O. (2006), Aid or trade, or aid and trade? *The Australian Economic Review* 39, 78–88.

Mosley, P., Hudson, J., Horrell, S. (1987), Aid, the public sector and the market in less developed countries. *Economic Journal* 97, 616–641.

Osei, R., Morrissey, O., Lloyd, T. (2005), The fiscal effects of aid in Ghana. *Journal of International Development* 17, 1037–1054.

Rodrik, D. (2003), *In Search of Prosperity: Analytic Narratives on Economic Growth*. Princeton University Press, Princeton, NJ.

Roodman, D. (2004), *The anarchy of numbers: aid, development and cross-country empirics*. Centre for Global Development, Washington, DC, mimeo.

Ryan, T. (2002), Policy timeline and time series data for Kenya: an analytical data compendium. *KIPPRA Special Report*, No. 3, Kenya Institute for Public Policy Research and Analysis, Nairobi.

World Bank (1998), *Assessing Aid: What Works, What Doesn't, and Why*. Oxford University Press for the World Bank, Washington, DC.

CHAPTER 17

What Does Aid to Africa Finance?[*]

Shantayanan Devarajan, Andrew Sunil Rajkumar and Vinaya Swaroop

The World Bank, Washington, DC 20433, USA

Abstract

The recent increase in aid to Africa, alongside increases in special-purpose aid, has revived interest in the question of the fungibility of aid – the notion that, if a donor gives aid for a project that the recipient government would have undertaken anyway, then the aid is financing some expenditure other than the intended project. That aid in this sense may be "fungible", while long recognized, has recently been receiving some empirical support. This paper focuses on sub-Saharan Africa, the region with the largest GDP share of aid. It presents results indicating that aid may be partially fungible, and suggests some reasons why.

Keywords: Foreign aid, fungibility, developing countries, public expenditure, sub-Saharan Africa

JEL classifications: E62, O23

1. Introduction

Two of the more significant developments in foreign aid over the last five years have been the increase in aid volumes to sub-Saharan Africa, and the proliferation of single-purpose grants, including the Education for all initiative and the Global Fund for AIDS, TB and Malaria. The juxtaposition of these two developments has revived interest in the question of whether earmarked aid is "fungible".

The concept of fungibility can best be illustrated with an example. Suppose an aid donor gives money to build a primary school in a poor country. If the recipient government would have built the school anyway, then the consequence of the aid is to release resources for the government to spend on other items. Thus, while the primary school

---

[*] The findings, interpretations, and conclusions expressed in this paper are entirely those of the authors. They do not necessarily represent the views of the World Bank, its Executive Directors, or the countries they represent. The authors acknowledge helpful comments they received from Alan Gelb, Rino Schiavo-Campo, Howard Pack, Lant Pritchett, and seminar participants at AERC, IFPRI and the World Bank.

THEORY AND PRACTICE OF FOREIGN AID
VOLUME 1   ISSN: 1574-8715
DOI: 10.1016/S1574-8715(06)01017-7

may still get built, the aid is financing some other expenditure (or tax reduction) by the government. This could be problematic, especially from the donor's perspective, if the released resources of the government end up financing "unproductive" public expenditures.

That foreign aid is in this sense "fungible" has been recognized for a long time. In 1947, Paul Rosenstein-Rodin, then Deputy Director of the World Bank's Economics Department, noted: "When the World Bank thinks it is financing an electric power station, it is really financing a brothel". In the mid-1950s, some of the Bank's member countries asked for a revision of its policy of lending only for infrastructure because they wanted to borrow for health and education projects. The World Bank's president responded that they could finance their health and education projects with the funds that were released by the Bank's financing of infrastructure.

In light of the increased focus on sub-Saharan Africa, both as the recipient of scaled-up aid, as well as a major destination of single-purpose grants (such as GFATM), this paper examines the extent of aid fungibility in Africa. Before proceeding, we note that the two anecdotes above illustrate some important aspects of fungibility. First, the question of what aid ultimately finances is interesting only if the preferences of the donor are different from those of the recipient. If they had identical preferences, then it would not matter if the aid were given to a specific project or as budgetary support. Second, when donor and recipient preferences differ, it is still not clear whether the presence of fungibility is good or bad. It all depends on what the government does with the resources that are released by the aid projects – whether it builds pyramids or health clinics. Third, regardless of what the government does with the released resources, aid fungibility has important implications for how donors evaluate the impact of their aid. To the extent that aid is fungible, the development impact of the electric power station loan is not captured by the rate of return of that project (Devarajan *et al.* (1997)).

Despite its importance to policy, the question of the fungibility of aid remained at the level of anecdotes for over four decades. Recently, however, there has been a flurry of quantitative work, triggered on the one hand by heightened concern over the effectiveness of foreign aid (Boone (1995), World Bank (1998), Easterly *et al.* (2004), Asra *et al.* (2005), Easterly (2005)), and on the other hand, by the availability of data (Cashel-Cordo and Craig (1990), Gang and Khan (1991), Pack and Pack (1990, 1993, 1996), Khilji and Zampelli (1994), Feyzioglu *et al.* (1998), Swaroop *et al.* (2000), Njeru (2003), and Cratty and Van de Walle (2005)).

The recent work has shown that foreign aid is fungible in certain countries and in certain sectors. For instance, Pack and Pack find that aid is totally fungible in the Dominican Republic, nonfungible in Indonesia and partially fungible in Sri Lanka. Swaroop *et al.* (2000) show that aid to India is fungible at the national level, but non-fungible at the state level. Using a panel data set, Feyzioglu *et al.* (1998) find that foreign aid is fungible in agriculture, education and health, partially fungible in power and non-fungible in transport and communication. Njeru (2003) found that increases in foreign aid to Kenya resulted in less than one-for-one increases in overall public spending. Cratty and Van de Walle (2005) found evidence of partial fungibility in

World Bank financing for a rural road rehabilitation project in Vietnam. None of these authors has offered a reasonable explanation for their results.

No region will be more affected by the recent changes to foreign aid than sub-Saharan Africa, which receives three times more foreign aid per capita than other developing countries. Some of the disappointing results on the effectiveness of aid in Africa may be due to its fungibility. Yet, none of the above mentioned studies on aid fungibility has focused on Africa, except for the paper by Njeru (2003) which looked only at fungibility at the macroeconomic level in Kenya and not between sectors.

The purpose of this paper is to fill these two lacunae in our understanding of the fungibility of foreign aid: why aid is fungible or nonfungible, and the extent of aid fungibility in Africa at the macroeconomic level as well as between sectors. In Section 2, we present a model of aid fungibility. In Section 3, we estimate the model using data from Africa. Our estimates permit us to compare the extent of aid fungibility in Africa with respect to other countries, as well as identify some of the reasons why aid may or may not be fungible in Africa. Section 4 presents some concluding remarks about the implications of our results for policy and future research.

2. A model of semi-fungible aid

In this section, we present a simple model that illuminates why aid may or may not be fungible. A variant of the models in Pack and Pack (1993) and Feyzioglu *et al.* (1998), the model incorporates the essential element in any discussion about fungibility, namely, a difference in the objective functions of the recipient and donor. Consider, therefore, an aid recipient with an objective function over two types of expenditure, g_1 and g_2, and domestic revenue R. In the absence of aid, the recipient's problem is to maximize

$$U(g_1, g_2) = g_1^{\alpha} g_2^{1-\alpha} \quad \text{subject to}$$

$$R = p_1 g_1 + p_2 g_2.$$

The recipient's problem gives rise to the standard optimal solutions, g_1^* and g_2^*. Now suppose the donor has a different objective function over the recipient's expenditure on g_1 and g_2:

$$U(g_1, g_2) = g_1^{\beta} g_2^{1-\beta} \quad \text{with } \beta > \alpha > 0.$$

Thus, the donor would like the recipient to spend more on good 1 than the recipient would otherwise. For example, good 1 could be education, which the donor has targeted as a priority sector. The donor's aid policy, then, is to give the recipient $(\beta - \alpha)R$ to spend on g_1.[1]

---

[1] As noted above, we are only modeling foreign aid in the case when there is a difference in the objective functions of the recipient and the donor. Thus, $\beta \neq \alpha$. Note that even with this aid, the recipients' expenditure on good 2 may not be optimal from the donor's perspective. However, what we are modeling here is the fact that we observe aid directed at particular sectors, that is, projects.

Given the difference in objective functions, the recipient would like to treat this aid as budgetary support. But there are costs to treating earmarked aid as fully fungible. For instance, it could lead to a cutback in aid the following year. We assume these costs (or, equivalently, the donor's ability to monitor expenditures) are a function of the deviation between the donor's desired total expenditure on good 1, $p_1 g_1^{**}$, and the actual amount spent on that good. The recipient's new optimization problem, therefore, is to maximize

$$U(g_1, g_2) = g_1^\alpha g_2^{1-\alpha} \quad \text{subject to}$$
$$R + (\beta - \alpha)R = p_1 g_1 + p_2 g_2 + \theta(p_1 g_1^{**} - p_1 g_1)$$

where θ is the cost of treating earmarked aid as fully fungible. Although this cost is probably borne in the future (in terms of less foreign aid than would otherwise have been given), we incorporate it as a charge today by considering the present value of this future cost.

An interior solution to the above problem exists if $\theta < (\beta - \alpha)/\beta$:

$$p_1 g_1^{***} = \frac{\alpha(1 - \beta\theta)}{1 - \theta} R + \frac{\alpha}{1 - \theta} AID \tag{1}$$

where $AID = (\beta - \alpha)R$. If $\theta \geq (\beta - \alpha)/\beta$, the cost of treating earmarked aid as fully fungible is so prohibitively high that $p_1 g_1^{***} = p_1 g_1^{**} = \alpha R + (\beta - \alpha)R$, i.e., aid is spent on g_1 as desired by the donor. On the other hand, when $\theta = 0$, there is no penalty for treating aid as budgetary support, so the coefficient for R becomes the same as that for AID. These two scenarios are illustrated in Figure 1.

The most important feature, however, is that Equation (1) lends itself to econometric estimation, since the variables R and AID are in principle observable. By estimating a variant of Equation (1), in the next section, we attempt to estimate how fungible aid is in different sectors.

Before proceeding to the empirical estimation, we treat one other issue that is often raised in discussing aid fungibility: the possibility that aid does not release resources for other expenditures but instead reduces tax effort. From the reasoning of the previous section, if the aid were earmarked for some expenditure that would have taken place anyway, the recipient government could use the funds released for some other spending or to reduce the amount of taxes it collects. In fact, if the marginal cost of taxation is high, this may be a prudent strategy for the recipient. To capture this possibility, we rewrite the recipient's utility function as

$$U(g_1, g_2, 1 - R)$$

where the $(1 - R)$ term represents the share of gross domestic product (GDP) available to the private sector. The recipient's problem now is to maximize

$$U(g_1, g_2, 1 - R) = g_1^{\alpha_1} g_2^{\alpha_2} (1 - R)^{\alpha_3} \quad \text{subject to}$$
$$R = p_1 g_1 + p_2 g_2.$$

The first-order conditions to this problem yield $R = 1 - \alpha_3$. When the country receives aid in the amount a (assume it is intended for budgetary support), the solution to the

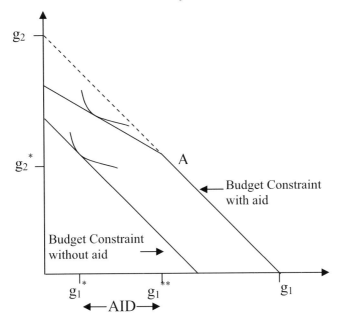

Fig. 1. A model of semi-fungible aid.

new maximization problem yields $R = 1 - \alpha_3 - \alpha_3 a$. Thus, the amount of aid that is diverted for reducing tax effort will be a function of the relative weight of the tax distortion (α_3) compared with the productivity of the other two expenditures in the utility function. In short, the recipient has the same incentive to divert aid toward tax reduction as towards other expenditures: the amount of diversion depends on the productivity of expenditures and the costs of taxation.

The above model describes fairly closely the situation of several African countries. In the past several decades, sub-Saharan Africa has received more foreign aid – both in gross as well as net terms – than any other region. Between 1970 and 1995, average per capita aid to all sub-Saharan African countries was US$23 (measured in current dollars); the average for all other developing countries was less than US$8. A number of studies have documented the aid experience of Africa.[2] In analyzing the growth performance of sub-Saharan Africa, Easterly and Levine (1993) looked at, among other variables, the impact of external income. Their main finding was that an annual increase in external income – from better terms of trade and transfers (grants and loans) – equal to 1 percentage point of gdp raises growth by 0.6 percentage points. Helleiner (1992) and Demery and Hussain (1993) have argued that during the 1980s foreign aid to sub-Saharan Africa financed imports and aid was instrumental in allowing several

---

[2] See World Bank (1994) for a review.

countries to move out of the import-compression phase. Were aid flows to Africa financing expenditures that would otherwise not be made? Were aid-financed imports truly marginal? Has aid to sub-Saharan Africa been fungible? If so, why, and if not, why not? These are the issues to which we now turn.

3. Empirical analysis

The model in Section 2 develops links between foreign aid and fiscal variables. In our empirical analysis, we examine these links. Using a panel database from 18 sub-Saharan African countries (more on this below), we first estimate the statistical relationship between foreign assistance, measured in gross terms, and total public spending. To determine which expenditure items were funded by foreign aid, we examine the link between total foreign aid and various public-spending activities. The impact of earmarked sector-specific aid on sectoral spending is estimated next. Finally, we examine whether the "fungibility coefficient" is affected by donors' monitoring costs. Specifically, we assess whether the number of aid donors in a particular country – a proxy for monitoring costs – affects the fungibility analysis.

3.1. Empirical research on aid fungibility

Empirical research on the fungibility of aid has looked at individual countries as well as a cross-section of countries. In the former category, Gang and Khan (1991), Gupta (1993), Swaroop *et al.* (2000), McGuire (1978), Pack and Pack (1990, 1993, 1996), among others, have analyzed aid fungibility across the sectoral classification of expenditures. In a study of foreign aid to Indonesia, Pack and Pack (1990) did not find any evidence of fungibility across sectoral expenditures. On the other hand, in the Dominican Republic they (Pack and Pack (1993)) found evidence of substantial diversion of foreign aid away from its intended purposes. The main innovation in Swaroop *et al.* (2000) is to incorporate the intergovernmental fiscal link in examining economic fungibility of external assistance in India. Using data on India, a federal country, they find that external assistance intended for development purposes merely substitutes for spending that governments – central and states – would have undertaken anyway; the funds freed by aid are spent on nondevelopment activities in general and administrative services in particular. Moreover, in passing external assistance to states, the central government makes a reduction in other transfers to states.

More recently, Njeru (2003) found that an additional shilling of foreign aid in Kenya led to just 88 cents more in overall public spending. However, an additional shilling in domestic resources was found to result in 1.11 shilling more of public spending. The study by Cratty and Van De Walle (2005) concluded, after controlling for endogeneity bias, that about a third of World Bank financing for a rural road rehabilitation project had in effect been used for purposes other than that intended.

The individual country studies, while important, do not allow any cross-country generalization, which could be useful information to the donor community. The study by Feyzioglu *et al.* (1998) uses a cross-country panel data set to analyze the relationship between sector-specific foreign aid and government expenditure on the agriculture, defense, education, energy, health, and transport/communications sectors. They find that developing country governments receiving earmarked concessionary loans for agriculture, education and energy, reduce their own resources going to these sectors and use it elsewhere; only loans to the transport and communication sector are fully spent on purposes intended by donors. There are a few other cross-country studies that have analyzed the issue of fungibility. Cashel-Cordo and Craig (1990) used a sample of 46 developing countries to analyze whether or not foreign aid changes the composition of government expenditure. The expenditure components in their analysis are, however, limited to defense and nondefense spending. The study by Khilji and Zampelli (1994) also looks at defense and nondefense expenditures in examining the fungibility of U.S. aid among eight major aid recipient countries.

3.2. Data, choice of variables and sample statistics

Our empirical analysis is based on a panel database that has annual observations on 18 sub-Saharan African countries from 1971 to 1995. The countries included in the sample are: Botswana, Burkina Faso, Cameroon, Ethiopia, Ghana, The Gambia, Kenya, Liberia, Lesotho, Madagascar, Malawi, Mauritius, Nigeria, Sudan, Swaziland, Zaire, Zambia, and Zimbabwe. The sample choice – number of countries and time period – was based on data availability for all the relevant variables, subject to the constraint that at least 10 years of complete data had to be available for each country in the sample. (For more information on the sample selection method and data sources, see the Data Appendix A.) The panel data are organized along three dimensions: (i) foreign aid variables; (ii) fiscal variables (public spending and revenue); and (iii) income and control variables.

(i) *Foreign aid data.* Our main aid variable is the total annual gross disbursement of Official Development Assistance (ODA) by all bilateral and multilateral sources, reported in an aid publication of the Organization of Economic Co-operation and Development (OECD). ODA has two components: grants and concessionary loans. To examine the impact of sector specific aid on sectoral spending, we had to use concessionary loans as the aid variable since no sector-specific information on grants is available. The data on sector-specific concessionary loans are available from the World Bank database. Data on total aid were also used to derive the variable we used as a proxy for the level of monitoring exerted on aid recipients.

(ii) *Fiscal data.* Our main source of fiscal data (public spending and revenue) is the International Monetary Fund's (IMF) database on Government Finance Statistics. In the definition of total public spending, we have included principal payments on concessionary loans. This adjustment was made because we were interested in finding out how much, if at all, aid was being used to finance principal payments due on past loans. For this reason, we also measure foreign aid in gross (as opposed to net) terms though we do not know if part of the aid was given for debt rescheduling or was an untied budgetary support. In terms of the composition of public spending we collected data for our sample countries on current, capital, and loan repayments on the one hand, and sectoral (agriculture, education, energy, health, industry, transport and communication) spending on the other. We were also interested in finding out if any of the aid money was channeled towards interest payments on foreign debt. We therefore obtained information on this variable for each country from the OECD database.

(iii) *Data on income and control variables.* The database includes data on GDP, infant mortality, gross primary and secondary school enrollment rates, population and the share of agriculture in national income.

Table 1 shows the summary statistics for the 18-country sample. Measured in 1995 U.S. dollars the mean per capita GDP over the period 1970 through 1995 is US$837. Over this period, the cross-country means range from a low of $178 (Ethiopia) to $1,951 (Mauritius).

The mean size of government (measured as the share of total government spending in GDP) in these countries is close to 28 percent. Once again we see a large variation in terms of cross-country means: The range is from 11.2 percent for Burkina Faso to 52.7 percent for Lesotho. The average share of foreign aid in GDP for this group of sub-Saharan African countries is 10 percent. Nigeria, a major oil producer and exporter, is at the lower end (0.2 percent of GDP). When aid is measured as a percentage of GDP,

Table 1. Summary statistics (constant per capita 1995US$, except ratios which are in percent)

Variable	Sample mean	Standard deviation	Minimum [country mean]	Maximum [country mean]
1. Government expenditure				
Total expenditure	249	233	39 (Burkina Faso)	691 (Botswana)
Capital expenditure	58	58	5 (Burkina Faso)	252 (Botswana)
Current expenditure	185	188	32 (Burkina Faso)	525 (Botswana)
Repayments on concessionary loans	5	11	0.50 (Zaire)	12 (Swaziland)
Share of total expenditure in GDP	27.8	11.8	11.2 (Burkina Faso)	52.7 (Lesotho)
2. Foreign aid				
Total aid	62	46	2 (Nigeria)	151 (Botswana)
Concessionary loans	21	19	1 (Nigeria)	40 (Swaziland)
Grants	40	36	2 (Nigeria)	119 (Botswana)
Share of total aid in GDP	10.0	8.0	0.2 (Nigeria)	20.8 (Gambia)
3. Gross domestic product	837	627	178 (Ethiopia)	1,951 (Mauritius)

Note:

1. The above numbers are for our sample of 280 observations, from 18 sub-Saharan African countries. (See Data Appendix A for more details.)
2. Foreign aid above refers to Official Development Assistance as reported by OECD.

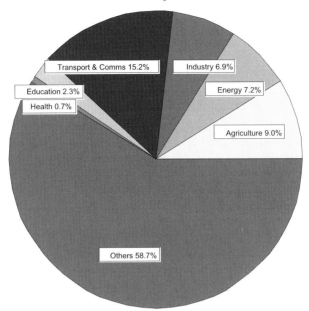

Fig. 2.   Breakdown of concessionary loans.

The Gambia is the largest recipient. However, in per capita terms, Botswana is the country in the sample that received the highest foreign aid. Finally, roughly two-thirds of total aid is in the form of grants for this group of countries.

Figures 2 and 3 show the sectoral breakdown of concessionary loans and government expenditure, respectively.[3] Almost 40 percent of the concessionary loans have gone to four sectors: agriculture, energy, industry, and transport and communications. It is clear from the figure that there were not too many concessional loans to education and health.[4] Among the six sectors, education accounts for most of the public spending. Next are transport and communication and agriculture. As a crude indicator, these figures signal that donor and recipient preferences may not be identical.

3.3. Regression analysis

Foreign aid fungibility is analyzed by estimating the following three equations:

$$G_{i,t} = \alpha_{0,i} + \alpha_1 Aid_{i,t} + \alpha_2 GDP_{i,t-1} + \varepsilon_{i,t} \tag{2}$$

for country i ($i = 1, \ldots, I$) at time t ($t = 1, \ldots, T$);

---

[3] Concessionary loans to "other" sectors include multi-sector loans, balance of payments support, administrative budget support, and loans to sectors that cannot be identified.

[4] It is possible that a lot of assistance was given to education and health sectors in the form of grants. Lack of data precludes us from analyzing the composition of grants.

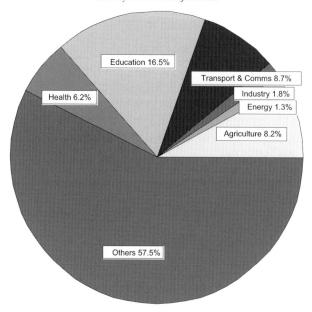

Fig. 3. Breakdown of government expenditure.

$$G_{i,t}^{E_j} = \delta_{0,i} + \delta_1 GDP_{i,t-1} + \delta_2 Aid_{i,t} + \delta_3\left(G_{i,t}^N - \bar{G}_{i,t}^N\right) + v_{i,t} \tag{3}$$

where E_j $\{j = 1, 2, 3\}$ are current, capital and principal repayment expenditures and G^N is total domestic resources defined as total expenditures net of foreign aid. $G_{i,t}^N$ is estimated as

$$\bar{G}_{i,t}^N = \beta_{0,i} + \beta_1 Aid_{i,t} + \beta_2 GDP_{i,t-1}. \tag{3'}$$

This two-stage estimation procedure is used because foreign aid affects the composition of public spending directly as well as indirectly (more on this below). Similarly, for each sector s $(s = 1, \ldots, S)$ we have:

$$G_{i,s,t} = \lambda_{0,i,s} + \lambda_{1,s} GDP_{i,t-1} + \lambda_2 Cloan_{i,s,t} + \lambda_{3,s}\left(G_{i,s,t}^N - \bar{G}_{i,s,t}^N\right)$$
$$+ \lambda_{4,s}(Tloan_{i,t} - Cloan_{i,s,t}) + \lambda_{5,s} TGrants_{i,t} + \eta_{i,s,t} \tag{4}$$

where is estimated as:

$$\bar{G}_{i,s,t}^N = \phi_{0,i,s} + \phi_{1,s} GDP_{i,t-1} + \phi_2 Cloan_{i,s,t} + \phi_{3,s}(Tloan_{i,t} - Cloan_{i,s,t})$$
$$+ \phi_{4,s} TGrants_{i,t}. \tag{4'}$$

Equation (2) examines the impact of total foreign aid on the government's budget. This model incorporates the possibility that if the aid was earmarked for some expenditure that would have taken place anyway, the recipient government could use the funds released for some other spending or to reduce the amount of taxes it collects.

In Section 2, we derived the condition that links public spending on good i with domestic revenue R and foreign aid (for example, see Equation (1)). Equations (3) and (4) estimate this relationship for various types of public expenditure. However, we know that domestic resources may change with a change in foreign aid. Since we are interested in the effects on public expenditure of domestic resources and foreign aid, independently of each other, we control for the impact of aid on total domestic resources. This is done using a two-stage estimation process. Equation (3′) indicates the first stage estimation for capital and current expenditure, and for principal repayments. The residuals from Equation (3′) are then used in place of in Equation (3), which is the second-stage estimation. Similarly, the residuals from Equation (4′) are used in place of G^N in Equation (4), which estimates the impact of sector aid and domestic resources on sector expenditure.

The variables in the above mentioned three regressions are (all measured in 1995 US\$, per capita terms):

$GDP_{i,t}$: Gross domestic product for country i at time t;
$G_{i,t}$: Total government expenditure;
$G^N_{i,t}$: Total government expenditure (net of foreign aid);
$G^{E_j}_{i,t}$: Government expenditure for current, capital or principal repayment purposes, where E_j $\{j = 1, 2, 3\}$ is current, capital or principal repayment expenditure, respectively;
$G_{i,s,t}$: Government expenditure in sector s;
$Aid_{i,t}$: Total gross ODA disbursement;
$CLoan_{i,s,t}$: Gross concessionary loan disbursement to sector s;
$TLoan_{i,t}$: Total concessionary loans to all sectors;
$TGrants_{i,t}$: Total grants to all sectors;
$\varepsilon_{i,t}, v_{i,t} \& \eta_{i,s,t}$: White noise error terms for the three equations.

We would ideally like to include sector-specific grants in Equation (4). However, data on grant disbursements are available only at the aggregate level, and not by sector (see Section 3.2 above). Thus we have to use concessionary loans as our sector-aid variable.

Loans to a particular sector may be correlated with loans to other sectors and with grants. To avoid bias in our estimates, we include the latter as additional right-hand side variables in Equations (4′) and (4), although these are not the variable coefficients we are primarily interested in.

Table 2 presents the estimates of Equations (2), (3) and (3′) which are all estimated under the null hypothesis that the coefficient of the country dummy variable, $\alpha_{0,1}$, is a fixed parameter. If, however, the Hausman test rejects the null hypothesis that the appropriate model is fixed effects then the random effects model is estimated.[5]

---

[5] In the fixed effects model, α_0, i, the country dummy parameter, is a fixed coefficient. In the random effects model these parameters are assumed to be independent random variables with a fixed mean and variance, i.e., $\alpha_{0,i} = \alpha_0 + \varepsilon_0$. Hausman has developed a test, which shows that under the null hypothesis

Table 2. Least squares regressions: government expenditure on foreign aid

Equation	(2.1)	(2.2)	(2.3)	(2.4)	(2.5)
Dependent variable	Total expenditure	Domestic resources[2]	Capital expenditure[3]	Current expenditure[3]	Principal repayments[3]
Constant	2.59	2.59	0.93	1.93	−0.25
	(0.84)	(0.84)	(0.69)	(1.37)	(−0.39)
GDP_{t-1}	0.11	0.11	0.03	0.08	0.001
	(4.89)	(4.89)	(3.21)	(7.81)	(0.25)
Foreign aid[4]	0.89	−0.11	0.28	0.30	0.31
	(5.89)	(−0.72)	(4.30)	(4.31)	(10.07)
Residuals from regression (2.2)			0.28	0.72	0.007
			(10.03)	(24.75)	(0.56)
Overall R-squared	0.22	0.14	0.34	0.74	0.29
Model[5]	Fixed	Fixed	Random	Random	Random

Notes:

1. Before regressing, all variables were converted to constant 1995 US$ per capita. Regressions were done in first differences based on a sample of 280 observations, from 18 countries (see Data Appendix A for more details). Parentheses indicate t-statistics.
2. The variable "Domestic Resources" is defined as all expenditure financed from domestic resources, i.e., total expenditure minus foreign aid.
3. Total expenditure is divided into three components: capital, current, and principal repayments. The latter include only repayments on foreign concessionary loans.
4. Foreign aid is defined as Official Development Assistance (the definition used by the Organization for Economic Co-operation and Development).
5. Model indicates whether the country dummies in the regression represent a fixed effects or a random effects model. The Hausman test statistic was used to select the appropriate model.

Regression (2.1) shows a positive and statistically significant relationship between total public spending and the total gross disbursement of ODA. The regression shows that a dollar increase in foreign aid leads to an increase of 0.89 cents in total government spending; the remaining aid is used for tax relief.[6] Moreover, a dollar increase in last year's GDP leads to an increase of 11 cents in government expenditures. This evidence suggests that in this sample of 18 sub-Saharan African countries, very little aid, if any, is being used for tax relief. At the margin, most

---

the fixed effects model is appropriate and the preferred estimator is least squares with dummy variables. If, however, the fixed effects model is rejected in favor of the random effects model then the preferred estimator is generalized least squares. For details, see Hausman (1978).

[6] In some developing countries, not all foreign aid goes through the budget. Our aid data (from OECD sources) are likely to be different from that of budgetary aid receipts of the sub-Saharan African governments. It is therefore possible that some of the other 11 cents of the marginal dollar in aid represents extra-budgetary aid.

Table 3. Least squares regressions: government expenditure on concessionary loans and grants

Equation	(3.1)	(3.2)	(3.3)	(3.4)	(3.5)
Dependent variable	Total expenditure	Domestic resources[2]	Capital expenditure[3]	Current expenditure[3]	Principal repayments[3]
Constant	2.59	2.59	0.95	2.01	−0.36
	(0.84)	(0.84)	(0.70)	(1.44)	(−0.63)
GDP_{t-1}	0.11	0.11	0.03	0.08	0.001
	(4.88)	(4.89)	(3.21)	(7.95)	(0.20)
Concessionary loans[4]	0.89	−0.11	0.32	0.51	0.06
	(3.81)	(−0.44)	(3.20)	(4.89)	(1.30)
Grants[4]	0.89	−0.11	0.25	0.14	0.51
	(4.42)	(−0.52)	(2.87)	(1.54)	(13.67)
Residuals from regression (3.2)			0.28	0.72	0.01
			(10.02)	(25.07)	(0.61)
Overall R-squared	0.22	0.14	0.34	0.74	0.43
Model	Fixed	Fixed	Random	Random	Random

Notes:

1. See notes 1, 2, 3, and 5 of Table 2.
2. Official Development Assistance is the aid variable. It is subdivided into its two components: grants and concessionary loans.

aid is associated – in a statistical sense – with an increase in government spending.

Regression (2.2) is estimated to control for the effect of foreign aid and GDP on the domestic resources of the government. The residuals of this equation are used as an exogenous variable in the subsequent equations reported in this table. In turn, this variable represents the true exogenous shock to a country's domestic resources. Regression (2.3), which includes expenditure according to the economic classification of IMF's Government Financial Statistics, indicates that roughly 28 cents of an additional dollar in ODA is spent on government's capital expenditure. Moreover, the coefficient of ODA in regression (2.4) shows that 30 cents of the dollar increase in aid goes toward current expenditure. These findings may not be necessarily bad for at least two reasons. First, parts of foreign aid could be designed for current expenditure related activities. Second, several components of current expenditure, such as operations and maintenance, may have higher rates of return than capital expenditure.[7] Finally, the aid coefficient in regression (2.5) shows that 31 cents of the marginal dollar are being used to finance principal repayments on the foreign concessionary loans. A comparison of

[7] In a study of 43 developing countries over 20 years, Devarajan *et al.* (1996) show that the only broad public expenditure category that is associated with higher economic growth is the current expenditure.

Table 4. *Panel data regressions: sectoral expenditure and concessionary loans*

Equation	(4.1)	(4.2)	(4.3)	(4.4)	(4.5)	(4.6)	(4.7)	(4.8)	(4.9)
Dependent variable	Total	Agriculture	Energy	Industry	T&C	Education[2]	Education without Botswana[2]	Health	Other[3]
Constant	2.59	−1.21	−0.04	−0.23	−0.11	0.26	3.00**	−0.62	2.41**
	(0.84)	(−0.92)	(−0.15)	(−0.68)	(−0.13)	(0.17)	(2.08)	(−1.20)	(2.30)
GDP_{t-1}	0.11**	0.01	0.002	0.004	0.01*	0.02**	0.01**	0.004**	0.06*
	(4.89)	(1.33)	(1.25)	(1.61)	(1.82)	(5.20)	(3.78)	(3.20)	(8.27)
Foreign aid	0.89**								
	(5.87)								
Concessionary loans to sector		−0.04	0.13*	0.11	0.36**	−0.80**	0.98**	0.26	0.65**
		(−0.45)	(1.72)	(1.57)	(2.62)	(−2.93)	(2.10)	(0.66)	(6.50)
Concessionary loans to all other sectors		0.11**	0.004	0.002	−0.03	−0.05	−0.06*	0.002	0.13
		(2.63)	(0.24)	(0.07)	(−0.50)	(−1.60)	(−1.77)	(0.15)	(1.26)
Total grants (to all sectors)		0.10**	−0.03	0.01	0.09*	0.08**	0.07*	0.03**	0.12*
		(2.78)	(−1.64)	(0.58)	(1.67)	(2.50)	(1.89)	(2.80)	(1.80)
Agriculture as share of GDP_{t-1}		0.05							
		(1.14)							
Primary school enrolment rate$_{t-1}$						0.03	−0.007		
						(1.17)	(−0.28)		
Secondary school Enrolment rate$_{t-1}$						−0.06	−0.11**		
						(−1.25)	(−2.42)		
Infant mortality rate$_{t-1}$								0.008*	
								(1.72)	

Table 4. *(Continued)*

Equation	(4.1)	(4.2)	(4.3)	(4.4)	(4.5)	(4.6)	(4.7)	(4.8)	(4.9)
Dependent variable	Total	Agriculture	Energy	Industry	T&C	Education[2]	Education without Botswana[2]	Health	Other[3]
Residuals from domestic resources regression		0.07** (6.66)	0.01** (2.50)	0.02** (2.87)	0.13** (7.44)	0.14** (13.19)	0.12** (10.75)	0.04** (10.46)	0.57** (26.90)
R-squared	0.22	0.20	0.06	0.06	0.23	0.49	0.40	0.36	0.78
Model	Fixed	Random	Random	Random	Random	Random	Random	Random	Random

Notes:

1. The large negative coefficient of "concessionary loans to sector" in the education regression is reversed when Botswana is dropped. Botswana is hence an outlier; the analysis in the text focuses on regression (4.7), without Botswana in the sample.
2. Other expenditure is defined as total expenditure less spending on the six sectors.

*Indicates the same at the 10 percent significance level.

**Indicates that a coefficient is statistically different from zero at the 5 percent significance level.

the coefficients on the aid variable with the coefficients on the variable "residuals of total spending net of aid" suggests that at the margin more money is spent on current expenditure if the financing is from own domestic sources. For capital spending, however, the source of additional resources do not matter; be it foreign or domestic, 28 cents of an additional dollar is spent. Regression (2.5) indicates that none of the additional domestic resources is used to finance debt repayments.

Table 3 provides the estimates of the same equations as reported in Table 2 except that the aid variable in these equations is broken in its two components: concessionary loans and grants. As indicated in Equation (3.1), the impact of the two aid variables on total public expenditure is remarkably identical. In their analysis of 14 developing countries (of which four were in sub-Saharan Africa), Feyzioglu *et al.* (1998) found that disbursement of concessionary loans were far more stimulative of total government expenditures than was total aid. As conjectured in their paper, however, the difference in the two coefficients could be due to the bias introduced in the estimate of concessionary loans for not including data on grants. An important finding reflected in Equation (3.5) of our Table 3 is that it is only grants and not loans that are used to repay the principal on loans. Moreover, concessionary loans are used more for current than capital purposes (regressions (3.3) and (3.4)).

Table 4 reports the estimates of regression (3.3). Regressions reported in this table examine the link between the gross disbursement of concessionary loans to a particular sector and public spending in that sector.

In each of the six sectoral regressions – one each for agriculture, energy, industry, transport and communication, education and health – the coefficient on the variable "residuals of total spending net of aid" indicates how the government distributes an additional dollar that it gets from all resources net of concessionary loans. Comparing these coefficients with the coefficients on the sectoral-aid variable (loans to sector) indicate the level of fungibility at the sectoral level. Only concessionary loans to the education, energy, and transport and communication sectors[8] show a positive and statistically significant relationship with their respective sectoral spending. The regression on the energy sector shows that a dollar increase in sectoral aid leads to an increase of 13 cents in energy sector spending; the remaining aid is used elsewhere. Moreover, when governments get an extra dollar in domestic resources they only spend, on average, 1 cent on the energy sector. Comparing the two coefficients suggests that aid to the energy sector is partially fungible. Evidence from the transport and communication sector (T&C) reveals a similar story. The increase in sectoral spending from own resources is 13 cents but it jumps to 36 cents from aid resources, thus indicating a case of partial fungibility. Aid to education, however, is being spent almost fully in the sector. Since in education, teacher wages are nearly 95 percent of the budget, it is likely that aid finances nearly everything else at the margin. Other

---

[8] As noted at the bottom of Table 4, Botswana is evidently an outlier for the education regression. The analysis in the text focuses on regression (4.7), without Botswana in the sample.

sectoral regressions – agriculture, health, and industry – indicate that there is no evidence from this group of countries that aid to these sectors is increasing spending in the sectors for which it was intended.

3.4. Regression analysis: What determines the level of fungibility?

The sector regressions in the previous section assume that the level of fungibility, which is captured by the parameter θ in Equation (1), is the same across countries. A more realistic approach may be to allow the coefficient of the sector-aid variable in the regressions – which is positively related to θ (see Equation (1) – to be a function of the degree of monitoring exerted by aid donors on the recipient country. Since we cannot observe this degree of monitoring, we use a proxy for it: the total number of aid donors. A donor would have greater difficulty monitoring his aid program if he is one of several donors in the country, compared with the case if he is the only donor. Given a particular level of aid to a country (for any given sector), we would expect the number of donors to be inversely correlated with the level of monitoring, and hence with the coefficient of the sector aid variable in the regressions.

To test this hypothesis, we modify Equation (4), allowing the coefficient of our sector-specific aid variable, $\lambda_{2,i,s,t}$,[9] to be a linear function of the total number of aid donors to country i, $Nd_{i,t}$:

$$\lambda_{2,i,s,t} = h_{0,i,s} + h_{1,s} Nd_{i,t}. \tag{5}$$

In this flexible specification, $h_{0,i,s}$ is allowed to vary across the 18 countries. However, $h_{1,s}$ is the same for all countries (for any given sector).[10] The parameter $h_{1,s}$ measures the relationship between *changes* in the number of donors ($Nd_{i,t}$) and changes in the coefficient of sector aid ($\lambda_{2,i,s,t}$).

Using Equation (5) to substitute into (4) we get the following estimable equation:

$$\begin{aligned} G_{i,s,t} = {} & \lambda_{0,i,s} + \lambda_{1,s} GDP_{i,t-1} \\ & + \sum_{j=1}^{18} h_{0,i,s} (CDummy_j Cloan_{i,s,t}) + h_{1,s} (Nd_i.Cloans_{i,s,t}) \\ & + \lambda_{3,s} \left(G_{i,s,t}^N - \hat{G}_{i,s,t}^N \right) + \lambda_{4,s} (Tloan_{i,t} - Cloan_{i,s,t}) \\ & + \lambda_{5,s} TGrants_{i,t} + \eta_{i,s,t} \end{aligned} \tag{6}$$

---

[9] In Equation (4) this coefficient only had the subscripts 2 and s. Now it is allowed to vary across countries and across time (see Equation (5)). Thus we add i and t as subscripts.

[10] Alternatively, $h_{0,i,s}$ could be made constant across countries, dropping the i subscript. However, this does not allow for the possibility that $\lambda_{2,i,s,t}$ is affected by other country specific factors besides the number of donors.

Table 5. **Estimates for $h_{1,s}$, or the impact of the number of donors on the level of fungibility**

Equation	(5.2)	(5.3)	(5.4)	(5.5)	(5.6)	(5.7)	(5.8)	(5.9)
Dependent variable	Agriculture	Energy	Industry	T&C	Education	Education without Botswana	Health	Other
Number of donors × concessionary loans to sector (estimated coefficient or $\hat{h}_{1,s}$)	−0.07 (−1.21)	−0.02 (−0.69)	0.01 (0.44)	−0.12** (−2.39)	−0.17 (−0.90)	−0.38* (−1.67)	−0.36 (−1.34)	−0.10** (−2.24)

Note: The information in this table comes from estimating Equation (6) in the text, for each sector. Due to the large number of regressors, only $\hat{h}_{1,s}$, or the coefficient of "number of donors × concessionary loans to sector", is reported for each sector regression. For notes 2 to 4 see Table 4.

where $CDummy_j$ is a country dummy for country j.[11] This equation includes 19 interaction terms on the right-hand side: (i) $CDummy_j \times Cloan_{i,s,t}$ (country dummy $\times$ concessionary loans to sector), using in turn each of the 18 country dummies; and (ii) $Nd_{i,t} \times Cloan_{i,s,t}$ (number of donors $\times$ concessionary loans to sector). The other right-hand side variables in Equation (6) also appear in Equation (4).

Equation (6) was estimated for each of the defined sectors. The key results are shown in Table 5. Given the large number of regressors, we only report the estimated value (with t-statistic) of the coefficient we are mainly interested in, that of $Nd_{i,t} \times Cloan_{i,s,t}$ (number of donors $\times$ concessionary loans to sector). We thus present estimates for $h_{1,s}$ in Equations (5) and (6), for each sector.

There is evidence that the number of donors has an impact on the level of fungibility (i.e., that $h_{1,s}$ is different from zero), but only for the transport and communications (T&C) and education sectors.[12] The regression results in the previous sub-section showed that: (i) aid is fully fungible ($\hat{\lambda}_{2,s} = 0$) in the agriculture, industry and health sectors, and: (ii) aid is partially fungible ($0 < \hat{\lambda}_{2,s} < 1$) in the energy, transport and communications (T&C) and education sectors. According to the results shown in Table 5, the partial fungibility of aid in the T&C and education sectors is negatively related to the number of aid donors to a recipient country. This supports our hypothesis that the number of donors has an inverse relationship with, and is a proxy for, the degree of monitoring exerted by donors, at least for the T&C and education sectors.[13]

4. Conclusion

This paper set out to explore two issues: (i) the extent of aid fungibility in sub-Saharan Africa; and (ii) reasons why aid was fungible or not. In terms of the first question, we find that the broad pattern of aid fungibility observed in cross-country and country-specific studies is reflected in our analysis of African countries. Specifically, we find relatively little evidence that aid leads to greater tax relief in Africa; every dollar of aid leads to an increase in government spending of 90 cents. We reiterate that the implications of this result are by no means clear-cut. If the marginal cost of taxation is exceptionally high – and there is some evidence that this is so in African countries (see Devarajan *et al.* (2001)) – then using aid for tax relief may well be the best use of foreign resources. The effect of aid on the composition of public spending between current and capital expenditures is also broadly consistent with international evidence. Aid in Africa leads to an increase in current and capital spending in equal amounts. Again, we note that, even if all aid was intended to finance capital expenditures, the

---

[11] The country dummies operate in the usual way: $CDummy_j$ takes the value 1 for country j, and 0 otherwise.

[12] As noted at the bottom of Table 4, Botswana is evidently an outlier for the education regression. The analysis in the text focuses on regression (5.7), without Botswana in the sample.

[13] Using a similar procedure, we tested for the possibility that the level of fungibility may change over time. We did not find any such evidence for the six sectors.

reallocation to current spending may not necessarily be harmful. One of Africa's problems is the chronic underspending on operations and maintenance. Interestingly, we find that an almost equal amount of aid goes towards repaying the principal on past loans. On the surface, this appears to be a striking result. Very few donors would have explicitly given aid in order to repay loans. But on further reflection, this is not so surprising. The inability to meet debt-service payments threatened many African countries with a complete cut-off from foreign capital. The use of aid resources to relax this constraint could have been quite rational. Moreover, the fungibility of loans intended for particular sectors in Africa roughly mirrors a pattern found with a broader sample of countries, with some exceptions. Aid to energy and transport and communication sectors lead to some increase in public spending in those sectors, but it is by no means one-for-one. By contrast, in the worldwide sample, aid to transport and communications was almost fully nonfungible.[14] Finally, aid to the education sector – which had no discernible effect on education spending in the global sample – has an almost one-for-one effect on education sector spending in Africa. In any event, even in these partially fungible sectors, governments spend more out of aid resources than they do out of their own resources at the margin. Aid to Africa is partially fungible: governments do not spend all sectoral aid in that sector, nor do they treat such aid as merely budgetary support.

Our answers to the second question shed light on the findings about partial fungibility. We find that as the number of donors to a country increases, aid is more likely to be fungible. If we accept the notion that the number of donors represents a proxy for monitoring costs, then it is not surprising that most aid is partially fungible. Recipients are trading off the benefits of full fungibility with the costs. When these costs are low, such as when there are a large number of donors in a country, we observe greater fungibility.

The implications of these results are threefold. First, the development community seems to have swung from a denial of the existence of fungibility (with some notable exceptions) to the other extreme of accepting that all aid is fungible. The facts seem to indicate, though, that aid is partially fungible. On the one hand, this strengthens the conclusion that donors should be concerned with the quality of the overall public expenditure program of the recipient country. It also confirms the importance of donor coordination. On the other hand, our results seem to indicate that aid to particular sectors does have an influence on the composition of public spending, so that sectoral aid programs and projects have a role to play in development assistance. Second, our preliminary findings about the influence of the number of donors on fungibility suggest that further work on the costs of fungibility to the recipient may be a fruitful area of research. Third, countries that are highly aid dependent and where aid is fungible would be hurt most if the level of aid is reduced. This is because in the case of aid being fungible, its reduction would be equivalent to a decrease in the country's own revenue. Another issue, hitherto unstudied, is fungibility across donors: in a country,

---

[14] Though nonfungibility of aid to a sector as a whole does not preclude aid fungibility within the sector.

does increased aid from one donor increase or decrease aid from other donors? These issues are probably best addressed in individual country studies. But, for policy purposes, it is also useful – not to say essential – to pull these studies together into a cross-country analysis, as we have attempted here.

Data Appendix A

A.1. Sample: Size and selection

The sample used in the empirical analysis comprises 280 observations from 18 sub-Saharan African countries, from the years 1971 to 1995. The 18 countries are: Botswana, Burkina Faso, Cameroon, Ethiopia, Ghana, The Gambia, Kenya, Liberia, Lesotho, Madagascar, Malawi, Mauritius, Nigeria, Sudan, Swaziland, Zaire, Zambia, and Zimbabwe.

Sample size and selection were based entirely on data availability. We started by collecting all available data on the relevant variables for sub-Saharan African countries, for the years 1971–1995 (see sources listed below; 1971 is the first year and 1995 is the last year, for which sector-specific loan data is available). A country was included in the sample if it had complete information on all variables (aggregate as well as sector-specific) for at least 10 years of the chosen time period.

All aid and government expenditure/revenue variables, as well as gross domestic product, were converted to 1995 US$. Conversion from local currency units to US$ was done using World Bank conversion factors (which in most cases are the same as the official exchange rates reported in the *International Financial Statistics* of the International Monetary Fund).

A.2. Data sources

Data on foreign aid are from *Geographical Distribution of Financial Flows to Aid Recipients* (OECD, 1998) and from World Bank's database

- Data on principal repayments on concessional loan and interest payments on foreign debt are from OECD (1998).
- Data on government expenditure, excepting concessional loan repayments, are from *Government Finance Statistics* (International Monetary Fund, various years).
- Data on gross domestic product, agricultural output as a share of GDP, and exchange rates are from the *World Development Indicators* (World Bank); World Bank conversion factors were used for exchange rates.
- Data on infant mortality rates and gross enrollment rates in primary and secondary schools are from United Nations Social Indicators.

References

Asra, A., Estrada, G., Kim, Y., Quibria, M.G. (2005), Poverty and Foreign Aid Evidence from Recent Cross-Country Data. *Economics and Research Department Working Paper*, No. 65 (March). Asian Development Bank. Manila, Philippines.

Boone, P. (1995), *Politics and the Effectiveness of Foreign Aid*. London School of Economics and Center for Economic Performance.

Cashel-Cordo, P., Craig, S.G. (1990), The public sector impact of international resource transfers. *Journal of Development Economics* 32, 17–42.

Cratty, D., Van de Walle, D. (2005), Do donors get what they paid for? Micro-evidence on the fungibility of development project aid. *World Bank Policy Research Working Paper* 3542.

Demery, L., Hussain, I. (1993), *Assessment of the interrelation between adjustment financing and economic performance in SPA countries*. Africa Region, World Bank, Washington, DC.

Devarajan, S., Swaroop, V., Zou, H.-F. (1996), The composition of public expenditure and economic growth. *Journal of Monetary Economics* 37, 313–344.

Devarajan, S., Squire, L., Suthiwart-Narueput, S. (1997), Beyond rate of return: Reorienting project analysis. *The World Bank Research Observer* 12 (1), 35–46.

Devarajan, S., Suthiwart-Narueput, S., Thierfelder, K. (2001), The marginal cost of public funds in developing countries. In: Fossati, A., Wiegard, W. (Eds.), *Policy Evaluations with Computable General Equilibrium Models*. Routledge Press.

Easterly, W. (2005), What did structural adjustment adjust? The association of policies and growth with repeated IMF and World Bank adjustment loans. *Journal of Development Economics* 76 (1), 1–22.

Easterly, W., Levine, R. (1993), *Is Africa different? Evidence from growth regressions*. Policy Research Department, World Bank, Mimeograph.

Easterly, W., Levine, R., Roodman, D. (2004), Aid, policies and growth: comment. *American Economic Review* 94 (3), 774–780.

Feyzioglu, T., Swaroop, V., Zhu, M. (1998), A panel data analysis of the fungibility of foreign aid. *The World Bank Economic Review* 12 (January), 29–58.

Gang, I.N., Khan, H.A. (1991), Foreign aid, taxes and public investment. *Journal of Development Economics* 34, 355–369.

Gupta, K.L. (1993), *Sectoral fungibility of foreign aid: evidence from India*. Mimeograph, University of Alberta, Alberta.

Hausman, J.A. (1978), Specification tests in econometrics. *Econometrica* 46, 1251–1272.

Helleiner, G.K. (1992), The IMF, the World Bank and Africa's adjustment and external debt problems: an unofficial view. *World Development* 20 (June), 779–792.

Khilji, N.M., Zampelli, E.M. (1994), The fungibility of U.S. military and non-military assistance and the impacts on expenditures of major aid recipients. *Journal of Development Economics* 43, 345–362.

McGuire, M.C. (1978), A method for estimating the effect of a subsidy on the receiver's resource constraint: with an application to the U.S. Local governments 1964–1971. *Journal of Public Economics* 10, 355–369.

Njeru, J. (2003), The impact of foreign aid on public expenditure: the case of Kenya. *African Economic Research Consortium (AERC) Paper* 135 (September). AERC, Nairobi.

Organisation for Economic Co-operation and Development (1998), *Geographical distribution of financial flows to aid recipients*. Paris, France, CD-ROM.

Pack, H., Pack, J.R. (1990), Is foreign aid fungible? The case of Indonesia. *Economic Journal* 100, 188–194.

Pack, H., Pack, J.R. (1993), Foreign aid and the question of fungibility. *Review of Economics and Statistics* 75 (May), 258–265.

Pack, H., Pack, J.R. (1996), *Foreign Aid and Fiscal Stress*. The University of Pennsylvania, Philadelphia, PA.

Swaroop, V., Jha, S., Rajkumar, A.S. (2000), Fiscal effects of foreign aid in a federal system of governance: the case of India. *Journal of Public Economics* 77 (3), 307–330.

World Bank (1994), *Adjustment in Africa: Reforms, Results, and the Road Ahead. A World Bank Policy Research Report*. Oxford University Press.

World Bank (1998), *Assessing Aid: What Works, What Doesn't and Why*. A World Bank Policy Research Report. Oxford University Press.

CHAPTER 18

Aid Effectiveness in the Education Sector: A Dynamic Panel Analysis

Katharina Michaelowa and Anke Weber

University of Zurich, Institute of Political Science: Political Economy and Development, Mühlegasse 21, CH-8001 Zurich, Switzerland
E-mail addresses: katja.michaelowa@pw.unizh.ch; anke.weber@pw.unizh.ch

Abstract

Applying the general question of aid effectiveness to the sector of education, this paper provides some evidence for a positive effect of development assistance on primary enrolment and completion. However, even the most optimistic estimates clearly show that at any realistic rate of growth, aid will never be able to move the world markedly closer towards the internationally agreed objective of "Education For All". Universal primary education requires increased efficiency of educational spending by donors and national governments alike. Moreover, there is some evidence that the recipient countries' general political and institutional background matters. Under conditions of bad governance, the impact of aid on enrolment can actually turn negative.

Keywords: Aid effectiveness, primary education, good governance

JEL classifications: F350, O150, I220

1. Introduction

In the late 1990s, the World Bank study on aid effectiveness (World Bank, 1998) provoked a general debate, both among aid agencies and in academia, on the effectiveness and the efficiency of development assistance. Evidence available at micro-level typically provides strong support for the effectiveness of aid. Donor agencies tend to carry out regular project evaluations and publish overall statistics in which the share of "successful" projects generally varies between 70 and 90% (Michaelowa and Borrmann, 2006).

At macro-level, however, the available evidence leads to results which are less robust by far. Empirical investigations have often failed to find a significantly positive link between aid and economic development. Boone (1996) even provides convincing evidence for a negative rather than a positive relationship. The World Bank study as

THEORY AND PRACTICE OF FOREIGN AID
VOLUME 1   ISSN: 1574-8715
DOI: 10.1016/S1574-8715(06)01018-9

well as Burnside and Dollar's (2000) paper resuming the study's main arguments conclude that the missing link between aid and growth may be due to donors' insufficient attention to governance issues within recipient countries. In fact, their econometric results show a positive effect of aid on growth wherever good governance is prevailing. One major argument in this context is the fungibility of resources. In recipient countries with "bad governance" governments might substitute the aid funds for national public expenditure in the sectors towards which the aid flows are directed, and use the released national funds for unproductive expenditure such as the purchase of arms or increased consumption. Hansen and Tarp (2001) contradict these results on econometric grounds and provide evidence for an overall positive effect of aid. At the same time, Easterly (2001, 2002, 2003, 2006) questions the effectiveness of aid altogether, independently of governance in the recipient countries, arguing, inter alia, on the basis of inefficiencies on the donor side. Harms and Lutz (2004) as well as Doucouliagos and Paldam (2005) present a comprehensive overview of the literature available so far.

It is the objective of this paper to evaluate the apparently contradictory evidence on aid effectiveness at the example of a specific sector: education. A sectoral approach avoids the extremely high complexity of macro-level evaluations in which it is virtually impossible to acknowledge for all factors with potential impacts on the link between aid and economic development. At the same time, as opposed to micro-level project assessments, sectoral analysis should be able to reveal the relevance of fungibility and the impact of good governance. Finally, sectoral data can be drawn from international statistics which appear to be more reliable than micro-level project evaluation data generated by bilateral development agencies.

The advantage of the education sector is primarily that development objectives in this field have been set out very clearly and have been agreed upon among all international donors at various occasions. Declarations adopted at the "Education For All" (EFA) international fora in Jomptien 1990 and Dakar 2000, as well as the "Millennium Development Goals" (MDGs) adopted both at the UN level and in the framework of the Development Assistance Committee (DAC) of the OECD donor countries (OECD/DAC, 2001, p. 18), all call for universal primary education as a major priority of poverty alleviation and general development policy.

In this paper, the impact of aid for education on the development of primary enrolment rates will be assessed in a dynamic panel analysis for about 120 low- and lower-middle income countries. While Section 2 discusses the data used for the econometric analysis, Section 3 describes the econometric approach and presents the results under different empirical assumptions and based on two different data sets: a long-term structural panel (five-year averages, 1975–2000) and a short-term annual panel (1993–2000). Section 4 draws some conclusions of this sectoral study in the context of the wider debate on aid effectiveness.

2. Data and variable selection

In order to carry out the analysis outlined above, information is required on primary education outcomes as well as on aid allocated to education in the different recipient countries. Moreover, various control variables related to the recipient countries' national education expenditure, specificities of the local education systems, the overall level of economic development, and some indicators of governance, need to be introduced.

In particular, reliable data on development cooperation are crucial for the assessment of aid effectiveness. Generally, this type of information can be drawn from the International Development Statistics (IDS) compiled by the DAC secretariat (OECD/DAC, 2004). Typically, aid data are provided either in terms of commitments or in terms of disbursements. As commitments do not always translate into actual flows of resources and as, even if they do, the delay does not always follow a systematic pattern, the aid data used should be preferably based on disbursements. However, information on disbursements by sector of development assistance is available only from 1990 onwards. Similarly, for technical cooperation which, according to the DAC statisticians, is more accurate in terms of the sectoral break up, data are available only since 1992. For this reason, both of these series can be used only for an analysis of the impact of aid within the 1990s. In order to increase the number of observations, the panel based on this dataset uses annual observations, even though one-year steps may not be sufficient to show the impact of structural variables with little variation over time.

In order to assess long-term developments and the impact of structural variables, the only alternative is to use the data on aid commitments which are available throughout the 1970s, 1980s and 1990s. Unfortunately, until recently, donor reporting to this database (Creditor Reporting System, CRS) has remained incomplete; a fact that becomes most obvious when the total amount reported to the CRS database is compared to the total amount published in general DAC statistics. However, under the assumption that the sectoral share as provided in the CRS data is correct, an approximation of the true commitment data can be derived using the correct total from DAC statistics. This transformation is equivalent to a simple expansion of the sectoral information available from CRS:

$$EDUCAID = EDUCAID_{CRS} + \left(\frac{EDUCAID_{CRS}}{TOTALODA_{CRS}} \right)$$
$$\times (TOTALODA_{DAC} - TOTALODA_{CRS})$$
$$\iff EDUCAID = EDUCAID_{CRS} \left(\frac{TOTALODA_{DAC}}{TOTALODA_{CRS}} \right) \quad (1)$$

where EDUCAID = aid for education; TOTALODA = total official development assistance. The subscripts denote the respective sources (DAC versus CRS databank).

All other variables can be directly drawn from international databases.

As far as the measurement of progress towards universal primary education is concerned, the indicators to be used have been agreed internationally along with the definition of the MDGs' goal No. 2 on education. They include the net primary enrolment rate, persistence to grade 5 and the primary completion rate. Persistence to grade 5 always requires a simultaneous consideration of enrolment because it is defined only with respect to those students who initially enter the education system. The combination of both aspects is captured in the completion rates which relate the number of students completing primary education to the total number of children of the corresponding age group. The only disadvantage is that for completion (just as for enrolment) there is no specific final grade level identified, so that different durations of primary education may distort international comparability for those countries which significantly differ from the typical duration of five or six years. Nevertheless, the net enrolment rate (NER) and the primary completion rate (COMPLETION) appear to be the most appropriate variables in the context of our analysis.

Unfortunately, there are considerable problems of data availability. The only educational indicator for which a reasonably complete coverage exists over the years is gross primary enrolment. However, its message is difficult to interpret as more than 50% of the observations exceed 100%. The reason is that, as opposed to the net enrolment rate which only considers pupils of the appropriate age, the gross enrolment rate considers pupils of *any* age and compares them to the (much more restricted) number of children of official primary school age. Thus the gross enrolment rate is inflated by late enrolment and grade repetition which is substantial in some countries, notably in Africa and Latin America, and its increase may reflect an increase in inefficiency rather than a true increase in enrolment.

Fortunately, the simultaneous consideration of direct information on the efficiency of the education system (e.g. persistence and repetition rates) can mitigate this deficiency. Moreover, even the gender balance (in both primary and secondary education) provides complementary information. Note that whenever there is close to universal enrolment, the gender-ratio must be close to one, which is generally not the case otherwise.

For the purpose of this study, we thus combine all the information available on gross enrolment and on the additional indicators mentioned above, and use it to derive revised and more comprehensive data on NER and COMPLETION. All imputations are based on linear regressions with subsequent trimming to ensure that the imputed values are in the support of the underlying variables.

All relevant educational indicators are available from the UNESCO-UIS (2006) statistical database. For convenience, they can also be drawn together with other macroeconomic variables from the World Bank's World Development Indicators (WDI). However, the most recent WDI database (World Bank, 2005) does no more include the older UNESCO statistics (up to 1997), so that it has to be used jointly with the WDI 2003 database (World Bank, 2003).

In order to characterize the national education systems in recipient countries, information on current education expenditure in percent of GNI (EXPEDUC), the pupil–teacher ratio in primary education (PTR), and the share of children and youths aged 0–14 as a percentage of overall population (YOUNG-POP) are selected as potentially relevant variables. GDP per capita (GDPcap) is added as a variable controlling for the recipient countries' general income level. Information on each of these variables is available from the WDI database (World Bank, 2005).

Note that in order to measure national resources allocated to education, current expenditure is preferred to the overall education budget because the latter may in some cases include the aid resources taken into account separately here.[1] This problem can be avoided for current educational expenditure as – until recently – donors argued that regular payments were to be financed locally in order to ensure sustainability.

Finally, four variables are introduced to assess the impact of good governance. Following Burnside and Dollar (2000, p. 851), relevant policies considered are the budget surplus in percent of GDP (BUDGET), the rate of inflation (INFLATION), and openness (OPEN) calculated as the sum of exports and imports as a percentage of GDP. Based on these three variables, Burnside and Dollar create a policy index using weights specifically derived for growth regressions. As these weights are not applicable to education, this paper does not recur to the index but considers each variable separately. Again, all necessary data is provided by the WDI database (World Bank, 2005).

As the above variables merely refer to economic aspects of good governance, they are complemented by the Freedom House index of political rights and civil liberties (FREE) which covers the broader political and institutional environment. This index is based on the evaluation of: free elections, the real power of elected political representatives, the de facto power of the opposition, the right to organize in groups, freedom of domination by the military or other powerful groups, and self determination rights of minority groups (political rights), as well as freedom of expression and belief, association and organizational rights, rule of law and human rights, and personal autonomy and economic rights (civil liberties). The index is measured on a one-to-seven scale, with one representing the highest degree of freedom and seven the lowest (Freedom House, 2005). Alternative indices such as the more recent World Bank governance indicators computed by Kaufmann *et al.* (2003, 2005) have also been considered, but have been finally rejected due to the limited length of available time series.[2]

As the overall data set contains a considerable number of missing values, imputations were carried out for all explanatory variables. With the exception of FREE, these imputations were based on linear regression using related variables, i.e. their own lags as well as other macroeconomic indicators in the case of macroeconomic variables, and different types of aid data including information on related sectors such a health in the case of EDUCAID. When information was missing for the Freedom House Index, the observation was replaced by the highest (i.e. worst) value available over time for the country concerned. For all variables, missing value indicators were computed and integrated in the econometric estimation equations in order to avoid or reduce potential bias created by these imputations.

---

[1] In fact, UNESO-UIS questionnaires require the inclusion of aid resources into the national education budget. However, in practice, bilateral project aid cannot generally be expected to be included in these figures. In many cases, national education ministries were not even informed about the volumes concerned. Transparency improved when budget financing and the financing of sector programs were introduced at the turn of the century. Nevertheless, according to information from UNESCO-UIS, even budget aid has not been consistently included into the national figures yet.

[2] For the data, see World Bank (2006).

Countries were included in the sample if they belonged (i) to the group of low- or lower-middle income countries as defined by the World Bank (2003) as well as (ii) to the group of developing countries (Part I of DAC aid recipients) according to DAC statistics. The latter condition excludes several lower middle income countries, particularly in Eastern Europe. This selection is based on the idea that countries above a certain development threshold have generally reached universal primary education so that they are of no interest for the analysis in this paper. Overall, over 120 low- and lower-middle income countries are covered by the following econometric analysis.

Note that the data set deliberately ends in 2000 although some more recent data is available. The reason is that with the beginning of the 21st century, budget aid and sector program support have been introduced in many countries so that a distinction between aid resources and the recipient governments' own spending on education has become blurred even with respect to current education expenditure which was traditionally fully left to the responsibility of local governments.

3. *Econometric analysis*

As there is strong evidence of an autocorrelation of educational outcomes both in terms of enrolment and completion, the econometric analysis is carried out using the GMM dynamic panel estimators suggested by Arellano and Bond (1991), Arellano and Bover (1995) and Blundell and Bond (1998). While Arellano and Bond (1991) use a first differenced estimator to avoid the correlation of the lagged dependent variable with the individual effect included in the error term, Arellano and Bover (1995) reinclude levels equations in combination with suitable lags of first differenced variables as instruments. Blundell and Bond (1998) demonstrate that these additional levels restrictions remain informative even if the restrictions in first differences encounter the weak instruments problem discussed by Staiger and Stock (1997). Moreover, they show that adding the levels equations considerably increases the precision of the estimator, especially when the autocorrelation of the dependent variable is relatively high.

At the same time, the overall number of instruments becomes disproportionally high in some regressions, sometimes higher than the number of countries included in the panel. Due to the additional levels restrictions, this problem arises more often with the Blundell–Bond than with the Arellano–Bond estimator. Roodman's (2005) implementation of both estimators in Stata suggests an easy way to mitigate this problem through a limitation of the lags to be considered as instruments (collapse option). In our analysis, this option is used in some regressions in order to improve overall regression statistics, in particular the test for validity of the overidentifying restrictions (Hansen test). Note that for both Arellano–Bond and Blundell–Bond estimation, one-step and two-step options are available. Arellano and Bond's (1991) simulations suggest that the two-step option may increase the precision of coefficient estimates and considerably improve overall regression statistics in case of heteroscedasticity, but that standard errors tend to be systematically underestimated. This systematic bias is taken into account by the robust version of the estimators implemented by Roodman (2005) which include Windmeijer's (2005) finite-sample correction for the two-step covariance matrix.

An additional methodological issue is that EDUCAID cannot be realistically considered as an exogenous variable. It is highly plausible that exogenous shocks like droughts or earthquakes simultaneously influence aid inflows and development outcomes like educational enrolment and completion rates. For this reason, EDUCAID is instrumented in all regressions, generally using its own lag as an instrument.

To some extent, one might expect the same argument to be true for national resources allocated to education (EXPEDUC). As we are measuring current expenditure flows which are, by definition, more stable than capital investment, the problem may be less relevant though. In any case, in order to check the robustness of our results, we will also instrument EXPEDUC by its lag in some regression specifications.

Generally, the choice of a lagged explanatory variable as its own instrument has the advantage of a strong correlation with the initial variable. However, it is sometimes difficult to argue that it is truly uncorrelated with the error term, i.e. that it satisfies the second requirement for a valid instrumental variable (IV). In particular, a problem arises when the endogeneity of the original variable is caused by reverse causation, i.e. by an influence of the dependent variable on the regressor concerned. This may be an alternative reason for the endogeneity of EDUCAID as it is not implausible to assume that donors purposefully orient their educational aid resources towards recipient countries most in need of these resources, i.e. to countries with low net enrolment and completion rates. Obviously, if current aid is influenced by current educational outcomes, lagged aid is influenced by lagged educational outcomes. As in our case, educational outcomes are autocorrelated over time, lagged aid is indirectly also related to current educational outcomes, and hence to the error term of the current period.[3]

To give due attention to the possibility of reverse causation, we spent considerable time to think of instruments for EDUCAID that would remain valid in this case. In order to find alternative instruments, development assistance channelled to other sectors such as health, water and sanitation, infrastructure, industry, energy, agriculture and government/civil service was examined with respect to the criteria set out in Angrist *et al.* (1996). Almost all of these variables are significantly correlated with educational aid, but there appears to be a certain trade-off between the strength of the correlation and the potential endogeneity of the instrument itself. The most extreme case is aid for health which is highly correlated with aid for education both across countries and across time. Partial R^2s using the commitment data from the 1970s onwards and control variables as in the regressions discussed in the following section are: 27% (within),

---

[3] Only under very specific assumptions about the relationship between the error term of the regression equation and the error term of the equation specifying the (reverse) effect of educational outcomes on aid, it is still possible to construct a situation in which the lagged EDUCAID is uncorrelated with the error term.

59% (between) and 40% (overall).[4] At the same time, it can be expected that outcomes in both sectors are similarly correlated. Generally unsatisfactory social sector development may enhance donor spending on health and education simultaneously. Therefore, using health as an instrumental variable may not solve the endogeneity problem.

Moreover, aid for health might raise enrolment rates independently of aid for education as healthier children may have a higher likelihood to attend school. It is therefore inappropriate as an instrument for EDUCAID.

An alternative instrument which can probably be considered as truly exogenous is energy aid. Energy aid comprises all assistance allocated to the production of energy, energy sector policy planning, institution building and distribution management. It does not include the extraction of raw materials for power generation (OECD/DAC, 2004).

Unfortunately, the correlation between energy aid and educational aid is much lower than in the case of health. While the cross-country correlation is acceptable, the correlation within countries over time is almost negligible. Partial R^2s for the regression of EDUCAID on ENERGYAID and all other control variables as in the regression tables discussed below are: 3% (within), 31% (between) and 24% (overall).[5] Nevertheless, the relationship between EDUCAID and ENERGYAID is significant at the 1% level in this model. A graphical representation is provided in Figure 1.

The graph shows that some positive relationship exists, but it is not very clear and blurred by several outliers. Shea (1997, pp. 348f.) notes that as long as the instruments are perfectly exogenous, coefficient estimates remain consistent, but their precision is reduced. However, as within each country only few time series observations are available, finite sample properties are more relevant here. Staiger and Stock (1997) emphasize the important bias which can arise if the relevance of the instruments is weak, and show that the endogeneity bias in the simple OLS regression might in some cases be lower. The above discussion shows that ENERGYAID belongs to these relatively weak instruments, in particular when we consider the within country relationship. Nevertheless, ENERGYAID appears to be the best instrument available and will be retained in the analysis for some regressions as an alternative to the lagged EDUCAID.

The results of the different regressions will be discussed in two settings: a long term structural model (Section 3.1) and an annual model for the 1990s (Section 3.2). While the former is theoretically more appealing, the latter benefits from the availability of more reliable data.

---

[4] The computation of partial R^2s here and elsewhere in this paper is based on the analysis suggested by Shea (1997). However, to adjust to the panel structure of the data, OLS regressions in each step were substituted by random effects regressions. Similarly, the final correlation of residuals (step 4, p. 349) was replaced by a bivariate random effects regression in order to derive partial R^2s distinguishing between the correlations within and between countries. Note that the correlation tests were carried out before the EDUCAID variable was imputed so as to properly distinguish between the different sector variables.

[5] The exact figures refer to the case in which aid is measured as a percentage of GDP (EDUCAIDg) as discussed below. The partial R^2s of analogous regressions for the corresponding equations in Tables 1 and 2 are somewhat lower, and ENERGYAID is less highly significant.

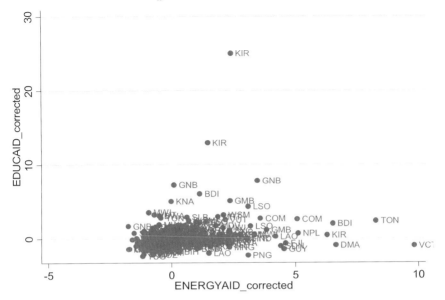

Note: Both EDUCAID and the instrumental variable (IV) are corrected for the influence of all other explanatory variables included in Tables 1–3.

Fig. 1. Energy aid as an instrument for educational aid.

3.1. Results for the structural panel

The basic idea of the structural panel is that educational outcomes such as enrolment will tend to react on long-term developments of resource availability, the education system and the policy environment rather than on short-term variation of any of these variables. From this perspective, annual data create unnecessary noise which can be avoided if the data are smoothed over several years. For the purpose of this study, available information on all variables was simply averaged over the five-year periods 1971–1975 until 1996–2000.

For the early years, information on COMPLETION is extremely scarce, so that about two thirds of the data would have to be imputed. We therefore confine the analysis of the structural panel to the determinants of NER. Results are presented in Table 1.

As the effect of a given aid volume depends upon the size of the recipient country, examining the effect of aid flows in absolute numbers does not seem adequate. We propose two different ways to adjust these numbers to country size:

Education aid relative to the population of the recipient country (*EDUCAIDn*), and

(i) Education aid in % of recipient countries' GDP (*EDUCAIDg*).
(ii) While the former takes into account the number of people who effectively have to share the amount of aid received, the latter reflects the relevance of aid as compared to the recipient countries' own resources.

Table 1. Results for the structural panel using EDUCAIDn

Dependent variable: NER	(1) Arellano&Bond IV: L.EDUCAIDn	(2) Arellano&Bond, robust IV: L.EDUCAIDn	(3) Blundell&Bond, robust IV: L.EDUCAIDn	(4) Blundell&Bond, robust IV: L.EDUCAIDn L.EXPEDUC	(5) Blundell&Bond, robust IV: ENERGYAID
L.NER	0.74***	0.55**	0.39	0.57	0.24
	(0.005)	(0.012)	(0.165)	(0.171)	(0.359)
EDUCAIDn commitments	0.15**	0.01	0.12	0.08	−0.23
	(0.019)	(0.909)	(0.371)	(0.539)	(0.308)
EXPEDUC	0.13	−0.73	2.07*	5.30	1.04
	(0.934)	(0.629)	(0.071)	(0.688)	(0.523)
PTR	0.30**	0.44***	−0.24	−0.11	−0.27*
	(0.018)	(0.000)	(0.205)	(0.637)	(0.093)
YOUNG-POP	−0.00	0.02	0.01	0.01	0.07
	(0.979)	(0.855)	(0.896)	(0.884)	(0.489)
GDPcap	0.001	0.001	0.002**	0.002	0.003**
	(0.486)	(0.378)	(0.043)	(0.278)	(0.013)
BUDGET	−0.26**	−0.18	−0.07	−0.11	−0.01
	(0.028)	(0.132)	(0.582)	(0.554)	(0.955)
INFLATION	0.001	0.000	0.000	0.000	0.000
	(0.220)	(0.693)	(0.726)	(0.904)	(0.768)
OPEN	−2.08	−0.47	−1.23	−4.78	0.83
	(0.221)	(0.769)	(0.329)	(0.732)	(0.620)
FREE	0.06	−0.66	−0.89	−0.85*	−1.71***
	(0.936)	(0.323)	(0.107)	(0.069)	(0.003)

Table 1. *(Continued)*

Dependent variable: NER	(1) Arellano&Bond IV: L.EDUCAIDn	(2) Arellano&Bond, robust IV: L.EDUCAIDn	(3) Blundell&Bond, robust IV: L.EDUCAIDn	(4) Blundell&Bond, robust IV: L.EDUCAIDn L.EXPEDUC	(5) Blundell&Bond, robust IV: ENERGYAID
Wald	chi2(18) = 7878.3 (0.000)	chi2(18) = 203.4 (0.000)	chi2(18) = 531.21 (0.000)	chi2(18) = 1940.5 (0.000)	chi2(17) = 247.47 (0.000)
Hansen	chi2(6) = 8.60 (0.197)	chi2(18) = 17.04 (0.520)	chi2(8) = 6.84 (0.554)	chi2(12) = 10.22 (0.597)	chi2(4) = 1.17 (0.883)
AR1	z = −2.28 (0.022)	z = −1.88 (0.060)	z = −1.77 (0.076)	z = −1.74 (0.081)	z = −2.24 (0.025)
AR2	z = 1.02 (0.307)	z = 1.21 (0.225)	z = 1.03 (0.304)	z = 1.05 (0.292)	z = 1.25 (0.213)
N	382	382	520	520	442
Countries	122	122	129	129	124

Notes: P values in parentheses. The prefix L. denotes a lagged variable. Constant term and missing value indicators not presented here. For an overview of variable definitions and sources, see Appendix A.

*Significant at 10%.

**Significant at 5%.

***Significant at 1%.

Table 1 presents five regressions using always the same set of explanatory variables but different estimation techniques. Regression (1) shows the simple Arellano–Bond model, regression (2) the Arellano–Bond model with Windmeijer's robust variance-covariance matrix, and regression (3) the robust Blundell–Bond estimation. In all of these, EDUCAID is instrumented using its own lag (L.EDUCAID) so that we have an additional restriction added to the moment restrictions of the original GMM estimator. Regressions (4) introduces lagged national current expenditure on education as an additional IV variable for EXPEDUC and regression (5) uses ENERGYAID instead of L.EDUCAID to instrument for aid to education.

All estimations are carried out with both aid variables EDUCAIDn and EDU-CAIDg alternatively. As results turn out to be very similar, the following presentation for the structural panel will be confined to EDUCAIDn. The corresponding tables for EDUCAIDg can be obtained from the authors upon request.

Results are far from robust across the different regression techniques. EDUCAID, our main variable of interest, shows a significantly positive coefficient only in one regression (regression (1)). Unfortunately, as discussed above, this specification is the least reliable with respect to significance levels. As soon as the structural bias of standard errors is taken into account using Windmeijer's robust variance-covariance matrix, no significant effect can be distinguished any more.

Interestingly, there is no improvement with respect to the evidence for any significant impact of aid even in regression (5). If donors distributed aid for education according to need, i.e. in response to low enrolment rates, we should expect the coefficients of regressions (1)–(4) to be biased downwards, but regression (5) to show the true effect of aid. However, in Table 1 the opposite happens: Rather than to increase and to become significant, the coefficient in fact turns negative. Thus there is no evidence that the missing link between aid resources and educational outcomes could be due to reverse causation.

With respect to national current education expenditure, we do not find any more positive result, either. This variable is significantly positive only in one regression, too (regression (3)), and only at the 10% level. We thus do not find any evidence for a greater effectiveness of national as compared to foreign resources. As far as our other control variables with respect to the national education are concerned, the pupil-teacher ratio (PTR) is positive and strongly significant in all Arellano–Bond regressions. This effect is highly plausible in a situation of under-supply in which (at a given level of resources and their distribution) enrolment can only be increased by accepting more children within each class (see (Mingat and Tan, 2003; Mingat and Suchaut, 2000) and (MINEDAF, 2002) for further discussion). Our Arellano–Bond coefficient estimates imply that increasing the PTR by 10 students goes hand in hand with an increase of the net enrolment rate by 3–4 percentage points. At the same time, we cannot observe this effect in our Blundell–Bond estimations where the coefficient turns negative although it remains insignificant except for regression (5), where it becomes marginally significant at the 10% level.

Surprisingly, the share of children within the total population (YOUNG-POP) does not show any significant effect although one would expect that a higher share of school aged children puts additional strain on the education system. An explanation may be that the long run relationship may be blurred through a correlation of YOUNG-POP with other factors such as the development of infrastructure which are not taken into account here. In this case, we should observe a significant relationship in Section 3.2 when we will discuss the results of the annual panel for the 1990s.

The control variable for the general income level shows the expected positive coefficients. The effect remains moderate, however, as educational expenditure is already controlled for, and is significant only in specifications (3) and (5).

Finally considering the governance variables leads to a more interesting result. None of the variables related to economic aspects of good governance appear to be positively related to education outcomes. Inflation (INFLATION) and openness (OPEN) are insignificant throughout and a budget surplus (BUDGET) has a negative rather than a positive effect, if at all. Possibly, this reflects that budgetary austerity might go hand in hand with cuts in national educational investment which is not taken into account elsewhere in the regression if it is not financed by aid. But the result with respect to BUDGET is not very convincing as it is clearly significant only in regression (1) and this regression suffers from a downward biased standard errors as explained above.

However, as opposed to the economic variables, the political and institutional aspects captured by the Freedom House index (FREE) do show some relationship between good governance and student enrolment, at least in the (rather more reliable) robust Blundell–Bond regressions. Coefficients are significant in regressions (4) and (5). According to the corresponding coefficient estimates, a one-point increase on the seven-point scale towards oppression goes hand in hand with a reduction of primary enrolment rates by 0.9–1.7 percentage points.

This shows that the role of institutional factors frequently demonstrated in a more general context of development (see e.g. (Rodrik *et al.*, 2002; World Bank, 2001)) also appears to be somewhat relevant for the specific sector of education. At the same time, the relevance of economic as opposed to political governance seems to be limited to economic development measured by variables such as growth.

Overall, the regression results for the structural panel appear plausible, though not very stable when changing the estimation techniques applied. While there are certain advantages of the Blundell–Bond system GMM as compared to the Arellano–Bond estimator, and a clear underestimation problem of standard errors in the non-robust specification of the latter, any further judgment about the reliability of the different regressions is difficult to establish.

3.2. Results for the annual panel

To complement our analysis by the estimation of a short term relationship, we can now turn to an annual database for the 1990s which is more complete and reliable, both with respect to educational outcomes and with respect to aid to EDUCAID. Only information for ENERGYAID is still very limited.

For educational outcomes, we can now use either the NER or the completion rates (COMPLETION), and for EDUCAID we can use either disbursements or technical cooperation. Adding the remaining choice between EDUCAIDg and EDUCAIDn, we have eight different options for each regression. To simplify the presentation, we limit the rest of the analysis to EDUCAIDg because the corresponding point estimates are easier to interpret and to compare with the values of the coefficient for EXPEDUC which is expressed as a percentage of GNI. Moreover, Table 2 only displays the results for regressions using COMPLETION and disbursements (with regression specifications as in Table 1) while Table 3 shows all other possible combinations of aid and educational outcome variables using a single (preferred) estimation technique.

In the setting of Table 2, EDUCAID turns out to be positive and significant throughout, except for the regression in which it is instrumented by ENERGYAID. Coefficients are always higher than those for current national education expenditure, and the latter are not significant in any of the five regressions. The highest point estimates for the coefficient of EDUCAID in those regressions in which it is significant is 2.5 (regression (4)), which indicates that an increase in aid for education by 1% of GDP implies an increase in primary completion rates by 2.5 percentage points.

The control variables for the context of the national education system PTR and YOUNG-POP are now consistently significant as well (except for regression (2) in the case of the PTR). The share of the population under 15 years of age shows the expected negative impact on the capacity of the education system to accommodate all children, an effect for which the evidence was lacking in the structural panel discussed earlier. As opposed to the structural panel, the effect of the PTR is now negative throughout. This may indicate that in the short run, demand-side effects dominate over supply-side restrictions. Thus the negative coefficient can be interpreted as an indication that parents do not send their children to school (or take them out again rather early) if class size is so big that they do not expect much positive result from the children's attendance.

GDP per capita does not appear to be relevant in the short run, once all the other variables are controlled for. It is significant only in regression (1) where standard errors are known to be biased.

With respect to the economic governance indicators, estimation results are similar to those of the structural panel. Again, no significant and positive relationship between good economic governance and educational outcomes can be found.

The only variable which is significant in at least one regression is INFLATION (regression (5)), but again the coefficient indicates the opposite of what would typically be expected as an effect of good governance, as inflation seems to be positively rather than negatively related to primary completion. If at all this effect can be taken seriously, it might have to be interpreted in relation to teacher salaries. As mentioned in the previous section, the latter make up for the bulk of current educational expenditure and increased enrolment and completion are very difficult to achieve under conditions of relatively high salaries (Mingat *et al.*, 2002). At the same time, nominal teacher salaries, just as the salaries of any civil servants, have been relatively sticky, at least until the late 1990s. From that perspective, inflation may have reduced the financing needs of the education system through an effective reduction of real salaries.

In any case, this effect, if any, has nothing to do with a potential effect of good economic governance. At the same time, as opposed to Table 1, evidence for a positive impact of good political governance is not convincing either in Table 2.

Overall regression statistics are again generally acceptable although in regression (3), the validity of overidentifying restrictions can only be accepted if the significance level is reduced to 5%. Despite this problem, we select this regression for further analysis with varying combinations of educational outcome and aid variables. The reasons for this choice are the following:

(i) As explained above, Blundell–Bond estimation is generally preferable to the original Arellano–Bond estimation.

(ii) Among the Blundell–Bond regressions, the additional instrumentation of EXPEDUC in regression (4) does not change much of the results, both with respect to the regression coefficients of the significant variables and with respect to overall regression statistics. While the Hansen test slightly improves, the AR2 test is rather close to rejecting the hypothesis of no 2nd order serial correlation. Using L.EXPEDUC as an IV thus does not seem to lead to an improvement of the initial specification.

(iii) The replacement of L.EDUCAID by ENERGYAID as an IV for EDUCAID in regression (5) does lead to some improvement of the overall regression statistics. However, the number of observations decreases by 1/3 due to the missing value problem with respect to ENERGYAID already discussed above. Taking together the evidence from the structural and the annual panel presented so far, results for regression (5) often diverge from results of the other regressions, but not in the sense expected if there were reverse causation which the IV approach would take care of. There rather seems to be some risk that the results of regression (5) are suffer from sample selection bias induced by a nonrandom selection of observations into the model when all the missings for ENERGYAID cannot be considered.

(iv) Finally, as compared to most of the other regressions, regression (3) shows a relatively high and significant impact of EDUCAID. In case of doubt, we tend to select those specifications which are more favorable for a positive impact of aid. By doing so, we attempt to ensure that our final results indicate the most optimistic, rather than the most pessimistic results for the effect of aid on educational outcomes.

Table 3 therefore takes regression (3) from Table 2 as a basis. We first keep COMPLETION as the dependent variable and replace only the disbursements by technical cooperation for EDUCAID (regression (1)). We then show the results for disburse-

Katharina Michaelowa and Anke Weber

Table 2. *Results for the annual panel using EDUCAIDg/disbursements*

Dependent variable: NER	(1) Arellano&Bond IV: L.EDUCAIDg	(2) Arellano&Bond, robust IV: L.EDUCAIDg	(3) Blundell&Bond, robust IV: L.EDUCAIDg	(4) Blundell&Bond, robust IV: L.EDUCAIDg L.EXPEDUC	(5) Blundell&Bond, robust IV: ENERGYAID
L.COMPLETION	−0.07***	−0.07	0.12	0.16	0.04
	(0.000)	(0.379)	(0.329)	(0.138)	(0.805)
EDUCAIDg disbursements	0.83***	0.83*	2.22**	2.53**	31.37
	(0.000)	(0.069)	(0.041)	(0.021)	(0.151)
EXPEDUC	0.29	0.29	0.68	2.13	2.04
	(0.279)	(0.799)	(0.828)	(0.588)	(0.637)
PTR	−0.07***	−0.07	−0.68***	−0.64***	−0.69***
	(0.003)	(0.561)	(0.000)	(0.000)	(0.003)
YOUNG-POP	−2.19***	−2.19***	−1.08***	−1.07***	−1.63***
	(0.000)	(0.001)	(0.000)	(0.000)	(0.000)
GDPcap	−0.003***	−0.003	0.000	−0.000	0.002
	(0.001)	(0.309)	(0.915)	(0.977)	(0.202)
BUDGET	0.03	0.03	−0.02	0.08	0.22
	(0.259)	(0.772)	(0.884)	(0.577)	(0.435)
INFLATION	0.000	0.000	−0.000	−0.000	0.003**
	(0.639)	(0.837)	(0.690)	(0.670)	(0.030)
OPEN	0.32	0.32	1.55	−0.07	0.89
	(0.140)	(0.417)	(0.611)	(0.985)	(0.838)
FREE	−1.05***	−1.05	−0.87	−0.41	0.81
	(0.000)	(0.252)	(0.208)	(0.511)	(0.497)

Table 2. *(Continued)*

Dependent variable: NER	(1) Arellano&Bond IV: L.EDUCAIDg	(2) Arellano&Bond, robust IV: L.EDUCAIDg	(3) Blundell&Bond, robust IV: L.EDUCAIDg	(4) Blundell&Bond, robust IV: L.EDUCAIDg L.EXPEDUC	(5) Blundell&Bond, robust IV: ENERGYAID
Wald	chi2(19) = 41455 (0.000)	chi2(19) = 49.93 (0.000)	chi2(19) = 253.52 (0.000)	chi2(19) = 293.79 (0.000)	chi2(18) = 2744 (0.000)
Hansen	chi2(88) = 87.08 (0.508)	chi2(88) = 87.08 (0.508)	chi2(18) = 28.23 (0.059)	chi2(27) = 34.77 (0.145)	chi2(9) = 11.99 (0.214)
AR1	$z = -4.13$ (0.000)	$z = -3.20$ (0.001)	$z = -3.63$ (0.000)	$z = -3.89$ (0.000)	$z = -2.74$ (0.006)
AR2	$z = 0.09$ (0.925)	$z = 0.08$ (0.940)	$z = 1.35$ (0.177)	$z = 1.58$ (0.114)	$z = -0.30$ (0.763)
N	822	822	999	999	664
Countries	124	124	128	128	112

Notes: *P* values in parentheses. The prefix L. denotes a lagged variable. Constant term and missing value indicators not presented here. For an overview of variable definitions and sources, see Appendix A.

* Significant at 10%.
** Significant at 5%.
*** Significant at 1%.

Table 3.   Alternative education and aid variables

Blundell&Bond, robust IV: L.EDUCAIDg	(1) Dep. var.: COMPLETION	(2) Dep. var.: NER	(3) Dep. var.: NER
L.COMPLETION	0.14		
	(0.257)		
L.NER		0.21	0.22
		(0.258)	(0.360)
EDUCAIDg technical coop.	−0.54		0.90**
	(0.272)		(0.015)
EDUCAIDg disbursements		−1.11	
		(0.209)	
EXPEDUC	−0.47	1.26	10.36**
	(0.804)	(0.345)	(0.015)
PTR	−0.68***	−0.31**	−0.25
	(0.000)	(0.030)	(0.180)
YOUNG-POP	−1.02***	−0.68***	−0.90***
	(0.000)	(0.002)	(0.006)
GDPcap	−0.000	0.001	0.000
	(0.630)	(0.423)	(0.642)
BUDGET	−0.00	0.17	0.08
	(0.980)	(0.185)	(0.570)
INFLATION	−0.000	0.000	−0.001
	(0.488)	(0.629)	(0.665)
OPEN	2.68	0.65	−8.91**
	(0.146)	(0.588)	(0.032)
FREE	−1.14*	−0.86*	−1.07
	(0.099)	(0.073)	(0.144)
Wald	chi2(19) = 278.46	chi2(19) = 178.42	chi2(18) = 2634.56
	(0.000)	(0.000)	(0.000)
Hansen	chi2(18) = 28.41	chi2(18) = 26.06	chi2(19) = 19.79
	(0.056)	(0.098)	(0.407)
AR1	z = −3.58	z = −2.55	z = −1.89
	(0.000)	(0.011)	(0.059)
AR2	z = 1.45	z = 1.50	z = 1.61
	(0.148)	(0.133)	(0.108)
N	999	999	697
Countries	128	128	113

Notes: P values in parentheses. The prefix L. denotes a lagged variable. Constant term and missing value indicators not presented here. For an overview of variable definitions and sources, see Appendix A.
* Significant at 10%.
** Significant at 5%.
*** Significant at 1%.

ments, but with NER instead of COMPLETION as the dependent variable (regression (2)). Finally, in regression (3), technical cooperation is combined with NER as the dependent variable.

Neither the relationship between technical cooperation and primary completion rates, nor the relationship between disbursements and net enrolment rates turn out to be significant. Coefficient estimates even turn negative. However, regression (3) which estimates the effect of technical cooperation in the education sector on primary net enrolment shows a positive and significant impact of 0.9 percentage points induced by an increase in aid by 1% of GDP. Similarly, current national expenditure is insignificant in regressions (1) and (2), but significant with a strong positive effect in regression (3). In fact, in this particular specification, the effect of EXPEDUC is extremely strong and about 11 times higher than the effect of technical cooperation.

All other results are similar as before. We again find a negative effect of a high pupil–teacher ratio and of a high share of children within the population. The negative effect of bad political governance which had been less obvious in Table 2 is again found here and significant at the 10% level in two out of three regressions. Among our variables for economic governance, now openness to trade shows the only significant effect (in one regression), but again, the negative coefficient estimate contradicts rather than confirms any positive effect of good economic governance.

It should be noted that overall regression statistics tend to be less convincing for this table, than in the other regression tables discussed before.

Comparing the results of the structural panel with the results of the annual panel for the 1990s, we do not observe major changes with respect to the effect of most of the explanatory variables. While it was expected that due to their limited change over time, especially the macroeconomic and governance variables, but also variables characterizing the education system would not reveal much impact in the annual panel, we actually observe that those which appear relevant in one case, also appear relevant in the other case.

However, we observe that overall, the annual panel appears to show a much more convincing effect of aid. In those regressions in which it is significant, it is estimated to lie at a gain in enrolment or completion by between 0.8 and 2.5 percentage points for an increase of aid by 1% of the GDP in recipient countries. However, looking at resources currently allocated to aid for education, this effect appears only very small. On average during the 1990s and across the countries considered here, aid to education as a share of GDP was 0.3% for disbursements and 0.5% for technical cooperation.[6] Therefore, in the most optimistic case, to reach an aid induced increase in primary completion rates by 2.5 percentage points, we would need to increase aid allocated to education by 200%. Thus, neither in our structural analysis since the early 1970s, nor in our annual analysis for the 1990s, aid appears to be a strongly relevant determinant

---

[6] Calculated on the basis of the imputed dataset. Note that the higher percentage for technical cooperation may be explained either by the fact that information on this variable is more complete or by the (partial) inclusion of commitments which may not always have led to actual disbursements (see Section 2).

of educational outcomes. Moreover, there is no clear evidence with respect to the effectiveness of aid as compared to the effectiveness of current national education expenditure.

However, so far, we have not considered non-linearities and potential interaction effects. This may lead to a bias of our previous results and will be considered in detail in the following section.

3.3. Testing for non-linearities and the possible interaction of aid and governance

Non-linearities could be imagined with some plausibility for most of the explanatory variables in the regression. The wider aid effectiveness literature shows some strong evidence for decreasing returns of aid (see e.g. (Hansen and Tarp, 2001)), and decreasing returns seem plausible as well for GDP per capita and the different variables introduced to measure good governance. It might well be that some of the potentially relevant relationships have been underestimated or not even been discovered yet because of the limitations of the linear model.

Moreover, as Burnside and Dollar's (2000) seminal paper on aid effectiveness suggests that aid may have a relevant impact only under conditions of good governance, the interaction between aid and governance will also be examined here. Possibly, our initial results on aid effectiveness in the education sector are underestimated because this interaction is not taken into account. Moreover, even if the average effect remains small, the effect of aid could be very high in a suitable political and economic environment.

Hansen and Tarp's (2001) critique of the Burnside and Dollar (2000) results on aid effectiveness shows that the issue of interaction terms and non-linearities of individual variables should not be treated separately. According to Hansen and Tarp, the relevance of the interaction term between aid and governance in the Burnside–Dollar model is simply a reflection of decreasing returns to aid, or, put differently, to an omitted variable bias due to the omission of a relevant quadratic term.

In this study, in order ensure that potential non-linearities are taken into account, each structural or political variable, including aid to education, is inserted into the model as a quadratic function. To avoid overloading the model with too many variables, this procedure is repeated one by one for each variable separately, whereby the quadratic term is retained in the overall model only if significant. In a second step, following the same procedure, each of the governance variables is inserted into the model with an interaction term with educational aid and retained in the model if significant. This procedure is carried out based on the annual panel for the 1990s and for all combinations of COMPLETION and NER with disbursements and technical cooperation. The base equation to which the quadratic and interaction terms are added is again regression (3) from Table 2, i.e. the same regression underlying Table 3.

As presented in Table 4, we find some evidence for both, decreasing returns of aid and an interaction between aid and good governance, albeit the former is statistically significant only when aid is expressed in terms of disbursements and educational outcomes in terms of NER (regressions (2) and (7)) while the latter is significant only when aid is expressed in terms of technical cooperation (regressions (3), (4) and (6)). While the relevance of the interaction term was tested for all governance variables (not shown), the only significant effect was found with respect to political governance expressed in terms of the Freedom House Index. FREE by itself then turns insignificant (although it remains close to significant in regression (5)).

Note that the first four regressions of Table 4 all use the same explanatory variables and only differ with respect to the use of COMPLETION or NER for educational outcomes, and disbursements or technical cooperation for EDUCAIDg. They all include both a square term for EDUCAIDg and the interaction term between FREE and EDUCAIDg. Regressions (5) and (6) additionally introduce a square term for FREE into the two regressions using technical cooperation, in which the interaction effect with FREE was significant. This leads to some reduction of the estimated strength of the relationship, but the latter remains significant at the 10% level, at least in regression (6). Regression (7) finally omits the interaction term from the equations based on disbursements and NER, in which only the quadratic impact of aid was significant. This change does not alter the evidence for decreasing returns of aid.

Let us now more closely examine the coefficient estimates. The evidence on diminishing returns from regression (7) suggests that the quadratic aid function has its maximum at about 5% of a recipient country's GDP. This implies that the effect of higher disbursements gradually decreases up to this point and then turns negative. 5% is more than 10-times higher than average disbursements, but still exceeds the actual amount in some individual country-cases so that its effect is rather questionable. In those countries which receive relatively little aid, however, the added value of an increase of aid resources may be marked. According to regression (7) the effect for countries with initial aid to education of between 0.1 and 0.5% of national GDP is more than twice as high as estimated in the most optimistic results from Tables 2 and 3.

In all other regression models of Table 4, the effect of aid cannot be determined independently of the recipient country's political environment. This variable also influences the threshold after which increasing aid has a negative impact. Computing the maximum amount of aid with a positive effect from regression (4) where both EDUCAIDg by itself and the interaction term with FREE are significant we obtain 10% of GDP for a country with an ideal situation of political rights and civil liberties (FREE = 1), but only 0.4% (i.e. close to the current average) for a country with a rather difficult situation (FREE = 5). For countries with an even worse situation (FREE = 6 or 7) any positive amount of aid to education appears to have a negative, rather than a positive effect on educational outcomes. These results suggest that aid resources may indeed be fungible, so that under adverse external circumstances, even if they are directly allocated to a specific purpose like education, they may indirectly fuel other activities harmful to development. In the other two regressions in which the interaction term is significant, the influence of political freedom on the impact of aid is of similar (regression (6)) or even greater magnitude (regression (3)). In the latter,

Table 4. *Diminishing returns and the interaction of aid and political governance*

Blundell&Bond, robust IV: L.EDUCAIDg	(1) Dep. var: COMPLETION	(2) Dep. var: NER	(3) Dep. var: COMPLETION	(4) Dep. var: NER	(5) Dep. var: COMPLETION	(6) Dep. var: NER	(7) Dep. var: NER
L.COMPLETION	0.11 (0.378)		0.21** (0.029)		0.20** (0.041)		
L.NER		0.29* (0.098)		0.31** (0.029)		0.30** (0.044)	0.30* (0.088)
EDUCAIDg disbursements	9.31 (0.142)	8.13*** (0.005)					6.24** (0.016)
EDUCAIDg² disbursements	−0.50 (0.273)	−0.70*** (0.003)					−0.67** (0.011)
Disbursements × FREE	−2.71 (0.164)	−1.36 (0.166)					
EDUCAIDg technical coop.			4.46 (0.134)	4.34* (0.087)	2.95 (0.319)	3.62 (0.138)	
EDUCAIDg² technical coop.			−0.18 (0.236)	−0.16 (0.222)	−0.12 (0.436)	−0.13 (0.301)	
Technical coop. × FREE			−1.02* (0.075)	−0.84** (0.043)	−0.70 (0.194)	−0.69* (0.075)	
EXPEDUC	0.17 (0.962)	−0.05 (0.971)	−0.18 (0.944)	0.24 (0.886)	−0.36 (0.889)	0.28 (0.868)	0.26 (0.837)
PTR	−0.70*** (0.000)	−0.26* (0.064)	−0.64*** (0.000)	−0.20* (0.081)	−0.64*** (0.000)	−0.22* (0.074)	−0.29** (0.039)
YOUNG-POP	−1.07*** (0.000)	−0.60*** (0.005)	−0.91*** (0.001)	−0.68*** (0.006)	−0.91*** (0.000)	−0.64*** (0.007)	−0.58* (0.012)
GDPcap	0.000 (0.713)	0.001 (0.316)	0.000 (0.988)	0.001 (0.467)	−0.000 (0.695)	0.000 (0.661)	0.001 (0.323)

Table 4. *(Continued)*

Blundell&Bond, robust IV:L.EDUCAIDg	(1) Dep. var.: COMPLETION	(2) Dep. var.: NER	(3) Dep. var.: COMPLETION	(4) Dep. var.: NER	(5) Dep. var.: COMPLETION	(6) Dep. var.: NER	(7) Dep. var.: NER
BUDGET	0.00	0.05	0.02	0.05	-0.03	0.02	0.09
	(0.977)	(0.678)	(0.895)	(0.725)	(0.865)	(0.883)	(0.484)
INFLATION	-0.0001	0.0001	-0.0001	0.0001	-0.0001	0.0001	0.0001
	(0.719)	(0.405)	(0.521)	(0.494)	(0.437)	(0.604)	(0.490)
OPEN	1.89	1.93	2.07	1.54	2.25	1.50	1.68
	(0.596)	(0.092)*	(0.395)	(0.391)	(0.397)	(0.410)	(0.128)
FREE	-0.35	-0.54	-0.55	-0.51	-5.21	-3.25	-0.50
	(0.626)	(0.320)	(0.400)	(0.387)	(0.107)	(0.167)	(0.365)
FREE^2					0.54	0.32	
					(0.149)	(0.257)	
Wald	chi2(21) = 283.03	chi2(21) = 228.94	chi2(21) = 397.42	chi2(21) = 364.84	chi2(22) = 398.09	chi2(22) = 364.59	chi2(20) = 247.35
	(0.000)	(0.000)	(0.000)	(0.000)	(0.000)	(0.000)	(0.000)
Hansen	chi2(26) = 36.12	chi2(36) = 41.68	chi2(36) = 41.42	chi2(36) = 45.02	chi2(36) = 40.46	chi2(36) = 45.76	chi2(27) = 38.39
	(0.089)	(0.238)	(0.246)	(0.144)	(0.280)	(0.128)	(0.072)
AR1	z = -3.46	z = -2.93	z = -3.93	z = -3.19	z = -3.85	z = -3.10	z = -2.98
	(0.001)	(0.003)	(0.000)	(0.001)	(0.000)	(0.002)	(0.003)
AR2	z = 1.14	z = 1.54	z = 1.69	z = 1.47	z = 1.65	z = 1.54	z = 1.58
	(0.256)	(0.124)	(0.091)	(0.142)	(0.099)	(0.124)	(0.115)
N	999	999	999	999	999	999	999
Countries	128	128	128	128	128	128	128

Notes: P values in parentheses. The prefix L. denotes a lagged variable. Constant term and missing value indicators not presented here. For an overview of variable definitions and sources, see Appendix A.

* Significant at 10%.
** Significant at 5%.
*** Significant at 1%.

Table 5.   *Simulations of the impact of aid to education at different levels of political freedom and aid*

Freedom House index (FREE)	1	2	3	4	5	6	7
			decreasing political freedom				→
EDUCAIDg (technical coop.)							
0.1% of GDP	3.40	2.38	1.36	0.34	−0.68	−1.70	−2.72
0.5% of GDP	3.26	2.24	1.22	0.20	−0.82	−1.84	−2.86
1% of GDP	3.08	2.06	1.04	0.02	−1.00	−2.02	−3.04
2% of GDP	2.72	1.70	0.68	−0.34	−1.36	−2.38	−3.40
5% of GDP	1.64	0.62	−0.40	−1.42	−2.44	−3.46	−4.48

Note: Numbers indicate the partial derivative ∂COMPLETION/∂EDUCAIDg for different initial values of EDUCAIDg and FREE based on coefficient estimates from regression (3), Table 4.

only up to a situation of moderate political freedom (FREE = 4) aid to education can exert any positive effect, while the effect is unambiguously negative in all situations in which oppression is stronger (FREE $\geq$ 5). Table 5 presents an overview over the simulation results based on regression (3) with varying degrees of political freedom and initial aid.

It follows that under very positive political conditions, aid to education in the relevant range always has a positive effect while its effect is always negative under situations of extreme oppression. In between, i.e. in the ranges of FREE from 3 to 4, the effect of aid turns negative if aid is relatively high.

The above discussion provides a more refined picture of the impact of aid. However, overall, the effect of aid still seems to be very moderate. While the evidence on the diminishing returns of disbursements indicated that in cases of little initial aid, the impact of additional aid could be about twice as high as expected from the previous section, results for the interaction with political rights and civil liberties appear to be relatively close to the initial results, even for the best initial situations. Obviously, some of this result may be due to the low quality of the data at hand. As mentioned earlier, information on disbursements is far from complete while information on technical cooperation covers only parts of donor activity and does not clearly distinguish between disbursements and commitments. These problems may lead to downward biased coefficient estimates. However, it may also be that aid to education is not effectively oriented towards the central objective of universal primary education. This may be reflected in major parts of EDUCAID being oriented towards secondary and tertiary, rather than primary education. Specific data for development assistance allocated to primary education is available only for commitments and only after 1975 (and with many missing values).[7] As far as information is available, we

---

[7] The DAC statistics include some inconsistent data with figures for aid to primary education higher than total aid to education. To calculate the above means, these values were adjusted to the maximum possible share of 100%. Without this adjustment, the means would appear substantially higher.

find that its share is indeed rather small: On average, it is 44% of total aid to education for the late 1970s and early 1980s, and about 35% thereafter (OECD/DAC, 2004). Especially after 1990, when the EFA-objectives had been internationally declared in Jomptien, one might have expected a stronger orientation towards primary education. However, it seems that the share has in fact been decreasing relative to earlier years.

4. Conclusions

Analyzing aid effectiveness at the sectoral level provides some interesting evidence both with respect to the general debate on aid effectiveness and with respect to the interaction between aid and governance. Despite some differences in the results based on different data and estimation methods, the empirical application to the education sector provides allows us to conclude that aid to education increases primary education in developing countries (measured both in terms of enrolment and completion rates). We thus indeed observe a positive effect of aid at the sector level.

At the same time, coefficient estimates for the impact of aid are rather small. In the most optimistic case, they imply that an increase of the current aid by 200% would lead to a rise of net primary enrolment by 2.5 percentage points. Only where aid to education is relatively low at the outset, there may initially be a higher impact (about twice as high). All in all, this result demonstrates that, at any realistic rate of growth of aid to education, universal primary education will not be reached by this means. This holds at least as long as development assistance is not spent much more efficiently than it currently is. In fact, strikingly, despite the fact that universal primary education has been made a central international objective repeated over and over again on international conferences on poverty and on education, the average share of donors' aid to education effectively committed to primary education has only been about 1/3 in recent years.

Unfortunately, there is no compelling evidence that national education expenditure in developing countries shows any greater impact on education outcomes. Only in one regression specification, we obtain a rather high positive and significant coefficient implying that an increase of current education expenditure by 1% of GNI leads to a rise in net primary enrolment by 10%. Generally, coefficient estimates are much lower and insignificant. This confirms parts of the educational development literature which suggests that inefficiencies in national education expenditure are so important that results are only loosely related to financial inputs, at least in a cross-country comparison.

Moreover, it comes out rather clearly that the structural parameters of the education system such as the number of young people in the country and the pupil–teacher ratio also play a crucial role when it comes to finding sustainable solutions for the financing of primary education. In the long run, countries in which population growth is high apparently have to accept equally high pupil–teacher ratios to achieve education for all. In the short run, however, high pupil–teacher ratios may reduce the demand for education.

Finally, the study suggests that national policies do not matter in the education sector alone. While good governance in economic terms (trade openness, budgetary austerity, price stability) does not show any significant positive effect on primary education enrolment, general political and institutional governance clearly does. Lack of political freedom and civil liberties is quite consistently negatively related to enrolment.

In addition, at least in the short run, the effects of development assistance and governance seem to be interrelated. It turns out that under very bad political and institutional conditions, aid can have a negative, rather than a positive impact on primary enrolment and completion. This may be interpreted as an indication of fungibility of resources, whereby more aid frees government resources for activities that are detrimental to the country's overall development.

Simulations provide some evidence that the impact of aid to education is highest when (i) aid resources remain a rather limited share of national resources (diminishing returns) and (ii) good governance in terms of political rights and civil liberties provide a positive environment for learning and its application in the society and on the labor market. Nevertheless, even under very positive circumstances, the average effect of aid remains rather small.

With this result, our evidence for the education sector comes quite close to the conclusion one might draw from the general aid effectiveness literature. While getting conceptionally closer to the micro-level than the macroeconomic studies on aid and growth, we are far from obtaining the highly optimistic results suggested by project evaluations. Given that our results on the impact of aid are as weak as at the macro-level, despite the considerable reduction of complexity in the relationships to be considered, these results do not seem to be a simple reflection of omitted variable bias. It remains that our study suffers from imprecise and incomplete information on many variables, which could only be taken into account by imputations and the inclusion of missing value indicators in our regressions. This may imply that the actual effect of aid is somewhat underestimated here. However, as long as the potential bias is not really substantial, this would not alter our general conclusions.

Acknowledgements

We would like to thank Simone Kirasic for useful research assistance, and Julia Benn (OECD/DAC) and Michael Bruneforth (UNESCO-UIS) for their support with respect to the interpretation of the DAC and UNESCO statistics. Moreover, we are grateful for helpful comments and suggestions by Jean Bourdon, Michael Funke, Ashok Parikh, Smita Sirohi, Matthias Lutz and the participants of a research seminar at IREDU (University of Burgundy, Dijon).

Appendix A. List of variables

Variable name	Definition	Sources
NER	net primary enrolment (%)	WDI (World Bank, 2003, 2005)
COMPLETION	primary completion rate, total (% of relevant age group)	WDI (World Bank, 2006)
EDUCAID	aid allocated to education (constant 2001 US$, millions)	commitments: IDS/CRS, Table 1
EDUCAIDn	EDUCAID (constant 2001 US$) / population	disbursements: IDS/CRS, Table 5
EDUCAIDg	EDUCAID (US$) / GDP · 100	technical cooperation: IDS/DAC, Table 5a (OECD/DAC, 2004)
EXPEDUC	national education expenditure (% of GNI)	WDI (World Bank, 2003)
PTR	pupil–teacher ratio in primary education	WDI (World Bank, 2003, 2005)
YOUNG-POP	population aged 0–14 (% of total population)	WDI (World Bank, 2003, 2005)
GDPcap	GDP per capita (constant 2000 US$)	WDI (World Bank, 2003, 2005)
BUDGET	budget surplus (% of GDP)	WDI (World Bank, 2005)
INFLATION	inflation (consumer prices, % annual)	WDI (World Bank, 2003, 2005)
OPEN	openness (export + import, % of GDP)	WDI (World Bank, 2003, 2005)
FREE	Freedom House index of political rights and civil liberties (1–7, whereby 1 shows the highest degree of freedom)	Freedom House (2005)
ENERGYAID	aid allocated to energy production and planning (constant 2001 US$, millions)	commitments: IDS/CRS, Table 1 disbursements: IDS/CRS, Table 5 technical cooperation: IDS/DAC, Table 5a (OECD/DAC, 2004)

References

Angrist, J., Imbens, G., Rubin, D. (1996), Identification of causal effects using instrumental variables. *Journal of the American Statistical Association* 91, 444–455.

Arellano, M., Bond, S. (1991), Some tests of specification for panel data: Monte Carlo evidence and an application to employment equations. *Review of Economic Studies* 58, 277–297.

Arellano, M., Bover, O. (1995), Another look at the instrumental variable estimation of error-components models. *Journal of Econometric* 68, 29–51.

Blundell, R., Bond, S. (1998), Initial conditions and moment restrictions in dynamic panel data models. *Journal of Econometrics* 87, 115–143.

Boone, P. (1996), Politics and the effectiveness of aid. *European Economic Review* 40, 289–329.

Burnside, C., Dollar, D. (2000), Aid, policies and growth. *American Economic Review* 90, 847–868.

Doucouliagos, H., Paldam, M. (2005), The aid effectiveness literature: the sad result of 40 years of research. *Working Paper*, No. 15, University of Aarhus, Department of Economics.

Easterly, W. (2001), *The Elusive Quest for Growth. Economists' Adventures and Misadventures in the Tropics*. MIT Press, Cambridge.

Easterly, W. (2002), The cartel of good intentions: bureaucracy versus markets in foreign aid. *Working Paper*, No. 4. Center for Global Development, Institute for International Economics. Washington (revised version, May).

Easterly, W. (2003), Can foreign aid buy growth? *Journal of Economic Perspectives* 17, 23–48.

Easterly, W. (2006), *The White Man's Burden. Why the West's Effort to Aid the Rest Have Done so Much Ill and so Little Good*. Penguin, New York.

Freedom House (2005), Freedom House Country Ratings. http://www.freedomhouse. org/ratings/index.htm (29/05/06).

Hansen, H., Tarp, F. (2001), Aid and growth regressions. *Journal of Development Economics* 64, 547–570.

Harms, P., Lutz, M. (2004), The macroeconomic effects of foreign aid: A survey. *Discussion Paper*, No. 11, University of St. Gallen, Department of Economics.

Kaufmann, D., Kraay, A., Mastruzzi, M. (2003), Governance matters III: governance indicators for 1996–2002. World Bank Policy Research. *Working Paper*, No. 3106, Washington, DC.

Kaufmann, D., Kraay, A., Mastruzzi, M. (2005), Governance matters IV: governance indicators for 1996–2004. World Bank Policy Research. *Working Paper*, No. 3630. Washington, DC.

Michaelowa, K., Borrmann, A. (2006), Evaluation bias and incentive structures in bi- and multilateral aid agencies. *Review of Development Economics* 10, 313–329.

MINEDAF (2002), *Universal Primary Education: Goal for All*. Statistical Document MINEDAF, vol. VIII. UNESCO, Dar-Es-Salaam.

Mingat, A., Suchaut, B. (2000), *Une analyse économique comparative des systèmes éducatifs africains*. De Boeck, Paris.

Mingat, A., Tan, J.-P. (2003), On the mechanics of progress in primary education. *Economics of Education Review* 22, 455–467.

Mingat, A., Rakotomalala, R., Tan, J.-P. (2002), *Achieving Education for All by 2015. Simulation Results for 33 African Countries*. World Bank, Washington, DC.

OECD/DAC (2001), *DAC Guidelines on Poverty Reduction*. Paris.

OECD/DAC (2004), International development statistics (IDS) databank. http://www.oecd.org/dataoecd/50/17/5037721.htm (20/01/04).

Rodrik, D., Subramaniam, A., Trebbi, F. (2002), Institutions rule: The primacy of institutions over integration and geography in economic development. *IMF Working Paper*, No. 02/189. Washington, DC.

Roodman, D. (2005), xtabond2: stata module to extend xtabond dynamic panel data estimator. Center for Global Development. Washington, DC. http://econpapers.repec.org/software/bocbocode/s435901.htm (10/04/06).

Shea, J. (1997), Instrument relevance in multivariate linear models: a simple measure. *The Review of Economics and Statistics* 79, 348–352.

Staiger, D., Stock, J. (1997), Instrumental variables regressions with weak instruments. *Econometrica* 65, 557–586.

UNESCO-UIS (2006), World Education Indicators. http://www.uis.unesco.org/en/stats/statistics/indicators/indic0.htm (23/05/06).

Windmeijer, F. (2005), A finite sample correction for the variance of linear efficient two-step GMM estimators. *Journal of Econometrics* 126, 25–51.

World Bank (1998), *Assessing aid*. Washington, DC.

World Bank (2001), Building institutions for markets. *World Development Report* 2002. Washington, DC.

World Bank (2003), *World development indicators*. Washington, DC, CD-ROM.

World Bank (2005), *World development indicators*. Washington, DC, CD-ROM.

World Bank (2006), Governance matters IV: governance indicators for 1996–2004. http://www.worldbank.org/wbi/governance/pubs/govmatters4.html (20/05/06).

CHAPTER 19

The Determinants of Aid in the Post-Cold War Era

Subhayu Bandyopadhyay[a,b] and Howard J. Wall[c]

[a]*Department of Economics, College of Business and Economics,*
PO Box 6025, West Virginia University, Morgantown, WV 26506-6025, USA
[b]*Research Fellow, IZA, Bonn, Germany*
E-mail address: bandysub@mail.wvu.edu
[c]*Research Division, Federal Reserve Bank of St. Louis,*
PO Box 442, St. Louis, MO 63166-0442, USA
E-mail address: wall@stls.frb.org

Abstract

This paper estimates the responsiveness of aid to recipient countries' economic and physical needs, civil/political rights, and government effectiveness. We look exclusively at the post-Cold War era and use fixed effects to control for the political, strategic, and other considerations of donors. We find that aid and per capita income have been negatively related, while aid has been positively related to infant mortality, rights, and government effectiveness.

Keywords: Foreign aid

JEL classifications: F35

1. Introduction

This paper estimates the extent to which aid, or official development assistance, is related to measures of recipient-countries' physical and economic needs, human rights, and government effectiveness. We examine the post-Cold War era, which thus far has not been the focus of substantial research, although there are fairly obvious reasons to believe that the differences in the geopolitics between the pre- and post-Cold War eras amount to a structural difference in terms of aid allocation.

There are many reasons why we should be interested in the determinants of aid levels. First, because aid is an important means by which donor countries and agencies try to alleviate poverty, we should care about whether aid is being directed towards those most in need of it. Similarly, we should also be interested in whether aid tends to

THEORY AND PRACTICE OF FOREIGN AID
VOLUME 1   ISSN: 1574-8715
DOI: 10.1016/S1574-8715(06)01019-0

go more towards where it might be most effective, as measured by the effectiveness of the recipient government in making use of the aid or in fostering economic growth.[1]

Early studies of aid allocation tend to apply some version of the McKinlay and Little (1979) dichotomy – recipient needs versus donor interests – to models of aid allocation. As laid out by Maizels and Nissanke (1984), in the recipient-needs model, "aid is given to compensate for the shortfalls in domestic resources", whereas in the donor-interests model, aid serves donors' "political/security, investment, and trade interests". Maizels and Nissanke found that multilateral aid tended to follow the recipient-needs model, while bilateral aid tended to follow the donor-interests model, although there were elements of each model in both types of aid.[2]

Subsequent research has added two other categories – human rights and recipient-country institutions – to the McKinlay and Little dichotomy, although not all papers deal with all four categories simultaneously.[3] For example, Wall (1995) found that countries with lower per capita incomes tended to receive higher levels of aid per capita, although aid was not related to infant mortality or to civil/political rights. On the other hand, Trumbull and Wall (1994) found that, when recipient-country fixed effects are included to control for donor interests, aid levels respond to changes in infant mortality and rights, but not to changes in per capita income.

Alesina and Dollar (2000) included a variety of variables, such as trade openness, colonial history, and friendliness at the UN, to capture the effects of donor interests. They concluded that, although aid is related to per capita income and democracy (but not to civil rights), it is as much directed by political and strategic considerations. A pair of recent studies focus on the institutions of the recipient countries: Alesina and Weder (2002) found that corrupt governments do not tend to receive less aid than clean governments, and Dollar and Levin (2004) found that, over time, aid has become directed more towards countries with sound institutions and policies, although there were differences across bilateral donors and multilateral agencies.

In a series of papers, Eric Neumayer provided a detailed analysis of the relationship between aid and human rights.[4] In Neumayer (2003a), UN agencies were found to respond to economic and possibly human-development needs, but not necessarily to political freedom and corruption. There is some evidence in Neumayer (2003b) that high levels of rights or improvements in rights mean higher bilateral aid, but Neumayer concluded that the role of rights is limited and did not increase after the end of the Cold War. Finally, Neumayer (2003c) found that although respect for rights tends to play a role at the selection stage, there is significant inconsistency in the application of rights to the determination of the levels of bilateral aid.

---

[1] See Boone (1996) and Kosack (2003) for discussions of the links between institutions and aid effectiveness. Also, in Burnside and Dollar (2000, 2004) the impact of aid on growth depends on the quality of recipient-state institutions and policies; although Easterly *et al.* (2004) and Rajan and Subramanian (2005) found little or no evidence of this.

[2] See also Dowling and Hiemenz (1985).

[3] Neumayer (2003b) provided an excellent survey of the literature.

[4] See also Neumayer (2003d).

This paper focuses on three of the four categories of aid determinants – recipient needs, human rights, and recipient-government effectiveness – while following Trumbull and Wall (1994) in using fixed effects to control for the fourth category, the strategic and political interests of donor countries. The advantage of this approach is that, because we do not have to choose strategic/political variables explicitly, we avoid the problems that can arise if there are excluded variables that determine both the level of aid and one or more of our other explanatory variables. This means that we do not run the risk of heterogeneity bias because of omitted time-invariant factors related to history, geography, culture, etc. If these factors, which are primarily the sort of factors that are used to measure donor interests, are not completely specified and they are correlated with aid and one or more of the included explanatory variables, then heterogeneity bias is the result. The relative shortness of our sample provides comfort that fixed effects provide a useful control for donor interests.

While our fixed-effects approach follows Trumbull and Wall (1994), there are two main differences between our analysis and theirs. The first and more obvious difference is that we are able to look at a more recent time period, so our results should be more relevant for understanding the present situation. Second, because we use a quadratic rather than a log-linear functional form, we are able to provide a richer analysis of the functional relationship between aid and the variables of interest.

2. Empirical model and data

Our dependent variable, Aid_{it}, is real net official development assistance from all sources for country i in year t. Data are taken from the World Bank and are denominated in constant 2000 \$US. We estimate the following reduced-form regression, in which i denotes the recipient country and t denotes time:

$$
\begin{aligned}
Aid_{it} = {} & \alpha_0 + \alpha_i + \gamma_t \\
& + \beta_1 GDPpercapita_{it} + \beta_2 GDPpercapita_{it}^2 \\
& + \delta_1 InfantMortality_{it} + \delta_2 InfantMortality_{it}^2 \\
& + \lambda Civil/PoliticalRights \\
& + \omega GovernmentEffectiveness \\
& + \theta_1 Population_{it} + \theta_2 Population_{it}^2 + \varepsilon_{it}.
\end{aligned}
$$

The intercept includes a component, α_0, that is common to all recipient countries, and a recipient-country fixed effect, α_i, that is specific to each recipient country but fixed over the sample period. We also include a period effect, γ_t, that is common to all countries in the sample but varies over time. Our two recipient-needs variables are real GDP per capita and infant mortality, both of which are from the World Bank.[5] We think it is important to include both of these variables because each captures a different

---

[5] Per capita GDP is converted into \$US using purchasing-power-parity exchange rates.

Table 1. Sample statistics

	Mean	Standard deviation
Real aid ($millions)	356.93	439.26
Real GDP per capita ($thousands)	4.96	4.54
Infant mortality	52.33	39.56
Civil/political rights	8.29	3.39
Government effectiveness	−0.30	0.67
Population (millions)	36.25	139.51

element of recipient need: Per capita income captures economic need while infant mortality represents physical need. While clearly correlated in the long run, economic and physical needs do not necessarily move in the same direction over shorter periods of time, and aid is clearly meant to respond to both.

For our rights variable, we use the sum of the civil liberties and political rights indices produced by Freedom House. For each category, the Freedom House index scores countries from 1 to 7, with 1 being the most free and 7 being the most restrictive. For the regression here, we have reversed the order, so that the level of rights increases with the index. Our measure of recipient-government effectiveness is from the World Bank's Governance Indicators (see Kaufmann et al., 2006), which scores governments between −2.5 and 2.5 on the basis of the "competence of their bureaucracy and the quality of public service delivery". Finally, we include recipient-country population to capture differences in recipient-country size. The quadratic specification enables us to consider the extent of population bias, by which the per capita aid allocation falls with country size: a concave relationship between the level of aid and population is consistent with a population bias.

We have three years of data, 1995, 2000, and 2003. After eliminating observations for which data are incomplete and countries for which there are fewer than two useful observations, we are left with 135 recipient countries and 395 observations. The sample statistics for all variables are provided in Table 1 and the country averages of the variables are provided in the data appendix.

The distribution of average aid to countries in our sample is illustrated by Figure 1. The mean country in our sample received $357 million per year in aid, although the median country, Yemen, received only $226 million, indicating that aid was skewed toward a few countries. Specifically, there were 13 countries that received more than $1 billion in aid per year, the top five of which were China, Poland, Congo, Indonesia, and Russia. At the other extreme, four countries in our sample – Singapore, the Bahamas, St. Kitts, and Kuwait – averaged less than $10 million in aid receipts per year.

Figure 2 provides a different angle on the distribution of aid across countries by showing the shares of total aid received. The three countries receiving the most aid – China, Poland, and Congo – alone accounted for 13 percent of the total. These countries plus the 10 countries that received between $900 million and $1800 million per

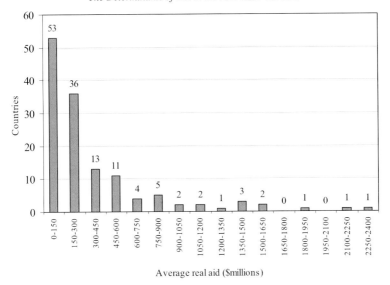

Fig. 1.   *Distribution of average aid.*

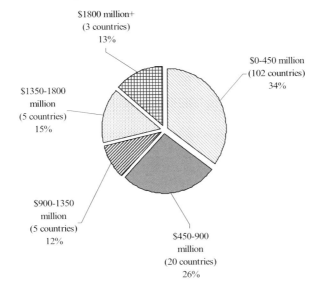

Fig. 2.   *Shares of world aid.*

year accounted for a larger share of aid (40 percent) than did the 102 countries that received less than $450 million per year.

   To get a clear picture of how aid is distributed, we need to control for the sizes of the recipient countries, so Figure 3 plots the within-country averages of our explanatory

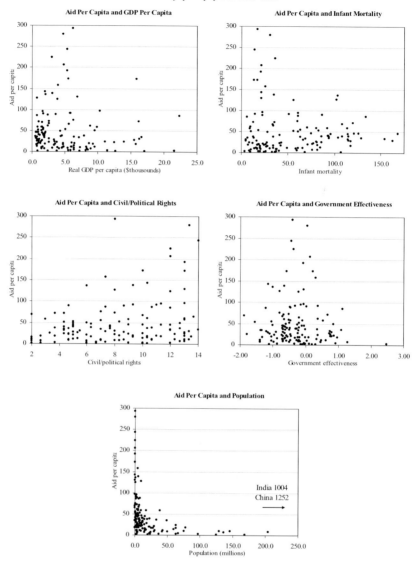

Fig. 3.   Aid per capita and the explanatory variables (country averages).

variables against per capita aid. These plots serve to illustrate the simple correlations
between the dependent and independent variables as well as the distribution of the
values of our independent variables.

Note that the vast majority of our recipient countries had average per capita incomes
around or below $10,000, although there were nine countries with average incomes
above $15,000: Israel and Singapore were the richest of these countries, followed by

Kuwait, Malta, Slovenia, Bahrain, Seychelles, the Bahamas, and the Czech Republic. There was a general tendency for relatively poor countries to receive more aid per capita, but some countries' receipts were well in excess of the sample average. For example, eight countries – Tonga, Cape Verde, Dominica, Vanuatu, Samoa, St. Vincent, St. Lucia, and Seychelles – saw average per capita aid that was more than two standard deviations above the mean. At the other extreme, six countries – Nigeria, China, Brazil, Kuwait, India, and Saudi Arabia – received less than $2 per capita.

From the second panel in Figure 3, it is clear that the eight countries listed above as having the highest per capita aid allocation also tended to have relatively low rates of infant mortality. Also note from this panel that there was a negative correlation between average per capita aid and infant mortality, and that the three countries with the highest average infant mortality rates – Sierra Leone, Niger, and Angola – received only about the average level of aid per capita.

As the third panel of Figure 3 shows, our civil/political rights variable was pretty evenly distributed across the countries in our sample, and there was a general positive correlation between per capita aid allocation and rights. In fact, of the eight countries listed above as receiving the most aid per person, only two – Tonga and Seychelles – had civil/political rights scores below 12. Glancing at the fourth panel, there was no apparent correlation between aid per capita and the effectiveness of recipient-country governments. Also, the governments were clustered below the mediocre score of +1, with Singapore as the lone really effective government. Still, there is significant variation among countries, with many scoring worse than −1. Finally, consistent with the notion of population bias, the fifth panel illustrates the tendency for the smallest (largest) countries to receive the highest (lowest) levels of aid per capita.

3. Empirical results

While the distributions and correlations discussed above are suggestive, they are, of course, inadequate for addressing whether aid is responsive to needs, rights, government effectiveness, and/or donor interests. Instead we need to control for all four categories of variables simultaneously, as in our regression equation above, to determine the influence of each category individually on aid.

We first estimate the model under the restriction that fixed effects, which we use to control for donor interests and other omitted factors, do not matter ($\alpha_i = 0 \ \forall i$), and then without these restrictions. So that we can control for recipient-specific heteroskedasticity, we estimate both models with Feasible Generalized Least Squares. Table 2 provides the regression results for both models, while Table 3 provides the Wald tests for the joint significance of those explanatory variables with quadratic specifications. For each estimation, we have produced a set of figures (Figures 4 and 5) to illustrate the shapes of the estimated relationships between aid and the five explanatory variables. Table 4 reports for the two models the effect on aid of one-standard-deviation increases in each of the five explanatory variables for the average country.

Table 2.   Regression results: dependent variable = level of real aid

	No fixed effects			With fixed effects		
	Coeff.	Std. Err.	t-statistic	Coeff.	Std. Err.	t-statistic
Common intercept	564.693*	48.850	11.56	400.684*	126.088	3.18
Recipient fixed effects	no			yes		
2000 dummy	−56.913*	12.688	−4.49	−82.195*	6.984	−11.77
2003 dummy	−18.343	12.985	−1.41	−11.714	10.667	−1.10
Real GDP per capita	−78.178*	5.955	−13.13	−116.490*	8.848	−13.17
Real GDP per capita squared	2.646*	0.268	9.86	3.927*	0.387	10.14
Infant mortality	−3.053*	0.693	−4.41	3.632*	1.291	2.81
Infant mortality squared	0.022*	0.004	5.75	−0.015*	0.008	−1.95
Civil/political rights	0.212	1.841	0.12	8.940*	2.486	3.60
Government effectiveness	114.432*	13.934	8.21	82.453*	12.856	6.41
Population (millions)	7.497*	0.394	19.01	13.419*	2.815	4.77
Population squared	−0.005*	0.000	−10.78	−0.012*	0.002	−6.95
Log likelihood		−2563.56			−2264.07	
Number of observations		395			395	
Number of recipient countries		135			135	
Estimated coefficients		11			145	

Estimated using Feasible Generalized Least Squares, allowing for recipient-specific heteroskedasticity. An "*" indicates statistical significance at the 10 percent level.

Table 3.   Wald tests of joint significance

	No fixed effects		With fixed effects	
	χ^2	Prob. $> \chi^2$	χ^2	Prob. $> \chi^2$
Real GDP per capita	202.53	0.000	174.00	0.000
Infant mortality	46.40	0.000	8.37	0.015
Population	388.91	0.000	49.34	0.000

Table 4.   Responsiveness of aid to explanatory variables

	No fixed effects	With fixed effects
Real GDP per capita	−90	−135
Infant mortality	−19	27
Civil/political rights	1	29
Gov't effectiveness	75	54
Population	1013	1734

Change in aid ($millions) for the average country from a one-standard-deviation increase in the explanatory variable.

3.1. Model without fixed effects

In the estimation without fixed effects, the effects of all of our explanatory variables except for the civil/political rights variable are statistically different from zero. This is according to the *t*-statistics for the coefficients on the variables with linear specifications, and according to the Wald tests in Table 3 for the variables with quadratic specifications. Thus, according to this model, the level of aid is responsive to recipient needs (as measured by per capita income and by infant mortality), the effectiveness of recipient-country governments, and population, but not to civil/political rights.

For the nature of these relationships, refer to Figure 4, which illustrates the U-shapes of the relationships between aid and both needs variables; i.e., from high levels of need (low income and high infant mortality) an increase in need brings an increase in aid. On the other hand, at low levels of need, an increase in need brings a decrease in aid. This rather peculiar result is not much of a concern when looking at per capita income, however, because there are very few countries with incomes on the upward sloping portion of the relationship. As reported in Table 4, a one-standard-deviation increase in per capita GDP (about $4500) from the average (about $5000) means a decrease in aid of $90 million. The U-shape of the relationship for infant mortality is more troubling because the majority of countries have infant mortality levels that would place them on the downward-sloping portion of the relationship (see Figure 3). For example, for a country with the sample average rate of infant mortality (about 52), a one-standard-deviation increase in infant mortality (about 40) means a *decrease* in aid of $19 million.

The two other statistically significant explanatory variables are worth noting. First, in this model, aid is fairly responsive to government effectiveness: The difference between the least-effective government and the most-effective government is close to $550 million. Put another way, a one-standard-deviation increase from the average level of government effectiveness (-0.30) to the still-mediocre level of 0.37 means a $75 million increase in aid. And, finally, the hill shape of the relationship between aid and population confirms the oft-observed population bias, i.e., per capita aid falls with population. In fact, the bias is strong enough that for countries with populations above around 700 million (just India and China) an increase in population means a decrease in the level of aid, not just per capita aid.

3.2. Model with fixed effects

When we do not impose the restrictions that the fixed effects are all zero (i.e., the intercepts are the same for all recipients), we find that all five explanatory variables are statistically significant in explaining levels of aid. Further, a likelihood-ratio test easily rejects the null hypothesis that the fixed effects are all zero, meaning that this is the statistically preferred model. Because there are no theory-based reasons to impose these restrictions, it is also the preferred model in terms of theory. The rejection

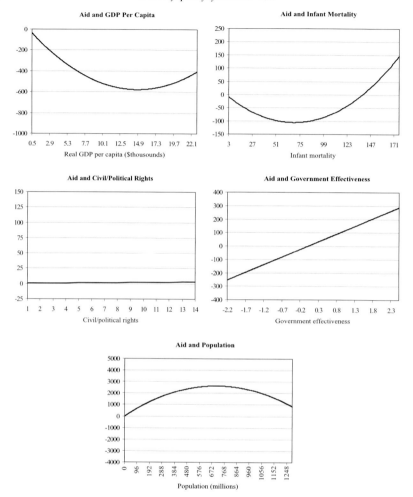

Fig. 4.   Relationships without fixed effects.

of these restrictions on the fixed effects has important implications for our interpretation of the relationships between aid and the explanatory variables, and highlights the
importance of controlling for donor interests.

Comparing Figures 4 and 5, for which axes in corresponding figures have the same
scale, it is clear that the estimated relationships between aid and each of the variables
differ importantly between the two models. Even though per capita income, infant
mortality, government effectiveness, and population are statistically significant in both,
the actual responsive of aid differs between models.

The relationship between aid and per capita GDP has the same U-shape as in the
previous model, with the upward sloping portion where there are very few recipient

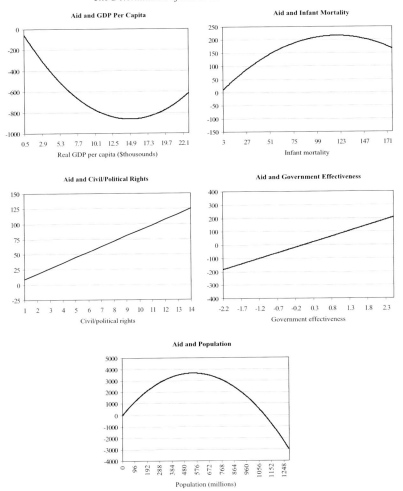

Fig. 5. *Relationships with fixed effects.*

countries. In this model, however, aid is more responsive to per capita income: A one-standard-deviation increase in per capita GDP means a $135 million decrease in aid for the average country, which is 50 percent higher than with the previous model (see Table 4).

The relationship between aid and infant mortality differs a great deal between the two models. Recall that in the first model, the relationship was U-shaped and most countries' levels of infant mortality put them on the downward sloping portion of the curve. But in the preferred model, the relationship is hill-shaped and is upward-sloping for all but a handful of countries. For the average country, a one-standard-deviation increase in infant mortality means a $27 million increase in aid. One might expect that the relationship between aid and infant mortality, if positive, would be convex rather than concave as we have found. One reason for the concavity is that, while higher levels of infant mortality indicate greater need, they might also indicate health-care systems that are less effective at making use of any money that they receive. If so, donors might then be allocating more of their limited aid budgets to countries with better health-care systems, where each dollar of aid might have a larger impact on well-being. At the extreme, for those countries with the very highest levels of infant mortality and least effective health-care systems, this concavity might make the relationship between aid and infant mortality a negative one.

An increase in the civil/political rights variable means an increase in aid according to the preferred model, in contrast with the no-fixed-effects model, for which it was statistically insignificant. A one-standard-deviation increase in civil/political rights means an increase in aid of $29 million. Recipient-government effectiveness matters in both models, although it matters somewhat less in the model with fixed effects. A one-standard-deviation increase in government effectiveness means a $54 million increase in aid, which is $21 million less than from the first model. Finally, because the estimated relationship between aid and population is concave, we find a population bias, which is somewhat larger than in the first model. Per capita aid falls more than twice as fast in this model, and the peak of the relationship is at a lower population level.

4. Conclusions

In this paper, we have estimated the responsiveness of total aid in the post-Cold War era to the needs, civil/political rights, and government effectiveness of recipient countries. To do so, we used the approach espoused in Trumbull and Wall (1994) to use fixed effects to control for donor interests. We have found that aid in this era generally responded negatively to per capita GDP and positively to infant mortality, rights, and government effectiveness. This is in contrast with much of the existing literature, which, while tending to find a positive link between aid and per capita income, has been decidedly more mixed in terms of the other variables.

Acknowledgements

This paper was written while Howard Wall was a visiting scholar at the Institute for Economic and Monetary Studies at the Bank of Japan. He would like to express his appreciation for their resources and hospitality. The authors also would like to thank Kristie Engemann for her research assistance. The views expressed are those of the authors and do not necessarily represent official positions of the Federal Reserve Bank of St. Louis or the Federal Reserve System.

Appendix A.   Country averages

Country	Real aid per capita ($)	Real aid ($mils.)	Real GDP per capita ($thous.)	Infant mortality	Civil/ political rights	Gov't effective- ness	Popula- tion
Albania	88.9	280.0	3.6	23.0	8.7	−0.49	3.2
Algeria	8.3	247.9	5.4	38.3	4.7	−0.69	30.1
Angola	33.8	410.6	1.9	154.0	4.3	−1.33	12.3
Argentina	3.1	111.8	11.5	18.7	12.0	0.11	36.5
Armenia	72.3	228.7	2.6	35.7	8.0	−0.52	3.2
Azerbaijan	22.7	182.9	2.6	77.3	4.7	−0.96	8.0
Bahamas, The	17.9	5.2	15.8	17.0	13.5	0.96	0.3
Bahrain	71.9	46.0	16.2	13.0	4.3	0.66	0.7
Bangladesh	10.1	1297.0	1.5	58.3	8.7	−0.59	129.7
Belarus	10.3	104.0	4.7	14.0	4.7	−1.04	10.0
Belize	64.4	15.4	5.6	34.3	13.7	−0.20	0.2
Benin	45.1	273.5	1.0	96.0	12.0	−0.12	6.1
Bolivia	87.0	711.1	2.4	60.7	10.7	−0.47	8.2
Botswana	33.4	52.3	7.2	68.7	12.0	0.73	1.6
Brazil	1.8	299.5	7.2	36.3	10.3	−0.14	168.7
Bulgaria	34.4	275.4	6.4	13.3	12.0	−0.22	8.1
Burkina Faso	39.5	431.8	1.0	108.0	7.7	−0.49	11.1
Burundi	31.3	205.6	0.6	114.0	4.3	−1.20	6.7
Cambodia	40.3	494.0	1.8	93.3	4.3	−0.57	12.4
Cameroon	37.7	565.6	1.8	94.0	3.7	−0.70	14.9
Cape Verde	279.6	119.1	4.7	31.0	13.3	0.04	0.4
Central African Republic	29.0	101.9	1.1	115.0	7.3	−1.15	3.7
Chad	27.3	206.9	1.0	117.0	5.0	−0.64	7.7
Chile	6.6	97.2	9.0	10.3	12.7	1.27	15.1
China	1.8	2252.6	3.8	33.0	2.7	0.19	1252.0
Colombia	8.7	376.8	6.4	20.7	8.0	−0.18	41.8
Comoros	54.8	29.1	1.7	63.0	7.0	−1.04	0.6
Congo, Dem. Rep.	34.7	1826.4	0.8	129.0	7.0	−1.38	48.7
Congo, Rep.	24.5	78.5	1.0	81.0	3.3	−1.79	3.4
Costa Rica	6.9	25.2	8.4	10.7	13.0	0.46	3.7
Cote d'Ivoire	43.8	635.7	1.5	114.0	5.0	−0.65	15.5
Croatia	17.7	79.4	9.3	7.7	10.3	0.09	4.5
Czech Republic	27.5	282.4	15.5	5.0	13.0	0.72	10.3
Djibouti	136.1	86.3	2.1	103.3	6.0	−1.00	0.7
Dominica	243.9	17.6	5.3	14.3	14.0	−0.45	0.1
Dominican Republic	10.6	85.9	6.0	34.7	10.7	−0.28	8.3
Ecuador	15.4	186.6	3.4	28.3	10.3	−0.86	12.3
Egypt, Arab Rep.	23.6	1454.0	3.4	43.0	4.3	−0.10	63.2
El Salvador	37.9	228.0	4.6	34.7	10.7	−0.28	6.1
Equatorial Guinea	68.7	28.9	1.5	108.0	2.0	−1.89	0.4
Eritrea	51.5	209.4	1.0	56.0	4.3	−0.50	4.0
Estonia	49.9	69.0	9.6	10.3	12.7	0.84	1.4
Ethiopia	16.2	1024.4	0.7	117.0	6.3	−0.63	63.1
Fiji	52.3	42.0	5.1	18.3	8.3	−0.20	0.8
Gabon	75.2	84.0	6.3	60.0	7.0	−0.79	1.2

(*continued on next page*)

Appendix A.   (continued)

Country	Real aid per capita ($)	Real aid ($mils.)	Real GDP per capita ($thous.)	Infant mortality	Civil/ political rights	Gov't effective-ness	Popula-tion
Gambia, The	40.9	52.1	1.7	92.7	5.0	−0.20	1.3
Georgia	42.2	201.5	2.0	41.0	7.7	−0.62	4.8
Ghana	37.5	721.2	1.9	63.3	10.3	−0.02	19.3
Grenada	129.6	13.1	6.9	21.7	13.0	−0.07	0.1
Guatemala	21.7	241.6	3.8	41.0	8.0	−0.60	11.2
Guinea	39.2	276.7	1.9	115.0	5.0	−0.71	7.3
Guinea-Bissau	86.4	115.4	0.8	133.7	7.3	−1.21	1.3
Guyana	124.5	94.2	3.9	56.0	12.0	−0.23	0.8
Haiti	52.8	395.1	1.7	82.7	5.0	−1.54	7.9
Honduras	66.9	419.3	2.5	34.0	10.0	−0.71	6.4
Hungary	24.2	243.4	13.9	8.5	13.0	0.76	10.1
India	1.4	1421.4	2.4	68.3	10.0	−0.09	1004.2
Indonesia	7.7	1573.4	3.1	37.3	7.0	−0.23	204.6
Iran, Islamic Rep.	2.5	154.5	5.8	37.3	3.7	−0.34	63.0
Israel	85.0	526.7	22.3	6.0	12.0	1.12	6.2
Jamaica	17.5	43.7	3.6	17.0	11.3	−0.19	2.6
Jordan	157.5	768.3	4.0	25.7	7.3	0.30	4.8
Kazakhstan	11.3	171.3	4.8	61.0	5.0	−0.70	15.3
Kenya	20.4	588.6	1.0	76.3	6.0	−0.70	29.6
Kuwait	1.7	3.5	17.1	9.7	6.7	0.29	2.1
Kyrgyz Republic	49.3	236.9	1.5	60.7	6.0	−0.61	4.9
Lao PDR	58.2	299.7	1.5	92.3	3.0	−0.52	5.2
Latvia	37.4	89.1	7.9	13.0	12.7	0.35	2.4
Lebanon	48.3	206.2	4.3	28.3	5.0	−0.25	4.3
Lesotho	45.7	78.3	2.1	74.7	9.0	−0.05	1.7
Lithuania	61.2	215.0	8.9	10.0	13.0	0.37	3.5
Macedonia, FYR	91.8	186.0	5.8	15.0	9.3	−0.33	2.0
Madagascar	25.2	386.3	0.8	85.7	10.0	−0.46	15.2
Malawi	45.8	463.0	0.6	120.7	10.0	−0.69	10.2
Malaysia	3.9	88.9	8.5	8.7	6.7	0.91	22.9
Mali	45.7	482.0	0.8	125.7	11.3	−0.70	10.7
Malta	35.0	13.6	16.7	7.0	14.0	1.08	0.4
Mauritania	89.8	230.5	1.7	86.7	4.7	0.02	2.6
Mauritius	19.9	22.9	8.7	18.5	13.0	0.75	1.2
Mexico	2.8	257.8	8.2	26.5	10.0	−0.01	96.7
Moldova	23.7	101.4	1.4	27.3	9.0	−0.73	4.3
Mongolia	95.1	226.6	1.6	61.0	11.3	−0.15	2.4
Morocco	17.1	483.6	3.5	42.7	6.3	−0.01	28.4
Mozambique	58.2	1002.7	0.9	113.3	9.0	−0.47	17.4
Namibia	91.9	166.3	5.8	51.0	11.0	0.37	1.9
Nepal	19.3	433.4	1.3	71.3	8.3	−0.56	22.7
Nicaragua	138.2	685.9	3.1	35.0	9.3	−0.65	5.0
Niger	29.7	312.4	0.8	163.0	8.0	−0.90	10.5
Nigeria	1.9	238.3	0.9	106.7	6.0	−1.11	124.9
Oman	21.7	50.5	12.5	12.3	4.7	0.86	2.4

Appendix A. (continued)

Country	Real aid per capita ($)	Real aid ($mils.)	Real GDP per capita ($thous.)	Infant mortality	Civil/ political rights	Gov't effective- ness	Popula- tion
Pakistan	6.4	868.9	1.9	81.7	6.0	−0.50	136.3
Panama	10.6	29.5	6.0	20.3	12.3	−0.21	2.8
Papua New Guinea	60.2	295.6	2.5	70.3	10.3	−0.66	5.1
Paraguay	18.8	93.7	4.7	26.3	9.3	−1.04	5.2
Peru	16.6	426.2	4.8	34.7	9.3	−0.32	25.6
Philippines	10.2	752.6	3.9	31.0	10.7	0.04	75.5
Poland	57.4	2212.6	9.9	9.3	13.0	0.52	38.5
Romania	19.9	441.8	6.5	19.3	11.0	−0.46	22.3
Russian Federation	10.3	1500.2	7.3	17.3	7.0	−0.47	145.7
Rwanda	71.0	465.9	1.1	120.0	3.7	−0.67	7.3
Samoa	206.6	35.2	4.8	21.3	12.0	0.13	0.2
Saudi Arabia	1.1	23.5	12.7	24.3	2.0	−0.04	20.5
Senegal	57.7	523.7	1.5	80.7	9.0	−0.09	9.4
Seychelles	172.2	13.7	15.9	13.3	10.0	−0.59	0.1
Sierra Leone	46.2	229.1	0.6	168.0	6.3	−1.01	5.0
Singapore	2.7	9.6	21.5	3.5	6.0	2.47	3.8
Slovak Republic	23.0	123.6	11.1	8.7	12.3	0.37	5.4
Slovenia	30.2	60.1	16.3	5.0	13.3	0.79	2.0
Solomon Islands	143.1	59.1	2.0	21.7	10.3	−1.15	0.4
South Africa	11.6	500.1	9.6	49.3	13.0	0.48	43.0
Sri Lanka	27.6	504.6	3.3	16.7	8.7	−0.25	18.3
St. Kitts and Nevis	96.2	4.1	10.4	23.0	13.0	−0.06	0.0
St. Lucia	172.6	25.8	5.5	17.0	13.0	0.21	0.2
St. Vincent & the Grenadines	192.0	21.3	5.3	20.7	13.0	−0.09	0.1
Sudan	11.3	358.5	1.7	65.7	2.0	−1.39	31.0
Swaziland	35.3	34.0	4.4	93.7	4.7	−0.50	1.0
Syrian Arab Republic	15.3	233.3	3.3	20.3	2.0	−0.64	15.9
Tajikistan	17.9	110.6	0.9	81.7	3.7	−1.32	6.1
Tanzania	35.5	1183.9	0.5	103.7	7.7	−0.63	33.1
Thailand	13.5	805.0	6.4	27.0	10.0	0.33	59.7
Togo	26.0	107.0	1.6	80.3	5.3	−1.10	4.4
Tonga	292.9	29.0	6.2	17.3	8.0	−0.42	0.1
Tunisia	20.5	197.7	6.0	23.3	5.0	0.78	9.5
Turkey	4.2	274.8	6.3	40.3	7.3	−0.04	66.6
Turkmenistan	6.4	29.2	4.1	76.0	2.0	−1.39	4.6
Uganda	38.6	877.5	1.2	86.0	6.3	−0.31	22.9
Ukraine	8.0	397.8	4.5	17.3	8.3	−0.70	49.8
Uruguay	10.9	35.6	8.3	15.7	13.3	0.61	3.3
Uzbekistan	6.2	153.5	1.5	59.3	2.7	−0.96	24.3
Vanuatu	224.2	41.9	3.0	36.3	12.0	−0.38	0.2
Venezuela, RB	2.8	67.3	5.5	20.0	9.0	−0.87	24.0
Vietnam	18.1	1420.6	2.0	24.7	2.7	−0.23	77.6
Yemen, Rep.	13.1	226.0	0.8	85.0	5.3	−0.70	17.3
Zambia	126.7	1177.6	0.8	102.0	8.0	−0.80	9.7
Zimbabwe	30.3	355.9	2.6	66.5	5.5	−0.69	12.1

References

Alesina, A., Dollar, D. (2000), Who gives foreign aid to whom and why? *Journal of Economic Growth* 5 (1), 33–63.

Alesina, A., Weder, B. (2002), Do corrupt governments receive less foreign aid? *American Economic Review* 92 (4), 1126–1137.

Boone, P. (1996), Politics and the effectiveness of foreign aid. *European Economic Review* 40 (2), 289–329.

Burnside, C., Dollar, D. (2000), Aid, policies, and growth. *American Economic Review* 90 (4), 847–868.

Burnside, C., Dollar, D. (2004), Aid, policies, and growth: revisiting the evidence. *World Bank Policy Research Working Paper* 3251.

Dollar, D., Levin, V. (2004), The increasing selectivity of foreign aid, 1984–2002. *World Bank Policy Research Working Paper* 3299.

Dowling, J.M., Hiemenz, U. (1985), Biases in the allocation of foreign aid: some new evidence. *World Development* 13 (4), 535–541.

Easterly, W., Levine, R., Roodman, D. (2004), Aid, policies, and growth: comment. *American Economic Review* 94 (3), 774–780.

Kaufmann, D., Kraay, A., Mastruzzi, M. (2006), Governance matters V: aggregate and individual governance indicators for 1996–2005. *World Bank Policy Research Working Paper* 4012.

Kosack, S. (2003), Effective aid: how democracy allows development aid to improve the quality of life. *World Development* 31 (1), 1–22.

Maizels, A., Nissanke, M.K. (1984), Motivations for aid to developing countries. *World Development* 12 (9), 879–900.

McKinlay, R.D., Little, R. (1979), The US aid relationship: a test of the recipient need and the donor interest models. *Political Studies* 27 (2), 236–250.

Neumayer, E. (2003a), The determinants of aid allocation by regional multilateral development banks and united nations agencies. *International Studies Quarterly* 47 (1), 101–122.

Neumayer, E. (2003b), Is respect for human rights rewarded? An analysis of total bilateral and multilateral aid flows. *Human Rights Quarterly* 25 (2), 510–527.

Neumayer, E. (2003c), Do human rights matter in bilateral aid allocation? A quantitative analysis of 21 donor countries. *Social Science Quarterly* 84 (3), 650–666.

Neumayer, E. (2003d), *The Pattern of Aid Giving: The Impact of Good Governance on Development Assistance*. Routledge, London.

Rajan, R.G., Subramanian, A. (2005), Aid and growth: what does the cross-country evidence really show? *NBER Working Paper* 11513.

Trumbull, W.N., Wall, H.J. (1994), Estimating aid-allocation criteria with panel data. *Economic Journal* 104 (July), 876–882.

Wall, H.J. (1995), The allocation of official development assistance. *Journal of Policy Modeling* 17 (3), 307–314.

CHAPTER 20

Foreign Aid, History, and Growth

Scott Gilbert and Kevin Sylwester

Department of Economics, MC 4515, Southern Illinois University, Carbondale, IL 62901, USA
E-mail addresses: gilberts@siu.edu; ksylwest@siu.edu

Abstract
Recent work focuses on long-run historical factors in promoting economic growth and
raising income. Other work considers whether the inflow of foreign aid works better
in countries having good policies or good institutions. A problem with the latter is the
endogeneity of policies and institutions since these are mutable. This paper combines
the two approaches and asks whether aid (representing an inflow of resources) is better at promoting economic growth in historically "advantaged" (as identified by the
literature) as opposed to "disadvantaged" ones. It finds that history still does matter
but understanding why is less clear.

Keywords: Foreign aid, economic growth, historical determinants

JEL classifications: O40, O19

1. Introduction

Does foreign aid boost growth? Few questions raise such vociferous debate. For one,
hundreds of millions of people live in poverty and so the possibility of aid raising economic growth in poor countries presents tremendous welfare implications. Moreover,
whether aid is beneficial or not matters for the appropriateness of developed countries to continue to allocate billions of dollars to foreign aid budgets, at least without
major structural changes in how aid is distributed. Early studies produced ambiguous conclusions and no consensus arose as to foreign aid's efficacy in raising growth
rates of income per capita in poor countries.[1] Later work stressed various contingen-
cies as to whether aid was effective or not in boosting growth. Burnside and Dollar
(2000) [BD] provide the most conspicuous example. They find that aid spurs growth

---

[1] See Boone (1996), Hansen and Tarp (2000), and White (1992a, 1992b) for surveys of this earlier theoretical and empirical literature.

but only in countries enacting good economic policies such as low inflation, low budget deficits, and trade openness. Their results were quickly challenged by others who showed that their findings were not robust to the use of different measures of macroeconomic policy, different sets of observations either across time or space, or different model specifications.[2]

These recent studies examining whether aid is effective in good policy environments employ a common empirical methodology. Economic growth is regressed upon several control variables and foreign aid. The measure of foreign aid enters the empirical specification both singularly and as part of an interactive term with a measure of government policy. A large, positive coefficient on the interactive term (with higher values of the policy variable denoting better policies) is evidence that aid works better in countries practicing good policies.[3]

However, problems with this specification arise. For one, the policy variable could be endogenous as countries might enact specific policies to attract aid. Receiving large quantities of aid could also make enactment of good policies easier. For example, aid could be used to compensate those negatively affected by switching policies. Moreover, growth outcomes could be important for not only what policies are enacted but also for the values that measures of policy take. A quickly growing economy could boost tax revenue and thereby lower the budget deficit regardless of the intentions of policy makers. In cases where the policy variable is actually a measure of contemporary institutions, then the evolution of these institutions could also depend on the prevalence of foreign aid although not in a clear manner. Tavares (2003) reports that foreign aid decreases the prevalence of corruption. However, Bräutigam and Knack (2004) find that foreign aid diminishes the quality of governance in Africa. Institutions could also be influenced by economic causes. Chong and Calderón (2000) find that economic growth granger-causes institutional outcomes.

Second, the receipt of foreign aid could also be endogenous, especially if donors are more likely to send aid to slow growing economies. Countries suffering some natural disaster which slows economic growth could also be prime candidates for inflows of foreign aid.

This paper takes a different approach than have most studies in this literature. Several studies have developed theories where historical or geographic factors influence institutional development which then influences economic outcomes such as income per capita. One example is from Acemoglu *et al.* (2001) [AJR] who argue that the mortality of European settlers centuries ago determined current institutional structures and thereby economic outcomes. Other studies consider different predeterminants.

---

[2] See Burnside and Dollar (2004), Collier and Dollar (2001, 2002, 2004), Collier and Hoeffler (2004), Dalgaard *et al.* (2004), Easterly (2003), Easterly *et al.* (2004), Guillaumont and Chauvet (2001), Hansen and Tarp (2000, 2001a, 2001b), Hudson and Mosley (2001), Lensink and White (2001), Lu and Ram (2001), Ram (2004), and World Bank (1998) for examples and discussion of this debate.

[3] A measure of macroeconomic policy has not been the only interactive term considered as to how aid impacts growth. Boone (1996) considers distinctions between liberal and repressive regimes. Islam (2003) examines distinctions within this latter group, namely between tinpot and totalitarian rulers.

According to these various perspectives, some countries had historical or geographic advantages (although which specific advantages differ across theories) that allowed them to sustain long-run economic growth, at least more so than in less advantaged countries. Here, we consider whether the effectiveness of foreign aid in raising growth is higher in advantaged countries by interacting foreign aid with measures of these historical and geographic characteristics.

An advantage of examining how differing histories potentially affect the effectiveness of foreign aid is that historical factors are exogenous and not driven by inflows of foreign aid in the recent past. Moreover, given that these historical factors potentially matter for a wide range of institutional and policy outcomes, they also allow for a parsimonious way to consider various factors at once. Such an examination can also shed light on results from Dalgaard *et al.* (2004) [DHT] who consider a climate-foreign aid interactive term and find that aid promotes growth for temperate countries but does not do so in tropical countries. Roodman (2004) reports that this finding is robust to various changes in the empirical methodology. However, whether their results suggest that it is some aspect of climate itself that makes aid less effective or that distinctions in the effectiveness of aid arise because institutional outcomes are dependent on climatic differences is not clear. This paper can help address this issue.

Of course, weaknesses from this methodology also arise. First, if countries differing in one or two historical characteristics evolve policies and institutions differing along many dimensions, then what institutions or policies are most important in determining the effectiveness of foreign aid becomes less clear. Likewise, these historical measures are indirect indicators as to why aid might be more effective in some countries than in others at raising economic growth and income levels. They are not measures of the institutions or policies themselves. More generally, these historical characteristics could also be important in determining (or at least being associated with) noninstitutional factors as to why aid works better in some countries than in others. Second, when applying these characteristics to the issue of how effective foreign aid is in raising growth, then the applicable sample contains countries that receive foreign aid and so are lower income countries. If these countries are poor primarily because they all manifest to similar extents the same historical or geographic disadvantages, then considering how the effectiveness of aid differs across these countries is a nonstarter. Thus, we can only examine historical and geographic factors that sufficiently differ across low income countries.

Third, if long-run historical factors become less important for current outcomes as time goes on, then the strength of associations will diminish over time. Nevertheless, the work cited above often finds that associations between what happened decades and even centuries ago and current outcomes persist. Finally, measurement errors are likely to be more prevalent with historical data and measures of historical characteristics than with more contemporaneous variables. Given these shortcomings, this methodology should be seen as complementary with other work, providing advantages over past work in some areas (especially in regards to endogeneity issues) but inferior in others.

The rest of the paper is organized as follows. Section 2 summarizes recent contributions in the literature regarding historical factors and institutional and economic outcomes. Section 3 presents the methodology. Section 4 discusses the results and Section 5 offers conclusions.

2. Historical factors and economic outcomes

A recent trend in the economic growth and development literature focuses on long-ago historical factors and their relevance for economic outcomes today. Hall and Jones (1999) assert that contact with Europe in the 19th century provided long-run institutional benefits that contribute to higher productivity and income today. AJR argue that European influence is too broad a concept as types of contact differed across colonies. Where Europeans settled was where beneficial protective institutions arose as colonists wanted to keep their property from being extracted by the mother country. Such protective institutions did not arise where Europeans did not settle. AJR further argue that institutions persist over time and so distinctions between settlement colonies and extractive colonies arising from where Europeans decided to settle matter for institutions and economic outcomes today.

DHT suggest that one explanation for their finding that climate influences the effectiveness of aid is that climate influenced institutional outcomes and that this is actually what their climate variable (percentage of land in the tropics) is capturing since Europeans tended not to settle in tropical regions. However, DHT do not claim this explanation as a correct or dominant interpretation behind their findings, only a possible one. To better gauge whether this is a correct interpretation or not, one needs to find historical or geographic characteristics that matter for institutions. To the extent that historical variables stem from climatic causes (such as patterns of European settlement as in AJR), then the effectiveness of aid stemming from climate should no longer be significant once controlling for the interaction between aid and European settlement.

These are not the only theories linking history or geography to contemporary outcomes. Acemoglu *et al.* (2002) take a slightly different perspective. They argue that places with large indigenous populations were more subject to exploitation than were sparsely populated areas. Such subsequent exploitation fomented institutions that not only persisted over time but were less conducive to raising income levels. Engerman and Sokoloff (1997) consider other factor endowments as to why many Latin American regions began richer than North America but later fell behind. Easterly and Levine (2003) consider how various geographic characteristics also matter for institutional outcomes. Sylwester (2003, 2004) examines how some of these same factors matter for income inequality within countries.

The above theories consider how factor endowments or geography/climate influence institutional outcomes. Other views on the importance of history influencing current distributions of income across the world do not rely on such foundations. Englebert (2000a, 2000b) considers whether the state is "legitimate". Illegitimate states arise when there are conflicts between precolonial and postcolonial institutions at least as viewed by the post-independence population. No such conflicts arise for countries that were never colonies or where indigenous populations were mostly wiped out. In many cases, countries with illegitimate states are ones with borders created by external forces such as European governments partitioning Africa in the late 1800's. Often, these borders comprised groups having little, if any, previous history of shared governance or common political structures. Leaders in illegitimate states are less able to create institutions or enact policies beneficial to economic growth because they must first assuage powerful political players or constituencies within the country to survive.

Bockstette *et al.* (2002) consider how long a country has had state-level institutions. Having such states in the past could be important for learning-by-doing benefits of governance, creating hierarchical attitudes important for state effectiveness, fomenting trust across groups, and forming cultural and linguistic unity. Any of these, they argue, could make current institutions more effective at promoting development today.

3. Empirical methodology

We use the approach found in BD, DHT, and Easterly *et al.* (2004). A panel dataset is employed for N aid receiving countries for T periods of four years each. The empirical model, in its most general form, takes the following specification:

$$\text{GROWTH}_{it} = a_t + b_i + B \cdot \text{GDP}_{it} + D \cdot \text{POL}_{it}$$
$$+ \text{AID}_{it}[e + F \cdot \text{POL}_{it} + G \cdot \text{GEO}_i + H \cdot \text{HIST}_i] + u_{it} \qquad (1)$$

where i denotes the country and t the time period. GROWTH denotes the growth rate of real GDP per capita (adjusted for purchasing power parity). GDP denotes the natural log of GDP per capita (GDP) at the beginning of the period and can control for the level of development. Its inclusion can also control for convergence effects as poorer countries could have greater potential to grow than initially higher income countries although GDP differences across countries are not as great here as in samples including high-income countries. POL denotes a policy (or a set of policies if POL is a vector) deemed to be important for economic growth. In some specifications, BD construct a single index using the inflation rate, the budget balance ratio to GDP, and the Sachs–Warner (SW) measure of openness. Here, we focus on use of only SW since inflation rates and budget deficits can also be seen as outcome measures and not only of the policies chosen by the government.

AID denotes the level of foreign aid a country receives during some period. Under a most general specification, AID's effect on growth is allowed to vary across countries depending on the policies that are run as in BD, on various geographic (GEO) factors such as whether the country lies in the tropics (TROP) as in DHT, and on some set of historical characteristics, HIST, such as settler mortality rates (MORT) from AJR or state legitimacy (LEGIT) from Englebert (2000a, 2000b).

The last term, u_{it}, is a regression error having unconditional expectation $\mathrm{E}u_{it} = 0$ for all i and t, finite variance, and zero cross sectional correlation, $\mathrm{E}u_{it}u_{jt} = 0$ for all $i \neq j$.

Such a specification will not only better identify what conditions make aid more or less effective in certain countries but can also shed light on previous findings. For example, if g loses significance once MORT is included, then the interpretation of the findings in DHT becomes clearer as then TROP appears to be capturing geographic factors that led to different degrees of European settlement and, hence, institutional development. However, if g remains significant when MORT or other historical variables are included then it becomes more likely that geographic factors directly influence the effectiveness of aid in boosting growth rates perhaps through agricultural productivity or determining the disease environment. Finally, if H is significant when other, more contemporaneous interactive terms are also included, then the results provide evidence that long-run historical factors still matter for how the receipt of foreign aid affects growth today.

As with most other studies in this literature, we employ period fixed effects to take into account period-specific global shocks. However, unlike most of these studies, we also include country fixed effects. Including these fixed effects provides a parsimonious way to capture various factors that influence economic growth, including important geographic, historical, and cultural factors. This is especially important in our study. Since we want to determine whether such characteristics are important in influencing the effectiveness of foreign aid, we want to control for any direct effect that these factors have on growth. Employing country fixed effects allows us to simultaneously control for all the direct effects from these time invariant factors across all our specifications.

A problem with estimating (1) by OLS is the potential for several right-hand side variables to be endogenous. An obvious candidate is for AID to be endogenous as countries with poor growth performances might be the first to attract foreign aid. Policies might also be endogenous, especially when outcome measures are used to try to proxy for policies since these outcomes can be influenced by the growth rate of the economy. Of course, this is not the only reason why policies could be endogenous. Countries might run policies in hopes to attract aid. BD consider the possible endogeneity of foreign aid but argue that policies are not endogenous. DHT consider the endogeneity of both aid and policies. Like DHT we estimate (1) by GMM where instruments are one period lags of the right-hand side variables. However, we employ fewer instruments so as to obtain a more parsimonious specification.[4]

Details regarding the data along with sources are given in Appendix A. Much of the data comes from DHT and we use their sample. Namely, we consider 47 countries (for which MORT is available) and 6 four-year periods: 1974–1977, 1978–1981, 1982–1985, 1986–1989, 1990–1993, and 1994–1997.

---

[4] DHT include in their model period fixed effects but not cross-section fixed effects, and in their error specification they allow unrestricted error correlation across time. This effects their GMM implementation and instrument weighting matrix. By comparison, we use both period and cross-section fixed effects, with the latter a possible proxy for low-frequency autocorrelation, and to implement these effects we apply a two-stage least squares instrument weighting matrix.

4. Results

We begin with a simple specification where HIST in (1) contains MORT and the POL and GEO interaction terms are empty. We focus on MORT for two reasons. For one, MORT has received a great deal of attention in the historical and institutional determinants literature, more so than other historical determinants of institutions. Second, DHT speculate that one reason for their finding that foreign aid works less well in the tropics is that tropical climates proved more deadly to European colonists and so these countries never developed institutions conducive to economic growth. Use of MORT allows us to directly examine this conjecture.

The first column of Table 1 presents least squares results from (1). The coefficient for AID*MORT is negative but is not significantly different from zero, providing no strong evidence that aid works differently where settler mortality rates were high. However, a potential problem with this specification is the potential endogeneity of AID. For example, donors may target aid to the neediest countries, that is, where growth prospects are poor.[5]

Table 1. **Baseline regressions (dependent variable is GROWTH)**

	(1) OLS	(2) GMM	(3) GMM	(4) GMM	(5) GMM
GDP	−1.468	6.115	4.894	7.701	6.278
	(1.355)	(4.970)	(4.374)	(5.877)	(5.212)
SW	1.133	3.607	3.428	3.964	3.392
	(0.739)	(2.700)	(2.477)	(2.871)	(2.563)
AID	0.091	4.155*	11.105**	4.696*	3.895*
	(0.360)	(2.159)	(5.256)	(2.429)	(1.994)
AID*MORT	−0.020	−0.308**		−0.327**	−0.408**
	(0.039)	(0.129)		(0.137)	(0.173)
AID*LMORT			−1.559**		
			(0.705)		
AID*WA					1.953
					(1.650)
Instruments		Z	Z	Z	Z
# of obser.	276	276	276	260	276

Standard errors in parentheses. Z denotes GDP and one-period lags of other right-hand side variables. Country and period fixed effects suppressed to ease presentation.
*Denotes significance at 10% significance level.
**Denotes significance at 5% significance level.

---

[5] We performed Durbin–Wu–Hausman tests to examine endogeneity of the right-hand side variables under several specifications. Results were not identical across specifications. In some cases, the null of exogeneity was not rejected. In others, it was. Given that some evidence for endogeneity exists, we treat aid as endogenous throughout the remainder of the paper.

Column (2) presents GMM coefficient estimates using the lags of SW, AID, and AID*MORT as instruments for these potentially endogenous variables. The coefficient on the interaction term increases in magnitude (becomes more negative) to −0.31 and now evidence becomes stronger that foreign aid works less effectively where settler mortality was high. To see the economic magnitudes of these coefficients, consider the following example of a country receiving foreign aid totaling 1% of its GDP. This amount is less than the sample average of 1.36% but more than the median of 0.76%. In cases where MORT = 0, the effect is to raise growth by 4.2 percentage points, or a little over one standard deviation. This effect, if true, suggests that foreign aid has been effective in promoting economic growth. Now consider a country where MORT equals its average of three. The effect is to reduce aid's effectiveness by 0.93 percentage points. For most countries, the combined effect of aid on growth remains positive. For the combined effect to be negative with foreign aid of one percent of GDP, MORT must exceed 13.5. The highest value of MORT in the sample is Mali's 29.4.

Before trying to uncover economic reasons for the above results, the remaining columns in Table 1 provide some robustness checks to see if the above findings are spurious. For one, values for MORT are skewed across countries with many low values and a few extreme ones. Column (3) replaces MORT with its log to diminish the effect of these outliers. The general conclusions still hold. Column (4) removes observations where foreign aid is negative or where foreign aid exceeds 7% of GDP. After removing these outliers, coefficient estimates remain similar as before.[6] Finally, MORT is generally highest for countries of western and central Africa. Column (5) adds the interaction term, WA*AID, where WA = 1 for a country of this region and zero otherwise. If the experiences of these countries are primarily driving the results, then the coefficient on AID*MORT should diminish when including this additional interaction term. However, the coefficient on AID*MORT increases in magnitude.

How can one explain these findings? Several possibilities arise. For one, MORT as argued by AJR could have determined future institutional outcomes and so be a proxy for contemporary institutions. If so, then the results suggest that foreign aid works better in countries that enjoy institutions more conducive to growth. But a second possibility is that environments that contributed to settler mortality hundreds of years ago remain deleterious to the potential benefits of foreign aid in raising economic growth, perhaps due to a greater prevalence of disease or poorer soil quality. Of course, neither explanation might be as important as something else associated with settler mortality. Perhaps places where few Europeans settled were unable to increase human capital levels as quickly as could other countries. Or, perhaps European settlers provided other benefits to their posterity besides those mentioned above. The remaining parts of this paper explore these possibilities.

---

[6] Using the log of the mortality rate for this diminished sample also does not change the findings.

4.1. Institutional explanations

Table 2 considers institutional explanations behind these results. The first column adds ICRGE*AID to the specification where ICRGE is the measure of institutions used by both BD and by DHT. Does aid perform better in countries having better institutions? Theoretically, one would think so. Much of the literature has found that countries with better institutions grow faster and so countries receiving an injection of resources should then be able to direct these resources to more beneficial uses. Moreover, if MORT is primarily capturing institutional factors, then the coefficient on AID*MORT should diminish when ICRGE*AID is included in the specification.

However, once ICRGE*AID is included the coefficient on AID*MORT slightly increases in magnitude as shown in column (1). When AID*MORT is removed from the specification as in column (2), the coefficient on ICRGE*AID is negative, albeit insignificant. There is no strong evidence that foreign aid is more effective in countries with better institutions.[7] Of course, institutional outcomes could themselves be

Table 2. Institutional regressions (dependent variable is GROWTH)

	(1) GMM	(2) GMM	(3) GMM	(4) GMM	(5) GMM
GDP	6.153 (4.692)	3.769 (3.500)	5.762 (4.308)	2.829 (3.335)	1.656 (2.756)
SW	3.603 (2.519)	2.702 (2.016)	3.212 (2.269)	1.178 (1.835)	2.078 (1.788)
AID	1.843 (1.978)	2.773* (1.547)	−1.211 (5.730)	6.124 (3.966)	0.624 (1.215)
AID*MORT	−0.396*** (0.147)		−0.500* (0.292)		
AID*ICRGE	0.673 (0.433)	−0.0017 (0.0012)	1.506 (1.773)	−0.106 (0.772)	
AID*LEGIT					1.442 (1.281)
Instruments	Z	Z	Z^a	Z^b	Z
# of obser.	276	276	276	276	276

Standard errors in parentheses. Z denotes GDP and one-period lags of other right-hand side variables. Country and period fixed effects suppressed to ease presentation.
[a] Also includes lags of AID*DEN and AID*LEGIT.
[b] Also includes lags of AID*DEN, AID*LEGIT, and AID*MORT.
*Denotes significance at 10%, significance level.
***Denotes significance at 1% significance level.

[7] AJR use the extent of property expropriation as their measure of institutions. Using such a measure does not alter the findings.

endogenous. Columns (3) and (4) use other historical factors argued to be important for institutions to instrument for ICRGE, namely population density in 1500 from Acemoglu *et al.* (2002) and Englebert's measure of state legitimacy. In neither specification, with or without AID*MORT, is the coefficient on the ICRGE*AID interaction term significant. In fact, without AID*MORT, the coefficient on ICRGE*AID is negative. Finally, column (5) replaces MORT with another historical factor of institutions, LEGIT from Englebert (2000a), which takes the value one for countries that had what he classifies as legitimate states at independence and zero for illegitimate ones. An advantage of using LEGIT is not only its availability but this measure is not directly derived from geographic predeterminants of institutions. Therefore, a positive and significant coefficient for AID*LEGIT would more clearly suggest that institutions as opposed to other factors, are important for the effectiveness of aid. However, the coefficient on AID*LEGIT is not significant.[8]

Given these results, it becomes less likely that MORT is capturing important historical factors that helped determine contemporary institutions which are important for the effectiveness of foreign aid. It then becomes less likely that a similar explanation is behind the findings in DHT. In a nutshell, there is no evidence that countries having better institutions today use aid more effectively to promote economic growth.

4.2. Geographic explanations

If not institutions, then perhaps MORT captures geographic characteristics still prevalent today. Table 3 considers some of these factors. Column (1) replaces MORT with TEMP from DHT. There is some evidence that aid is less effective in hotter climates. However, the coefficient on AID*TEMP in column (2) decreases in magnitude and becomes insignificant once AID*MORT is included although the size of the coefficient on AID*MORT is slightly smaller than in other specifications.[9] Therefore, it does not appear that MORT is solely capturing direct effects from generally hotter climates.

Columns (3) and (4) consider specifications using other geographic variables. ME is a malarial ecology index from Kiszewski *et al.* (2003). It captures not the prevalence of malaria in the population which might be endogenous to levels of development but conditions of the environment which make incidences of malaria more likely (hot climates, suitability for mosquitoes, etc.). Including this interaction term along with AID*MORT does not change the coefficient on the latter nor is it statistically significant without AID*MORT in the specification (available from the authors upon

---

[8] Coefficients on interaction terms using other historical determinants of institutions such as population density in 1500 from Acemoglu *et al.* (2002) and state history from Bockstette *et al.* (2002) were also not significant.

[9] We do not use AID*TROP from DHT as GMM results become highly nonsensical when it is included in specifications with country fixed effects. Standard errors are huge and so no inferences can be drawn. Still, temperatures are hotter in the tropics and so TEMP should be an appropriate proxy.

Table 3. Geography regressions (dependent variable is GROWTH)

	(1) GMM	(2) GMM	(3) GMM	(4) GMM	(5) GMM	(6) GMM
GDP	0.765	5.449	6.555	5.134	4.912	8.651
	(2.189)	(4.533)	(5.397)	(4.872)	(4.292)	(7.372)
SW	1.928	3.806	3.463	3.647	3.308	4.109
	(1.811)	(2.593)	(2.602)	(2.520)	(2.267)	(3.356)
AID	11.087	10.368	3.893*	0.088	6.483*	3.519
	(8.130)	(7.845)	(1.983)	(5.356)	(3.045)	(3.414)
AID*MORT		−0.282**	−0.413**	−0.379***		−0.406*
		(0.111)	(0.180)	(0.108)		(0.245)
AID*TEMP	−0.399	−0.259				
	(0.315)	(0.296)				
AID*ME			0.113			
			(0.102)			
AID*SOIL				0.113		
				(0.124)		
AID*MORT70					−0.978**	0.372
					(0.453)	(0.838)
Instruments	Z	Z	Z	Z	Z	Z
# of obser.	272	276	276	276	270	270

Standard errors in parentheses. Z denotes GDP and one-period lags of other right-hand side variables. Country and period fixed effects suppressed to ease presentation.
*Denotes significance at 10% significance level.
**Denotes significance at 5% significance level.
***Denotes significance at 1% significance level.

request).[10] Column four considers soil suitability since tropical climates often have soils of poorer quality than do more temperate regions. Poor soil could have contributed to higher mortality rates in the past as well as retard the effectiveness of aid in promoting agricultural and economic development. SOIL denotes the fraction of land of excellent or moderate quality. However, the inclusion of this interaction term does not diminish the coefficient on AID*MORT nor is the coefficient on AID*SOIL significant when included without AID*MORT in the specification.[11]

[10] Using other measures of malaria such as the proportion of each country's population that live with a high risk of contracting malaria, MAL94P, and another measure that considers more fatal strains of malaria, MALFAL, do not drastically change the results. Although MAL94P*AID is significant and negative without AID*MORT in the specification, it loses its significance once the latter is included. The coefficient on AID*MORT retains its significance.
[11] We also interacted AID with value added per agricultural worker in 1970 (from the World Bank's World Development Indicators) but this also was not significant, either with or without AID*MORT in the specification.

Scott Gilbert and Kevin Sylwester

Finally, the last two columns of Table 3 consider the mortality rate of males in 1970, MORT70. We consider 1970 so that this variable is not affected by inflows of aid or by economic growth since the start of the sample period. Although not directly capturing the disease environment, mortality should be associated with the prevalence of many serious diseases in addition to malaria, not only now but possibly centuries ago.[12] The correlation between MORT and MORT70 is 0.55. In column (4) the coefficient on AID*MORT70 is significant and negative when included without other interaction terms. However, it loses its significance and even changes sign when AID*MORT is included in the specification while the latter retains statistical significance. This provides further evidence that the association of MORT with the effectiveness of foreign aid is not due to more contemporaneous factors stemming from geography.

4.3. Other explanations

Glaeser *et al.* (2004) argue that settler mortality might not have determined institutional outcomes so much as educational ones. That is, it is true that Europeans settled where their mortality rates were low, but the most important long-run effect of extensive settlement was to increase human capital in these locales which then perpetuated across centuries. If true, then there is another explanation for the above findings. Perhaps MORT is correlated with higher human capital which is able then to use foreign aid more effectively.

To test this proposition, one would want data on human capital levels within the population. Unfortunately, stock data is unavailable for many countries in this sample. Instead, we use enrollment data and assume that schooling is high where stocks of human capital are also high. Nevertheless, we remain mindful that important distinctions remain between the two. We use enrollment in primary education, PRIM, as our human capital measure. Nevertheless, MORT remains significant when it is included as shown in column (1) of Table 4.[13] The coefficient on AID*PRIM is negative. Although the weaknesses of using enrollment rates temper any strong conclusions, there is no evidence that the potential for MORT to proxy for current human capital levels can explain these results.

Many countries where MORT is high are former French colonies, especially ones in western Africa. However, adding the interaction term PARIS*AID where PARIS takes the value one for a former French colony and zero otherwise does not change the results.[14]

---

[12] Of course, this is not to suggest that settlers and indigenous populations are identically susceptible to local diseases.

[13] We also used the 1970 enrollment rate for all time periods to better control for endogeneity of the human capital measure and since enrollment in 1970 should more directly influence human capital levels in later years of the sample. However, findings did not differ under this change. Using secondary enrollment rates also does not change the findings.

[14] Replacing PARIS with a dummy for membership in the franc zone region also does not alter the conclusions.

Table 4.   Other candidates (dependent variable is GROWTH)

	(1) GMM	(2) GMM	(3) GMM	(4) GMM	(5) GMM	(6) GMM
GDP	5.778	8.180	5.949	9.102	6.489	3.374
	(5.781)	(8.101)	(4.961)	(9.856)	(5.374)	(3.656)
SW	3.667	4.780	4.726*	3.886	4.139	3.686
	(2.947)	(4.397)	(2.784)	(3.684)	(3.348)	(2.634)
AID	5.513	4.215*	3.890*	6.923	4.406*	6.954
	(4.980)	(2.468)	(2.137)	(5.591)	(2.299)	(5.825)
AID*MORT	−0.312**	−0.329**	−0.301**	−0.483	−0.268***	−0.209**
	(0.154)	(0.158)	(0.128)	(0.340)	(0.096)	(0.101)
AID*PRIM	−0.016					0.020
	(0.037)					(0.035)
AID*PARIS		2.322				
		(2.536)				
AID*ENG			6.628***			
			(1.311)			
AID*EUR				−3.907		
				(5.113)		
AID*SW					−0.532	−0.699
					(0.676)	(0.811)
AID*TEMP						−0.269
						(0.214)
AID*ICRGE						0.309
						(0.322)
Instruments	Z	Z	Z	Z	Z	Z
# of obser.	267	276	276	276	276	276

Standard errors in parentheses. Z denotes GDP and one-period lags of other right hand side variables. Country and period fixed effects suppressed to ease presentation.
*Denotes significance at 10% significance level.
**Denotes significance at 5% significance level.
***Denotes significance at 1% significance level.

Hall and Jones (1999) use percentages of the population that speak a European language as a measure of influence on these societies. Aid could work better in such places since a higher percentage of the population that speaks a western European language could indicate more human capital, more complete integration with the world economy, and customs/institutions that are more conducive to growth. We let EUR denote the fraction of the population that speaks a European language and ENG denote the fraction of the population speaking English. Columns (3) and (4) present the results. The AID*ENG interaction term is highly significant and suggests that aid is more beneficial in countries with large English-speaking populations. However and as stated above, several stories could explain the association between the two. Nevertheless, AID*MORT remains significant. On the other hand, AID*MORT is no longer

significant when EUR*AID is included. Although the coefficient for AID*MORT increases in magnitude, the higher standard errors create less precise estimates. Given
that European languages are more likely to persist in countries having large populations of European descent, it is not unlikely that the two are associated. The correlation
between MORT and EUR is −0.31. The coefficient on AID*EUR is negative, albeit
insignificant, and so different in sign from that of AID*ENG. Perhaps there are differences among which European populations settled various regions although it is not
clear what aspect of European influence matters.

Column (5) interacts aid with the measure of policy, SW. Perhaps countries where
Europeans were more likely to settle enact better policies today. However, the coefficient on AID*MORT remains significant. Although this is a much different specification than the one employed in BD, there is no evidence that running better policies
raises the effectiveness of aid.

Finally, column (6) shows results from our most complete specification as aid is
interacted with a host of variables: institutions, human capital, policy, and geography.
The coefficient on AID*MORT remains negative and significant.

5. Conclusion

This paper answers a question with another question. DHT speculate that perhaps
their findings regarding the significance of TROP in determining the effectiveness of
foreign aid could be that tropical climates influenced European settlement and so influenced later development and perhaps characteristics that determine the efficacy of
foreign aid. We do find that settler mortality influences the effectiveness of aid today (although our specification does not find similar associations between tropical
– or hot – climates and the effectiveness of aid as does DHT). On the other hand,
this paper does not conclusively determine why. Various historical, geographic, and
contemporary explanations were considered but findings regarding AID*MORT are
robust to their inclusion, contrary to what one would expect if these explanations are
correct. One possibility is that many of these characteristics are poorly measured and
so this measurement error prevents true effects from surfacing. This could be especially true with human capital measures and so a human capital explanation behind
the AID*MORT results could still be found once better data is obtained. Nevertheless,
better understanding why settler mortality is associated with the effectiveness of aid is
a goal of later research.

On a final note, the coefficient on AID is not robust across specifications. Sometimes it is significant and sometimes not. Sometimes it is large in magnitude but in
other cases near zero. Unfortunately, such inconstancy regarding whether foreign aid
is generally effective or not raises fundamental questions. The interactive terms test if
aid works differently across countries and this paper does find evidence of one distinction. However, the paper cannot say conclusively whether aid works in raising growth
rates in most countries yet is less beneficial in countries where settler mortality was
high OR whether aid does not boost growth rates in many countries and actually low-

ers growth where settler mortality was high. Many other studies do not find clear associations between aid and growth and our paper does not resolve this issue.

Acknowledgements

The authors would like to thank seminar participants at Southern Illinois University for their comments.

Appendix A

The sample of countries comes from DHT along with the six four-year periods considered: 1974–1977, 1978–1981, 1982–1985, 1986–1989, 1990–1993, and 1994–1997.

Countries in the sample include: Algeria, Argentina, Burkina Faso, Bolivia, Brazil, Chile, Cote d'Ivoire, Cameroon, Congo, Colombia, Costa Rica, Dominican Republic, Ecuador, Egypt, El Salvador, Ethiopia, Gabon, Ghana, Gambia, Guatemala, Honduras, Haiti, Indonesia, India, Jamaica, Kenya, Morocco, Madagascar, Mexico, Mali, Malaysia, Niger, Nigeria, Nicaragua, Pakistan, Peru, Paraguay, Senegal, Sierra Leone, Sri Lanka, Togo, Trinidad and Tobago, Tunisia, Uganda, Uruguay, Venezuela, and the Democratic Republic of Congo (formerly Zaire).

From DHT:

GROWTH – Average growth rate of real GDP per capita adjusted for purchasing power parity;
GDP – natural log of real GDP per capita at beginning of period adjusted for purchasing power parity;
SW – Sachs Warner Index of trade openness;
ICRGE – Measure of institutional quality from Knack and Keefer (1995). Higher values denote better institutions;
AID – Effective development assistance as a percentage of GDP, originally from Chang *et al.* (1998).

From AJR:

MORT – Settler Mortality, number of deaths per 10 settlers.

From McArthur and Sachs (2001):

TEMP – Average annual temperature (Celsius).

From Englebert (2000a):

LEGIT – = 1 if state is classified as legitimate, = 0 otherwise.

From Acemoglu *et al.* (2002):

DEN – Population density in 1500.

From Sachs (2003):

ME – Index of malaria ecology, higher values denote a higher natural prevalence of malaria (originally from Kiszewski *et al.* (2003));
MAL94P – Percentage of population which faces a high risk of transmitting malaria;
MALFAL – MAL94P times the fraction of malaria cases involving Plasmodium falciparum, an especially fatal type of malaria.

From Gallup *et al.* (2001):

SOIL – Percentage of soil that is of excellent or moderate quality (SOILSUI1 + SOILSUI2 from dataset).

From World Bank's World Development Indicators:

PRIM – Gross enrollment rate in primary education. To avoid using enrollment rates in the middle of a period, values for the six sample periods come from the years: 1970, 1975, 1980, 1985, 1990, and 1990, respectively;
MORT70 – Mortality rate in 1970 per 10 male adults.

From Hall and Jones (1999):

EUR – Fraction of the population that speaks a western European language;
ENG – Fraction of the population that speaks English.

References

Acemoglu, D., Johnson, S., Robinson, J.A. (2001), The colonial origins of comparative development: an empirical investigation. *American Economic Review* 91, 1369–1401.

Acemoglu, D., Johnson, S., Robinson, J.A. (2002), Reversal of fortune: geography and institutions in the making of the modern world income distribution. *Quarterly Journal of Economics* 117, 1234–1291.

Bockstette, V., Chanda, A., Putterman, L. (2002), States and markets: the advantage of an early start. *Journal of Economic Growth* 7, 347–369.

Boone, P. (1996), Politics and the effectiveness of foreign aid. *European Economic Review* 40, 289–329.

Bräutigam, D.A., Knack, S. (2004), Foreign aid, institutions, and governance in sub-Saharan Africa. *Economic Development and Cultural Change* 52, 255–285.

Burnside, C., Dollar, D. (2000), Aid, policies, and growth. *American Economic Review* 90, 847–868.

Burnside, C., Dollar, D. (2004), Aid, policies, and growth: reply. *American Economic Review* 94, 781–784.

Chang, C.C., Fernandez-Arias, E., Serven, L. (1998), Measuring aid flows: a new approach. *Working Paper*. The World Bank.

Chong, A., Calderón, C. (2000), Causality and feedback between institutional measures and economic growth. *Economics and Politics* 12, 69–81.

Collier, P., Dollar, D. (2001), Can the world cut poverty in half? How policy reform and effective aid can meet international development goals. *World Development* 29, 1787–1802.

Collier, P., Dollar, D. (2002), Aid allocation and poverty reduction. *European Economic Review* 45, 1–26.

Collier, P., Dollar, D. (2004), Development effectiveness: What have we learnt. *Economic Journal* 114, F244–F271.

Collier, P., Hoeffler, A. (2004), Aid, policy and growth in post-conflict societies. *European Economic Review* 48, 1125–1145.

Dalgaard, C., Hansen, H., Tarp, F. (2004), On the empirics of foreign aid and growth. *Economic Journal* 114, F191–F216.

Easterly, W. (2003), Can foreign aid buy growth. *Journal of Economic Perspectives* 17, 23–48.

Easterly, W., Levine, R. (2003), Tropics, germs, and crops: how endowments influence economic development. *Journal of Monetary Economics* 50, 3–39.

Easterly, W., Levine, R., Roodman, D. (2004), Aid, policies, and growth: comment. *American Economic Review* 94, 774–780.

Engerman, S.L., Sokoloff, K.L. (1997), Factor endowments, institutions, and differential paths of growth among new world economies. In: Haber, S.H. (Ed.), *How Latin America Fell Behind*. Stanford University Press, Stanford CA, pp. 260–304.

Englebert, P. (2000a), *State Legitimacy and Development in Africa*. Lynne Rienner Publishers, Boulder, CO.

Englebert, P. (2000b), Solving the mystery of the AFRICA dummy. *World Development* 28, 1821–1835.

Gallup, J.L., Mellinger, A.D., Sachs, J.D. (2001), *Geography Datasets*. Center for International Development, Harvard University.

Glaeser, E.L., La Porta, R., Lopez-de-Silanes, F., Shleifer, A. (2004), Do institutions cause growth? *Journal of Economic Growth* 9, 271–303.

Guillaumont, P., Chauvet, L. (2001), Aid and performance: a reassessment. *Journal of Development Studies* 37, 66–92.

Hall, R.E., Jones, C.I. (1999), Why do some countries produce so much more output per worker than others. *Quarterly Journal of Economics* 114, 83–116.

Hansen, H., Tarp, F. (2000), Aid effectiveness disputed. *Journal of International Development* 12, 375–398.

Hansen, H., Tarp, F. (2001a), Aid and growth regressions. *Journal of Development Economics* 64, 547–570.

Hansen, H., Tarp, F. (2001b), On aid, growth and good policies. *Journal of Development Studies* 37, 17–41.

Hudson, J., Mosley, P. (2001), Aid policies and growth: in search of the holy grail. *Journal of International Development* 13, 1023–1038.

Islam, M.N. (2003), Political regimes and the effects of foreign aid on economic growth. *Journal of Developing Areas* 37, 35–53.

Kiszewski, A., Mellinger, A., Malaney, P., Spielman, A., Ehrlich, S., Sachs, J. (2003), *A global index representing the stability of malaria transmission*. Center for International Development, Harvard University.

Knack, S., Keefer, P. (1995), Institutions and economic performance: cross-country tests using alternative measures. *Economics and Politics* 7, 207–227.

Lensink, R., White, H. (2001), Are there negative returns to aid. *Journal of Development Studies* 37, 42–65.

Lu, S., Ram, R. (2001), Foreign aid, government policies, and economic growth: further evidence from cross-country panel data for 1970–93. *Economia Internazionale* 54, 15–29.

McArthur, J.W., Sachs, J.D. (2001), Institutions and geography: comment on Acemoglu, Johnson, and Robinson (2000). *NBER Working Paper* 8114, Cambridge, MA.

Ram, R. (2004), Recipient country's 'policies' and the effect of foreign aid on economic growth in developing countries: additional evidence. *Journal of International Development* 16, 201–211.

Roodman, D. (2004), The anarchy of numbers: aid, development, and cross-country empirics. *Working Paper Number* 32, Center for Global Development.

Sachs, J.D. (2003), Institutions don't rule: direct effects of geography on per capita income. *NBER Working Paper* 9490, Cambridge MA.

Sylwester, K. (2003), Income inequality and population 1500 AD: a connection. *Journal of Economic Development* 28, 61–82.

Sylwester, K. (2004), A note on geography, institutions, and income inequality. *Economics Letters* 85, 235–240.

Tavares, J. (2003), Does foreign aid corrupt. *Economics Letters* 79, 99–106.

White, H. (1992a), The macroeconomic impact of development aid: a critical survey. *Journal of Development Studies* 28, 163–240.

White, H. (1992b), What do we know about aid's macroeconomic impact? An overview of the aid effectiveness debate. *Journal of International Development* 4, 121–137.

World Bank (1998), *Assessing Aid: What Works, What Doesn't, and Why?* Oxford University Press, New York.

CHAPTER 21

Foreign Aid and Export Performance:
A Panel Data Analysis of Developing Countries

Jonathan Munemo[a], Subhayu Bandyopadhyay[b] and Arabinda Basistha[b]

[a]*World Bank, 1818 H St., NW, Washington, DC 20433, USA*
E-mail addresses: jmunemo@worldbank.org
[b]*Economics Department, West Virginia University, Morgantown, WV 26506-6025, USA*
E-mail addresses: bandysub@mail.wvu.edu; arbasistha@mail.wvu.edu

Abstract

The effect of foreign aid on economic activity of a country can be dampened due to potentially adverse effects on exports through a real exchange rate appreciation. In this study we examine the long-term relationship between export performance and foreign aid in developing countries while accounting for other factors. The estimates of direct effect of foreign aid on exports are imprecise. However, the effect of the quadratic term of foreign aid on exports is negative and precise. This implies large amount of foreign aid does adversely affect export performance. The results are robust to the use of two different export performance measures and different sub-samples.

Keywords: Foreign aid, export performance, developing countries

JEL classifications: F35, O24

1. Introduction

The relationship between export performance and foreign aid of a country depends upon several factors. The traditional justification for foreign aid is that it eases the resource constraint of the developing economies, especially on the supply side. These supply factors include investment, infrastructure, geography, and quality of institutions. Investment and improvements in trade facilitating infrastructure such as roads, ports, and telecommunications are important for enhancing the supply response of exports (World Bank, 2004). Geographical factors such as distance to the coast or access to sea-navigable rivers directly affect transport costs, and trade is very sensitive to transport costs (Gallup *et al.*, 1999). The quality of institutions too affects the investment climate, which in turn affects the supply response of the economy (World Bank, 2004).

THEORY AND PRACTICE OF FOREIGN AID
VOLUME 1   ISSN: 1574-8715
DOI: 10.1016/S1574-8715(06)01021-9

However, foreign aid can also harm export performance of an economy through real exchange rate appreciation. A number of studies have shown that aid inflows indirectly eroded the export competitiveness of developing countries by causing real exchange rate appreciation (Van Wijnbergen, 1986; Younger, 1992; White and Wignaraja, 1992; Elbadawi, 1999). Because foreign aid raises the domestic demand for goods and services, it drives up prices in the non-traded sector and causes the real exchange rate to appreciate – a "Dutch disease" effect which causes aid to have an anti-export bias. Recently, Rajan and Subramanian (2005a, 2005b) and Mavrotas (2007) have also pointed out that this channel is a potential reason for quantitatively small effect of foreign aid on economic performance of a country.

This paper seeks to examine the above hypothesis of negative effect of foreign aid on export performance of a country. We use a panel of 84 developing countries to estimate the effect of foreign aid on export performance measures after controlling for the additional factors that may affect exports. The results do show a negative effect of a quadratic term of foreign aid on long term performance of exports when we account for possible endogeneity. The results are also robust to two different export measures and different sub-samples. We interpret these estimates as evidence favoring the importance of the real exchange rate channel effect of foreign aid on export performance in the long run.

The rest of the paper proceeds as follows: Section 2 describes the specification of the model to be estimated, the data used in the analysis and estimation issues. Basic results of the estimation are presented in Section 3, results from sub-sample estimations in Section 4 and conclusions in Section 5.

2. Model specification, data, and estimation

2.1. Model specification

We use a simple linear model for estimating the effect of foreign aid on exports but do allow for a quadratic foreign aid term in it. The other potentially important factors are proxies for supply constraints, country size, economic well being of the country and institutional risks. The following equation specifies our empirical model:

$$\log(\textit{Export Performance})_{it}$$
$$= \beta_0 + \beta_i + \beta_t + \beta_1 \cdot \log(\textit{Aid})_{it} + \beta_2 \cdot \left(\log(\textit{Aid})_{it}\right)^2$$
$$+ \beta_3 \cdot \log(\textit{Imported Capital})_{it} + \beta_4 \cdot \log(\textit{Teledensity})_{it}$$
$$+ \beta_5 \cdot \log(\textit{Population})_{it} + \beta_6 \cdot \log(\textit{Lagged per Capita Income})_{it}$$
$$+ \beta_7 \cdot \log(\textit{Financial Risk})_{it} + \beta_8 \cdot \log(\textit{Political Risk})_{it} + \varepsilon_{it}.$$

In the above equation, we allow for country (indexed by i) fixed effects and time (indexed by t) fixed effects.[1] The country fixed effects should capture the potential country heterogeneity biases like geographical location, distance to coast etc. The time fixed effects should capture the global biases like implementation of global trade agreements etc. The imported capital (initial) and teledensity are our proxies for supply and infrastructural constraints. Population captures the country size issue and initial per capita income should capture the countries well being at the beginning of the period. It also serves as a proxy for infrastructural constraints as relatively richer countries are less likely to have poor infrastructure. Finally, the financial risk and the political risk variables serve as proxies for institutional risks.

2.2. Data

Data on total net ODA in current US dollars were obtained from the OECD-DAC database and the unit-value of imports price index was obtained from the IMF International Financial Statistics database. Data on non-oil trade and capital imports were obtained from the World Bank's WITS database. Political and financial risk data were obtained from the PRS Group. The remaining data were obtained from the World Bank's WDI and GDF databases.

Two measures of export performance are used in estimating our equation: the share of each country's non-oil exports in total world non-oil imports, and total exports of goods and services as a percent of GDP. We use the standard measure of real per-capita foreign aid which is total net Official Development Assistance (ODA) as our 'aid' variable. As in Burnside and Dollar (2000), data on net ODA was converted into constant 2000 dollars using the unit-value of imports price index. We divided the real aid figure for each country by the country's total population to obtain real aid per capita. Another measure of foreign aid used in the regressions is the aid as a percentage of GDP.

Imported capital is measured by imports of machinery and transport equipment as a percent of GDP. Based on Moran (1989), many developing countries are highly dependent on imported capital goods for production and investment. The teledensity variable is mainline teledensity and the population is total population. The real lagged per capita income is PPP based (constant 2000 dollars). The measures of financial risk rating and political risk rating imply, in both cases, the higher the rating the lower the risk. The political risk rating is derived from governance indicators such as government stability, control of corruption, law and order, ethnic tensions, democratic accountability, bureaucracy quality, and the influence of military in politics. The financial risk rating is based on trade related indicators including exchange rate stability.

---

[1] We also experimented with allowing for lags of foreign aid in the regression. The results were largely similar though imprecise.

Table 1. Countries included in the estimation

Least developed countries	Other low income countries (per capita GNI <$825 in 2004)	Middle income developing countries (per capita GNI $826 – $10,065 in 2004)
Angola*	Cameroon*	Algeria
Bangladesh	Congo, Rep.*	Argentina
Benin*	Cote d'Ivoire*	Belize
Burkina Faso*	Ghana*	Bolivia
Burundi*	India	Brazil
Cambodia	Kenya*	Chile
Central African Republic*	Mongolia	China
Chad*	Nicaragua	Colombia
Congo, Dem. Rep*	Nigeria*	Costa Rica
Djibouti*	Pakistan	Dominican Republic
Equatorial Guinea*	Papua New Guinea	Ecuador
Gambia, The*	Vietnam	Egypt, Arab Rep.
Guinea*	Zimbabwe*	El Salvador
Guinea-Bissau*		Gabon
Haiti		Guatemala
Laos		Guyana
Madagascar*		Honduras
Malawi*		Indonesia
Mali*		Iran
Mauritania*		Jamaica
Mozambique*		Jordan
Nepal		Lebanon
Niger*		Malaysia
Rwanda*		Mexico
Senegal*		Morocco
Sierra Leone*		Oman
Sudan*		Panama
Tanzania*		Paraguay
Togo*		Peru
Uganda*		Philippines
Yemen		Saudi Arabia
Zambia*		Sri Lanka
		Syrian Arab Republic
		Thailand
		Trinidad and Tobago
		Tunisia
		Turkey
		Uruguay
		Venezuela

Note: Based on DAC list of ODA Recipients, effective from 2006. The asterisked countries are least developed and low income African countries.

2.3. Estimation issues

There are a few estimation issues that are worth discussing at this point. The first relates to the sample of developing countries in the panel data for the period 1980–2003. The use of panel data makes it possible to account for fixed effects in the model. The data are averaged into five year periods (to account for long term variation) for each country (except for 2000–2003, which has 4 periods). The total number of developing countries in our sample is 84. The sample includes both low income and middle income countries, some of which are Least Developed Countries (LDCs), and some of which are non-LDCs (Table 1). However, there are three countries[2] that have negative foreign aid per capita numbers in their sample which rules out the use of logarithms for those data points. We decided to treat those datapoints as missing, thereby making the full sample an unbalanced panel in our primary estimation. Similarly, there were twelve datapoints missing for aid GDP ratio. The summary statistics for the variables are presented in Table 2. Secondly, the data on financial and political risk were available for only 72 countries.

Finally, we tackle the issue of potential endogeneity in the regressions by using instrumental variables technique. The biggest source of potential endogeneity is probably omitted variables – mostly from inadequate number of supply side constraints. There are two types of instruments that we use in the IV estimation. The first are three dummy variables: Friend of UK (FUK), Friend of France (FF), and Friend of US (FUS). The literature has shown that the key determinants of foreign aid allocation are initial income per capita, population, and political or strategic interests of donors (Boone, 1996; Burnside and Dollar, 2000; Alesina and Dollar, 2000;

Table 2. Summary statistics of variables

Variable	Mean	Standard deviation
Based on 84 countries		
World export market share	0.175	0.578
Exports as a percent of GDP	29.057	18.333
Real aid per capita	0.376	0.425
Aid GDP ratio (in percentages)	7.86	9.50
Mainlines teledensity	38.438	53.760
Population, total	45.921	157.836
Real per capita income, PPP (initial)	3182.627	2795.528
Imported capital (initial)	8.903	10.891
Based on 72 countries		
Financial risk	27.158	7.791
Political risk	53.606	12.203

---

[2] Chile, Malaysia, Trinidad and Tobago.

Bandyopadhyay and Wall, 2006). Following Boone (1996) and Rodrik (1995), these dummies are set to one if a recipient country receives more than one percent of the donor's total aid budget allocated to developing countries.

The significance of political and strategic considerations in aid allocation is shown by the fact that more US aid is provided to important allies such as Egypt and Israel, while the UK and France allocate most of their aid to former colonies. Following Rajan and Subramanian's (2005a, 2005b) argument that these types of strategic factors are unrelated to economic performance and can be used as instruments for aid in IV estimation, we use the dummy variables as instruments for aid in our regressions. Our second type of instruments is the initial aid per capita or initial aid GDP ratio that are predetermined variables at each time period and improve the fit of a linear aid regression considerably. However, our results are not very sensitive to the exclusion of this second type of instruments.

3. Primary empirical results

3.1. Full sample estimation results

We start out by documenting the relationship between export performance and foreign aid. The top panels in Figure 1 show a negative relation between aid GDP ratio and two export measures. However, the slope of the linear fit varies between the panels. The bottom left panel in Figure 1 also shows a negative relationship between log of world export market share and log of foreign aid per capita. When we use log export to GDP ratio instead of export market share in the bottom right panel, it shows a positive relationship. Overall, the linear relation between aid and exports vary depending on the measures of aid and exports.

In the first column of Table 3 we present the pooled OLS results with additional control variables. The top panel uses aid GDP ratio and the bottom panel uses aid per capita. The result of negative relationship between foreign aid and export performance is imprecise in the top panel and disappear in the bottom panel. The quadratic term also switches sign. The coefficients of imported capital and initial per capita income are positive and significant. We re-estimate the equation after allowing for country and time fixed effects and report the results in the second column. The linear effect of foreign aid is negative for aid GDP ratio and positive for aid per capita.

The last column reports the fixed effects IV estimation. We instrument for both the linear and the quadratic term of foreign aid using the strategic dummies, initial foreign aid and initial foreign aid squared as instruments. The point estimate of linear effect of foreign aid is negative and imprecise. More importantly, the effect of the quadratic foreign aid term is negative and significant for both the regressions. This implies large amount of foreign aid is likely to adversely affect the export performance of a country; confirming the Rajan and Subramanian (2005a, 2005b) reasons for poor economic performance of the aid recipient countries. A similar discussion of adverse effects of foreign aid via exchange rate channel is also presented in Mavrotas (2007).

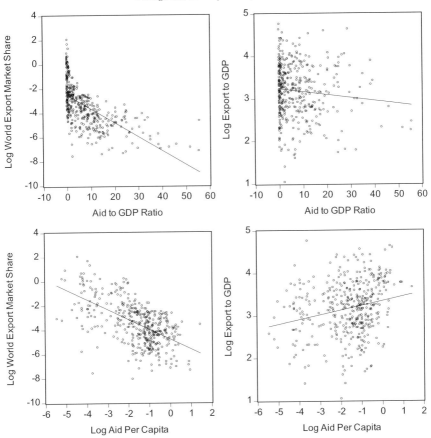

Fig. 1.   Scatter diagram of exports and aid.

We see a similar picture when we examine the estimates in Table 4 using export to GDP ratio. The pooled OLS results in the first column and fixed effects result in the second column report a mostly positive linear effect of foreign aid on export performance. The quadratic effect estimates are mixed and mostly imprecise. Using instrumental variables in the last column, we see mixed results for the linear effect of foreign aid. However, the quadratic term of foreign aid is negative and significant for both regressions and confirms our Table 3 results using a different export performance measure.

3.2. Estimation results from the sub-sample of 72 countries

We now examine the estimation results from a sub-sample of 72 countries and with institutional risks data in an unbalanced panel. We also concentrate on using just aid

Table 3.   Regression results for the full sample using world export market share

Explanatory variables	POLS	FE	FE-IV
Aid GDP ratio	−0.002	−0.012	−0.023
	(0.04)	(0.05)	(0.05)
Aid GDP ratio squared	−0.029***	0.004	−0.038**
	(0.01)	(0.01)	(0.02)
Log of imported capital (initial)	0.436***	0.277***	0.253***
	(0.07)	(0.06)	(0.06)
Log of mainlines teledensity	−0.015	0.392***	0.319***
	(0.06)	(0.09)	(0.09)
Log of population	0.824***	0.930*	0.604
	(0.03)	(0.51)	(0.46)
Log of real per capita income (initial)	1.124***	0.542***	0.520**
	(0.13)	(0.15)	(0.21)
Log of real per-capita aid	0.123	0.129*	−0.050
	(0.11)	(0.08)	(0.09)
Log of real per-capita aid squared	0.004	0.006	−0.035*
	(0.03)	(0.02)	(0.02)
Log of imported capital (initial)	0.439***	0.330***	0.343***
	(0.07)	(0.07)	(0.08)
Log of mainlines teledensity	0.007	0.400***	0.384***
	(0.06)	(0.08)	(0.08)
Log of population	0.901***	1.320***	1.189**
	(0.03)	(0.50)	(0.49)
Log of real per capita income (initial)	1.191***	0.563***	0.540***
	(0.09)	(0.16)	(0.17)

Note: The dependent variable is log of world export market share. The data is an unbalanced panel of 84 countries. The regressions include a constant. White's standard errors are in the parentheses.
*Implies the coefficient significant at the 10% level.
**Implies the coefficient is significant at the 5% level.
***Implies significance at the 1% level.

GDP ratio as our foreign aid variable due to space considerations. The pooled OLS results with additional controls in the first columns of Tables 5 and 6 show mixed results for linear effects of foreign aid but negative and significant effects of the quadratic term. We get a similar picture when we compare the results of second and third columns of Tables 5 and 6. Allowing for cross section and time fixed effects in the second columns, the results for the quadratic term are still negative but insignificant. Fixed effects IV regressions in the third column show mixed and insignificant estimates for the linear foreign aid term. The quadratic aid term shows negative and significant estimates.

Overall, the results from the full sample unbalanced panel and the panel of 72 countries are largely similar. Both show that the linear effect of foreign aid on export performance is mixed and imprecise. The results also show that the quadratic term

Table 4. Regression results for the full sample using export to GDP ratio

Explanatory variables	POLS	FE	FE-IV
Aid GDP ratio	−0.022	0.113***	0.105***
	(0.02)	(0.03)	(0.03)
Aid GDP ratio squared	−0.022***	0.001	−0.024*
	(0.01)	(0.01)	(0.01)
Log of imported capital (initial)	0.552***	0.292***	0.270***
	(0.04)	(0.04)	(0.04)
Log of mainlines teledensity	−0.011	−0.002	−0.053
	(0.03)	(0.05)	(0.05)
Log of population	−0.094***	0.349	0.071
	(0.02)	(0.26)	(0.24)
Log of real per capita income (initial)	0.122*	0.417***	0.408***
	(0.07)	(0.09)	(0.10)
Log of real per-capita aid	0.014	0.075	−0.033
	(0.03)	(0.05)	(0.07)
Log of real per-capita aid squared	0.002	−0.004	−0.025*
	(0.01)	(0.01)	(0.01)
Log of imported capital (initial)	0.526***	0.335***	0.350***
	(0.04)	(0.05)	(0.05)
Log of mainlines teledensity	0.004	0.002	−0.011
	(0.02)	(0.05)	(0.05)
Log of population	−0.069***	0.463*	0.327**
	(0.01)	(0.25)	(0.16)
Log of real per capita income (initial)	0.164***	0.288***	0.269***
	(0.01)	(0.07)	(0.07)

Note: The dependent variable is log of export to GDP ratio. The data is an unbalanced panel of 84 countries. The regressions include a constant. White's standard errors are in the parentheses.
*Implies the coefficient significant at the 10% level.
**Implies the coefficient is significant at the 5% level.
***Implies significance at the 1% level.

of foreign aid is important. Its effect is negative and significant when the endogeneity problem in the regressions is addressed using instrumental variables. The results imply that large amount of foreign aid will negatively affect exports of a country.

4. Empirical results from least developed economies and low income African countries

In this section we subdivide our sample into two sub-samples. The first is the set of 32 least developed countries as listed in Table 1. The second is the set of 33 low income African countries also listed in Table 1 and asterisked. These two samples have special significance given the very low level of development in those countries. The fixed effects and fixed effects IV estimation results for the least developed countries are presented in Table 7 using both measures of export performance. The results show all

Table 5. Regression results for 72 countries using world export market share

Explanatory variables	POLS	FE	FE-IV
Aid GDP ratio	0.003	−0.046	−0.017
	(0.05)	(0.03)	(0.04)
Aid GDP ratio squared	−0.031***	−0.001	−0.031*
	(0.01)	(0.09)	(0.02)
Log of imported capital (initial)	0.378***	0.203***	0.220***
	(0.08)	(0.05)	(0.06)
Log of mainlines teledensity	−0.079	0.350***	0.304***
	(0.05)	(0.09)	(0.09)
Log of population	0.813***	0.576	0.645
	(0.04)	(0.45)	(0.44)
Log of real per capita income (initial)	1.179***	0.592***	0.672***
	(0.13)	(0.17)	(0.17)
Log of financial risk	−0.296	0.353***	0.377***
	(0.19)	(0.11)	(0.12)
Log of political risk	0.451*	−0.285	−0.316*
	(0.25)	(0.16)	(0.17)

Note: The dependent variable is log of world export market share. The data is an unbalanced panel of 72 countries. The regressions include a constant. White's standard errors are in the parentheses.
*Implies the coefficient significant at the 10% level.
**Implies the coefficient is significant at the 5% level.
***Implies significance at the 1% level.

positive and precise estimates of linear effect of foreign aid on exports. However, the quadratic term is also always negative and mostly significant. The evidence supports our hypothesis that large volume of aid adversely affects exports.

Similar results for low income African countries are in Table 8. Again the estimated effects of the linear aid terms are positive and the quadratic terms are negative. However, the estimates are significant only for export to GDP ratio as the dependant variable. Imported capital is positive and significant in the exports to GDP ratio regressions but not in case of world export market share. The real initial per capita income coefficients are always positive and significant. Overall, the sub-sample results are largely similar to our full sample results and lend support to the hypothesis that large amount of aid has negative effect on the exports of a country.

5. Conclusion

In this paper, we analyzed whether aid adversely affects the long term export performance of a country due to an appreciation of real exchange rate while taking into account various supply and other factors. Our results show that large amount of foreign aid adversely affects export performance of developing countries but the effect is not clear for smaller amounts.

Table 6. *Regression results for 72 countries using export to GDP ratio*

Explanatory variables	POLS	FE	FE-IV
Aid GDP ratio	−0.022	0.094***	0.106
	(0.023)	(0.03)	(0.03)
Aid GDP ratio squared	−0.022***	−0.001	−0.026*
	(0.01)	(0.01)	(0.01)
Log of imported capital (initial)	0.477***	0.247***	0.266***
	(0.04)	(0.04)	(0.05)
Log of mainlines teledensity	−0.055*	−0.019	−0.093
	(0.03)	(0.05)	(0.06)
Log of population	0.118***	0.249	0.157
	(0.02)	(0.25)	(0.25)
Log of real per capita income (initial)	0.098	0.424***	0.512***
	(0.06)	(0.10)	(0.10)
Log of financial risk	0.331***	0.053	0.029
	(0.10)	(0.08)	(0.08)
Log of political risk	0.272*	−0.047	−0.033
	(0.11)	(0.11)	(0.11)

Note: The dependent variable is log of export to GDP ratio. The data is an unbalanced panel of 72 countries. The regressions include a constant. White's standard errors are in the parentheses.
*Implies the coefficient significant at the 10% level.
**Implies the coefficient is significant at the 5% level.
***Implies significance at the 1% level.

Table 7. *Regression results for least developed economies*

Explanatory variables	FE	FE-IV	FE	FE-IV
	World export market share		Export to GDP ratio	
Aid GDP ratio	1.120***	1.1836**	0.837***	0.621*
	(0.42)	(0.53)	(0.24)	(0.36)
Aid GDP ratio squared	−0.220***	−0.302**	−0.153***	−0.158
	(0.07)	(0.12)	(0.05)	(0.08)
Log of imported capital (initial)	0.306***	0.359***	0.279***	0.300***
	(0.10)	(0.13)	(0.07)	(0.08)
Log of mainlines teledensity	0.154	−0.070	−0.075	−0.198**
	(0.17)	(0.18)	(0.09)	(0.10)
Log of population	1.571	0.153	−0.317	−1.002
	(1.54)	(1.82)	(0.65)	(0.77)
Log of real per capita income (initial)	0.966***	0.847***	0.717***	0.542***
	(0.20)	(0.24)	(0.12)	(0.16)

Note: The dependent variables are log of world export market share (first two columns) and log of export to GDP ratio (last two columns). The data is an unbalanced panel of 32 countries. The regressions include a constant. White's standard errors are in the parentheses.
*Implies that the coefficient significant at the 10% level.
**Implies the coefficient is significant at the 5% level.
***Implies significance at the 1% level.

Table 8.   *Regression results for low income African economies*

Explanatory variables	FE	FE-IV	FE	FE-IV
	World export market share		Export to GDP ratio	
Aid GDP ratio	0.090	0.140	0.329***	0.337***
	(0.10)	(0.10)	(0.07)	(0.10)
Aid GDP ratio squared	−0.033	−0.020	−0.047***	−0.058**
	(0.02)	(0.03)	(0.02)	(0.02)
Log of imported capital (initial)	0.093	0.068	0.190***	0.196***
	(0.08)	(0.08)	(0.06)	(0.07)
Log of mainlines teledensity	−0.053	−0.009	−0.115	−0.143*
	(0.11)	(0.12)	(0.09)	(0.08)
Log of population	2.044*	2.349*	0.566	0.398
	(1.21)	(1.31)	(0.63)	(0.68)
Log of real per capita income (initial)	0.620***	0.705***	0.568***	0.552***
	(0.17)	(0.19)	(0.13)	(0.15)

Note: The dependent variables are log of world export market share (first two columns) and log of export to GDP ratio (last two columns). The data is an unbalanced panel of 33 countries. The regressions include a constant. White's standard errors are in the parentheses.
*Implies the coefficient significant at the 10% level.
**Implies the coefficient is significant at the 5% level.
***Implies significance at the 1% level.

Acknowledgements

The views expressed here are those of the authors and should not be attributed to the World Bank. The authors would like to thank the Editor, Sajal Lahiri, for comments and suggestions. Usual disclaimers apply.

References

Alesina, R., Dollar, D. (2000), Who gives foreign aid to whom and why? *Journal of Economic Growth* 5, 33–63.

Bandyopadhyay, S., Wall, H. (2006), The determinants of aid in the Post Cold-War era. *Working Paper*, Federal Reserve Bank of St. Louis.

Boone, P. (1996), Politics and the effectiveness of foreign aid. *European Economic Review* 40, 289–329.

Burnside, C., Dollar, D. (2000), Aid, policies, and growth. *American Economic Review* 90, 847–868.

Elbadawi, I. (1999), External aid: help or hindrance to export orientation in Africa? *Journal of African Economies* 8, 578–616.

Gallup, J., Sachs, D., Mellinger, A. (1999), Geography and economic development. *Working Paper* 1, CID.

Mavrotas, G. (2007), Scaling up of foreign aid and the emerging new agenda. In: Lahiri, S. (Ed.), *Frontiers of Economics and Globalization: Theory and Practice of Foreign Aid*. Elsevier, Amsterdam.

Moran, C. (1989), Imports under a foreign exchange constraint. *World Bank Economic Review* 3, 279–295.

Rajan, R., Subramanian, A. (2005a), What undermines aid's impact on growth. *Working Paper* 11657, NBER.

Rajan, R., Subramanian, A. (2005b), Aid and growth: what does the cross-country evidence really show? *Working Paper* 11513, NBER.

Rodrik, D. (1995), Why is there multilateral lending? *Working Paper* 5160, NBER.

Van Wijnbergen, S. (1986), *Aid, Export Promotion, and the Real Exchange Rate: An African Dilemma*. Center for Economic Policy Research, London.

White, H., Wignaraja, G. (1992), Exchange rates, trade liberalization, and aid: the Sri-Lankan experience. *World Development* 20, 1471–1480.

World Bank (2004), *World Development Report: a Better Investment Climate for Everyone*. World Bank, Washington, DC.

Younger, S. (1992), Aid and the Dutch disease: macroeconomic management when everybody loves you. *World Development* 20, 1587–1597.

SUBJECT INDEX

marginal utility of income, 11
market failures, 296
Marshall Plan, 156
Marshall–Lerner condition, 164, 166
military conflicts, 13
military hardware, 6, 13
Millennium Development Goals, 212–214,
    216–218, 221, 223–226, 296, 302, 358
Millennium Summit, 302
mortality of European settlers, 404
Mozambican experience, 236, 276
multilateral institutions, 303

negative externality, 6
neoclassical growth theory, 290
net gain function, 6
net gain of land, 6
New Economic Geography, 32
no-black-hole condition, 39
nominal exchange rate, 158
non-government organizations (NGOs), 27
nutrition
– aid impact on, 204–207

optimal quota, 178–180, 182
ownership, 301, 304

Pareto-improving foreign aid, 131, 132, 140
Paris Club, 303
pipeline approach
– to aid impact, 195
polarization, 293
policies, 298, 300
policy conditionality, 304
policy coordination, 270
pollution abatement, 85–97, 99, 100
poverty, 18, 25
– reduction, 296
– trap, 294
PRGF, 300, 301
primary completion rate, 359
primary enrolment rate, 359
production externality, 174
project aid, 248
proliferation of donors, 235
propensity score matching, 195, 205, 206
protect the lives, 7
protection of the lives, 12

quota, 175, 180–182
quota rents, 177

randomized evaluation, 193–195
real exchange rate, 421, 422, 430
recipient country, 164, 166, 167
redistributive politics, 18–21, 24–27
regional public goods, 296
regression based approach
– to aid impact, 195–203
remittances, 105–107, 114, 115
rent seeking, 117
reparation payments, 31
resource rich countries, 293
revenue functions, 7
role of aid, 235, 236

Samaritan's Dilemma, 305
savings rates, 298
scaled-up aid, 334
scaling-up ODA, 216, 219–221, 226
sector wide approaches (SWAPs), 303
selection bias
– in impact evaluation, 192, 193
self-fulfilling expectation, 133, 147
settlement, 406
settler mortality, 410, 414, 416, 417
short-run, 35
shortage of demand, 165
single-purpose grants, 333, 334
soldiers, 5, 6, 9
special-purpose, 333
spreading, 37
stable, 39
stagnation, 165
steady state, 139, 140
stickiness, 117, 118
structural adjustment programmes, 299
sub-Saharan Africa, 333, 335, 337, 351
sustain point, 43
sustained aid, 235, 280, 281
syndromes, 294

tax effort, 315
technological progress, 290, 298
terms of trade, 31, 173, 337
tied aid, 174, 175, 179–182
time series country analysis, 315
trade-off between foreign aid and foreign
    investment, 58
transaction costs, 299, 301
transboundary pollution, 85–88
transfer paradox, 44, 131, 132, 157, 173